DELIVER ME!
DELIVER ME
DEC 25 2018

LIVIN' THE DREAM.

Created, written, and drawn by

Terry Flippo

"Neither snow nor rain nor heat nor gloom of night, yadda yadda yadda..."

We've all heard the unofficial motto of the United States Postal Service by now. But to quote one of the strips in this book, "I'd like to meet the guy who came up with that slogan and kick his @$$."

Really!?

Have you ever carried mail in two feet of snow?

No picnic.

Seriously though, postal work is no joke. Delivering mail is a stressful, physically demanding, deadline-oriented job. On your feet all day, climbing stairs, jumping fences, delivering 40-pound boxes of dog food and kitty litter. I compare it to being a professional athlete, except you're an athlete whose career spans 35 years, not 10.

Postal workers are some of the hardest-working, most dedicated people you'll meet. Despite doing this high-pressure job, or maybe because of it, they also tend to have a great sense of humor about what they do. When I first started writing and drawing *Deliver Me!** I wasn't sure how long I would be doing it. I didn't know if I could come up with enough material to keep it going. Surprisingly, once I started posting the strips online I began to receive suggestions from fellow postal workers...

"How about a strip about doggy doo?"

"Did you do a strip about Forever stamps?"

"Do one about 'or current resident.'"

I'll admit, it's the support and enthusiasm that has kept the strip (and me) going. It feels like I'm telling "our story." So this book is dedicated to all the guys and gals in Postal Blue. *Deliver Me!* wouldn't exist without you.

Carry on!

--Terry Flippo

*Originally titled *Postage Due*, until I stumbled across a comic already using that name.

Thanks to all who have suggested strip ideas: Misden Forrestal, Patrick McGrath, Michelle Mobilio, Mollie Easter, Jose Molina, Kara Foote, Cathy LaRoche Rupert, Fran Kelly Clark, Chris Wiles, Tee Smith, Josh Madison, Kim Robbins, Holli Wood, James White, Anita Bromfield, Billy Wilson, Mike Meier, Ron Reader, Dana Cantrell, Kyle Konetzke, Kay Foot, Betsy Myers, Andy Durbin, Maxine Conti, Ken Howser, Scott Horn, Ron Crump, Stephanie Saunders, Lisa McLean Ozeretny, Denise Huffman, Eugene Topkins, and Lenny Skibicki. Thanks also to Mike Hall for technical and design assist in assembling this collected edition.

POSTAGE DUE

by flip

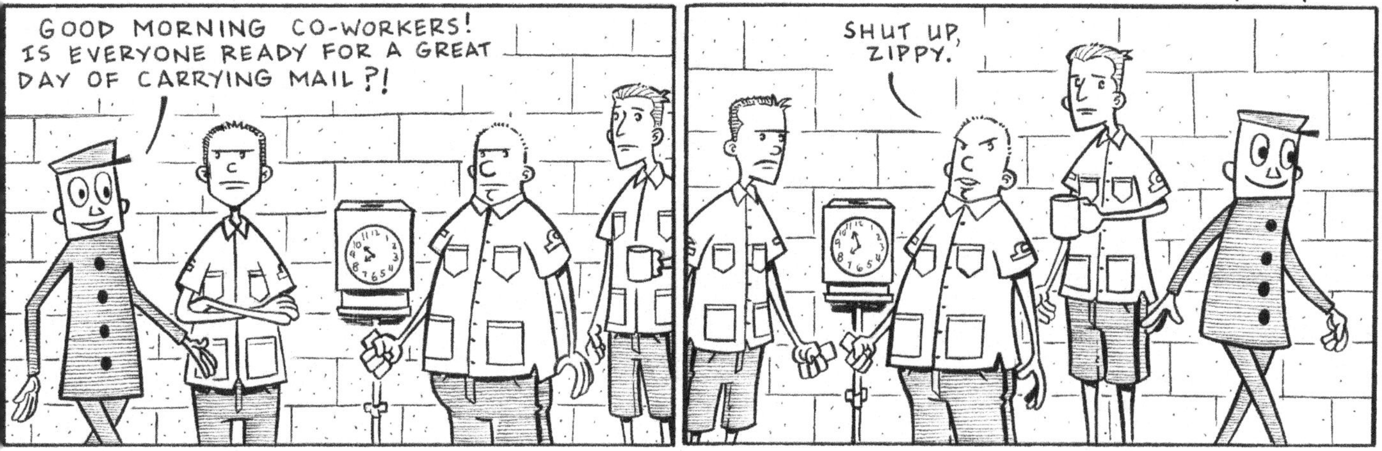
GOOD MORNING CO-WORKERS! IS EVERYONE READY FOR A GREAT DAY OF CARRYING MAIL?!
SHUT UP, ZIPPY.

POSTAGE DUE

by flip

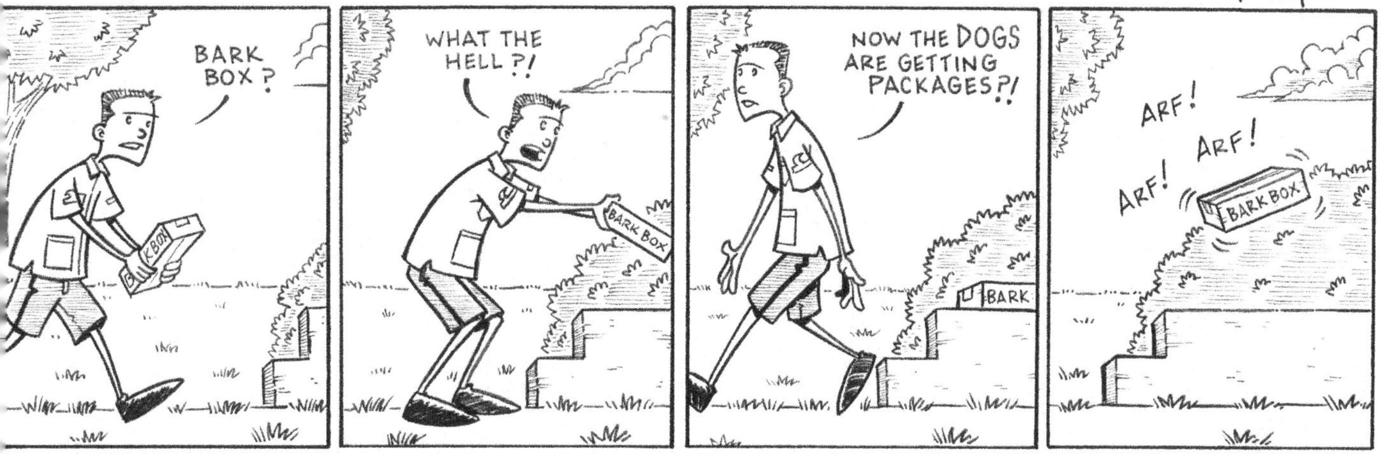
BARK BOX?
BARK BOX
WHAT THE HELL?!
BARK BOX
NOW THE DOGS ARE GETTING PACKAGES?!
BARK
ARF!
ARF!
ARF!
BARK BOX

POSTAGE DUE by flip

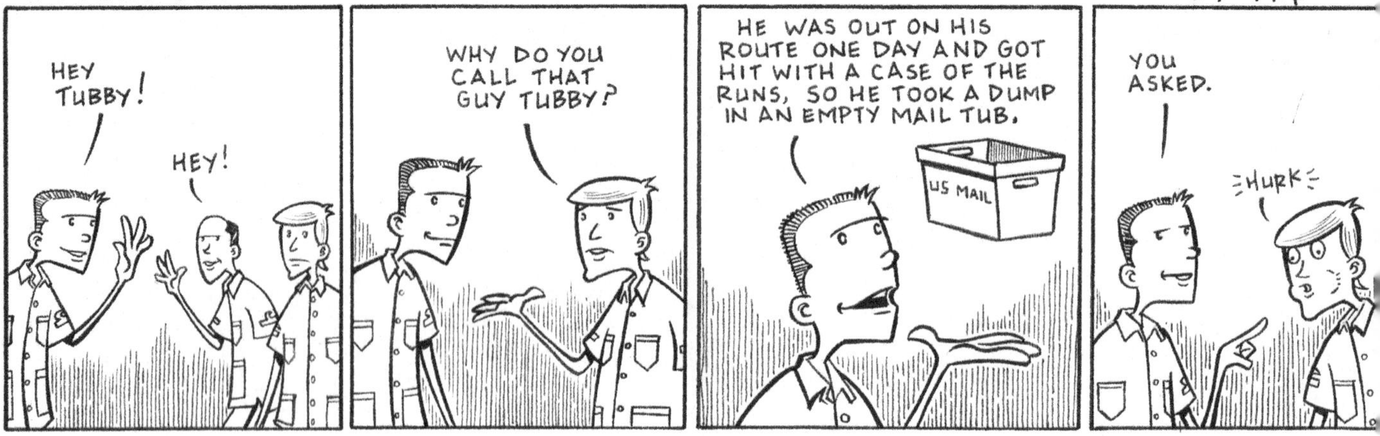
HEY TUBBY!
HEY!
WHY DO YOU CALL THAT GUY TUBBY?
HE WAS OUT ON HIS ROUTE ONE DAY AND GOT HIT WITH A CASE OF THE RUNS, SO HE TOOK A DUMP IN AN EMPTY MAIL TUB.
US MAIL
YOU ASKED.
HURK

POSTAGE DUE by flip

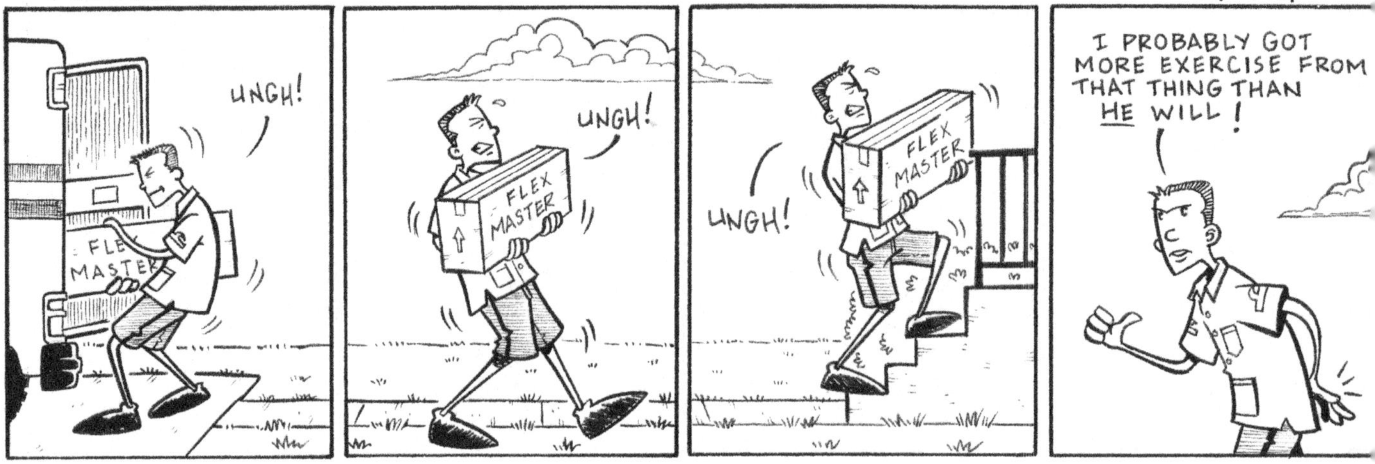
UNGH!
FLEX MASTER
UNGH!
FLEX MASTER
UNGH!
FLEX MASTER
I PROBABLY GOT MORE EXERCISE FROM THAT THING THAN HE WILL!

DELIVER ME! by flip

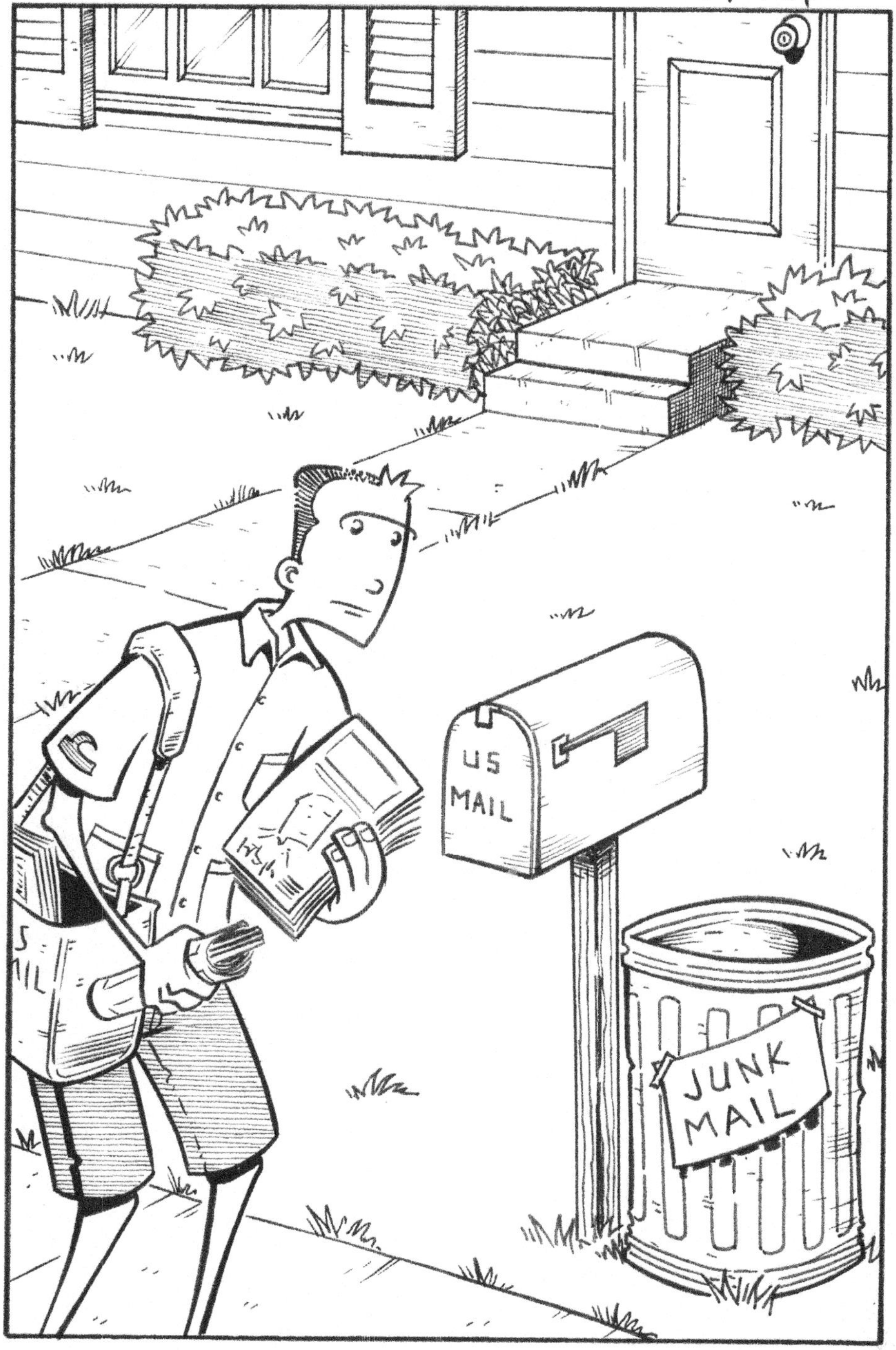
US MAIL
JUNK MAIL

POSTAGE DUE by flip

THERE ARE THREE WAYS A LETTERCARRIER CAN TELL FALL IS ON THE WAY...
1. PUMPKIN SPICE LATTE' IS BACK.
MMM...
2. THE AIR IS COOL AND THE TREES ARE SHEDDING THEIR LEAVES.
US MAIL
3. WE HAVE MAIL-ORDER CATALOGS OUT THE WAZOO!

POSTAGE DUE by flip

US MAIL
WOULDN'T WANT YOUR JOB TODAY!
I DON'T WANT IT EITHER.
US M

POSTAGE DUE

by flip

SPLORTCH
?
DAMMIT.
IF THERE'S A DOG TURD WITHIN FIVE MILES, I'LL FIND A WAY TO STEP IN IT!

POSTAGE DUE

by flip

KNOCK KNOCK
OH.
IT'S JUST THE MAILMAN.
ODDLY ENOUGH, THAT'S THE SAME RECEPTION I GET AT HOME.

DELIVER ME! by flip

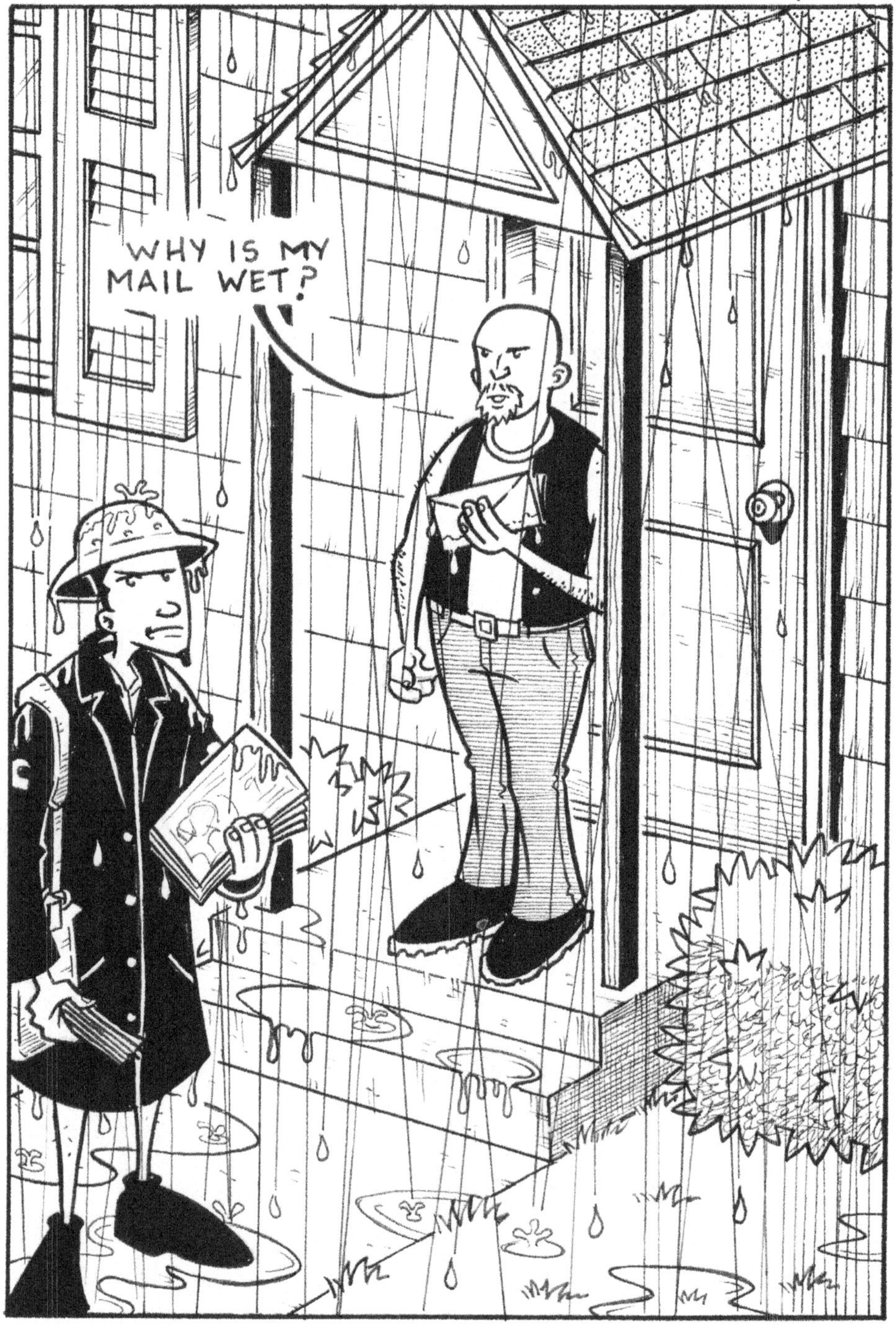
WHY IS MY MAIL WET?

POSTAGE DUE

by flip

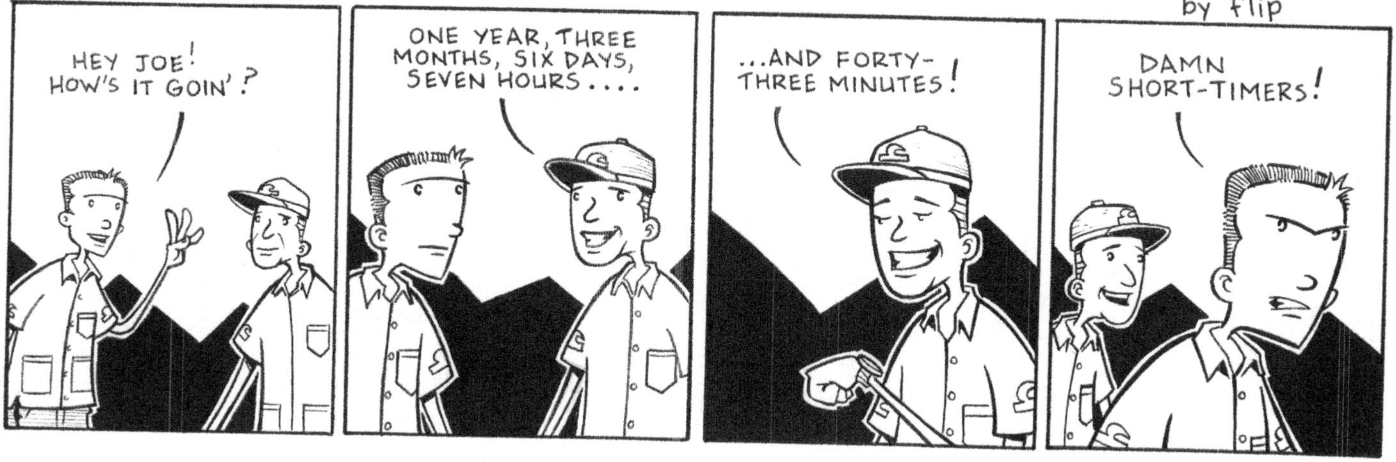
HEY JOE! HOW'S IT GOIN'?
ONE YEAR, THREE MONTHS, SIX DAYS, SEVEN HOURS....
...AND FORTY-THREE MINUTES!
DAMN SHORT-TIMERS!

POSTAGE DUE

by flip

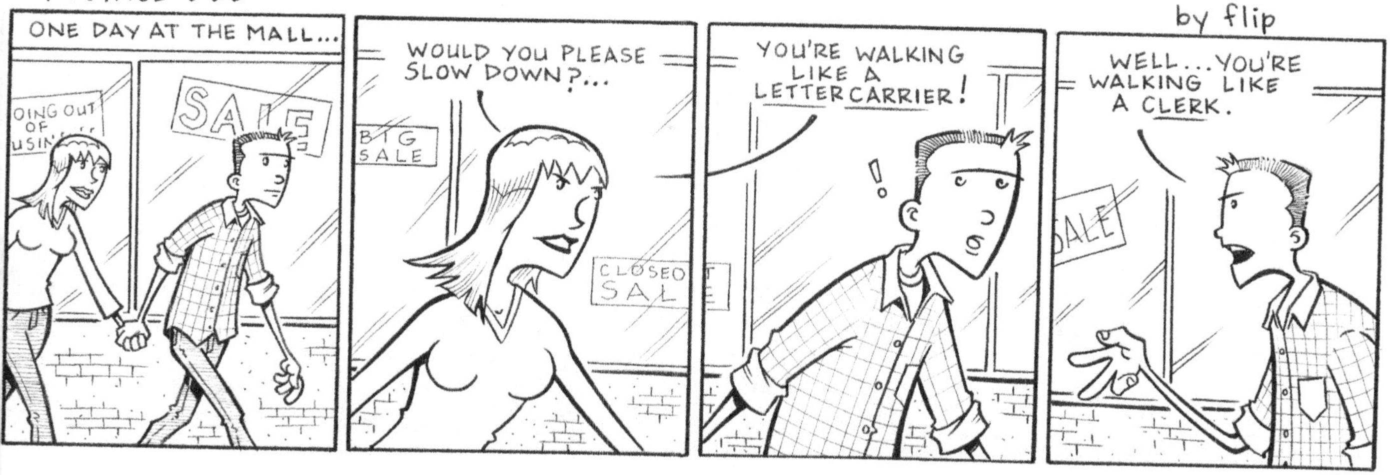
ONE DAY AT THE MALL...
SALE
WOULD YOU PLEASE SLOW DOWN?...
BIG SALE
YOU'RE WALKING LIKE A LETTER CARRIER!
WELL... YOU'RE WALKING LIKE A CLERK.
SALE

POSTAGE DUE

by flip

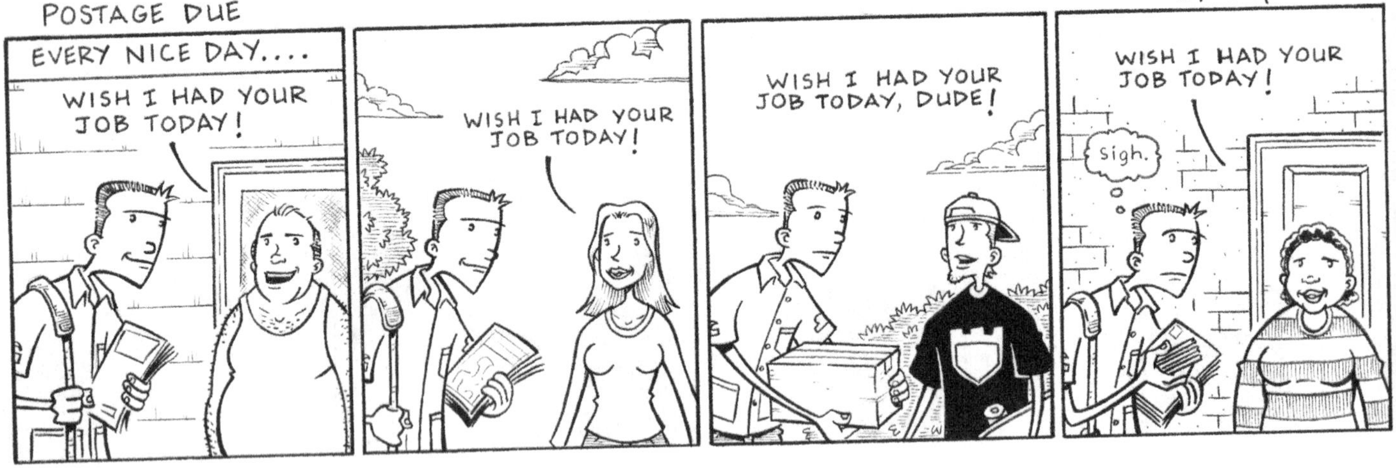
EVERY NICE DAY....
WISH I HAD YOUR JOB TODAY!
WISH I HAD YOUR JOB TODAY!
WISH I HAD YOUR JOB TODAY, DUDE!
Sigh.
WISH I HAD YOUR JOB TODAY!

POSTAGE DUE

by flip

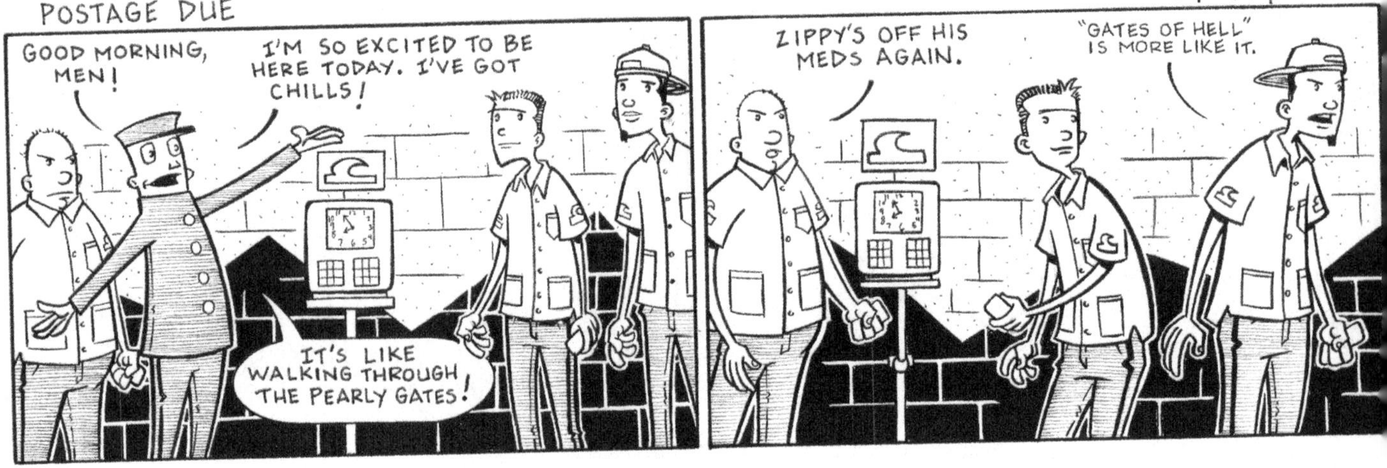
GOOD MORNING, MEN!
I'M SO EXCITED TO BE HERE TODAY. I'VE GOT CHILLS!
IT'S LIKE WALKING THROUGH THE PEARLY GATES!
ZIPPY'S OFF HIS MEDS AGAIN.
"GATES OF HELL" IS MORE LIKE IT.

POSTAGE DUE

by flip

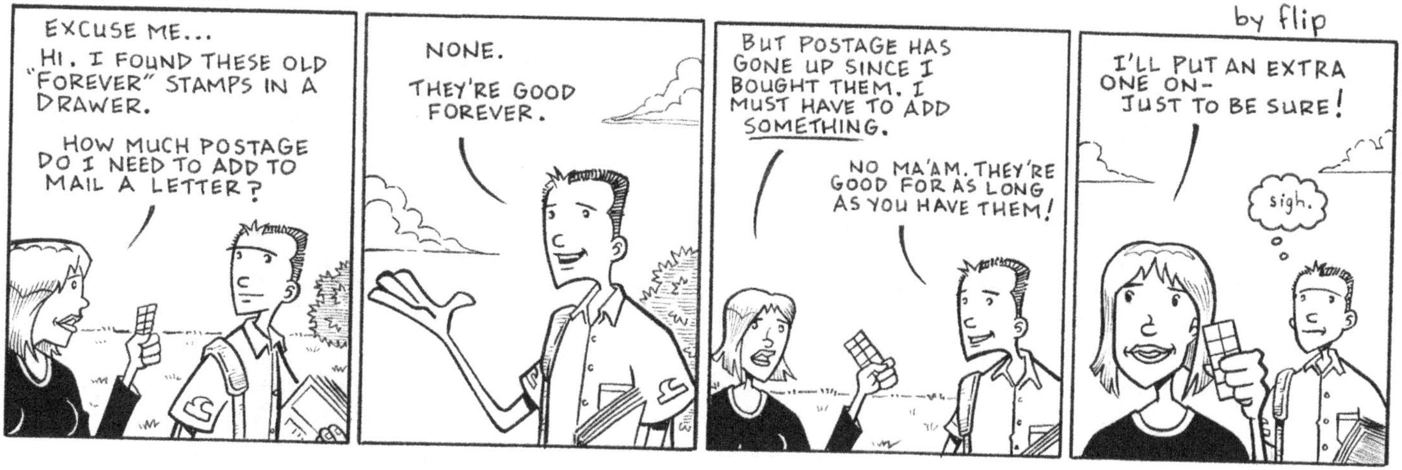
EXCUSE ME...
HI. I FOUND THESE OLD "FOREVER" STAMPS IN A DRAWER.
HOW MUCH POSTAGE DO I NEED TO ADD TO MAIL A LETTER?
NONE.
THEY'RE GOOD FOREVER.
BUT POSTAGE HAS GONE UP SINCE I BOUGHT THEM. I MUST HAVE TO ADD SOMETHING.
NO MA'AM. THEY'RE GOOD FOR AS LONG AS YOU HAVE THEM!
I'LL PUT AN EXTRA ONE ON- JUST TO BE SURE!
sigh.

POSTAGE DUE

by flip

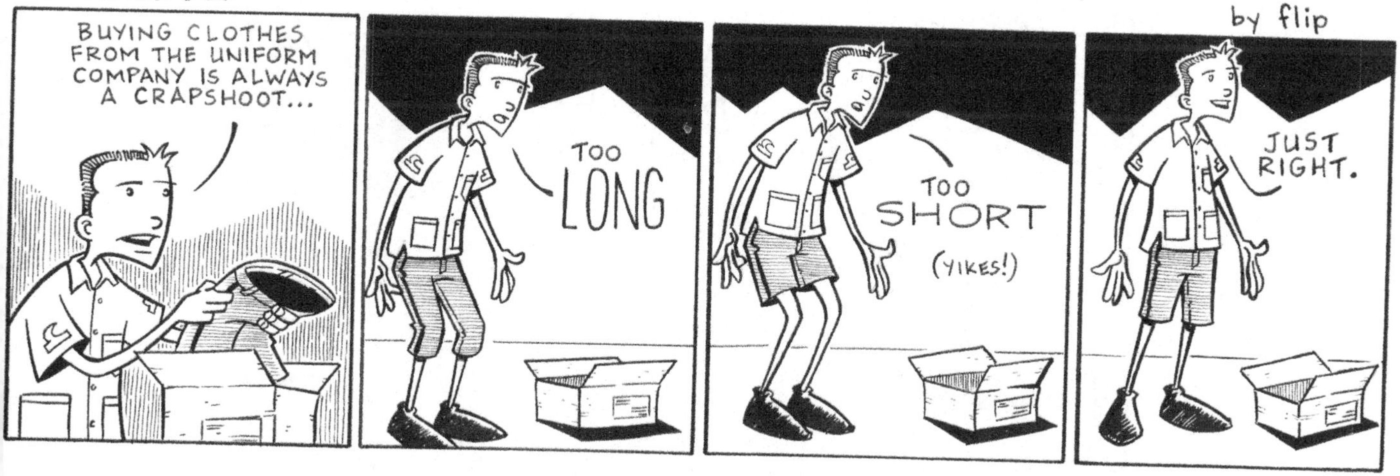
BUYING CLOTHES FROM THE UNIFORM COMPANY IS ALWAYS A CRAPSHOOT...
TOO LONG
TOO SHORT
(YIKES!)
JUST RIGHT.

DELIVER ME!

by flip

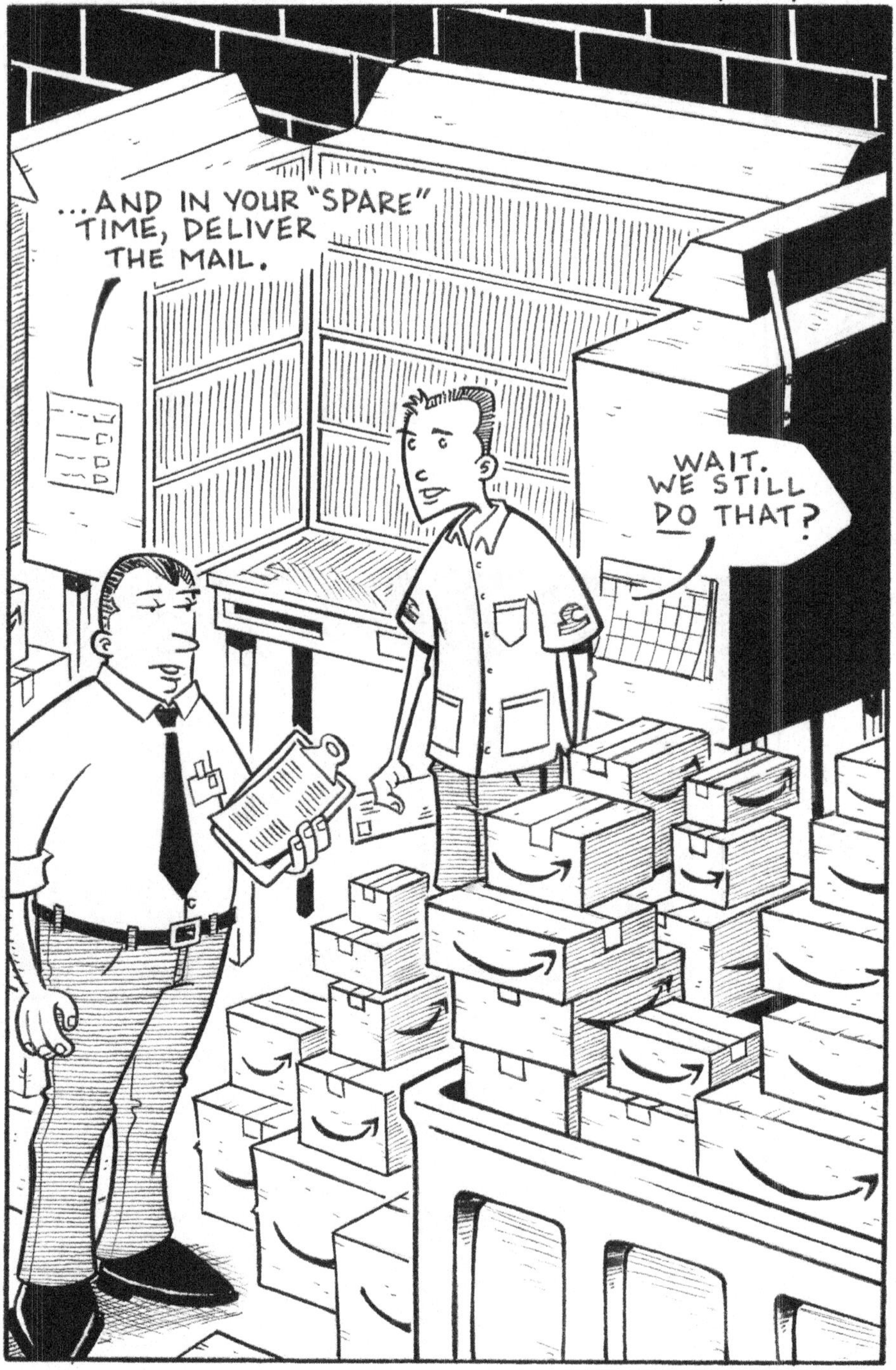
...AND IN YOUR "SPARE" TIME, DELIVER THE MAIL.
WAIT. WE STILL DO THAT?

POSTAGE DUE

by flip

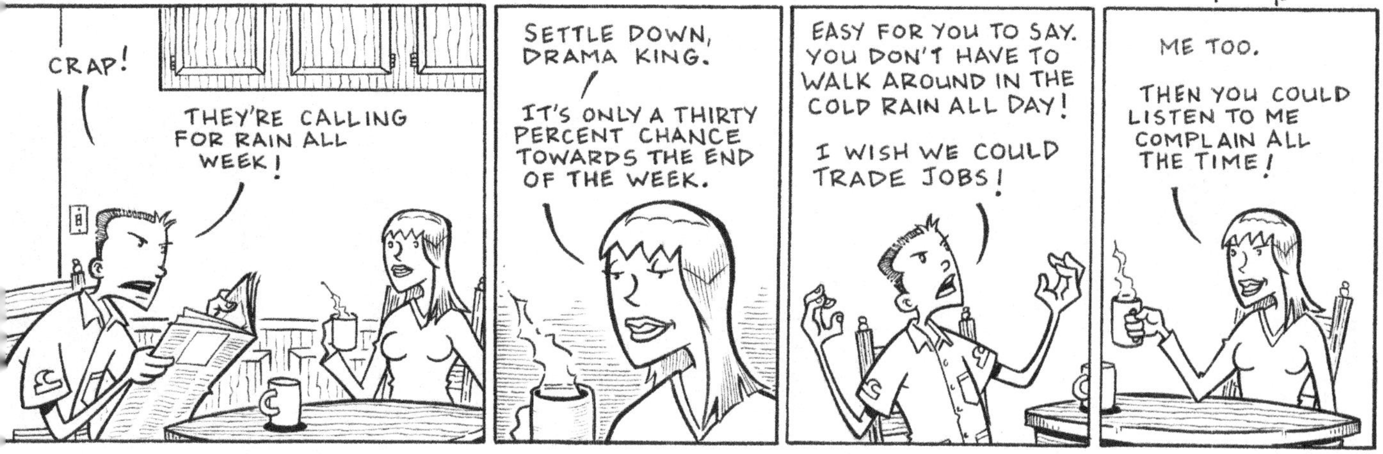
CRAP!
THEY'RE CALLING FOR RAIN ALL WEEK!
SETTLE DOWN, DRAMA KING.
IT'S ONLY A THIRTY PERCENT CHANCE TOWARDS THE END OF THE WEEK.
EASY FOR YOU TO SAY. YOU DON'T HAVE TO WALK AROUND IN THE COLD RAIN ALL DAY!
I WISH WE COULD TRADE JOBS!
ME TOO.
THEN YOU COULD LISTEN TO ME COMPLAIN ALL THE TIME!

POSTAGE DUE

by flip

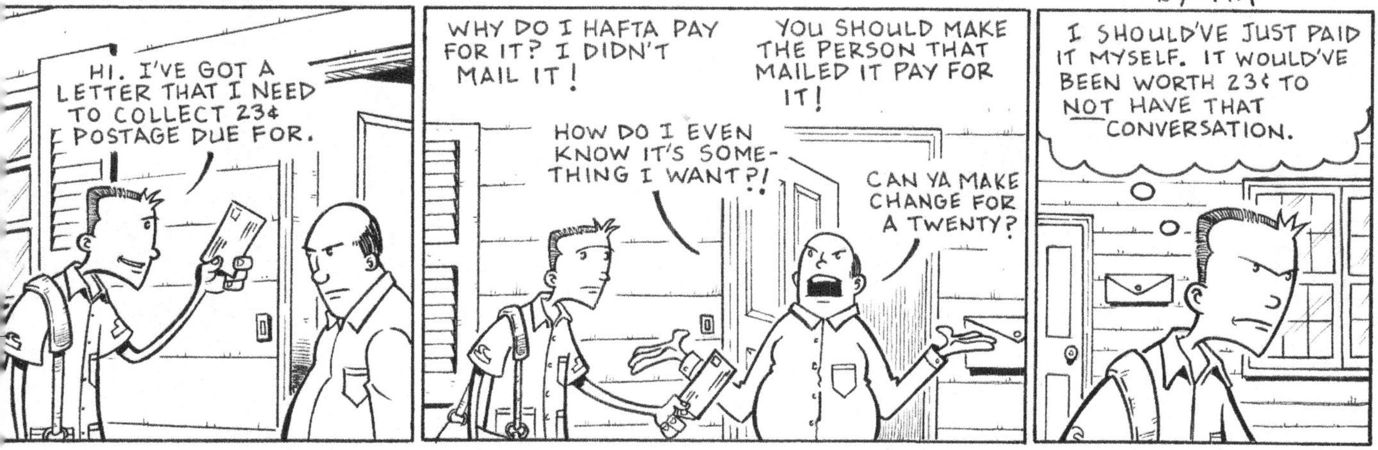
HI. I'VE GOT A LETTER THAT I NEED TO COLLECT 23¢ POSTAGE DUE FOR.
WHY DO I HAFTA PAY FOR IT? I DIDN'T MAIL IT!
YOU SHOULD MAKE THE PERSON THAT MAILED IT PAY FOR IT!
HOW DO I EVEN KNOW IT'S SOMETHING I WANT?!
CAN YA MAKE CHANGE FOR A TWENTY?
I SHOULD'VE JUST PAID IT MYSELF. IT WOULD'VE BEEN WORTH 23¢ TO NOT HAVE THAT CONVERSATION.

DELIVER ME!

by flip

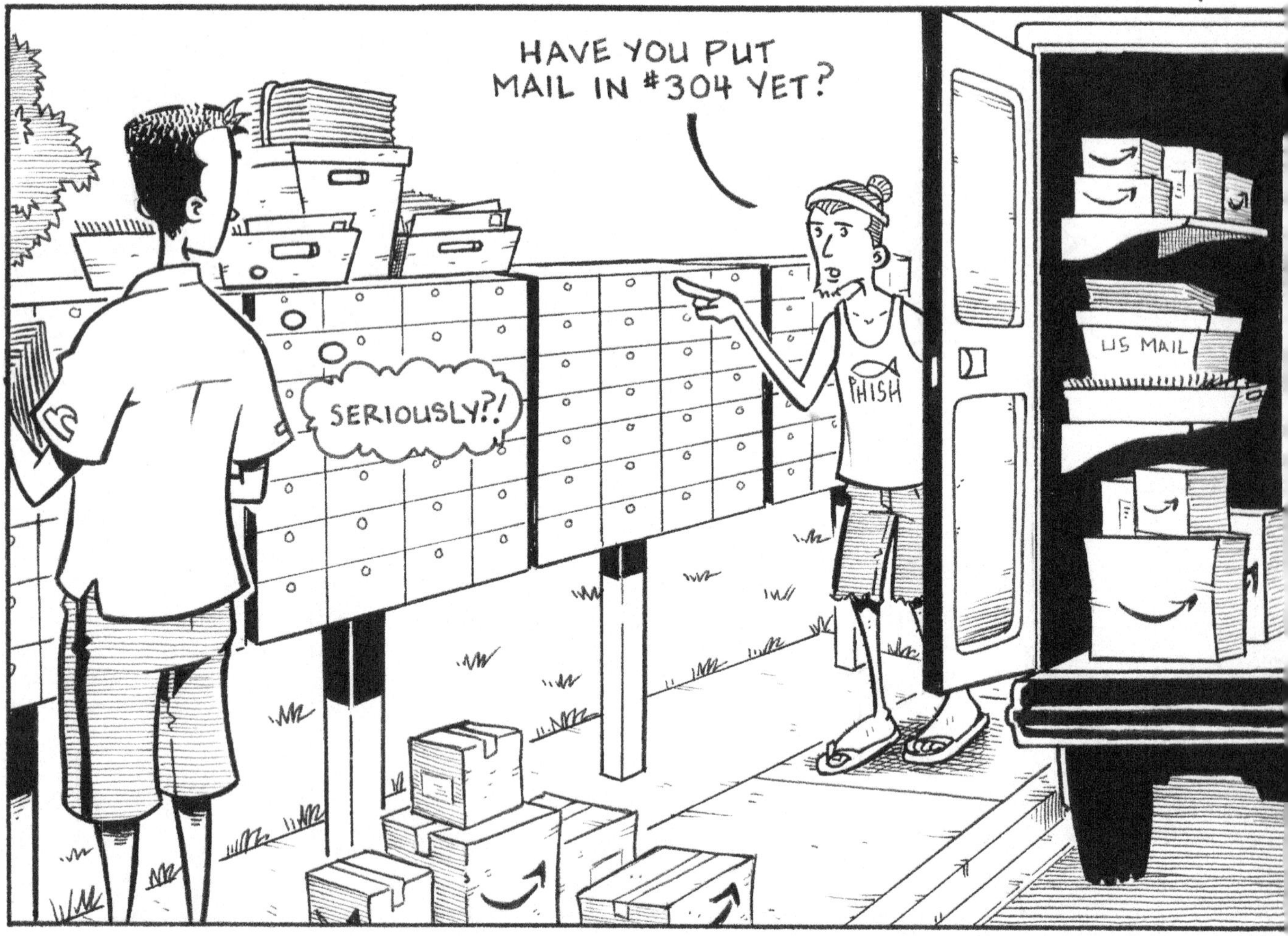

HAVE YOU PUT MAIL IN #304 YET?
SERIOUSLY?!
PHISH
US MAIL

POSTAGE DUE

by flip

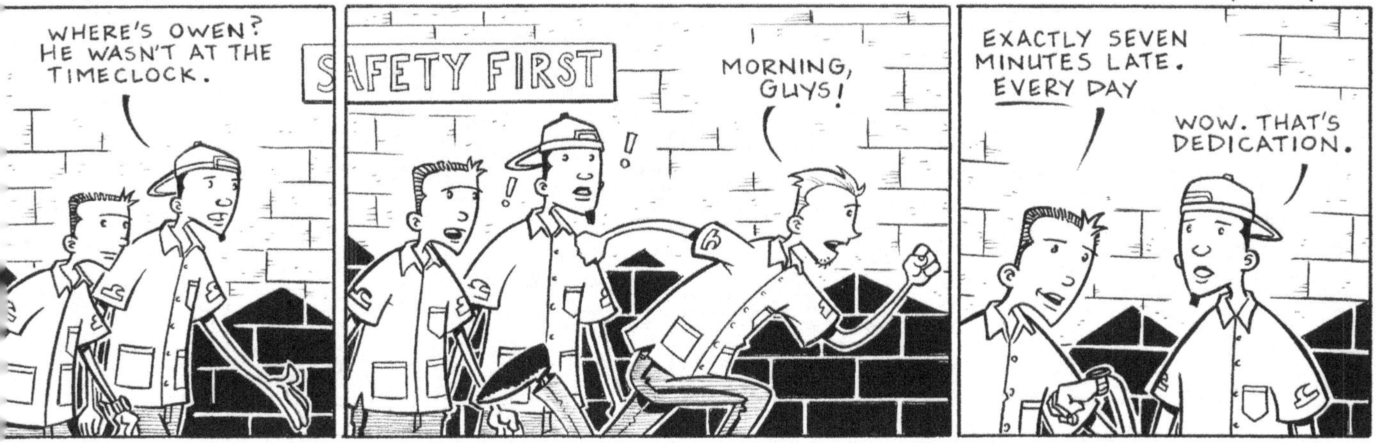
WHERE'S OWEN? HE WASN'T AT THE TIMECLOCK.
SAFETY FIRST
MORNING, GUYS!
!
!
EXACTLY SEVEN MINUTES LATE. EVERY DAY
WOW. THAT'S DEDICATION.

POSTAGE DUE

by flip

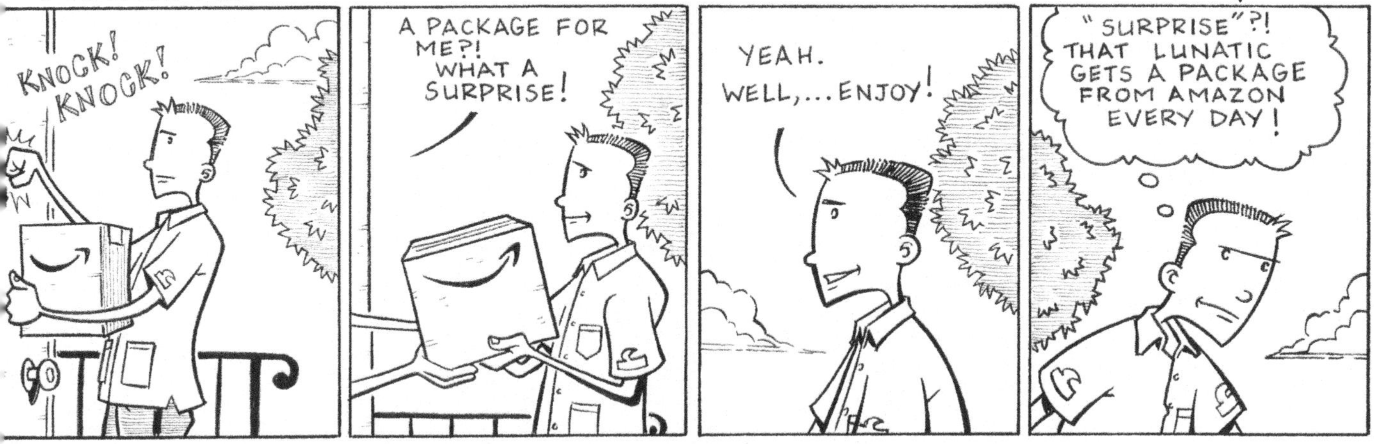
KNOCK! KNOCK!
A PACKAGE FOR ME?! WHAT A SURPRISE!
YEAH. WELL,... ENJOY!
"SURPRISE"?! THAT LUNATIC GETS A PACKAGE FROM AMAZON EVERY DAY!

POSTAGE DUE

by flip

IT'S MY THREE-DAY WEEKEND!
SEE YA MONDAY, CHUMPS!
HONEY DO LIST
IS IT MONDAY YET?
PAI

POSTAGE DUE

by flip

GOOD MORNING HON DID YOU SEE WHERE THE TELEPHONE COMPANY CAME AND DUG UP THE YARD TO PUT IN NEW CABLE? THEY TORE UP ALL THE SOD WE JUST PUT D N AND I TOLD THEM IT'S NOT
RIGHT TO JUST THROW GRASS SEED DOWN WHEN THEY'RE DONE FILLING IN THE HOLE WE WORK HARD TO KEEP OUR YARD LOOKING NICE AND IT'S NOT FAIR I TO THE THEY HA O COM K A A
nod nod
US MAIL
BETTER JOB OF SEEDING THEY THINK IT'S ENOUGH TO JUST THROW STRAW DOWN BUT THE THE STRAW BLOWS ALL OVER THE PLACE AND THEY CRACKED THE SIDEWALK WIT IR BACKHOE AND LLED
nod nod
THE CITY AND THEY SAID THEY HAVE TO FIX THE SIDEWALK THEY'RE RESPONSIBLE FOR THAT NOT US AND THE KIDS ACROSS THE STREET KEEP HITTING THE CAR WITH R BALL AND THE
whew
US MAIL

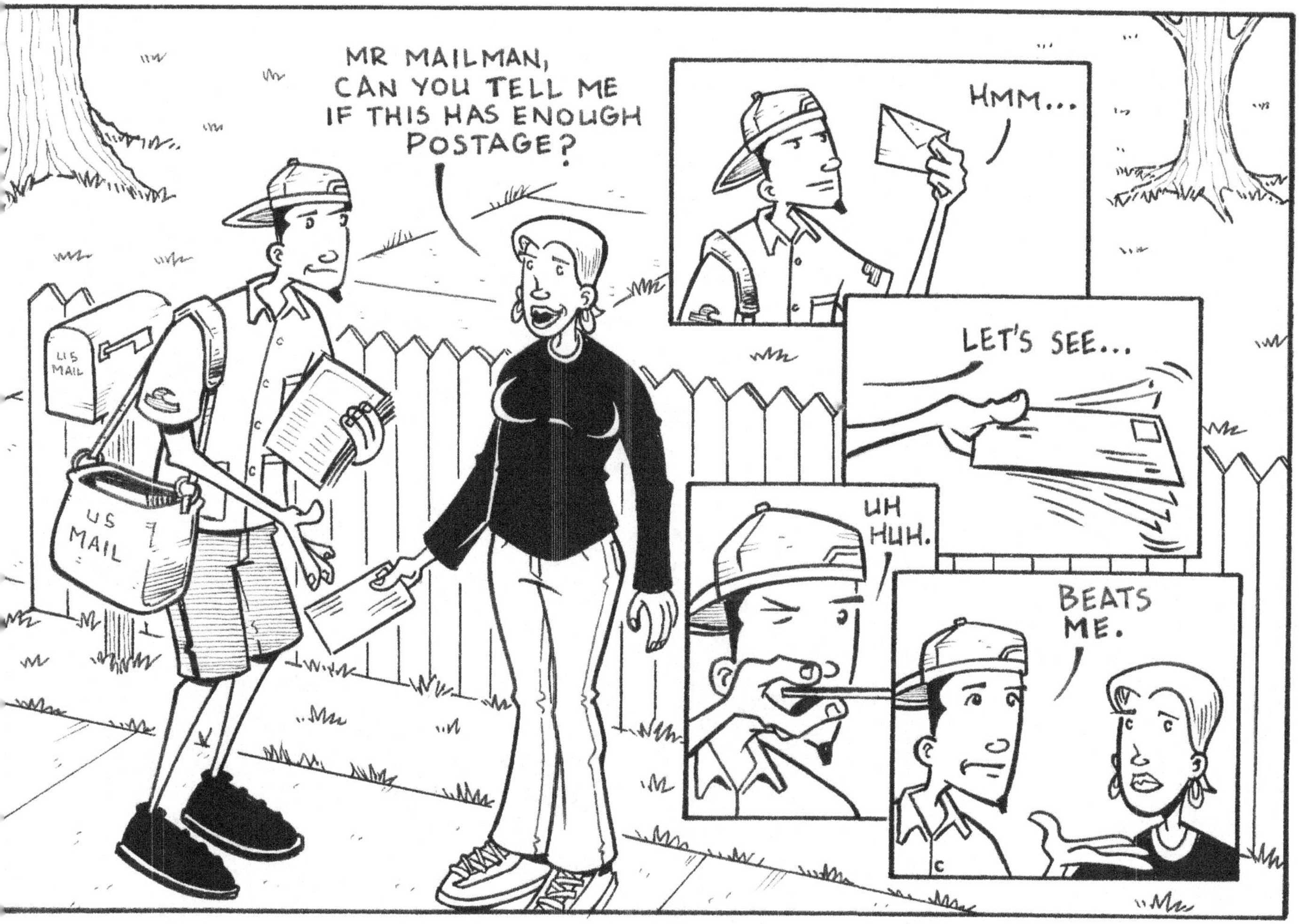
MR MAILMAN, CAN YOU TELL ME IF THIS HAS ENOUGH POSTAGE?
US MAIL
US MAIL
HMM...
LET'S SEE...
UH HUH.
BEATS ME.

DELIVER ME! by flip

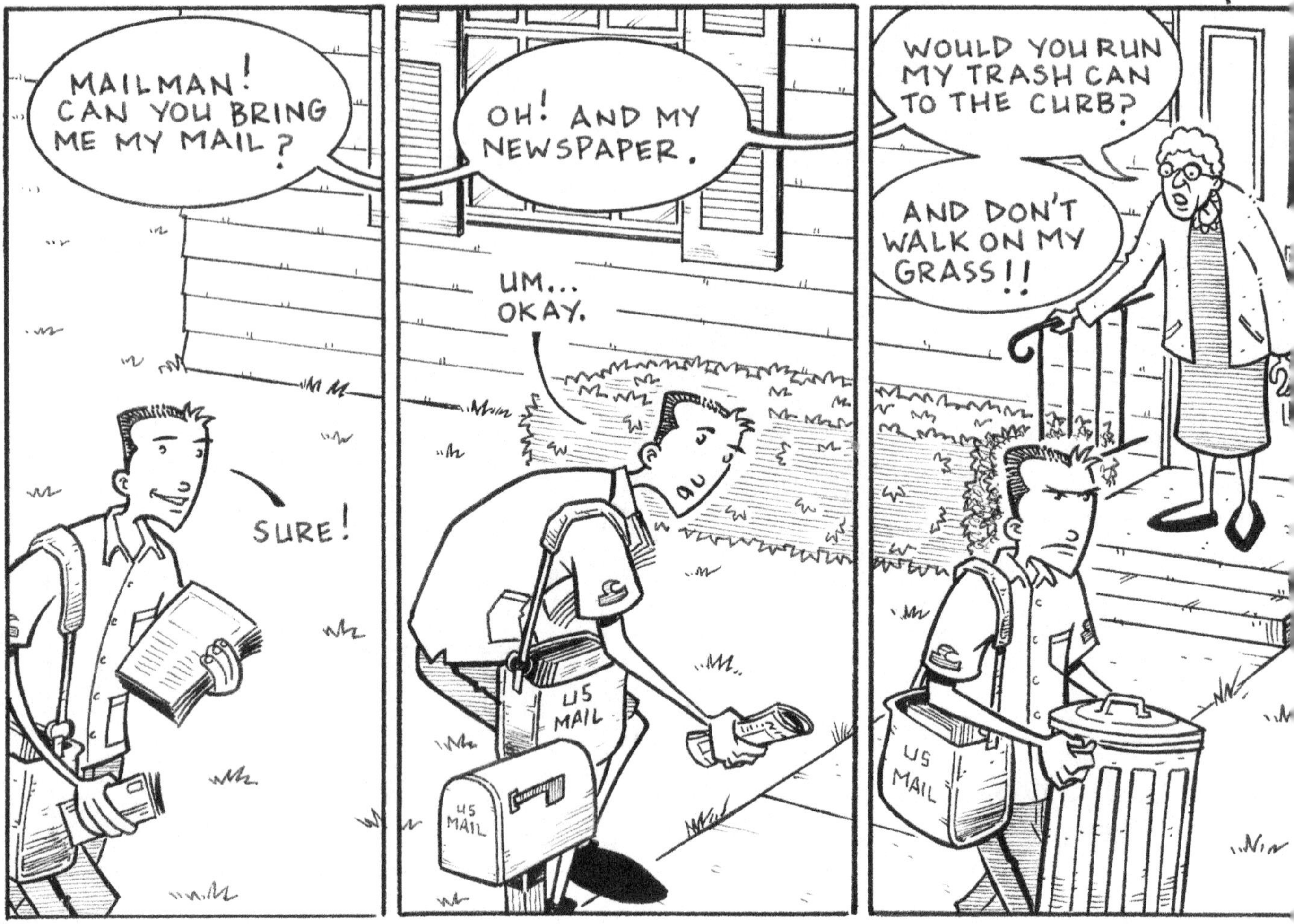
MAILMAN! CAN YOU BRING ME MY MAIL?
SURE!
OH! AND MY NEWSPAPER.
UM... OKAY.
US MAIL
US MAIL
WOULD YOU RUN MY TRASH CAN TO THE CURB?
AND DON'T WALK ON MY GRASS!!
US MAIL

POSTAGE DUE by flip

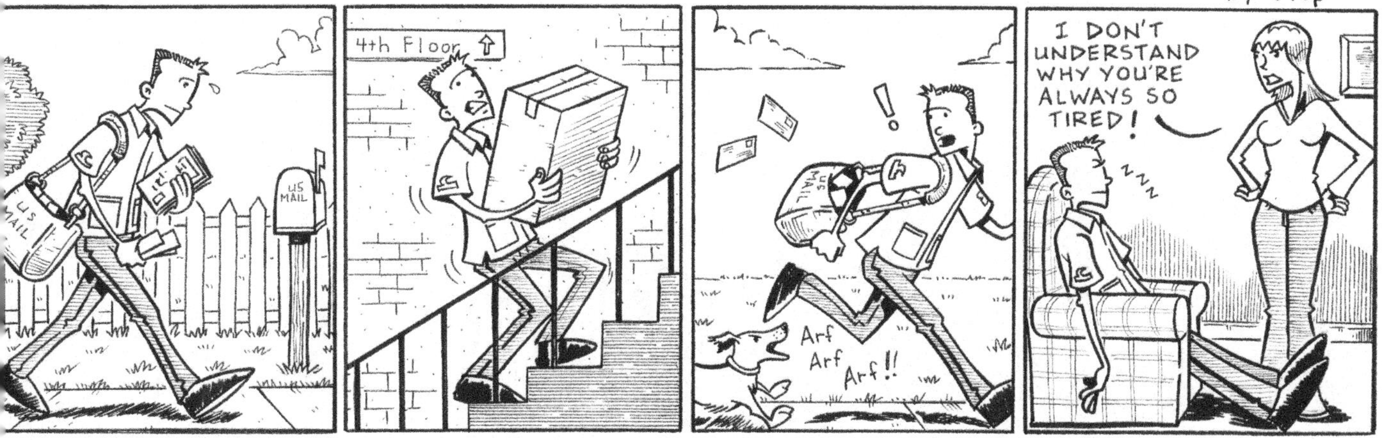
US MAIL
US MAIL
4th Floor
!
US MAIL
Arf
Arf
Arf!!
I DON'T UNDERSTAND WHY YOU'RE ALWAYS SO TIRED!
Z Z Z

POSTAGE DUE by flip

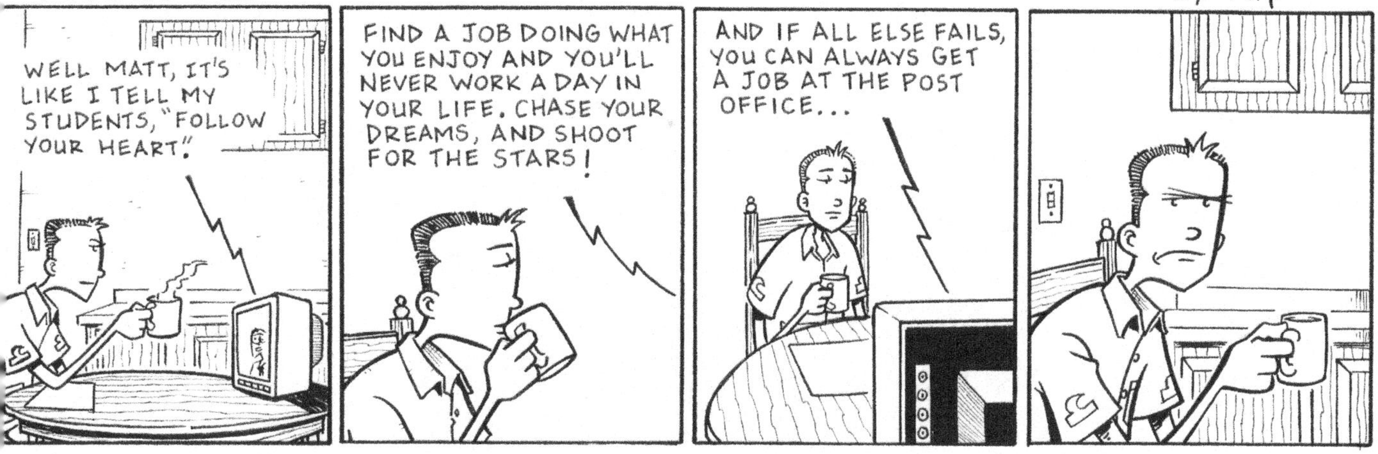
WELL MATT, IT'S LIKE I TELL MY STUDENTS, "FOLLOW YOUR HEART."
FIND A JOB DOING WHAT YOU ENJOY AND YOU'LL NEVER WORK A DAY IN YOUR LIFE. CHASE YOUR DREAMS, AND SHOOT FOR THE STARS!
AND IF ALL ELSE FAILS, YOU CAN ALWAYS GET A JOB AT THE POST OFFICE...

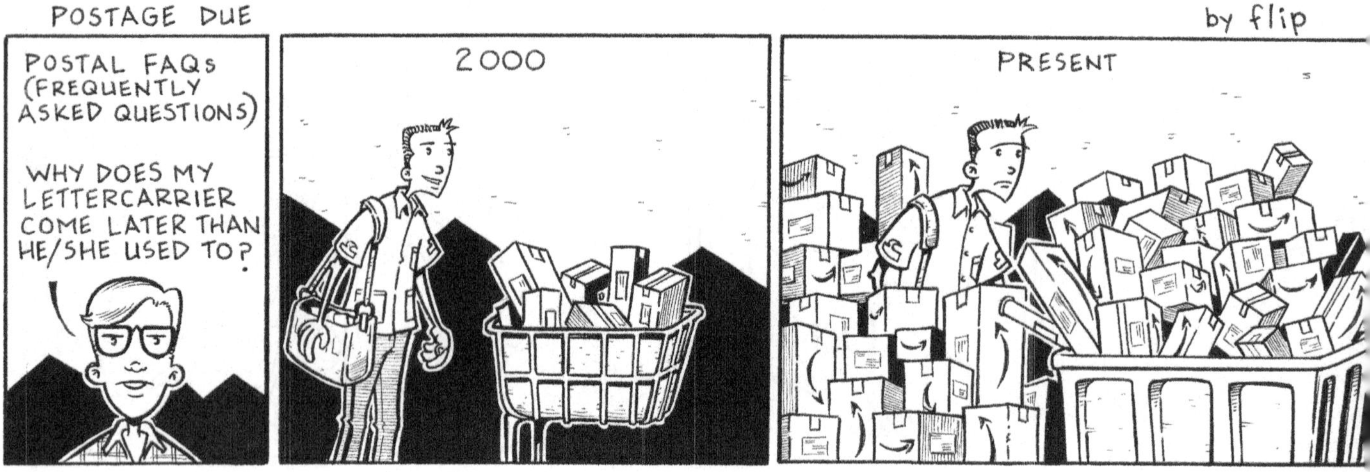
POSTAGE DUE
by flip
POSTAL FAQs (FREQUENTLY ASKED QUESTIONS)
WHY DOES MY LETTERCARRIER COME LATER THAN HE/SHE USED TO?
2000
PRESENT

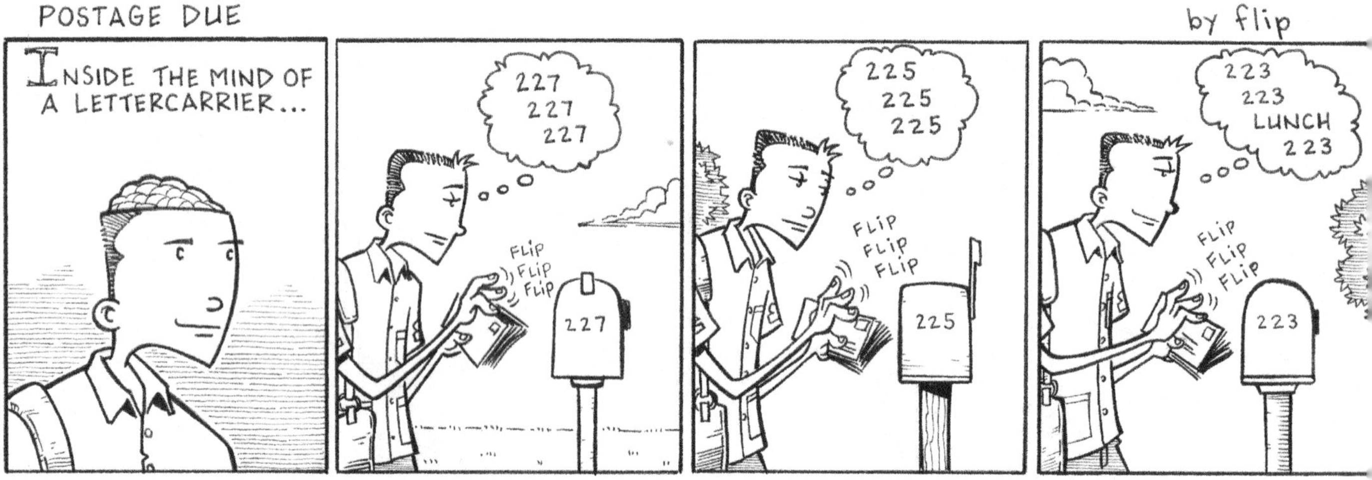
POSTAGE DUE
by flip
INSIDE THE MIND OF A LETTERCARRIER...
227 227 227
FLIP FLIP FLIP
227
225 225 225
FLIP FLIP FLIP
225
223 223 LUNCH 223
FLIP FLIP FLIP
223

DELIVER ME!

by flip

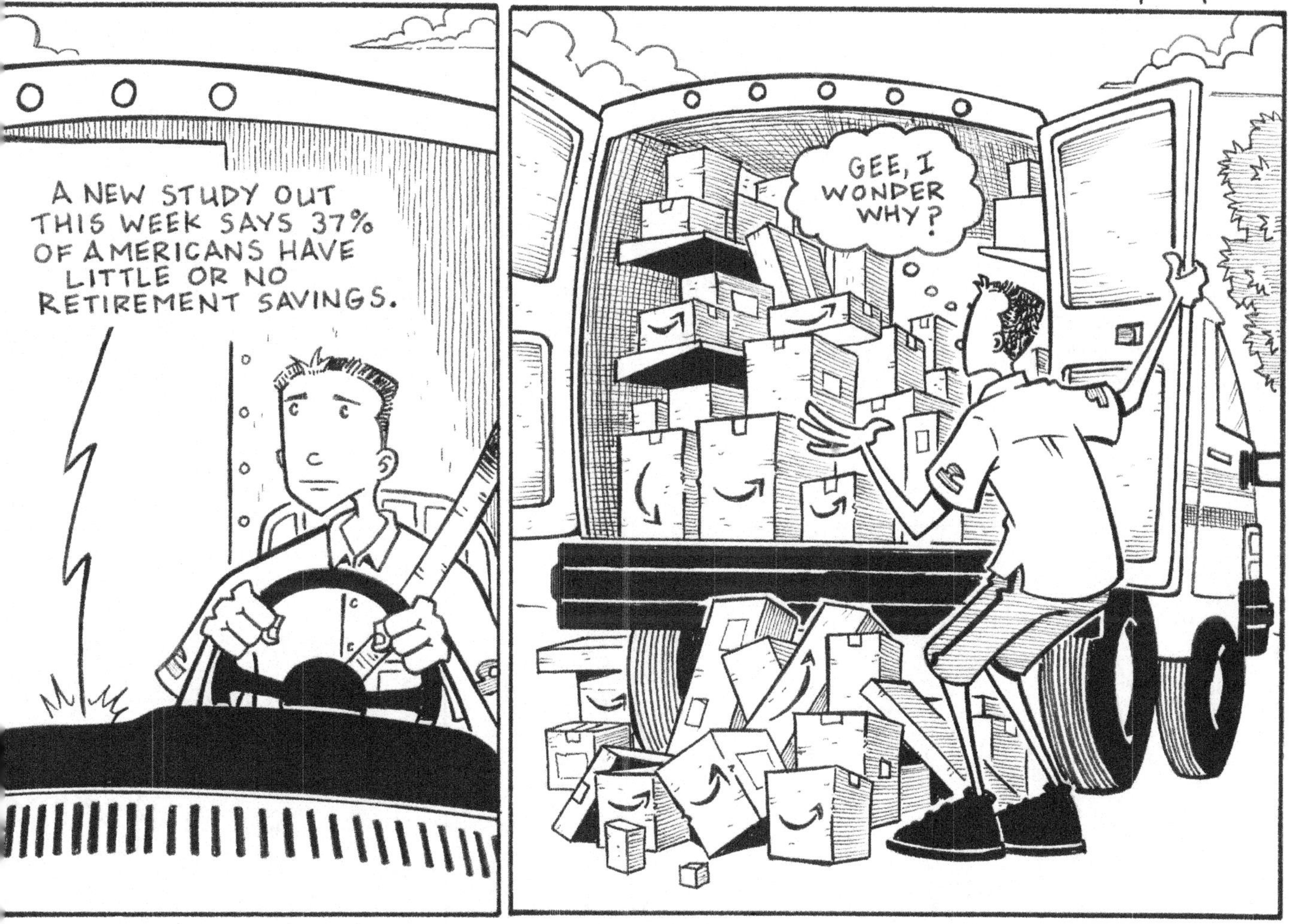
A NEW STUDY OUT THIS WEEK SAYS 37% OF AMERICANS HAVE LITTLE OR NO RETIREMENT SAVINGS.
GEE, I WONDER WHY?

POSTAGE DUE

by flip

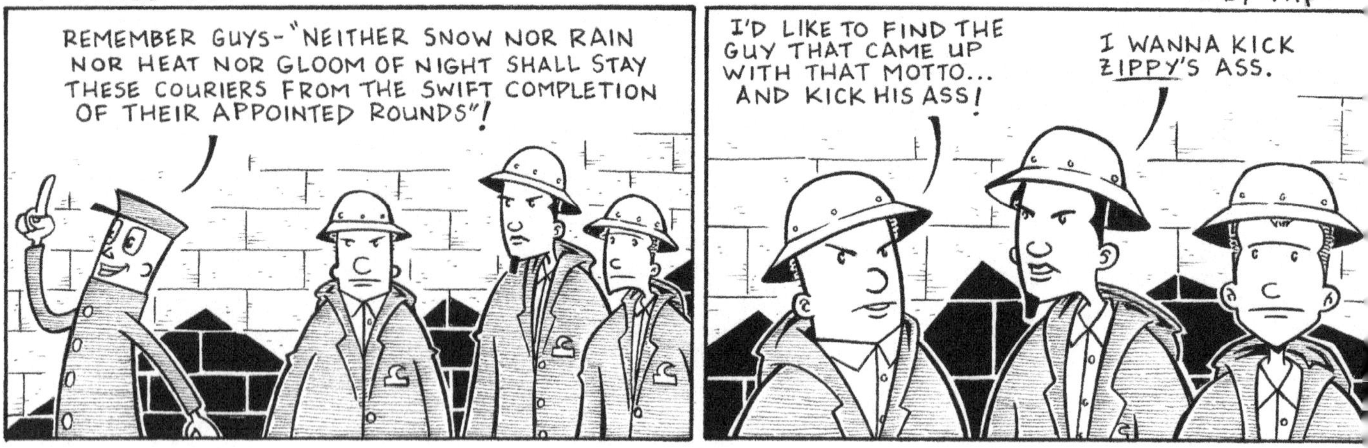

REMEMBER GUYS- "NEITHER SNOW NOR RAIN NOR HEAT NOR GLOOM OF NIGHT SHALL STAY THESE COURIERS FROM THE SWIFT COMPLETION OF THEIR APPOINTED ROUNDS"!
I'D LIKE TO FIND THE GUY THAT CAME UP WITH THAT MOTTO... AND KICK HIS ASS!
I WANNA KICK ZIPPY'S ASS.

POSTAGE DUE

by flip

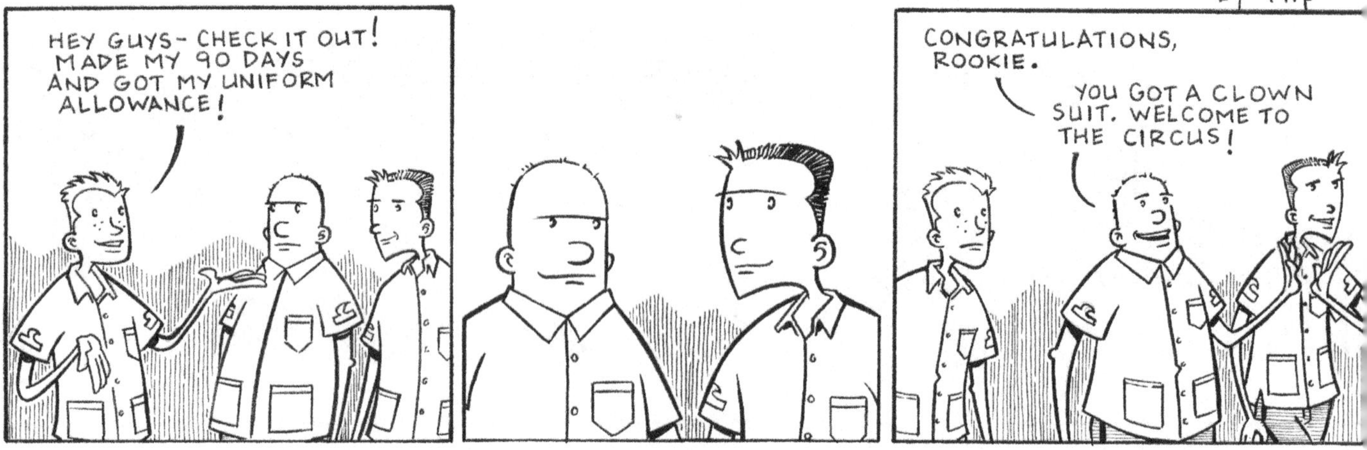

HEY GUYS- CHECK IT OUT! MADE MY 90 DAYS AND GOT MY UNIFORM ALLOWANCE!
CONGRATULATIONS, ROOKIE.
YOU GOT A CLOWN SUIT. WELCOME TO THE CIRCUS!

DELIVER ME! by flip

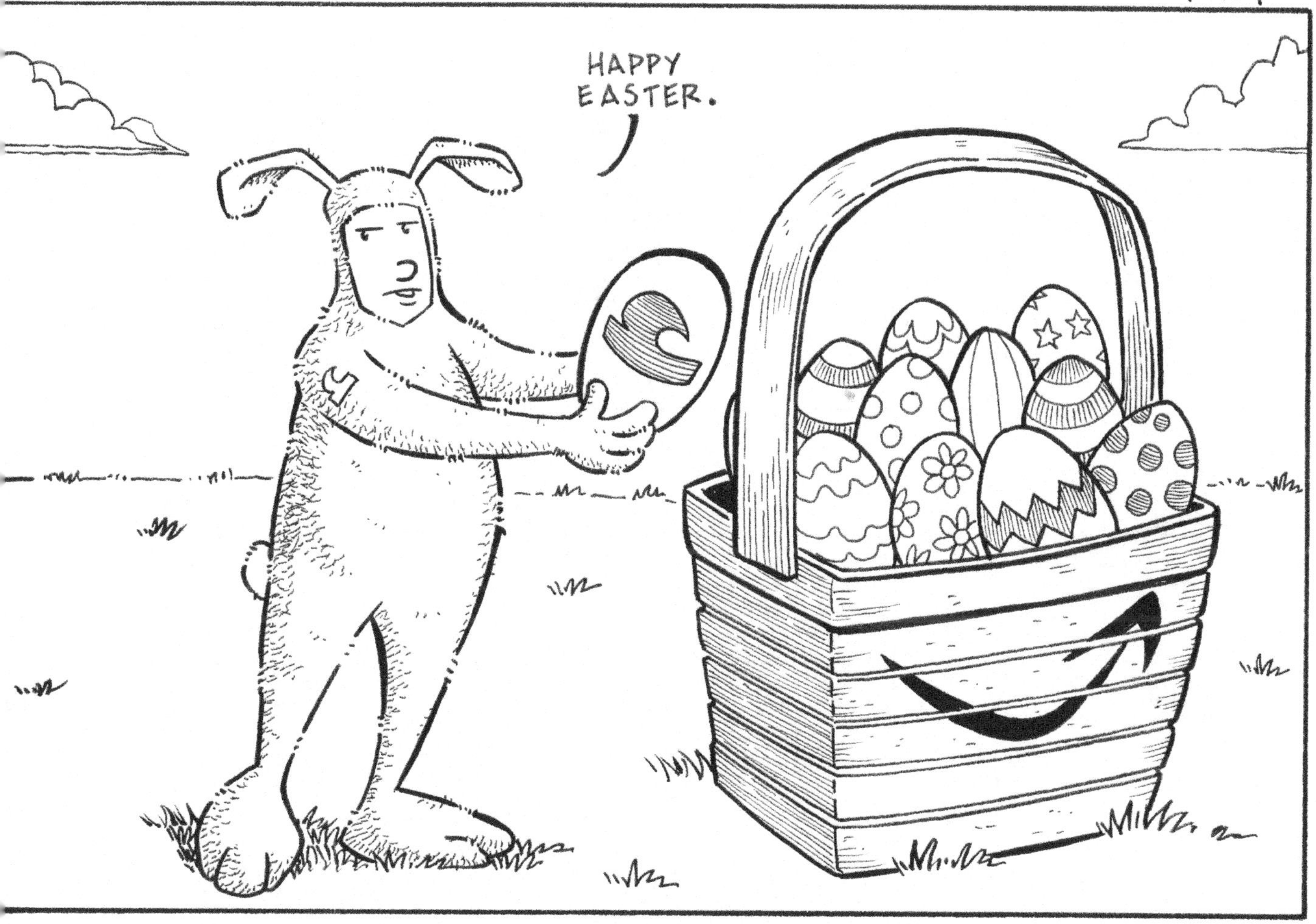
HAPPY EASTER.

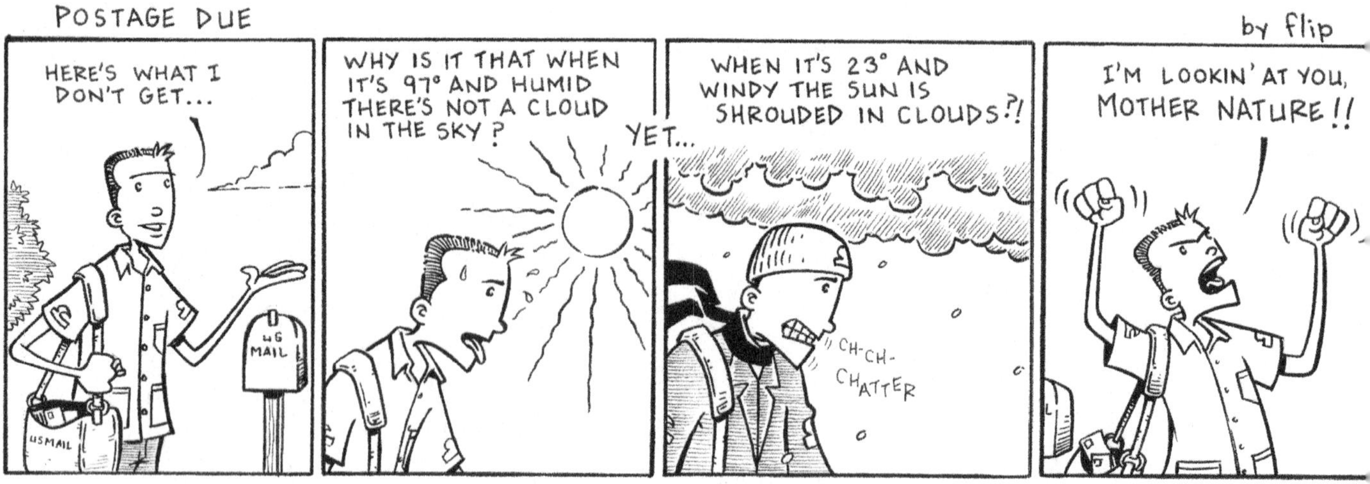
POSTAGE DUE
by flip
HERE'S WHAT I DON'T GET...
US MAIL
MAIL
WHY IS IT THAT WHEN IT'S 97° AND HUMID THERE'S NOT A CLOUD IN THE SKY?
YET...
WHEN IT'S 23° AND WINDY THE SUN IS SHROUDED IN CLOUDS?!
CH-CH-CHATTER
I'M LOOKIN' AT YOU, MOTHER NATURE!!

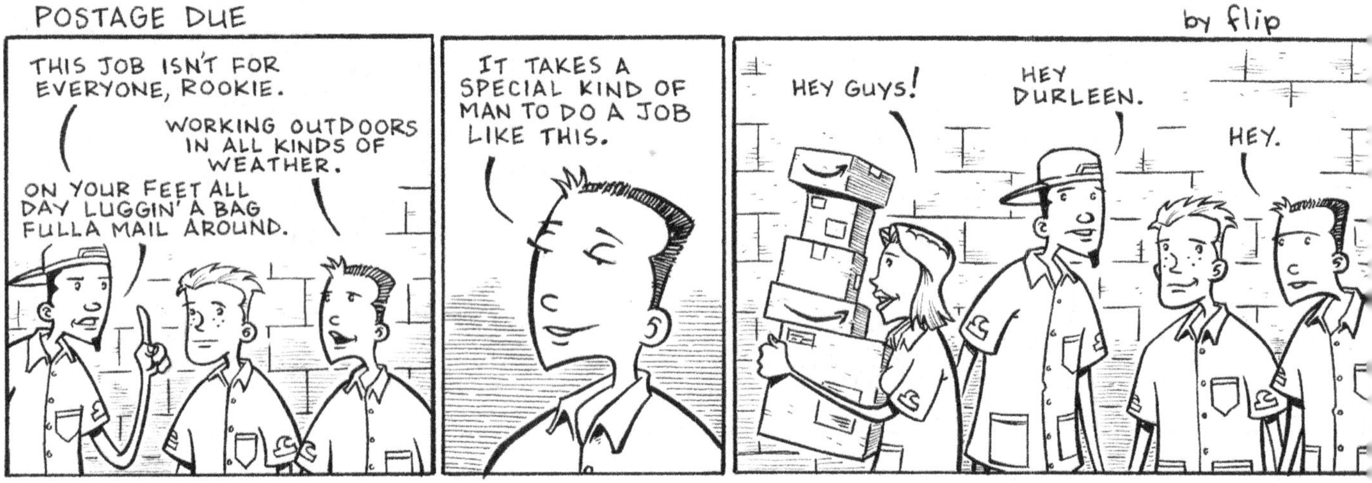
POSTAGE DUE
by flip
THIS JOB ISN'T FOR EVERYONE, ROOKIE.
ON YOUR FEET ALL DAY LUGGIN' A BAG FULLA MAIL AROUND.
WORKING OUTDOORS IN ALL KINDS OF WEATHER.
IT TAKES A SPECIAL KIND OF MAN TO DO A JOB LIKE THIS.
HEY GUYS!
HEY DURLEEN.
HEY.

DELIVER ME!

by flip

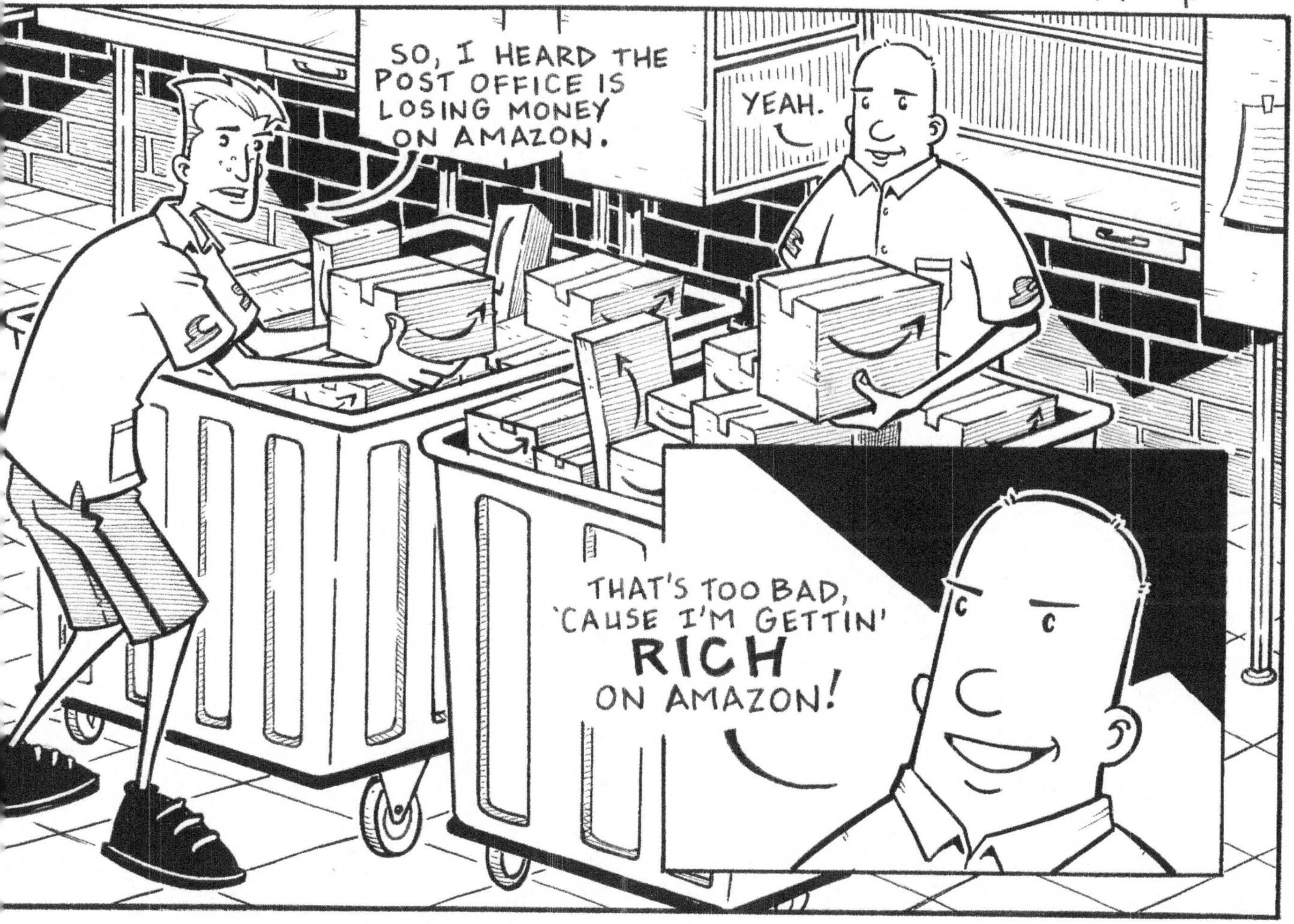

SO, I HEARD THE POST OFFICE IS LOSING MONEY ON AMAZON.
YEAH.
THAT'S TOO BAD, 'CAUSE I'M GETTIN' RICH ON AMAZON!

POSTAGE DUE

by flip

MAIL
US MAIL
WALK
WALK
WALK
WALK
WALK
US MAIL
WALK
WALK
WALK
US MAIL
US MAIL
WALK
WALK
OH, YOU'RE HOME!
WANNA GO FOR A WALK?

DELIVER ME!

by flip

FROM OUR DEPARTMENT OF MICRO-MANAGEMENT...
BIG BROTHER IS IN THE BUILDING AND THEY NOTICED YOU WERE HOLDING YOUR FLATS IN YOUR RIGHT ARM INSTEAD OF YOUR LEFT.
YEAH WELL, I'M LEFT-HANDED, SO IT'S QUICKER FOR ME TO RACK IT THIS WAY.
WELL THEY WANT IT DONE THEIR WAY.
OKAY. BUT EVERYTHING IS ALREADY RACKED NOW. SHOULD I PULL IT ALL OUT AND DO IT THE "RIGHT" WAY?
GRUMBLE GRUMBLE

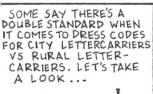

DELIVER ME!

SOME SAY THERE'S A DOUBLE STANDARD WHEN IT COMES TO DRESS CODES FOR CITY LETTER-CARRIERS VS RURAL LETTER-CARRIERS. LET'S TAKE A LOOK...

by flip

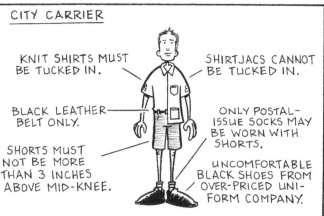

CITY CARRIER

KNIT SHIRTS MUST BE TUCKED IN.

SHIRTJACS CANNOT BE TUCKED IN.

BLACK LEATHER BELT ONLY.

ONLY POSTAL-ISSUE SOCKS MAY BE WORN WITH SHORTS.

SHORTS MUST NOT BE MORE THAN 3 INCHES ABOVE MID-KNEE.

UNCOMFORTABLE BLACK SHOES FROM OVER-PRICED UNIFORM COMPANY.

RURAL CARRIER

WHAT'EVS, DUDE.

DELIVER ME!

by flip

HI! PARCEL FOR YOU.

OUT OF CURIOUSITY, WHAT DOES "POW" STAND FOR?

IT'S THE PACKAGE-OF-THE-WEEK CLUB. FOR A MONTHLY FEE THEY SEND ME A BOX FULL OF STUFF I NEITHER NEED NOR WANT, EVERY WEEK!

POW.

WOW.

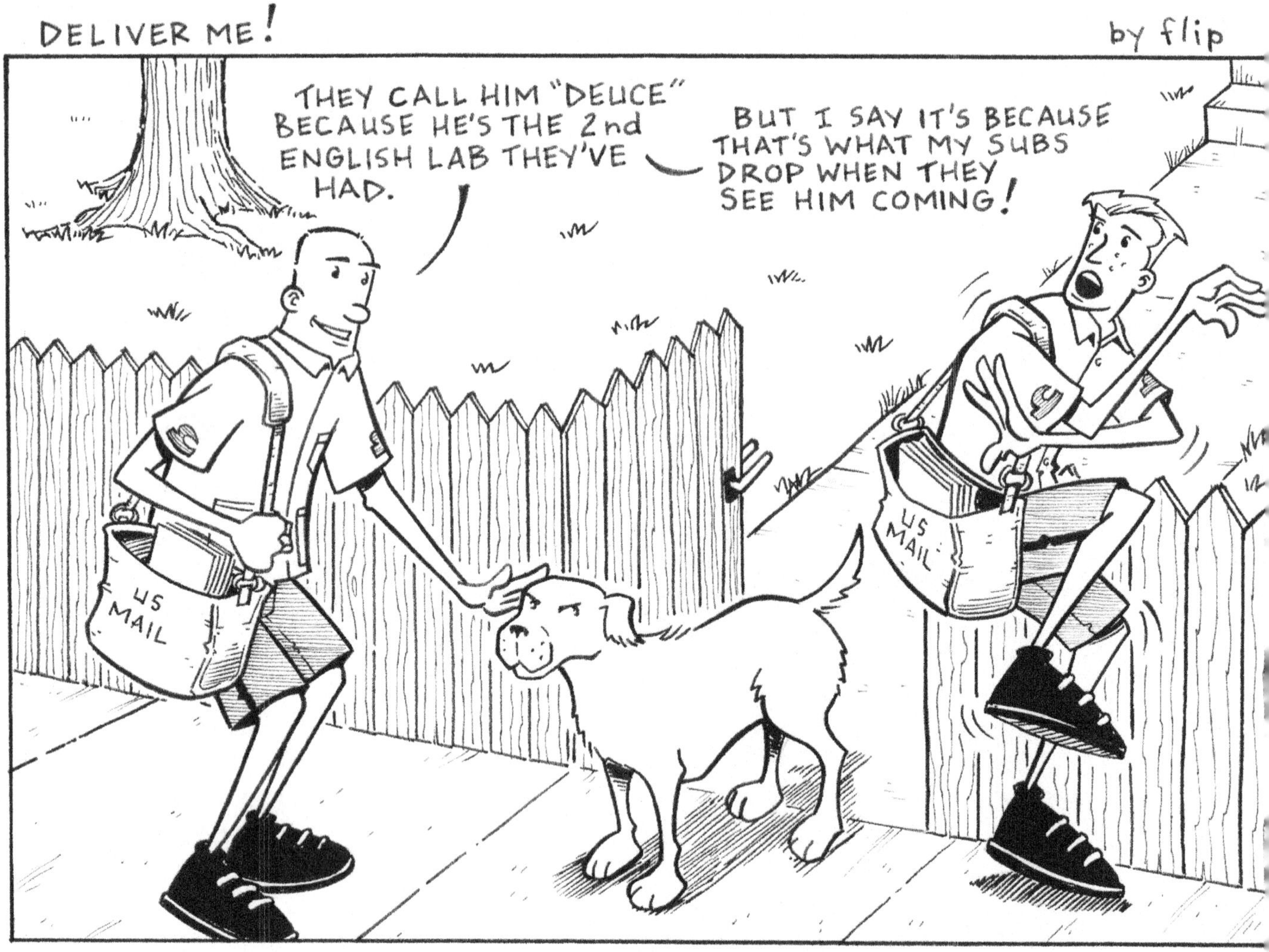
DELIVER ME!
by flip
THEY CALL HIM "DEUCE" BECAUSE HE'S THE 2nd ENGLISH LAB THEY'VE HAD.
BUT I SAY IT'S BECAUSE THAT'S WHAT MY SUBS DROP WHEN THEY SEE HIM COMING!
US MAIL
US MAIL

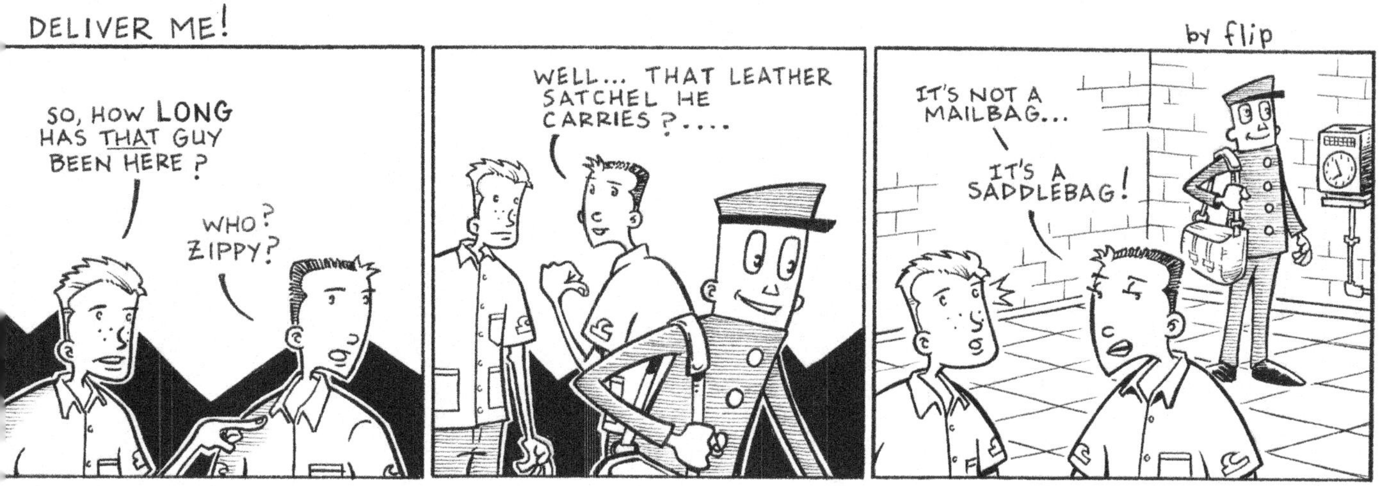
DELIVER ME!
by flip
SO, HOW LONG HAS THAT GUY BEEN HERE?
WHO? ZIPPY?
WELL... THAT LEATHER SATCHEL HE CARRIES?....
IT'S NOT A MAILBAG...
IT'S A SADDLEBAG!

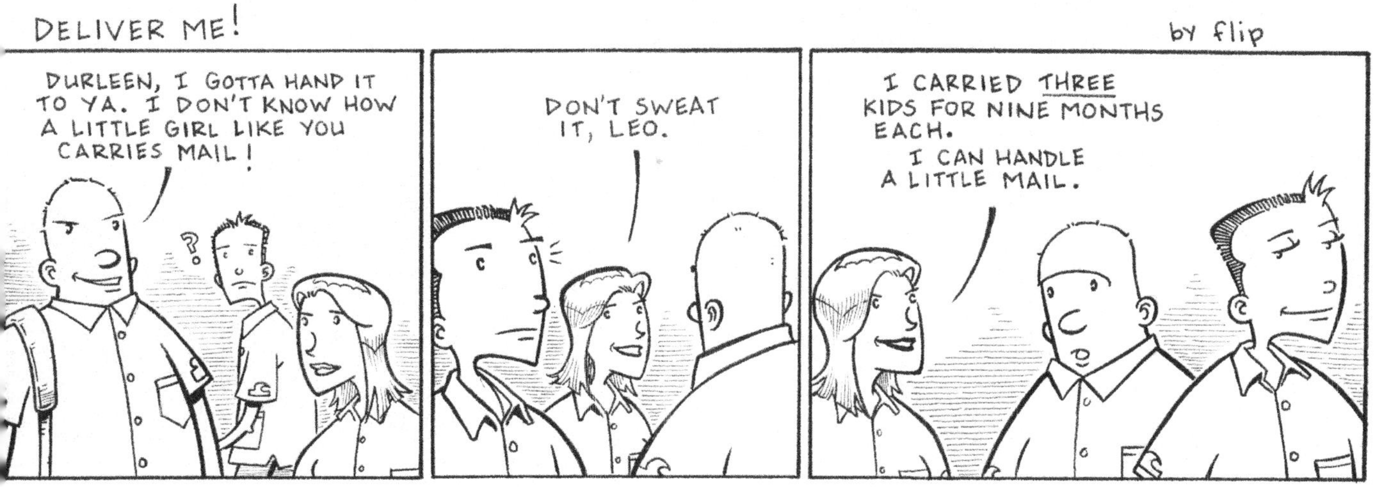
DELIVER ME!
by flip
DURLEEN, I GOTTA HAND IT TO YA. I DON'T KNOW HOW A LITTLE GIRL LIKE YOU CARRIES MAIL!
?
DON'T SWEAT IT, LEO.
I CARRIED THREE KIDS FOR NINE MONTHS EACH.
I CAN HANDLE A LITTLE MAIL.

DELIVER ME!

by flip

OUR OFFICE IS IN THE PROCESS OF IMPLEMENTING AN AUTOMATED SICK CALL SYSTEM....

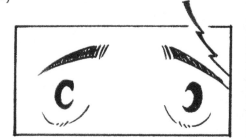

THANK YOU FOR CALLING THE POSTAL SERVICE SICK CALL CENTER.

IF YOU ARE TIRED OF BEING FORCED TO CARRY YOUR ROUTE AND PART OF ANOTHER EVERY DAY, PRESS "1"

IF YOUR FEET ARE SORE FROM WALKING 5 MILES A DAY IN UNCOMFORTABLE UNIFORM COMPANY SHOES, PRESS "2"

IF YOUR SON/DAUGHTER HAS A BALL GAME TODAY, PRESS "3"

UB,... I'B JUS' SICK?

32

DELIVER ME!

by flip

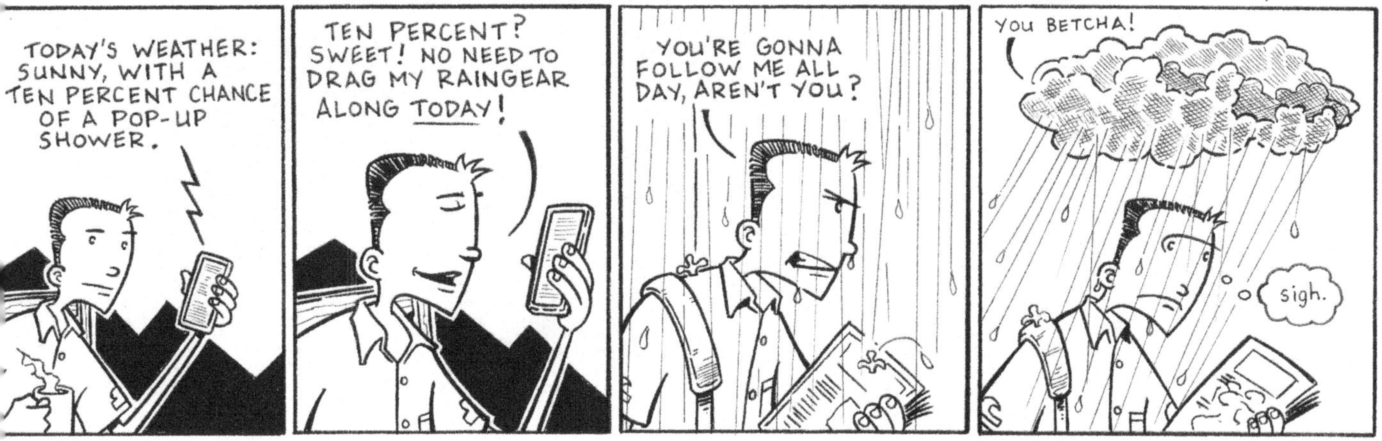

TODAY'S WEATHER: SUNNY, WITH A TEN PERCENT CHANCE OF A POP-UP SHOWER.
TEN PERCENT? SWEET! NO NEED TO DRAG MY RAINGEAR ALONG TODAY!
YOU'RE GONNA FOLLOW ME ALL DAY, AREN'T YOU?
YOU BETCHA!
sigh.

DELIVER ME!

by flip

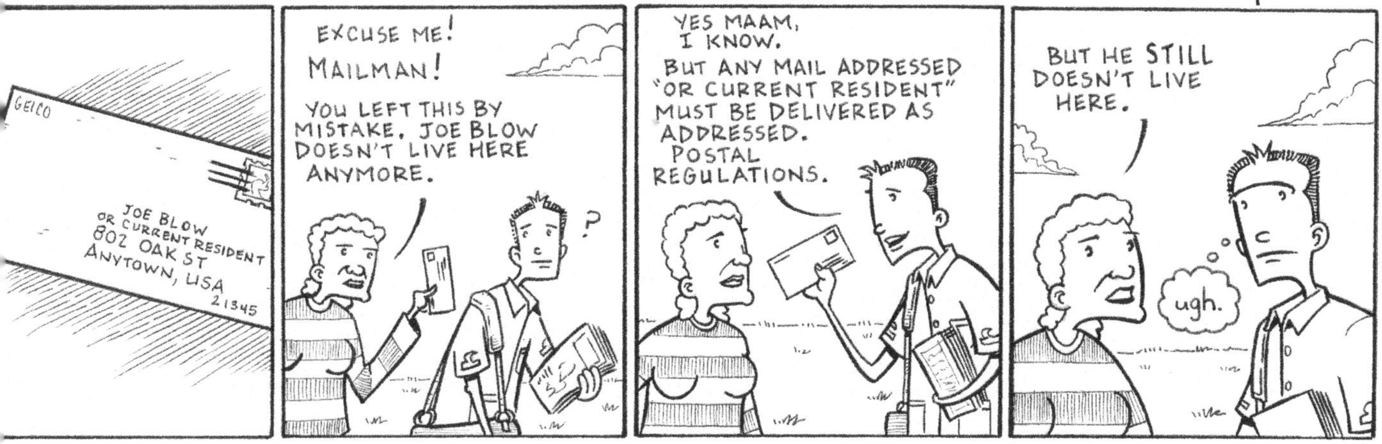

GEICO
JOE BLOW OR CURRENT RESIDENT 802 OAK ST ANYTOWN, USA 21345
EXCUSE ME!
MAILMAN!
YOU LEFT THIS BY MISTAKE. JOE BLOW DOESN'T LIVE HERE ANYMORE.
?
YES MAAM, I KNOW.
BUT ANY MAIL ADDRESSED "OR CURRENT RESIDENT" MUST BE DELIVERED AS ADDRESSED. POSTAL REGULATIONS.
BUT HE STILL DOESN'T LIVE HERE.
ugh.

DELIVER ME!

by flip

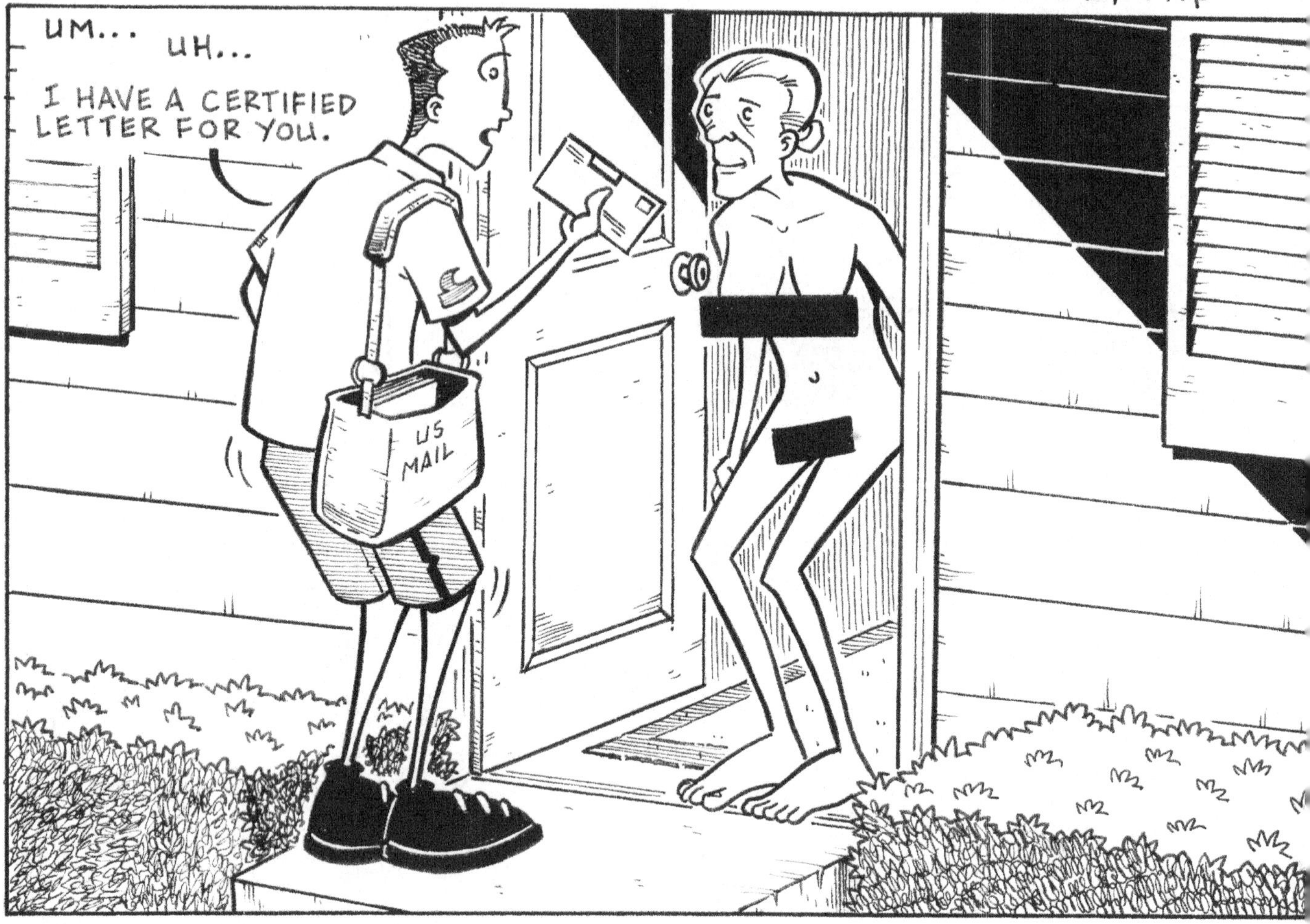
UM... UH...
I HAVE A CERTIFIED LETTER FOR YOU.
US MAIL

DELIVER ME!

by flip

I CAN'T WAIT FOR MY DAY OFF.
I NEED YOU TO WORK YOUR DAY OFF.
I CAN'T WAIT FOR MY HOLIDAY OFF!
I NEED YOU TO WORK YOUR HOLIDAY.
I CAN'T WAIT FOR....
OH FORGET IT!!

DELIVER ME!

by flip

redplum IS A WEEKLY MAILING CONSISTING OF STORE ADS SLOPPILY PUT TOGETHER. LETTERCARRIERS DREAD REDPLUM DAY. HERE'S WHY...
redplum
PIZZA!
TYPICAL DAY....
SHOOBY DOOBY DO
US MAIL
redplum DAY...
UNGH! I THINK I JUST STRAINED MY REDPLUMS!
US MAIL

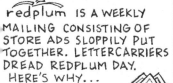

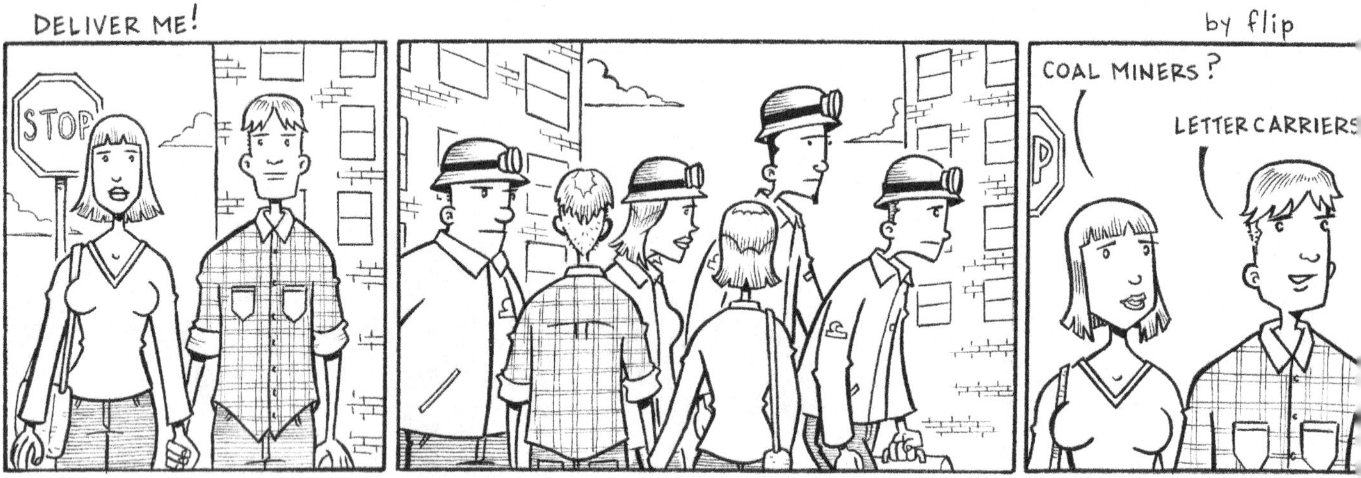
DELIVER ME!
by flip
STOP
COAL MINERS?
LETTER CARRIERS

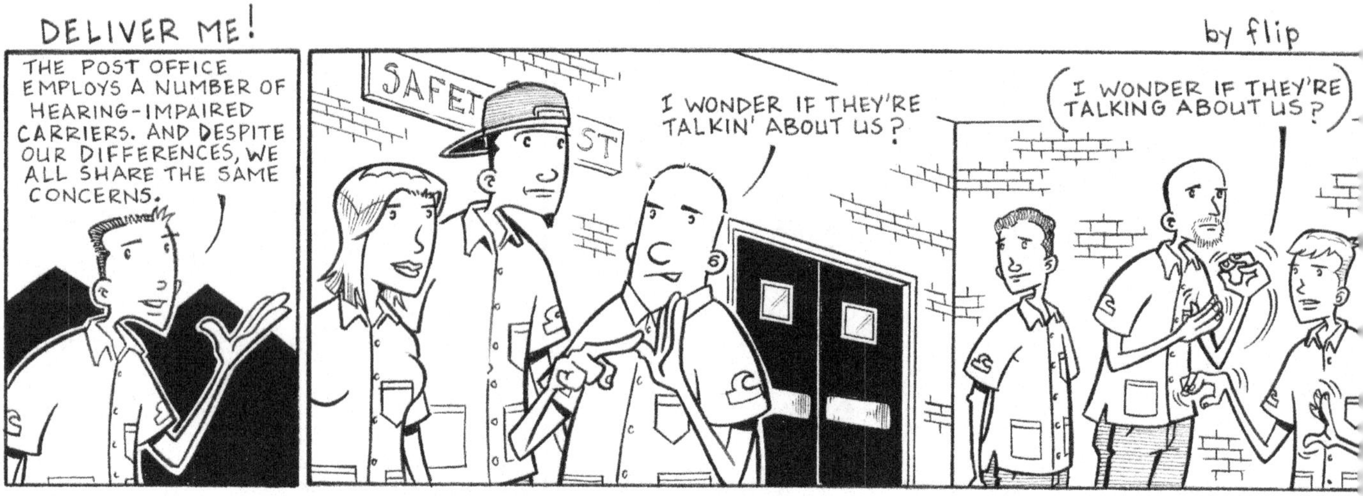
DELIVER ME!
by flip
THE POST OFFICE EMPLOYS A NUMBER OF HEARING-IMPAIRED CARRIERS. AND DESPITE OUR DIFFERENCES, WE ALL SHARE THE SAME CONCERNS.
I WONDER IF THEY'RE TALKIN' ABOUT US?
I WONDER IF THEY'RE TALKING ABOUT US?

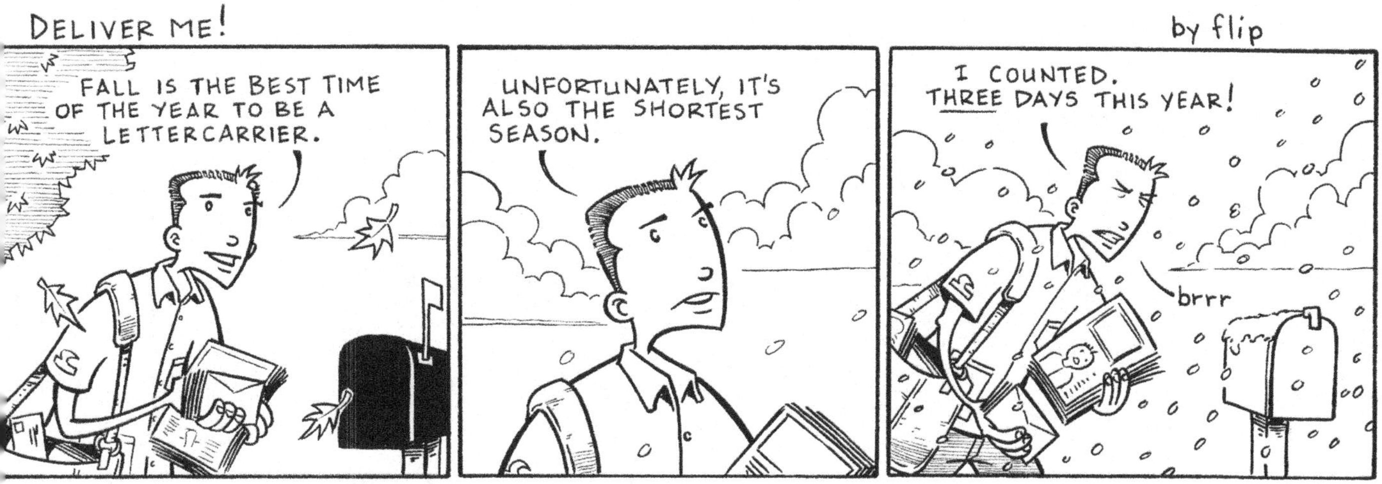
DELIVER ME!
by flip
FALL IS THE BEST TIME OF THE YEAR TO BE A LETTERCARRIER.
UNFORTUNATELY, IT'S ALSO THE SHORTEST SEASON.
I COUNTED. THREE DAYS THIS YEAR!
brrr

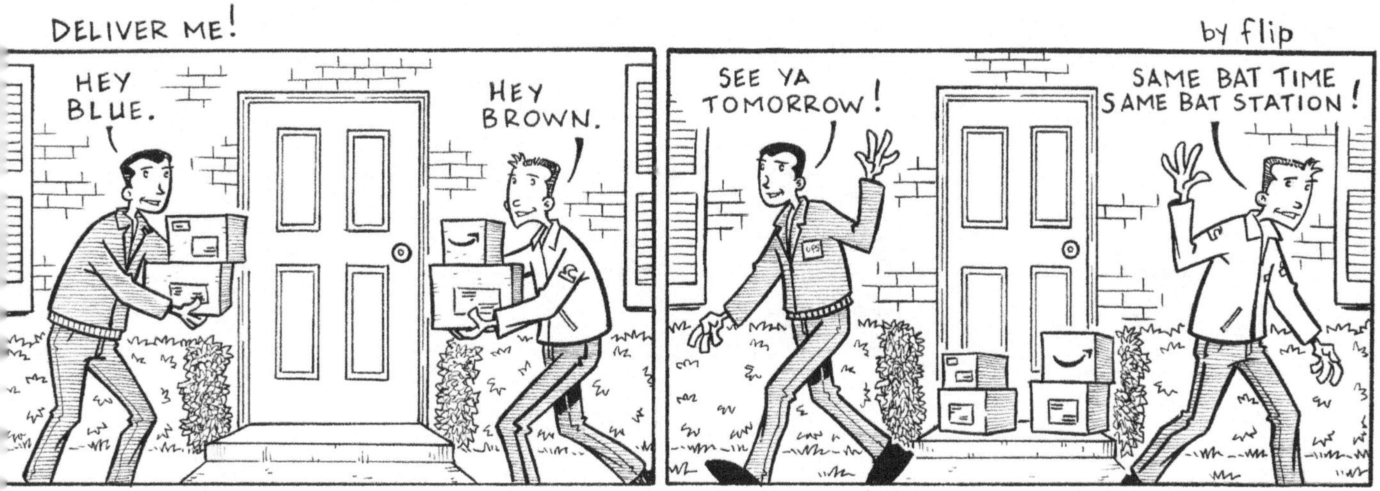
DELIVER ME!
by flip
HEY BLUE.
HEY BROWN.
SEE YA TOMORROW!
SAME BAT TIME SAME BAT STATION!

DELIVER ME! by flip

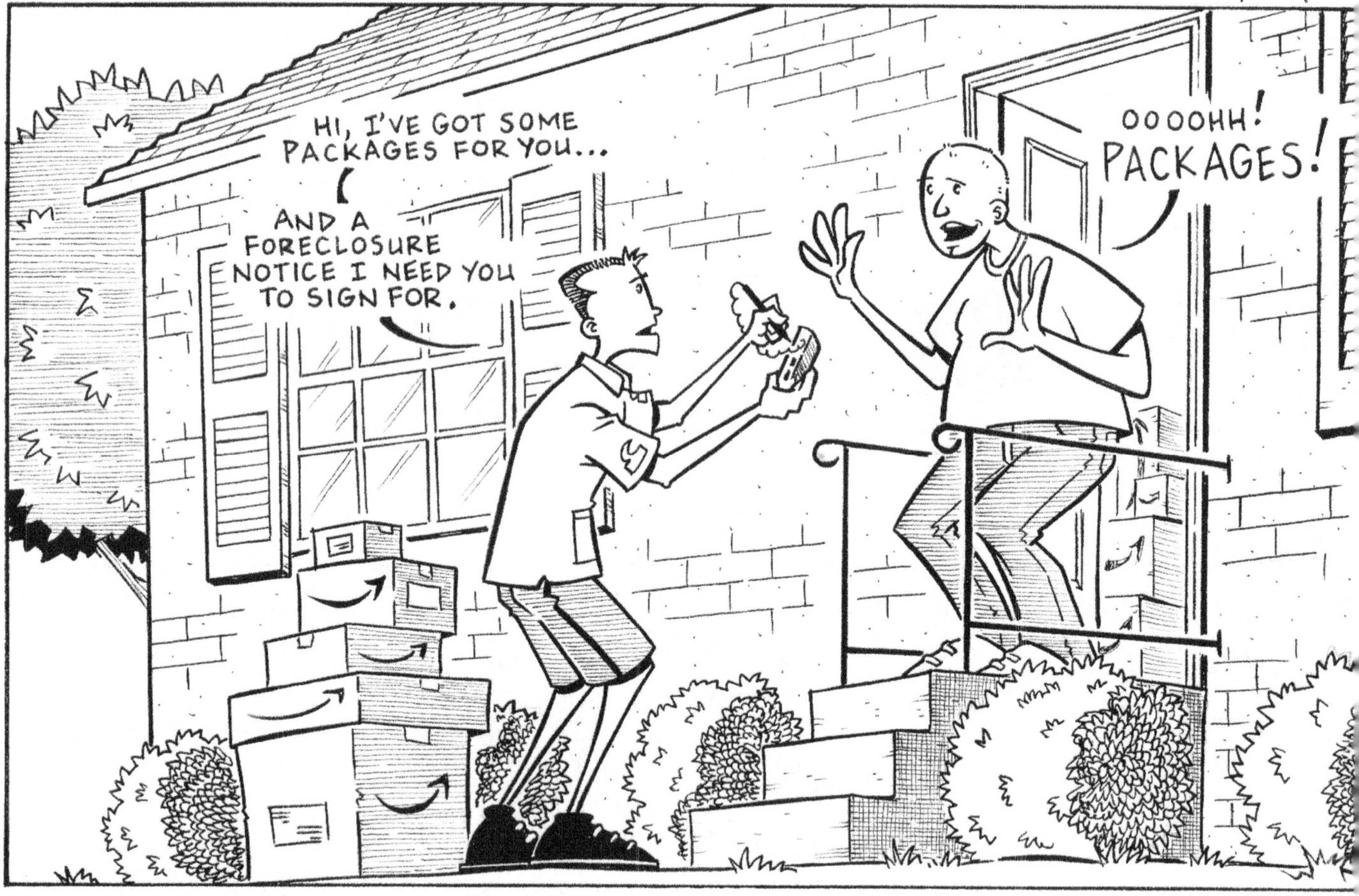
HI, I'VE GOT SOME PACKAGES FOR YOU...
AND A FORECLOSURE NOTICE I NEED YOU TO SIGN FOR.
OOOOHH! PACKAGES!

DELIVER ME! by flip

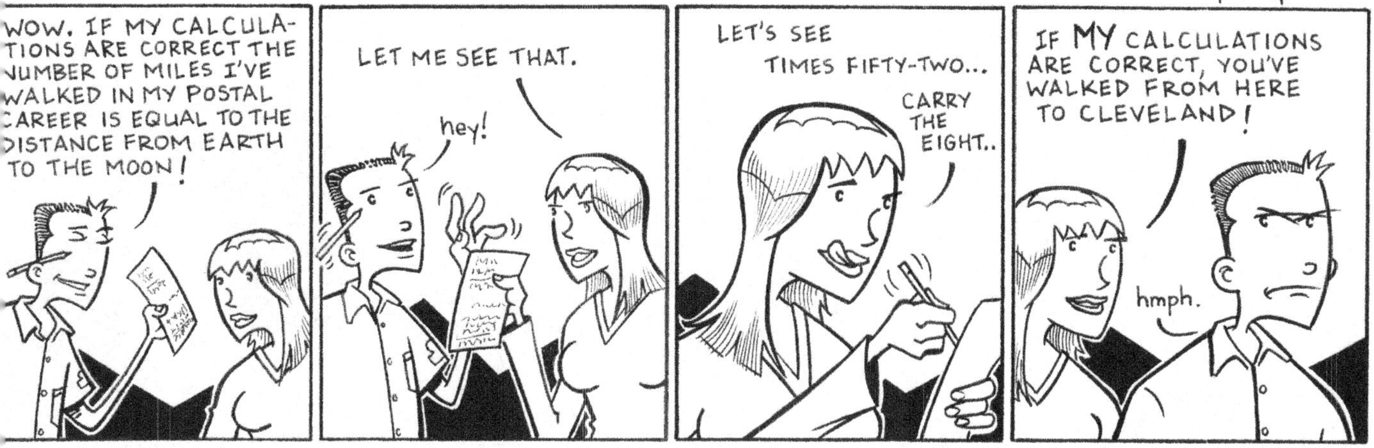

WOW. IF MY CALCULATIONS ARE CORRECT THE NUMBER OF MILES I'VE WALKED IN MY POSTAL CAREER IS EQUAL TO THE DISTANCE FROM EARTH TO THE MOON!
LET ME SEE THAT.
hey!
LET'S SEE
TIMES FIFTY-TWO...
CARRY THE EIGHT..
IF MY CALCULATIONS ARE CORRECT, YOU'VE WALKED FROM HERE TO CLEVELAND!
hmph.

DELIVER ME! by flip

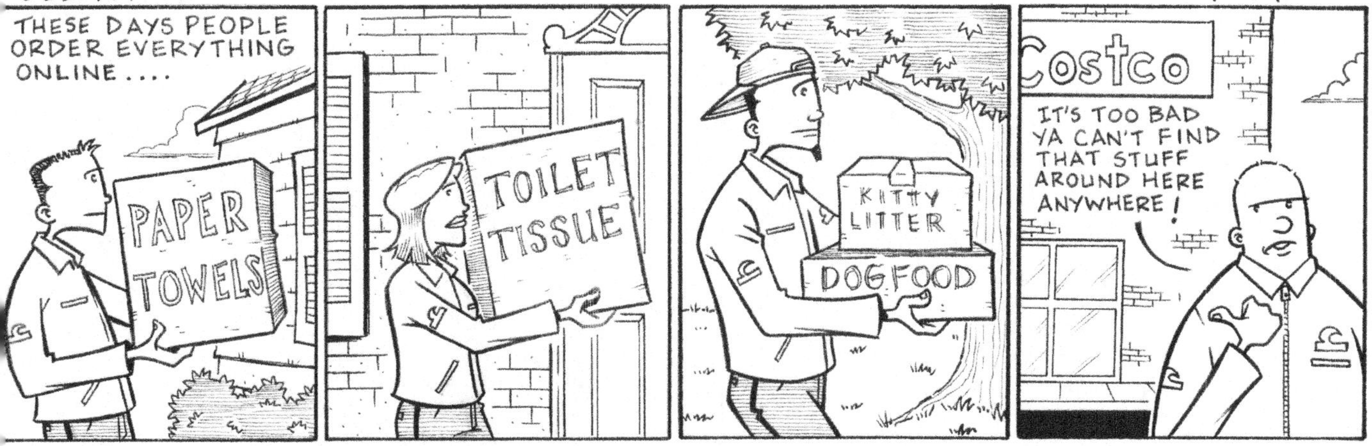

THESE DAYS PEOPLE ORDER EVERYTHING ONLINE....
PAPER TOWELS
TOILET TISSUE
KITTY LITTER
DOG FOOD
Costco
IT'S TOO BAD YA CAN'T FIND THAT STUFF AROUND HERE ANYWHERE!

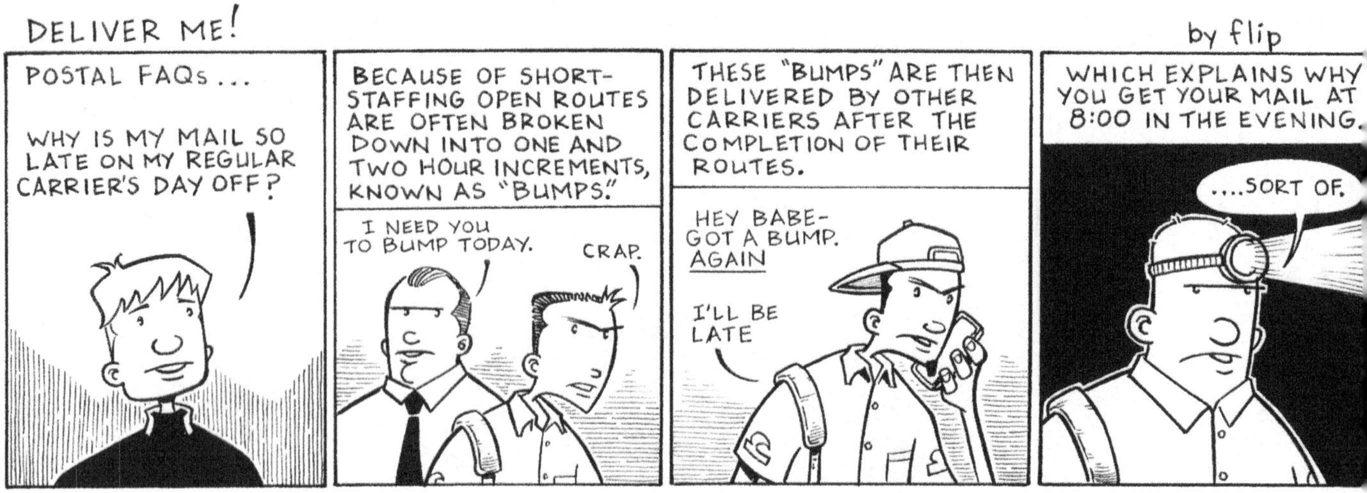
DELIVER ME!
by flip
POSTAL FAQs...
WHY IS MY MAIL SO LATE ON MY REGULAR CARRIER'S DAY OFF?
BECAUSE OF SHORT-STAFFING OPEN ROUTES ARE OFTEN BROKEN DOWN INTO ONE AND TWO HOUR INCREMENTS, KNOWN AS "BUMPS."
I NEED YOU TO BUMP TODAY.
CRAP.
THESE "BUMPS" ARE THEN DELIVERED BY OTHER CARRIERS AFTER THE COMPLETION OF THEIR ROUTES.
HEY BABE- GOT A BUMP. AGAIN
I'LL BE LATE
WHICH EXPLAINS WHY YOU GET YOUR MAIL AT 8:00 IN THE EVENING.
....SORT OF.

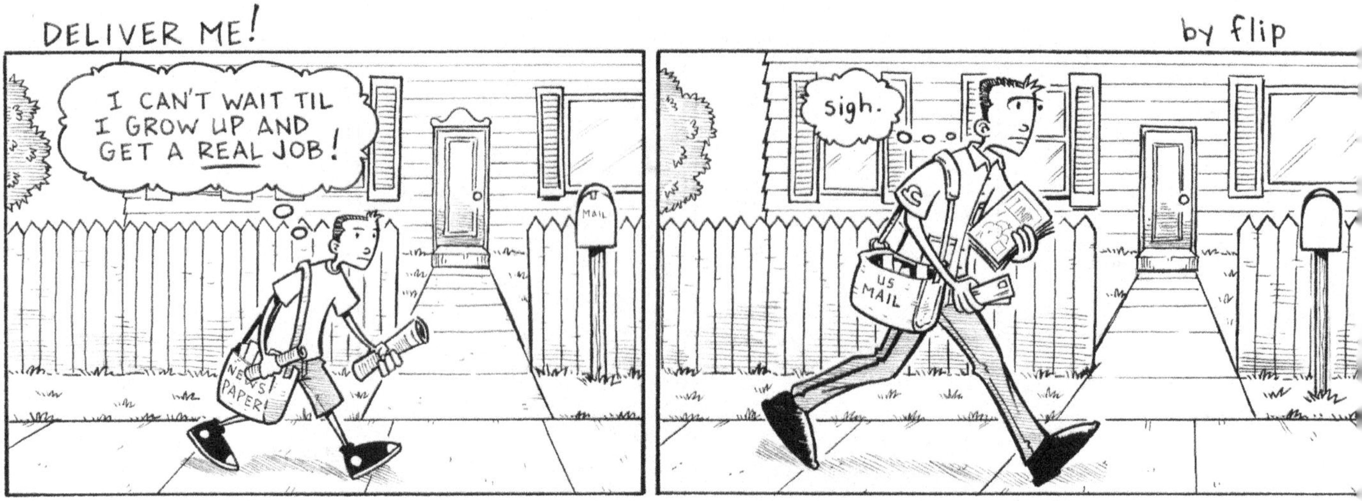
DELIVER ME!
by flip
I CAN'T WAIT TIL I GROW UP AND GET A REAL JOB!
MAIL
NEWS PAPER
sigh.
US MAIL

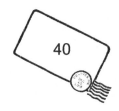

DELIVER ME! by flip

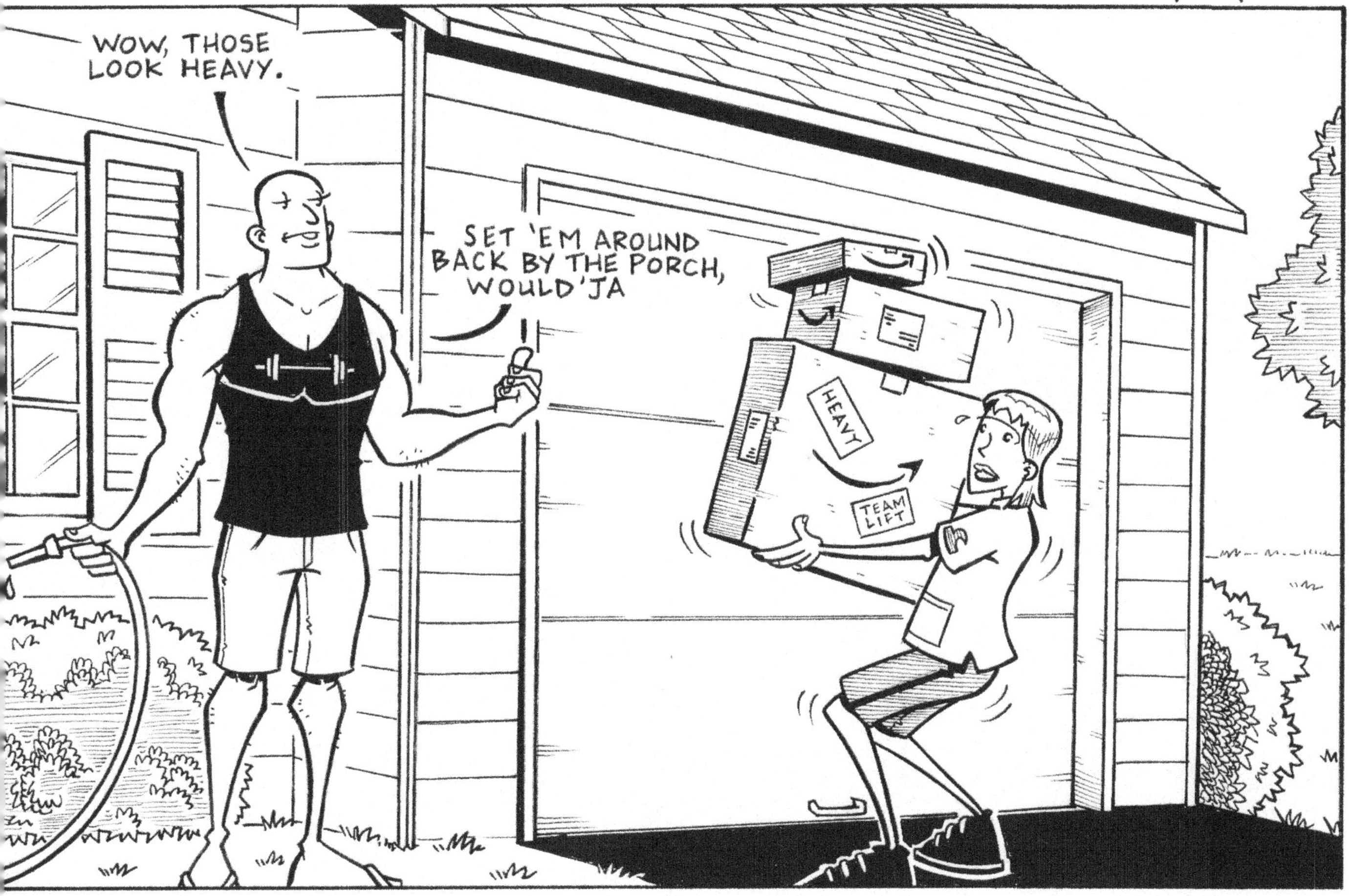
WOW, THOSE LOOK HEAVY.
SET 'EM AROUND BACK BY THE PORCH, WOULD'JA
HEAVY
TEAM LIFT

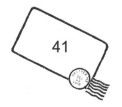

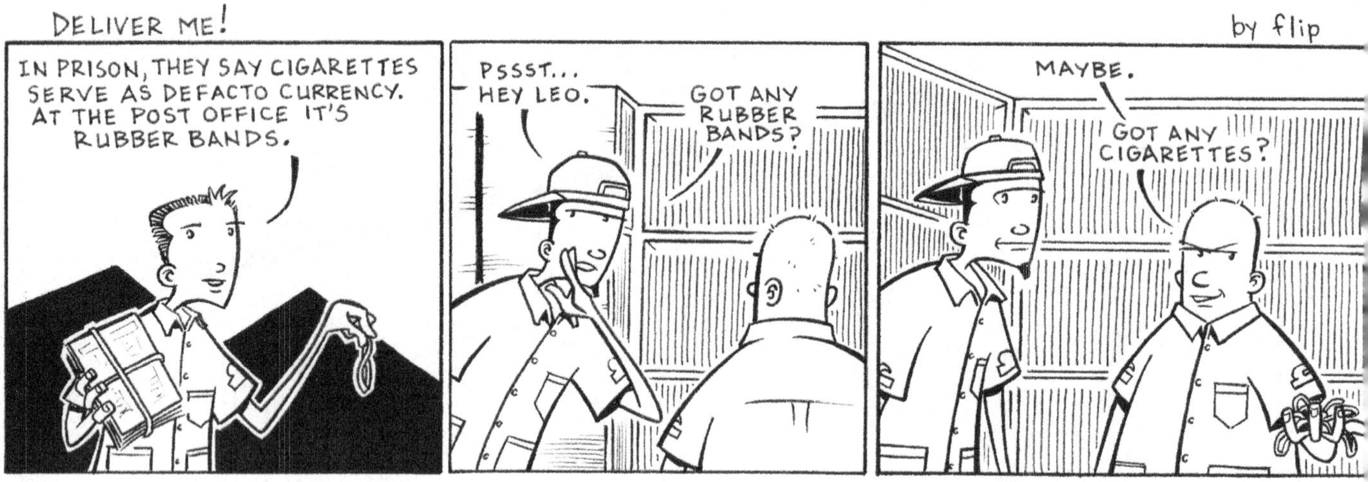
DELIVER ME!
by flip
IN PRISON, THEY SAY CIGARETTES SERVE AS DEFACTO CURRENCY. AT THE POST OFFICE IT'S RUBBER BANDS.
PSSST... HEY LEO.
GOT ANY RUBBER BANDS?
MAYBE.
GOT ANY CIGARETTES?

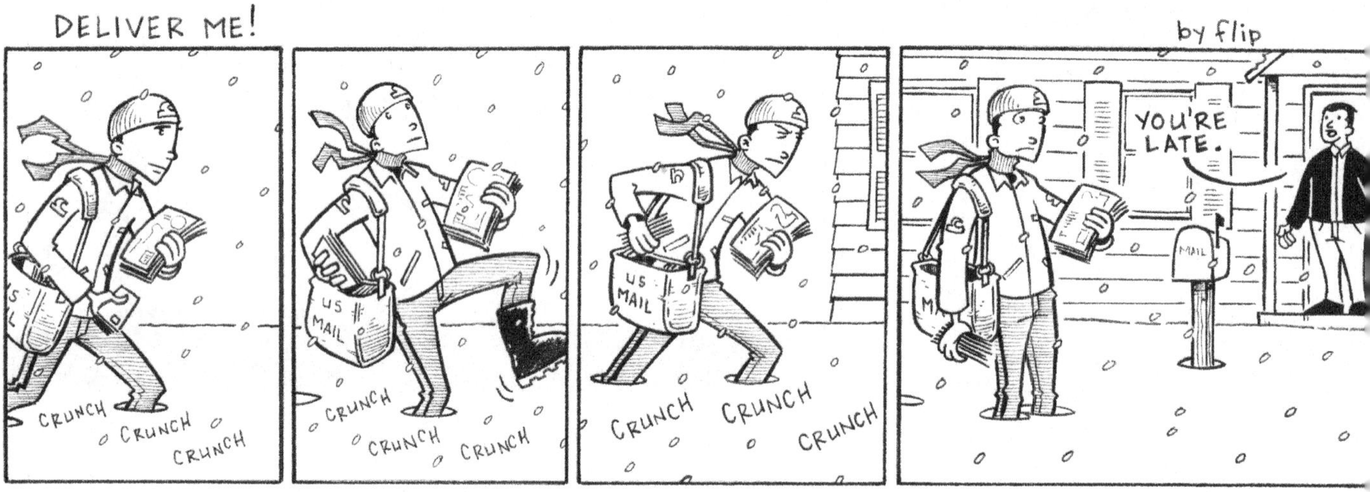
DELIVER ME!
by flip
US MAIL
CRUNCH CRUNCH CRUNCH
CRUNCH CRUNCH CRUNCH
CRUNCH CRUNCH CRUNCH
MAIL
YOU'RE LATE.

DELIVER ME! by flip

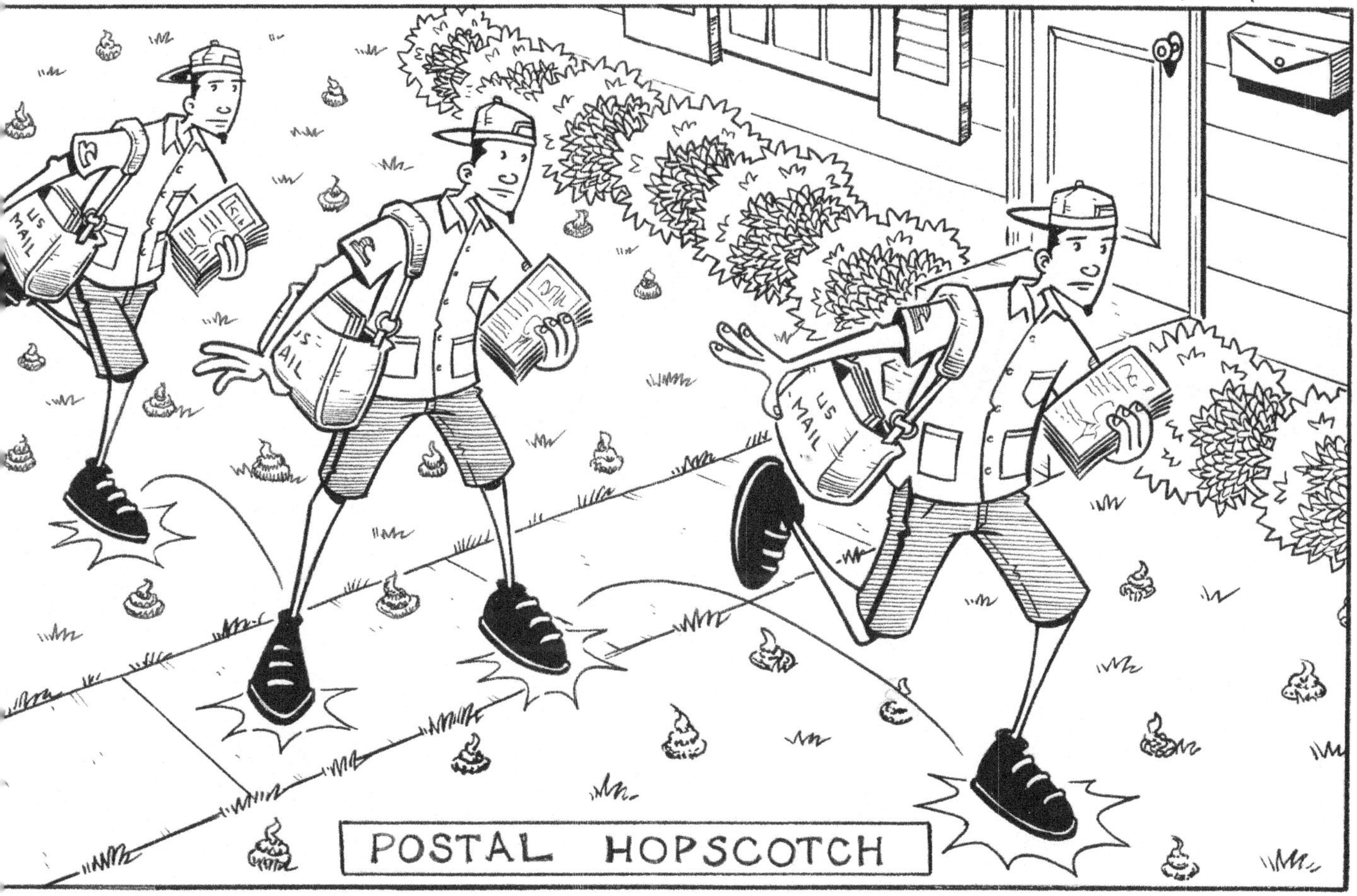

US MAIL
US MAIL
US MAIL
POSTAL HOPSCOTCH

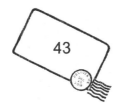

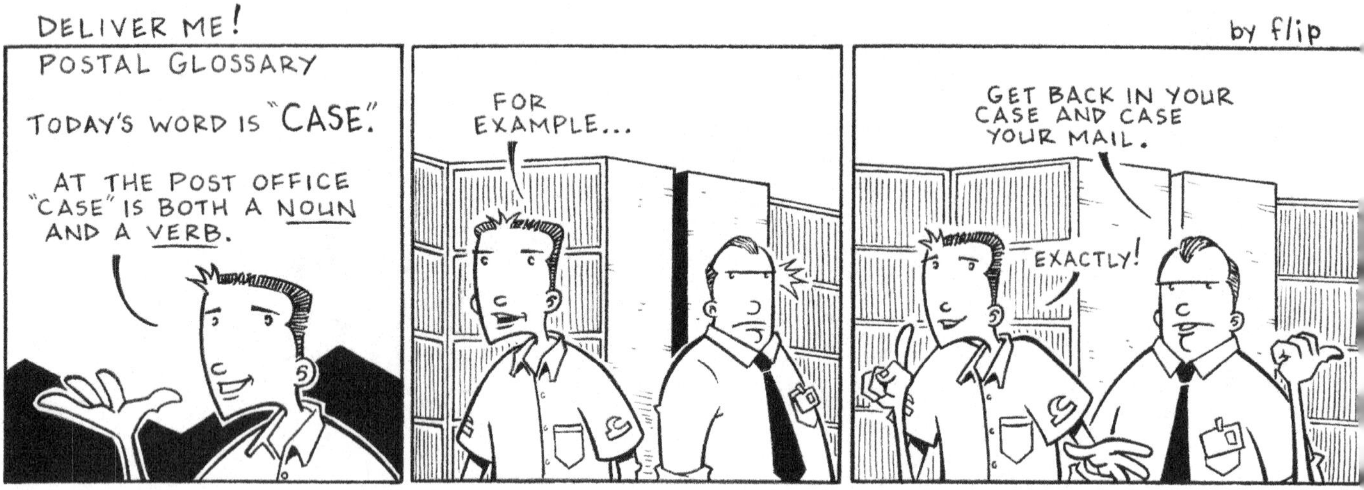
DELIVER ME!
by flip
POSTAL GLOSSARY
TODAY'S WORD IS "CASE."
AT THE POST OFFICE "CASE" IS BOTH A NOUN AND A VERB.
FOR EXAMPLE...
GET BACK IN YOUR CASE AND CASE YOUR MAIL.
EXACTLY!

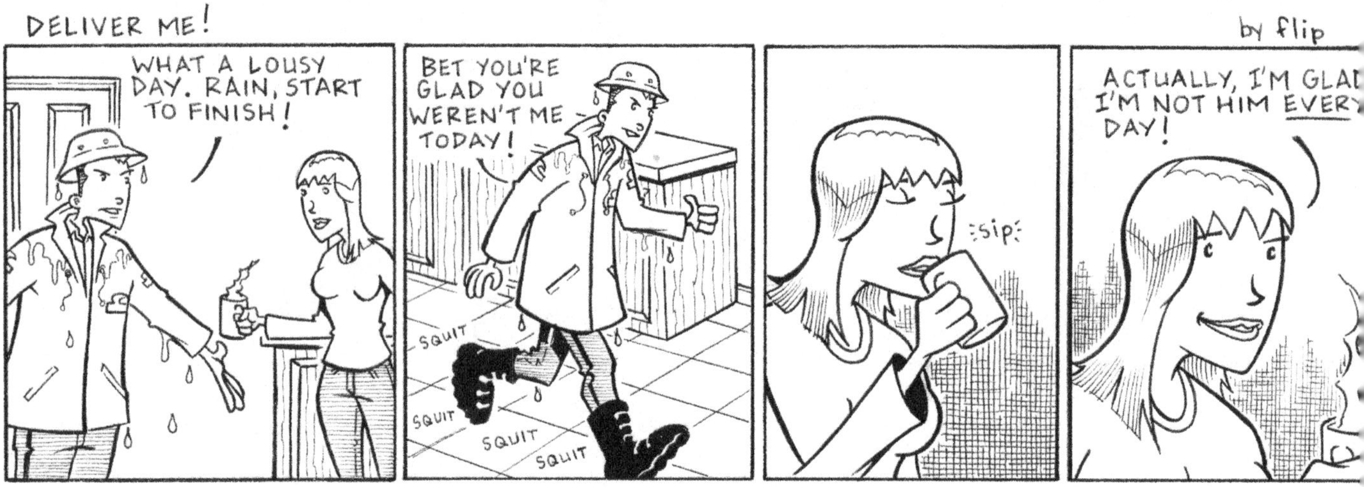
DELIVER ME!
by flip
WHAT A LOUSY DAY. RAIN, START TO FINISH!
BET YOU'RE GLAD YOU WEREN'T ME TODAY!
SQUIT
SQUIT
SQUIT
SQUIT
sip
ACTUALLY, I'M GLAD I'M NOT HIM EVERY DAY!

DELIVER ME! by flip

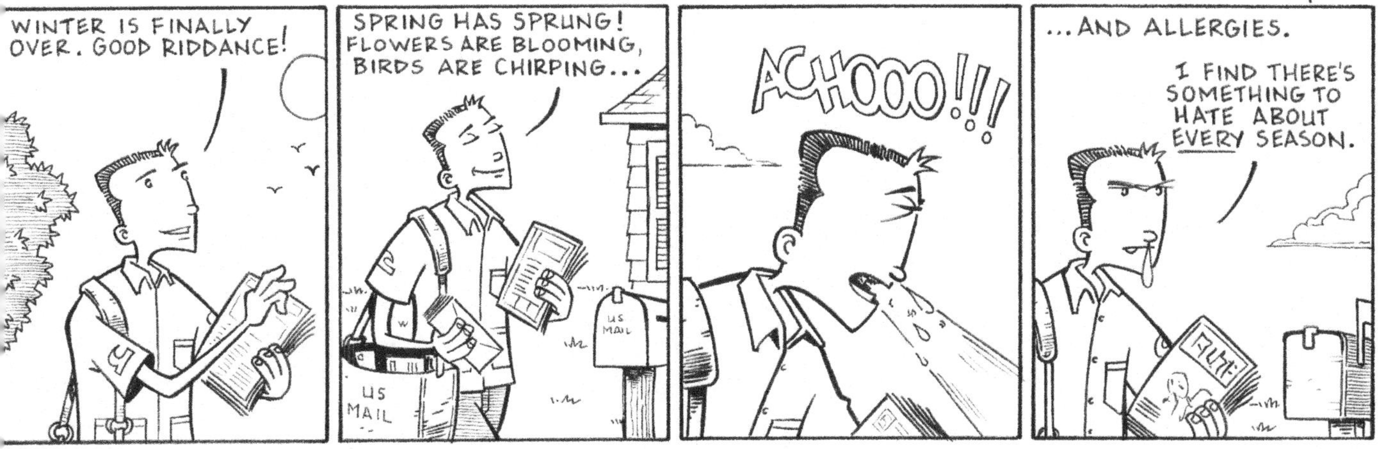
WINTER IS FINALLY OVER. GOOD RIDDANCE!
SPRING HAS SPRUNG! FLOWERS ARE BLOOMING, BIRDS ARE CHIRPING...
US MAIL
US MAIL
ACHOOO!!!
...AND ALLERGIES.
I FIND THERE'S SOMETHING TO HATE ABOUT EVERY SEASON.

DELIVER ME! by flip

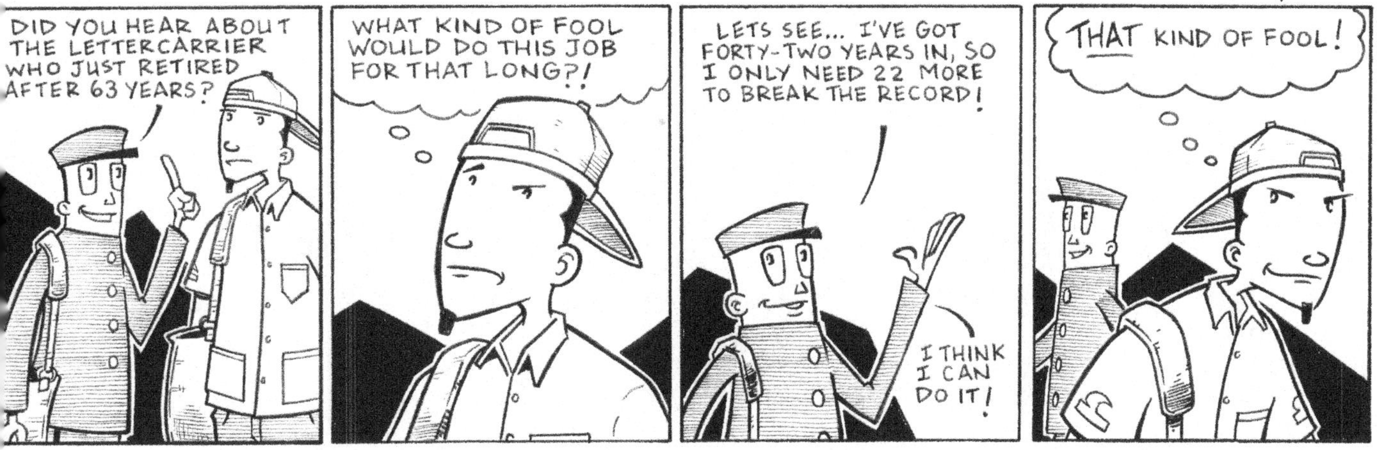
DID YOU HEAR ABOUT THE LETTERCARRIER WHO JUST RETIRED AFTER 63 YEARS?
WHAT KIND OF FOOL WOULD DO THIS JOB FOR THAT LONG?!
LETS SEE... I'VE GOT FORTY-TWO YEARS IN, SO I ONLY NEED 22 MORE TO BREAK THE RECORD!
I THINK I CAN DO IT!
THAT KIND OF FOOL!

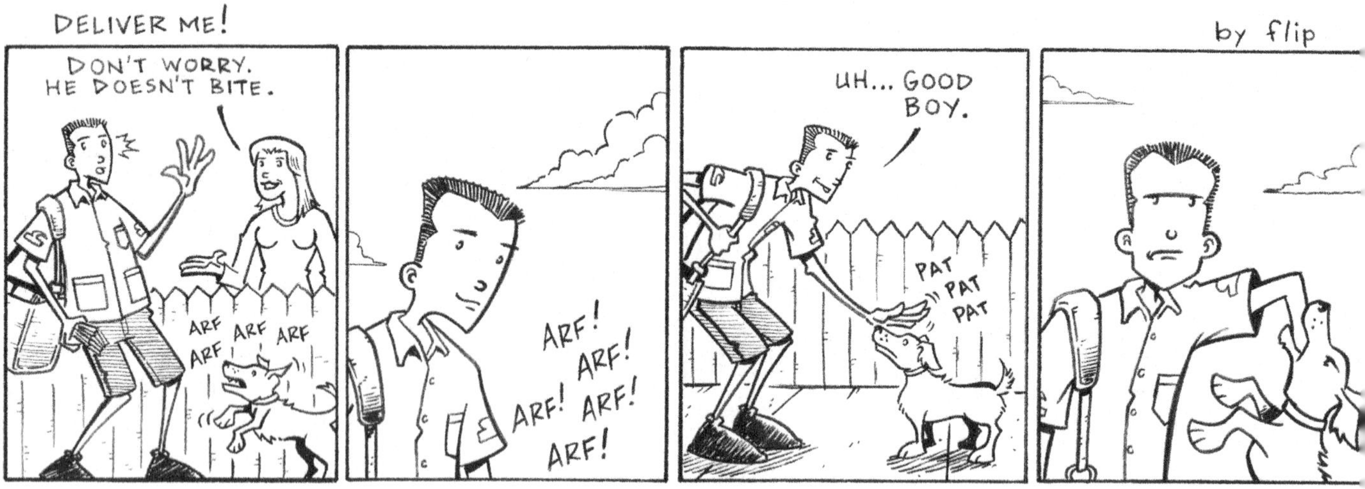
DELIVER ME!
by flip
DON'T WORRY. HE DOESN'T BITE.
ARF ARF ARF ARF ARF
ARF! ARF! ARF! ARF! ARF!
UH... GOOD BOY.
PAT PAT PAT

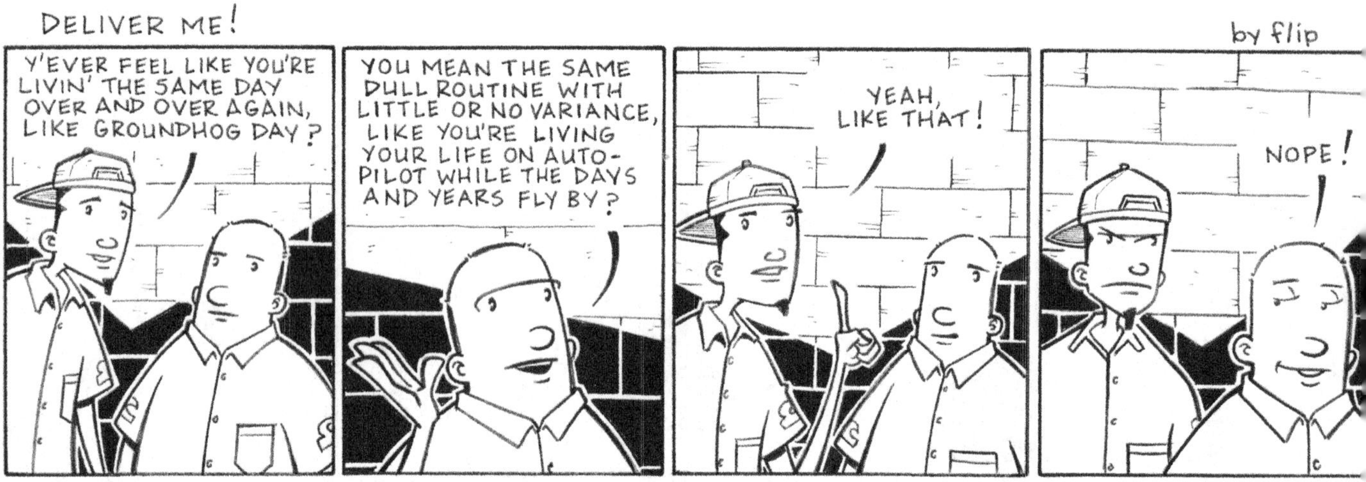
DELIVER ME!
by flip
Y'EVER FEEL LIKE YOU'RE LIVIN' THE SAME DAY OVER AND OVER AGAIN, LIKE GROUNDHOG DAY?
YOU MEAN THE SAME DULL ROUTINE WITH LITTLE OR NO VARIANCE, LIKE YOU'RE LIVING YOUR LIFE ON AUTO-PILOT WHILE THE DAYS AND YEARS FLY BY?
YEAH, LIKE THAT!
NOPE!

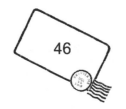

DELIVER ME!

by flip

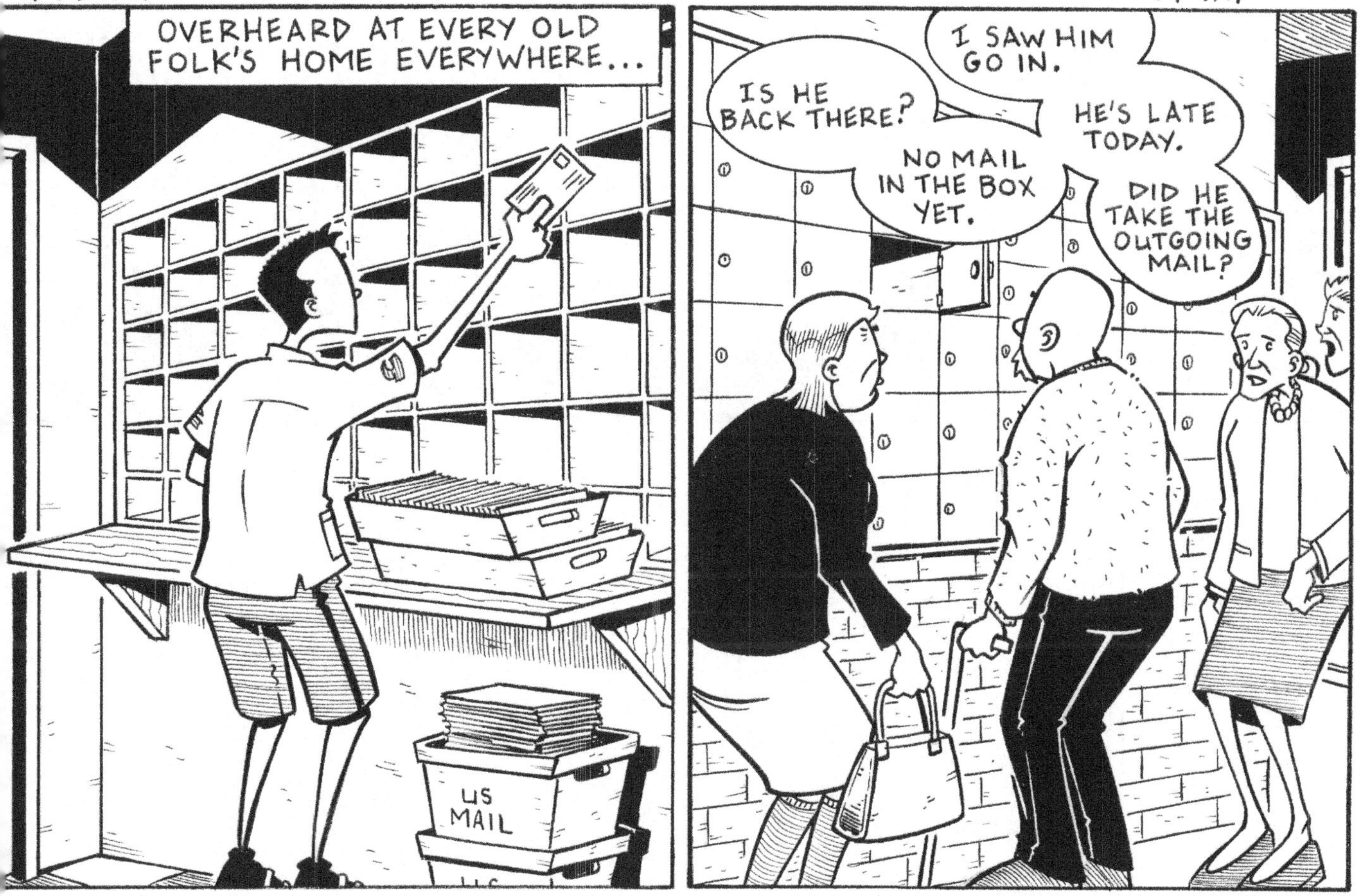
OVERHEARD AT EVERY OLD FOLK'S HOME EVERYWHERE...
US MAIL
IS HE BACK THERE?
I SAW HIM GO IN.
NO MAIL IN THE BOX YET.
HE'S LATE TODAY.
DID HE TAKE THE OUTGOING MAIL?

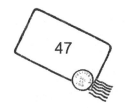

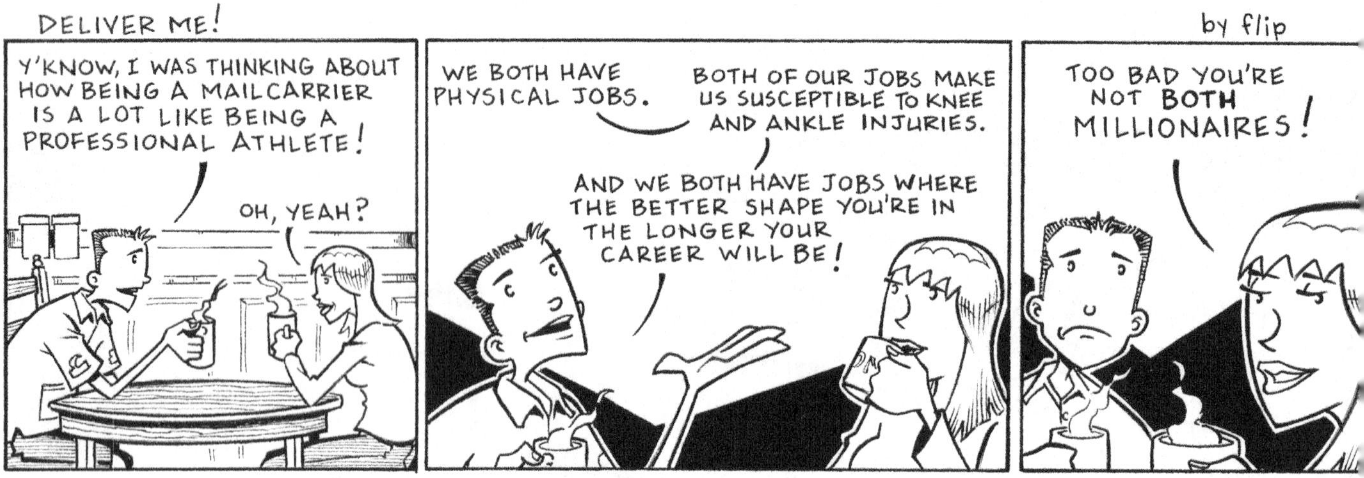
DELIVER ME!
by flip
Y'KNOW, I WAS THINKING ABOUT HOW BEING A MAILCARRIER IS A LOT LIKE BEING A PROFESSIONAL ATHLETE!
OH, YEAH?
WE BOTH HAVE PHYSICAL JOBS.
BOTH OF OUR JOBS MAKE US SUSCEPTIBLE TO KNEE AND ANKLE INJURIES.
AND WE BOTH HAVE JOBS WHERE THE BETTER SHAPE YOU'RE IN THE LONGER YOUR CAREER WILL BE!
TOO BAD YOU'RE NOT BOTH MILLIONAIRES!

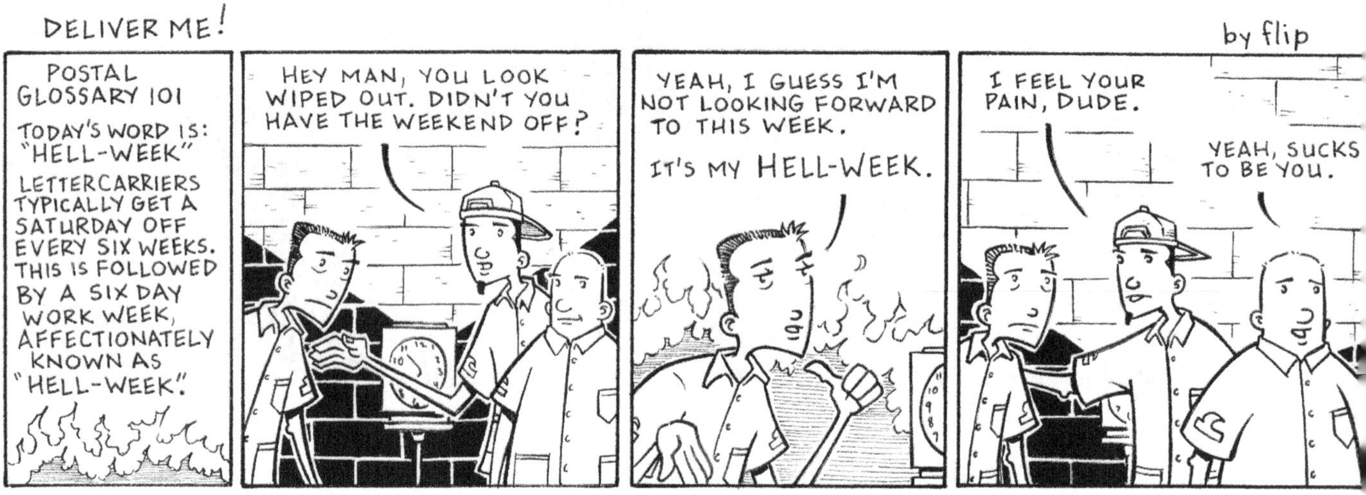
DELIVER ME!
by flip
POSTAL GLOSSARY 101
TODAY'S WORD IS: "HELL-WEEK"
LETTERCARRIERS TYPICALLY GET A SATURDAY OFF EVERY SIX WEEKS. THIS IS FOLLOWED BY A SIX DAY WORK WEEK, AFFECTIONATELY KNOWN AS "HELL-WEEK".
HEY MAN, YOU LOOK WIPED OUT. DIDN'T YOU HAVE THE WEEKEND OFF?
YEAH, I GUESS I'M NOT LOOKING FORWARD TO THIS WEEK.
IT'S MY HELL-WEEK.
I FEEL YOUR PAIN, DUDE.
YEAH, SUCKS TO BE YOU.

DELIVER ME!

by flip

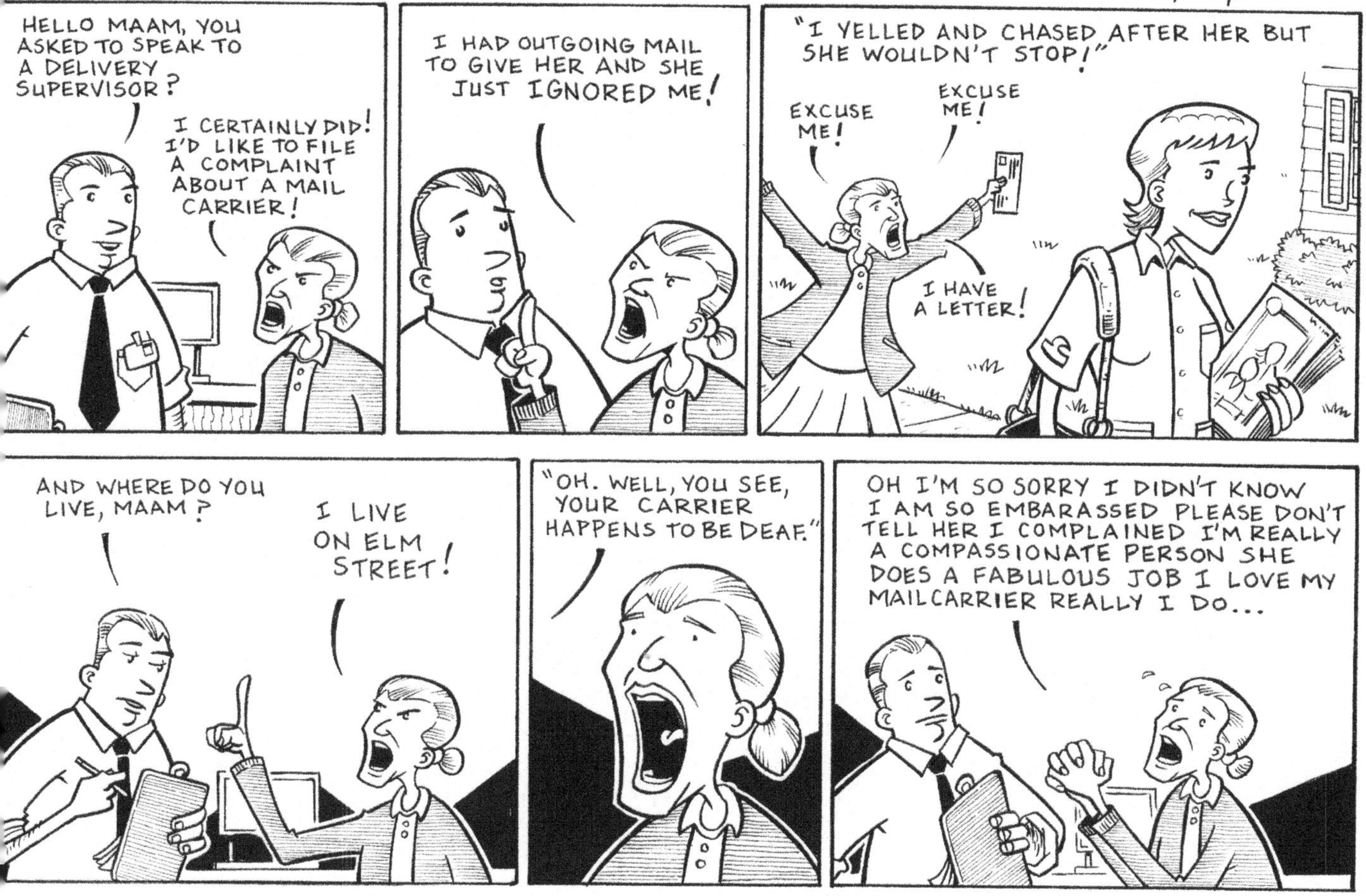

HELLO MAAM, YOU ASKED TO SPEAK TO A DELIVERY SUPERVISOR?
I CERTAINLY DID! I'D LIKE TO FILE A COMPLAINT ABOUT A MAIL CARRIER!
I HAD OUTGOING MAIL TO GIVE HER AND SHE JUST IGNORED ME!
"I YELLED AND CHASED AFTER HER BUT SHE WOULDN'T STOP!"
EXCUSE ME!
EXCUSE ME!
I HAVE A LETTER!
AND WHERE DO YOU LIVE, MAAM?
I LIVE ON ELM STREET!
"OH. WELL, YOU SEE, YOUR CARRIER HAPPENS TO BE DEAF."
OH I'M SO SORRY I DIDN'T KNOW I AM SO EMBARASSED PLEASE DON'T TELL HER I COMPLAINED I'M REALLY A COMPASSIONATE PERSON SHE DOES A FABULOUS JOB I LOVE MY MAILCARRIER REALLY I DO...

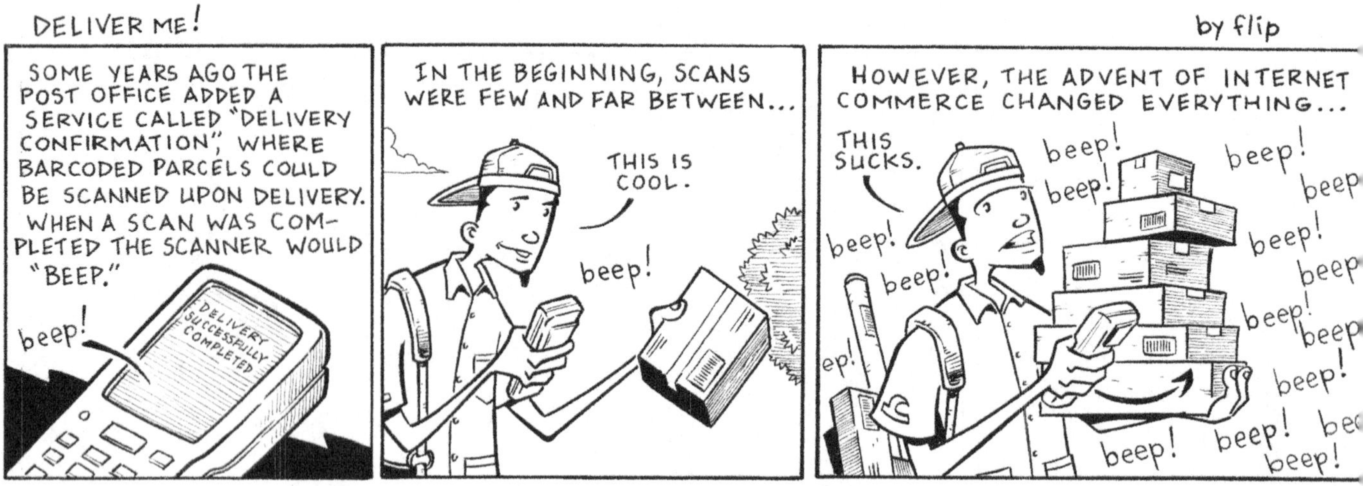
DELIVER ME!
by flip
SOME YEARS AGO THE POST OFFICE ADDED A SERVICE CALLED "DELIVERY CONFIRMATION", WHERE BARCODED PARCELS COULD BE SCANNED UPON DELIVERY. WHEN A SCAN WAS COMPLETED THE SCANNER WOULD "BEEP."
beep!
DELIVERY SUCCESSFULLY COMPLETED
IN THE BEGINNING, SCANS WERE FEW AND FAR BETWEEN...
THIS IS COOL.
beep!
HOWEVER, THE ADVENT OF INTERNET COMMERCE CHANGED EVERYTHING...
THIS SUCKS.
beep! beep! beep! beep! beep! beep! beep! beep! beep! beep! beep! beep! beep!

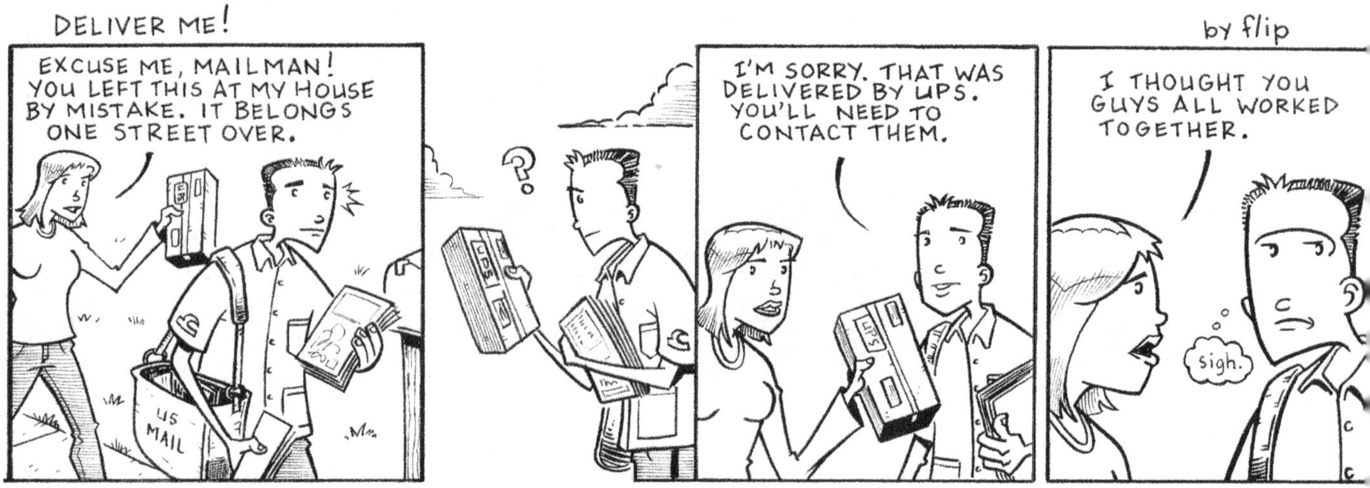
DELIVER ME!
by flip
EXCUSE ME, MAILMAN! YOU LEFT THIS AT MY HOUSE BY MISTAKE. IT BELONGS ONE STREET OVER.
US MAIL
?
UPS
I'M SORRY. THAT WAS DELIVERED BY UPS. YOU'LL NEED TO CONTACT THEM.
I THOUGHT YOU GUYS ALL WORKED TOGETHER.
sigh.

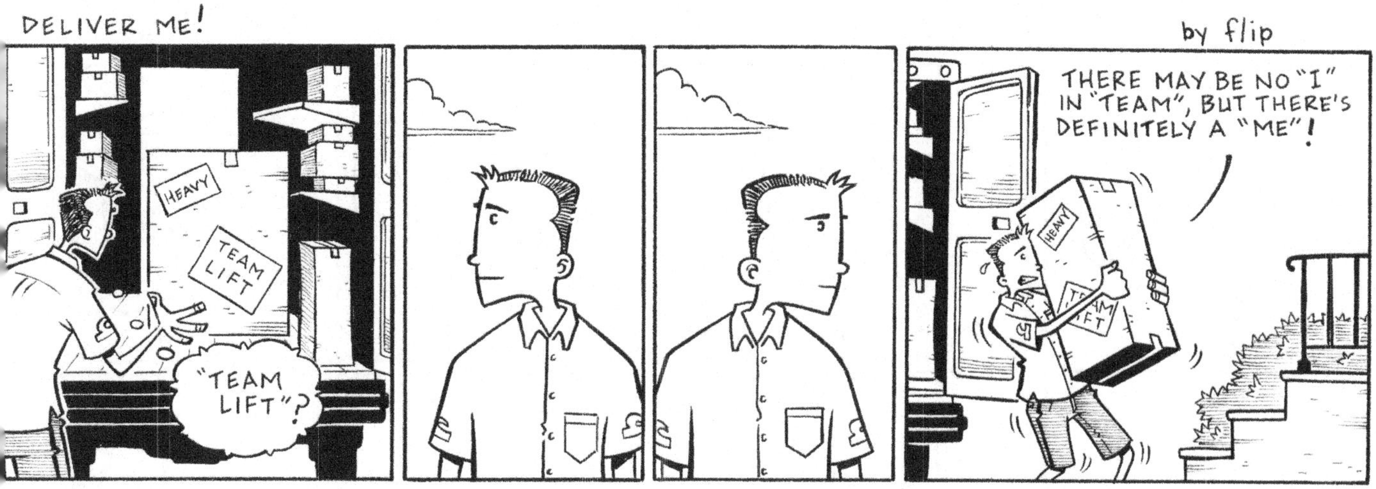
DELIVER ME!
by flip
HEAVY
TEAM LIFT
"TEAM LIFT"?
THERE MAY BE NO "I" IN "TEAM", BUT THERE'S DEFINITELY A "ME"!

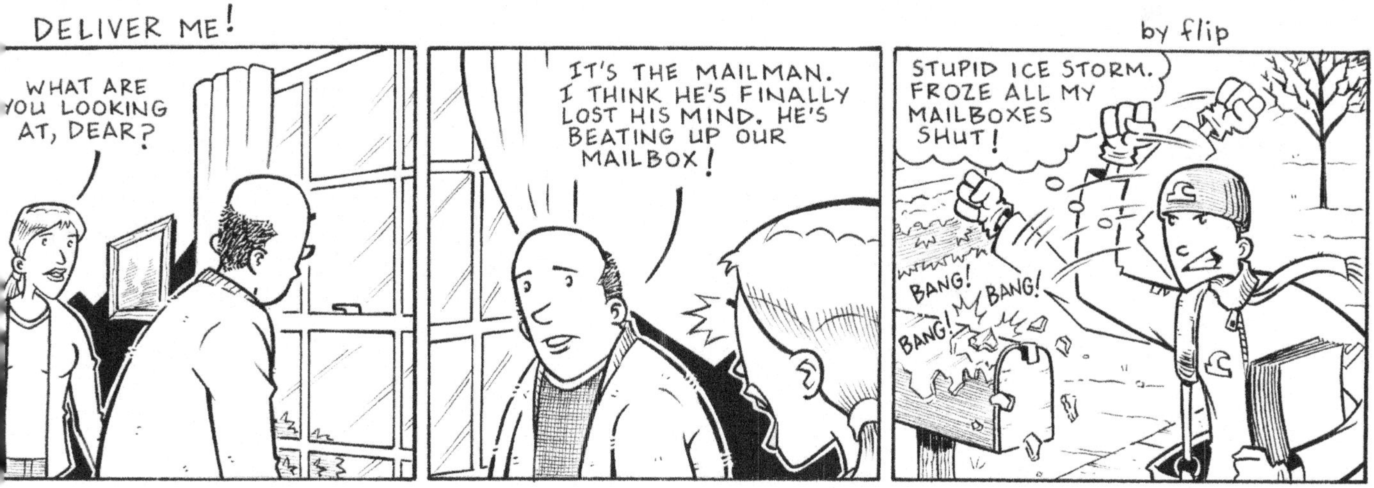
DELIVER ME!
by flip
WHAT ARE YOU LOOKING AT, DEAR?
IT'S THE MAILMAN. I THINK HE'S FINALLY LOST HIS MIND. HE'S BEATING UP OUR MAILBOX!
STUPID ICE STORM. FROZE ALL MY MAILBOXES SHUT!
BANG!
BANG!
BANG!

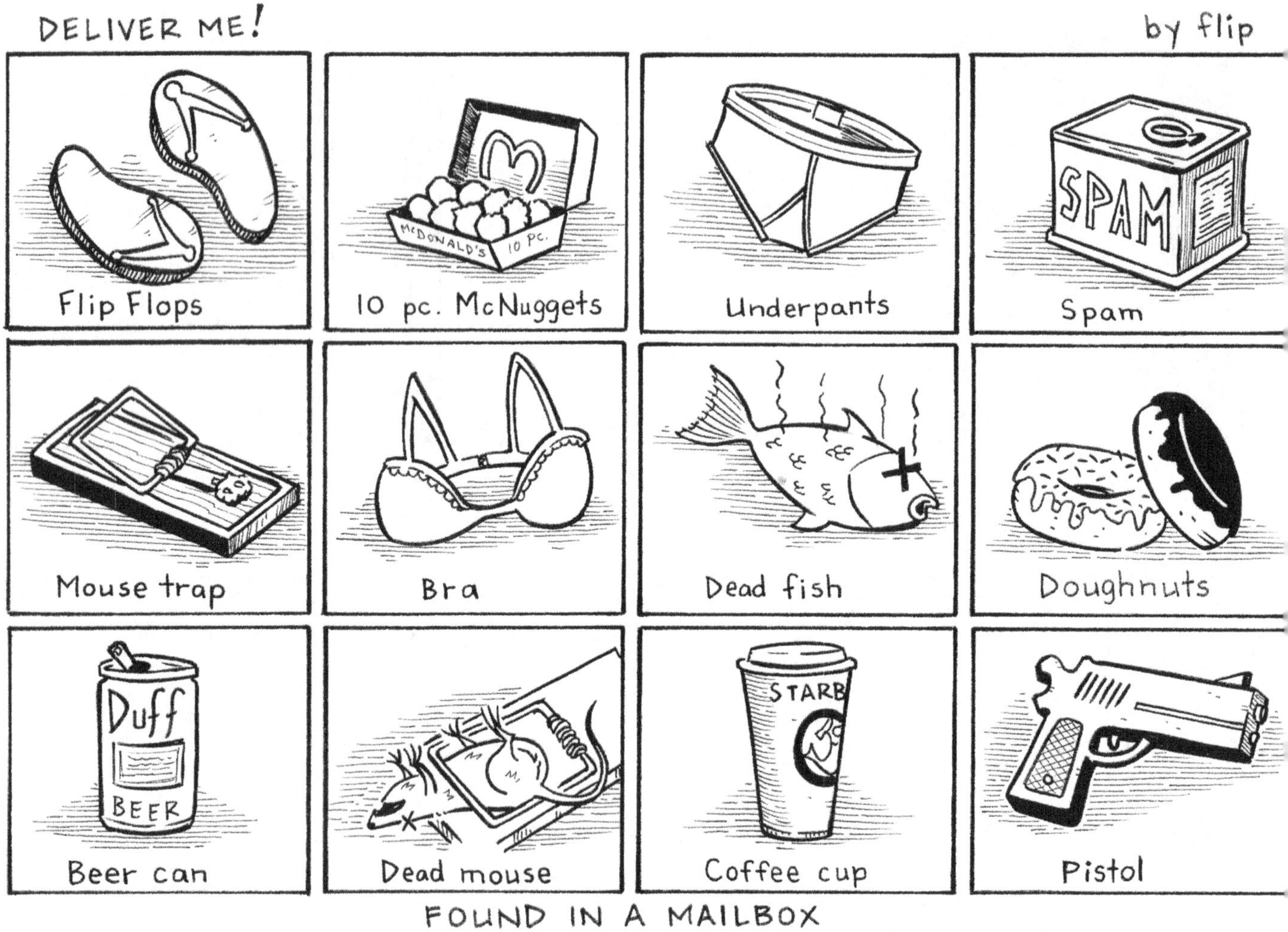
DELIVER ME!
by flip
Flip Flops
McDONALD'S
10 PC.
10 pc. McNuggets
Underpants
SPAM
Spam
Mouse trap
Bra
Dead fish
Doughnuts
Duff
BEER
Beer can
Dead mouse
STARB
Coffee cup
Pistol
FOUND IN A MAILBOX

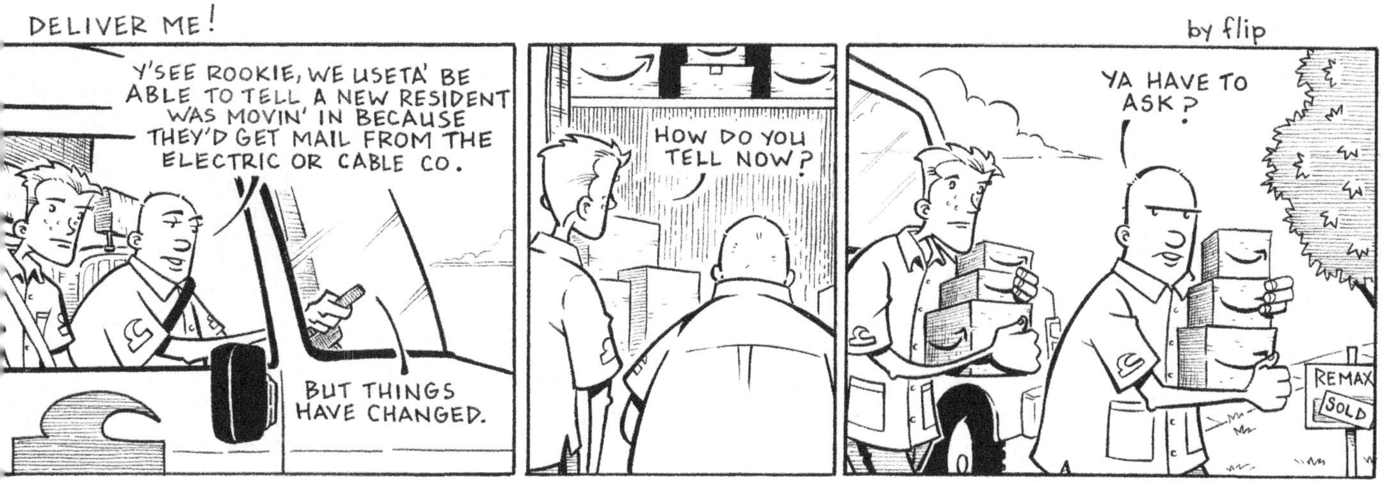
DELIVER ME!
by flip
Y'SEE ROOKIE, WE USETA' BE ABLE TO TELL A NEW RESIDENT WAS MOVIN' IN BECAUSE THEY'D GET MAIL FROM THE ELECTRIC OR CABLE CO.
BUT THINGS HAVE CHANGED.
HOW DO YOU TELL NOW?
YA HAVE TO ASK?
REMAX
SOLD

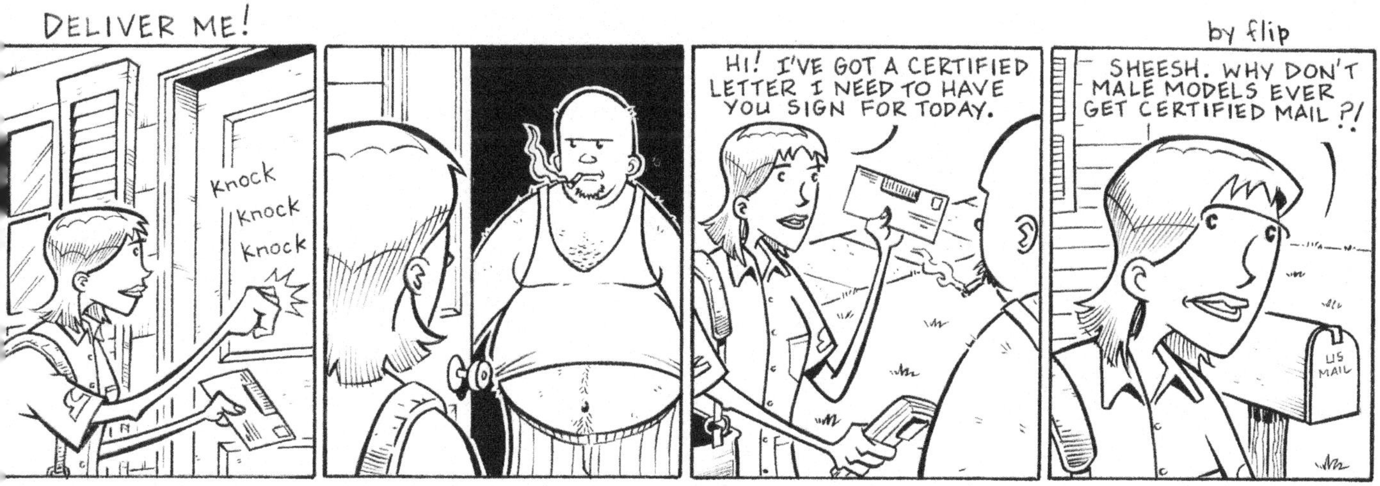
DELIVER ME!
by flip
Knock
Knock
Knock
HI! I'VE GOT A CERTIFIED LETTER I NEED TO HAVE YOU SIGN FOR TODAY.
SHEESH. WHY DON'T MALE MODELS EVER GET CERTIFIED MAIL?!
US MAIL

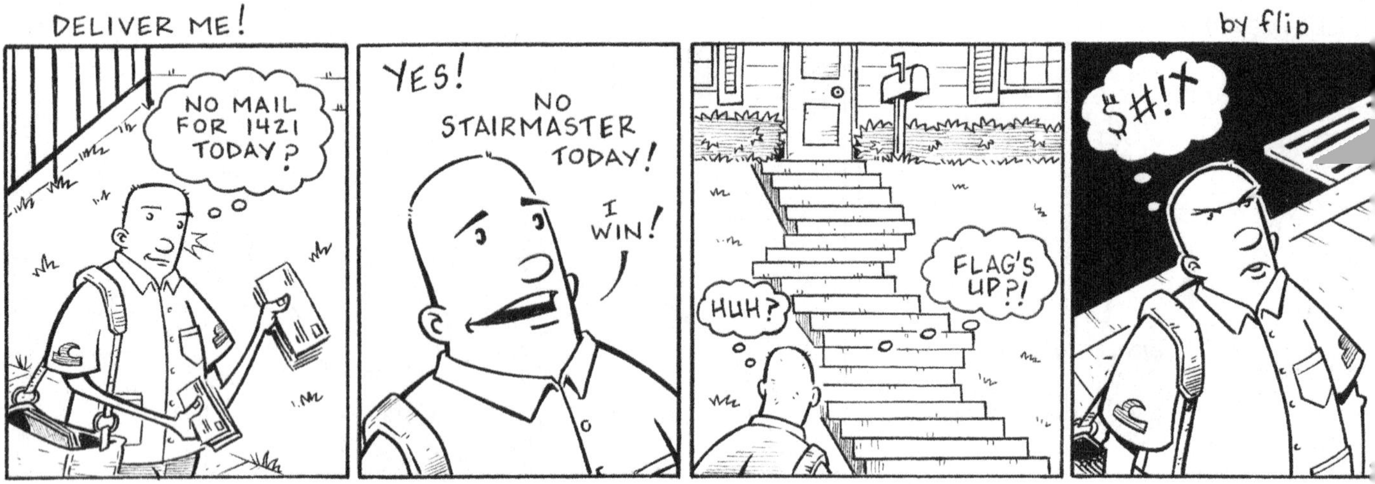
DELIVER ME!
by flip
NO MAIL FOR 1421 TODAY?
YES!
NO STAIRMASTER TODAY!
I WIN!
HUH?
FLAG'S UP?!
$#!X

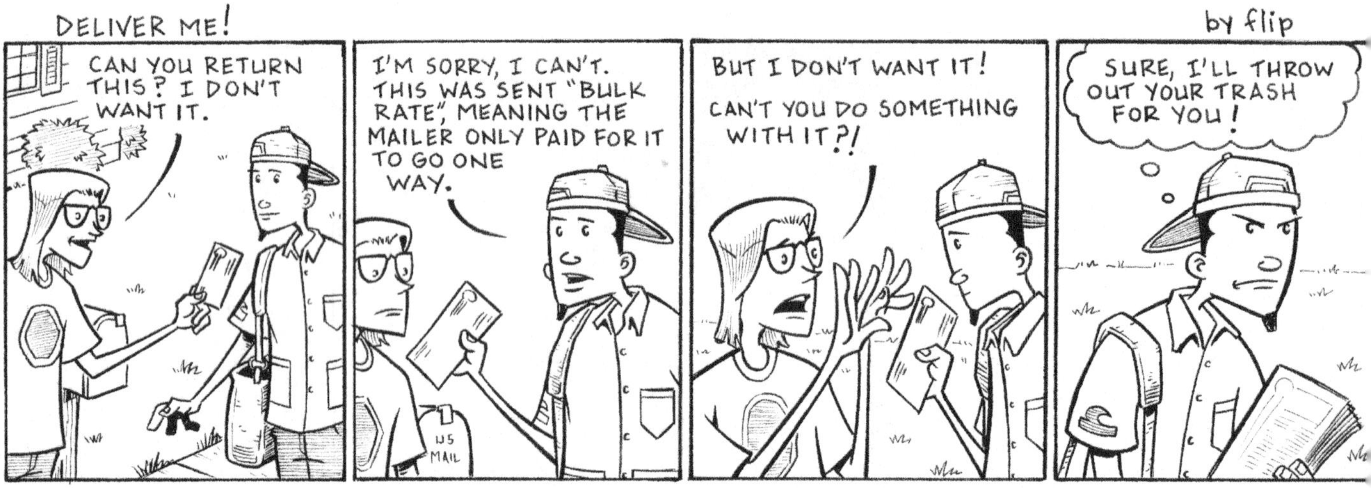
DELIVER ME!
by flip
CAN YOU RETURN THIS? I DON'T WANT IT.
I'M SORRY, I CAN'T. THIS WAS SENT "BULK RATE", MEANING THE MAILER ONLY PAID FOR IT TO GO ONE WAY.
US MAIL
BUT I DON'T WANT IT!
CAN'T YOU DO SOMETHING WITH IT?!
SURE, I'LL THROW OUT YOUR TRASH FOR YOU!

DELIVER ME! by flip

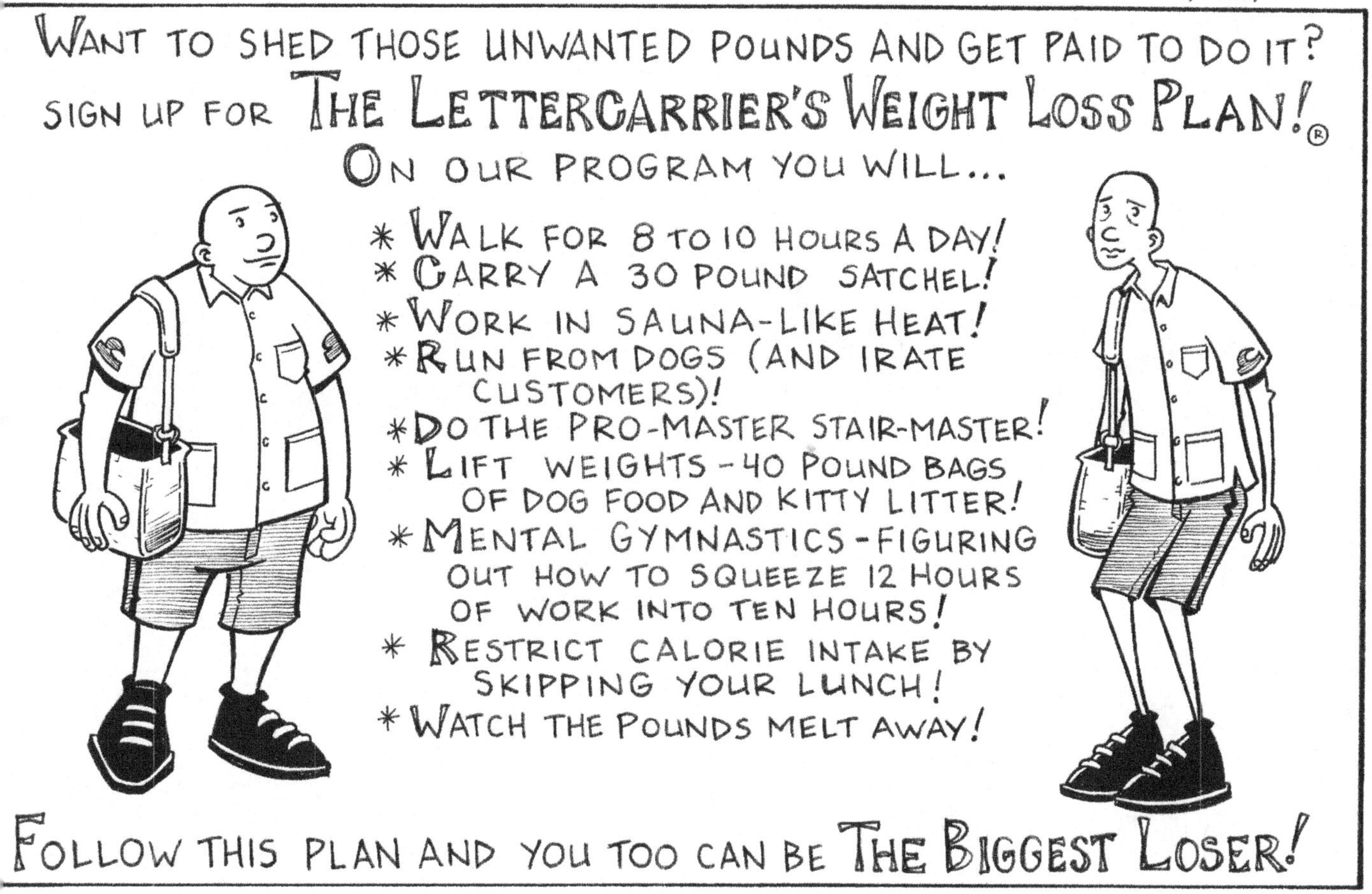
WANT TO SHED THOSE UNWANTED POUNDS AND GET PAID TO DO IT?
SIGN UP FOR THE LETTERCARRIER'S WEIGHT LOSS PLAN!®
ON OUR PROGRAM YOU WILL...
* WALK FOR 8 TO 10 HOURS A DAY!
* CARRY A 30 POUND SATCHEL!
* WORK IN SAUNA-LIKE HEAT!
* RUN FROM DOGS (AND IRATE CUSTOMERS)!
* DO THE PRO-MASTER STAIR-MASTER!
* LIFT WEIGHTS - 40 POUND BAGS OF DOG FOOD AND KITTY LITTER!
* MENTAL GYMNASTICS - FIGURING OUT HOW TO SQUEEZE 12 HOURS OF WORK INTO TEN HOURS!
* RESTRICT CALORIE INTAKE BY SKIPPING YOUR LUNCH!
* WATCH THE POUNDS MELT AWAY!
FOLLOW THIS PLAN AND YOU TOO CAN BE THE BIGGEST LOSER!

DELIVER ME!

by flip

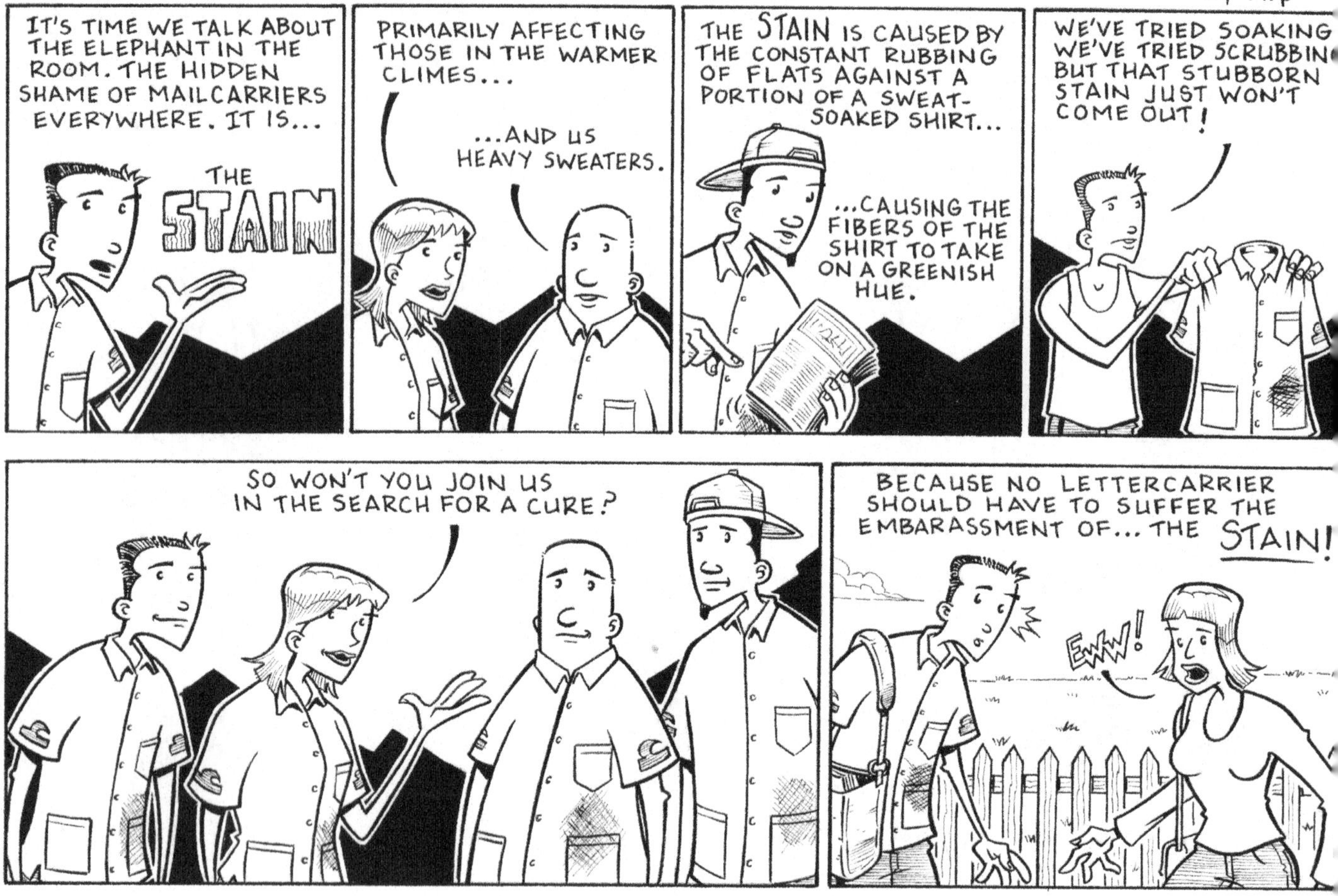

IT'S TIME WE TALK ABOUT THE ELEPHANT IN THE ROOM. THE HIDDEN SHAME OF MAILCARRIERS EVERYWHERE. IT IS...
THE STAIN
PRIMARILY AFFECTING THOSE IN THE WARMER CLIMES...
...AND US HEAVY SWEATERS.
THE STAIN IS CAUSED BY THE CONSTANT RUBBING OF FLATS AGAINST A PORTION OF A SWEAT-SOAKED SHIRT...
...CAUSING THE FIBERS OF THE SHIRT TO TAKE ON A GREENISH HUE.
WE'VE TRIED SOAKING WE'VE TRIED SCRUBBIN BUT THAT STUBBORN STAIN JUST WON'T COME OUT!
SO WON'T YOU JOIN US IN THE SEARCH FOR A CURE?
BECAUSE NO LETTERCARRIER SHOULD HAVE TO SUFFER THE EMBARASSMENT OF... THE STAIN!
EWW!

DELIVER ME!

by flip

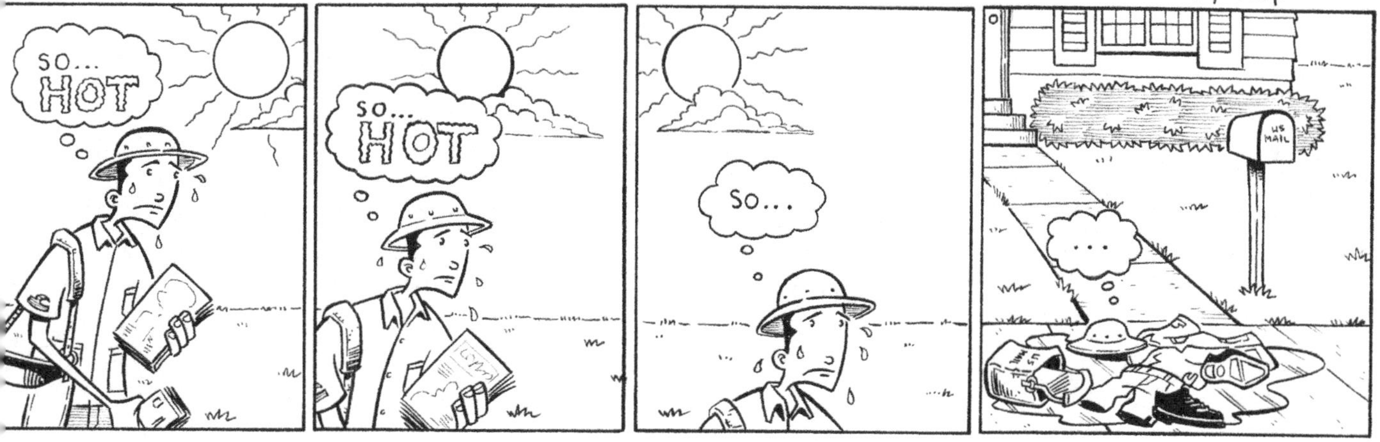
SO... HOT
SO... HOT
SO...
...
US MAIL

DELIVER ME!

by flip

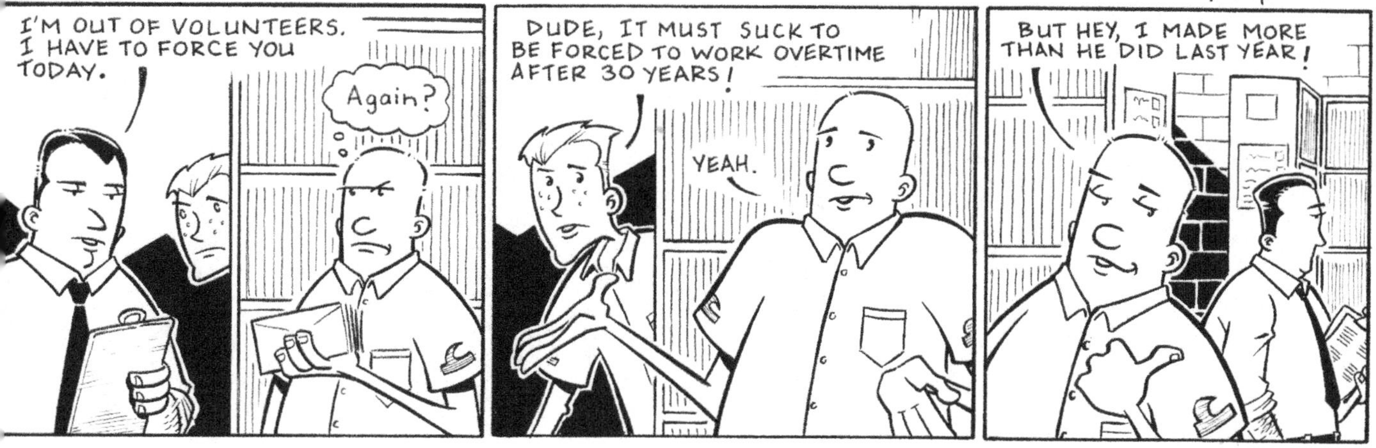
I'M OUT OF VOLUNTEERS. I HAVE TO FORCE YOU TODAY.
Again?
DUDE, IT MUST SUCK TO BE FORCED TO WORK OVERTIME AFTER 30 YEARS!
YEAH.
BUT HEY, I MADE MORE THAN HE DID LAST YEAR!

DELIVER ME! by flip

SQUEAK! SQUEAK! SQUEAK!
WHY DOESN'T HE OIL THAT SQUEAKY CART?!
IT'S NOT THE CART.
SQUEAK!

DELIVER ME! by flip

arf! arf! arf! arf! arf! arf! arf! arf! arf! arf!
BARK! BARK! BARK! BARK!
ruff! ruff! ruff! ruff! ruff! ruff!
SOUNDTRACK OF MY LIFE.

DELIVER ME!

by flip

We're here today to talk about an invaluable tool in the letter carrier toolbox...

The SWEAT FLAT!

When it's Summertime and you're sweating buckets you need something to keep the mail dry.

The sweat flat is just the ticket!

By placing a piece of "No Obvious Value" mail (that would normally be discarded) on the bottom of your bundle of flats, you can save that bottom piece of mail from becoming saturated with sweat.
Then all you need to do is switch out your sweat flat before it gets funky!

Come ta' think of it, I could use one a' these in my pants!

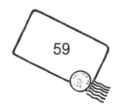

59

DELIVER ME! by flip

YOW! WHO MADE THE COFFEE TODAY?!
HIGH OCTANE, EH?
ZIPPY MADE IT.
THAT EXPLAINS A LOT!
YOU HAVE A GOOD WEEK END?! I HAD A GREAT WEEKEND!! I WASHED MY UNIFORMS AND SHINED MY SHOES AND PUT A NEW STRA ON MY ILBAG A
MILK

DELIVER ME! by flip

HEY GUYS- WHAT DO YA THINK MY CHANCES ARE OF GETTING NEXT SATURDAY OFF?
HA HA HA HA HA HA HA HA HA HA HA HA HA HA
SILLY ROOKIE. YOU WORK AT THE POST OFFICE NOW. YOU NEED A SATURDAY OFF, YOU GOTTA PUT IN FOR IT SIX MONTH IN ADVANCE!

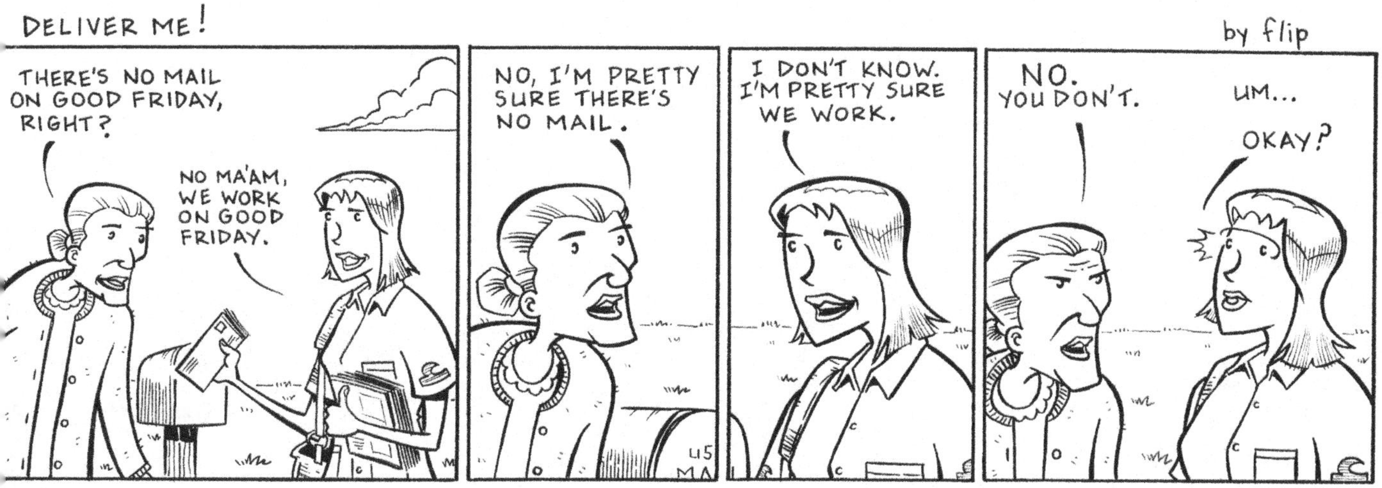
DELIVER ME!
by flip
THERE'S NO MAIL ON GOOD FRIDAY, RIGHT?
NO MA'AM, WE WORK ON GOOD FRIDAY.
NO, I'M PRETTY SURE THERE'S NO MAIL.
I DON'T KNOW. I'M PRETTY SURE WE WORK.
NO. YOU DON'T.
UM...
OKAY?

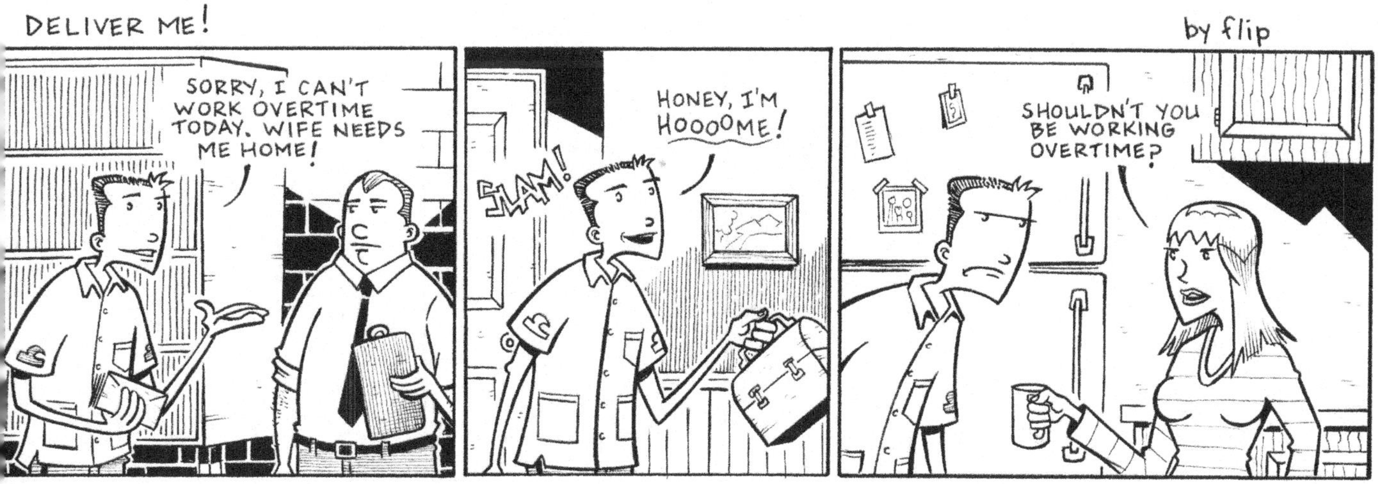
DELIVER ME!
by flip
SORRY, I CAN'T WORK OVERTIME TODAY. WIFE NEEDS ME HOME!
SLAM!
HONEY, I'M HOOOOME!
SHOULDN'T YOU BE WORKING OVERTIME?

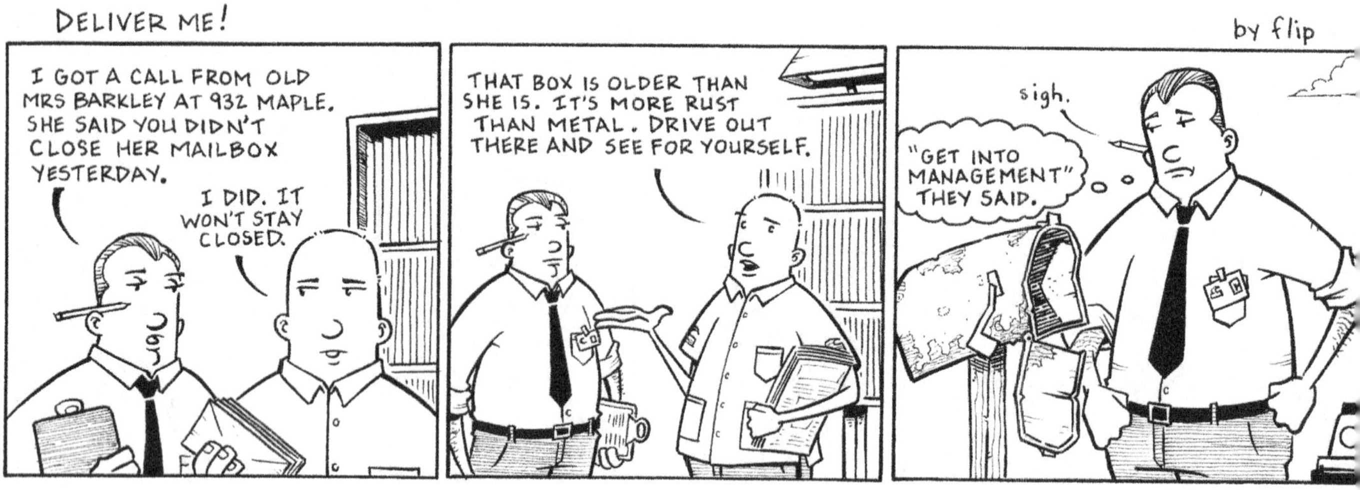
DELIVER ME!
by flip
I GOT A CALL FROM OLD MRS BARKLEY AT 932 MAPLE. SHE SAID YOU DIDN'T CLOSE HER MAILBOX YESTERDAY.
I DID. IT WON'T STAY CLOSED.
THAT BOX IS OLDER THAN SHE IS. IT'S MORE RUST THAN METAL. DRIVE OUT THERE AND SEE FOR YOURSELF.
sigh.
"GET INTO MANAGEMENT" THEY SAID.

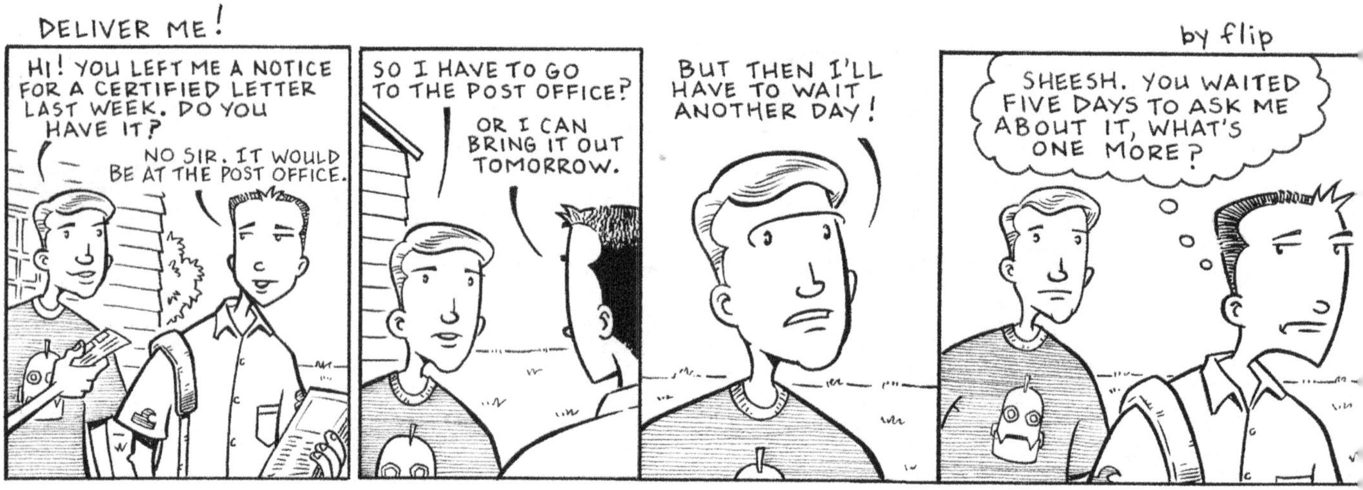
DELIVER ME!
by flip
HI! YOU LEFT ME A NOTICE FOR A CERTIFIED LETTER LAST WEEK. DO YOU HAVE IT?
NO SIR. IT WOULD BE AT THE POST OFFICE.
SO I HAVE TO GO TO THE POST OFFICE?
OR I CAN BRING IT OUT TOMORROW.
BUT THEN I'LL HAVE TO WAIT ANOTHER DAY!
SHEESH. YOU WAITED FIVE DAYS TO ASK ME ABOUT IT, WHAT'S ONE MORE?

DELIVER ME! by flip

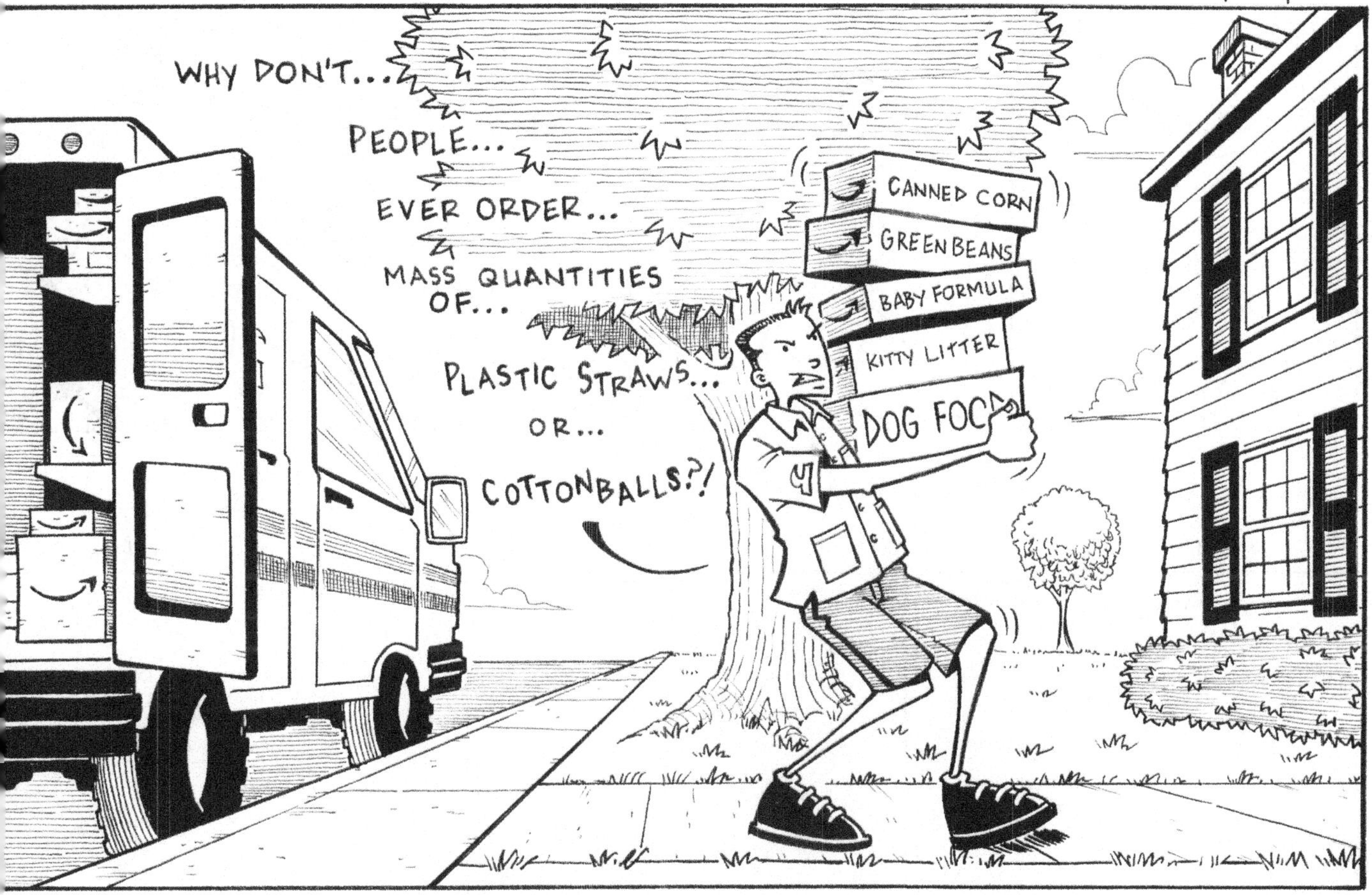
WHY DON'T...
PEOPLE...
EVER ORDER...
MASS QUANTITIES OF...
PLASTIC STRAWS...
OR...
COTTONBALLS?!
CANNED CORN
GREEN BEANS
BABY FORMULA
KITTY LITTER
DOG FOO

DELIVER ME!

by flip

WORKING SATURDAYS...
>SNIFF<
>SNIFF<
>SNIFF<
>SNIFF<
>SNIFF<
>SNIFF<
PEANUT BUTTER
GRAPE JELLY
>CHOMP<
>CHOMP<
>CHOMP<

DELIVER ME!

by flip

EXPRESSO MAIL FOR YOUR ROUTE. VERY IMPORTANT THAT IT'S DELIVERED BY NOON.
GOT IT!
Expresso-mail
WHEW! I HAD TO STOP WHAT I WAS DOING AND RACE OVER HERE, BUT I MADE IT!
THREE DAYS LATER...
WOW. THAT "VERY IMPORTANT" MAIL IS STILL IN THE BOX.
TIME

DELIVER ME! by flip

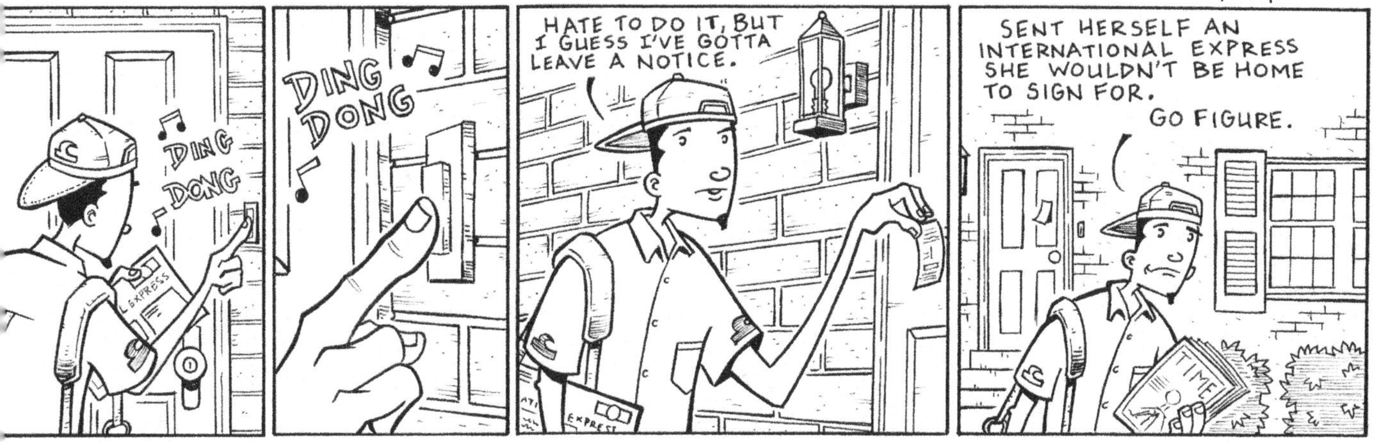
DING DONG
EXPRESS
DING DONG
HATE TO DO IT, BUT I GUESS I'VE GOTTA LEAVE A NOTICE.
EXPRESS
SENT HERSELF AN INTERNATIONAL EXPRESS SHE WOULDN'T BE HOME TO SIGN FOR.
GO FIGURE.
TIME

DELIVER ME! by flip

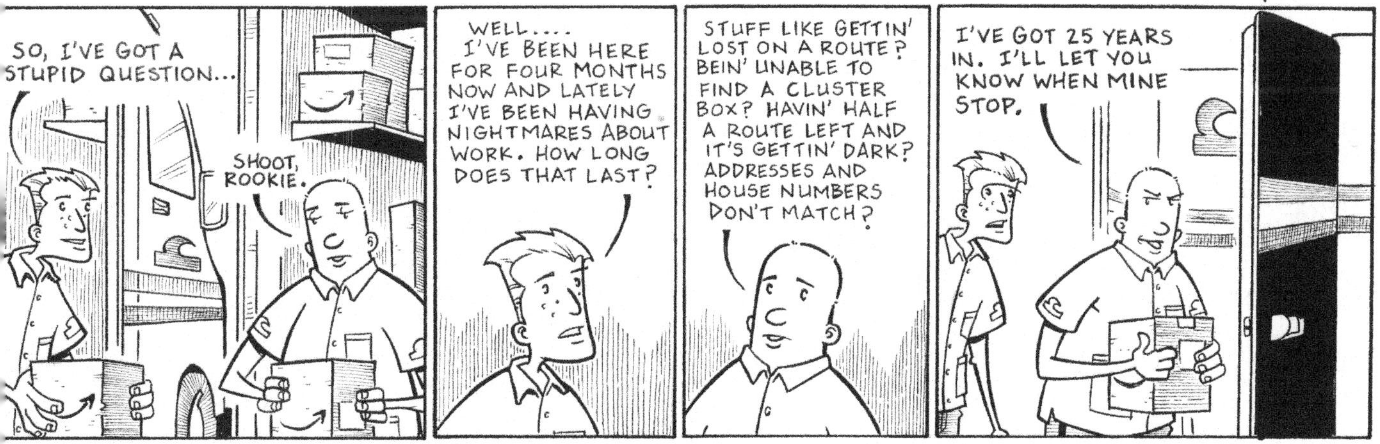
SO, I'VE GOT A STUPID QUESTION...
SHOOT, ROOKIE.
WELL.... I'VE BEEN HERE FOR FOUR MONTHS NOW AND LATELY I'VE BEEN HAVING NIGHTMARES ABOUT WORK. HOW LONG DOES THAT LAST?
STUFF LIKE GETTIN' LOST ON A ROUTE? BEIN' UNABLE TO FIND A CLUSTER BOX? HAVIN' HALF A ROUTE LEFT AND IT'S GETTIN' DARK? ADDRESSES AND HOUSE NUMBERS DON'T MATCH?
I'VE GOT 25 YEARS IN. I'LL LET YOU KNOW WHEN MINE STOP.

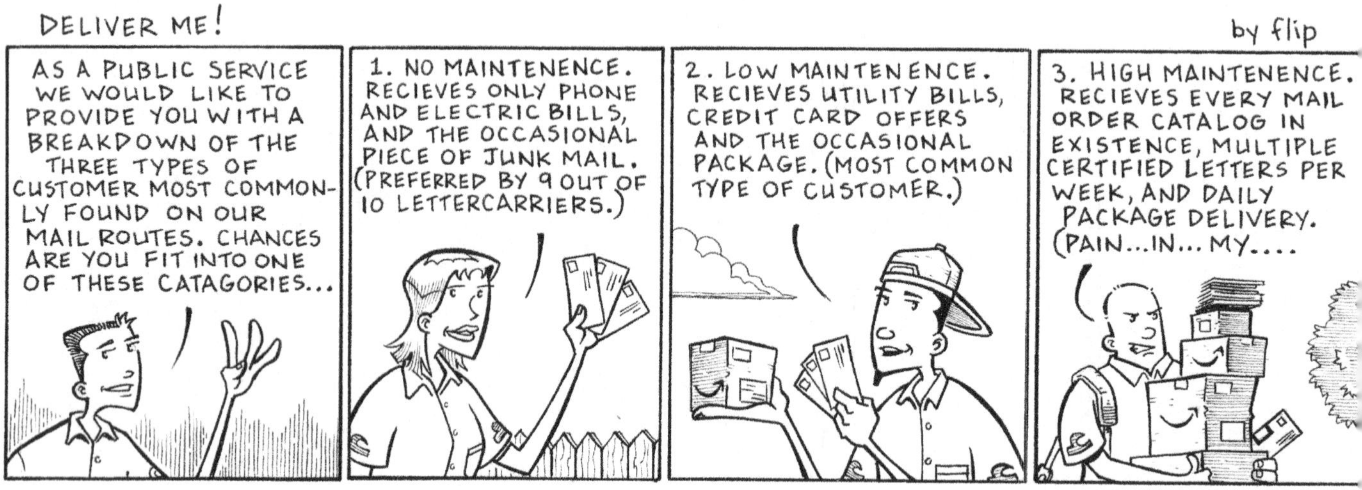
DELIVER ME!
by flip
AS A PUBLIC SERVICE WE WOULD LIKE TO PROVIDE YOU WITH A BREAKDOWN OF THE THREE TYPES OF CUSTOMER MOST COMMONLY FOUND ON OUR MAIL ROUTES. CHANCES ARE YOU FIT INTO ONE OF THESE CATAGORIES...
1. NO MAINTENENCE. RECIEVES ONLY PHONE AND ELECTRIC BILLS, AND THE OCCASIONAL PIECE OF JUNK MAIL. (PREFERRED BY 9 OUT OF 10 LETTERCARRIERS.)
2. LOW MAINTENENCE. RECIEVES UTILITY BILLS, CREDIT CARD OFFERS AND THE OCCASIONAL PACKAGE. (MOST COMMON TYPE OF CUSTOMER.)
3. HIGH MAINTENENCE. RECIEVES EVERY MAIL ORDER CATALOG IN EXISTENCE, MULTIPLE CERTIFIED LETTERS PER WEEK, AND DAILY PACKAGE DELIVERY. (PAIN...IN... MY....

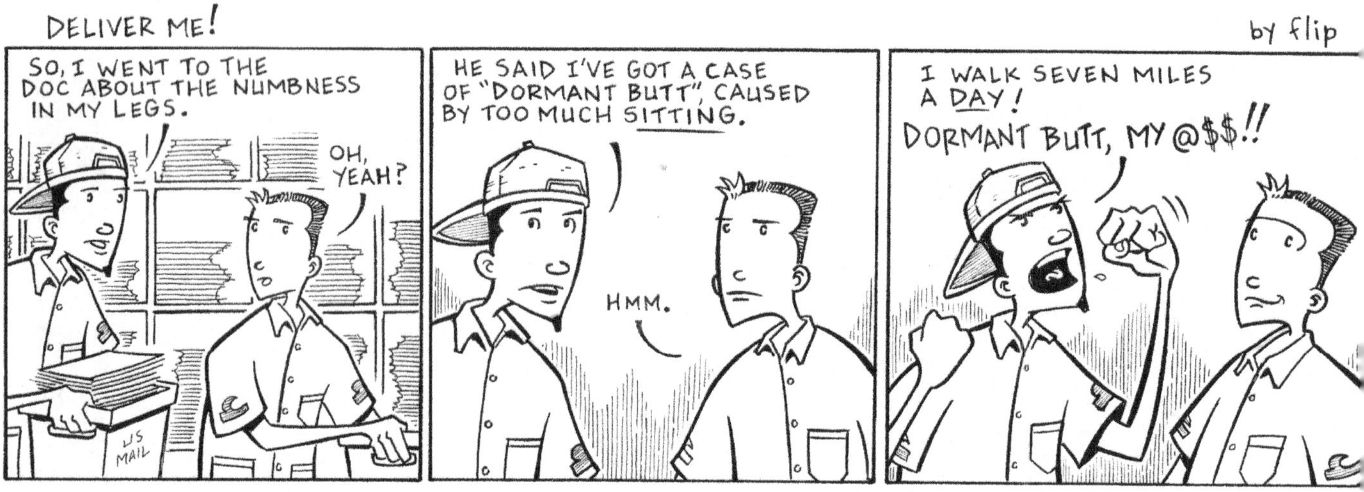
DELIVER ME!
by flip
SO, I WENT TO THE DOC ABOUT THE NUMBNESS IN MY LEGS.
OH, YEAH?
US MAIL
HE SAID I'VE GOT A CASE OF "DORMANT BUTT", CAUSED BY TOO MUCH SITTING.
HMM.
I WALK SEVEN MILES A DAY!
DORMANT BUTT, MY @$$!!

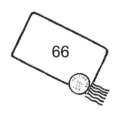

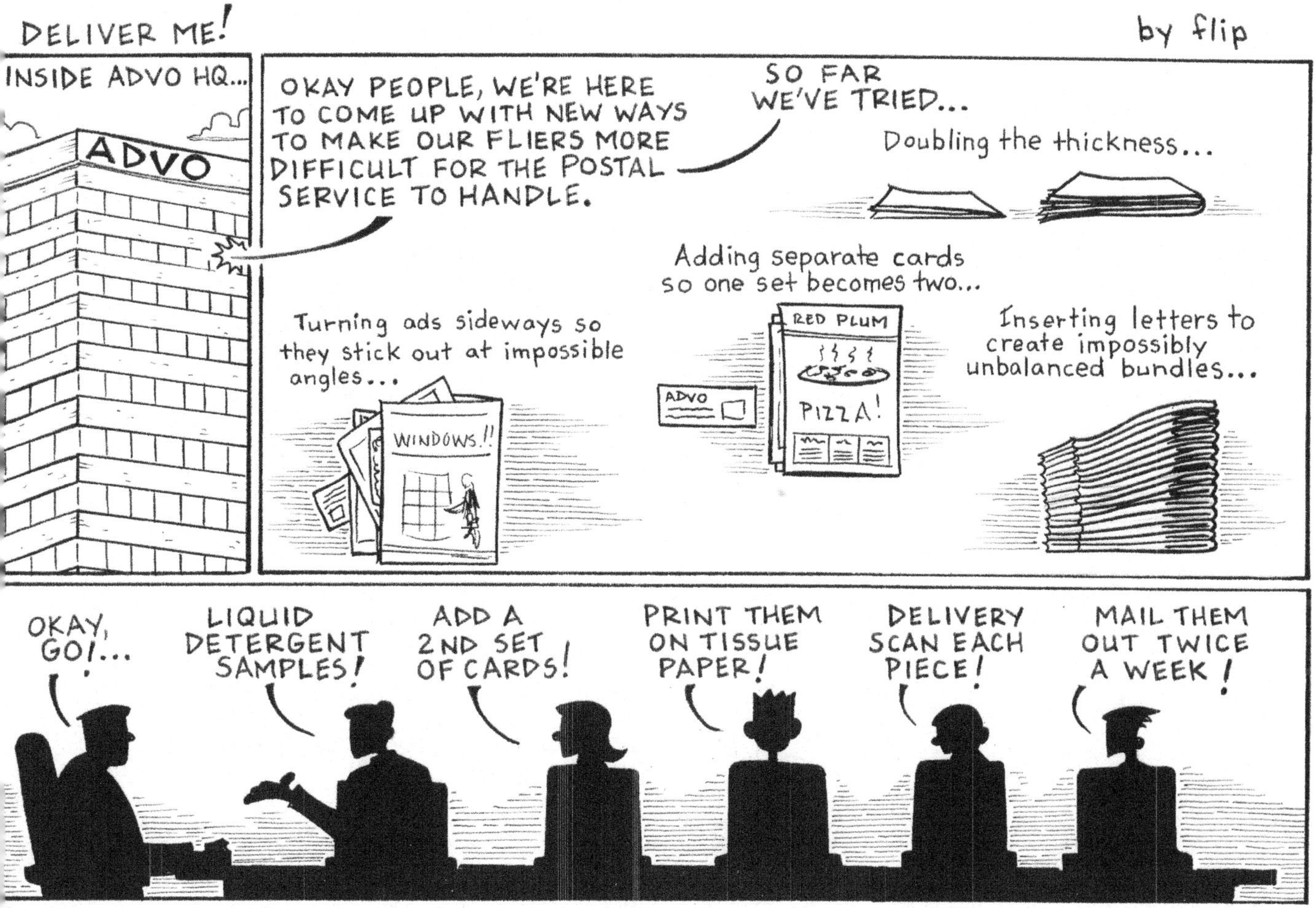
DELIVER ME!
by flip
INSIDE ADVO HQ...
ADVO
OKAY PEOPLE, WE'RE HERE TO COME UP WITH NEW WAYS TO MAKE OUR FLIERS MORE DIFFICULT FOR THE POSTAL SERVICE TO HANDLE.
SO FAR WE'VE TRIED...
Doubling the thickness...
Adding separate cards so one set becomes two...
Turning ads sideways so they stick out at impossible angles...
WINDOWS!!
RED PLUM
PIZZA!
ADVO
Inserting letters to create impossibly unbalanced bundles...
OKAY, GO!...
LIQUID DETERGENT SAMPLES!
ADD A 2ND SET OF CARDS!
PRINT THEM ON TISSUE PAPER!
DELIVERY SCAN EACH PIECE!
MAIL THEM OUT TWICE A WEEK!

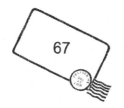

DELIVER ME! by flip

HEY MAILMAN, DO YOU HAVE A PACKAGE FOR ME?
NO, I DON'T THINK SO.
WELL MY PHONE SAYS YOU DO!
I'M PRETTY SURE I DON'T. BUT I'LL KEEP AN EYE OUT FOR IT.
UPS
FOUND IT.

DELIVER ME! by flip

ONCE AGAIN, IT'S DOG BITE PREVENTION WEEK.
ANYBODY NEED "MEAN DOG" SPRAY?
I DON'T KNOW ABOUT DOGS, BUT I COULD USE "MEAN CUSTOMER" SPRAY.

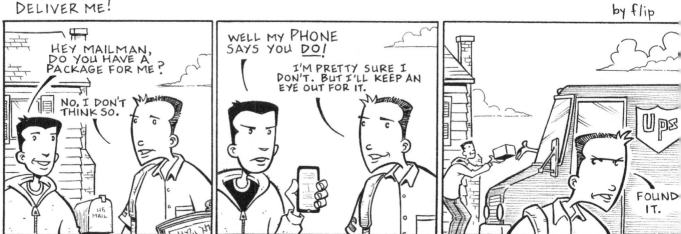

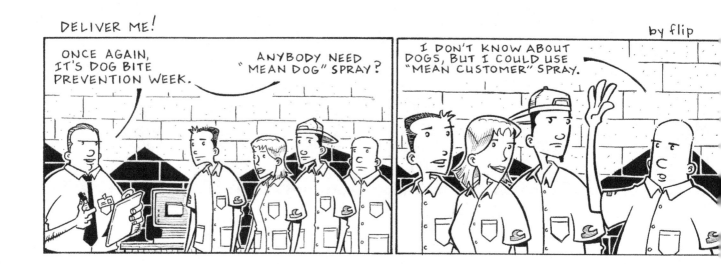

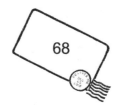

DELIVER ME!

by flip

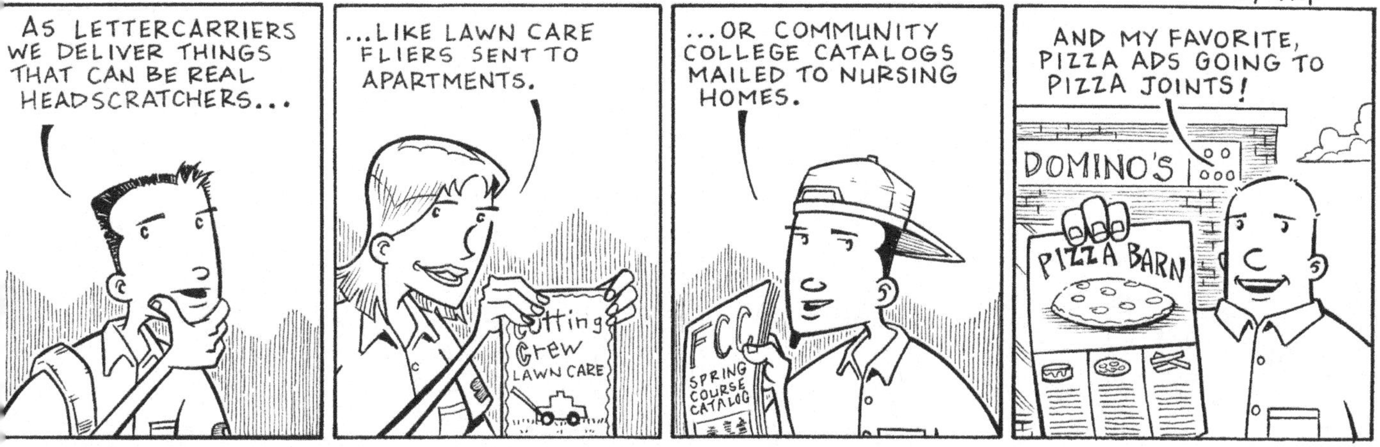
AS LETTERCARRIERS WE DELIVER THINGS THAT CAN BE REAL HEADSCRATCHERS...
...LIKE LAWN CARE FLIERS SENT TO APARTMENTS.
Cutting Crew LAWN CARE
...OR COMMUNITY COLLEGE CATALOGS MAILED TO NURSING HOMES.
FCC SPRING COURSE CATALOG
AND MY FAVORITE, PIZZA ADS GOING TO PIZZA JOINTS!
DOMINO'S
PIZZA BARN

DELIVER ME!

by flip

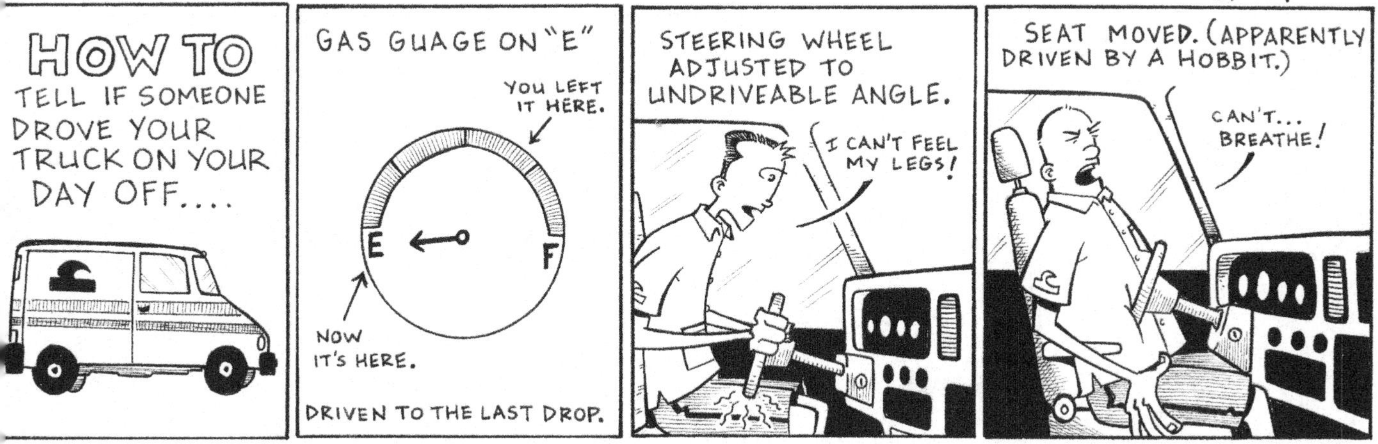
HOW TO TELL IF SOMEONE DROVE YOUR TRUCK ON YOUR DAY OFF....
GAS GUAGE ON "E"
YOU LEFT IT HERE.
E
F
NOW IT'S HERE.
DRIVEN TO THE LAST DROP.
STEERING WHEEL ADJUSTED TO UNDRIVEABLE ANGLE.
I CAN'T FEEL MY LEGS!
SEAT MOVED. (APPARENTLY DRIVEN BY A HOBBIT.)
CAN'T... BREATHE!

DELIVER ME! by flip

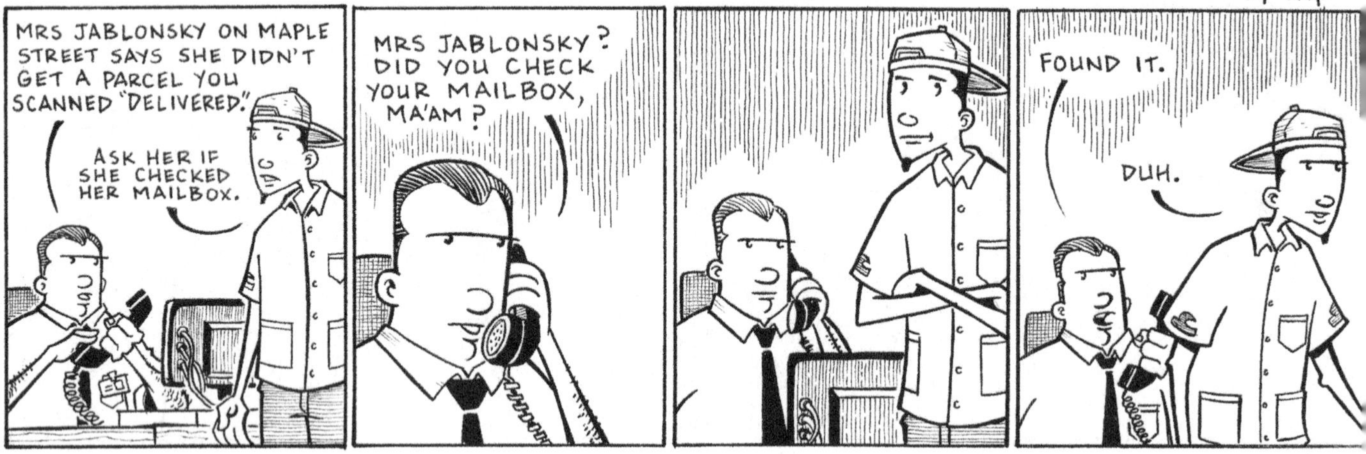
MRS JABLONSKY ON MAPLE STREET SAYS SHE DIDN'T GET A PARCEL YOU SCANNED "DELIVERED."
ASK HER IF SHE CHECKED HER MAILBOX.
MRS JABLONSKY? DID YOU CHECK YOUR MAILBOX, MA'AM?
FOUND IT.
DUH.

DELIVER ME! by flip

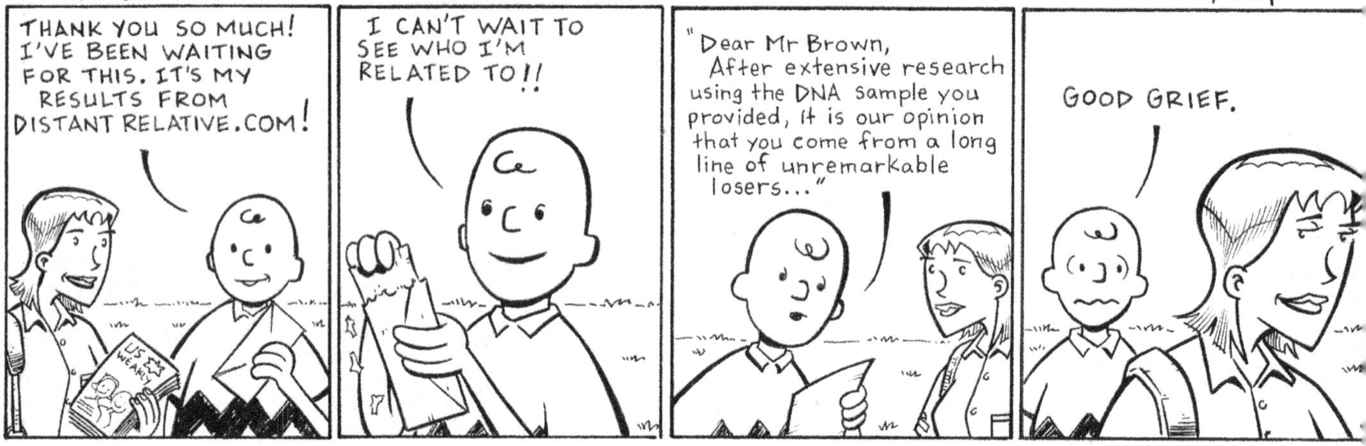
THANK YOU SO MUCH! I'VE BEEN WAITING FOR THIS. IT'S MY RESULTS FROM DISTANT RELATIVE.COM!
US WEEKLY
I CAN'T WAIT TO SEE WHO I'M RELATED TO!!
"Dear Mr Brown, After extensive research using the DNA sample you provided, it is our opinion that you come from a long line of unremarkable losers..."
GOOD GRIEF.

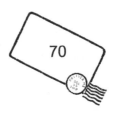

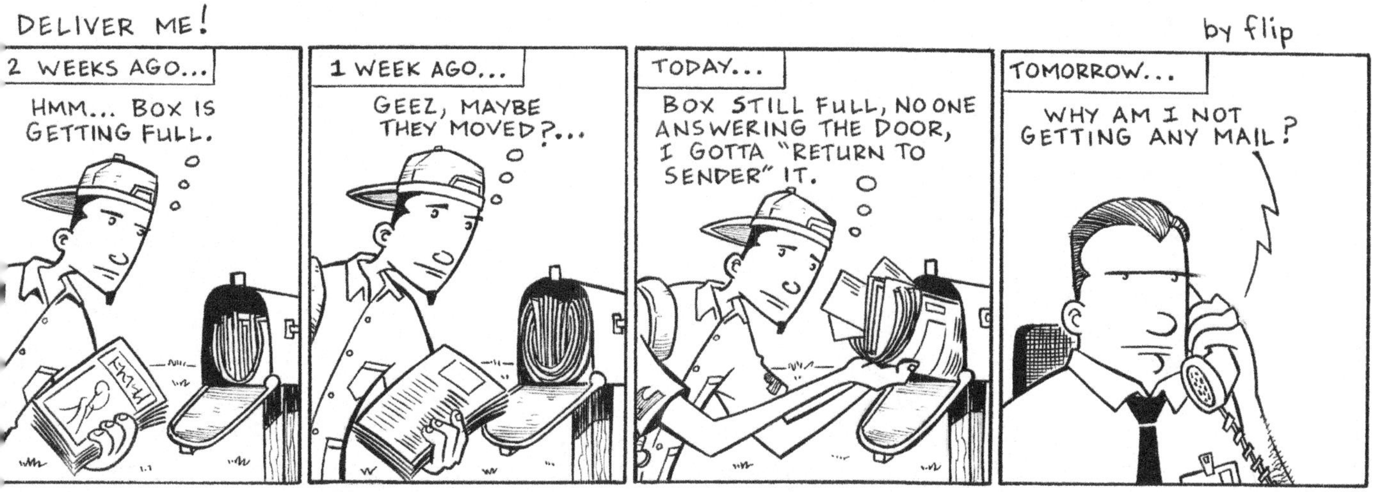
DELIVER ME!
by flip
2 WEEKS AGO...
HMM... BOX IS GETTING FULL.
1 WEEK AGO...
GEEZ, MAYBE THEY MOVED?...
TODAY...
BOX STILL FULL, NO ONE ANSWERING THE DOOR, I GOTTA "RETURN TO SENDER" IT.
TOMORROW...
WHY AM I NOT GETTING ANY MAIL?

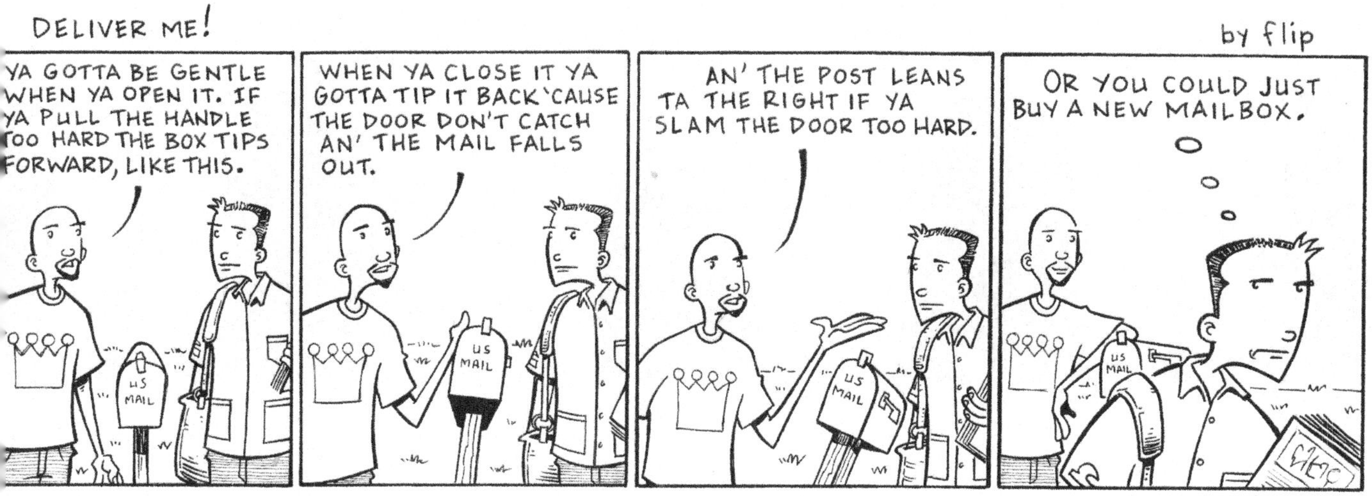
DELIVER ME!
by flip
YA GOTTA BE GENTLE WHEN YA OPEN IT. IF YA PULL THE HANDLE TOO HARD THE BOX TIPS FORWARD, LIKE THIS.
US MAIL
WHEN YA CLOSE IT YA GOTTA TIP IT BACK 'CAUSE THE DOOR DON'T CATCH AN' THE MAIL FALLS OUT.
US MAIL
AN' THE POST LEANS TA THE RIGHT IF YA SLAM THE DOOR TOO HARD.
US MAIL
OR YOU COULD JUST BUY A NEW MAILBOX.
US MAIL

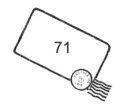

DELIVER ME! by flip

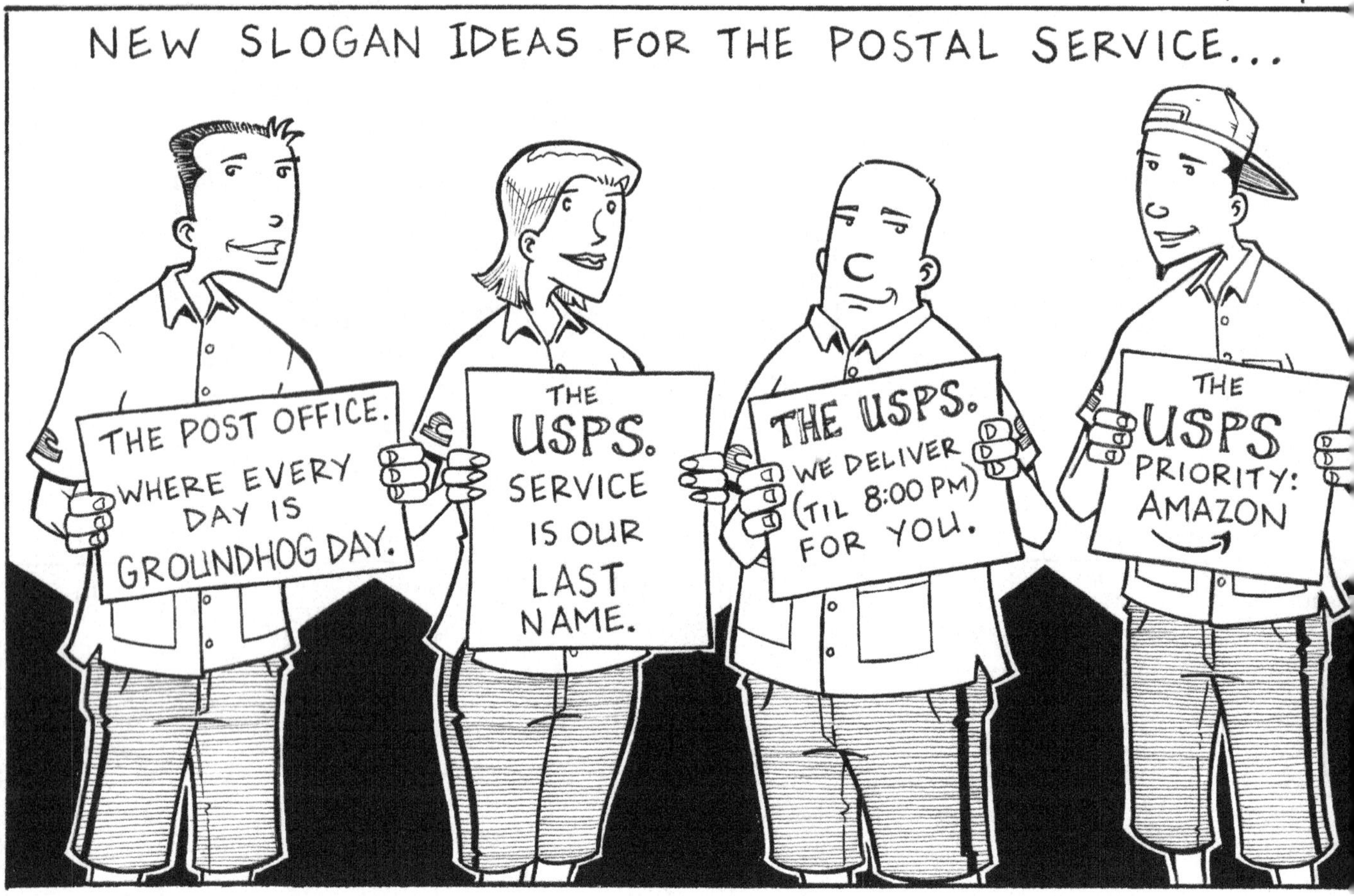
NEW SLOGAN IDEAS FOR THE POSTAL SERVICE...
THE POST OFFICE. WHERE EVERY DAY IS GROUNDHOG DAY.
THE USPS. SERVICE IS OUR LAST NAME.
THE USPS. WE DELIVER (TIL 8:00 PM) FOR YOU.
THE USPS PRIORITY: AMAZON

DELIVER ME!

by flip

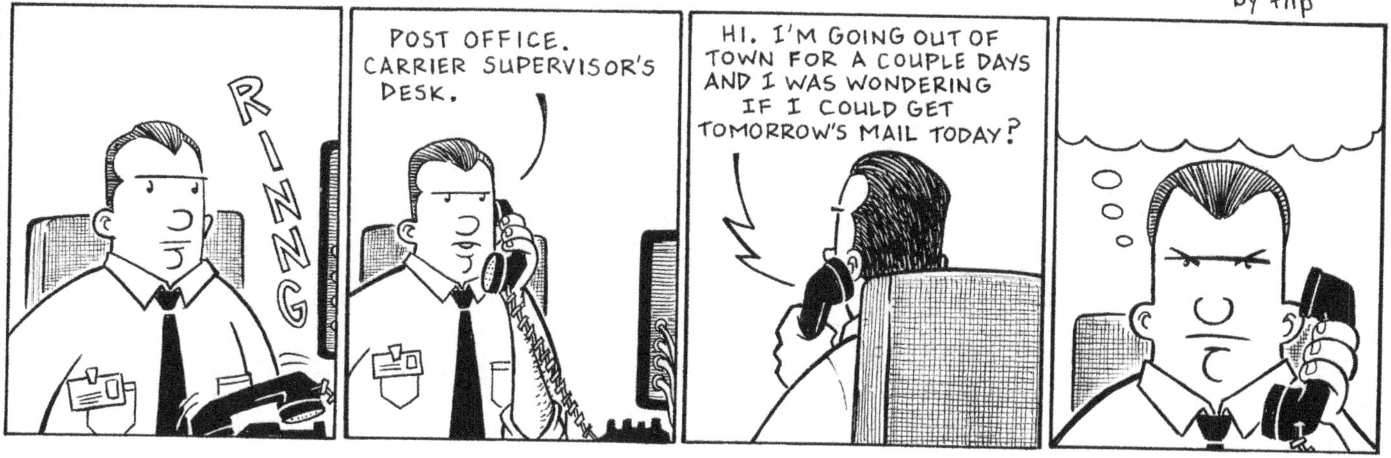
RINNG
POST OFFICE. CARRIER SUPERVISOR'S DESK.
HI. I'M GOING OUT OF TOWN FOR A COUPLE DAYS AND I WAS WONDERING IF I COULD GET TOMORROW'S MAIL TODAY?

DELIVER ME!

by flip

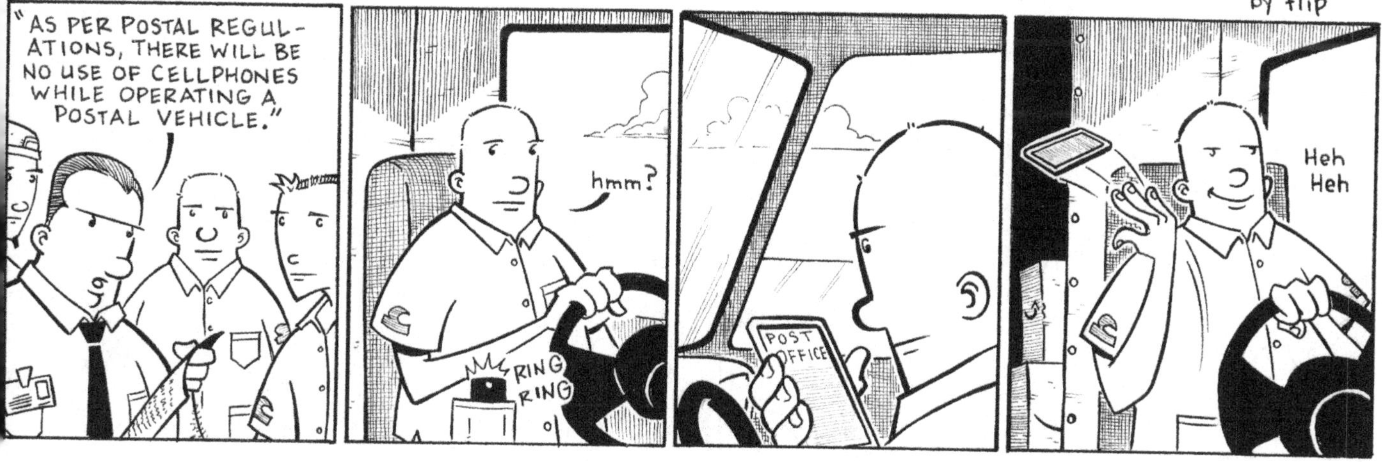
"AS PER POSTAL REGULATIONS, THERE WILL BE NO USE OF CELLPHONES WHILE OPERATING A POSTAL VEHICLE."
hmm?
RING RING
POST OFFICE
Heh Heh

DELIVER ME! by flip

Please please please...
Come on, baby...
CLUNK
CLUNK
NOOOOOOOOO!
US MAIL
US MAIL

DELIVER ME! by flip

FORREST GUMP FAMOUSLY SAID, "LIFE IS LIKE A BOX OF CHOCOLATES." WE'D LIKE TO ADD THAT SO IS DELIVERING MAIL IN THE SPRINGTIME.
HITMANS ASSORTED CHOCOLATES
WHETHER IT'S ANTS...
EWWW!
OR BEES....
GET OUT!
OR EVERYBODY'S FAVORITE... SPIDERS!
CHOCOLATES YOU SHOULDN'T HAVE!
"YOU NEVER KNOW WHAT YOU'RE GONNA GET!"

DELIVER ME!

by flip

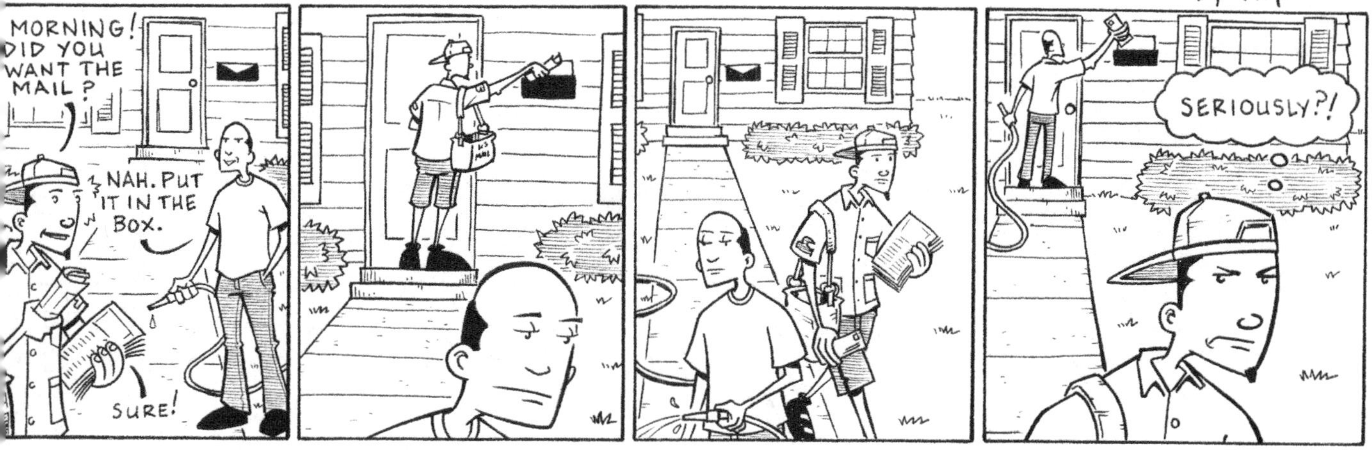
MORNING! DID YOU WANT THE MAIL?
NAH. PUT IT IN THE BOX.
SURE!
SERIOUSLY?!

DELIVER ME!

by flip

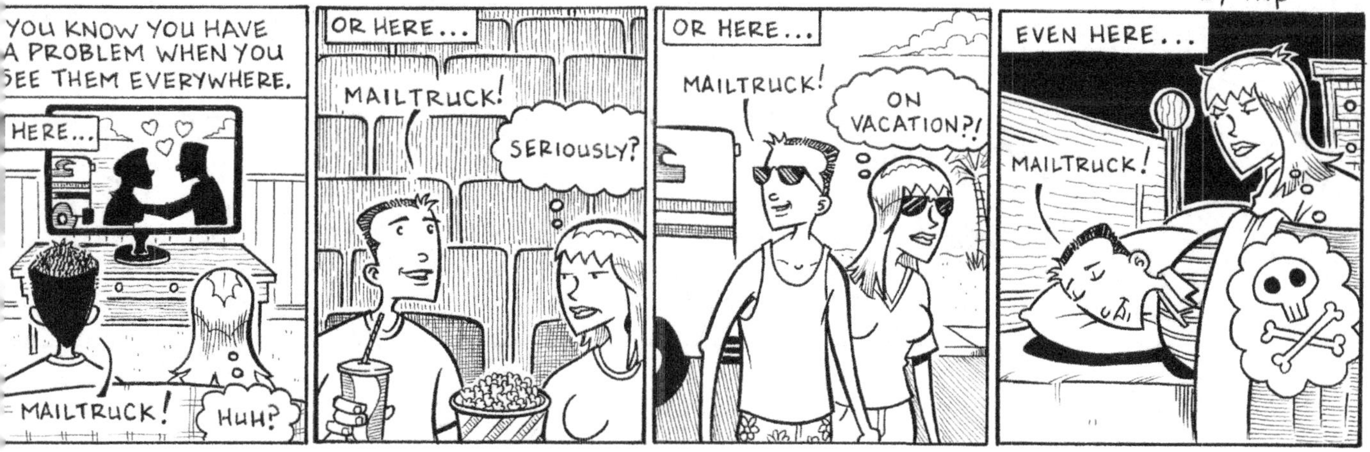
YOU KNOW YOU HAVE A PROBLEM WHEN YOU SEE THEM EVERYWHERE.
HERE...
MAILTRUCK!
HUH?
OR HERE...
MAILTRUCK!
SERIOUSLY?
OR HERE...
MAILTRUCK!
ON VACATION?!
EVEN HERE...
MAILTRUCK!

DELIVER ME! by flip

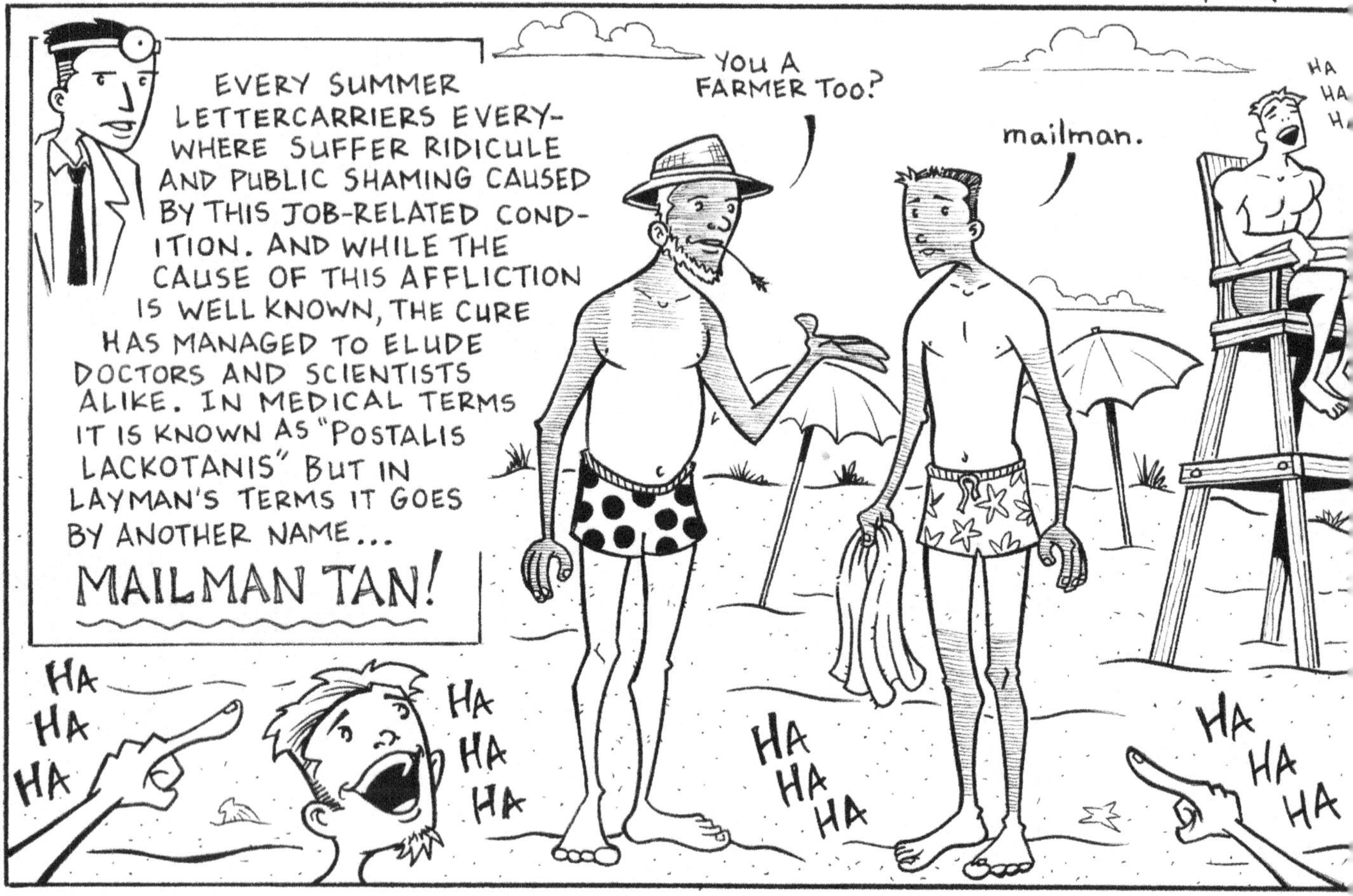

EVERY SUMMER LETTERCARRIERS EVERYWHERE SUFFER RIDICULE AND PUBLIC SHAMING CAUSED BY THIS JOB-RELATED CONDITION. AND WHILE THE CAUSE OF THIS AFFLICTION IS WELL KNOWN, THE CURE HAS MANAGED TO ELUDE DOCTORS AND SCIENTISTS ALIKE. IN MEDICAL TERMS IT IS KNOWN AS "POSTALIS LACKOTANIS" BUT IN LAYMAN'S TERMS IT GOES BY ANOTHER NAME...
MAILMAN TAN!
YOU A FARMER TOO?
mailman.
HA HA HA
HA HA HA
HA HA HA
HA HA HA
HA HA HA

DELIVER ME! by flip

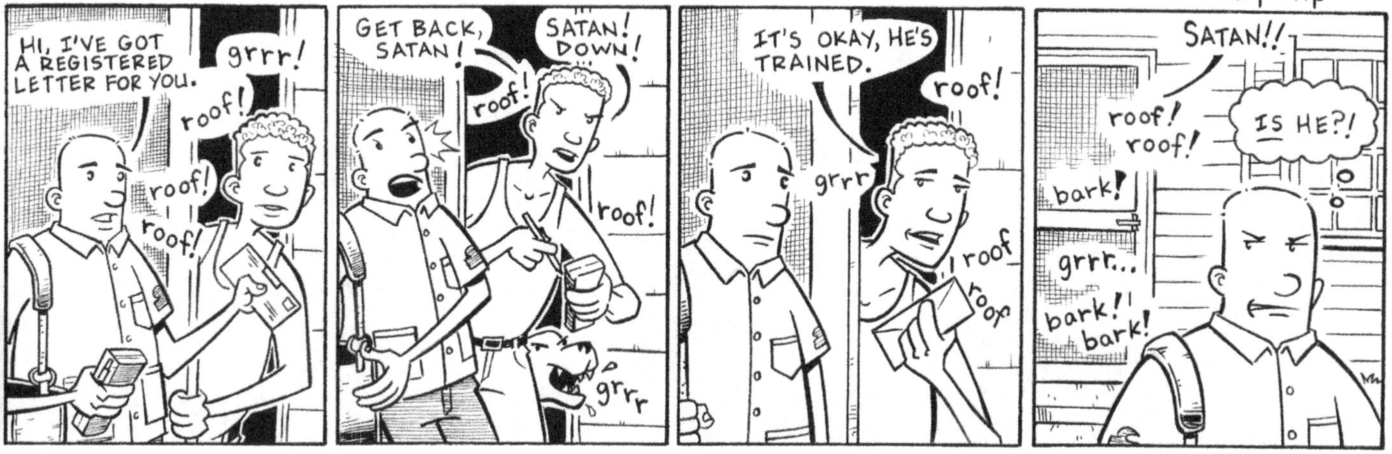
HI, I'VE GOT A REGISTERED LETTER FOR YOU.
grrr!
roof!
roof!
roof!
GET BACK, SATAN!
SATAN! DOWN!
roof!
roof!
grrr
IT'S OKAY, HE'S TRAINED.
roof!
grrr
roof
roof
SATAN!!
roof! roof!
IS HE?!
bark!
grrr...
bark!! bark!

DELIVER ME! by flip

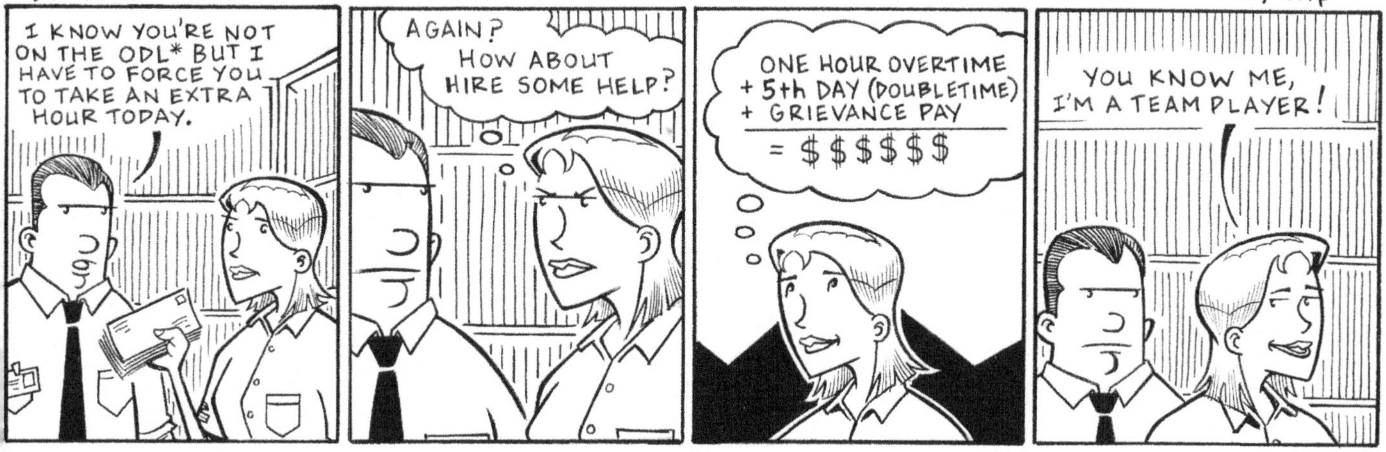
I KNOW YOU'RE NOT ON THE ODL* BUT I HAVE TO FORCE YOU TO TAKE AN EXTRA HOUR TODAY.
AGAIN? HOW ABOUT HIRE SOME HELP?
ONE HOUR OVERTIME
+ 5th DAY (DOUBLETIME)
+ GRIEVANCE PAY
= $$$$$$
YOU KNOW ME, I'M A TEAM PLAYER!

*OVERTIME DESIRED LIST

DELIVER ME! by flip

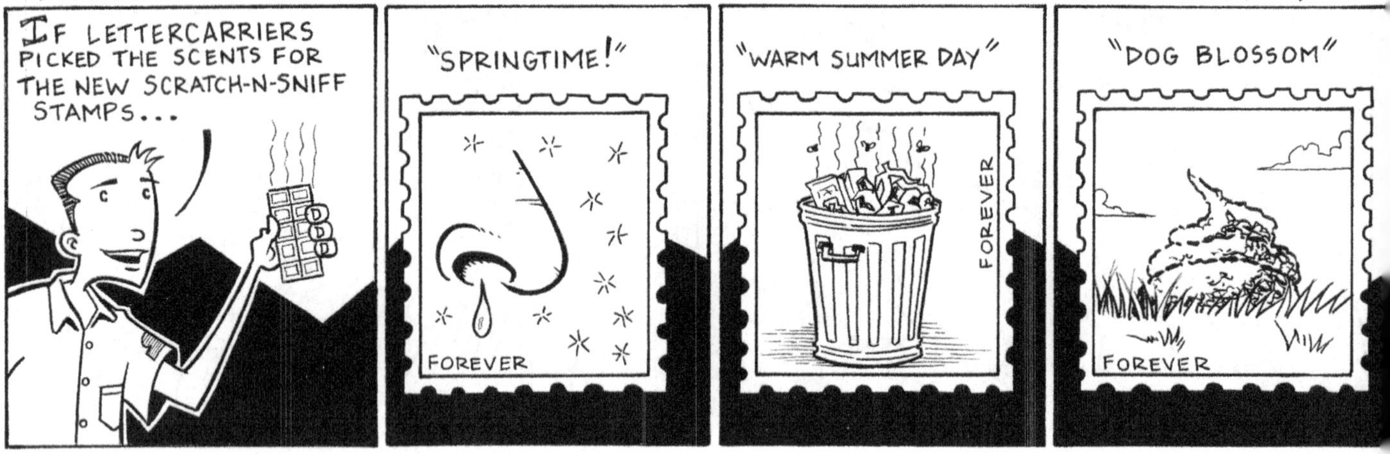
IF LETTERCARRIERS PICKED THE SCENTS FOR THE NEW SCRATCH-N-SNIFF STAMPS...
"SPRINGTIME!"
FOREVER
"WARM SUMMER DAY"
FOREVER
"DOG BLOSSOM"
FOREVER

DELIVER ME! by flip

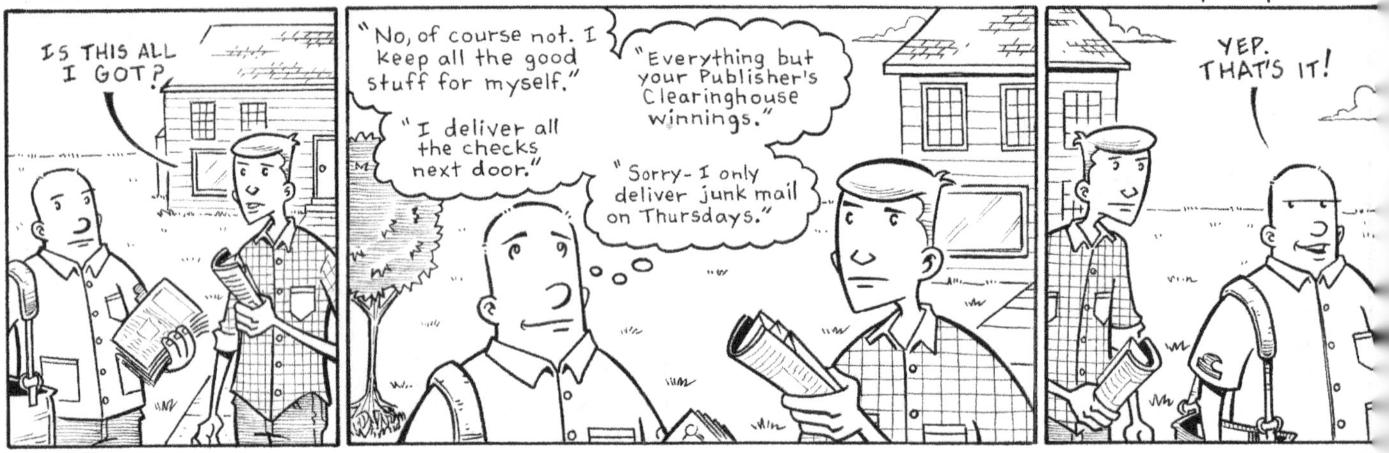
IS THIS ALL I GOT?
"No, of course not. I keep all the good stuff for myself."
"I deliver all the checks next door."
"Everything but your Publisher's Clearinghouse winnings."
"Sorry- I only deliver junk mail on Thursdays."
YEP. THAT'S IT!

DELIVER ME!

by flip

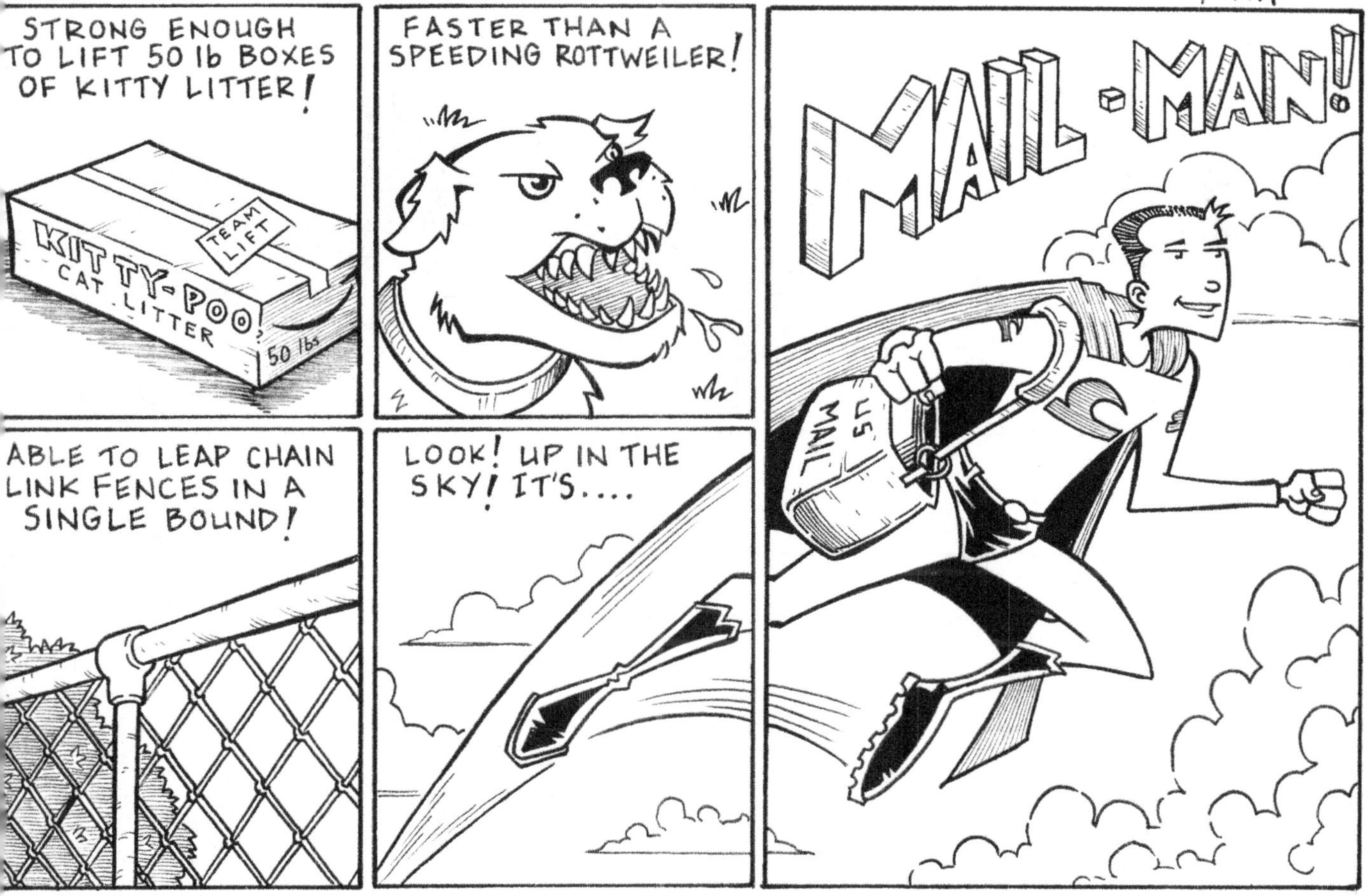
STRONG ENOUGH TO LIFT 50 lb BOXES OF KITTY LITTER!
KITTY-POO CAT LITTER
TEAM LIFT
50 lbs
FASTER THAN A SPEEDING ROTTWEILER!
ABLE TO LEAP CHAIN LINK FENCES IN A SINGLE BOUND!
LOOK! UP IN THE SKY! IT'S....
MAIL-MAN!
US MAIL

DELIVER ME! by flip

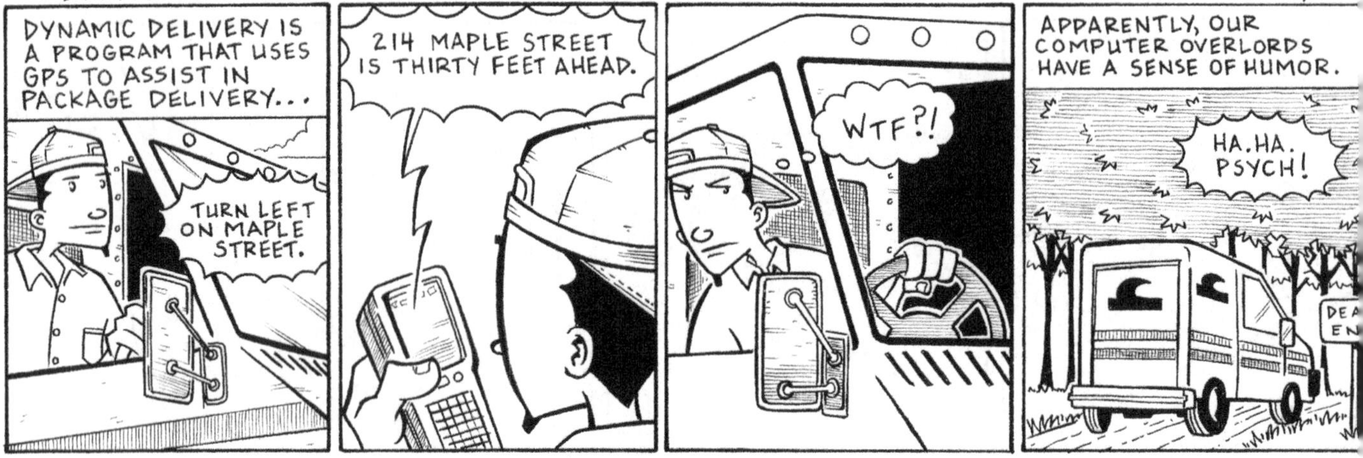

DYNAMIC DELIVERY IS A PROGRAM THAT USES GPS TO ASSIST IN PACKAGE DELIVERY...
TURN LEFT ON MAPLE STREET.
214 MAPLE STREET IS THIRTY FEET AHEAD.
WTF?!
APPARENTLY, OUR COMPUTER OVERLORDS HAVE A SENSE OF HUMOR.
HA.HA. PSYCH!

DELIVER ME! by flip

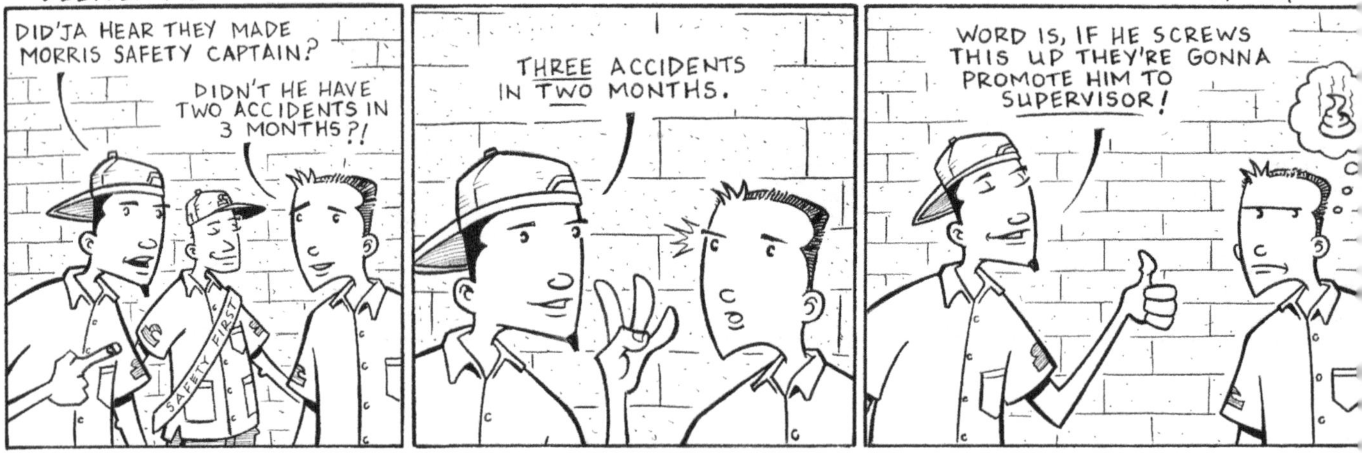

DID'JA HEAR THEY MADE MORRIS SAFETY CAPTAIN?
DIDN'T HE HAVE TWO ACCIDENTS IN 3 MONTHS?!
SAFETY FIRST
THREE ACCIDENTS IN TWO MONTHS.
WORD IS, IF HE SCREWS THIS UP THEY'RE GONNA PROMOTE HIM TO SUPERVISOR!

DELIVER ME! by flip

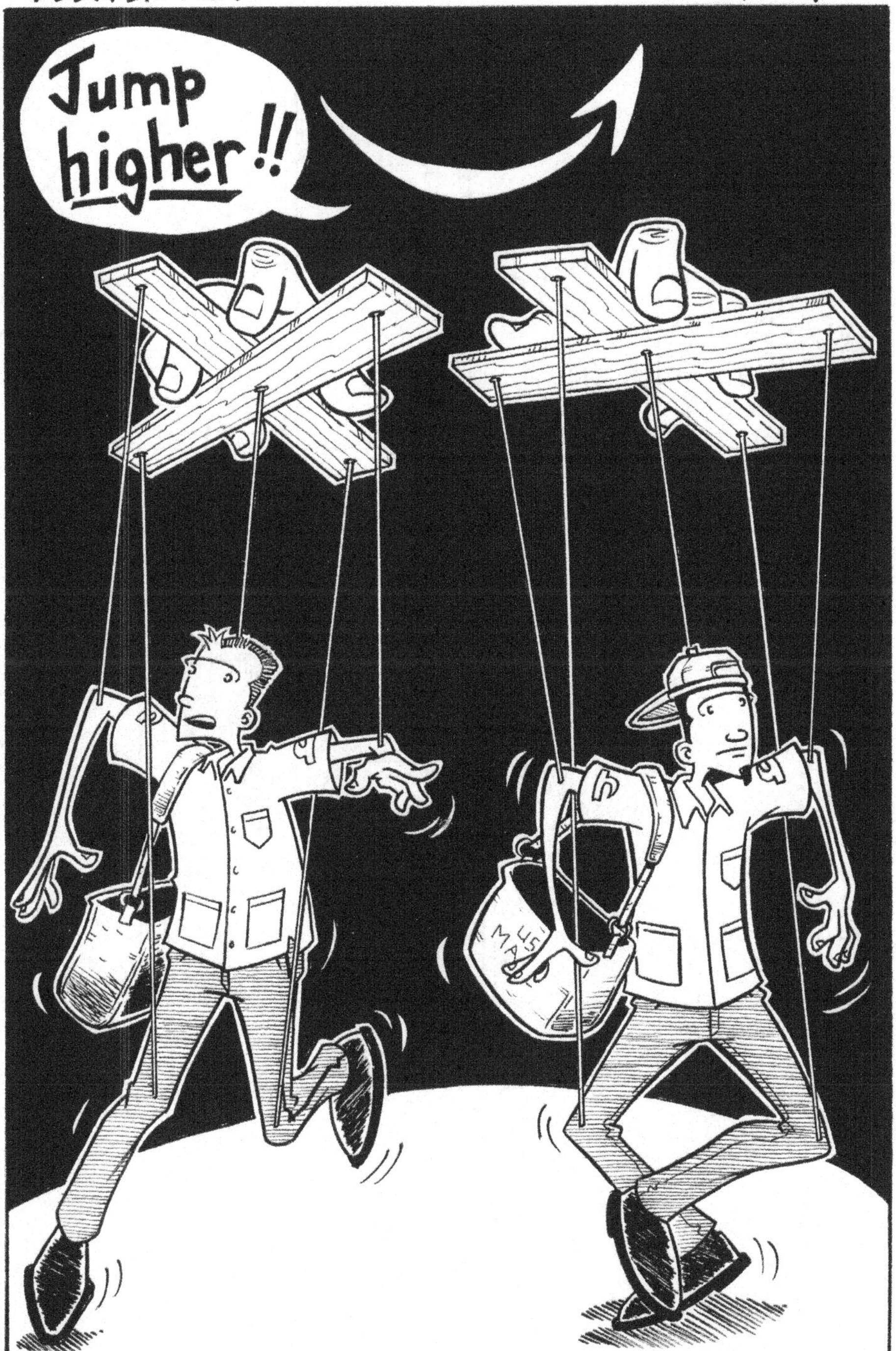
Jump higher!!

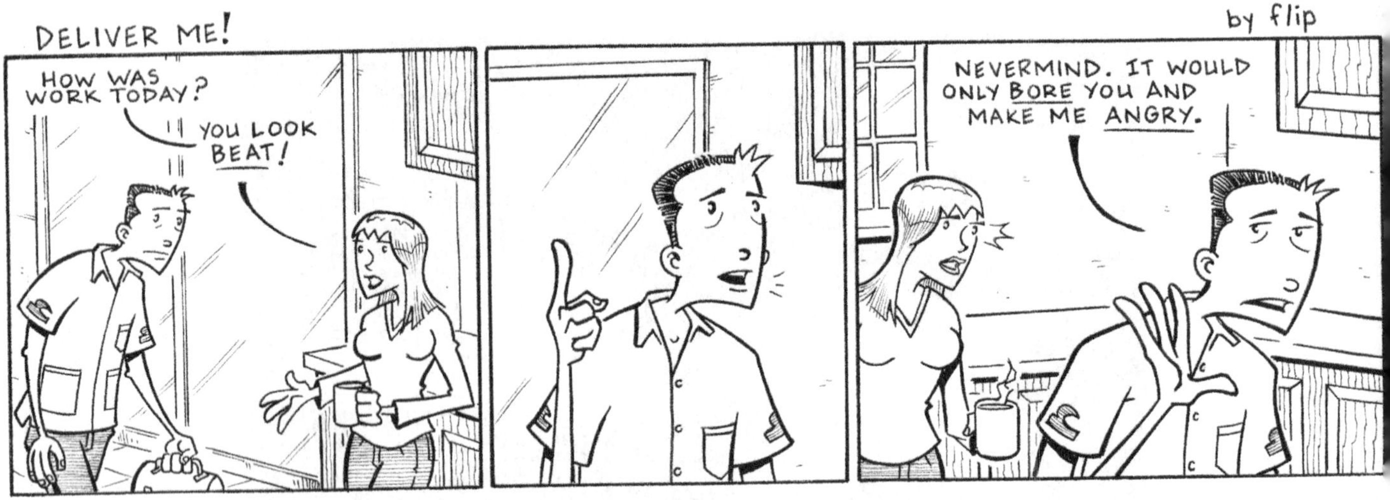
DELIVER ME!
by flip
HOW WAS WORK TODAY?
YOU LOOK BEAT!
NEVERMIND. IT WOULD ONLY BORE YOU AND MAKE ME ANGRY.

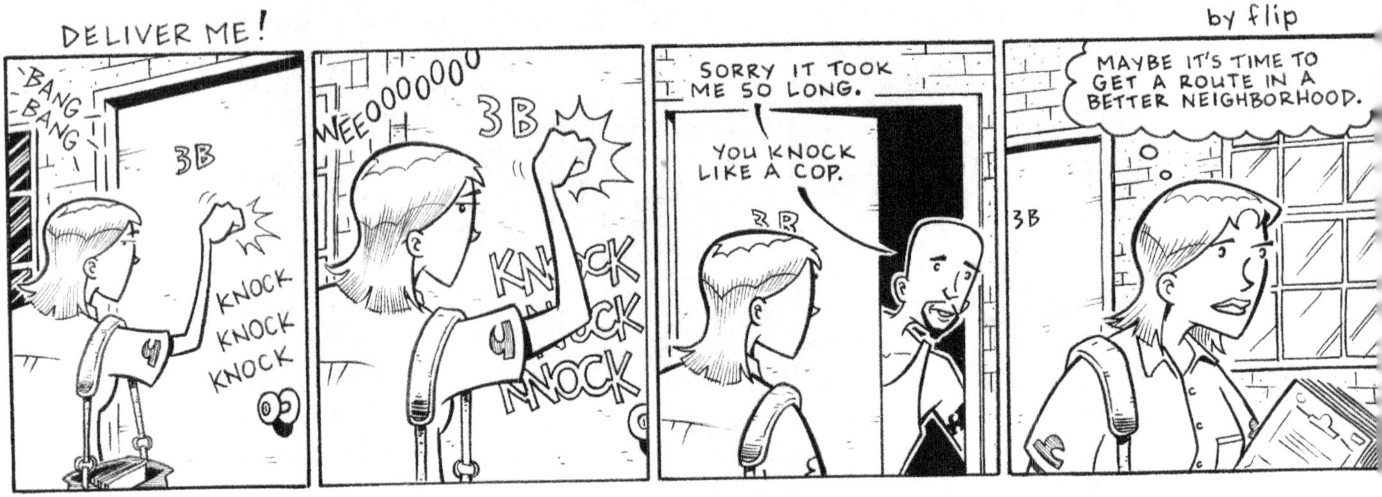
DELIVER ME!
by flip
BANG BANG
3B
KNOCK KNOCK KNOCK
WEEOOOOOOO
3B
KNOCK KNOCK KNOCK
SORRY IT TOOK ME SO LONG.
YOU KNOCK LIKE A COP.
3B
MAYBE IT'S TIME TO GET A ROUTE IN A BETTER NEIGHBORHOOD.
3B

DELIVER ME!

by flip

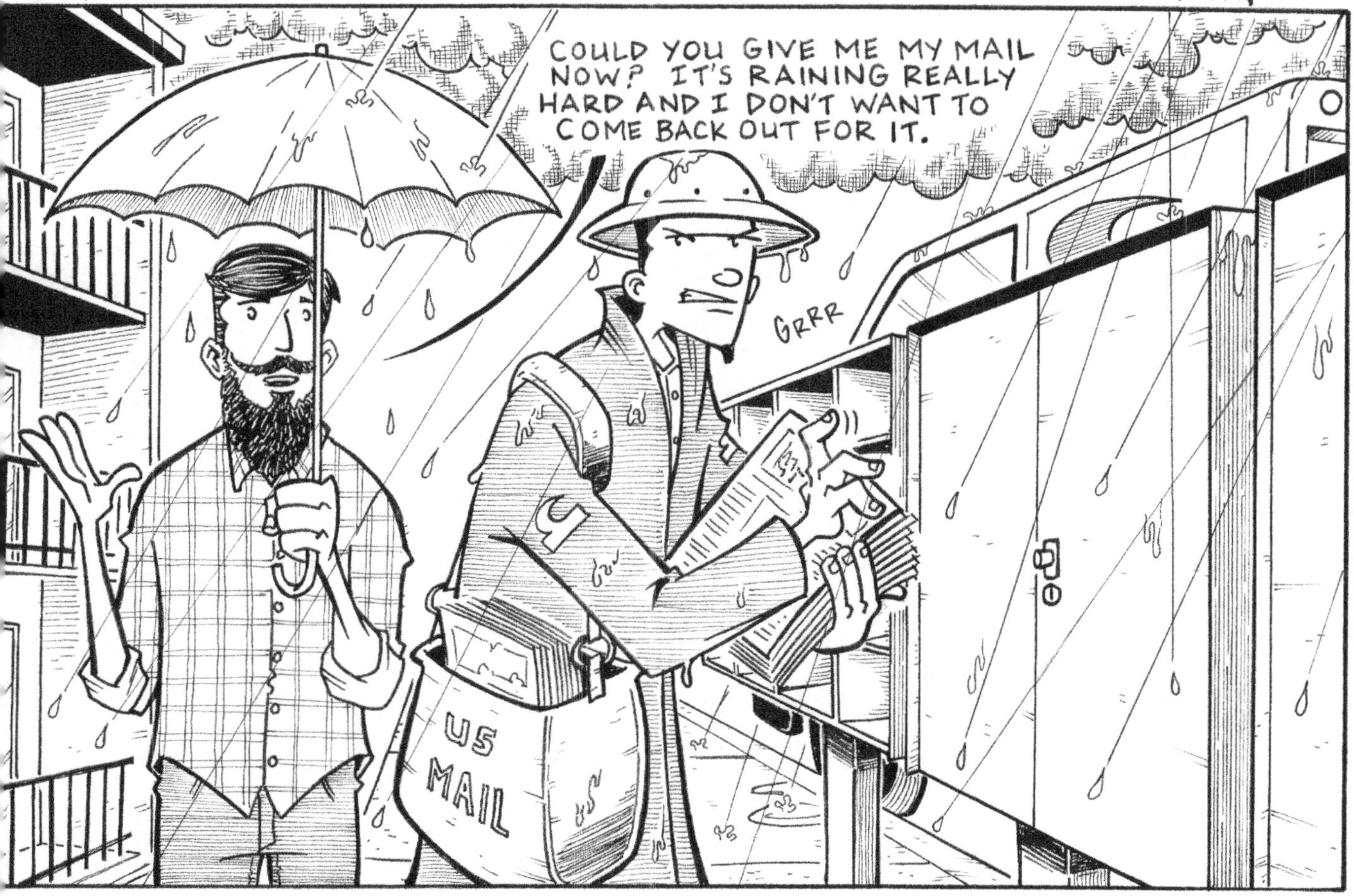
COULD YOU GIVE ME MY MAIL NOW? IT'S RAINING REALLY HARD AND I DON'T WANT TO COME BACK OUT FOR IT.
GRRR
US MAIL

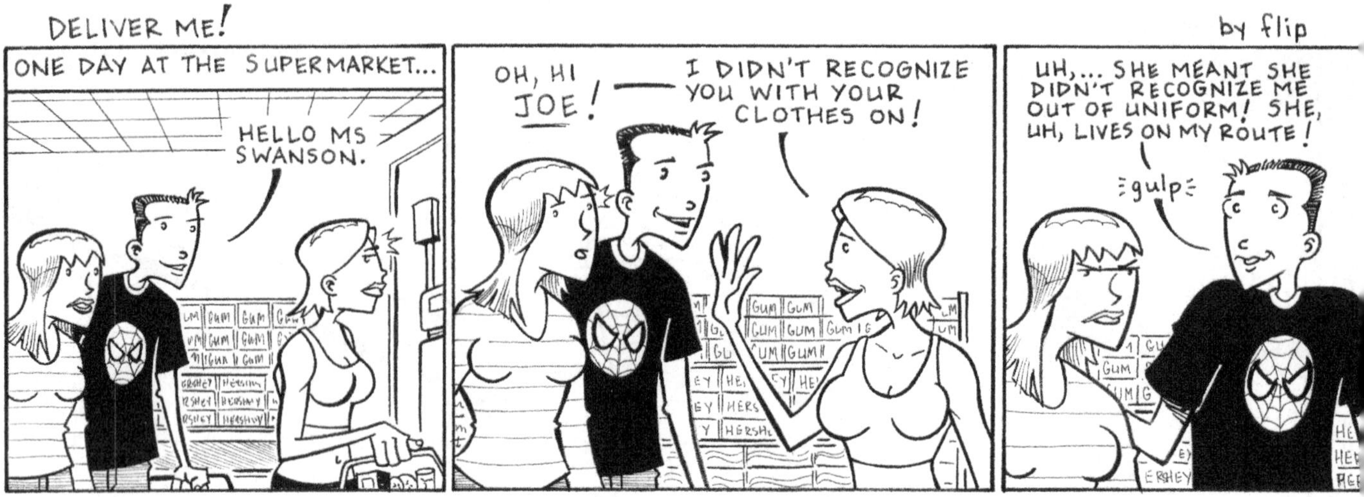
DELIVER ME!
by flip
ONE DAY AT THE SUPERMARKET...
HELLO MS SWANSON.
OH, HI JOE!
I DIDN'T RECOGNIZE YOU WITH YOUR CLOTHES ON!
UH,... SHE MEANT SHE DIDN'T RECOGNIZE ME OUT OF UNIFORM! SHE, UH, LIVES ON MY ROUTE!
gulp

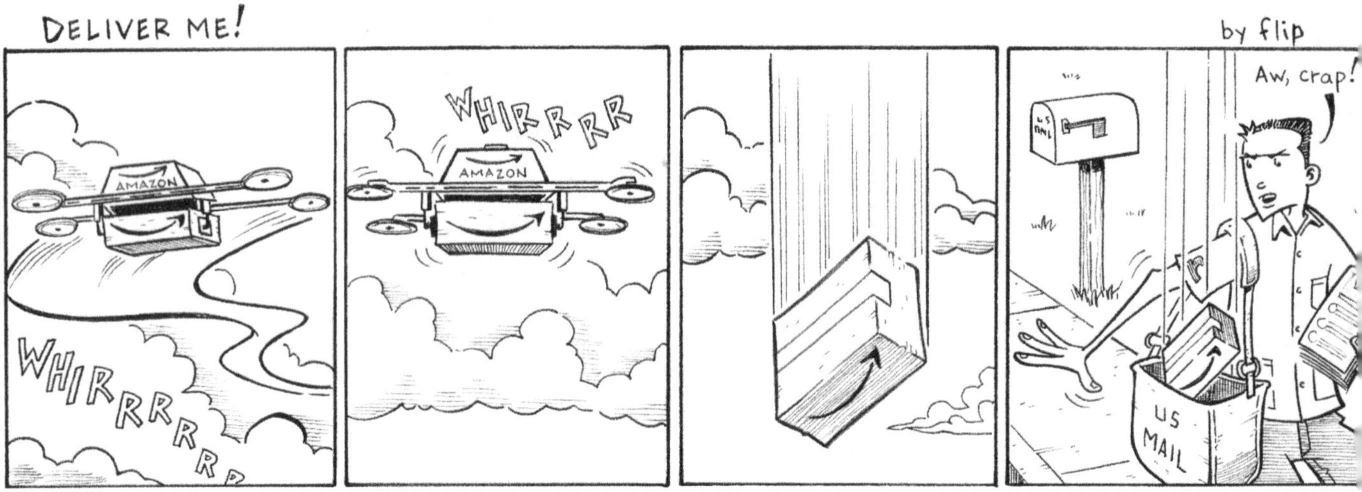
DELIVER ME!
by flip
AMAZON
WHIRRRRRRR
WHIRRRR
AMAZON
US MAIL
Aw, crap!

DELIVER ME! by flip

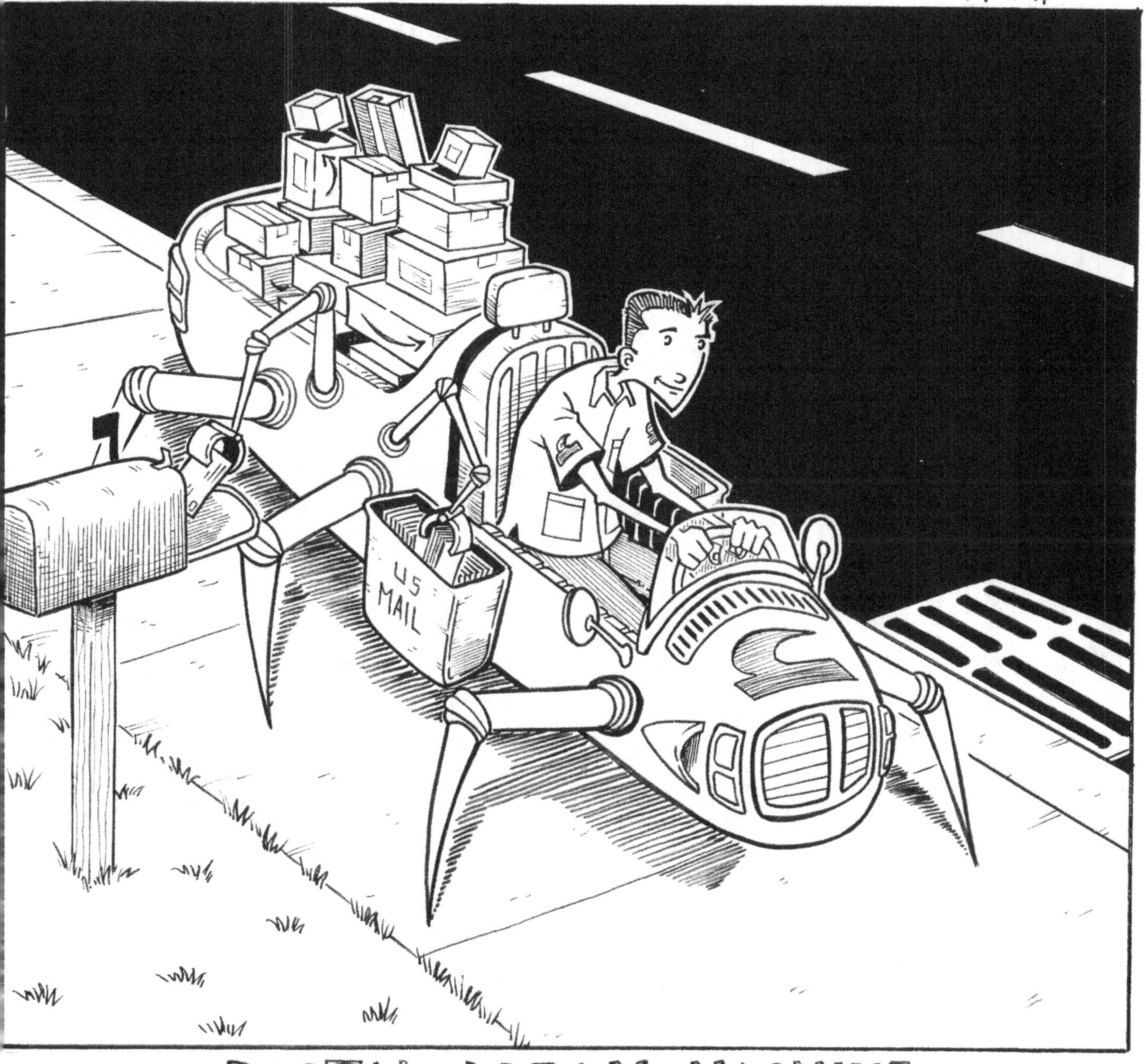
US
MAIL

POSTAL DREAM MACHINE

DELIVER ME! by flip

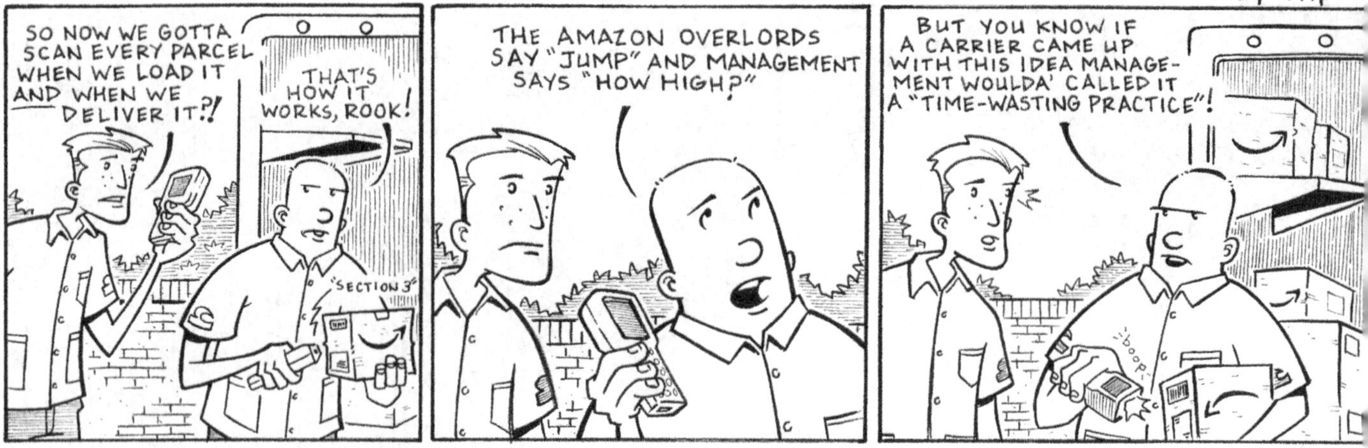
SO NOW WE GOTTA SCAN EVERY PARCEL WHEN WE LOAD IT AND WHEN WE DELIVER IT?!
THAT'S HOW IT WORKS, ROOK!
SECTION 3
THE AMAZON OVERLORDS SAY "JUMP" AND MANAGEMENT SAYS "HOW HIGH?"
BUT YOU KNOW IF A CARRIER CAME UP WITH THIS IDEA MANAGEMENT WOULDA' CALLED IT A "TIME-WASTING PRACTICE"!
boop

DELIVER ME! by flip

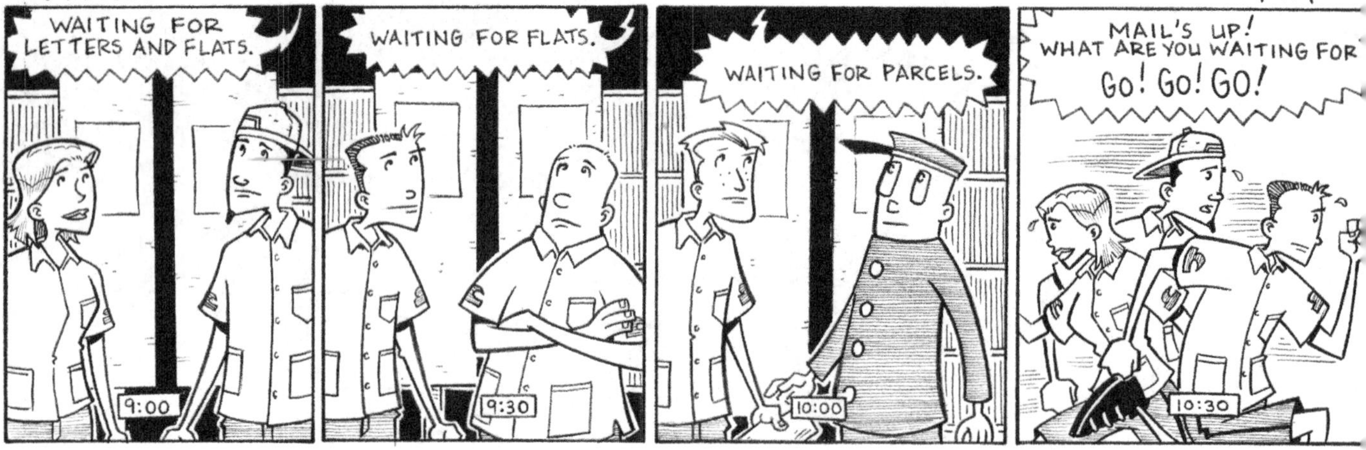
WAITING FOR LETTERS AND FLATS.
9:00
WAITING FOR FLATS.
9:30
WAITING FOR PARCELS.
10:00
MAIL'S UP! WHAT ARE YOU WAITING FOR
GO! GO! GO!
10:30

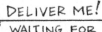

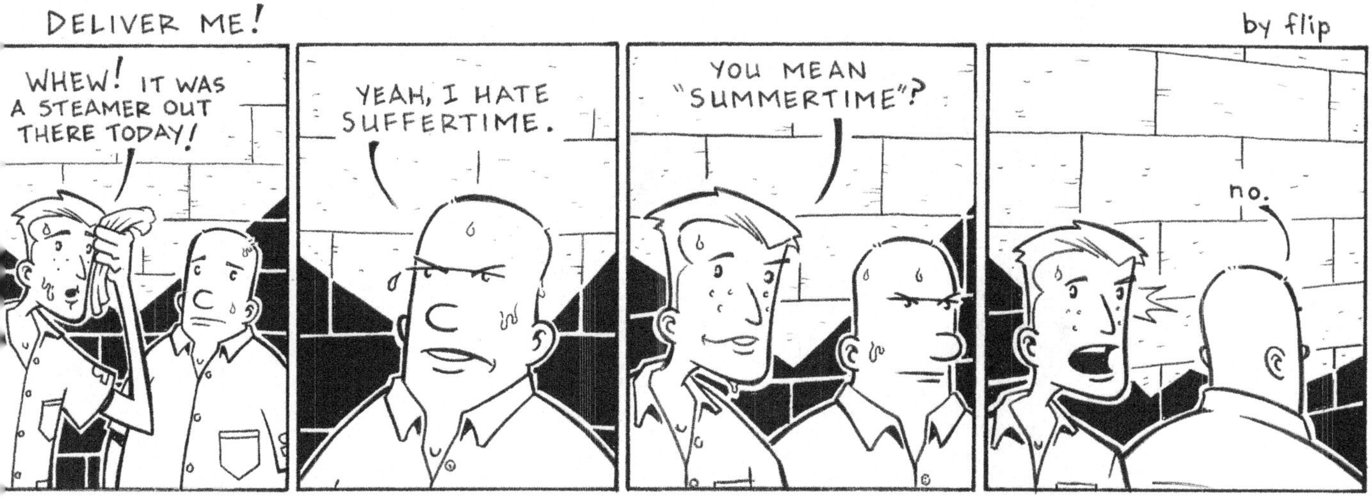
DELIVER ME!
by flip
WHEW! IT WAS A STEAMER OUT THERE TODAY!
YEAH, I HATE SUFFERTIME.
YOU MEAN "SUMMERTIME"?
no.

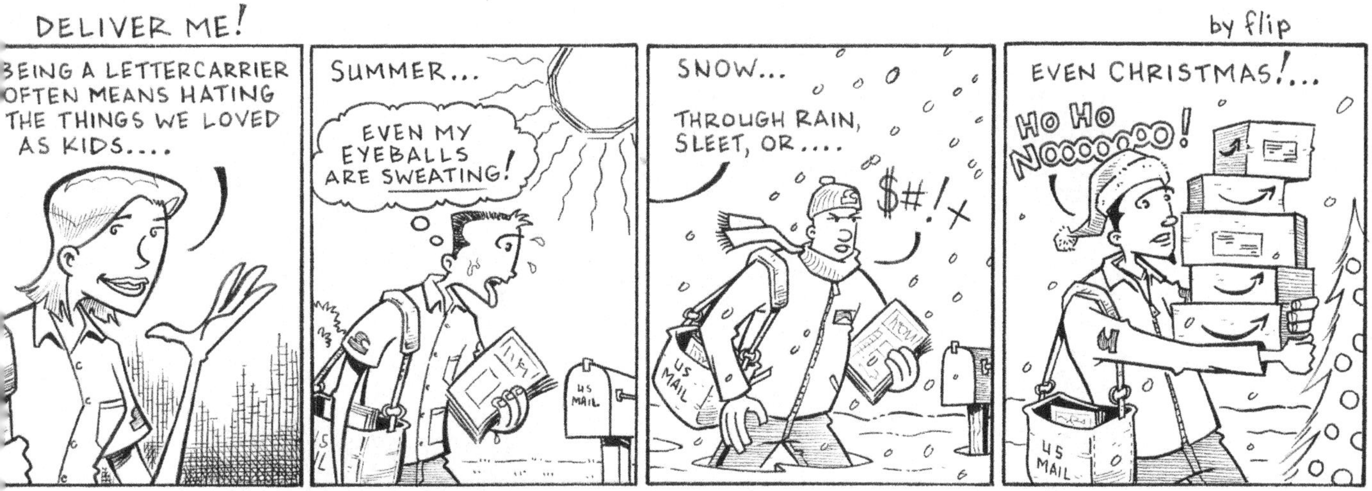
DELIVER ME!
by flip
BEING A LETTERCARRIER OFTEN MEANS HATING THE THINGS WE LOVED AS KIDS....
SUMMER...
EVEN MY EYEBALLS ARE SWEATING!
US MAIL
SNOW...
THROUGH RAIN, SLEET, OR....
$#!+
US MAIL
EVEN CHRISTMAS!...
HO HO NOOOOOOO!
US MAIL

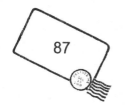

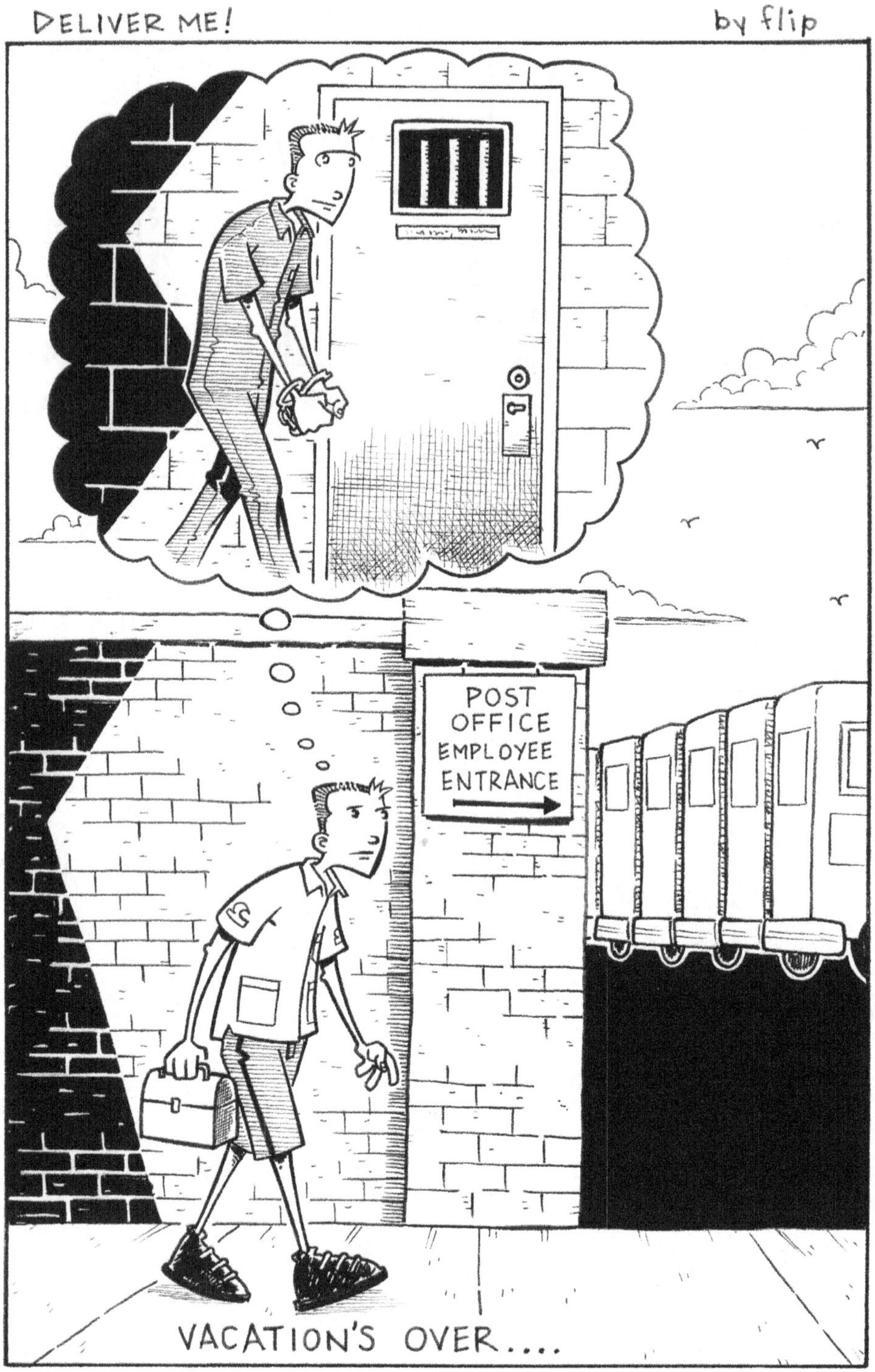
DELIVER ME!
by flip
POST
OFFICE
EMPLOYEE
ENTRANCE
VACATION'S OVER....

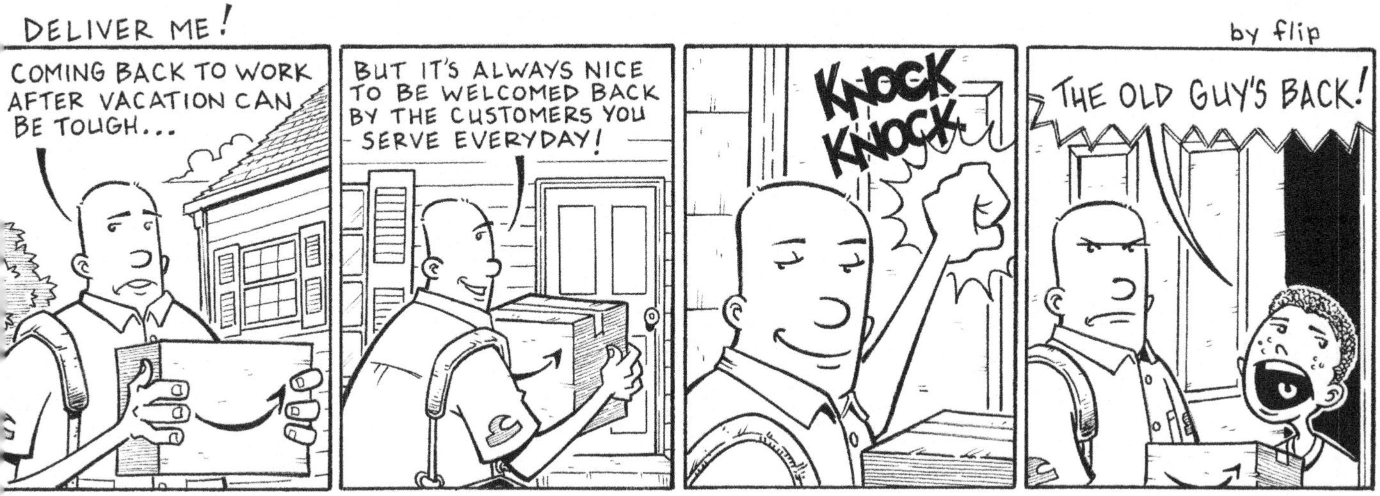
DELIVER ME!
by flip
COMING BACK TO WORK AFTER VACATION CAN BE TOUGH...
BUT IT'S ALWAYS NICE TO BE WELCOMED BACK BY THE CUSTOMERS YOU SERVE EVERYDAY!
KNOCK KNOCK
THE OLD GUY'S BACK!

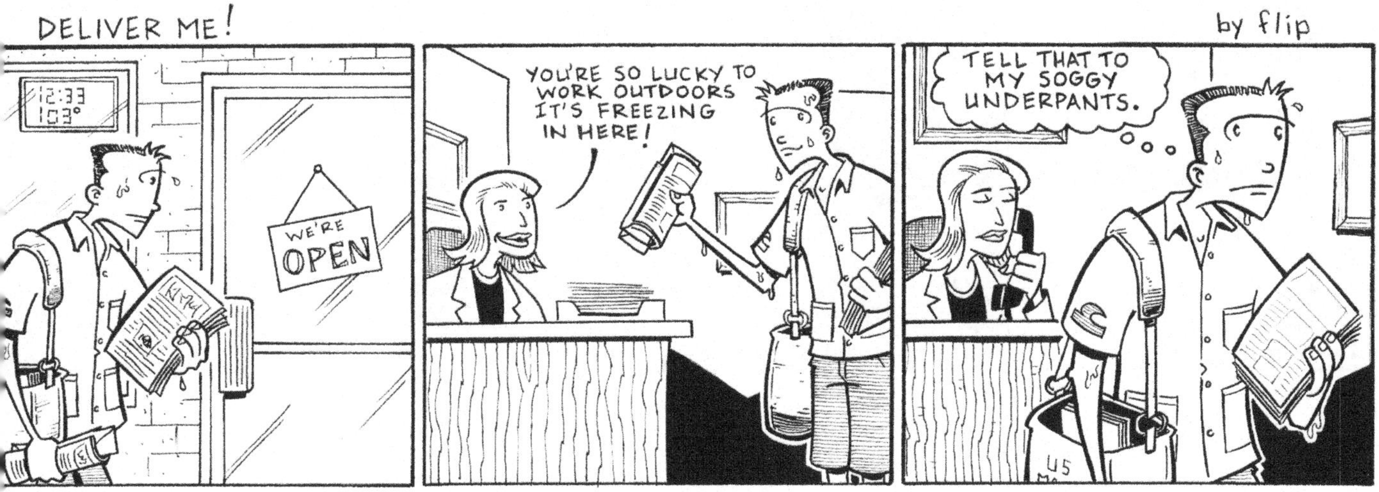
DELIVER ME!
by flip
12:33
103°
WE'RE OPEN
YOU'RE SO LUCKY TO WORK OUTDOORS IT'S FREEZING IN HERE!
TELL THAT TO MY SOGGY UNDERPANTS.

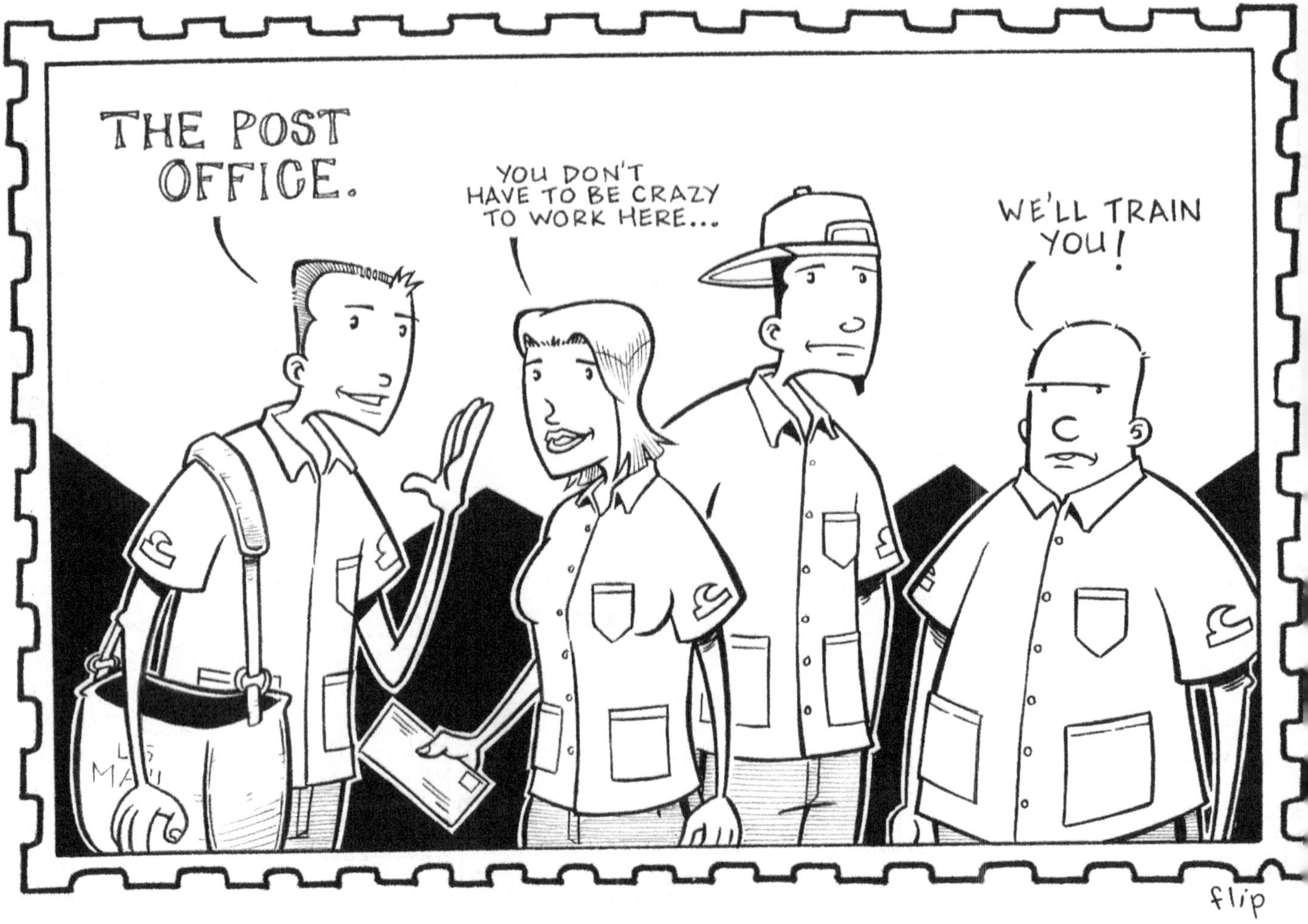
THE POST OFFICE.
YOU DON'T HAVE TO BE CRAZY TO WORK HERE...
WE'LL TRAIN YOU!
flip

Made in the USA
Coppell, TX
28 November 2020

42325912R00052

How and Why

1. Soaking the noodles first tenderizes them but still leaves them with a desirable chewiness. Lukewarm water helps the noodles absorb just the right amount.

2. Adding water as you stir-fry hydrates the noodles slowly, giving you control over how soft they become. Cooking is full of variables (air temperature, ingredient freshness, ingredient brand, thickness of noodles, size of pan used . . .). Resist adding too much water: Pad Thai is supposed to be a bit chewy.

3. Add some bean sprouts to the stir-fry, and also serve raw ones on the side for maximum crunch. Serving some crisp raw bean sprouts, Chinese chives and lime wedges with the dish gives these savory noodles a refreshing edge.

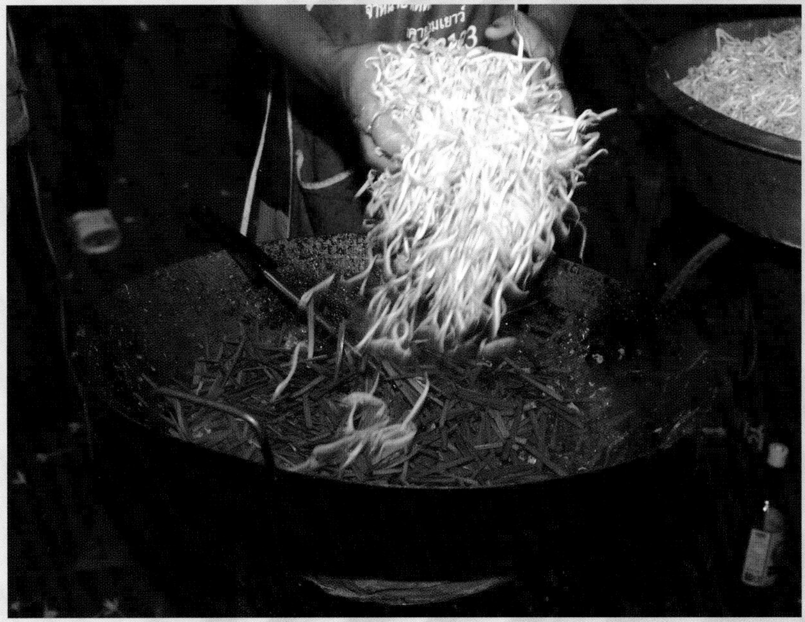

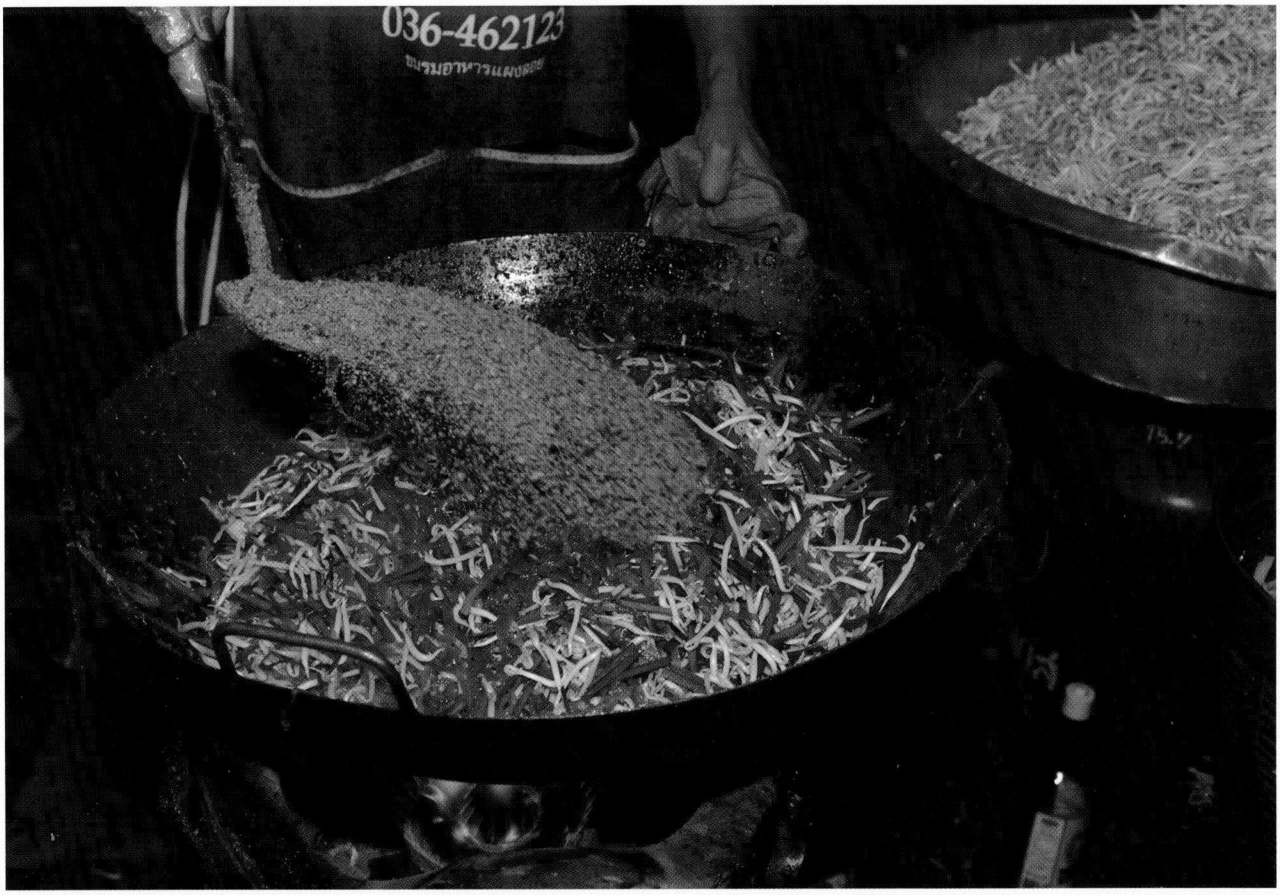
036-462123

Copious amounts of deep-roasted peanuts are an essential flavoring for Pad Thai noodles.

THAILAND

Drunken Rice Noodles with Pork, Basil and Oyster Sauce

Kuaytiaw Moo Pad Kee Mao

Literally translated as "drunk noodles," There is, oddly, no alcohol in the dish. The name is more suggestive of how you will feel after eating this spicy dish: drunk and they're often eaten by drunk people at late-night street stands so the name fits. This version is made with sliced pork, but ground pork or chicken can be substituted with equally tasty results.

Makes 4 to 6 servings as part of multi-dish meal

1/2 lb. (227 g.) Pork shoulder, butt, or leg bite size slices, about 1/8 inch (0.3 cm.) thick

4 Tbsp. Oyster sauce (divided use)

6–10 (1/8 oz. / 4 g.) Dried red chilies, stems and seeds removed

1 lb. (454 g.) Fresh flat rice noodles, 1/2 inch (1.3 cm.) wide (*sen kuaytiaw*) (pg. 66)

2 Tbsp. Rendered pork fat or vegetable oil

2 Tbsp. Minced garlic

2 Tbsp. Fish sauce (*nahm pla*)

2 tsp. Granulated sugar

1/2 cup Water

1 cup Long beans, cut into 1 1/2-inch (4 cm.) lengths (pg. 79)

3/4 cup Baby corn, fresh or canned, halved diagonally

1 Tbsp. Fresh or brined green peppercorns (drain and rinse briefly if brined) (pg. 42))

3/4 cup Bok choy or other leafy green, cut into 2-inch (5 cm.) pieces

1 cup Holy basil or other Asian basil leaves

1. Marinate pork in 2 Tbsp. oyster sauce 30 minutes. Soak chilies in 1/2 cup room temperature water 30 minutes, drain and squeeze out excess moisture then pound or chop into a semi-smooth paste. Soak rice noodles for 10 minutes in lukewarm water; separate into individual strands.

2. Stir-fry the noodles: Heat oil in a large sauté pan or wok over high flame; stir fry pork until cooked through (about 7 minutes). Add chilies and garlic; cook until fragrant (about 30 seconds). Add noodles, fish sauce, sugar, remaining 2 Tbsp. oyster sauce, and water; cook 30 seconds more. Add long beans, baby corn, and peppercorns; cook 1 minute. Add bok choy; cook until tender (about 30 seconds).

3. Add basil, cook for 10 seconds while gently stir-frying until wilted. Taste and adjust seasonings with fish sauce.

In Thailand, stalks of green peppercorns adorn the dish, allowing diners to regulate spice. Since fresh green peppercorns aren't available in most places, pickled ones are the most common substitute, cooked into the dish itself.

How and Why

1. Marinating pork in oyster sauce tenderizes and seasons the meat. This rich, multipurpose sauce contains cornstarch, salt, and sugar, which cure the meat. This ensures water retention and tenderness.

2. Add basil at the last moment to preserve its fragrance. Adding the basil too early will deaden its flavor and wilt it until it becomes lost in the dish.

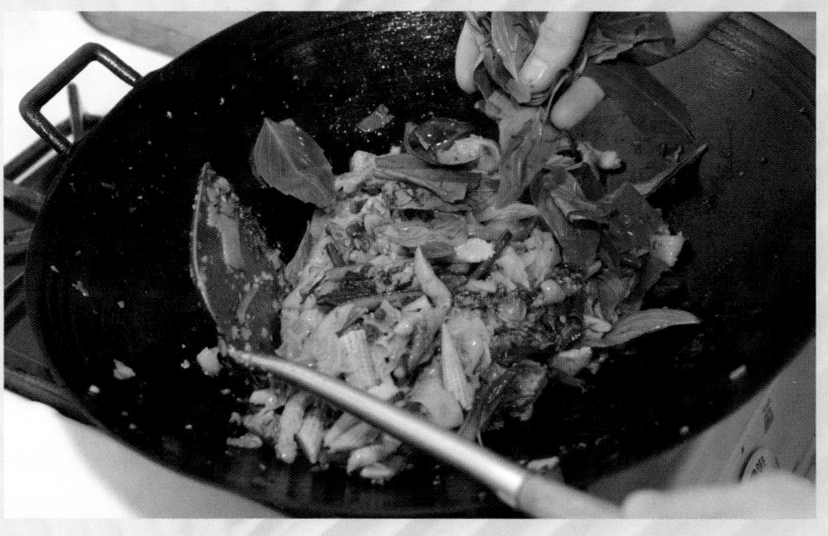

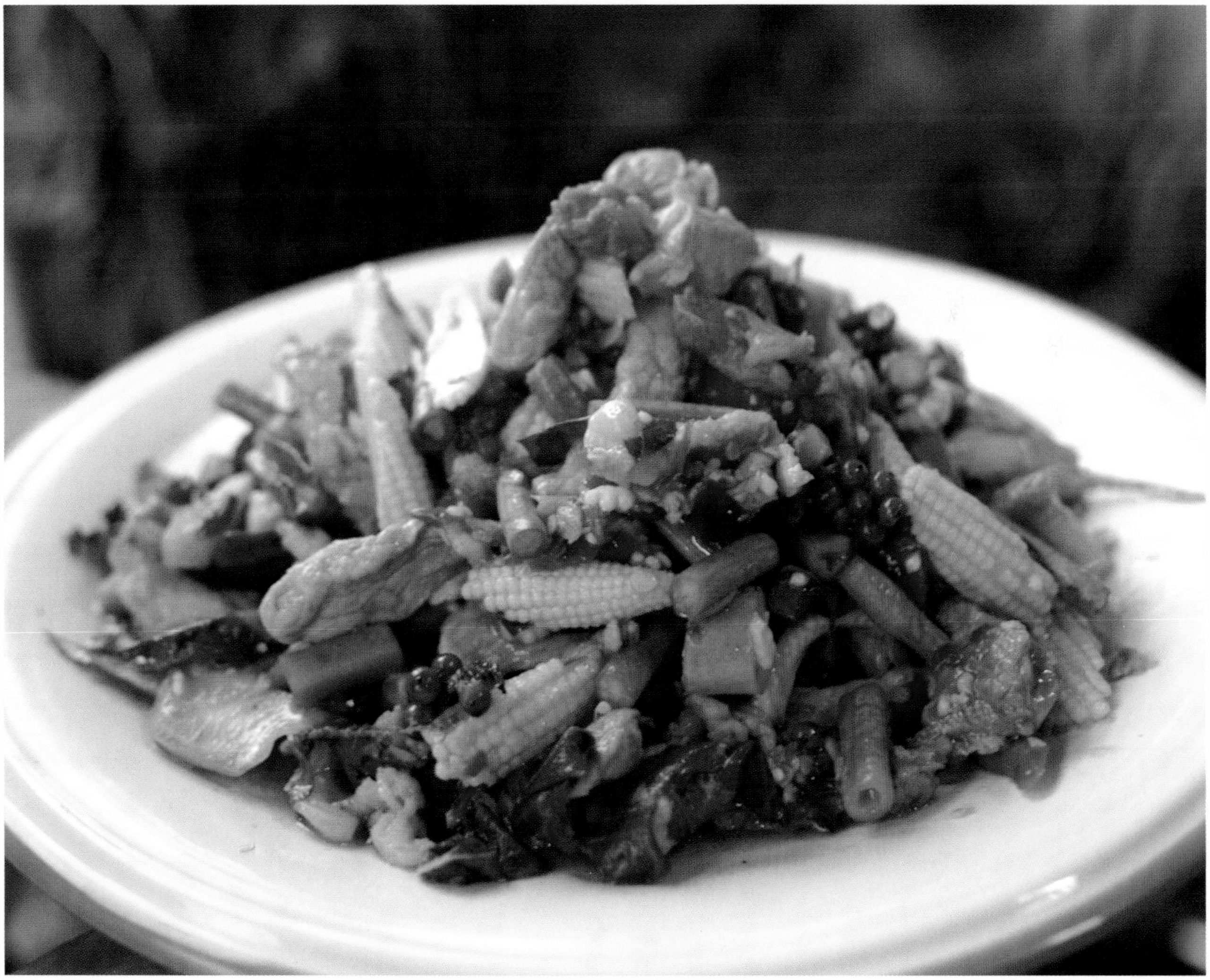

This version of Pad Kee Mao in Kanchanaburi was served as a side dish, absent of noodles.

Curry Coconut Broth with Chicken and Crispy Noodles
Kao Soi Gai

Thai mastery of complex flavors and textures finds its best showcase in this dish of resilient wheat noodles floating in rich scented coconut broth garnished with more crispy noodles. Thailand shares more than just a border with Myanmar (Burma). The nations have borrowed from each other in the evolution of dishes such as Kao Soi. Believed to be a hybrid of the Burmese word "khauk-hswe," which translates as "noodles," it also shows influences from Chinese style. A rich, coconut milk-based curry gravy bathes resilient flat noodles, pieces of chicken and a fascinating combination of raw shallots, cilantro, crispy fried noodles and pickled mustard greens. The pickled greens hail from China where they're essential to Chinese-Muslim cookery. A raw wedge of lime provides a final Thai touch to Kao Soi, squeezed in by the diner at the very last moment before he delves onto this textural culinary adventure.

Makes 4 to 6 bowls as a one-dish meal

FOR THE CURRY PASTE

6   cloves Garlic, roughly chopped
1   Tbsp. Grated ginger
1/2   tsp. Ground coriander
1/2   tsp. Ground turmeric
3   Tbsp. Red curry paste, (pg. 159) (add 1 more tablespoon if paste was made in blender) or store bought

FOR THE COCONUT GRAVY

2   cans (about 14 oz. or 414 ml. each) coconut milk, stirred (divided use)
5   cups (1.18 L.) Light chicken broth
1   lb. (454 g.) Chicken thigh meat, cut into bite size strips, about 1/4 inch (0.6 cm.) thick
2   Tbsp. Light brown palm sugar (pg. 58)
1   Tbsp. Soy sauce
1/4   cup Fish sauce (*nahm pla*)
2   Tbsp. Lime juice

CURRY GARNISHES

1   lb. (454 g.) Fresh wheat noodles, ideally flat
      (similar to fettuccini shape), cooked (pg. 116)

1/2   cup Pickled mustard greens, roughly chopped,
      1/2-inch (1.3 cm.) pieces (pg. 81)

3   small Shallots, sliced, about 1/4 inch (0.6 cm.) thick,
      (rinsed under cold water to reduce harshness)

1/4   cup Roughly chopped cilantro (leaves and stems)

2   cups Deep-fried wide, flat egg noodles (1/4 inch
      (0.6 cm.) wide) (pg. 116)—Cook from
      raw state into individual nests

2   medium Limes, cut into wedges (pg. 108)

1. Fortify the curry paste: In mortar or food processor, grind together garlic, ginger, coriander, turmeric and red curry paste.

2. Make coconut gravy: Heat 1 cup coconut milk in a wok or 4 qt. (4 L.) saucepan over medium heat. Cook, stirring often until it thickens substantially and oil begins to separate out, about 5 minutes. Stir in fortified curry paste; cook, stirring constantly for 2 minutes to develop the flavors.

3. Add chicken broth, chicken meat, and palm sugar; simmer 10 minutes. Add soy sauce, fish sauce, and remaining coconut milk; simmer 5 minutes more over low heat. Remove from heat; add lime juice. Adjust seasoning to taste with fish sauce, palm sugar, soy sauce, and salt if needed.

4. Assemble the soup: Reheat cooked noodles in boiling water; divide into serving bowls. Top each with a ladleful of coconut chicken gravy. Arrange mustard greens, shallots and cilantro atop the sauced noodles. Garnish the top with a nest of fried noodles, and then serve with lime wedges on the side.

How and Why

Fry the noodles into individual nest shapes for ease of service and best eye appeal. Frying small bundles of noodles allows you to drop each portion on top of the kao soi in each bowl.

Coconut Sticky Rice with Fresh Mangos
Khao Neow Mamuang

In Thailand, street stalls with tall piles of mangos signals a maker of this fruity, nutty delicacy. In that tropical land, the rice is served room temperature. But since our climate is cooler, keep the rice slightly warm (about 80° to 90°F or 27° to 32°C) for the most pleasant experience. This ensures tender rice and maximum flavor. If you can't find yellow mung beans, use toasted peanuts and/or sesame seeds instead.

Makes 4 to 6 servings as part of a multi-dish meal

1 1/2 cups White sticky "glutinous" rice (pg. 72)
1   Tbsp. Dried yellow mung beans (actually, skinned, split green mung beans) (pg. 74)

RICE SEASONING MIXTURE
1/2   cup Canned coconut milk, stirred well
1/2   cup Granulated sugar
1/2   tsp. Kosher salt
4   Pandan leaves, tied in knot (pg. 37)

COCONUT TOPPING
1   cup Canned coconut milk, stirred well
4   tsp. Light brown palm sugar (pg. 58)
1/8   tsp. Kosher salt
2   tsp. Rice flour
2 to 4 large Mangos, ripe, peeled and cut into thick slices

1. Soak sticky rice in room temperature water overnight, (or in lukewarm water for 1 hr), drain well. Soak mung beans in hot tap water for 1 hr (110°F or 34°C); drain well.

2. Toast beans in a dry wok or sauté pan (non-stick works best) over medium heat, stirring often until dry and golden brown.

3. Transfer drained rice to a Thai sticky rice steamer basket or any steamer lined with material to prevent rice from falling through (such as cheesecloth), cover and steam over boiling water for 30 to 45 minutes until cooked through.

4. In a small saucepan, combine 1/2 cup coconut milk, granulated sugar, 1/2 tsp. kosher salt, and pandan leaves; bring to a boil. Remove from heat, cool slightly; use a pair of tongs to squeeze out much juice as possible from the pandan leaves. Combine this mixture with cooked rice, folding the two together until thoroughly mixed. Cover, and set aside to rest for 15 minutes, allowing rice to absorb all of the seasonings.

5. Meanwhile, whisk together 1 cup coconut milk, palm sugar, 1/8 tsp. kosher salt, and rice flour until very smooth. Heat in a saucepan over medium heat, whisking constantly, until mixture thickens and comes to a boil.

6. Serve slightly warm or room temperature mounds of the rice with mango, drizzled with coconut sauce and sprinkled with toasted mung beans.

Sticky Rice steamer baskets stacked at the market.

Sticky rice vendors can be found in many cities.

How and Why

1. Soak glutinous rice overnight for the best texture. Sticky rice should be soft and chewy when properly cooked. Slow soaking allows a large amount of water Soak the rice before steaming.

2. Wet bamboo steamer and rest for 15 minutes before steaming. The helps prevent the rice from sticking to the bamboo.

3. Squeeze pandan to extract as much flavor as possible. Although the pandan readily releases much of its flavor into the coconut milk, a squeeze really makes a difference in the depth of flavor.

4. Whisk topping constantly as it cooks. The starchy rice flour will clump into large globules if the sauce is not continuously agitated as it cooks.

Thai Coffee
Gaa Faa Yen

When my sous chef Ari Slatkin and I traveled to Bangkok to work with Thai cuisine and culture expert David Thompson on his book, this coffee kept us alive and cooking. The bittersweet grounds the Thais use contain not only coffee, but also corn, soy, butter, and sugar. These added ingredients, incorporated during the roasting process, give the brew a toasty, nutty flavor. Each roaster has his proprietary mixture. In the U.S., I usually buy Pantainorasingh brand (pg. 362).

Makes: 4 to 6 servings

1 cup Thai coffee mixture (1¼ cup for iced coffee) (pg. 362)
4 cups Water, boiling
to taste (about 1 can) Sweetened condensed milk

1. Stir coffee grounds into boiling water. Brew 5 minutes.
2. Strain through a coffee filter, very fine wire mesh strainer or cheesecloth.

FOR HOT COFFEE
Fill each cup with 3 to 4 Tbsp. condensed milk; top with 1 cup hot coffee. Guests stir it to make it as sweet and creamy as they wish.

FOR ICED COFFEE
Stir brewed coffee and condensed milk together. Cool to room temperature, and then pour over crushed ice (about 1 cup ice per serving) in tall glasses.

How and Why
Use more coffee grounds for the best iced coffee. Pouring the coffee over the ice dilutes it, so starting with a stronger brew is best.

Thai Iced Tea
Chah Yen

This bright orange colored beverage is more popular in the U.S. than it is in Thailand. In it, raw tea leaves are combined with roasted corn, vanilla and, in most cases, orange food coloring. Evaporated milk (not to be confused with the sweetened condensed milk used in Thai coffee) is traditionally used in this intensely sweet, mega-strong tea infusion.

Makes: 4 to 6 servings

6 cups Water
2 cups Thai tea mixture (pg. 362)
1½ cups Granulated sugar
4 to 6 cups Crushed ice
2 to 3 cups Evaporated milk

1. Bring water and sugar to a boil in a large saucepan. Remove from heat; stir in tea powder. Brew for 10 minutes. Strain through coffee filter, fine mesh strainer, or several layers of rinsed cheesecloth. Cool to room temperature; cover and chill in refrigerator.
2. Fill 4 to 6 glasses with about 1½ cup of crushed ice each. Divide chilled sweetened tea over ice (about 1 cup of tea). Top with ¼ to ½ cup evaporated milk and serve.

How and Why
Crushed ice makes better Thai iced tea and coffee. The smaller piece's greater surface area quickly chills the tea. As you tilt back the glass, these cold jewels snuggle against your lips and maximize the sensory experience.

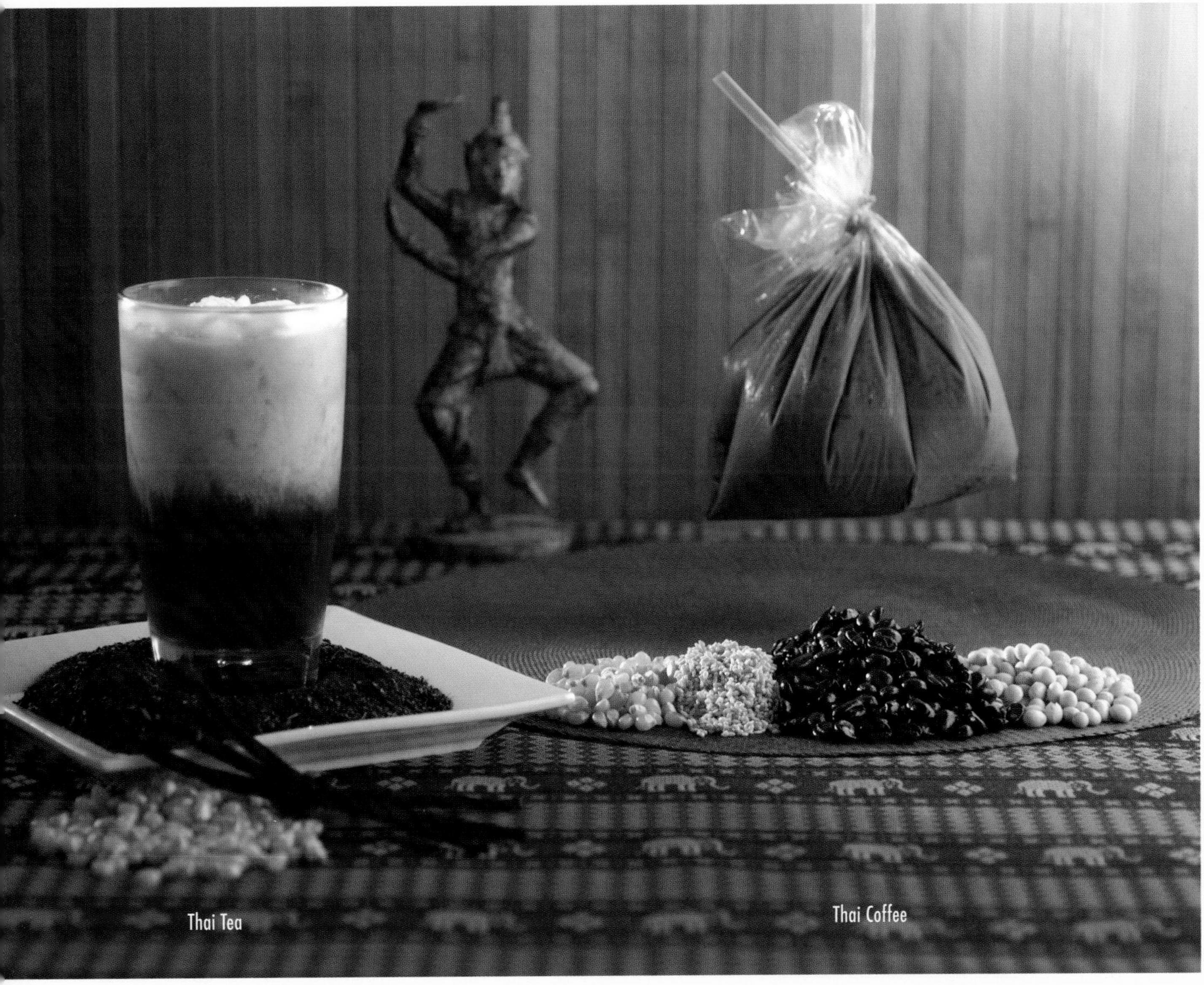
Thai Tea
Thai Coffee

Often street vendors fill a bag with ice laden coffee, wrap it to go and send you on your way.

Vietnam

HISTORY

Chinese Origins
French Colonized
Communist Rule

ETHNIC DIVERSITY

50+ Ethnic Tribes
Ancestor Worship

GEOGRAPHY

Extensive Coastline
Distinctive Regions
Mekong Delta

Authentic Recipes

CULINARY ETIQUETTE

Host Leads Meal
Table Salads
Chopsticks Reign

PREVAILING FLAVORS

Copious Herbs
Caramelized Sugar,
Black Pepper & Shallots
Fish Sauce, Lime
& Garlic

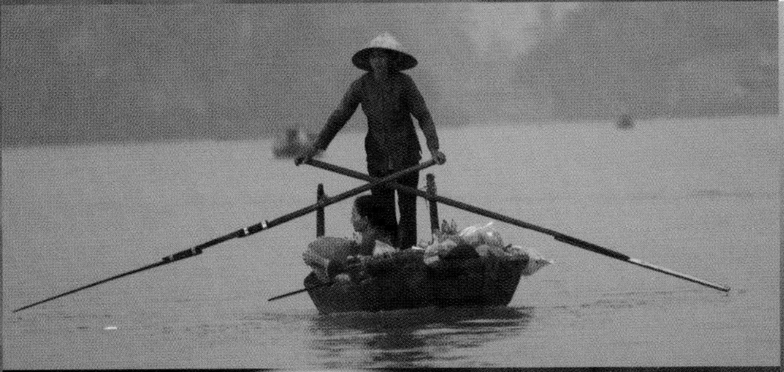

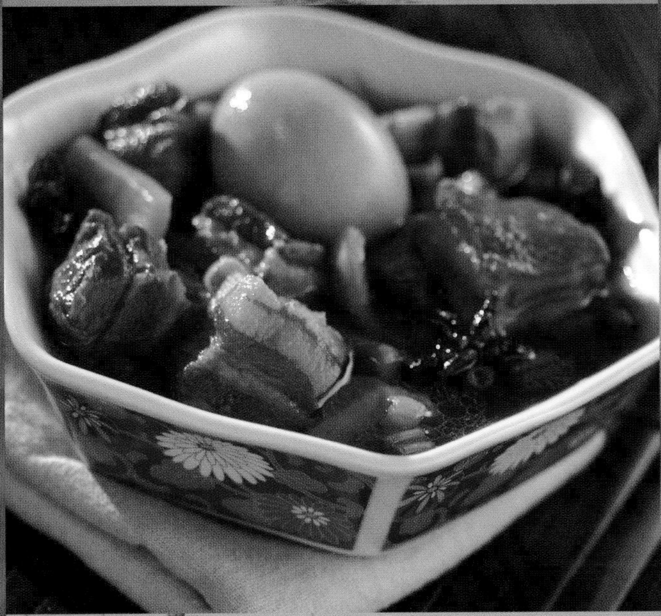

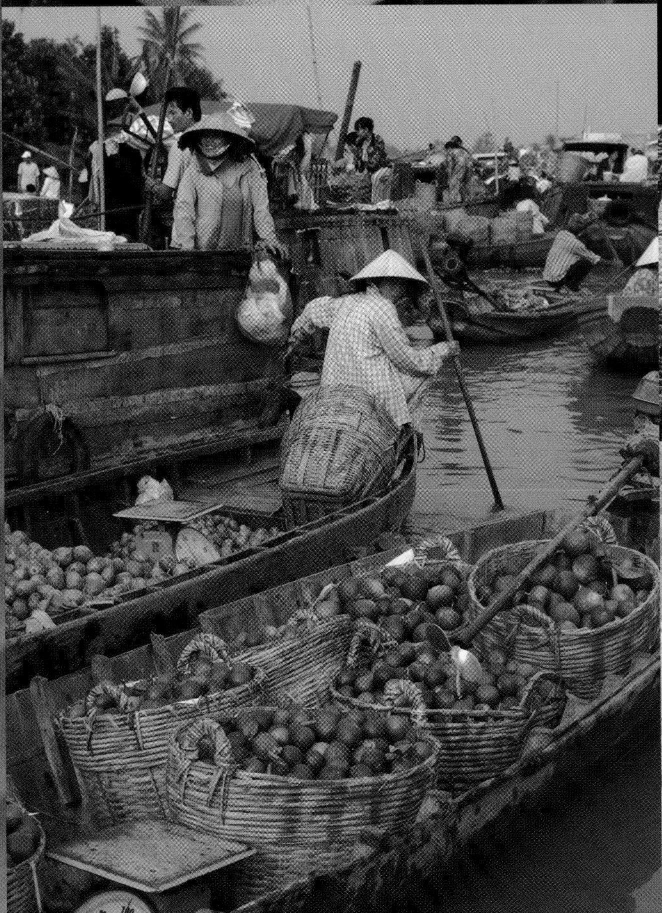

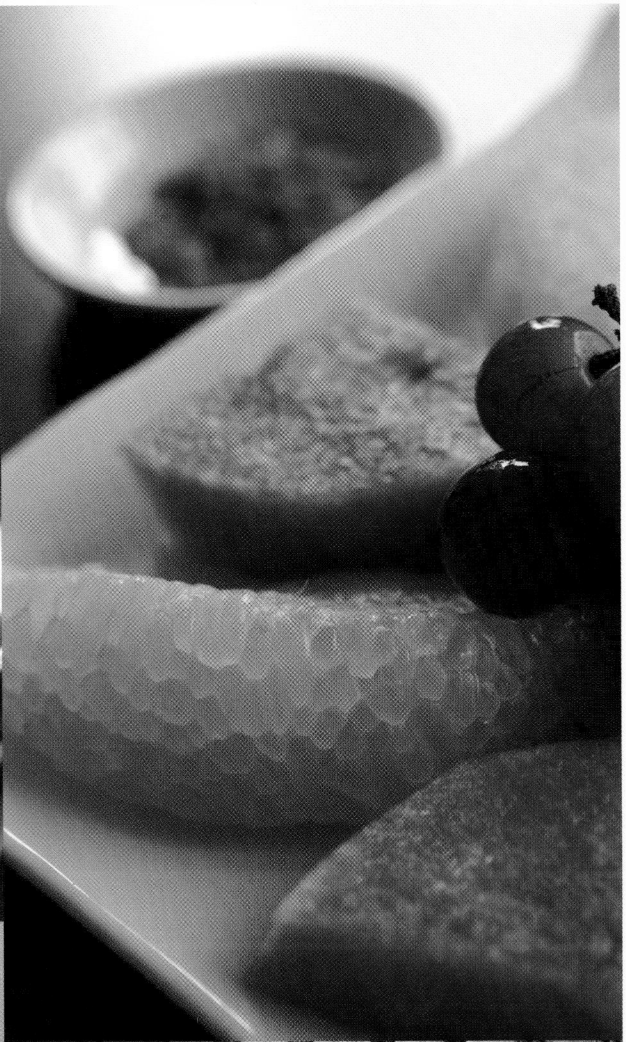

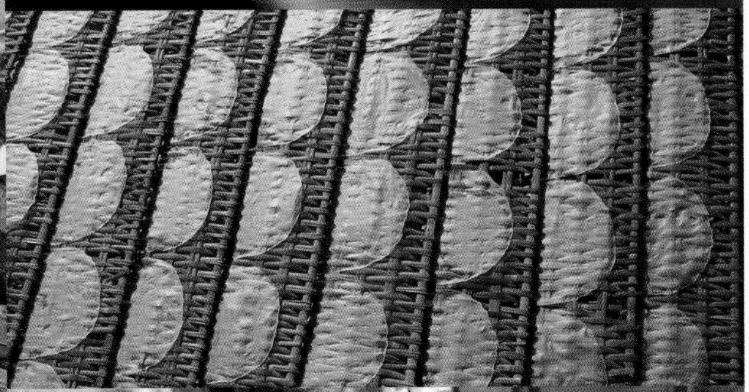

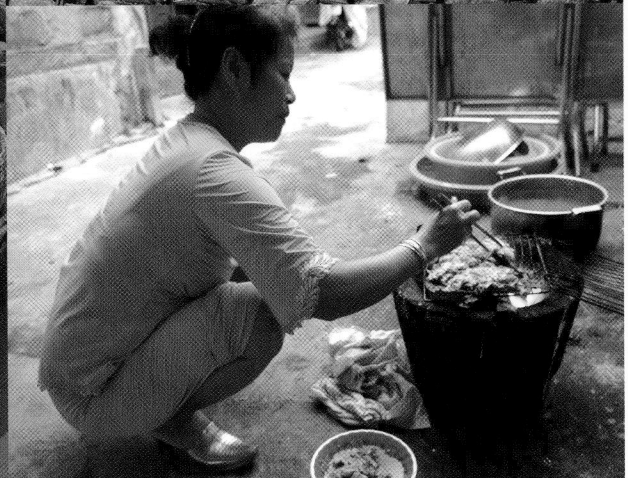

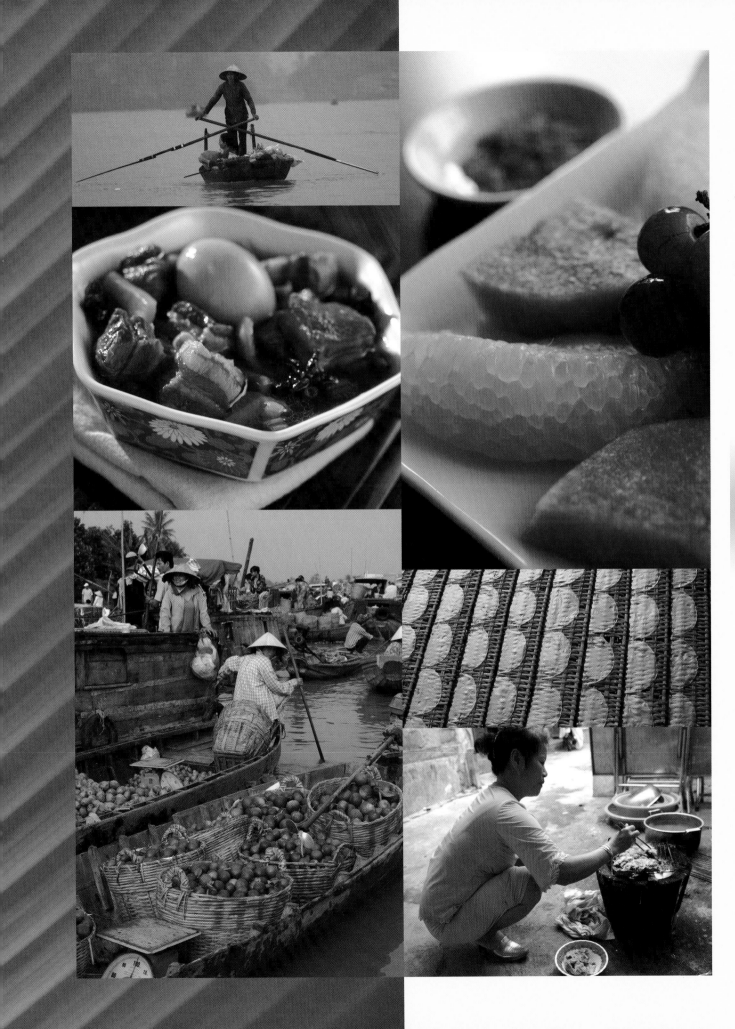

Annatto

I first went to Vietnam in 2001. I was teaching Asian cookery at the Culinary Institute of America, and I felt that firsthand experience of the culture of this cuisine would help me truly get my head around it and be able to teach it better. I also wanted to see how different it was from the culinary cultures of Malaysia, Singapore, and Thailand. A twenty-four–hour journey can seem daunting to even the most seasoned traveler, but one day seemed like a small price to pay for culinary paradise

Foods of Vietnam are generally subtler than neighboring cuisines, with less reliance on spice pastes. It's not so different from a comparison one could make between Japanese cuisine and the geographically adjacent food cultures of Korea and China. Much of the ingredient pantry is the same, yet the way in which cooks manipulate the ingredients and present dishes yields completely different cuisine. As in Japanese food, Vietnamese cuisine does not contain many spicy foods. When Vietnamese foods are spicy, they most often acquire their heat outside of the kitchen. Guests add sliced chilies to soups, dip roasted pork belly in chili-salt, or reach for chili sauce, *tương ớt tỏi Việt-Nam* (pg. 199), at the table. Contrary to the cuisines of Thailand and Malaysia, the red hue of grilled meats, stews, and fat-speckled soups comes not from chilies, but from flavorless yet colorful annatto seeds. Coconut milk is still part of the pantry but more relegated to sweets than savory dishes. Noodle soup broths are more often clear, not clouded by coconut milk as they are in Thai and Malaysian cooking. But Vietnamese stews do often incorporate the clear and faintly sweet juice from the center of young coconuts.

Vietnam is changing rapidly. My excursion in 2007 revealed dramatic changes from what I'd seen on my first two trips in 2001 and 2005. As the soles of my shoes touched the pavement (or lack thereof in spots) outside of Saigon airport, the entire feel of Vietnam was different. Over the previous couple of years, the country had gone through a cultural and technological metamorphosis, emerging from its cocoon as a butterfly of the twenty-first century. It felt more mature and refined, but still unmistakably Vietnamese.

The allure of Vietnam and its people is still very strong, and I am happy to see their food culture evolve with the rest of the world. Yet at the same time I wish that the unique cuisine and culture that has evolved there over the centuries will not be wiped away by a few decades of "progress." Community markets with fresh meats hanging in the open air, vibrant displays, vegetables being bartered for with vigor, avenues crowded with bicycles, and the iconic presence of beautiful long—*aó dài*—silk dresses on women, which tease with coy modesty—will Vietnam strike a happy balance between traditional and new? Will it preserve its unique identity, or be swallowed up by globalization? One thing is for sure: Vietnam is changing rapidly, and the authenticity of tomorrow is being created today.

Geography—A Journey from North to South

The shape of Vietnam is appropriately compared to an ancient yoke for shoulder-borne baskets, *đòn-gánh*. Like a yoke, it is bulbous on the ends and narrow in the middle. On the north is a border with China, and to the mountainous northwest is Laos. The Red River, *Sông Hồng*, flows in from the north, entering Vietnam from China's Yunnan province, through the mountainous highlands, through the northern capital city of Hà-nội. The heavy silt deposits are all but gone by the time it spreads out into the majestic waters of the Gulf of Tonkin. The country's expansive coastline runs 2,000 miles along its eastern side, with the narrowest point in central Vietnam just over thirty miles wide. Cambodia borders Vietnam in the southwest.

The Northern Culinary Star — *Hà-Nội*

The French quarter is filled with colonial architecture, Hoàn-Kiếm Lake hosts teams of the elderly practicing tai chi each morning, and the residents are found sipping tea and coffee in cafés. The North Star of the culinary sky is Hà-Nội; it is a point of reference for the origin of much of Vietnamese cuisine. Phở, often referred to as the national dish, is an amalgamation of steaming hot, spice-infused beef broth, silky-smooth rice noodles, various cuts of beef, and shaved onions (pg. 218). Northerners opt for black pepper instead of chili peppers, season their soups with less sugar, and still rely on fish sauce, but they use more salt than in the south.

The Imperial Central Region

If you move down south to the central region, make sure to stop in the culinary mecca of *Huế*. The former imperial city is home to superlative gastronomic experiences. Inject yourself into the street life by hailing a *cyclo* (pedicab). An afternoon can quickly escape your grasp as you are carted from the moat-encased Citadel, along the Perfume River, and into the depths of the *Đông-Ba* market.

The once-quaint town of Hội-An is a must-see, even though tour groups now mob the streets. Nowadays, I keep my head down and stay connected with the locals. Like Huế, Hội-An unravels slowly, revealing its culinary delights after a few hours of searching. Rice's versatility in the hands of Vietnamese cooks is again a culinary hit with *Bánh Bèo*, small rice flour cakes sprinkled with chopped pink shrimp and crispy pork cracklings (pg. 214), and they are at their best at Bà Đỏ restaurant.

IT USED TO BE REGIONAL

In northern Hà-Nội, where its roots still remain, the national noodle soup dish, *Phở* is now called *Phở bò* to indicate that it's made with beef, distinguishing it from the chicken version, *Phở gà*, that is now popular in the south. In the past, in cities like Hội-An, one only needed to ask for *Mì*, and it was understood to be the regional dish of *Mì Quảng*: flat rice noodles in a light curry broth (pg. 230). Now, since so many other types of noodles from other areas are available, the suffix of *Quảng* is needed.

"Huế UNDER WATER . . .
CRUNCHY PORK BELLY SATISFIES"

My guide, Mr. Công, had an appropriately scholarly appearance. He sated my curiosity again and again with historically detailed stories and personal anecdotes about his life as a Vietnamese teacher turned culinary adventurer. And he kept his promises. My heart jumped out from our car as we whizzed past a street vendor selling spit-roasted pork belly. I needed to taste the crackling golden skin that bubbled over those glowing knotty coals. He promised he would bring me back.

We returned the following day for what I now call "Way Under Water." (Huế is pronounced "way.") I have a pork belly epiphany in every country I visit, it seems. First, it was Malaysian sliced pork belly layered with slabs of steamed taro, bathed in sweet, dark, spiced soy sauce. Then it was the deep-fried Thai slab-o-crunchy-pork. Then, slices of marinated grilled pork in Singapore's Chinatown. But nothing could prepare me for this experience.

Our car stopped abruptly. I jumped hastily out armed with my camera, my appetite, and a grin of optimistic anticipation. Not a word was spoken as I approached crunchy hog heaven. Lusty salivation is a universal language. Mrs. Quy wordlessly assembled a sample for me to taste. She plucked a faintly bitter green leaf like *yu choy* (pg. 76) and folded in a small chunk of pork belly, a sliver of cucumber, a sprig of rau răm (Vietnamese coriander), and a tiny piece of fragrant Asian basil. Before relinquishing the delicacy, she anointed it with a squeeze of lime. Then, she rolled it up like a Cuban cigar, pressed it into my palm, and instructed me to dip it in chili-salt. The instant I placed this pleasure packet in my mouth, I began to undertake the multilayered flavor experience. My crisp-pork guru motioned to some fresh green peppercorns, clearly wanting me to pop some into my mouth. Wow. That spark elevated the pleasure sensations I was feeling to a whole new level.

I knew I had to convince Mrs. Quy to teach me the secret to this gustatory perfection. Guileless, she obligingly offered to lead me through the daylong process. But she warned me that she wakes each morning at 6:00 a.m. to the daily ritual of marinating the slabs of meat. "Time is no matter," I told her. This wouldn't be the first time I woke before dawn to get a once-in-a-lifetime recipe.

Crack of dawn the next morning, the typhoon was coming as my guru and I squatted on the floor of her bare-bones kitchen. The "sink" consisted of a spigot and a bucket. Great food needs no special kitchen, just heart, hands, and unrelenting attention. We chopped garlic, minced lemongrass, and blended seasonings with oyster sauce, soy sauce, and shameless spoonfuls of MSG. Then we turned to the pig. A splash of vinegar on the skin laid the foundation for our spices; next came a dousing of *shao xing,* Chinese rice wine, reminding me of the persistent Chinese influence on Vietnamese food and how this was similar to how they roasted meats to crackling perfection. The final seasoning paste was built in a bowl. The foundational seasonings of soy sauce and oyster sauce bound the aromatic five-spice powder and spicy coarse black peppercorns; the Southeast Asian iconic citrus like fragrant lemongrass perfumed the entire mixture. Then we slathered each slab of pork belly and waited for the marinade to do its magic. While the seasonings bewitched the meaty pig, my guru and I had time to talk over breakfast noodles in her modest home.

As we sat, ate, and talked, storm clouds grew more ominous. It began to rain in buckets. Roasted pork is not that uncommon, *Thịt Heo Quay* as it's known, but her version was different so I had asked her where she'd learned to make it. I expected a long yarn, but instead she simply said, "I learned it from life." Essentially, she'd invented it out of thin air. I knew I had to leave. I pledged that I'd return to her stall to sample the pork we'd made together. When I did, it was everything I remembered and more. I'll never forget Quy Lanh or the day she shared with me. And you will never experience another pig as special as hers, made by the recipe you'll find on page (pg. 250).

I'd promised to study with another local food master that night to learn the Huế Chicken Salad (pg. 238), but the typhoon was blowing full force. By evening I was walking through water up to my knees whilst, like a soldier protecting his rifle, I was precariously holding my camera, laptop, and other electronic gadgetry above the rising waters. I made it back, barely. Another episode of mayhem to bring home the true foods of Vietnam was over.

There's Nothing Like Southern Saigon (except *Hồ Chí Minh City*)

The southern cousin of beef noodle soup is chicken noodle soup. Here, *Phở gà* is lighter in flavor and sometimes served with shaved kaffir lime leaves (pg. 222). Generally the southern palate has a preference for sweeter foods and tends to rely on lime juice more than vinegar for an acidic accent. To get away fron the seemingly inescapable southern heat and humidity, locals and foreigners trek up to the south-central highlands of *Đà-Lạt*, an hour north of Hồ Chí Minh City (Saigon). The land is fertile and supports substantial agriculture. Root vegetables, ruby red strawberries, emerald green herbs, rich coffee, and tea flourish in the cool arid air there. It's also a favorite Vietnamese honeymoon getaway.

The Mekong Delta Wet Life

southeastasianflavors.com Go to...

The network of southern waterways that make up the Mekong Delta are host to numerous floating markets. The banks are lined with rice paddies and cottage-industry food manufacturing. The bountiful water supply enables Vietnam to practice extensive aquaculture of shrimp, clams, fish, and other crustaceans. Vietnam's once nearly non-navigable roads are being replaced with highways. Everything is available on the water, often for only a few thousand đồng (there are 15,000 VND to one U.S. dollar).

History

Vietnam has been occupied by many foreign powers and has assimilated some culinary traits from every one of them. The Portuguese, French, Americans, and Khmer have impacted the fundamentally Sino-culture (Chinese-based culture) there. China ruled this area for about one thousand years, beginning in 111 B.C. This primordial Chinese culinary culture had profound influence here. Rice-based cuisine took hold and never let go. Although both wheat and rice noodles are present, the Vietnamese eat more rice noodles than their northern mother.

The nearly one hundred years of French rule left behind thousands of architectural reminders, but I believe that the introduction of bread was their most significant lasting contribution. The Chinese may have taught the Vietnamese that a good broth makes good soup, but the French solidified this practice by emphasizing long-cooked stocks (a practice not seen much in Southeast Asia outside of Vietnam). Beef stew is still made using French methods, but the Vietnamese added the Chinese-influenced touches of star anise, cassia (cinnamon), and rock sugar to their slow-simmered meat dishes. Annatto seeds (pg. 40) inject a brilliant orange hue into the broth. Iconic Southeast Asian aromatic lemongrass is the finishing touch to their own rendition of beef stew, *Bò Kho* (pg. 260). The stew is served with plates of fresh herbs and baguettes for sopping up the sauce.

Bánh Xèo, sizzling rice flour pancakes (pg. 208) are probably adaptations of French crepes. The Vietnamese have taken these crepes to places the French never dreamed of. Ingredients like corn, avocados, and asparagus, introduced by the French, now find their way into indigenous dishes. Sauté pans, skillets, and fry pans are used as often as woks. Contemporary yet authentic Vietnamese beverages such as coffee and Cognac drinks further illustrate how French culture has been absorbed into the local cuisine.

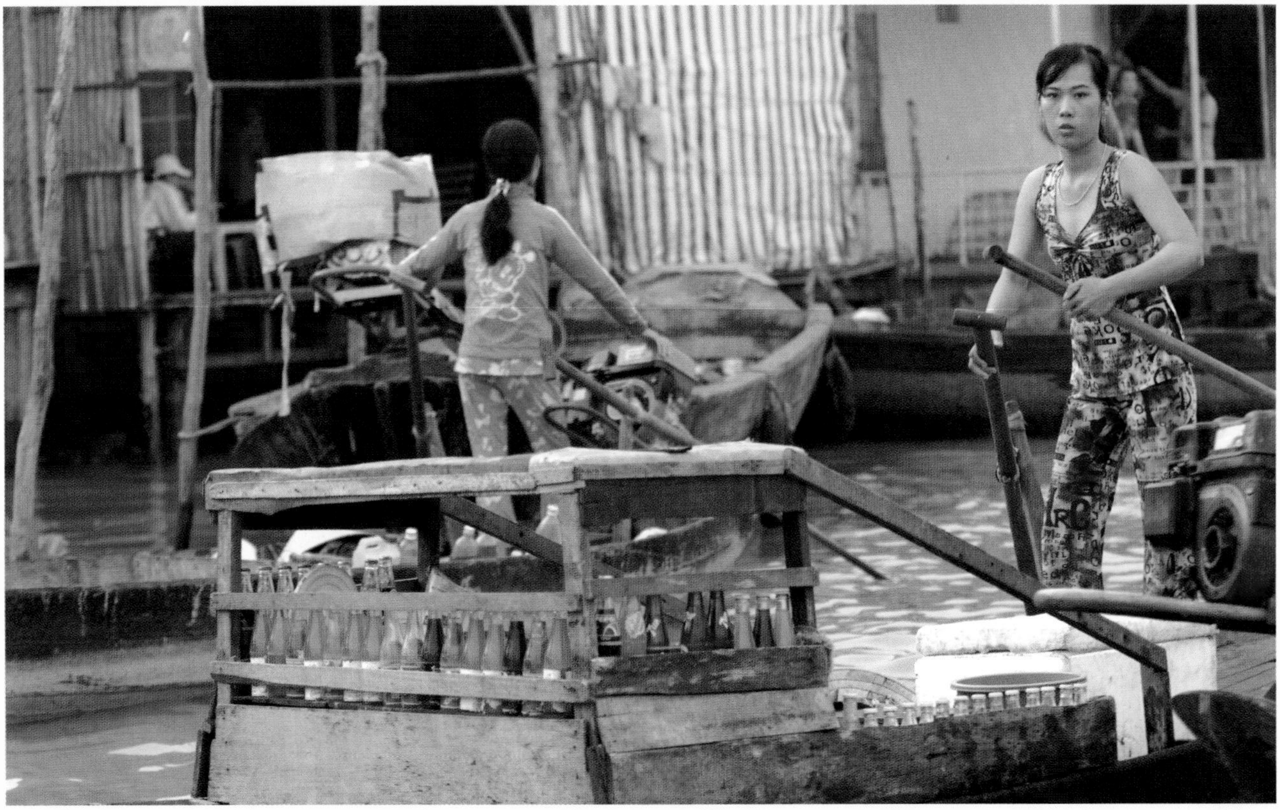

Communist Rule

The nightmares of the Vietnam War, which ended in victory for Hồ Chí Minh's communist forces, left clues to the sordid past. Resourceful Vietnamese utilize remnants of the battle. Spent army Jeep wheel rims are used as weighted bases for signs. Discarded bulletproof vests are taken apart and resewn into Kevlar bags that are filled with ice blocks and pounded to make crushed ice for drinks and snacks. (These bulletproof ice crushers are so effective that locals now sell newly fashioned bags from new material for this purpose. I brought back both a genuine recycled vest and a modern Kevlar crush bag, which I use for ice at home and while on the road teaching cooking classes.)

Ethnic Diversity in Vietnam

More than 80 percent of today's Vietnamese population is descended from ancient southern Chinese migrants from thousands of years ago. These modern Vietnamese are referred to as the *Kinh* or *Việt*. The vast array of ethnic tribes, estimated at fifty-four, is unparalleled in other parts of Southeast Asia. The majority of them live in the northwest highlands. Their rural communities have changed little over the centuries, but the past fifty years of foreign influences has created some odd dualities. Colorful hand-sewn fabric and ornate headdress worn by one villager is as common as a baseball cap and jeans on his neighbor. The familiar alphabet creates a false sense of familiarity to Westerners, who often commit gross mispronunciations. *Phở* is pronounced as "fuh," not "foe" as most newcomers to the cuisine exclaim as they revel in this noodle soup that has taken the foodie world by storm.

Although by some published statistics Buddhists officially make up the majority of the population, the popular ancestor worship is more prevalent than any of the six official religions of Vietnam. Festivals and spiritual celebrations are still prominent in today's modern culture. Tết, the Vietnamese New Year in

January or February (depending on the lunar calendar), is the most significant annual event and officially lasts for three days (although most businesses close for the week). Families and businesses ceremonially cleanse their places and then decorate them in red. Fresh fruits fill the altars, and children don new clothes. Not surprisingly, food is a major part of the holiday, so much so that some will say they "eat Tết" as opposed to "celebrate Tết."

Culinary Etiquette in Vietnam

Just as in most Asian dinner settings, the eldest are served first. Hosts take very personal care of guests, who are expected to eat with visible passion. Don't be surprised if your host uses his or her own chopsticks to serve you. He'll offer the prime morsels of each dish. Smile and eat each item promptly. At most meals food is brought whenever it's ready, without much attention to courses or order of service. They're not careless with food, just not overly formal. More attention is paid to food pairings than food order. Even at small roadside restaurants, they will organize foods that are intended to go together. There are often many accompaniments for each dish. Platters, plates, and bowls usually remain on the table and do not get passed around. If it must happen, make sure to pass the dish with both hands and look at them as the dish exchanges hands. Nod with your offering to show that it is gesture of

sharing, not just a labor of necessity. (See the Communal Table in the SEA Identity chapter on page 18.)

At the Vietnamese Table

The Vietnamese season dishes with gusto from numerous condiments set on the table: sliced chili peppers, cruets of fish sauce, chili sauce, salt, plates of herbs, and limes for squeezing.

They use chopsticks more than in any other Southeast Asian culture. Just as with all Asian cultures that use chopsticks, do not spear your food. Lifting a bowl toward your mouth is appropriate and very common. When eating a bowl of noodle soup, use the chopsticks in your dominant hand to wrangle supple noodles and other items in the soup and use a large soup spoon in your other hand for the broth. The fork and spoon combination typical of Malaysian and Thai tables is also employed for specific dishes. There's also plenty of finger food.

Prevailing Foods in Vietnam

Soups

Soups in Southeast Asia (Vietnam is no exception) are served throughout the day, including breakfast and late-night suppers. They can be a

one-dish meal or a course in a formal banquet (where they're called called "súp," and are usually more Western in style). They're sometimes a savory beverage to cleanse the palate between dishes. In *cháo* (also known in Asia as *congee*, *jook*, porridge, or gruel), rice and water are simmered together into a comforting, bland soup. Guests season this porridge to taste with garnishes like pickled vegetables, salted eggs, spicy ginger, pungent raw scallions, dried cured pork, and fragrant herbs.

Bún and Mì noodles each have their time to bask in broths of different origins. Phở Bò (pg. 218), is a spice-scented broth filled with silky-smooth flattened rice noodles referred to as Phở noodles. Bún, a thin, rounded rice noodle that comes from central and northern Vietnam, is often called "rice vermicelli" or "rice angel hair." The most famous dish with bún is *Bún Bò Huế* (pg. 226). The unusual recipe for the broth relies on a combination of simmered beef and pork and is then fortified with shrimp paste. These are only a couple of examples of the dozens of noodle soups that restaurants and street vendors ladle out daily. Look at the Asian noodles section (pg. 67) for a detailed description of the varieties of noodles used in Vietnam.

Đặc Biệt—THAT'S EXTRA SPECIAL

Although I haven't mastered any Southeast Asian languages, I always make sure to learn some food language basics. When ordering your food keep a sharp eye out for the words "Đặc Biệt." This term indicates that this is special version of the dish. The prized cuts of meat or the sheer variety of seafood can help a dish gain this coveted title.

Salads

The Vietnamese have developed an extensive canon of salads to enjoy their bountiful crops. Fruits like unripe green mangos, banana blossoms, and pummelos are deconstructed into small pieces and tossed with herbs and dressings. Dressings usually consist of fish sauce, sugar, wine, and chilies (pgs. 234, 236, 238, 241). Slender lotus rootlets pair with cucumbers and carrots for the salad *Gỏi Ngó Sen* (pg. 234). Imperial Huế chicken salad (*gỏi gà*) is a concoction of gently poached chicken pulled into supple strands and combined with shaved onions and copious amounts of *rau răm*, the pungent Vietnamese coriander (pg. 238).

Yin and yang, the balance of contrasting elements, is used throughout the Vietnamese kitchen. The multi-temperature noodle dishes are exquisite examples of this practice. Charred wafers of pork rest atop cool noodles in the dish, *Bún Thịt Nướng* (pg. 256) This dish is assembled in a large bowl as a single portion. Other items like *Chả Cá*, turmeric-tinted grilled fish with dill from Hà-Nội, are assembled by each guest from larger portions placed on the tabletop.

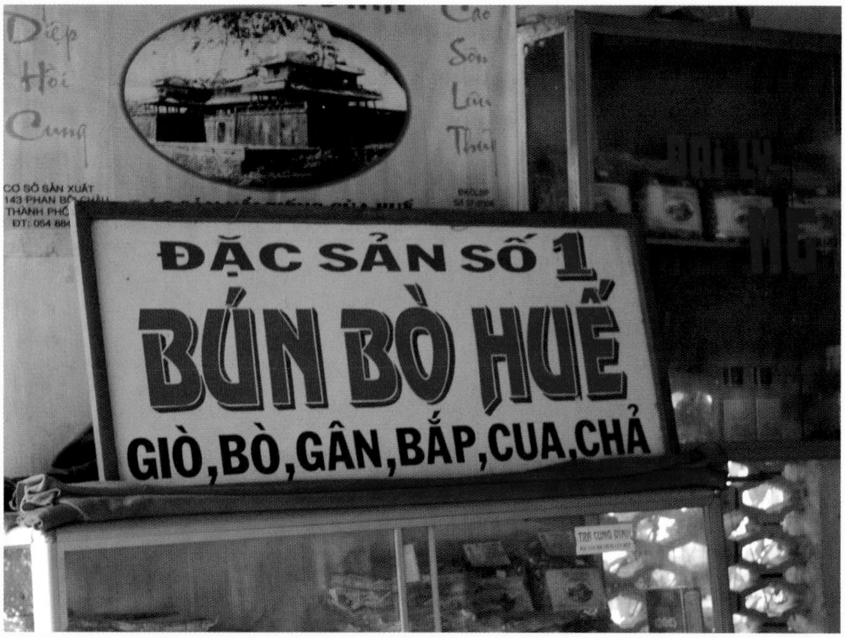
ĐẶC SẢN SỐ 1
BÚN BÒ HUẾ
GIÒ,BÒ,GÂN,BẮP,CUA,CHẢ

NOODLE KNOCKERS

When in the confines of the city, sounds bombard you around the clock. Unfortunately, the rhythm of the noodle knocker is slowly disappearing. Usually, children earn a little extra money for their families by running to shops to buy noodles for people who don't have time to go to the shop themselves. They knock a stick on a piece of wood as they walk, making a sound to signal to those that want a bowl of steaming noodles. Just tell these wandering hawkers what culinary delight you want, and they will run off and return with a delivery of pure flavor.

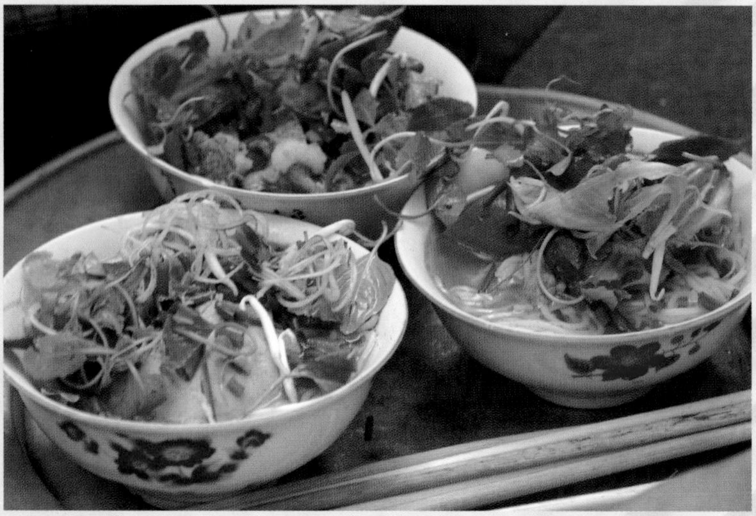

Rice

Rice is a primary food in the country, and the Vietnamese have figured out how to convert this precious grain into silky noodles, chewy spring roll wrappers called "rice paper," transcendental soups, savory and sweet dumplings, tender cakes, crisp breads, piquant vinegars, and intoxicating spirits. Long grain rice for everyday meals is cooked using the absorption method (pg. 106). Two varieties of glutinous (sticky) rice (*gạo nếp*) are grown: a short-medium grain variety and a long grain one (like Thailand). Both sticky rice varieties are soaked before being steamed. Rice flour is combined with wheat flour to make French-style baguettes especially light for the unique Bánh Mì Thịt sandwich (pg. 202).

Dominant Ingredients in Vietnam

FISH SAUCE (*nước mắm*) is the most essential seasoning in Vietnam. This shelf-stable, salty, protein-rich fermented seasoning adds depth of flavor to soups, salads, dipping sauces, marinades, and anything else except desserts. It's made the same way as Thai fish sauce (*nahm pla*), but Vietnamese fish sauce is more highly prized because its flavor is generally less pungent. For an extensive exploration of fish sauce, see the Southeast Asian Pantry (pg. 48).

VIETNAMESE CHARCUTERIE
"Giò"

Malaysian, Singaporean, and Thai cooks make sausages—mostly Chinese-style *lap cheong* in Malaysia and fermented pork sausages in Thailand. But the Vietnamese have really adopted the French practice of *charcuterie* (the art of making sausages, hams, pâtés, and other processed meat foods, usually from pork). Charcuterie, called *giò* in Vietnam, is clearly derived from French culinary presence in the region, as it is made in the same way as many French charcuterie products. The term *giò* is also a word used to describe the multipurpose pork paste used to create numerous Vietnamese charcuterie items. As Andrea Nguyễn explains in her book *Into the Vietnamese Kitchen* (Ten Speed Press 2006), "when ground meat is enhanced by other seasonings…rather than just boiled, it is elevated to the realm of *Tré,* a term for fancier charcuterie." Get a copy of Andrea's book to find out more about Vietnamese charcuterie.

Vietnamese Liver Pâté

Pa-Tê gan is not dissimilar to the French Pâté de Campagne, or country-style pâté, it's a little less spicy but otherwise contains pork, pork fat, pork liver, spices, and some binder such as tapioca starch. Baked in loaves, this spreadable forcemeat elevates the Vietnamese sandwich to higher levels, so try to get your hands on some for the *Bánh mì thịt* recipe (pg. 202).

FERMENTED SHRIMP PASTE is spoonable, and thinner than Thai or Malaysian versions. It's similar to China's southern style shrimp sauce. Shrimp sauce (*mắm tôm* or *mắm ruốc*) is such a central part of the cuisine that the term "mắm ruốc" is used to describe a light purple color, just as we refer to certain paint tints as "eggshell white" or "chocolate brown." In fact, fermented fish paste is a very savory, strongly umami, pungent seasoning that is not for the faint of heart. Used in small amounts, it imparts deep, complex layers of seafood nuance and even fruity notes to dishes. Used in liberal amounts, it could knock an uninitiated Westerner off his feet with its powerful odor of fermented fish.

Nước Chấm: THE ESSENTIAL DIPPING SAUCE

Vietnamese flavor combinations are more subtle than in neighboring countries: flavorful, yet not powerful; tart, not acidic; salted, not salty; sweet, but not cloying. Acute attention is paid to balance. Vietnamese finesse is evident in the ubiquitous *nước chấm* dipping sauce (pg. 198). It is the *de rigeur* dipping sauce for any spring rolls, whether soft-steamed or crispy-fried. It is poured over plates of rice vermicelli and grilled meats, anointed upon crunchy shrimp and mung bean cakes, and served with just about every type of grilled, roasted, fried, or broiled fish, meat, vegetable, or noodle in the land.

Nước chấm brings six ingredients into a harmonious statement. Fish sauce (*nước mắm*) is the foundation. Its salty, meaty (umami) flavor and heady fermented aroma cannot be duplicated by any other ingredient. Fresh lime juice provides crisp, palate-cleansing acidity, but its sharp edges are offset by a pinch of granulated cane sugar (never palm sugar, which would take over the flavor of the sauce). Minced garlic and chopped chilies introduce heat and oniony nuance. And sweet shreds of carrot impart their sweet, vegetable essence, plus appealing splashes of color and textural elements. Finally, the mixture is diluted to subtle dimensions with enough warm water to dissolve the sugar and soften the flavors. The result: a perfect sauce.

HERBS! Fresh herbs are used in such monstrous quantities in Vietnam that it takes some getting used to. Oh my goodness, the sheer variety is mind-blowing; one visit to a rural roadside restaurant allowed us the opportunity to have more than twenty-four different herbs to choose from, allowing us to customize our every bite. Three types of basil, two types of mint, sorrel, perilla, fish mint, and many more filled the platter.

My recipes use a recommended amount of sprigs (that vary in size). You can begin with this and then graduate to the copious amounts that the Vietnamese crave. Huế chicken salad (*gỏi gà*) (pg. 238) is an example of how mountains of fresh herbs can work their way into a dish. Phở is also served with an abundant plate of basil, chilies, cilantro, and occasionally other herbs for flavoring to taste.

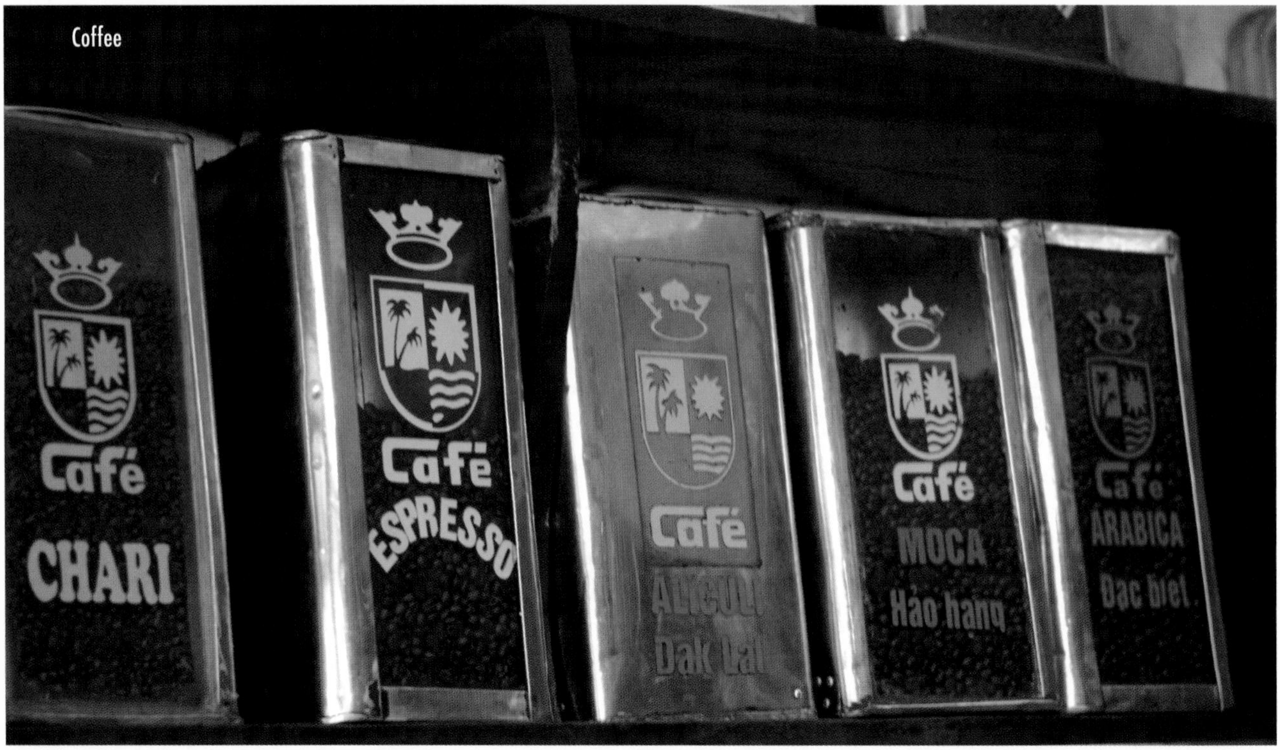
Café
CHARI
Café
ESPRESSO
Café
Café
MOCA
Hảo hạng
Café
ARABICA
Đặc biệt
Coffee

Presentation

Especially in the south and central regions, touching the food with your hands is an important part of the dining experience. It's not enough to sense a small piece of lettuce in the center of a chewy rice-paper-wrapped salad roll (*gỏi cuốn*) (pg. 206). Oh no, they want to extend the sensory experience: They'll utilize juicy lettuce leaves as a bed for aromatic herbs, crisp cucumbers, and crunchy bean sprouts which are used to create layers of texture and flavor with that salad roll and all of the other dishes served at the meal. The juxtaposition of hot, cooked foods with cold, raw table salads (*rau thơm*) is an essential characteristic of the Vietnamese meal.

Vietnamese Beverages

COFFEE

Not only is Vietnam the second largest exporter of coffee in the world after Brazil, but the Vietnamese themselves love it. Cafés are popular hangouts where young and old sit and sip the ultra-strong brew, *cà- phê*. In the past, the robusta variety of bean, usually called inferior, has been their bean of choice. But the Arabica bean is starting to gain some ground. *Trung Nguyên* is the most notable brand available in Vietnam (and also exported to the U.S.), but many Vietnamese Americans prefer the Café du Monde coffee from New Orleans,

Chè
A SWEET TREAT FOR ALL AGES

southeastasianflavors.com Go to...

On the sweet end of the spectrum, the Vietnamese have an entire category of sweet snacks referred to as *chè* (pronounced chay-ay). I recently traveled from the Mekong Delta all the way north to Hà-Nội. Along the way, we stopped in Danang, the hometown of my guide, Mr. Công, in the central region, and dedicated a day to a culinary exploration of chè. We found a special stall in the center of Đà-Nẵng's *Chợ Hàn* market that sold nothing but chè. Not exactly a cold soup and not exactly a pudding, chè is a chilled—often iced—composition of sweet ingredients served in glasses and eaten with spoons. It may contain any number of sweet ingredients such as sugared beans, chopped fruits, syrup-sweetened vegetables (like beets), crunchy seeds, and nuts. Many varieties of chè feature cubes of juice or sweet bean paste that have been gelled with agar-agar until they have a rubbery, resilient texture. Texture, in fact, is the main appeal of these confections.

When you go to a chè stall or café, expect to find dozens of choices. You can customize your own glass of chè, just as you would with toppings on an ice cream sundae. Simple versions are often seasonal: when corn is in season, *chè bắp* is made by simmering freshly shucked corn kernels, sugar, water, and tapioca to produce a gelatinous soup. In other seasons you'll see mashed avocado topped with crushed ice and coconut milk. Others may include elaborate layers of cut fruit with coconut, or my own favorite, bananas cooked with sweetened coconut milk and tapioca pearls. In the tropical heat, nothing beats chè for sweet, cool relief (pg. 264).

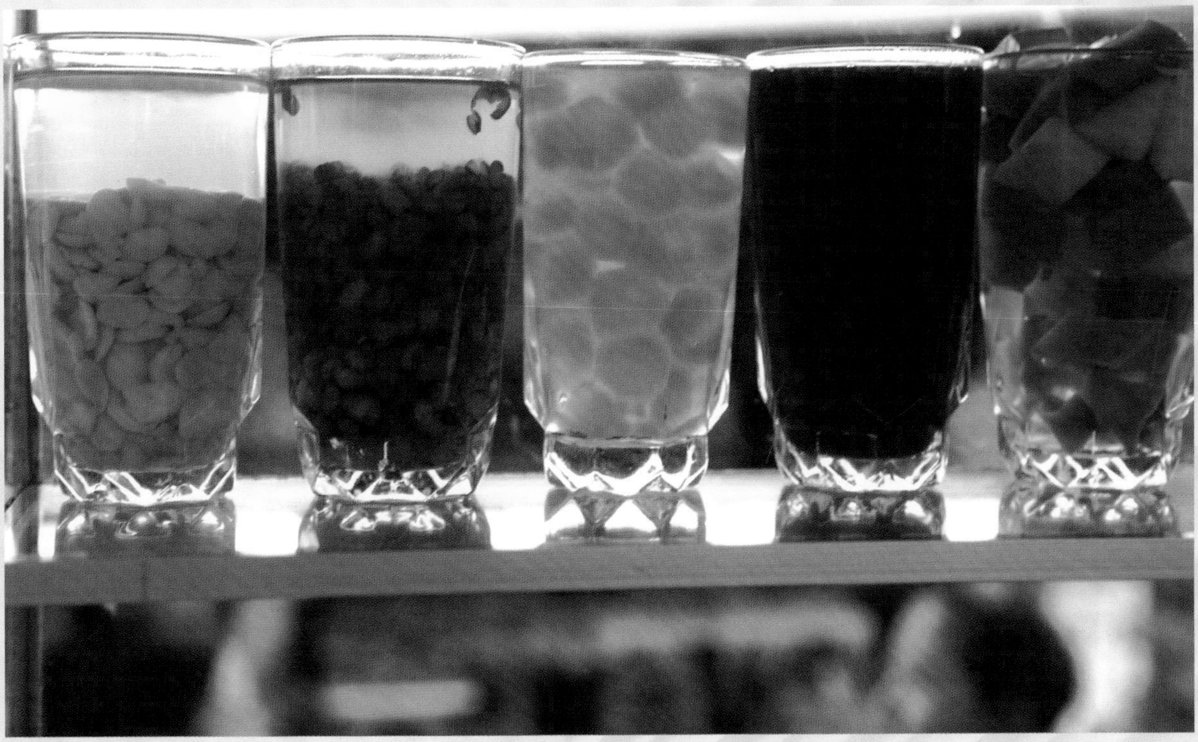

which has chicory root added to it. Either way, a dark roast and fine grind is essential to achieve the intensity for which Vietnamese coffee is famous.

There are a few primary decisions one must make before choosing a cup of Vietnamese coffee. Iced coffee is a choice at any time of year. As in the West, some drink it with milk, and others drink it black. Whatever you choose, you will be greeted with a powerful brew. There's a special device used for certain types of coffee. It's a single-serving metal brewer that perches right on the rim of the coffee cup or glass. At the top, a screened brewing chamber holds the dark grounds. Boiling water is added, and the coffee is left to brew for a few moments. Then, a twist of a screw in the center of the chamber releases the brewed coffee to filter slowly through a screen at the bottom, allowing the coffee to drip through into the cup or glass below. If you ask for coffee with milk, *cà-phê sữa*, a thick layer of condensed milk will be spooned into the bottom of the cup before the brewing device is affixed. The slow rain of rich, intense coffee drips directly onto the condensed milk. They begin to melt together as one rich mixture. Once all the coffee has dripped through, a few strokes of your spoon stir the sweet milk in, and a rich brown cup is ready for slow sipping. Pour this concoction over ice for an iced coffee. Mmmmm, I'll be right back. I need to go make myself a cup right now.

My hunger for new experiences is insatiable. But that does not mean that I'll eat anyting that's put in front of me. Intriguing as it may sound, I have never felt compelled to try the unique weasel shit coffee. Yes, you read that right. Weasel shit. *Cà-phê cứt Chồn* is brewed from beans that rodent connoisseurs of the beans have eaten and excreted. Oh, no worries, they are then "cleaned" off, processed and roasted to later brew into a rich cocoa-like coffee. No thanks.

A TEA CULTURE

As descendants of the Chinese, Vietnamese naturally value tea as an integral part of their world not only as a recreational beverage, but as a ceremonial elixir whose brewing skills are revered as art. Green tea and fermented black tea are both consumed in the home, at formal restaurant meals, with street food, and at cafés—pretty much everywhere by everyone. Serving tea upon welcoming someone to your home or a meeting is a gesture of hospitality and is expected even at the most nonformal engagements

Two teas (infusions) unique to Vietnam are made from dried artichokes and roasted beans. Artichokes came to be used in lean times when tea was in short supply. This thorny thistle provided an

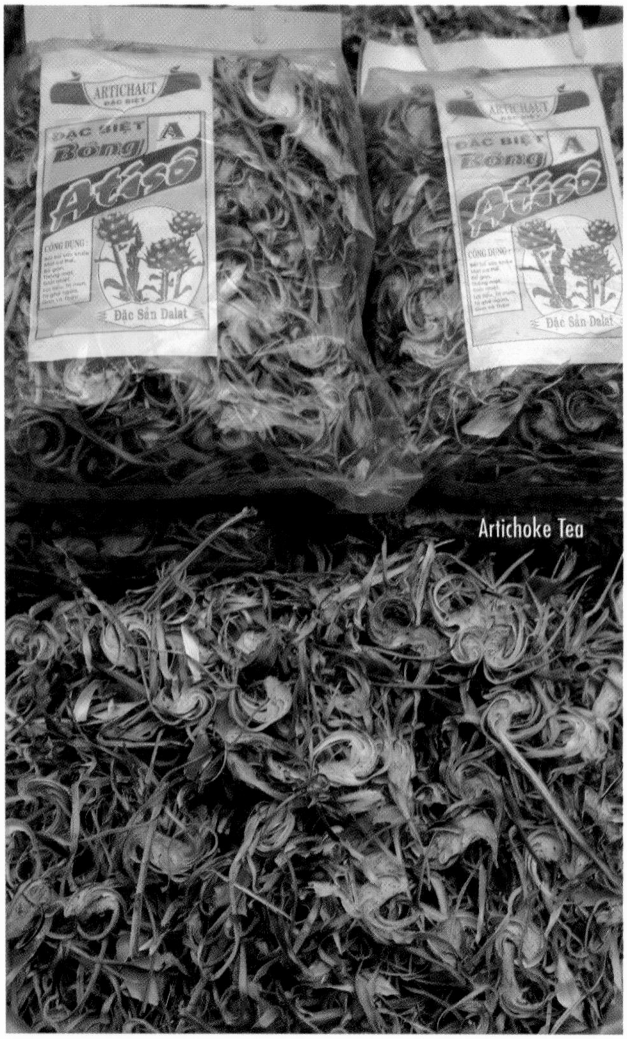
ARTICHAUT
Bông
Atisô
Đặc Sản Dalat
Artichoke Tea

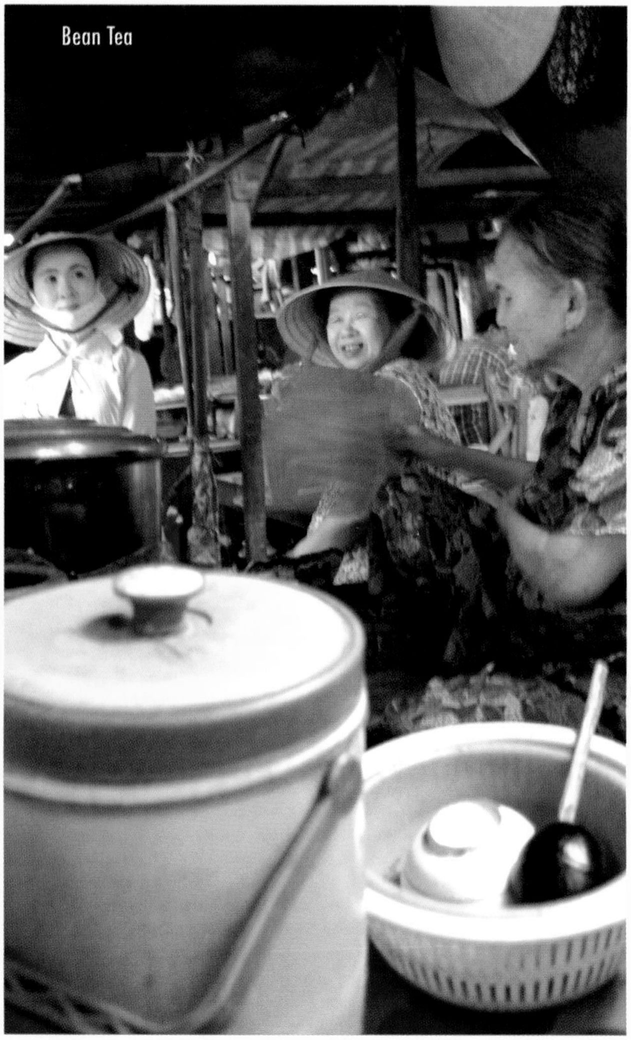
Bean Tea

astringent bitterness akin to tea. In Hội-An they have a unique tea made from roasted beans, *nước đậu ván*, that carries a deep flavor without caffeine. Even the busiest folks take time out of their day for a short repast of some wood-fired fresh brewed tea.

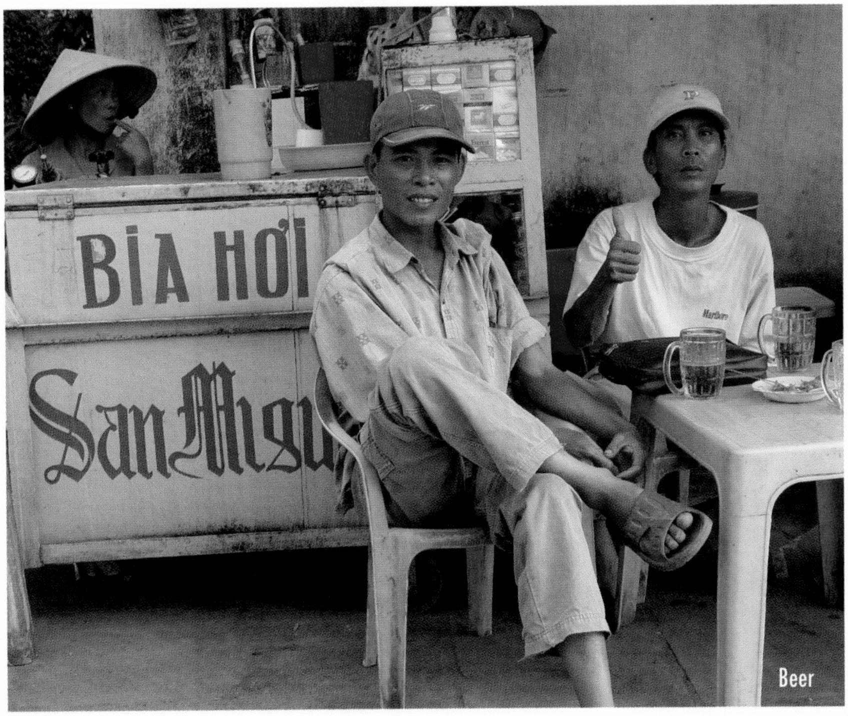
BIA HƠI
San Migu
Beer

FRESH BEER

On a hot day, as most days are in Vietnam, a freshly brewed beer is happiness. Like the locals, I find myself showering several times a day to cool down. When a shower is out of reach, an ice-cold beverage can satisfy. My engine's coolant is *bia hơi*, locally brewed fresh beer sold only in kegs. Very light in color (and, frankly, in flavor) it is refreshingly good. Drinking beer midday is not hard to get used to: I am quite proficient. However, drinking beer with large fragments of ice in it was a new experience (and truthfully, something I tried to avoid, though it was the lesser evil when warm beer was the only alternative).

SMOOTHIES OF THE EAST—*Sinh Tố*

The Western world is just catching up to Asian prowess in holistic health. "Sinh Tố" translates as "alive elements" or "vitamin." This illustrates how the Vietnamese value food for its health-giving properties. Health food stalls dot the streets and proudly display enormous varieties of fresh fruit for smooth shakes. An avocado smoothie is probably one of the most unusual for Westerners. It seems odd using something we usually serve as a savory treat in a sweet drink, but once you taste that thick creamy shake with condensed milk (pg. 266) you'll be a convert. It's just another way that Vietnam gets you to see food in a whole new light.

KEM

Calling it ice cream would not be accurate. This Vietnamese frozen confection is lighter in texture and contains no eggs. It evolved from a French creation, but suits the climate of Vietnam much better. There are versions based on cream and milk and others more like sorbet, based on sweetened fruit purées. Kem has become a passionate affair for the locals, especially the younger generation. As with ice cream, making kem requires specialized equipment, and so kem shops have become social gathering spots that proliferate across the land. Scoops of kem are served up to thousands every afternoon as school kids gather in local cafés.

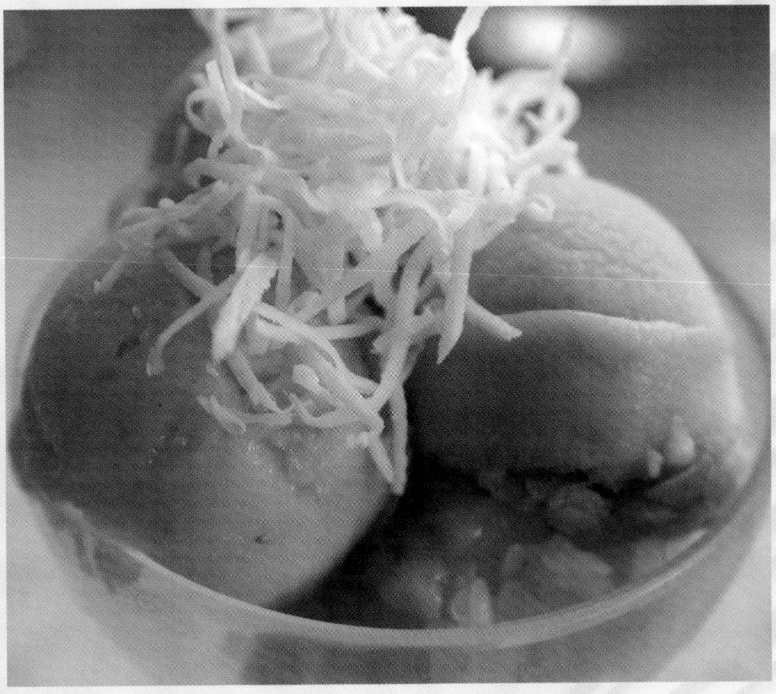

Lime and Garlic Dipping Sauce
Nước Chấm

Nước chấm is the most essential Vietnamese table condiment. It's a staple dipping sauce that is always at the ready to provide its fresh, salty and slightly sour accent to salad rolls (*goi cuon*) (pg. 206), to pour over some noodles and grilled pork (pg. 256), or simply place on the table as a condiment to perk up dishes that are missing that Umami kick, chili bite and citrus zest.

Every lime varies slightly in acidity. Chili heat varies. We all perceive taste differently (really!). The flavor of ingredients like limes is not consistent; sometimes they're more acidic than others. So adjust the flavors to suit yourself and your guests. Taste often and adjust as needed to achieve a balance of color, aromas, tastes, and textures.

Makes 3/4 cup

1 to 2 Thai bird chilies
1 clove Garlic, minced
1/4 cup Granulated sugar
1/2 cup Warm water
3 Tbsp. Lime juice with pulp
1/4 cup Fish sauce (*nước mắm*)
1 Tbsp. Finely shredded carrots (optional)

1. Cut one of chili into the thinnest rings possible; set aside for garnish. Mince the remaining chili.
2. Transfer minced chilies to a bowl, add the garlic, sugar, water, lime juice and fish sauce. Whisk until sugar is completely dissolved.
3. Add the reserved chili and carrots. Set aside for 10 minutes to let the flavors marry before tasting and adjusting seasoning.

How and Why

Using warm water makes a more rounded flavor. Warm water softens the garlic and helps dissolve the sugar faster.

Vietnamese Spicy Chili Sauce
Tương Ớt/đỏ

Vietnamese restaurants in the USA nearly all feature tall bottles of dazzling orange sauce on the table. It's actually Thai Sriracha Sauce (pg. 133). Here, I've provided a more traditional sauce, which is equally delicious, a bit coarser in texture, saltier, contains no fish sauce, and is not fermented (as its Thai counterpart often is).

Keep this on hand to spice up *Phở* (pg. 218). I add a touch to the broth, and keep a small dipping bowl on the side for adding zip to beef slices. Lemongrass Chicken Stir Fry with Tamarind (pg. 248) benefits immensely from a dash of this sauce. Watch out: it's habit-forming. Before long, red splashes of this fiery paste will be slathered on your burgers, chicken wings and fries. Like me, you'll be using it to spice up dressings and marinades too.

Makes 2 cups

1/4 cup (¼ oz. / 7 g.) Dried red chilies, remove stems and seeds
16   (¾ lb. or 340 g.) Long red chilies or other hot red chilies, roughly chopped
6   cloves Garlic, roughly chopped
1½   tsp. Kosher salt
2   tsp. Granulated sugar
1   cup Water
2   Tbsp. Distilled white vinegar

1. Bring all ingredients to a boil in a small saucepan, lower to a simmer, and cook gently for 5 minutes. Remove from heat; cool to room temperature. Puree in blender until very smooth.
2. Store in refrigerator. Bring to room temperature before serving. Keeps for up to three months, but tastes best within first three weeks.

How and Why

If substituting other chilies such as Red Fresno or Jalapenos, remove the seeds and discard them. These larger, thick-skinned chilies have harder seeds that do not puree well. To compensate for lost heat, add a few whole Thai bird chilies to the mix.

Scallion Oil
Hành Mở

The softer side of scallion's flavor is infused into the hot oil in this Vietnamese kitchen staple. The oil is slathered on grilled meats or seafood, or drizzled onto noodles. Look at the Grilled Shrimp Paste on Sugarcane (*chạo tôm*) recipe (pg. 242) to see how the oil aids in browning the shrimp. And check out the Rice Noodle Rolls (*bánh cuốn*) on page 212 to see how a brush of this oil adds a subtle oniony flavor without an overwhelming bite.

Makes ¹/₂ cup

¹/₂ cup Vegetable oil

2 Scallions, thinly sliced, about ¹/₄ inch (0.6 cm.) thick (about ¹/₂ cup)

1. In small pan, heat oil over medium heat, until it is hot enough to sizzle a piece of scallion on contact.

2. Add scallions and cook until scallions wilt slightly and change color (about 10 seconds).

3. Remove from, heat and set aside to rest for 30 minutes. Strain or scoop out scallions.

4. Store at room temperature for the day or refrigerate for up to 2 weeks.

How and Why

Slowly infusing the oil at a lower temperature brings out the most flavor. Instead of frying the scallions which drives off the water and much of the essential volatile, this method brings out the best aromas a slow infusion.

Vietnamese Peanut Sauce

Tương đậu phọng

A harmonious balance of sweet and salty, this sauce takes only minutes to make. It's the best complement to *Nước Chấm* with Vietnamese Salad Rolls (pg. 206), but is also delicious slathered on barbecued meats. The traditional version of this sauce is made fermented soybean sauce (*tương Bần*) (pg. 53), yet contemporary use of hoisin sauce in place of that rare ingredient, illustrates the close link between Chinese and Vietnamese cuisine. Compared to the long-cooked Malaysian peanut sauce, this is a snap to whip up and much less rich than the Thai coconut-enriched version.

Makes 1¹/₂ cups

1	Tbsp. Vegetable oil
2	tsp. Minced garlic
1	small Thai bird chili, minced
1	cup Hoisin sauce
¹/₄	cup Water
2	Tbsp. Rice vinegar (unseasoned)
1	Tbsp. Minced shallot
1	stalk Lemongrass, trimmed and minced
¹/₄	cup Canned coconut milk
¹/₂	cup Peanuts, roasted in dry pan (pg. 109)
2	Tbsp. Vietnamese Chili Sauce (*tương ớt/đỏ*) (pg. 199) or store-bought

1. Over a medium-low heat cook garlic in oil until aromatic—about 2 minutes. Add chilies, hoisin sauce, water, rice vinegar, shallots, and lemongrass; bring to a boil. Reduce heat; simmer 5 minutes.

2. Remove from heat, stir in coconut milk and half of peanuts. Cool to room temperature.

3. Transfer sauce to dish(s); garnish with remaining chopped peanuts and chili sauce.

How and Why

The sauce is cooked for a short time, so a quick, separate cooking of the garlic is needed to mellow its flavor, which softly pervades this condiment.

Vietnamese Sandwich with Grilled Pork, Pâté, Pickled Veggies
Bánh Mì Thịt

In Vietnam, an iconic culinary fusion is this multi-layered sandwich born of multicultural influences. The French introduced yeast-risen bread to Vietnam during their 100-year presence there. The Vietnamese tweaked the recipe, adding rice flour to make baguettes lighter and crisper. The French also brought pâté and butter as spreads for bread. Both ingredients have become integral, authentic parts of Vietnamese cuisine. In *Bánh Mì Thịt*, tender slices of simmered or grilled pork are stacked on French bread, with pâté, butter, pickled carrots, sweet scallions and fresh herbs.

Makes 4 to 6 sandwiches

CARROT AND DAIKON PICKLES

1/2   cup Distilled white vinegar
1/2   cup Sugar
1/2   tsp. Kosher Salt
1 1/2   cups Julienne daikon (large radish), about 1/8 inch
        (0.3 cm.) thick
1 1/2   cups Julienne carrots, about 1/8 inch (0.3 cm.) thick
        (pg. 108)

1. Whisk vinegar, sugar, and salt together until dissolved. Add daikon and toss well. Marinate for at least 30 minutes. These can be made a few days ahead, after that they begin to get limp (yet still tasty).

GRILLED PORK

1   Tbsp. Oyster sauce
2   tsp. Fish sauce (*nước mắm*)
1   Tbsp. Light brown palm sugar (pg. 58)
1/2   tsp. Ground black pepper
1   stalk Lemongrass, trimmed and minced
1   clove Garlic, minced
3/4   lb. (340 g.) Pork shoulder, butt, or leg, sliced
        about 1/8 inch (0.3 cm.) thick

1. Whisk all ingredients except pork together. Add pork and massage to coat well. Marinate for at least 30 minutes.
2. Grill pork until brown and cooked through. (You can also sauté if a grill is not available)

OTHER SANDWICH COMPONENTS

2   Thin crusted baguettes, *partially* split lengthwise
        (leave the spine uncut). The best is a baguette
        that has a thin crust and light center—
        "supermarket variety."
1/4   cup Mayonnaise (room temperature)
1/4   cup Salted butter (room temperature)
1/4   lb. (113 g.) Country style pate (French), beaten until
        spreadable (add butter, if needed, to soften)
6   leaves Green leaf lettuce
1   medium Cucumber, Kirby variety preferred, bite size
        julienne strips, about 1/8 inch (0.3 cm.) thick (pg. 81)
2   ea. Jalapeños, thinly sliced into rings, about 1/8 inch
        (0.3 cm.) thick
16   sprigs Cilantro sprigs (stem on)
1/4   cup Shaved scallions, thin as possible, about 2 inches
        (5 cm.) long
to taste Fish sauce (*nước mắm*)
1/4   cup Pork floss (also called "pork sung" or "this ruoc
        bong") (optional) (pg. 203)

ASSEMBLE SANDWICHES

1. Spread 1 to 2 tablespoons mayonnaise/butter on top half of bread. Spread pork pâté on bottom half of bread. Sprinkle one side with pork floss. Arrange the rest of the ingredient as evenly as possible: lettuce, cucumber, pork, jalapeños, cilantro, scallions pickled carrot and daikon (drained well), sprinkle with optional fish sauce then fold over top of baguette.

How and Why

Use a thin-crusted baguette. The thin crust keeps the balance of flavor and texture.

PORK FLOSS—NOT FOR YOUR TEETH

Ruốc (Northern); *Chà Bông* (Southern)

Misleading name, odd appearance. Pork "floss" is usually bought instead of being made at home. The Vietnamese call it "cotton pork"; the Chinese. "pork fu," but in English, the unfortunate term "pork floss" will get you what you want. Pork is simmered in seasoned water (fish sauce for Vietnamese, sweetened soy sauce for Chinese version) until tender, drained, pulled into thin shards, and then pounded until it resembles wool. It's dry roasted in a wok to steam out any excess moisture. The toasted dried pork is packed with flavor, and no longer needs refrigeration. If you're compelled to make some at home, look to Andrea Nguyễn's *Into the Vietnamese Kitchen* for the recipe (pg. 367).

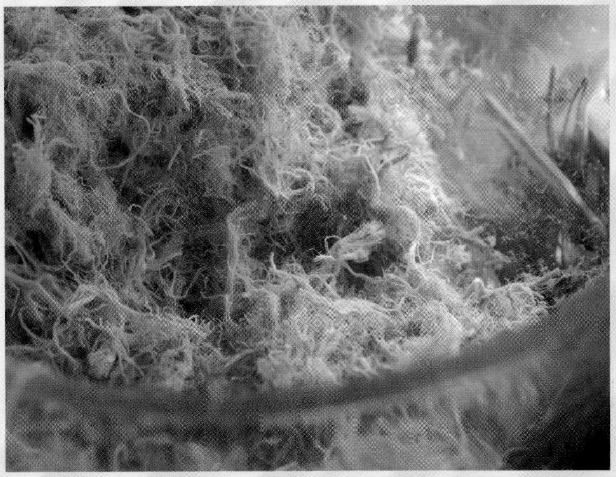

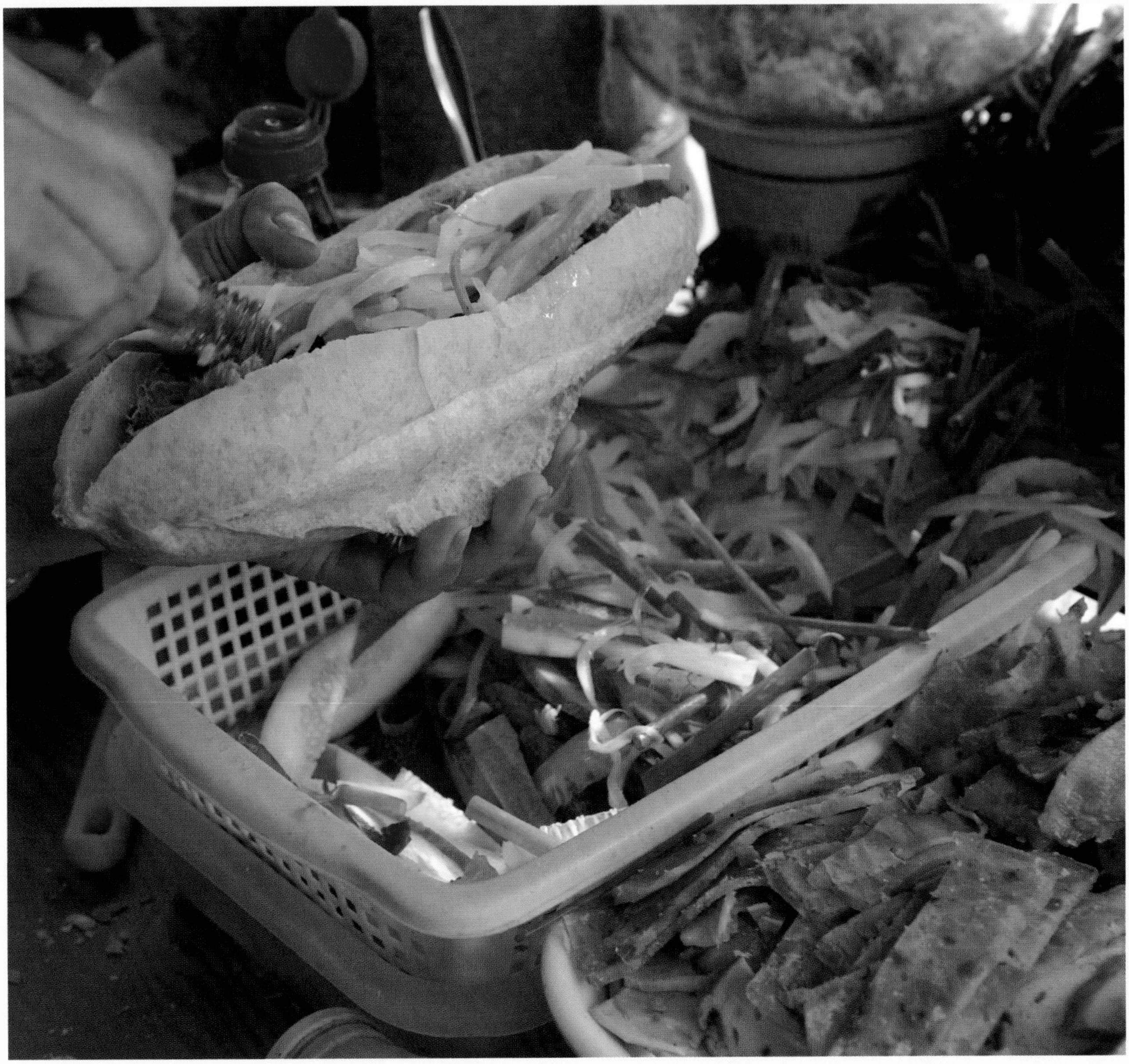

Vietnamese Sandwich with Grilled Pork, Pâté, Pickled Veggies

Bánh Mì Thịt

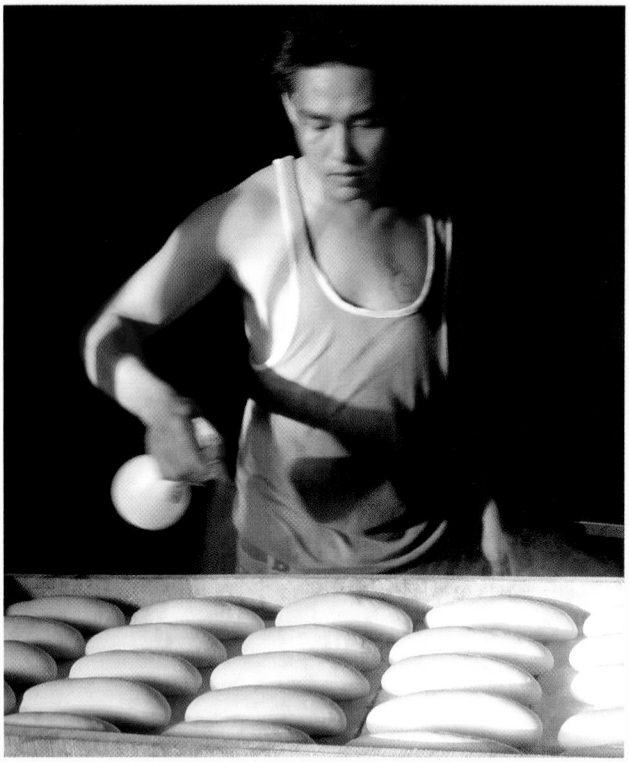

Bread rises and is sprayed with water to encourage a crunchy crust.

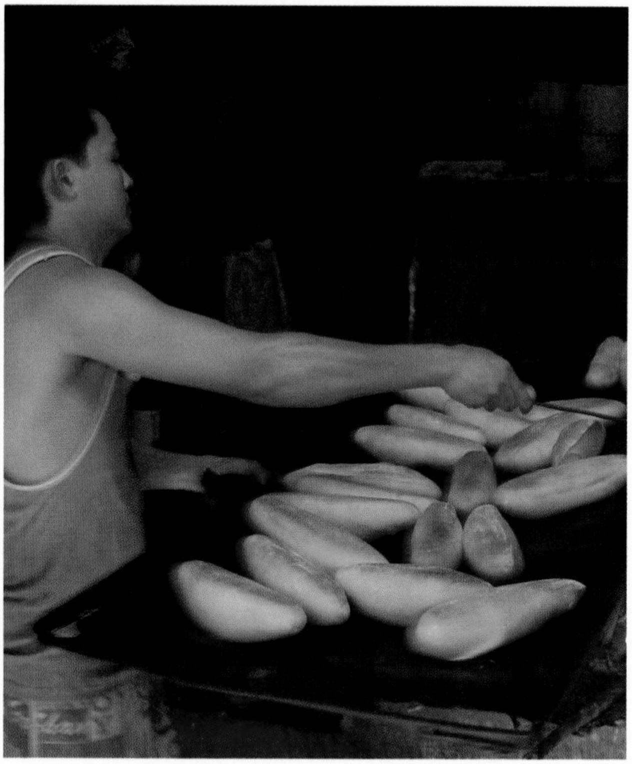

A wood fire oven adds an elusive flavor, artesian bread at it's best.

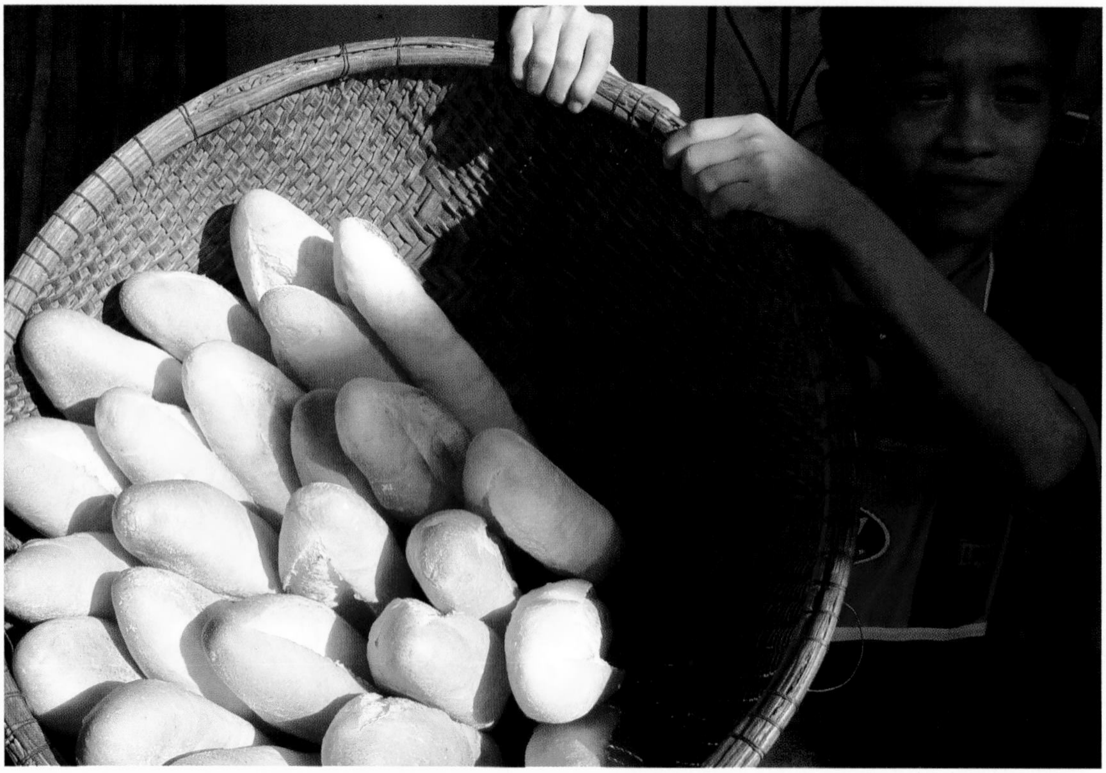

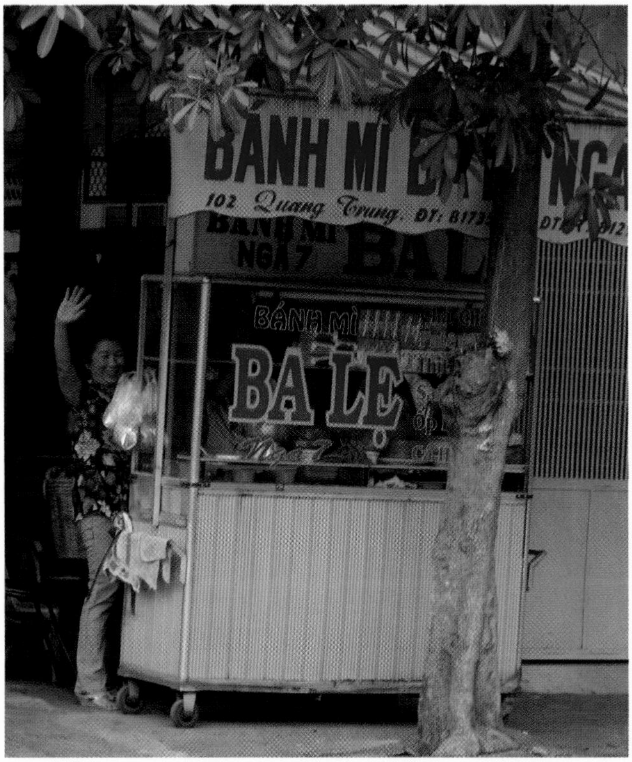
BÁNH MÌ
102 Quang Trung.

A welcoming smile calls you in for a bite.

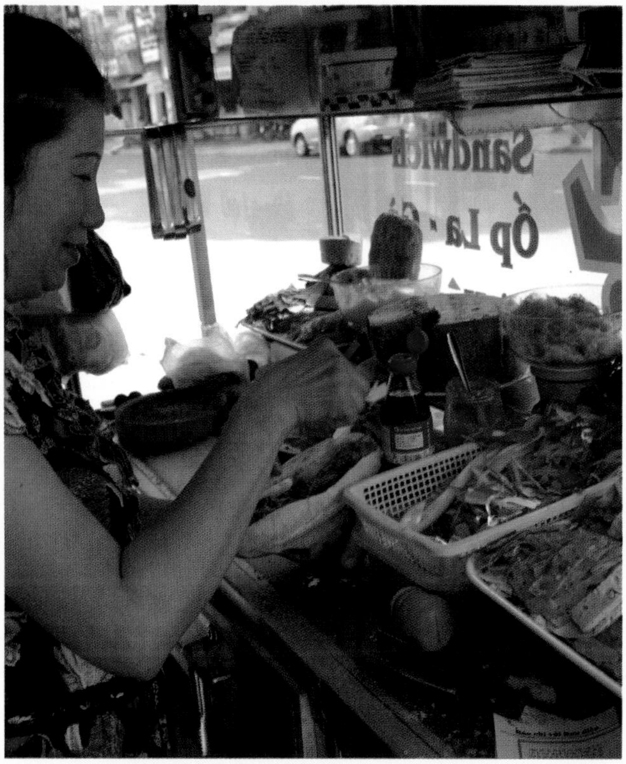

Each sandwich is built to order with what you request.

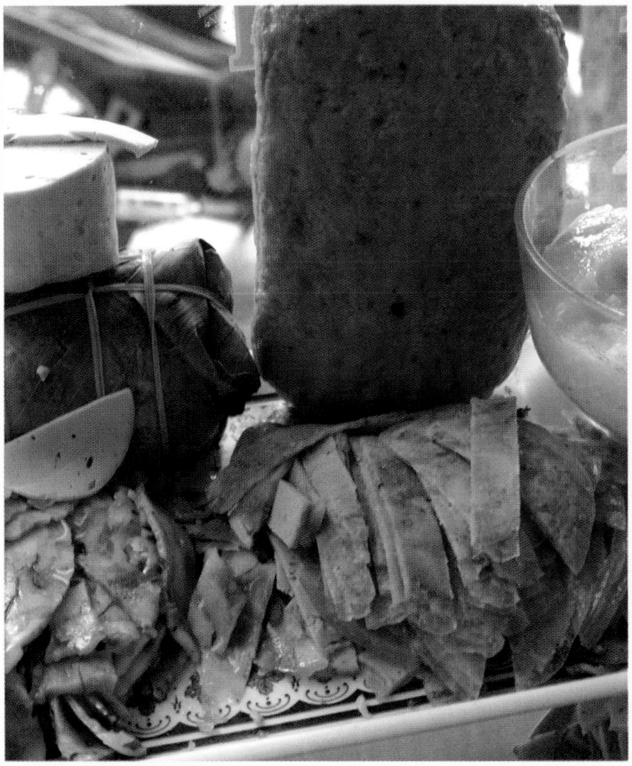

Various charcuterie and softened butter/margarine.

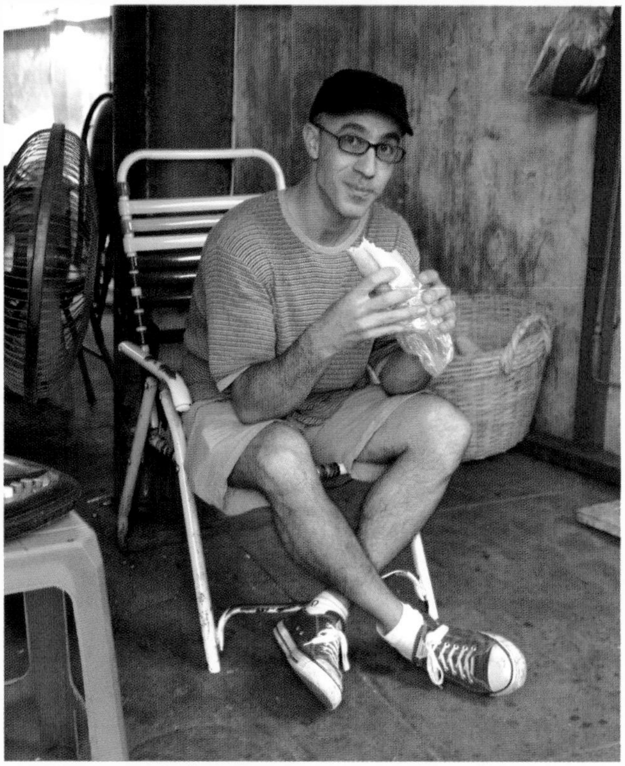

I finally get to sit down and devour my own sandwich.

Rice Paper Salad Rolls, Shrimp and Pork with Lime and Garlic Dipping Sauce

Gỏi Cuốn

Take note of the cross-thatched pattern on the rice paper. In Vietnam artisans make the rice paper by steaming rice flour batter on cloth over a caldron of water boiling over a fire of burning rice husks and peanut shells. The sheets are sun-dried on bamboo mats that create the pattern, a sign of hand-craftsmanship (pg. 70).

The rice paper is quite simple to work with once you've practiced with a few sheets. In Vietnam they eat them quite chewy, only rubbing the rice paper with water and never submerging in water as I recommend below. Make sure to only dip in water briefly, so they still have some bite. They are quite versatile: restaurants across the country are wrapping fillings that include grilled chicken and salmon. Try wrapping up other fillings yourself; such as vegetable slaw and grilled chicken.

Makes 15 rolls

4 oz. Dried rice vermicelli
1/4 lb. (113 g.) Lean pork, such as loin or leg, one piece about 1 inch (2.5 cm.) thick and 3 inches (7.5 cm.) long
15 Small shrimp, deveined with shell still on
20 to 25 leaves (2 heads) Green, red, butter or bibb lettuce (divided use)
1 medium Cucumber, Kirby variety preferred, bite size julienne strips, about 1/8 inch (0.3 cm.) thick
2 cups Bean sprouts, trimmed
15 Chinese chives, trimmed
1 cup Perilla (Vietnamese mint) or mint leaves
10 to 15 Round rice papers, 10 inches (25.4 cm.) in diameter
15 sprigs Cilantro sprigs
15 sprigs Perilla leaves sprigs
1 recipe Vietnamese peanut sauce (*tương đậu phọng*) (pg. 201) or Lime dipping sauce (*nước chấm*)

1. Prepare the Fillings: Soak the rice noodles in room temperature water until softened, about 30 minutes; drain. Boil soaked noodles until cooked through, 20 seconds to 1 minute depending on manufacturer and thickness of noodles. Immediately rinse with cool water, drain and reserve. In small saucepan, submerge pork in simmering water; gently cook until well-done through to 150°F or 65°C; plunge into ice water for 10 minutes. Remove, and cut into small slices, about 1/8 inch (0.3cm.) thick. Cook the shrimp in simmering salted water until just done, about 3 minutes. Cool in ice water 5 minutes. Shell, devein, and halve lengthwise. Rip 15 large tender 3 to 4-inch (71/2–10 cm) pieces of lettuce without ribs.

2. Set up for rolling: Fill a large mixing bowl or shallow basin that is wide enough to fit rice paper with warm water. Keep some boiling water handy to add to the bowl if the temperature drops below 100°F or 37.8°C. Choose an open area on the counter and arrange the lettuce, cucumbers, cooked noodles, bean sprouts, chives, pork and shrimp.

3. Make the Rolls:
- Dip a sheet of rice paper in the water for a few seconds. It should remain somewhat firm. Transfer it to a clean work surface. Set the fillings onto the bottom third of the sheet: a 2-inch × 3-inch (5 cm. × 71/2 cm.) piece of lettuce 6 strips of cucumber, about 1/4 cup noodles, 6 bean sprouts, and 2 to 3 leaves of Vietnamese mint.
- Begin to roll as if you were creating a burrito: fold rice paper from bottom over the filling, making sure rice paper is taught, then fold in each side to encase the fillings, but don't roll more than one turn up. Once you have the filling encased, then lay down two slices of pork, a single Chinese chive leaving 1 inch (2.5 cm.) protruding off one edge and roll a turn. Next, place two shrimp halves, bright colored side facing down (so that the shrimp can be seen through the rice paper). Now roll up the rest of the way. Repeat with remaining sheets and fillings.

4. Prepare Table Salad: Arrange remaining leaves of lettuce, cucumber, bean sprouts and Vietnamese herbs on a serving platter, adding any needed items.

5. Serving the Rolls: The guests places a lettuce leaf in the palm of her hand, lays a roll on top of that, and adds items from the table salad. She will fold this into a convenient shape, dip it in the sauce, and eat it out of hand.

How and Why

It is imperative that the paper finishes absorbing the water *after* it's taken from the warm soak. A brief soaking keeps the desirable chewy texture, results in rice paper that clings to itself, and keeps the rolls wrapped up tight.

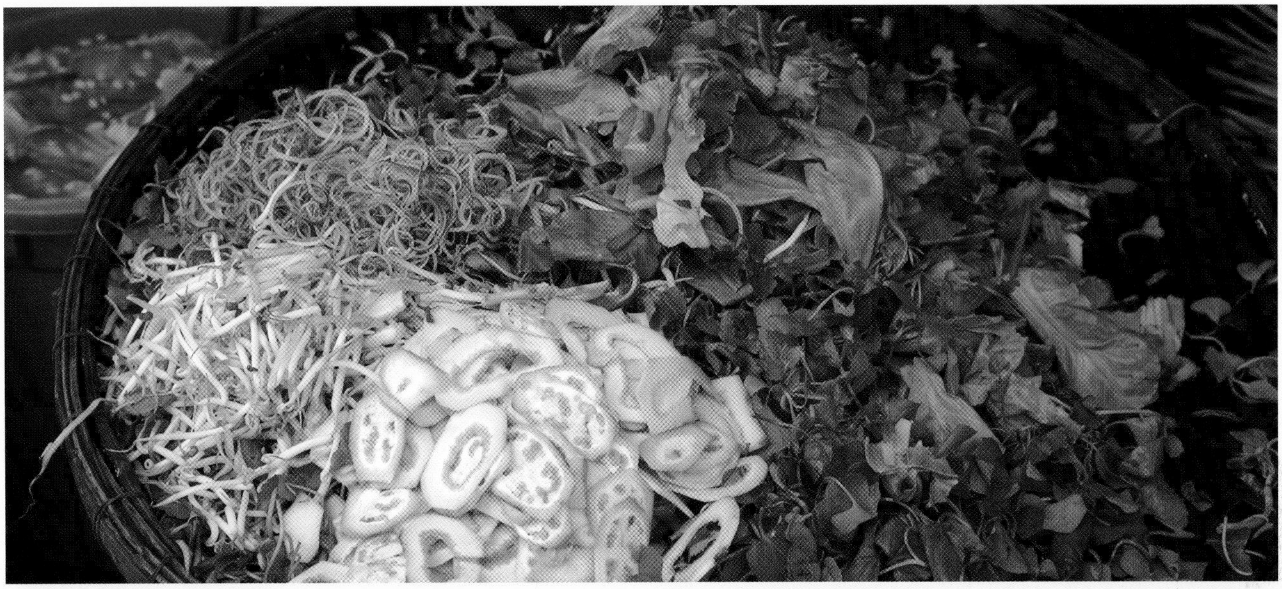

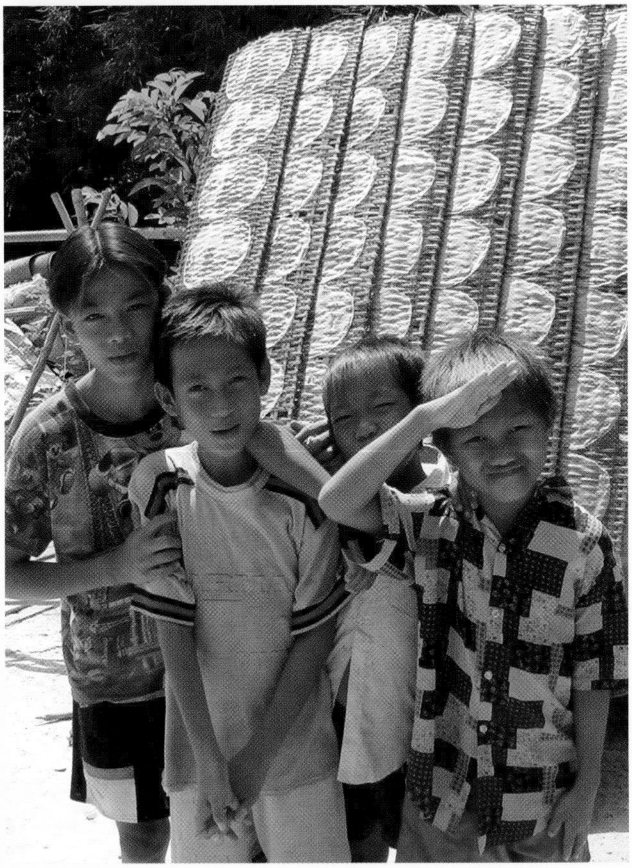

These boys followed me around the whole day as I learned the intricacies of making rice paper. See it drying on the mats behind them.

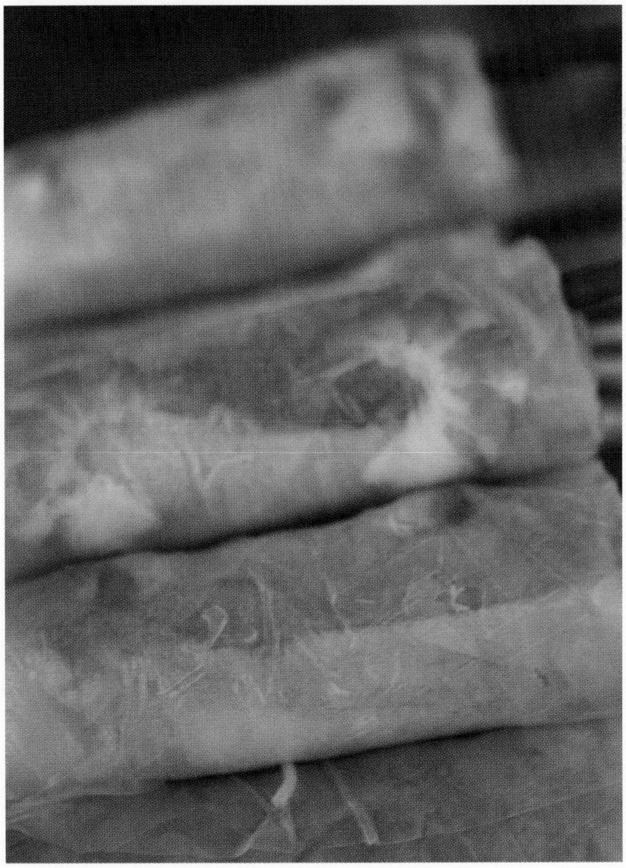

Crunchy Golden Coconut Crepes with Pork, Shrimp and Bean Sprouts

Bánh Xèo

You can hear these before you see them. Once I spot these frying on the coal stove of a Vietnamese street vendor, I rush over to feel the heat and enjoy the sizzling sounds that only get louder as I approach. The Vietnamese word "Xèo" translates as "sizzling," so these are commonly known as "sizzling Saigon crepes." They are thin, crunchy pancakes that radiate the yellow glow of turmeric, as they slowly crackle in savory pork fat. Although they look like omelets, there is no egg in them at all.

Once the crepe is cooked, it's packed with crunchy bean sprouts. To eat, the sprout-filled crepe is torn apart and wrapped up with lettuce leaves and herbs. It's dipped in a lime-dipping sauce (nước chấm). This recipe makes easily enough for a light lunch for six people.

Makes 6 ten-inch crepes, 6 to 8 servings as part of multi-dish meal

RICE CREPE BATTER

2	cups Rice flour
1/4	tsp. Ground turmeric (pg. 35)
1/2	tsp. Kosher salt
1 1/2	cup Water
3/4	cup Canned coconut milk
3	Scallions, thinly sliced on extreme angle, about 1/4 inch (0.6 cm.) thick

1. In a large bowl whisk together the rice flour, turmeric, and salt. Add water and oil. Whisk until mixture forms perfectly smooth batter (it will be very thin). If there are any lumps strain through a fine sieve. Set batter aside to rest for at least 30 minutes.

Gently fold the crepe. They are bound to have some cracks. Don't fret. You are going to rip them into pieces as you eat them anyway!

COOKED FILLINGS

1	cup Rendered pork fat, lard or vegetable oil
1/4	lb. (113 g.) Pork shoulder, small bite size thin slices, about 1/8 inch (0.3 cm.) thick
1/4	lb. (113 g.) Small shrimp, peeled and deveined, sliced in halves lengthwise
1/4	tsp. Kosher salt
1/2	cup Sliced yellow onion, about 1/8 inch (0.3 cm.) thick
1 to 2 med.	Long red chilies, sliced thinly into rings, about 1/8 inch (0.3 cm.) thick
3/4	cups Sliced mushrooms, 1/8-inch (0.3 cm.) slices
2	cups Bean sprouts, trimmed

1. Prepare your tools: Preheat oven to 250°F (121°C). Line a baking sheet with several layers of paper towels. Place 4 oz. ladle or 1/2 cup measuring cup with batter. Get a heat-proof rubber or wooden spatula.

2. Toss pork and shrimp in salt. Then divide into 6 small bowls, along with onions and mushrooms.

3. Make pancakes one by one (or use several pans at once):

A. Heat a 10-inch (25 cm.) non-stick sauté pan or cast-iron skillet (you will need a cover for this pan) over high heat. Add 1 Tbsp. lard, and then add one portion of pork, shrimp, onions and mushrooms. Stir-fry until pork and shrimp lose raw appearance. Distribute items on bottom of skillet evenly.

B. Stir batter to redistribute settled flour. Slowly ladle 1/2 cup of batter into pan, trying not to disturb the cooked items there. Swirl pan to coat bottom, allowing batter to ride 1/4–1/2 inch (0.6–1 cm.) up the side of pan. Stop swirling once the edges set. Immediately distribute bean sprouts over half the crepe. Cook until edges begin to dry up and peel back from pan. Drizzle 1 Tbsp. fat around outer edge of crepe, allowing it to run under crepe edges. Lower heat to medium.

C. Cover pan; cook 1 minute. Remove cover; continue to cook until edges begin to brown. Loosen pancake from bottom of pan with spatula. It should be sizzling; add oil if needed. Cook until bottom is light brown and crispy. Fold crepe to encase bean sprouts.

D. Transfer crepe to towel-lined pan; set in oven to keep warm. Repeat with remaining batter and fillings.

FOR THE TABLE SALAD AND DIPPING SAUCE

2	head Green and/or red leaf lettuce, separate leaves, wash and spin dry, then rip into 4 to 6-inch (10 to 15 cm) pieces
2	small Cucumber, Kirby variety preferred, cut into bite size julienne, about 1/8 inch (0.3 cm.) thick (pg. 81)
8	sprigs Asian basil
8	sprigs Perilla herb or mint (pg. 39)
1	recipe Lime dipping Sauce *Nước Chấm* (pg. 198)

1. Arrange all items decoratively on platter; cover and reserve at room temperature.

COOKING AND SERVING

1. Each person breaks one of the crepes into 6 to 8 pieces, places pieces crepe inside lettuce leaf. Tuck some leaves of each herb in there, and a few strips of cucumber. Wrap the lettuce leaf to encase fillings, dip in *nước chấm* sauce.

Crunchy Golden Coconut Crepes with Pork, Shrimp and Bean Sprouts

Bánh Xèo

On every trip to Asia I fall into a morning routine of visiting local markets, where I inevitably discover timeless regional specialties like the *bánh khoái*, known elsewhere in Vietnam as *bánh xèo*. They are hauntingly addictive taco-shaped sizzling crepes stuffed slivers of pork, sliced shrimp, and crisp bean sprouts (pg. 208). These crispy rice crepes look like omelets, since their batter is tinted with turmeric. In Hội-An, the *bánh khoái* are fried in pork fat and are made much smaller than the southern *bánh xèo*. They're eaten with the fingers by wrapping pieces in lettuce leaves with herbs, and then dipping them in *nước chấm* (pg. 198), the Vietnamese lime-laced fish dipping sauce.

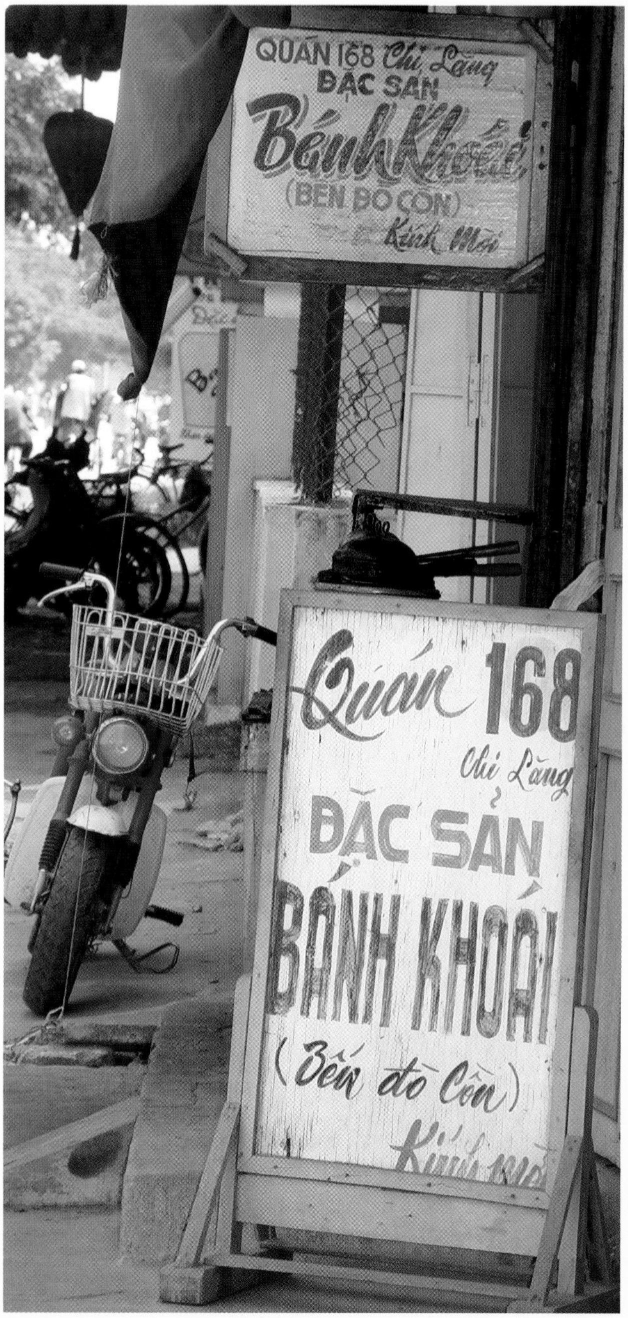
QUÁN 168 Chí Lăng
ĐẶC SẢN
Bánh Khoái
(BẾN ĐÒ CỒN)
Quán 168
Chí Lăng
ĐẶC SẢN
BÁNH KHOÁI
(Bến đò Cồn)

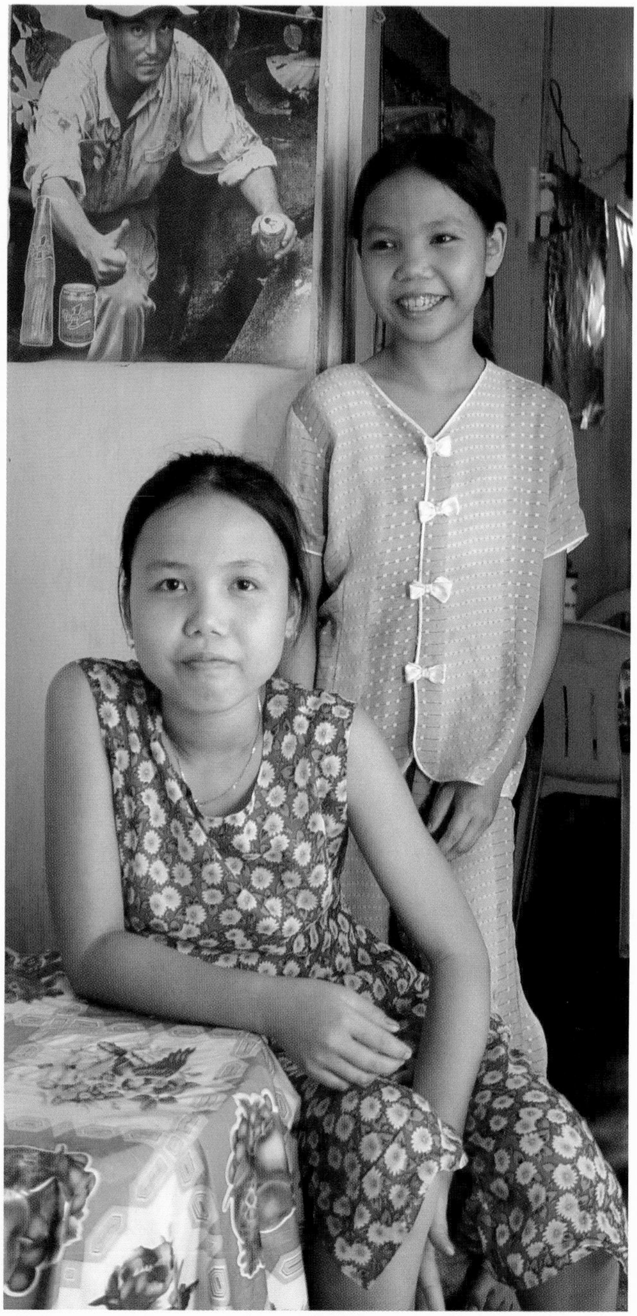

How and Why

1. Drizzling with the fat around edges gives that extra crunch. As the pancakes fry, they absorb some fat. It is necessary to add more fat as the crepe cooks, producing a better result than if you added all the fat at the beginning.

2. Covering pan briefly cooks the top of pancake and steams bean sprouts. The cover captures the steam.

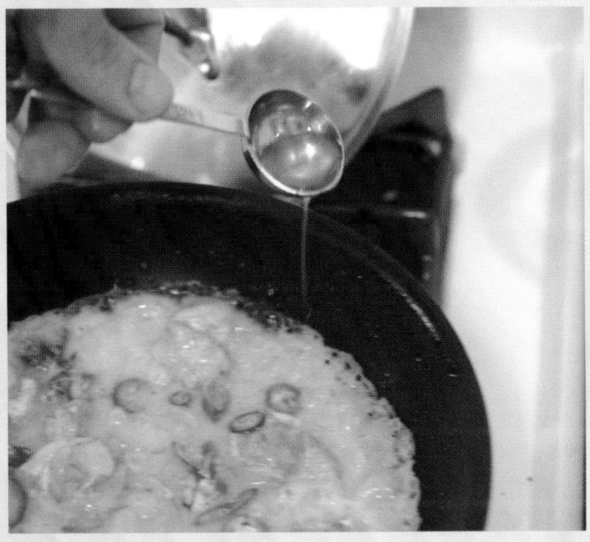

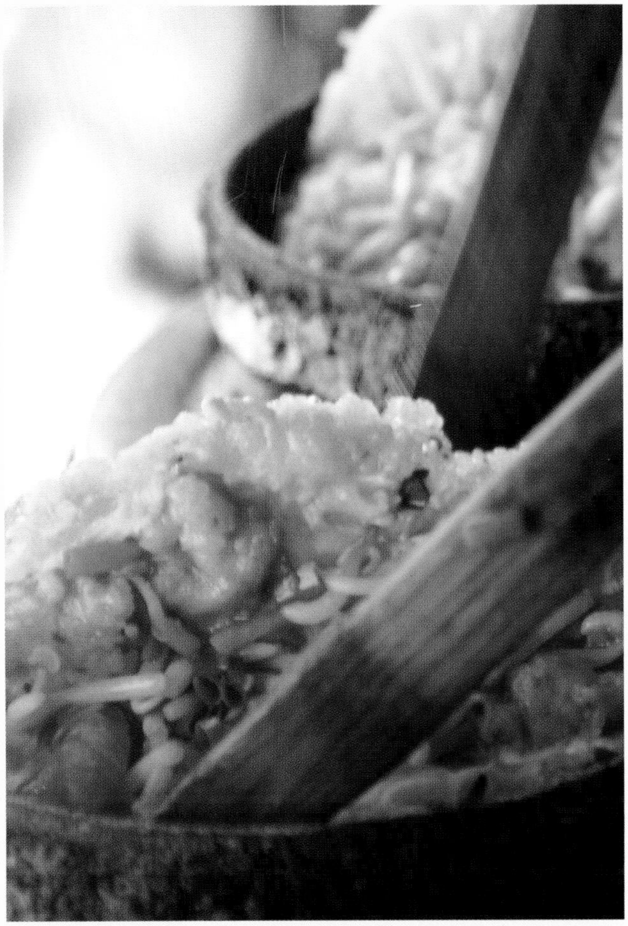

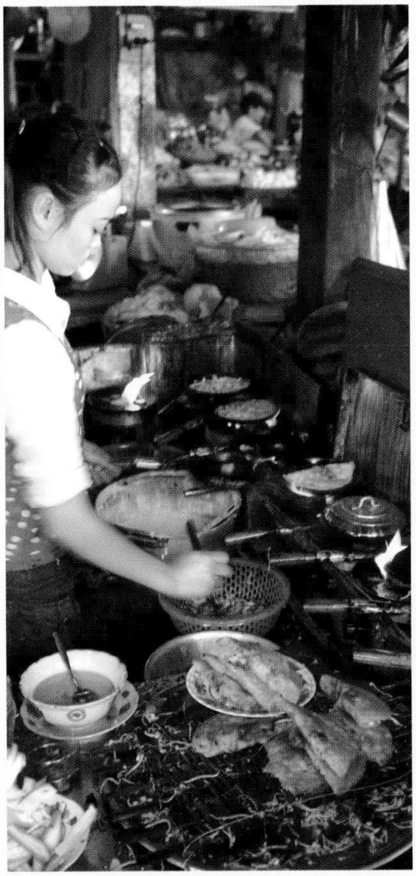

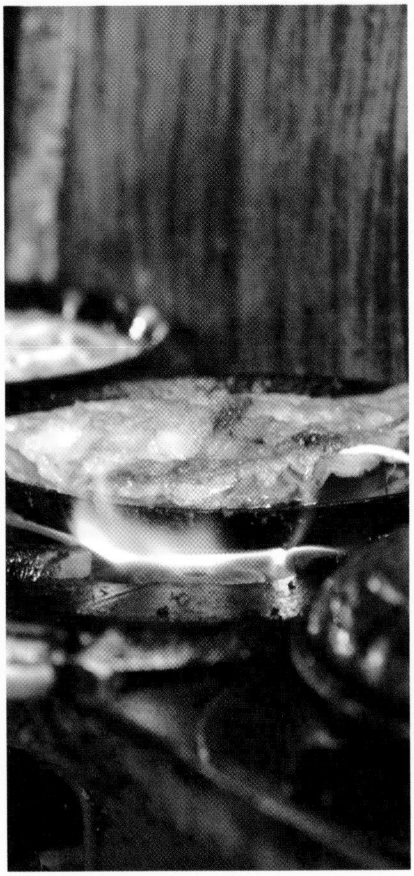

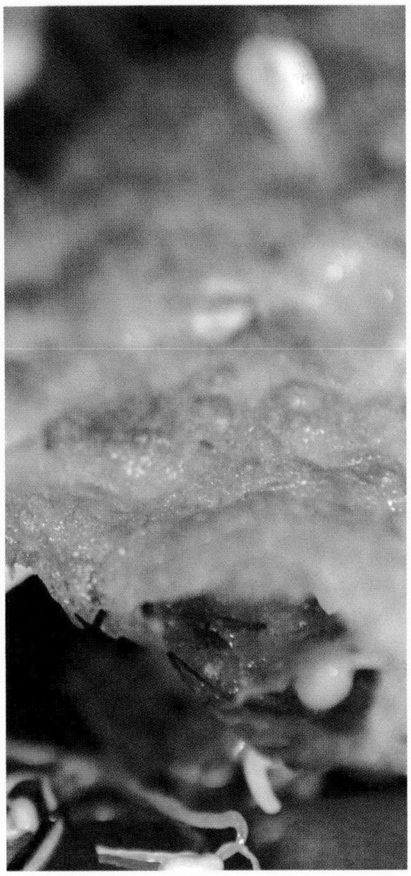

Rice Noodle Rolls with Pork, Shrimp and Wood Ear Mushrooms

Bánh Cuốn

These rolls use a special recipe for the noodle sheets (*bánh ướt*, as they are called in Vietnam). The tapioca flour added ensures the noodle sheet is very tender and elastic with a desirable stretch. The rolls hold together best when they're filled while the noodle is still warm. Though they're best eaten as soon as they're made, however they can be made ahead and steamed for a few minutes to bring them back to their original texture. A mixture of ground pork and ground shrimp makes the best filling.

Makes 10 rolls (3 bites each)

1¼ cup Rice flour
¼ cup Tapioca starch
¼ tsp. Kosher salt
2 cups Water
1 tsp. Vegetable oil
as needed Vegetable oil spray or extra oil for greasing
     the plate
2 pieces Dried wood ear mushrooms, about 2 inches
     (5 cm.) in diameter each
1 Tbsp. Vegetable oil
3 large Shallots, minced
½ lb. (227 g.) Coarsely ground pork and/or shrimp,
     ideally ¼-inch (0.6 cm.) grind
1 clove Garlic, minced
1 Tbsp. Fish sauce (*nước mắm*)
1 tsp. Granulated sugar
1 recipe Scallion Oil (pg. 200)
1 recipe Vietnamese Lime Dipping Sauce (*Nước Chấm*)
     (pg. 198)
¼ cup Mint leaves
¼ cup Cilantro leaves
¼ cup Fried shallots (pg. 119) or store bought

1. Prepare Rice Noodle Batter: In a large bowl whisk together the rice flour, tapioca starch, and salt. Add water and oil whisk until you have a perfectly smooth batter (it will be very thin, like milk). If there are any lumps strain through a fine wire mesh sieve. Set batter aside for at least 30 minutes.

2. Prepare filling: Soak mushrooms in warm water for 30 minutes. Drain, squeeze out excess moisture, trim any hard nodules; mince mushrooms. Marinate ground pork and shrimp with garlic, fish sauce and sugar. Heat small skillet over medium heat with vegetable oil. Add shallots and cook until translucent, add mushrooms, and pork; stir-fry until cooked through, making sure to break up pork if it sticks together into clumps.

3. Set up Work Area: Next to a burner on the stove, set up baking sheet coated liberally with oil, a small bowl with scallion oil, two medium plates (flat area 6 inches or 15 cm. in diameter) brushed with scallion oil, a heatproof brush or spray oil, a heat-proof rubber spatula, a small ladle or tablespoon, and a roll of plastic wrap.

4. Set up a steamer large enough to hold an 8-inch (20 cm.) diameter plate over the highest heat possible (pg. 101). You need to be able to steam a single layer on a plate. A makeshift steamer will also work fine. Place plate on steamer tray as level as possible, brush or spray with oil.

5. Make Noodles Sheets: Pre-heat plate in covered steamer for 3 minutes. Whisk batter to re-distribute settled flour. Spoon 3 to 4 tablespoons of batter of batter onto plate, use back of spoon to spread out into a very thin even layer, about 1/16–1/8 inch (0.1 cm. to 0.3 cm.) thick, adjusting plate level as needed. Cover steamer and cook 8 minutes or until you can press with tip of finger to feel bounce back. It will have an opaque appearance throughout. Carefully remove hot plate. Cool to room temperature.

6. Fill the Rolls as You Make Sheets: Place second plate in steamer to pre-heat and immediately fill the previously cooked sheet with 1 heaping tablespoon of filling. Place the filling in the center of bottom third of the sheet. Roll up like a spring roll or burrito, folding bottom over filling, and folding the sides in to center before rolling into a cylindrical shape. Transfer to scallion-oil brushed plate, repeat this process with remaining batter and filling, leaving ½ inch or 1.3 cm. between each roll, brushing each roll with scallion oil, and keeping them covered with plastic wrap.

7. Re-heat, Garnish and Serve: If you were able to resist eating all of them as you went, now is the time to re-heat them in the steam to bring back that soft, just-made texture. Only 3 to 5 minutes is needed in steamer. Sprinkle them with fried shallots before serving them with *Nước Chấm* sauce.

How and Why

1. Resting the batter for at least 30 minutes yields the most consistent results and resilient texture. Time resting allows the starch to hydrate evenly.

2. Keep the steamer filled with lots of water for a lot of steam. These require a wet environment of rapidly boiling water below.

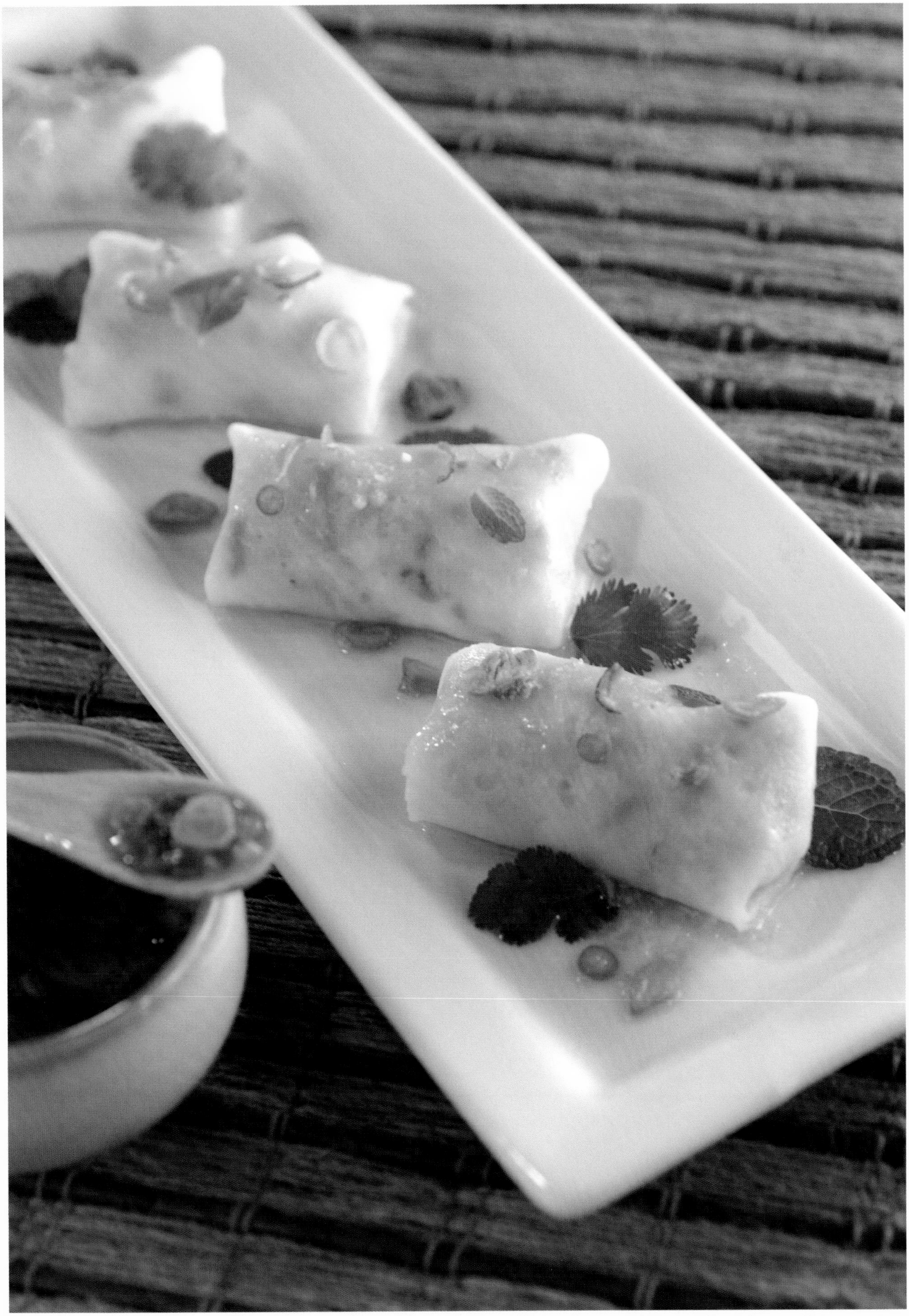

Tiny Steamed Rice Cakes with Shrimp and Crispy Pork Cracklings

Bánh Bèo

Each country in Southeast Asia has some delicious version of small rice pancakes. These bite-size cakes represent a blank canvas to create a myriad of snacks upon. A slight variation, such as small grilled shrimp with chili sauce, or minced pickled veggies make excellent choices. Be creative and make up your own version.

These Vietnamese steamed rice flour discs have little flavor of their own. The dish's flavor comes from fried shrimp and crisp pork cracklings, which are sprinkled on top. Piquant lime-chili sauce provides lively contrast. These are *mống*, the savory version. The sweet type is known as *Bánh bèo ngọt*. The steamed cakes can be prepared ahead and kept at room temperature for a few hours, before adding the shrimp topping.

You'll need 24 dipping-size cups to steam these individual cakes. You may already have some small dipping sauce dishes that will work. If not, go to a restaurant supply store or Asian market to pick up two dozen inexpensive tiny bowls.

Makes about 24 pieces

CAKES
1   cup Rice flour
1   Tbsp. Tapioca starch
1/8 tsp. Kosher salt

1¼ cups Water
2   tsp. Vegetable oil or rendered pork fat
12 to 24 Small dishes, about 1½ to 2 inches (3.8 cm. to
          5 cm.) wide and at least ½ inch (1.3 cm.) deep

SHRIMP TOPPING

2	tsp. Vegetable oil
2	tsp. Minced shallots
1/4	lb. (113 g.) Small shrimp, peeled, deveined, cut into 1/2-inch (1.3 cm.) pieces
1/2	tsp. Fish sauce (*nước mắm*)
1/4	tsp. Kosher salt
1/4	tsp. Granulated sugar
1/2	recipe Scallion oil (pg. 200)
1/2	recipe *Nước chấm* dipping sauce (pg. 198)
1	recipe Pork cracklings, broken into 1/4 to 1/2-inch (.6 cm. to 1.3 cm.) pieces (0.6 to 1 cm.) (pg. 121) or store-bought *chicarrones* (available at Latino takeout places)

1. Prepare the batter: In a large bowl, whisk together the rice flour, tapioca starch, and salt. Add water and oil; whisk until batter is perfectly smooth (it will be very thin, like milk). If there are any lumps, strain through a fine wire mesh sieve. Set batter aside to rest for at least 30 minutes.

2. Prepare shrimp topping: Heat a small skillet or wok over medium-low heat. Add oil and shallots; cook until translucent. Increase heat to medium-high; add shrimp, fish sauce, salt, and sugar. Mix well. Stir-fry until shrimp are cooked, excess moisture evaporates, and shrimp begin to brown. Shrimp will be well-done (some would call this "overcooked"). Transfer to bowl; allow to cool, uncovered. 15 minutes. Transfer to food processor; pulse until roughly chopped (or chop well by hand); set aside

3. Steam rice cakes: Set a steamer over boiling water at the highest heat possible. Place small cups into the steamer trays or baskets. Cover; steam to pre-heat for 2 minutes.. Whisk batter to re-distribute settled flour. With the cups as level as possible, carefully ladle 1 to 2 tablespoons of batter (depending on the width of the cups; you will need to fill them 1/4 to 1/2 inches or 0.6 to 1.3 cm. deep. Cover, and steam 8 to 10 minutes until they are firmly set (the center should bounce back when prodded). They should appear opaque. Carefully remove tray or basket from steamer; set aside to allow cakes to firm up at room temperature for a few minutes.

4. Loosen from cups: When cool enough to touch, loosen them around the edges with the tip of a small knife, so that they'll slide more easily from their dishes. Brush top of each cake with scallion oil. Keep covered until all cakes are cooked. If needed, clean cups and steam another batch in them.

5. Assemble the Cakes and Serve: Serve in cakes in their individual cups, or remove them from the cups and arrange them on serving platter. Place 1/2 teaspoon of shrimp mixture atop of each cake. Finish each with a piece of pork crackling. Serve with *Nước Chấm* sauce for dipping or drizzling (1/4 tsp. each).

How and Why

Shrimp are chopped or pounded, retaining a coarse texture.

Small dishes are used to steam each cake.

VIETNAM

215

Tiny Steamed Rice Cakes with Shrimp and Crispy Pork Cracklings

Bánh Bèo

Each time I visit the city of *Huế*, in central Vietnam, I make a pilgrimage is to *Quán Bánh Bà Đõ* Restaurant for their exceptional *bánh bèo*. If you visit Vietnam you must go taste them.

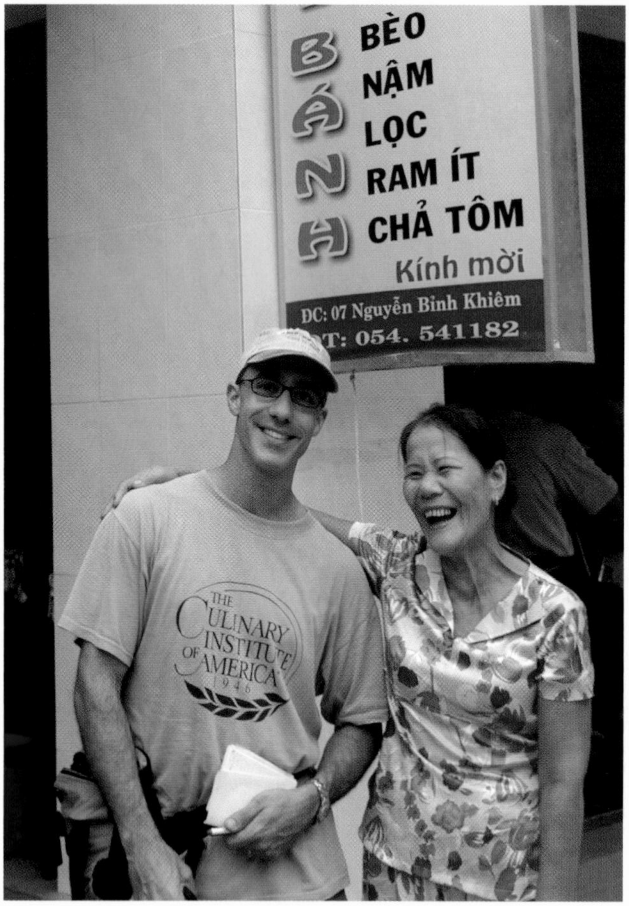
BÁNH
BÈO
NẬM
LỌC
RAM ÍT
CHẢ TÔM
Kính mời
ĐC: 07 Nguyễn Bỉnh Khiêm
T: 054. 541182
THE CULINARY INSTITUTE OF AMERICA
1946

The owner, Mrs. Đõ, and myself joke around in front of her legendary restaurant.

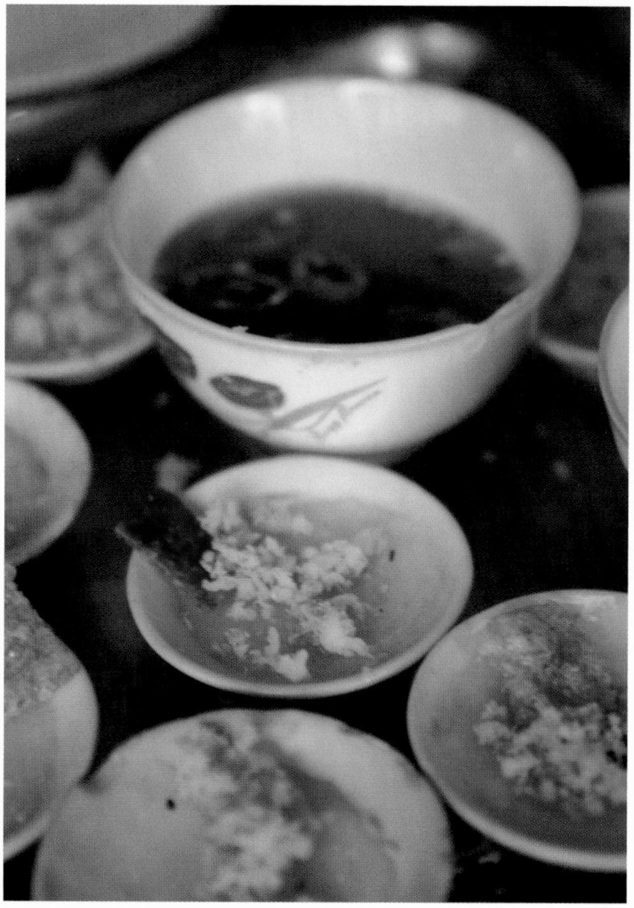

Crispy pork cracklings top the cakes juxtaposing the smooth texture of the cake.

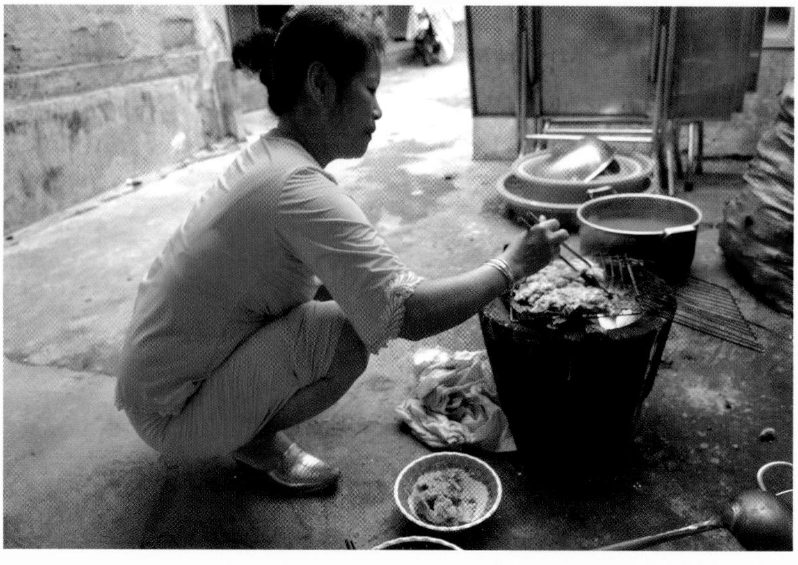

Marinated meats are grilled outside for the staff meal.

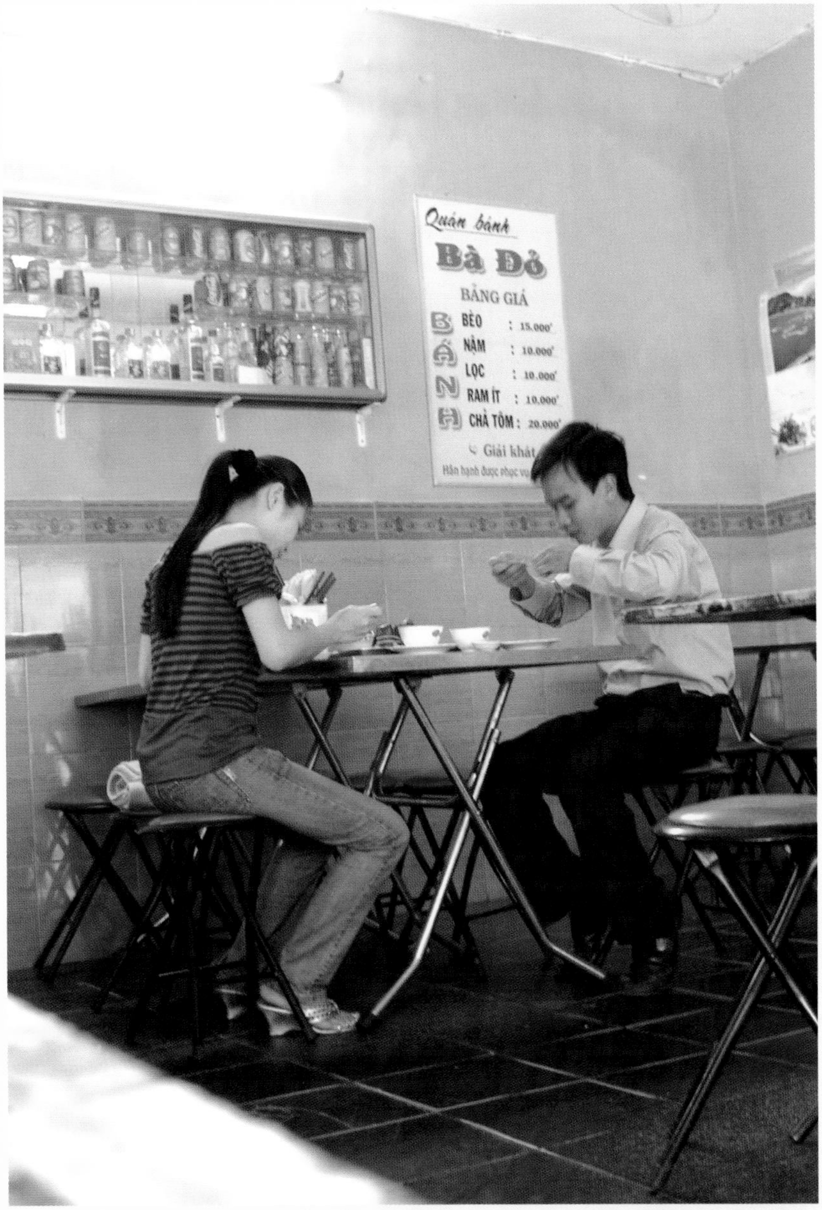
Quán bánh
Bà Đỏ
BẢNG GIÁ
BÁNH
BÈO : 15.000'
NẬM : 10.000'
LỌC : 10.000'
RAM ÍT : 10.000'
CHẢ TÔM : 20.000'
Giải khát

How and Why

1. Small shrimp impart a brighter orange color. In Vietnam, bright colored head-on shrimp are used. If you buy head-on shrimp, you can later use the heads to make Malaysian Prawn Noodles (pg. 304)!

2. Tapioca starch gives these cakes a resilient bite. Rice flour alone will work, but the tapioca (also known as cassava flour or yucca flour) creates a more pliable texture.

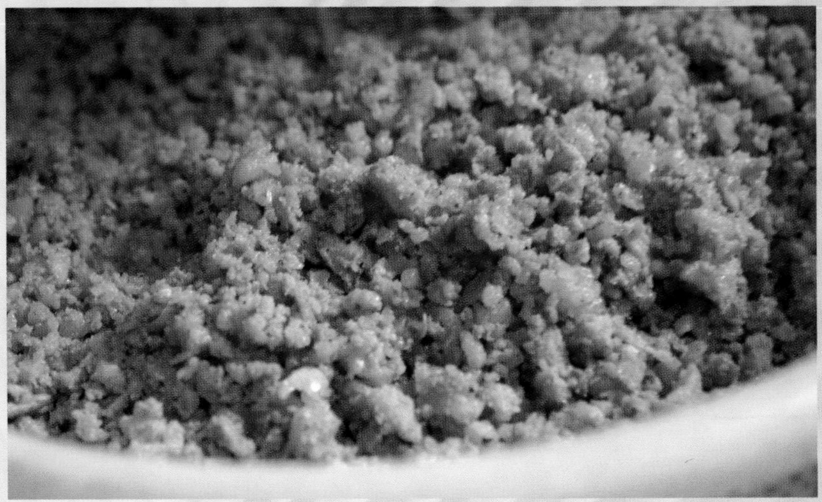

Aromatic Beef Broth with Rice Noodles, Shaved Onions, Lime Wedges and Fresh Herbs

Phở Bò

This one-dish meal is Vietnamese food culture in a bowl. *Phở*, pronounced as "fuh," not "foe" pairs delicate rice noodles with broth scented with star anise, cardamom, cloves, cassia, charred ginger and onions. The beef may be slow-simmered gelatinous beef tendon, poached beef brisket shavings, or raw beef sliced so thin that it cooks almost instantly in the hot broth.

In keeping with the Vietnamese tradition of finishing dishes at the table, each diner adds his own garnishes. In Vietnam it is usually simply sliced chilies, basil and some lime wedges. In the United States there seems to be (as with most everything) a necessity to add even more. Piles of Asian basil, bean sprouts, green chili rings, fresh lime wedges adorn the tables. Why doesn't the cook just add the vegetables to the soup? A couple reasons: First, it allows the guest to adjust the herbs, spices and seasonings that they want. Secondly, timing is everything. Vietnamese natives add bean sprouts and herbs to their *phở* regularly over the course of the meal. This ensures that the sprouts are always crisp, and that the herbs don't infuse the broth with too much of their flavor.

Phở is served with side sauces. In Vietnam a chili sauce (*tương ớt/đỏ*) (pg. 199) is at the ready to spice up the broth but in the US somehow two foreign sauces are always served. Hoisin sauce (from China) and Sriracha hot chili sauce (from Thailand). These can go directly to the broth with a squeeze of lime, or they can be used as dipping sauces for the dish's slices of meat, vegetables and noodles (my preference is not to add these to the broth, they can demolish the nuances of flavor in the long simmered broth).

Makes 4 to 6 bowls as a one-dish meal

BEEF BROTH: MAKES 3 QTS.

2	medium Yellow onions, skin-on, root trimmed, cut in half through the root end
4	inches Ginger
4	lb. (1.8 kg.) Beef marrow bones
2	lb. (.9 kg.) Beef Oxtails
4	piece Star anise
4	piece Cloves
1	piece Cassia (cinnamon), 3-inch (7.5 cm.) length

2	pods Black cardamom
1	lb Beef brisket or chuck, cut into pieces about 2 inches (5 cm.) wide, 2 inches (5 cm.) thick by 4 inches (10 cm.) long
1	Tbsp. Kosher salt
1/4	cup Fish sauce
	1-inch (2.5 cm.) piece Rock sugar, about a 1-oz. (28 gm) piece

1. Prepare Aromatics: Cut ginger and onions in half to create two flat sides. In a large skillet over high heat (cast iron works best), lightly char onions and ginger: place cut side down; cook until lightly blackened (onions about 5 to 8 minutes; ginger about 12 minutes). Heat a dry small sauté pan, over low heat; add star anise, cloves, cassia, and cardamom. Toast spices until fragrant and beginning to smoke; cool.
2. Prepare the Beef Broth: In a stockpot over high heat, cover marrow bones and oxtails with water; bring to a boil. Drain and discard liquid, rinse bones and wash pan to remove residual impurities. In a stockpot over high heat, combine bones with charred onions, charred ginger, star anise, cloves, cassia, beef, and enough water to cover by 1 inch; bring up a gentle boil. Lower heat; simmer 1 1/2 hours. Remove beef and check for doneness (this meat will be sliced and used in the soup). When meat is ready, plunge into iced water for 15 minutes. Wrap tightly to avoid a dry skin from forming; reserve in refrigerator.
3. Simmer broth for 1 1/2 to 2 hours more, adding water as needed to keep the bones barely covered. Skim fat and impurities from top as they collect. Taste for a rich flavorful stock.
4. Strain broth through very fine mesh strainer (or cheesecloth lined sieve). Add salt, fish sauce and sugar. Taste and adjust seasoning as needed. It should be salty then slightly sweet with aromatic background. The fish sauce should be understated, but subtly moving.

Beef Noodles Soup Accompaniments

INTERNAL GARNISHES

1/4 lb. (113 g.) Bottom round, top round, rib eye, or strip loin
1 lb. (454 g.) Dried flat rice noodles, 1/4 inch (0.6 cm.) width
1 small Yellow onion, sliced in half from top to bottom, then sliced paper thin into semi-circles, soaked in ice water for 30 minutes, drain very well
3 Scallions, chopped (For special touch, cut them where the white bottoms branch off into green tops. These highly prized parts of the scallion are called *hành trần*. Split them into 1 1/2-inch (3.8 cm.) pieces and cook them with the noodles)
2 Tbsp. Roughly chopped cilantro (leaves and stems)

1. Wrap raw beef in plastic; chill in freezer for 30 minutes or until semi-firm. Slice as thin as possible (1/16 of an inch 0.1 cm. is ideal). If meat begins to defrost while slicing, place back in freezer until firm. (Meat sliced this way is routinely available at Asian markets.)
2. Soak the rice noodles in warm (80° to 90°F or 27° to 32°C) water until softened, about 30 minutes; drain and set aside.
3. Slice the beef that was cooked in the broth into slivers, about 1/8 inch (0.3cm.) thick.

How and Why

1. Resting the batter for at least 30 minutes yields the most consistent results and resilient texture. Time resting allows the starch to hydrate evenly.

2. Keep the steamer filled with lots of water for a lot of steam. These require a wet environment of rapidly boiling water below.

TABLE SALAD AND SAUCES

8 sprigs Asian basil
8 to 12 leaves Sawleaf herb (*culanto*) (pg. 38)
1/4 cup Sliced hot chilies, green or red, about 1/8 inch (0.3 cm.) thick
3 cups Bean sprouts, trimmed, about 1/2 lb. (227 g.)
2 medium Lime, cut into Southeast Asian style wedges (pg. 108)
As needed Vietnamese chili sauce (*tương ớt tỏi*) (pg. 199) or store bought

1. Arrange all ingredients on plates or in bowls and place on table. Guest will add these by hand.

ASSEMBLE OF THE DISH

1. Have six Asian soup bowls and all garnishes ready. Bring broth up to a near boil. Taste and adjust spiciness as needed. Make sure broth is very hot, almost a full boil.
2. Bring a 1-gallon (4 L.) pot of water to a boil. Add softened noodles; cook for 15 seconds. Drain noodles, and distribute into bowls. Arrange the raw beef, cooked beef, onions, scallions, and cilantro atop the cooked noodles.
3. Ladle about 1 1/2 to 2 cups of broth into each bowl, making sure to pour some over the raw beef.
4. Serve with the table salad and chili sauce.

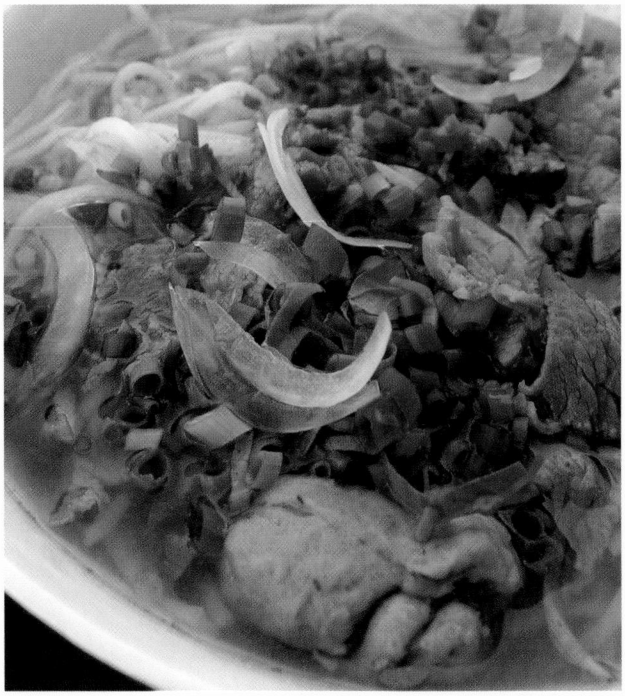

Aromatic Beef Broth with Rice Noodles, Shaved Onions, Lime Wedges and Fresh Herbs

Phở Bò

This steaming bowl of noodles fulfills my breakfast craving every time.

Herbs and shaved water spinach stems are added for texture and aroma as one head quickly towards the bottom of the bowl.

Pickled garlic slivers, sliced chilies, fresh limes and chili sauce allow you to customize the Phở's flavor to your liking.

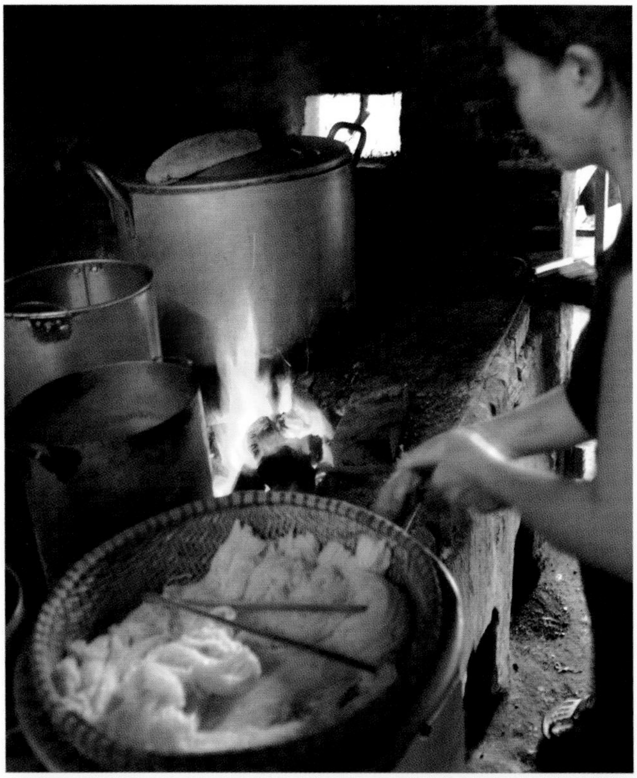

OPTIONAL COMPONENTS

Beef tendon may be the most misunderstood part of the animal. When cooked for hours, its tough rigid form softens into supple, gelatinous strands. I love it. Simmer tendons with the broth, and reserve them when you strain the broth. Slice them and add them along with the other soup garnishes.

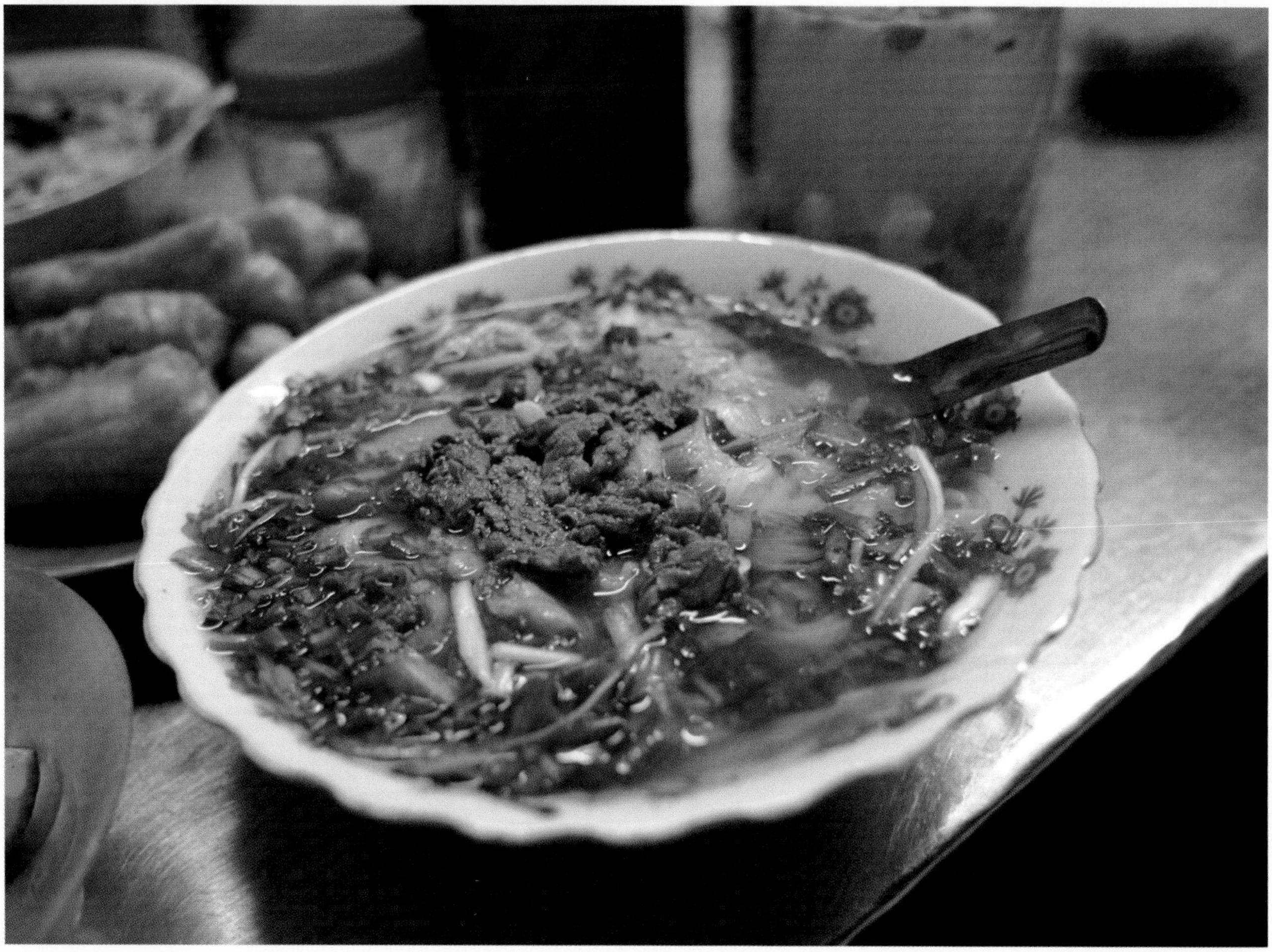

Aromatic Chicken Broth with Cellophane Noodles, Kaffir Lime Leaves and Fresh Herbs
Miến Gà

My latest culinary adventure was a mission to seek out *Phở Gà*, the lesser-known cousin of *Phở Bỏ* (beef noodle soup). There are many similarities, but chicken phở is lighter in color and taste, more delicately spiced. This close cousin to *Phở Gà* features aromatic kaffir lime leaves. The best I've ever tasted is served daily at *Quán Sơn Nga* in Saigon. Here they offer a variety of noodles. On my last trip, I choose transparent cellophane noodles made from mung bean starch. These delicate noodles were perfect for the chicken soup. I've translated it for the home kitchen.

Keeping with the Vietnamese tradition of adding the final touches at the table, this chicken noodle soup is served with shaved kaffir lime leaves, wedges of tart lime, a table salad of bean sprouts, basil leaves, and Perilla (Vietnamese mint), and spicy Vietnamese chili sauce for dipping (pg. 199).

Makes 4 to 6 servings a main dish

CHICKEN BROTH

1	medium Whole chicken (3 to 4 lbs or1.4 to 1.8 kg.), including gizzard and neck (but not liver and heart), rinsed
2	medium Yellow onions, skin-on, root trimmed, cut in half
4	inches (10 cm.) Ginger, lightly smashed

1	Tbsp. Coriander seeds
4	piece Star anise
1	piece Cassia (cinnamon), 3-inch (7.5 cm) length
2	tsp. Kosher salt
1/4	cup Fish sauce (*nước mắm*)

1-inch (2.5 cm.) piece Rock sugar, about 1 oz. (28 gm.)

1. Poach chicken: In a 2-gallon (8 L.) pot, combine chicken with just enough water to cover. Bring to a vigorous boil; lower to simmer. Skim off impurities; simmer 15 minutes. Remove from heat; cover and allow to rest at room temperature 45 minutes, until meat reaches 165°F or 74°C when checked with an instant-read thermometer. Remove chicken from poaching liquid, and plunge into ice water. Chill there 15 minutes to stop the cooking and firm up meat. Using your hands, pull off skin; discard. Pull meat from breast and thighs; tear into 1/4 to 1/2 inch (0.6 to 1.3 cm.) thick strips. Set meat aside. Reserve bones.

2. Prepare aromatics: Cut ginger and onions in half to create two flat sides. In a large skillet over high heat (cast iron works best), lightly char onions and ginger: place cut side down; cook until *lightly* blackened (onions about 5 to 8 minutes; ginger about 12 minutes). Heat a dry small sauté pan, over low heat; add coriander and toast until light brown, remove and reserve, then combine star anise, and cassia and toast spices until fragrant and beginning to smoke; cool.

3. Prepare broth: Recombine bones, chicken legs and poaching liquid; add charred ginger, onion, toasted spices, salt and place over high heat and bring up a soft boil, lower to simmer for 1 hour. Taste for a rich flavorful stock. At this point you are looking for chicken flavor. Seasoning will occur later. If broth is weak tasting continue to cook for additional 15 to 30 minutes. Strain broth through very fine mesh strainer (or cheesecloth lined sieve). Add fish sauce and sugar. Taste and adjust seasoning as needed. It should be salty then slightly sweet with aromatic background. It should be difficult to discern there is fish sauce.

Noodle Soup Accompaniments

GARNISHES

4   pkg. (about 2 oz. or 57 g. each) Cellophane noodles (*miến*) or 1 lb. or 454 g. rice noodles, fresh ribbon style, about 1/4 inch (0.6 cm.) wide (*Hủ tiểu dai*) store bought or homemade (pg. 117) or substitute dried rice noodles, cooked

1   small Yellow onion, sliced in half through the root, then sliced paper thin into semi-circles, soaked in ice water for 30 minutes, drain very well

2   Scallions, chopped, about 1/2-inch (1.3 cm.) pieces as prepared Pulled chicken meat from first step of recipe

1. In a bowl, submerge noodles in boiling water; soak 5 minutes. Rinse with cool water; drain well. Reserve. (If, desired snip them to shorten length and make eating them a bit easier.)

TABLE SALAD AND SAUCES

8   sprigs Perilla herb leaves (pg. 39) or mint leaves
8   sprigs Asian basil leaves
3   cups Bean sprouts, trimmed, about 1/2 lb. (227 g.)
2 to 3 medium Limes, cut into Southeast Asian style wedges (pg. 108)
6   Kaffir lime leaves, vein removed, sliced into very thin strips, 1/16 inch (.1 cm.) (0.2 cm.) thick
as needed Vietnamese chili sauce (*tương ớt*) (pg. 199)

1. Gently toss Perilla, basil and bean sprouts and pile on plate for center for the table.

2. Divide kaffir lime leaves among small bowls, one for each person, add one lime wedge per bowl.

ASSEMBLE THE DISH

1. Have six Asian soup bowls and all garnishes ready. Bring seasoned broth up to a near boil. Taste and adjust heat as needed. Make sure broth is very hot, almost a full boil.

2. Quickly cook noodles in 1 gallon (4 L.) of boiling water; drain and distribute into bowls.

3. Distribute pulled chicken meat, onions, and scallions atop the cooked noodles.

4. Ladle about 1 1/2–2 cups of broth into each bowl.

5. Serve with table salad, lime leaves and wedges, and chili sauce.

How and Why

Letting chicken cook slowly ensures moist meat. The slow cooking of the chicken prevents over coagulation of proteins that cause dry meat.

Aromatic Chicken Broth with Cellophane Noodles, Kaffir Lime Leaves and Fresh Herbs

Miến Gà

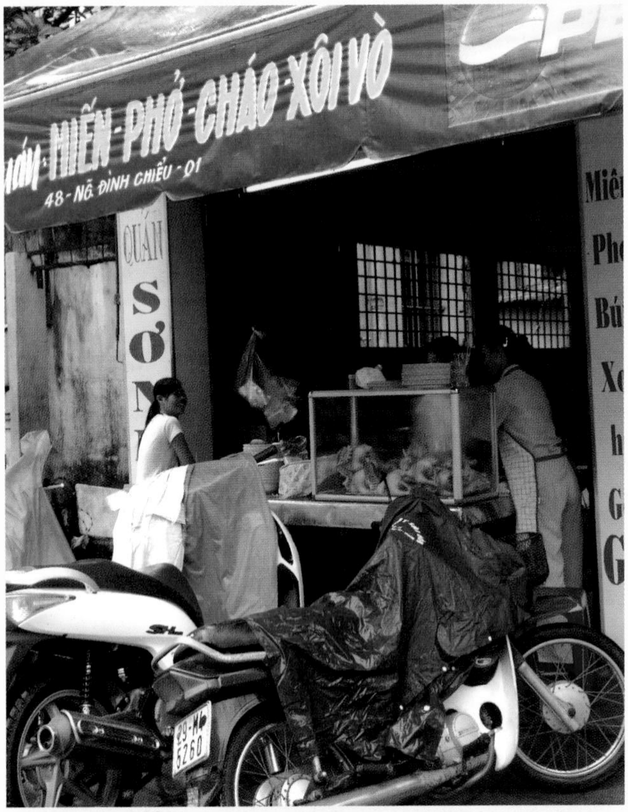
MIẾN-PHỞ-CHÁO-XÔI VÒ

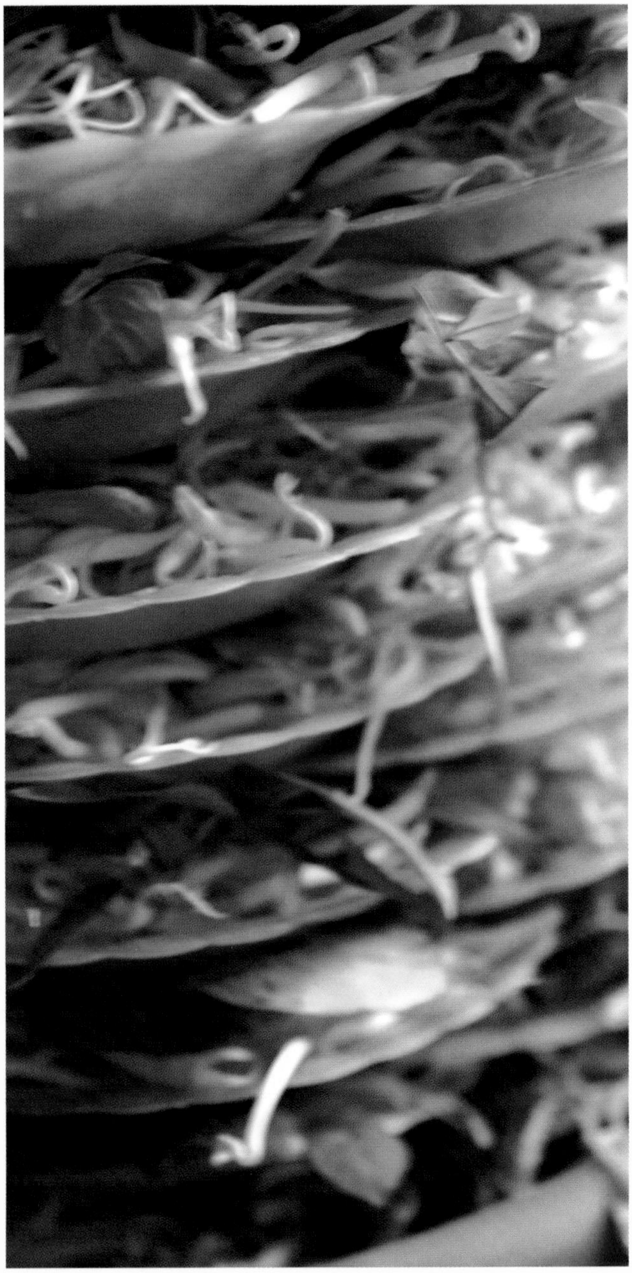

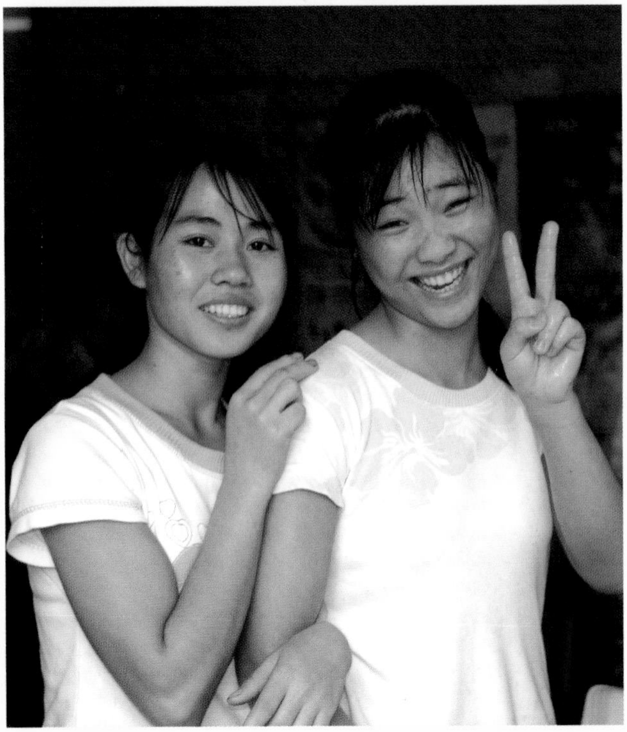

Upper left: *Make sure to seek out these noodles when you are in Saigon.*

Upper right: *Plates of table salads geared up for the lunch rush.*

Bottom left: *The staff are happy to serve you.*

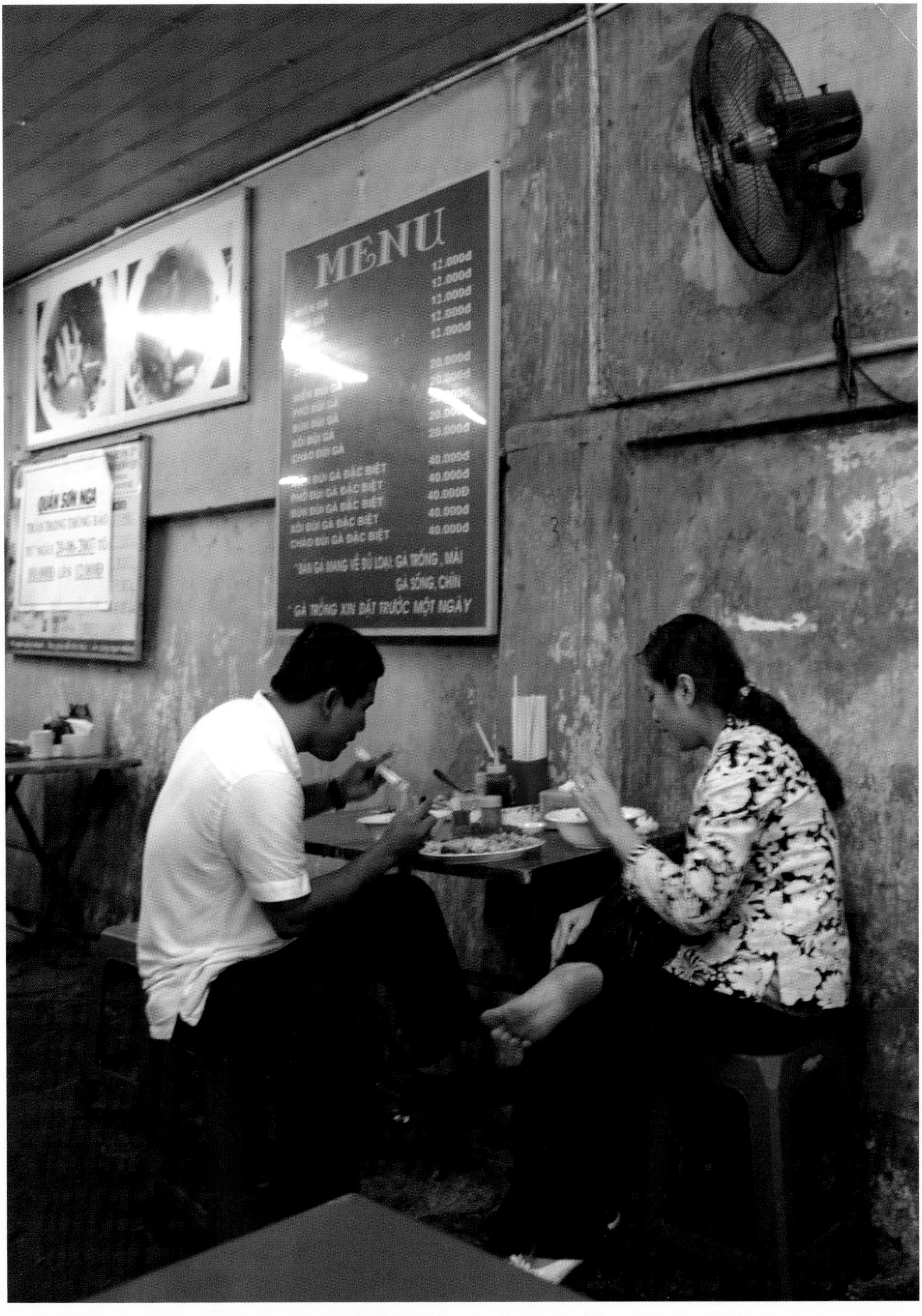
MENU
GÀ SỐNG, CHÍN
GÀ TRỐNG XIN ĐẶT TRƯỚC MỘT NGÀY

Take off your shoes and stay a while.

Imperial Spicy Pork and Beef Soup, with Shrimp Dumplings and Shaved Banana Blossoms

Bún Bò Huế

Aftcr tasting this soup from *Huế*, central Vietnam, you will begin to wonder why beef, pork and shrimp are not combined more often. Pork and beef bones, lemongrass, and chilies make a spicy broth. The addition of Vietnamese shrimp paste (*mắm ruốc* or *mắm tôm*) adds a depth of flavor that only fermented seafood can bring. Meaty pork bones work well in this broth, but fresh pigs feet create the best body. For the same reason, try to use beef shinbones. Marrow bones will make broth lacking in body, but they will definitely make up for it with a rich flavor. The soup's color has more bark than bite, since annatto seeds, not the chilies, are responsible for the red look of the broth.

To accompany this dish, the Vietnamese table salad includes shaved cabbage or lettuce, banana blossoms, crisp bean sprouts, piles of mint, and limes to brighten its flavor. Add small amounts of these to your soup as you continue your journey to the bottom of the bowl.

When you are in the mood for a *dặc biệt* (extra special) bowl of noodles, take the time to also prepare shrimp dumplings. These hearty seafood dumplings really add an authentic element not often found outside of Vietnam. Seafood dumplings are available at Asian markets, for those looking to save time on this recipe.

Makes 4 to 6 bowls as a one-dish meal

BEEF, PORK AND SHRIMP BROTH

3 lb./(1.4 kg.) Pork bones, about 2 to 3-inch (5 to 7.5 cm.) pieces (split fresh pig's feet if possible]

2 lb. (.9 kg.) Beef bones, about 2 to 3-inch (5 cm. to 7.5 cm) pieces (shin, marrow or knuckle bones)

1¹/2 lb.(700 g.) Pork hock, sliced, about ¹/2 inch (1.3 cm.) thick (butcher will do this for you)

1 Tbsp. Annatto seeds (pg. 40)

1 lb. (454 g.) Beef brisket or chuck, cut into pieces about 2 inches wide, 2 inches thick by 4 inches long (5 cm. wide, 5 cm. thick by 10 cm. long)

2 medium Yellow onions, cut in quarters

6 cloves Garlic, smashed

5 stalks Lemongrass, trim tip and root, cut the rest of stalk into 4-inch (10 cm.) lengths and bruise slightly

1 tsp. Black peppercorns, crushed

1 tsp. Kosher salt

1–2 Tbsp. Vietnamese style shrimp paste (pg. 52) (start with one and see if you can handle two, it is pungent really bolsters the overall flavor)

2 Tbsp. Fish sauce (*nước mắm*)

1-inch (2.5 cm.) piece Rock sugar, about 1oz. (28 gm.)

1. Blanch the Bones: In a large stockpot or Dutch oven, cover beef bones, pork bones and pork hock with water; bring to a boil over high heat. Drain; discard liquid, rinse bones, and wash out the pot to remove residual impurities.
2. Infuse oil with orange color: In the same stockpot, over medium-low heat, cook oil and annatto seeds, until they begin to sizzle (less than 1 minute). Remove from heat and set aside to rest for 10 minutes as the annatto color infuses into the oil. Strain or scoop out annatto seeds; discard them.
3. Add blanched bones, beef, onions, garlic, lemongrass and salt to the annatto oil. Add fresh water to cover by 1 inch (2.5 cm.). Over high heat, bring to a gentle boil, lower heat, and simmer for $1\frac{1}{2}$ hours. Remove beef and pork hock to separate containers; check them for doneness (this meat will be later sliced to garnish the soup). They should be tender. If not, continue to simmer until tender. When beef is ready, plunge into ice-water for 15 minutes. Wrap tightly in plastic wrap (to avoid dry skin forming), reserve in refrigerator for later use. Place pork in covered container to add to soup again later.
4. Simmer broth $1\frac{1}{2}$ to 2 hours more, adding water as needed to keep the bones barely covered. Skim fat and impurities from surface as they collect.
5. Strain broth through very fine mesh strainer (or cheesecloth-lined sieve). Add shrimp paste, salt, fish sauce and sugar. Taste and adjust seasoning as needed. It should be salty, then slightly sweet with an aromatic background.

Soup Accompaniments

NOODLE SOUP GARNISHES

$\frac{3}{4}$ lb. (340 g.) Dried large round rice noodles (not vermicelli—these are twice the thickness and sometimes available fresh. Substitute any other rice noodle.)
1 small Yellow onion, sliced in half through the root, then sliced into paper-thin semicircles, soaked in ice water 30 minutes, drained well
3 Scallions, white only, cut into $1\frac{1}{2}$-inch (3.8 cm.) pieces (For a special touch, make sure each bowl has a few pieces of the whitish bottoms that branch off into green tops, these are called *hành trần*)
$\frac{1}{4}$ cup Roughly chopped sawleaf herb (*culanto/ngò gai*) or cilantro (leaves and stems)
12 Shrimp and pork balls (optional, but recommended) (pg. 229)

1. Slice the reserved beef: Slice as thin as possible ($\frac{1}{16}$ inch (.1 cm.) is ideal). Place in container and cover with strained broth. (this will keep in moisture and infuse the beef with the broth's flavor)
2. Cook the noodles: Soak the rice noodles in room temperature water until softened, about 30 minutes; drain. Cook in rapidly boiling water until tender, rinse with cold water, drain and reserve.

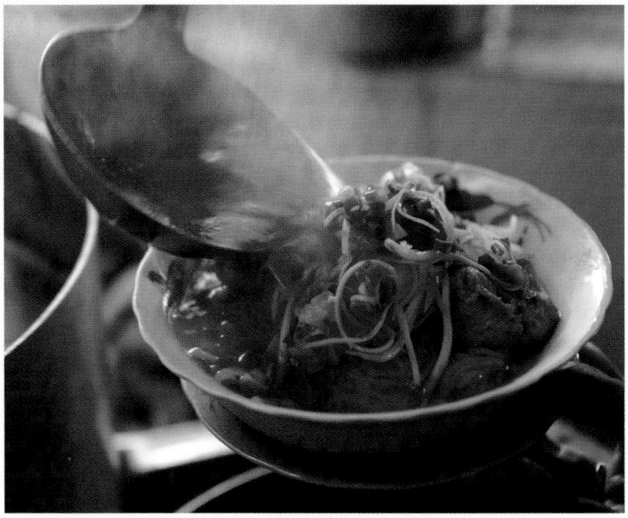

TABLE SALAD AND CONDIMENTS

1 cup Mint leaves
2 cups Bean sprouts, trimmed, about $\frac{1}{2}$ pound
1 cup Shaved green cabbage, about $\frac{1}{8}$ inch (0.3 cm.) thick or torn lettuce (romaine or escarole), bite size pieces
$\frac{1}{2}$ cup Shaved banana blossom, soaked in acidulated (lemony) water (pg. 108.)
2 to 3 medium Limes, cut into Southeast Asian style wedges (pg. 108)
$\frac{1}{2}$ cup Lemongrass-chili Oil (sidebar pg. 229) or Vietnamese chili sauce (*tương ớt/đỏ*) (pg. 199) or store bought chili sauce
if desired Vietnamese-style shrimp paste (*fine shrimp sauce*) (pg. 52)

1. Toss mint, bean sprouts, cabbage/lettuce, and banana blossoms until well mixed. Transfer to a serving platter, arranging limes around perimeter. Place on table along with shrimp sauce and chili sauce. Guests will add these as desired.

ASSEMBLY OF NOODLE BOWLS

1. Bring seasoned broth up to a near boil. Taste; adjust spiciness as needed. Add pork hocks, shrimp balls, and $1\frac{1}{2}$ inch (3.8 cm.) scallion pieces to cook them; bring back to a bare simmer.
2. Get noodle station set-up: Arrange 6 bowls, sliced cooked beef, sliced onions, and sawleaf herb on your work surface. Bring 1 gallon of water to a boil. Dip in cooked noodles to reheat;drain immediately, divide into bowls.
3. Distribute sliced beef, shaved onions, and sawleaf herb atop the noodles. Spoon a teaspoon of chili sauce on noodles. Add the pork hocks, cooked green onions, and shrimp balls from the broth. Ladle about $1\frac{1}{2}$ to 2 cups of broth into each bowl (it should be piping hot). Serve with table salad, shrimp sauce and extra chili sauce.

Imperial Spicy Pork and Beef Soup, with Shrimp Dumplings and Shaved Banana Blossoms

Bún Bò Huế

On one of my routine morning adventures, I stumbled upon this street vendor selling *Bún Bò Huế* for breakfast. It was 7 a.m. and I was really hungry.

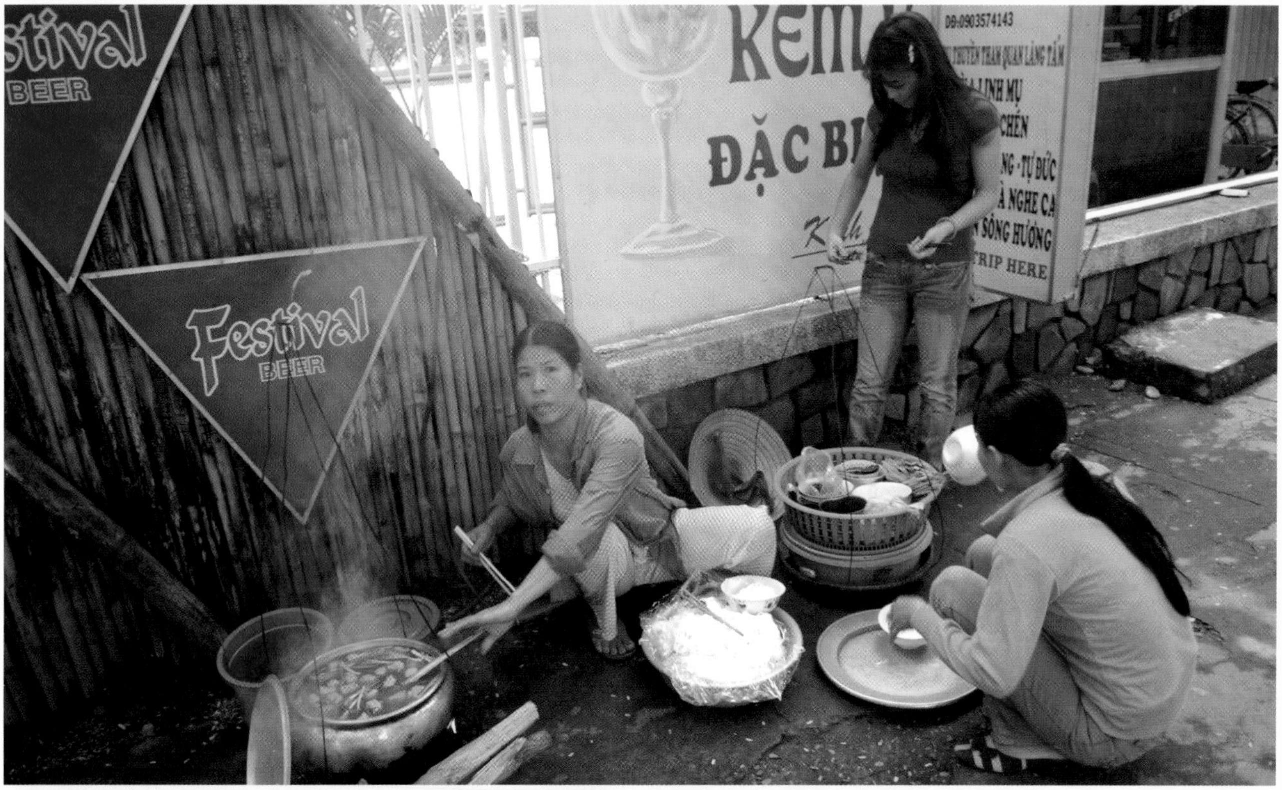
Festival
BEER

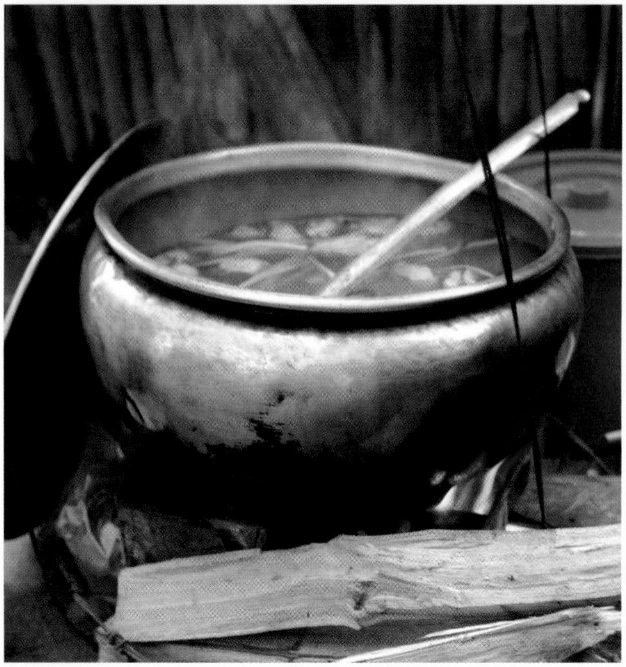

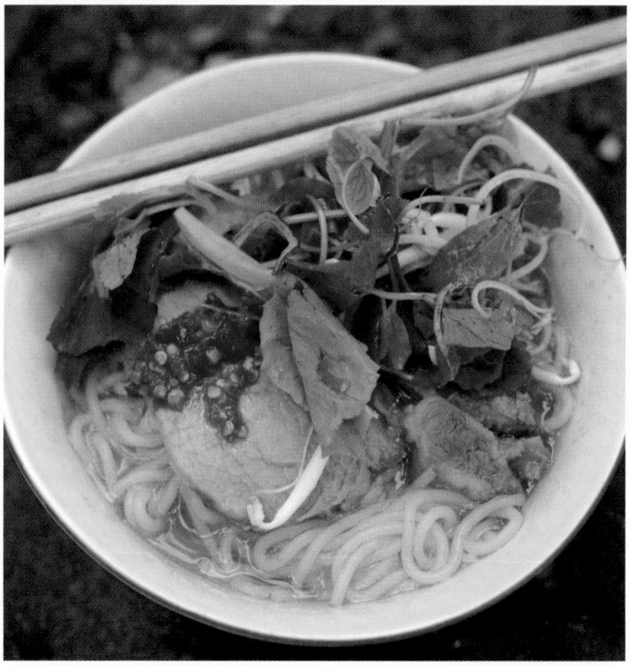

How and Why

1. Blanching the bones keeps the stock clear in color and flavor. This traditional step extracts much of the blood that coagulates in broth and onto bones. If left in, those impurities break off later and cloud the broth.

2. Simmer slowly to keep broth clear. If the soup boils rapidly the impurities boil back into broth and fat emulsifies (albeit temporarily) and clouds the broth.

LEMONGRASS-CHILI OIL

Combine 1/2 cup vegetable oil with 2 Tbsp. minced lemongrass (1 stalk, trimmed and minced) in small saucepan over medium heat. Heat until lemongrass aroma is released and it sizzles, about 30 seconds to one minute. Add 2 Tbsp. ground dried red chilies (hot) and cook for additional 15 seconds or until chilies also sizzle and get a shade darker. Remove from heat. Use this to top the noodles with oil before ladling in broth, and also serve some tableside for guest to add it as they want.

Đặc Biệt SHRIMP BALLS

1/2	lb. (227 g.) Small shrimp, peeled and deveined, roughly chopped
1/2	lb. (227 g.) Ground pork shoulder or other fatty part
2	cloves Garlic, minced
1	Tbsp. Minced shallots
1/2	tsp. Kosher salt
1	Tbsp. Fish sauce (*nước mắm*)
2	tsp. Granulated sugar
1	tsp. Coarsely ground black pepper
1	Tbsp. Finely ground roasted rice powder (pg. 244), rice flour, or cornstarch

1. Chill food processor working parts in freezer for 10 minutes. Do the same with the shrimp.

2. Combine ground shrimp, pork, garlic, shallots, salt, fish sauce, sugar, pepper and rice powder in chilled food processor. Puree shrimp mixture, stopping to scrape down bowl with rubber spatula a few times, until it is a semi-smooth paste Mixture should gather into a single mass as it whips around in the processor.

3. Sauté a 1 Tbsp. sample patty in a little oil until cooked through; taste and adjust seasoning as needed. Transfer mixture to container and refrigerate 30 minutes to allow mixture to set.

4. Drop tablespoon-size balls into the simmering broth to cook, about 3 minutes. Serve as a garnish for noodle bowl soups.

Rice Noodles in Curried Chicken Broth with Roasted Peanuts and Crispy Sesame Crackers
Mì Quảng

This authentic recipe calls for making the chicken broth from a whole chicken, and using some of the meat for the noodles. To streamline the process, you may choose to buy the chicken broth and meat separately and skip step one. The shaved banana blossom's astringent bite can be substituted by shaved green bananas or omitted completely without a detriment to the final flavor. Ground annatto seeds give the dish an attractive red hue without the heat of red chilies.

Another, lesser-known traditional element of the dish is a special noodle made specifically for this recipe. Ash or slaked lime is added to the rice flour batter for these noodles, turning them slightly yellow. This is why bright yellow colored noodles are often used in American Vietnamese restaurants (nice try, poor execution). I simply revel in the pure white noodles floating in the golden broth instead.

Makes 4 to 6 bowls as a one-dish meal

CHICKEN BROTH

2	lb. (.9 kg) Pork bones
1	Medium Whole chicken (3 to 4 lbs. or 1.4 to 1.8 kg.), or 1 lb. (454 g.) thigh meat and 3 lbs. (1.4 kg.) chicken bones
2-inch (5 cm.) piece Ginger, lightly smashed	

1	lg. Yellow onion, cut in quarters
4	cloves Garlic, smashed
10	Black peppercorns, crushed
1	tsp. Kosher salt
1-inch (2.5 cm.) piece Rock sugar, about 1oz. (28 gm.)	
2	Tbsp. Fish sauce (*nước mắm*)

230

1. Make Chicken Broth: In a soup pot over high heat, cover pork bones with water, and bring to a boil. Drain and discard liquid, rinse bones and wash pan to remove residual impurities. Remove thigh and legs from chicken, de-bone, and cut skinless thigh and leg meat into bite size strips, about 1/4 inch (0.6 cm.) thick (you'll need 1 lb. (454 g.) of total meat; use breast meat to make up the difference). Reserve these chicken strips in the refrigerator. Cut remaining chicken carcass, meat and all, into large pieces (3 to 4 inches each (7.6 to 10 cm.): the smaller the pieces the richer the broth). Place cut up chicken carcass and blanched pork bones in a 2-gallon (8 L.) pot; add just enough water to cover bones. Bring to a vigorous boil, lower to simmer, and skim off impurities that float to the surface. Add ginger, onion, garlic, peppercorns, salt, sugar, and fish sauce; simmer 1 1/2 hours to make a broth. Strain through fine wire mesh sieve.

Limes are an indispensable flavor booster for soups across Southeast Asia.

TO PREPARE THE CURRIED CHICKEN BROTH

2   tsp. Vietnamese curry powder (pg. 113) or store bought Vietnamese Curry Powder (pg. 362)
1/4   tsp. Annatto seeds, finely pounded or ground (pg. 40)
3   cloves Garlic, minced
1/4   tsp. Ground black pepper
1/2   tsp. Kosher salt
2   Tbsp. Vegetable oil or rendered pork fat

1. Marinate the Chicken: Toss reserved sliced chicken with curry powder, annatto, garlic, and salt. Marinate at least 30 minutes or overnight.
2. Make the Curried Broth: Heat oil in a wok or 4 quart (4 L.) saucepan over high heat. Add marinated chicken; stir-fry for 3 minutes, until chicken begins to lose raw appearance. Add 6 to 8 cups of chicken broth; bring to a gentle simmer for 5 minutes (to cook chicken and develop flavor of broth). Taste; adjust seasoning with salt.

Noodle Soup Accompaniments
CURRIED NOODLE SOUP GARNISHES

1   lb. (454 g.) Rice noodles, fresh ribbon style, about 1/4 inch (0.6 cm.) wide (bahn uot), store bought or homemade (pg. 117) (or substitute 1/2 lb. or 227 g. dried rice noodles, cooked)
2   Scallions, chopped
6   Tbsp. Peanuts, roasted in dry pan (pg. 109)
6   Tbsp. Fried shallots (pg. 119) or store-bought

1. Soak noodles in lukewarm water 10 minutes; drain. Separate into individual strands.
2. Heat a large saucepan of water for reheating the noodles.

TABLE SALAD

1/4   cup Mint leaves
2   cups Hand-torn lettuce leaves (green leaf or butter lettuce hearts are best), bite size pieces
1/2   cup Shaved banana blossom, soaked in acidulated (lemony) water (pg. 108)
2 to 3 medium Limes, cut into Southeast Asian style wedges (pg. 108)
4 to 6 small Long green chilies or other hot green chili
4 to 6 Vietnamese sesame rice and tapioca cracker (*bánh da* or *bánh tráng mè*), pre-toasted or toast over an open flame until puffed and slightly charred

1. Gently toss mint, lettuce and banana blossoms; arrange on serving platter.
2. Arrange lime wedges and chilies on a small plate.
3. Deep-fry or pan fry the rice/tapioca crackers until they puff (about 10 seconds); drain on paper towels, stack on a serving plate.

ASSEMBLY OF NOODLE BOWLS

1. Bring chicken and broth to a simmer.
2. Reheat noodles in boiling water, drain well, and divide among 4 to 6 bowls. Ladle simmering broth (with enough chicken for each serving) over the noodles.
3. Sprinkle with scallions, peanuts and shallots.
4. Serve with three side plates: chilies and limes; mixed mint and lettuce mixture; and a stack of fried crackers.

Rice Noodles in Curried Chicken Broth with Roasted Peanuts and Crispy Sesame Crackers

Mì Quảng

Upon arriving in *Hội-An*, a quaint town in central Vietnam, I asked locals where I could find the best maker of these mild curried noodles the city is famous for. I tried many, but none compared to the exceptional version made by *Nguyễn Thị Sinh*. I stayed at *Ms. Nguyễn's* kitchen for hours asking questions, taking notes, and snapping photos. See Web site for more photos of that special visit. This is her dish, wherein supple noodles float in a light curried broth, topped with roasted peanuts. At *Nguyễn Thị Sinh*, each table is treated to a few additional plates: one with greens and herbs to add as the noodles are eaten, another with limes for squeezing, green chilies for munching, and a pile of crunchy rice crackers to eat like croutons.

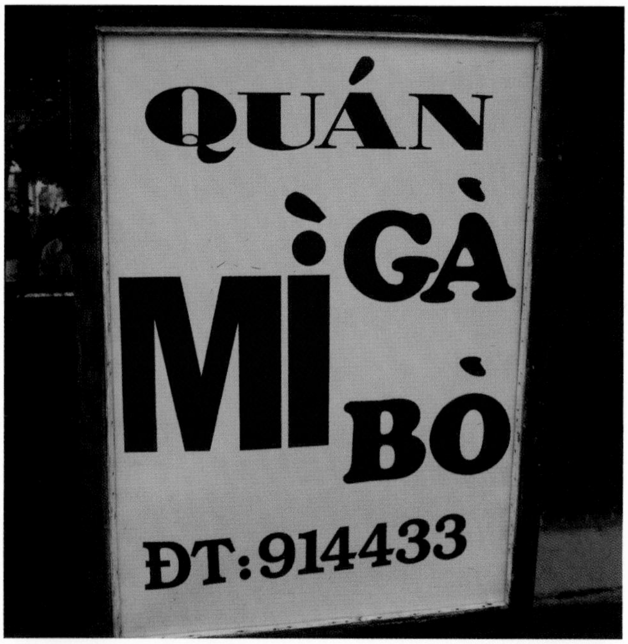
QUÁN
MÌ
GÀ
BÒ
ĐT:914433

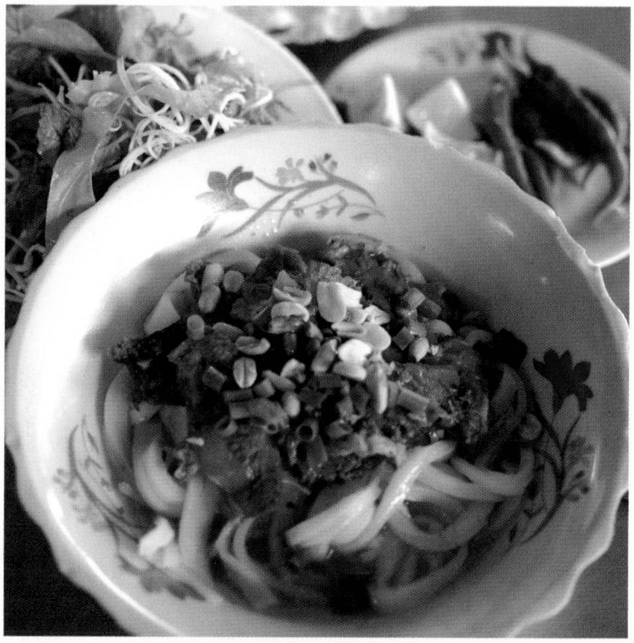

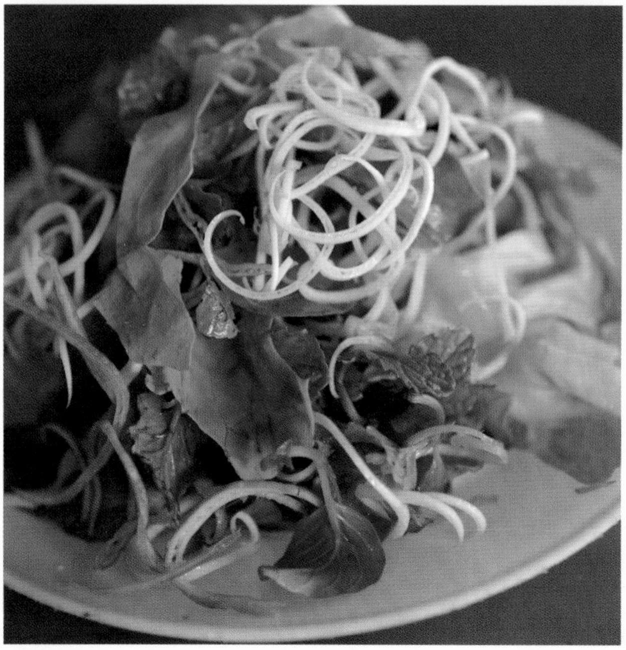

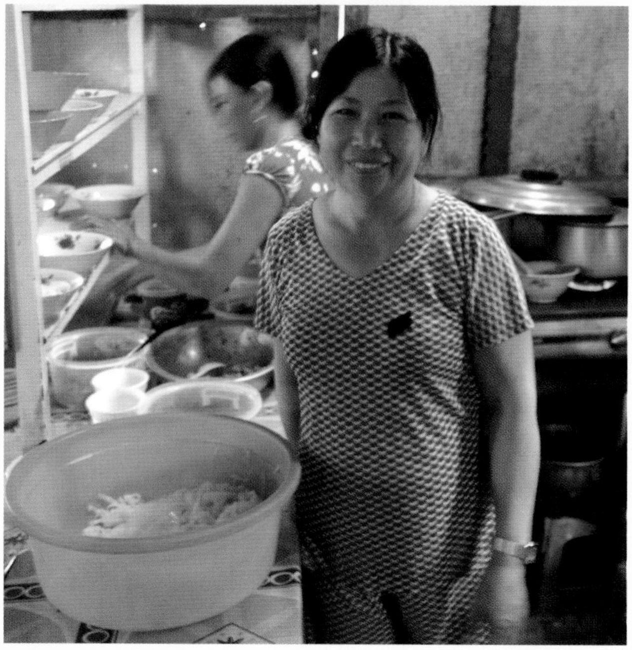

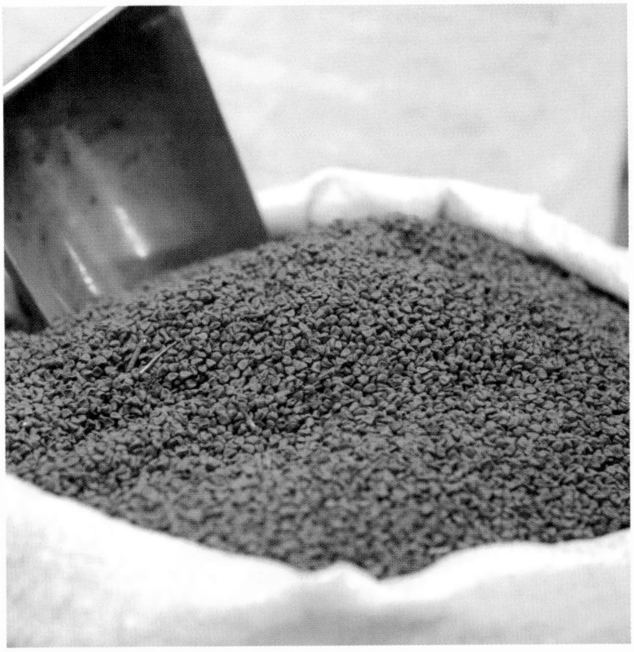

How and Why

1. Marinating the chicken gives the meat color and flavor. Take the time to infuse the meat with the curry powder flavor and color; this helps the salt to be absorbed.

2. The chicken is simmered with the broth for 5 minutes. This gives the broth time to acquire the color and flavor from the marinade.

At left: *Annotto seeds are gound up to add a burnt orange color.*

Below: *These inquisitive young staff members sat with us during lunch.*

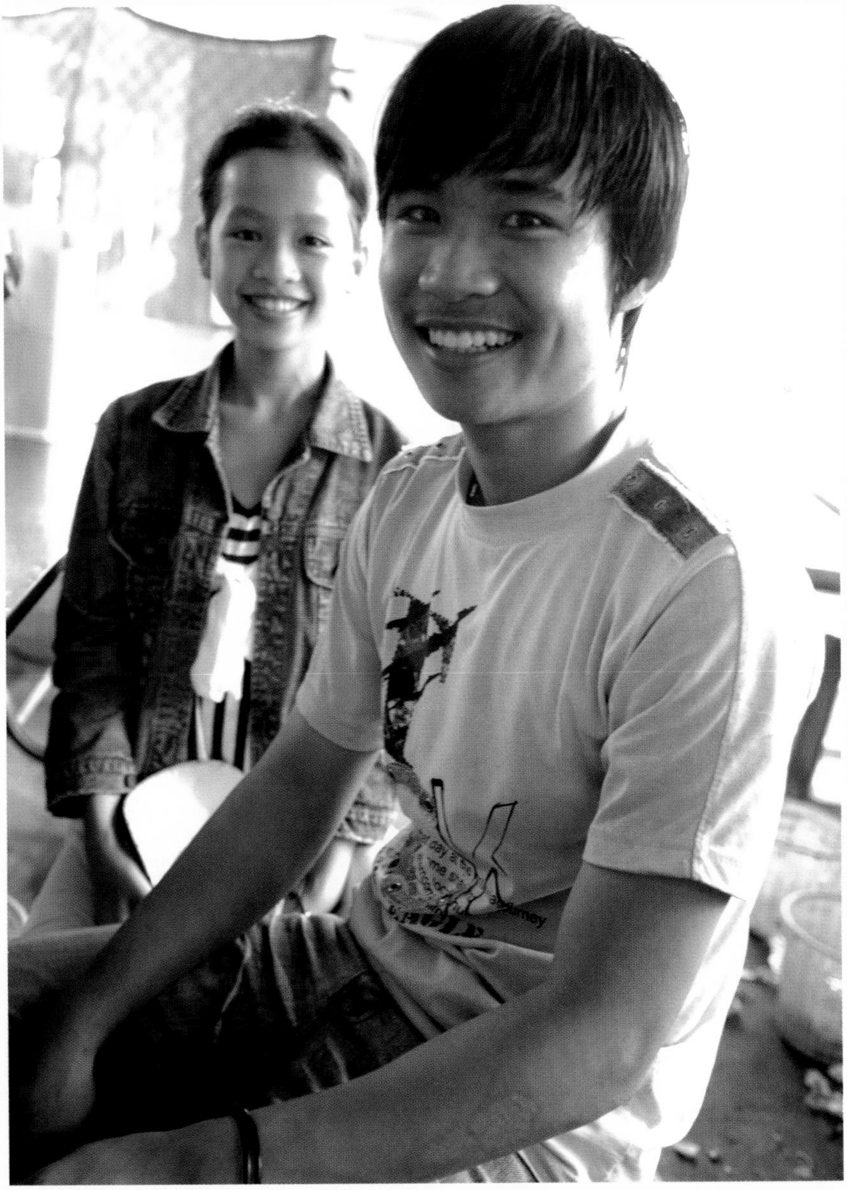

Lotus Rootlet and Cucumber Salad, Lime Dressing and Fried Shallots
Gỏi Ngó Sen

These tubular lotus roots are an excellent example of how keeping a well-stocked pantry allows you to quickly assemble Asian dishes "on the fly." All you need are fresh cucumbers, carrots, herbs and lime juice. The rest comes from the cabinets. If you find large, fresh lotus roots, they can be used in place of the canned ones I use here. Just peel them, slice them thinly, and then boil them for five minutes. The rest of the recipe remains the same.

If you want to make this into a vegetarian dish, replace the fish sauce with soy sauce. Conversely, adding cooked shrimp or chicken can elevate this to a main dish.

Makes 4 to 6 servings as part of a multi-dish meal

1   jar (16 oz. / 454 g.) Lotus rootlets (jarred) (pg. 79)
1   cup Cucumber strips, Kirby variety preferred,
         bite size strips about 1/4 inch (0.6 cm.) thick
1/4   cup Julienne carrots, Asian style (pg. 108),
         about 1/16 inch (.1 cm.) thick (0.2 cm)
1   medium Thai bird chilies, thinly sliced, about 1/8 inch
         (0.3 cm.) thick
2   cloves Garlic, minced
2   Tbsp. Fish sauce (*nước mắm*)
1/4   cup Lime juice
2   Tbsp. Granulated sugar
1/2   cup Vietnamese coriander leaves (*rau răm*) or
         mint leaves
1/4   cup Cilantro, roughly chopped
2   Tbsp. Fried shallots (pg. 119) or store bought

1. Empty jar of lotus rootlets (with liquid) into a large mixing bowl. Using wooden or bamboo chopsticks (chopsticks that have a coarse texture) stir the lotus rootlets to encourage their fine fibers to stick to the chopsticks, removing them from the rootlets. This will be awkward: Be persistent, and push them around for a few minutes.

2. Drain all of the liquid; cut the stems into 2 to 3 pieces each (about 1 1/2-inch lengths (3.8 cm). Into the bowl with the lotus rootlets, add the cucumbers, carrots, chilies, garlic, fish sauce, lime juice and sugar. Marinate 30 minutes at room temperature.

3. Taste the lotus rootlets; adjust seasoning as needed. Toss in the herbs. Transfer to serving bowl and garnish with the fried shallots.

Fresh lotus rootlets in a Vietnamese market. Jarred rootlets (page 179) are an excellent substitute.

How and Why

Go to... southeastasianflavors.com

1. Stir the lotus rootlets with chopsticks to avoid stringy pieces. As you stir lotus with wooden or bamboo chopsticks, some very fine fibers stick to rough surface of the sticks.

2. Make sure to marinate for the full 30 minutes. This step allows the seasonings to penetrate the lotus, cucumbers, and carrots.

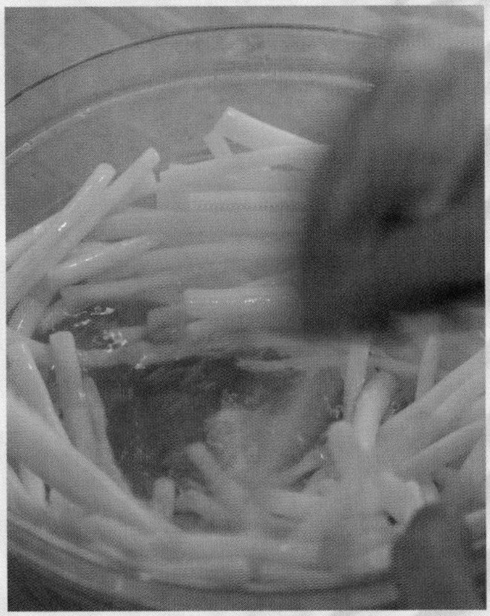

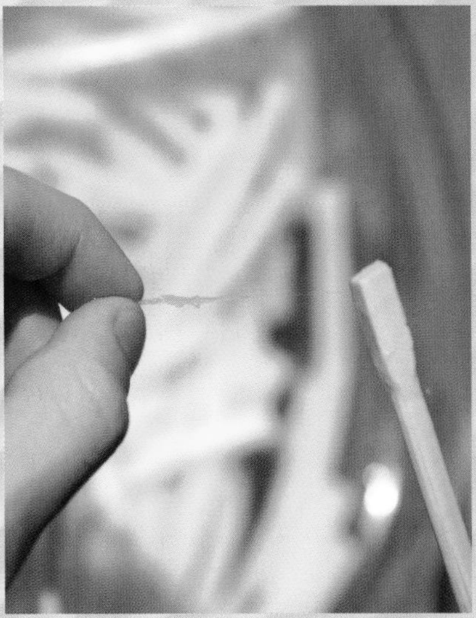

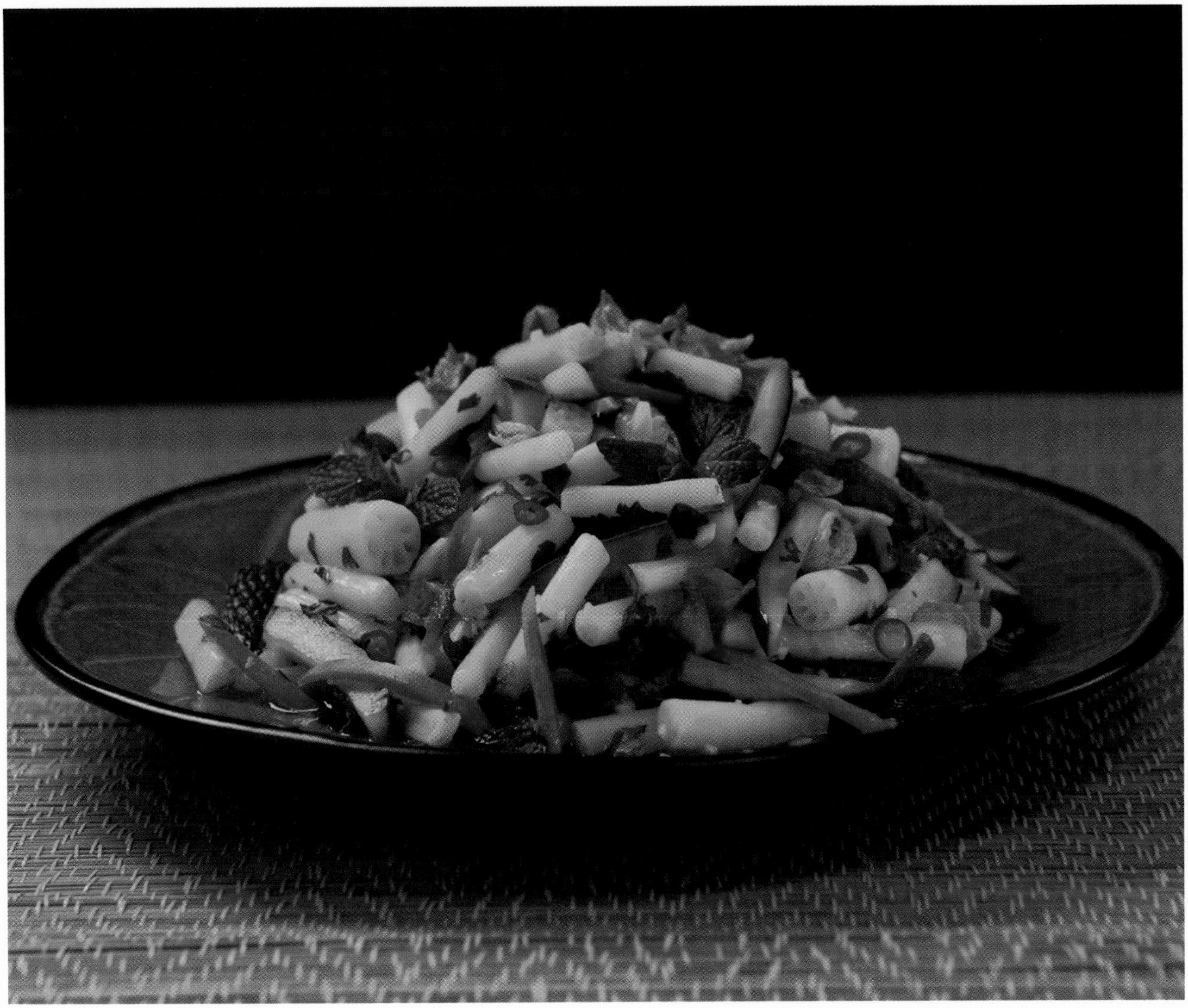

Green Mango Salad
Gỏi Xoài

Unripe mangos' pleasantly sour bite is balanced by a blend of sweet palm sugar in this salad, which is punctuated with the bright taste of mint and pan-roasted peanuts. In Vietnam this salad is paired with grilled beef (use same marinade from the pork for *bánh mì thịt*, page 202) or grilled shrimp. I love this refreshing treat all by itself.

Buy under-ripe mangos that are just beginning to turn color inside. They have the perfect balance of sweet and sour, and the aromatic qualities of the mango are beginning to develop. Since it's difficult to sample by cutting one open at the store, choose very firm green-skinned mangos that only give a little bit when pressed. Don't fret: whatever you bring home with will work. Either way green mangos crunch and flavor works best. If mangos are not at hand, use under-ripe papaya, chayote, or as some of my Vietnamese friends suggest, use green apples.

Like the pummelo salad on page 240, this dish can be served with shrimp chips to scoop up the pieces. If you do this, cut the mango into shorter (2-inch / 5 cm.) pieces so they fit on the crackers.

Makes 4 to 6 servings as part of a multi-dish meal

2	Tbsp. Lime juice
2	Tbsp. Fish sauce (*nước mắm*)
2	cloves Garlic, minced
2	Thai Bird Chilies, sliced into thin rings, about 1/16 inch (.1 cm.) thick
1	Tbsp. Dried shrimp, finely chopped or pounded
2	Tbsp. Light brown palm sugar (pg. 58)
4	lg. Unripe green mangos, peeled, seed removed and cut into julienne strips, about 1/8 inch (0.3 cm.) thick
1/2	cup Red onion, sliced 1/8 inch (0.3 cm.) thick, about 11/2- to 2-inch pieces (3.8 to 5 cm.) (rinsed in cool water if strongly flavored)
1/2	cup Asian basil leaves, sliced about 1/4 inch (0.6 cm.) thick
1/2	cup Mint leaves, sliced about 1/4 inch (0.6 cm.) thick
to taste	Kosher salt
1/4	cup Peanuts, roasted in dry pan (pg. 62)
2	Tbsp. Fried shallots (pg. 119) or store bought

1. In a large mixing bowl whisk together the lime juice, fish sauce, garlic, chilies, dried shrimp, and sugar until sugar dissolves. Add the mangos and onions and toss gently until it is coated well. Taste and adjust seasoning with sugar, fish sauce and salt.

2. Fold in basil and mint leaves; transfer to serving plate or bowl. Top with peanuts and fried shallots.

Unripe mangos are always green-skinned. However, beware since some varieties of mangos still have a green skin when ripe.

How and Why

Pounding the dried shrimp makes them more tender. The pestle opens up fibers as it strikes the shrimp, softening them and allowing their flavor to be better absorbed by the moist mango salad.

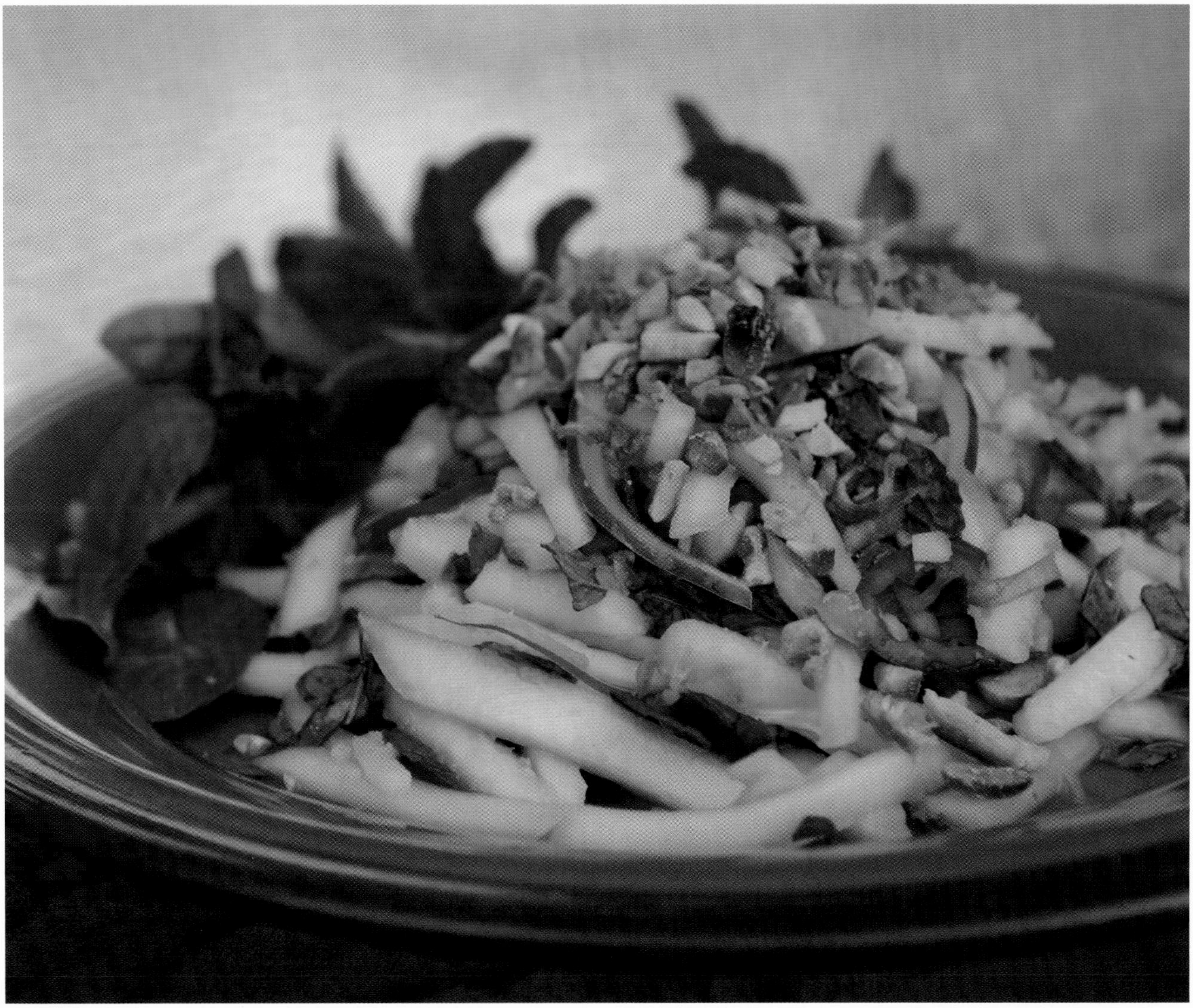

Poached Chicken and Cabbage Salad with Vietnamese Coriander

Gỏi Gà

*S*oft shreds of gently poached chicken intertwine with cool strips of cabbage, slivers of carrot, and loads of rau ram, an aromatic Vietnamese coriander. All bathe in the classic Vietnamese dressing of lime juice, fish sauce, chilies, garlic, and sugar. Topped with caramelized shallots, this fresh salad is a sure hit for a summer barbeque or dinner party.

If you want a quick tasty (albeit non-authentic) Vietnamese style salad, use a store-bought roasted chicken for this salad, and skip the poaching steps.

Makes 6 to 8 servings as part of a multi-dish meal

1	medium Whole chicken (3 to 4 lbs. or 1.4 to 1.8 kg.)
2	cups Green cabbage, cut into strips, about 2 inches (5 cm.) long and 1/2 inch (1.3 cm.) thick
1	tsp. Kosher salt
1	small Yellow onion, halved through the root end, sliced paper-thin into semi-circles, soaked in ice water 30 minutes, drained well
2	cloves Garlic, minced
1/4	cup Lime juice
2	Tbsp. Fish sauce (*nước mắm*)
2	Tbsp. Distilled white vinegar
1	tsp. Granulated sugar
1 1/2	tsp. Coarsely ground black pepper
1/2	cup Shredded or julienne carrot (pg. 108)
2	ea. Long red chilies or other hot red chilies, cut into julienne strips, about 1/8 inch (0.3 cm.)
3	cups Vietnamese coriander leaves (*rau răm*) (Substitute a mixture of mint and cilantro leaves)
1/4	cup Fried shallots (pg. 119) or store bought

1. Poach the chicken: In a 2-gallon (8 L.) pot, add enough water to cover chicken. Bring to a vigorous boil; lower to simmer. Skim off any impurities that rise to the surface; simmer 15 minutes. Remove from heat; cover pot and allow to rest at room temperature for 45 minutes, until chicken reaches an internal temperature of 165°F or 74°C. Carefully lift chicken from poaching liquid and plunge into ice water. Leave in water for 10 minutes (this stops the cooking and firms up the meat). Pull off skin and discard. Pull meat from the breast, thighs, and legs, tearing it into 1/4- to 1/2-inch (0.6–1.3 cm.) wide strips; set aside 1 lb. (454 g.) for salad. Transfer to covered container and reserve at room temperature. (Optional: recombine bones and poaching liquid, add a few aromatics such as onions, ginger, and lemongrass, and simmer one hour to make a stock for soup or other use).

2. Salt the Cabbage: Toss the cabbage and salt together, rest for fifteen minutes, squeeze out all excess moisture.

3. Make the Dressing: In large bowl, whisk together the garlic, lime juice, fish sauce, vinegar, sugar and black pepper.

4. Final Salad Preparations: Add sliced onions, carrots, cabbage, and chicken to the dressing; toss gently until well combined. Taste and adjust seasoning before adding the herbs. Fold in herbs. Transfer to platter, sprinkle with shallots.

My last trip to Huế in 2007 I met some amazing people, one such was Tường-Vi Nguyễn Thị. She also helped me query a street vendor about the details of an intoxicating spit-roasted pork (pg. 188). Vi is a passionate cook, and she revealed to me her most treasured recipe: this unforgettable chicken mélange. She took me on a guided tour through the local market, picked up all we needed for the dish, and took me to her family's home to teach me the dish in person. A delightful family and a delicious afternoon of flavors followed.

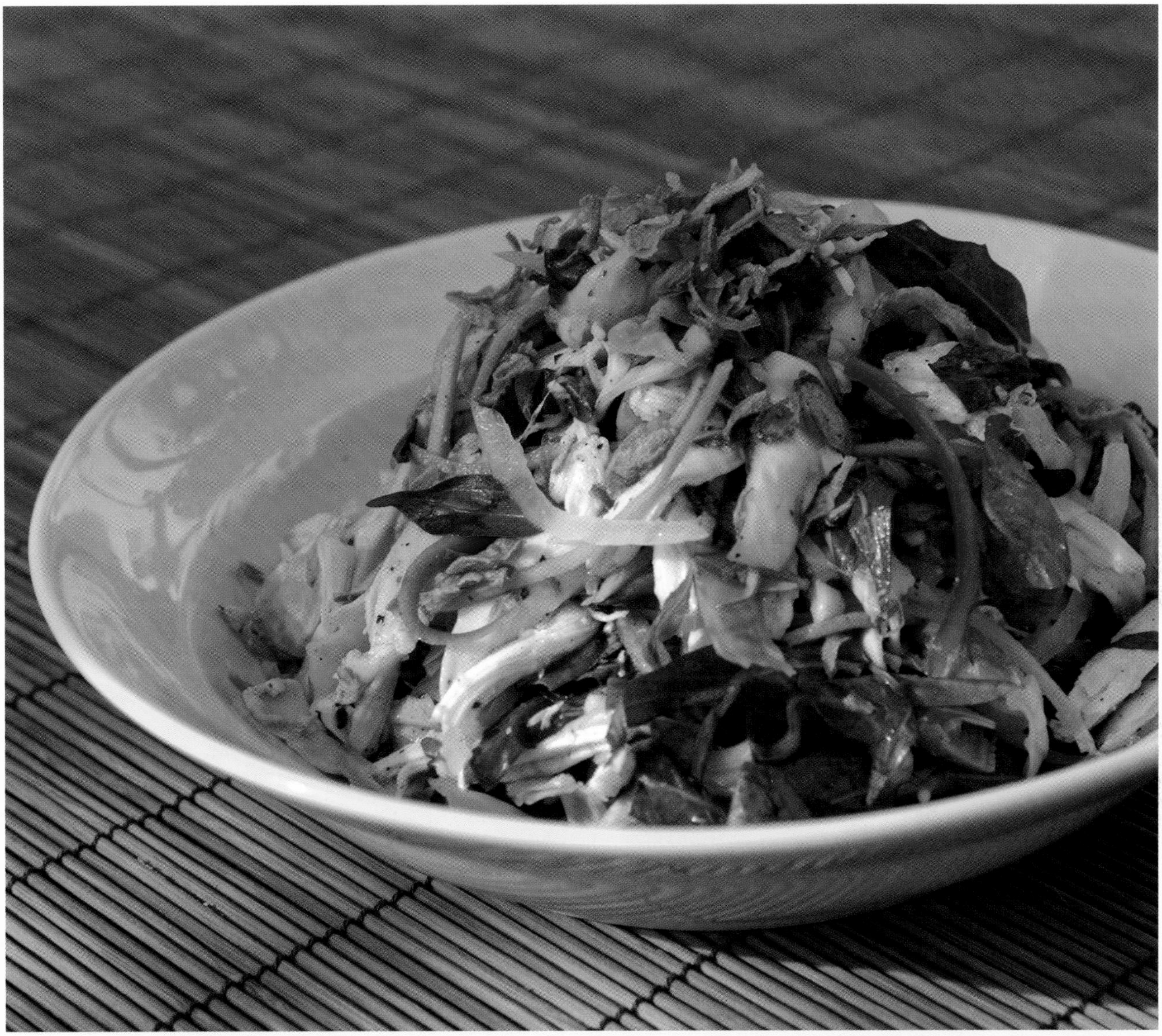

VIETNAM

How and Why

1. Letting chicken cook slowly ensures moist meat. The slow cooking of the chicken prevents over coagulation of proteins that causes dryness.

2. Salting the cabbage prevents a watery salad. Preliminary salting pulls out the excess moisture from the cabbage; this moisture is discarded before combining the cabbage with dressing.

3. Toss salad at the last moment for a supple texture. The acid and salt in the dressing will toughen the chicken and wilt the herbs as the salad sits, so toss them all right before eating. Yes, leftovers will be OK, just not as crisp.

Pummelo and Shrimp Salad
Gỏi Bưởi

Pummelo, a giant citrus fruit now available in the U.S., has an enticing sweet and sour flavor. The flesh, unlike an orange or grapefruit, is easily separated into individual juice-filled sacs. Piles of these fruits populate markets all over Vietnam, especially during at peak of their season from September through November. Dipped in the spicy chili salt (*muối tiêu*) (pg. 251), they are a typical Vietnamese snack.

To access the fruit inside these thick-skinned orbs, use a knife to cut through the fragrant peel down to the translucent yellow or pink flesh. For a detailed method how to peel and segment the cherished citrus see page 107. This salad is simple to make and refreshing to eat. Try pairing it with Chicken Stir-fry with Lemongrass, Chilies and Tamarind (pg.248) and steamed rice.

Makes 4 to 6 servings as part of multi-dish meal

1/4   lb. (113 g.) Lean pork, such as loin or leg, one piece, about 1 inch (2.5 cm.) thick and 3 inches (7.5 cm.) long

1/4   lb. (113 g.) Small shrimp, deveined with shell still on

2   Tbsp. Granulated sugar

1/4   tsp. Kosher salt

1   Tbsp. Fish sauce (*nước mắm*)

1   large Pummelo or 2 large grapefruits

1/2   cup Very fine julienne carrots, 1/16-inch (.1 cm.) thickness (pg. 108), about 2 inches long (5 cm.)

1/2   cup Mint leaves, sliced about 1/4 inch (0.6 cm.) thick

1/4   cup Cilantro, roughly chopped (leaves and stems)

2   Long red chilies, cut into thin rings or fine julienne 1/8 inch (0.3 cm.) thick

1/4   cup Peanuts, roasted in dry pan (pg. 109), roughly chopped

12 to 24 pieces Shrimp chips (*bánh phồng tôm*), deep-fried (optional)

1. Cook the pork and shrimp: In small saucepan, submerge pork in simmering water and gently cook until done through, 140°F. Plunge meat into ice water for 10 minutes. Drain and julienne, about 1/8 inch (0.3 cm.) thick. Cook the shrimp in simmering salted water until cooked, about 3 to 5 minutes. Cool in ice water for 5 minutes. Shell, de-vein, and halve lengthwise.

2. Make dressing: Combine sugar, salt and fish sauce in small pan. Simmer until sugar and salt dissolve; cool.

3. Prepare the Salad: Peel pummelo as shown (pg. 107). Peel off the membranes that encase each segment. Separate the pulp pods into individual or small bunches of pods, about 1/4-inch (0.6 cm.) pieces. Gently combine the pummelo with the pork, shrimp, carrots, mint, cilantro, and chilies. Drizzle with dressing and toss gently. Taste and adjust seasoning with sugar, salt and fish sauce. Transfer to serving bowl, garnish with peanuts.

4. Serve with shrimp chips on the side. The chips are used to scoop up the salad.

Vendor on the Mekong Delta sells her pummelos boat to boat.

How and Why

1. Cook the shrimp with the shell on for the best color, taste and texture. The shell protects the shrimp's flavor.

2. When cutting herbs, use a long stroke with your sharp knife. This helps reduce the bruising of the leaves, and prevent oxidation, which is unsightly and changes the flavor of the fresh herbs.

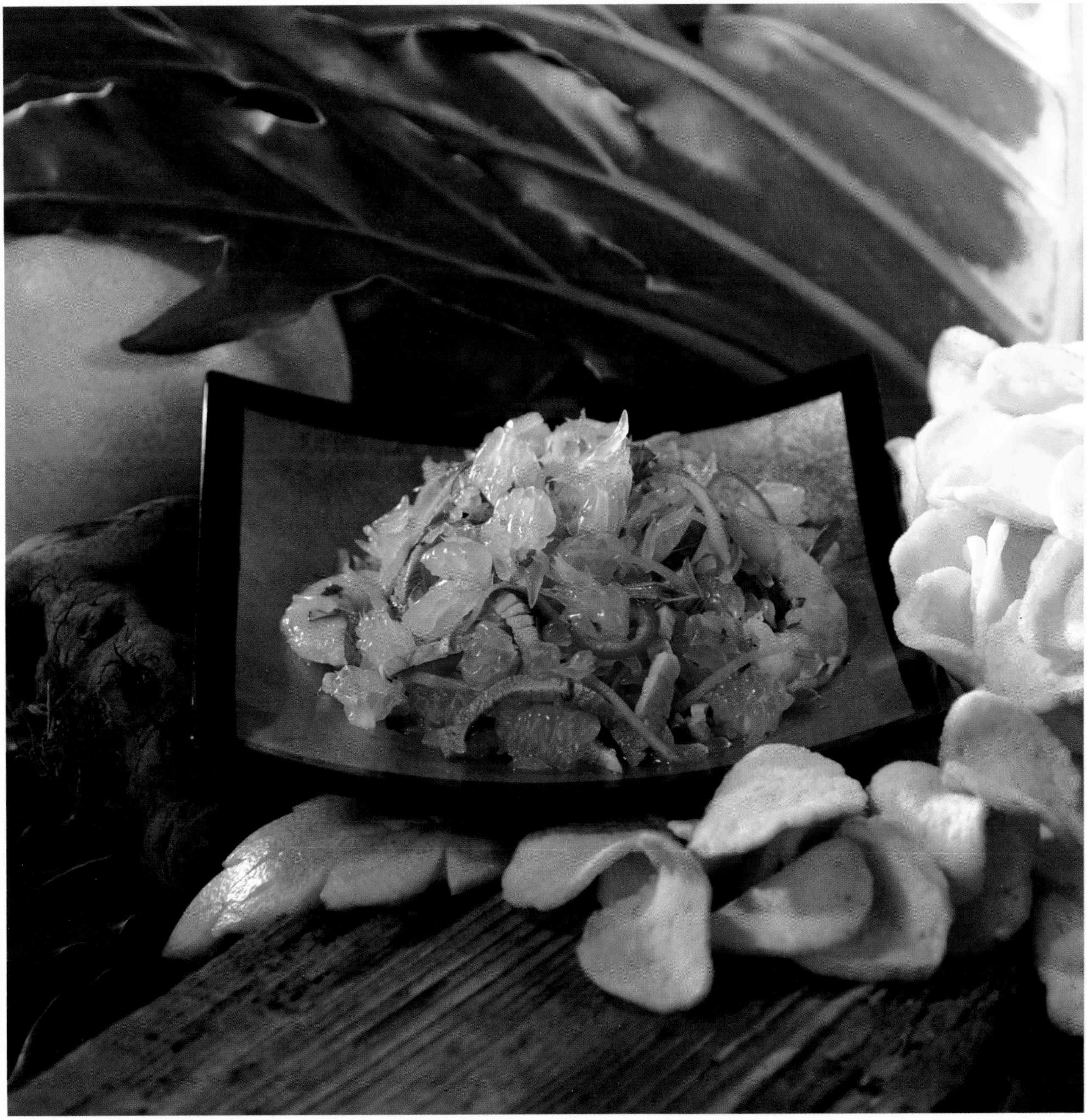

Grilled Shrimp Paste on Sugarcane
Chạo Tôm

This dish is eaten by breaking some of the grilled tender shrimp "mousse" from around the sugarcane stalks, bundling it in a lettuce leaf with a rice noodle sheet, herbs, and cucumber, and then dunking it into a lime dipping sauce. It originated in *Huế*, central Vietnam. A small amount of pork fat enriches the shrimp paste. Finely ground roasted rice powder (sidebar pg. 244) (*thính*) helps create the paste's unique texture. The paste is applied to sticks of sugarcane, steamed to firm it, and then grilled to concentrate its flavor and impart a smoky nuance.

Another serving option is to place these grilled skewers atop rice noodles with some shredded lettuce and a bowl of the lime dipping sauce. No sugarcane around? No worries. Just omit the sugarcane and make small patties instead.

Makes 4 to 6 servings as part of a multi-dish meal

2	oz. (57 g.) Minced pork fat, pork belly, or fatty trimmings from pork shoulder or butt
1	lb. (454 g.) Small shrimp, peeled, de-veined, and roughly chopped
2	cloves Garlic, minced
1	Tbsp. Shallot, minced
1/2	tsp. Kosher salt
2	tsp. Fish sauce (*nước mắm*)
2	tsp. Granulated sugar
1/2	tsp. Ground black pepper
1	Tbsp. Finely ground roasted rice powder (pg. 244) or store bought (substitute rice flour or cornstarch)
5	pieces Sugarcane, 4-inch (10 cm.) lengths, each stalk cut lengthwise into four sticks (about one 20 oz. (567 g.) can. If available, use fresh sugarcane: peel outer edges, then cut)
1	recipe Scallion oil (pg. 200]
1	head Green and/or red leaf lettuce—separate leaves, wash and spin dry, then rip into 4 to 6-inch pieces
1/2	lb. (227 g.) Fine rice vermicelli, cooked or rice paper sheets (pg. 117)
1	small Cucumber, Kirby variety preferred, bite size julienne strips, about 1/8 inch (0.3 cm.) thick
8 to 12	sprigs Cilantro
8 to 12	sprigs Mint
1	recipe Lime dipping sauce, *nước chấm* (pg. 198) and/or Vietnamese Peanut Sauce, *tương đậu phộng* (pg. 201)

1. Prepare and chill first ingredients: Simmer pork fat and two tablespoons of water in small pan over medium heat until water has evaporated and some of the fat has rendered, 5 minutes. Cool in the refrigerator. Place shrimp in work bowl of a food processor with blade and place; transfer this assembly to freezer for 10 minutes.

2. Make the shrimp paste: Restore chilled work bowl onto food processor base; add cooled pork fat, garlic, shallots, salt, fish sauce, sugar, pepper, and rice powder. Puree, stopping occasionally to scrape down bowl with a rubber spatula, until a semi-smooth paste is attained. (For correct texture see pg. 244.) Mixture should gather into a solid mass. Test the paste by frying a tablespoon-sized patty in a pan; adjust seasoning as needed. Transfer mixture to container and refrigerate 30 minutes to help mixture set.

3. Form the shrimp onto sugarcane sticks: Dampen a baking sheet, and then cover with plastic wrap. This will be your work surface. Divide shrimp paste into 2-Tbsp. portions (you should have about 12). Form them into tight balls. Push sugarcane sticks through center of each ball, and then use moistened hands (paste will not stick to hands this way) to mold shrimp paste around the sticks, leaving about 3/4–1 inch (1.9–2.5 cm.) of sugarcane exposed at each end. Arrange these in a single layer, spaced 1/2 inch (1.3 cm.) apart, into an oiled steamer basket.

4. Steam and grill the shrimp skewers: Steam shrimp skewers over rapidly boiling water for 3 minutes, until shrimp is partially cooked and firmly and adhered to the cane. Remove from heat, but keep them covered to prevent them from drying out. This recipe can be prepared up to this point hours or even one day ahead. Very lightly coat the shrimp paste with scallion oil. Grill shrimp skewers on pre-heated grill until golden brown and heated through, about 2 to 5 minutes.

5. Assemble the wraps: Arrange lettuce, noodles, cucumbers and herb sprigs on a platter. Each guest will begin with a swatch of lettuce, top with rice noodle, lay a piece of grilled shrimp paste on, personalize with his own choice of herbs and cucumbers, gather into a tight bundle and dip into lime dipping sauce (*nước chấm*).

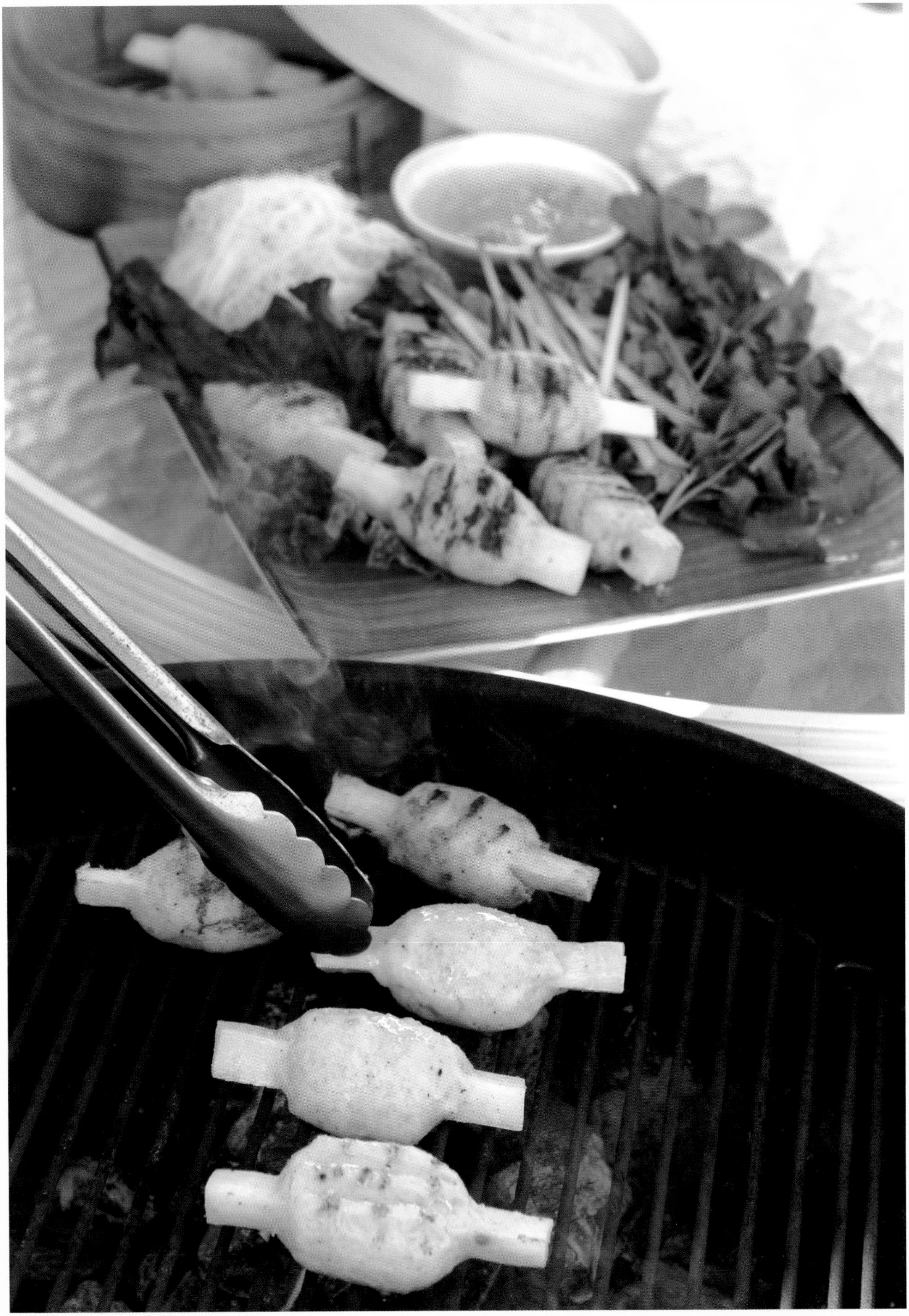

Grilled Shrimp Paste on Sugarcane

Chạo Tôm

How and Why

1. Chilling the food processor and shrimp ahead yields a resilient texture. To ensure a proper emulsion, having the ingredients very cold is essential.

2. Moisten your hands slightly to prevent sticking. Just keep them damp—too wet and the shrimp paste will not stick to the cane.

3. Leave enough room around each stalk so the steam evenly and do not stick. Having adequate space between skewers allows the steam to circulate properly and cook them evenly.

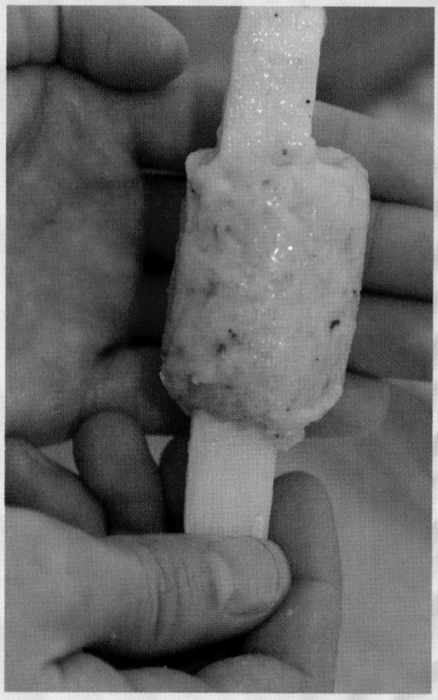

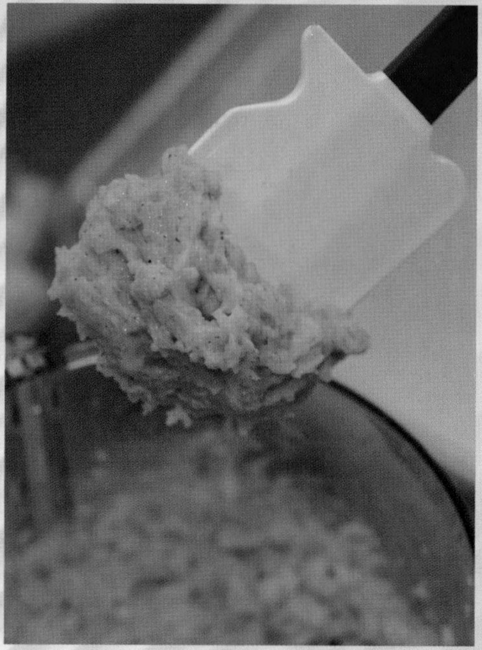

Roasted rice powder—known as *khao kua pon* in Thai and *thính* in Vietnamese, this pale cinnamon-colored powder is a traditional seasoning and binding agent. It's produced by pounding roasted long- or short-grain "sticky" rice. Roasted rice powder is commonly mixed with seasoned meats, fish, and or vegetables. It's used in northeastern Thai and Laotian salads such as *laarb*, and is sometimes sprinkled over spicy soups. Or finely ground to make the Vietnamese *Chạo Tôm* (pg. 242), Vietnamese: *Thính*

To make your own: Heat dry wok or sauté pan over medium heat, add long grain (sticky) glutinous rice. Cook, stirring often, until a deep golden brown color is achieved. Uneven appearance is expected. Judge color/doneness on darkest samples.

Dry roasted chili powder—remove stems from long dried chilies. Heat sauté pan over medium heat, add chilies in even single layer. Toast pressing down with back of spatula until they puff slightly and lighten in color. Cool in pan. Grind coarsely in spice grinder, pulsing to get the most even texture.

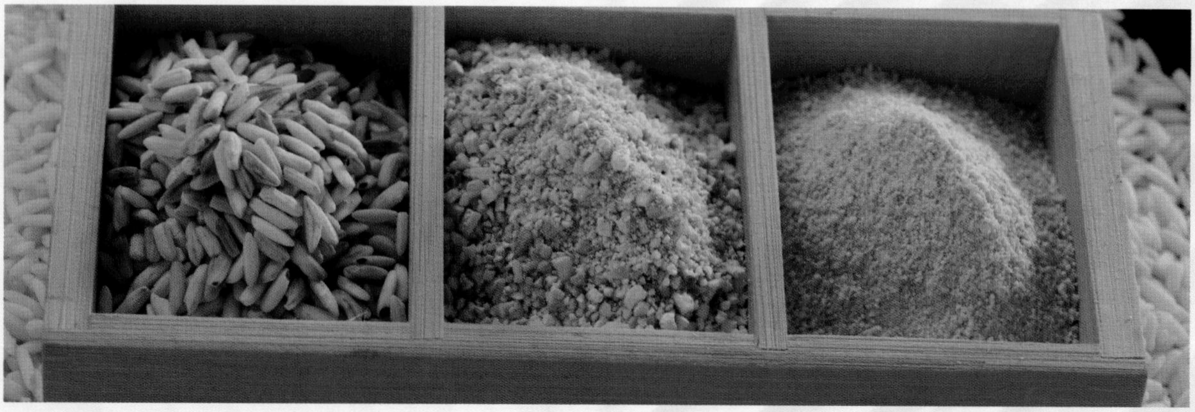

Caramel Shrimp with Black Pepper and Garlic

Tôm Kho

Kho, a term used for stews flavored with the deep brown caramel sauce (pg. 248) acquires an alluring color from that cooked sugar sauce. Although such stews are often prepared with river fish, or pork, I prefer shrimp.

Cẩm Vân Nguyễn, a Vietnamese celebrity chef, spent a day with me in her newly built cooking school in Saigon, teaching me recipes. This was one of them. In preparation for our lessons, her charming son *Khải* took me on the back of his scooter for an all-morning shopping trip for ingredients.

Makes 4 to 6 servings as part of a multi-dish meal

1/4 lb. (113 g.) Pork belly or shoulder, small bite-size slices, about 1/8 inch (0.3 cm.) thick
2 cloves Garlic, minced
1 Thai Bird Chili, minced
2 Tbsp. Fish sauce (*nước mắm*)
2 tsp. Granulated sugar
3 Tbsp. Vietnamese Caramel Sauce (pg. 248)
1/4 tsp. Coarsely ground black pepper
2 Tbsp. Water
1 lb. (454 g.) Medium shrimp, split down back and deveined with shell on
1/4 cup Chopped scallions

1. In a dry 2-quart (2 L.) pan over medium heat, cook pork, stirring often until it browns lightly and a few tablespoons of fat renders out, about 5 minutes. Add garlic and chilies; cook until aromatic, 30 seconds. Add fish sauce, sugar, caramel sauce, black pepper and water; bring to a boil. Add shrimp, toss to coat with sauce. Arrange them snugly. Cover, and place over low heat to simmer 3 minutes.

2. Remove cover; stir shrimp. Sauce should only come up about a half to three-quarters of the way up shrimp and be slightly thick. (If shrimp are fully cooked and sauce is too thin, transfer shrimp to serving bowl, cover to keep warm, and boil sauce rapidly to reduce and thicken; toss shrimp in reduced sauce.)

3. When sauce is the proper consistency, add the scallions, turn off heat, re-cover, and let rest for 30 seconds. Serve with steamed white rice.

How and Why

The right size pan ensures that there is the right shrimp to sauce ratio for cooking. If the pan is too wide the shrimp will not be simmering in the sauce, only on top of it, also it will have tendency to burn.

VIETNAM

245

Pork Belly Simmered in Coconut Juice and Caramel
Thịt Kho Nước Dừa

A glorious dish in the "kho" style, simmered with caramel, this dish gets added complexity from coconut juice, the liquid trapped in the center of young coconuts (not to be confused with coconut milk).

My friend Chris Rimlinger, a medical doctor by day, is an accomplished Vietnamese cook who taught me how to make this dish. This light version of kho has a very thin broth. If you like it more condensed, reduce the water by one cup. The intense sauce is pure comfort food when eaten over steamed jasmine rice. The pickled mustard greens' sour flavor echoes the way that the Malaysian chefs pair their brilliant yellow vegetable pickle, "acar awak," (pg. 324) with the deep brown savory chicken and mushroom stew, Pong Teh (pg. 322).

Makes 4 to 6 bowls as a one-dish meal

2	lb. (2 kg.) Pork belly, skin-on, 1¹/₂-inch (3.8 cm.) pieces (substitute pork shanks or shoulder (butt)
20	fl oz. Young coconut juice with meat, from fresh coconut, or buy frozen or canned (pg. 60)
3	cup (750 ml.) Water
2	medium Shallots, thinly sliced, about ¹/₄ inch (0.6 cm.) thick
3	cloves Garlic, smashed
6	Tbsp. Fish sauce (*nước mắm*)
1	tsp. Coarsely ground black pepper
4	pieces Star anise
¹/₄	cup Vietnamese caramel sauce (pg. 248)
4	lg. Hardboiled eggs
2-inch (5 cm.) piece Rock sugar, about 2oz. (56 gm.)	
4	Scallions, chopped
4	oz. Pickled mustard greens (*Dưa Cải Chua*), cut into bite size pieces (pg. 81)

1. Blanch the Pork: Cover pork with cold water, bring to a boil, drain and discard all liquid. Rinse pork briefly to wash off impurities.

2. Cook the Pork: In a saucepan, cover pork with coconut juice, 3 cups water, shallots, garlic, fish sauce, black pepper, star anise, and caramel sauce. Bring this mixture to a boil, lower to a simmer, and cook until pork is almost tender, about 1 to 1¹/₂ hrs.

3. Add hard boiled eggs; cover pot and simmer 20 minutes. Add rock sugar and stir to dissolve. Taste and adjust seasoning with salt, fish sauce, and sugar. Adjust color with additional caramel sauce—it should be a deep brown color.

4. Garnish with scallions, and serve bowl of mustard greens and steamed white rice. (pg. 106)

The lively throngs of the small waterways of the Mekong Delta are passageways for young coconut commerce.

How and Why

1. Blanch pork in water for clearer sauce and milder flavor. Excess blood is extracted from the pork during blanching.

2. Add the rock sugar at the end of simmering to avoid toughening the pork. Excessive sugar will toughen meats; the sugar pulls moisture from it.

Chicken Stir-Fry with Lemongrass, Tamarind and Chilies

Gà Xào Xả Ớt

Homes across Vietnam are filled with the sound of sizzling woks, filled with this quick chicken stir-fry. Lemongrass perfumes the spicy chili sauce. Pair it with other dishes for a balanced meal, as not many vegetables are included. If you are looking for more of a one-pot meal, toss in some chopped baby bok choy, maybe some bell peppers . . . be creative. Just make sure to add more of all of the seasonings to compensate for the additional ingredients.

Makes 4 to 6 servings as part of multi-dish meal

1	lb. (454 g.) Chicken thigh meat (boneless/skinless), bite size strips, about 1/2 inch (1.3 cm.) thick
4	tsp. Fish sauce, (*nước mắm*) (divided use)
1/2	tsp. Coarsely ground black pepper
1 to 2	Thai bird chilies, minced
2	stalks Lemongrass, trimmed and finely minced (pg. 102)
3	cloves Garlic, minced
2	Tbsp. Vegetable oil
1	small Onion, sliced into 2-inch (5 cm.) lengths, about 1/4 inch (0.6 cm.) thick
1	Tbsp. Vietnamese caramel sauce or dark brown sugar
1	Tbsp. Tamarind pulp (pg. 109)
1/4	cup Chicken broth or stock
1/4	cup Roughly chopped cilantro (leaves and stems)

1. Marinate chicken in 2 tsp. fish sauce, black pepper, chilies, lemongrass, and garlic for 15 minutes at room temperature.

2. Heat a large sauté pan (10 to 12 inch or 25 to 30 cm.) or wok over high heat; add oil and onions. Cook until translucent and begining to brown. Add chicken; stir occasionally until almost completely cooked, about 5 minutes. Add fish sauce, caramel sauce, tamarind, and chicken broth. Simmer 15 seconds; taste and adjust sauce with fish sauce and caramel.

3. Stir in cilantro, and remove from heat. Serve over steamed rice.

How and Why

Marinating the chicken ensures flavorful meat. The short cooking time and thin sauce mean that flavor would not adequately penetrate the chicken without the marinade.

CARAMEL SAUCE—*"Nuoc Mau"*
Yield: 1/2 cup

TRADITIONAL METHOD (less time, but fickle)

1/2 cup Sugar
1/4 cup Water

1. Place sugar in a dry, super-clean 2-quart saucepan. Heat over medium heat without stirring until sugar begins to liquefy and turn brown around perimeter of sugar—at least a 1/8 inch border of melted sugar.
2. Stir occasionally with a wooden spoon or heatproof spatula until it turns very deep brown. It will be foaming, and smoke will start to rise. Color should be reddish-black.
3. Stand back as you cautiously add water: it will boil vigorously and a lot of steam will rise. Be careful.
4. Whisk to dissolve any seized sugar. Cool, transfer to a container to use as needed.

CONTEMPORARY METHOD
(more hands-on time, but foolproof)

1/2 cup Sugar
1/2 cup Water (divided use)

1. Combine sugar and 1/4 cup of water in small saucepan until a smooth paste is formed.
2. Heat over medium heat until mixture begins to bubble and sugar is melted.
3. Continue to simmer without stirring until it turns very deep brown. It will be foaming and smoke will start to rise, color should be reddish-black.
4. Stand back as you cautiously add water: it will boil vigorously and a lot of steam will rise. Be careful.
5. Whisk to dissolve any seized sugar. Cool, transfer to a container to use as needed.

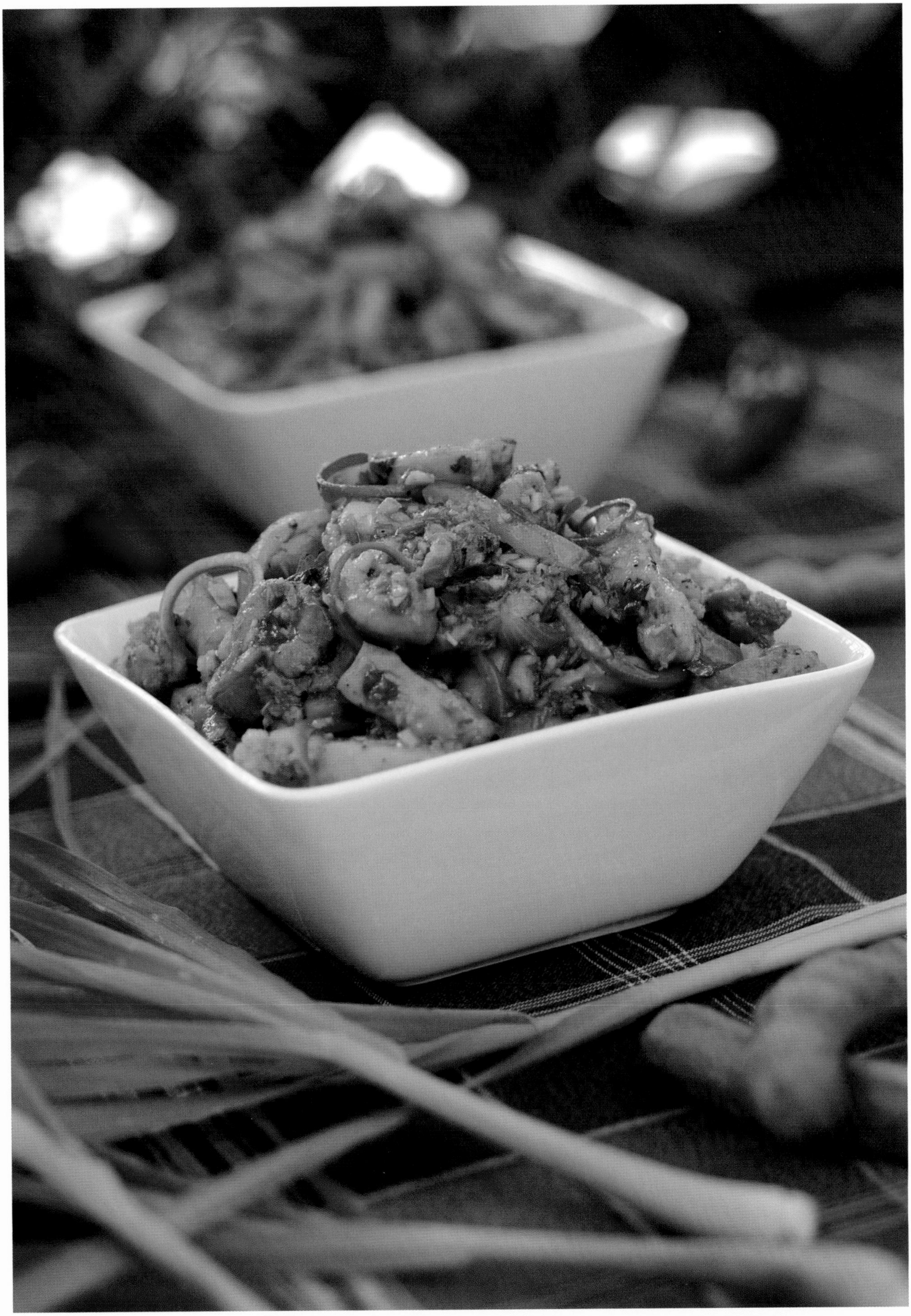

Packets of Crispy Roasted Pork Belly with Cucumber, Basil, Lime and Chili Salt

Thịt Heo Quay

In *Huế*, central Vietnam I experienced "pork belly lust" when I spotted a street vendor selling crispy, spit-roasted pig. Not a word was spoken as I approached crunchy hog heaven. Lusty salivation is a universal language. *Thịt Heo Quay*, read the sign. Ms. Quy wordlessly assembled a sample for me to taste. She plucked a faintly bitter green leaf of *yu choy* (pg. 76), into which she folded a small piece of pork belly, a sliver of cucumber, a sprig of Vietnamese coriander, and a fragrant leaf of Asian basil. Before relinquishing the delicacy, she anointed it with a squeeze of lime. Then, she rolled it up like a Cuban cigar, pressed it into my palm, and instructed me to dip it in chili-salt. The instant I placed this pleasure packet in my mouth, I took in the multi-layered flavor experience. My pork guru motioned to some fresh green peppercorns, signaling me to pop some into my mouth. WOW. That spark elevated the pleasure I was feeling to a whole other level. I knew I had to convince her to teach me the secret of this gustatory perfection. She did. So now I pass on the culinary treasure of roasted pork belly to you! See page 188.

If you have a rotisserie, this is the time to use it. I have a Ronco rotisserie that the ubiquitous Ron Popiel handed to me at his lavish home. It works very well for a home kitchen. This recipe calls for 2 lbs. (1 kg.) pork, which yields slightly more meat than you will be able to use in the packets. This allows you to choose the best morsels for serving. I always find that the extra roast pork disappears before we even get to assembling the bundles.

Makes 30 to 60 bite size pieces (plus extra pork for snacking)

ROASTED PORK

2   tsp. Chinese rice wine (*Shao Xing*)
3   Tbsp. Soy sauce
1   Tbsp. Oyster sauce
2   tsp. Sesame seeds
1   tsp. Five spice powder (pg. 43)
2   tsp. Ground black pepper
1   stalk Lemongrass, trimmed and minced
5   cloves Garlic, roughly chopped
2   lb. (.9 kg.) Pork belly, skin-on, boneless
1   Tbsp. Vegetable oil

1. Marinate the Pork: (4 hours or day ahead marinade). Score skin as seen in PHOTOs then rub pork skin with wine (skin side only!). Whisk together the soy sauce, oyster sauce, kosher salt, sesame seeds, five spice, black pepper, lemongrass, and garlic; rub over entire surface of the pork, lightly on the skin side. Transfer to a container, skin side up (so skin does not sit in marinade), and marinate in the refrigerator for minimum of 4 hours or overnight.
2. Roast the Pork:

- To Roast in Oven: Preheat oven to 325°F (163°C) with middle rack in place; place pork on roasting pan or large sauté pan with ovenproof handle. Roast in oven for 1¼ hrs, until meat is becoming tender, and skin is getting brown and crisp. Turn on broiler and watch carefully rotating pan as needed to get an evenly bubbled surface with a dark brown color, about 10 minutes. Cool to room temperature. Cut into bite-size pieces when everything else is ready.

- To Roast on a Rotisserie: Thread pork belly onto rack. Set rotisserie to medium temperature. Roast, 1½ hrs, or until pork belly is tender, and skin is deep brown and crisp. Cool to room temperature. Cut into bite-size pieces.

ACCOMPANIMENTS

1 to 2 bunches (30 to 60 leaves) *Choy sum, yu choy* or other slightly bitter greens (spinach is fine in a pinch)
1   small Cucumber, Kirby variety preferred, sliced into ⅛-inch (0.3 cm.) thick rounds
8 to 12 sprigs Vietnamese coriander (*rau răm*) or a mixture of mint and cilantro
8 to 12 sprigs Asian basil
6   cloves Garlic, sliced, about 1/18 inch (0.3 cm.) thick
2   Tbsp. Fresh or brined green peppercorns (drain and rinse if brined) (pg. 42)
2 to 3 medium Limes, cut into Southeast Asian style wedges (pg. 108)
2   Tbsp. Vietnamese Chili-salt (below)

1. Arrange choy sum leaves, cucumber slices, herb sprigs, garlic cloves and lime wedges on a large platter. Fill a small bowl with peppercorns and place on platter.
2. Add ½ tsp. sugar and 1 tsp. water to the 2 Tbsp. of chili salt. Fill small bowls (one per person) with a 1 tsp. of this mixture.

TO ASSEMBLE THE WRAPS:

1. Place leaf in the palm of one hand. Top with one piece of pork, a squeeze of lime, slice of cucumber, and a sprig of each herb. Roll up leaf.
2. Dip edge of wrap into chili-salt and eat entire packet in one bite.
3. Nibble on peppercorns and raw garlic slices as desired.

Chili Salt
Muoi Tieu

Synergy of flavors can take simplest combinations and elevate them to new levels. Numerous chili and salt mixtures adorn tables all over Vietnam. Small dishes of chili-salt accompany sliced fresh pineapple. A tiny dip of the luscious fruit into this salty powder makes the pineapple's flavor really "pop." This condiment works especially well for the Crispy Pork Belly. Add some coarsely ground black pepper for an earthy kick. Make small attractive piles in small dishes. Add a few wedges of lime for each person to squeeze, when serving chili salt with dishes like grilled shrimp or steamed crabs.

Makes 2 tablespoons

1-2   Thai bird chilies, preferably red, minced
2   Tbsp. Kosher salt

1. Combine in mortar and pestle or spice grinder combine salt and chilies and grind until a red powder is created.

How and Why

Uses kosher salt or coarse sea salt for the best taste and texture. Due to their coarse texture, these salts are most commonly sold without addition of iodine or anti-caking agents, which can give an acrid bite to simple table salt

Packets of Crispy Roasted Pork Belly with Cucumber, Basil, Lime and Chili Salt

Thịt Heo Quay

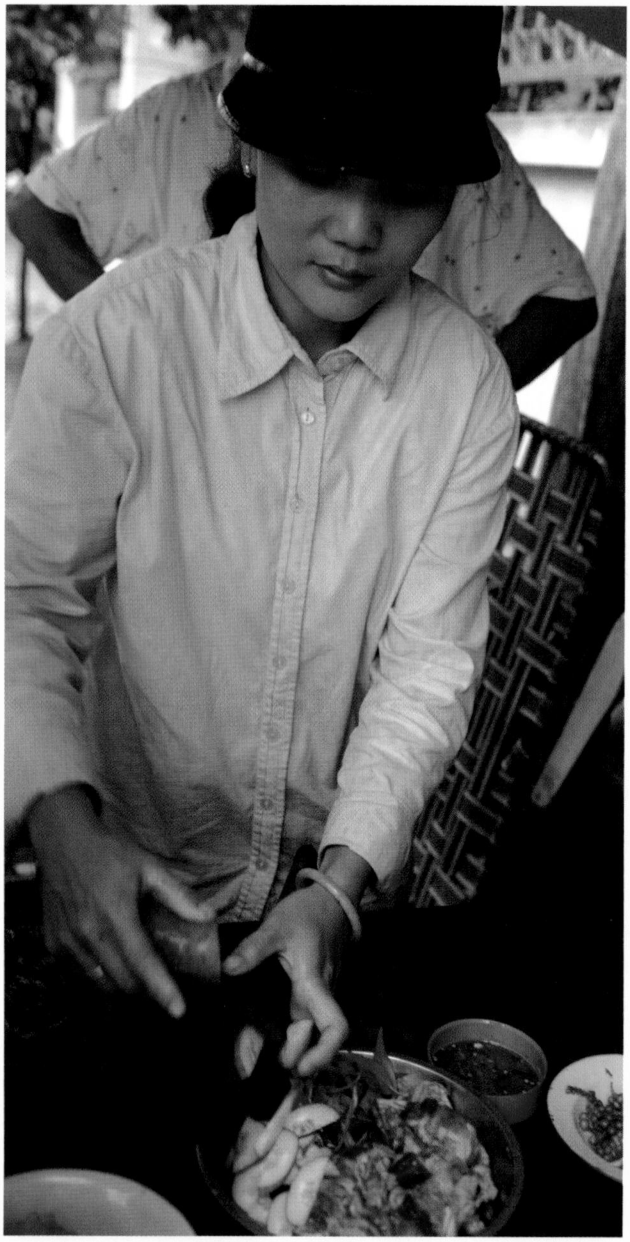

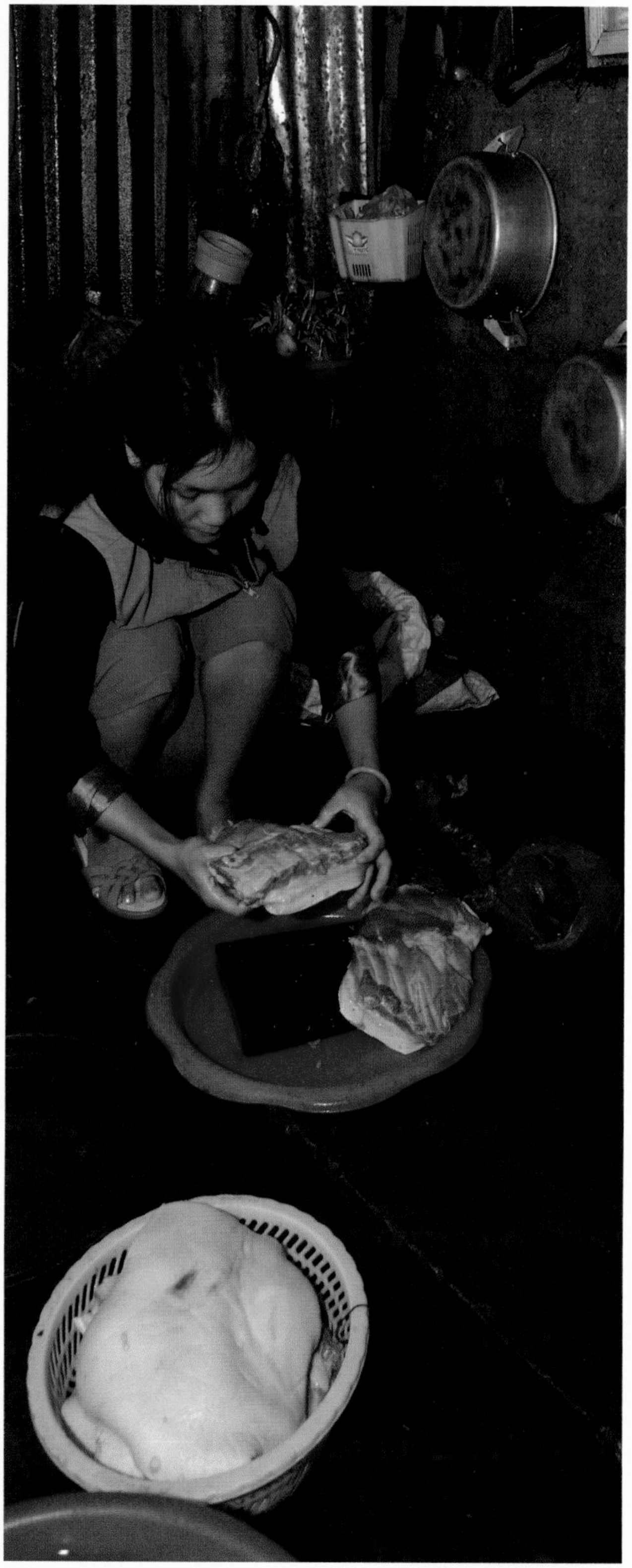

How and Why

Roasting first then broiling makes the skin more tender. The slow roast allows some of the fat to render then placing it under the broiler to create small bubbles that thin the skin and make it more tender (stay and watch this steps as it can burn easily).

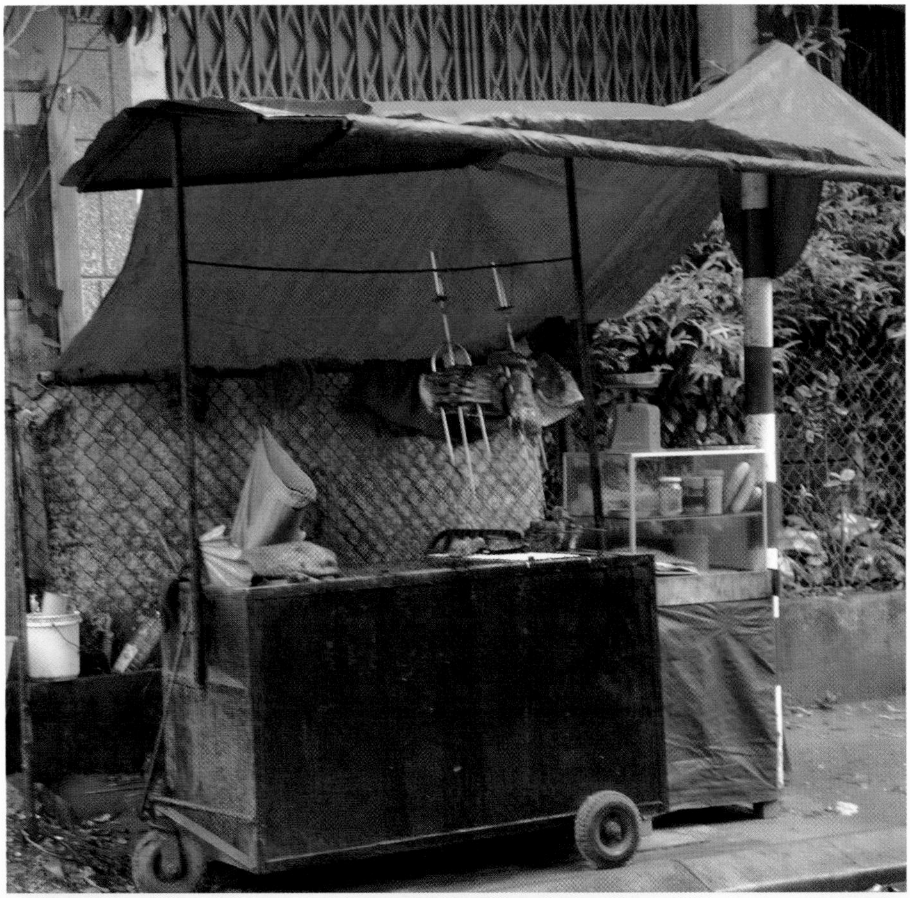

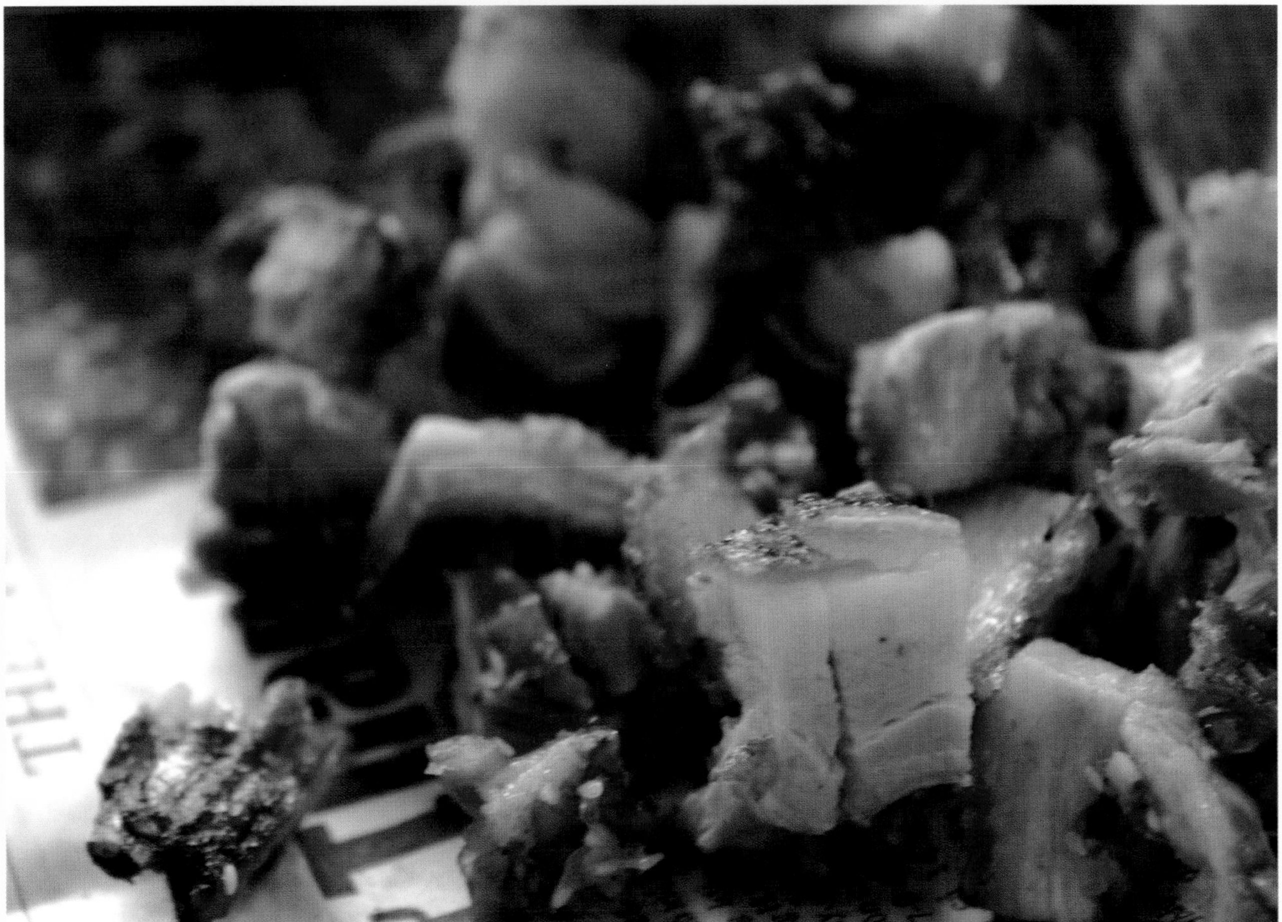

Corn with Pork Belly & Scallions
Bắp và Thịt Ba Rọi

Tucked into a small alley, the quaint, sparsely decorated home of Mr. Châu, whom we call "Captain Cook" (see Web site for story behind the name) hid one of the most vibrant kitchens in Vietnam. The Captain taught me how well corn, pork, and scallions go together. A short stop at the market left us armed with fatty fork, fresh corn, and spring onions. I balanced these treasures under my arms as I clung to the back of the Captain's scooter, speeding through the crowded Nha-Trang side streets.

His daughter, Hà Triêù Quyên and visiting cousin *Phương* helped as he whipped up an intriguing corn dish to eat with our crispy chicken wings and steamed fresh crabs. We sipped red wine while escaping the afternoon's brutal sun, hidden away in our back-alley cove.

Makes 4 to 6 servings as part of multi-dish meal

1/2 lb. (227 g.) Pork belly or fatty pork shoulder (butt), small bite-size pieces, about 1/8 inch (0.3 cm.) thick
1/4 cup Water
2 lg. Scallions, chopped (When in season substitute spring onions)
2 cloves Garlic, minced
1 Thai bird chili, minced
2 cups Corn kernels
1/2 tsp. Granulated sugar
pinch Ground black pepper
1 Tbsp. Fish sauce (*nước mắm*)

1. In a medium skillet or wok over medium heat, simmer pork and water, stirring often. Cook until water steams out and pork renders out about 1/4 cup of fat. It is okay for pork to brown slightly.

2. Add scallions, garlic, and chilies. Cook until aromatic, about 15 seconds. Add corn, sugar, pepper, and fish sauce. Cook, stirring constantly, until corn is tender.

3. Taste; adjust seasoning with fish sauce and sugar.

How and Why

Adding water to the pork at the beginning helps it to render more fat, creating a more luxurious sauce. The water conducts heat more evenly than the direct heat of the pan, so more fat renders and becomes part of the sauce.

Opposite page top left: *Captain Cook is in command of his kitchen.*

Opposite page top right: *Hà Triêù Quyên, blending a quick sauce.*

Opposite page bottom left: *Phuong's constant smiles in the kitchen are a delight.*

Opposite page bottom right: *We also steamed some live crabs with a lime-pepper dipping salt and fried chicken wings with chili sauce.*

Lemongrass Pork on Cool Rice Vermicelli with Herbs

Bún Thịt Nướng

These are a dining-out habit of mine. Although I love to cook Vietnamese food, I also go out to restaurants for it. These noodles are a frequent first choice. Vivid tastes, colors, and textures each add their own notes in the orchestra of flavors that unravels with each bite. The palate-tickling sensation of the angel-hair fine rice noodles becomes even more stimulating once the sweet-tart-savory dressing loosens their tangled filaments. They revel in a contrast of crunchy cool vegetables, chewy slivers of warm pork, and toothsome herbs.

Most places offer a few variations on this noodle bowl, topping the vermicelli and vegetables with grilled shrimp, fried spring rolls, or charred beef slices. Arm yourself with chopsticks and explore the terrain of Vietnamese cuisine.

Makes 4 to 6 bowls as a one-dish meal

1	Tbsp. Oyster sauce
2	tsp. Fish sauce (*nước mắm*)
1	Tbsp. Vegetable oil
1	Tbsp. Light brown palm sugar (pg. 58)
1/2	tsp. Ground black pepper
2	stalks Lemongrass, trimmed and minced
1	small Shallot, minced
1	clove Garlic, minced
3/4	lb. Pork shoulder, butt, or leg, sliced about 1/8 inch (0.3 cm.) thick
1	lb. (454 g.) Dried rice vermicelli

1/4	head Green or red leaf lettuce, shredded, about 1/2 inch (1.3 cm.) thick
1	small Cucumber, Kirby variety preferred, bite size julienne strips, about 1/8 inch (0.3 cm.) thick (pg. 81)
1/2	cup Carrots, shredded or fine julienne strips, about 1/16 inch (0.1 cm.) thick (pg. 108)
1/2	cup Perilla herb (pg. 38), sliced thinly, about 1/8-inch (0.3 cm.) slices
1/2	cup Roughly chopped cilantro, (leaves and stems)
3/4	cup Peanuts, roasted in dry pan (pg. 109)
1	recipe Lime dipping sauce (*nước chấm*) (pg. 198)

Some locals like to grind the pork instead of slicing it and grill the seasoned patties.

1. Marinate the Pork: In a medium bowl whisk together the oyster sauce, fish sauce, oil, palm sugar, pepper, lemongrass, shallots, and garlic. Add pork; massage to coat well. Marinate at least 30 minutes, overnight is even better.

2. Cook the Noodles: Meanwhile, soak rice vermicelli in room temperature water 15 minutes; drain. Cook noodles in 1 gallon (4 L.) of boiling water until tender yet resilient, anywhere from 20 seconds to 1 minute depending on thickness of noodles. Immediately rinse with cool water; drain well. Form the noodles into 4 to 6 bundles.

3. Set up the bowls: Divide lettuce among serving bowls; top with noodles. Cover, leave at room temperature until needed. The noodles will become a bit sticky but there's no need to do anything—they will loosen immediately when the sauce is added.

4. Cook the pork: Drain any excess marinade from pork. Grill pork slices until browned well and cooked through; reserve. (You may opt to sauté the pork instead).

5. Assemble the Noodle Bowls: Arrange cucumbers, carrots, mint and cilantro in bowl with noodles. Cut pork into bite size pieces and arrange atop noodles; sprinkle with roasted peanuts.

6. Serve with *nước chấm*. Divide sauce into 4 to 6 small bowls (4 to 6 Tbsp.). Each guest pours his sauce over his own dish and mixes before eating.

How and Why

To get the desired browning when sauteing, do not stir or move the pork often. Agitating the pork forces out juices that cool down the pan, causing the pan to brown more than the meat itself.

Soy Glazed "Shaking Beef" Salad with Pickled Onions

Bò Lúc-Lắc

*O*ften mistaken for a casual affair since it is so quick and easy to prepare, this stir-fry is really an elegant salad. Tender cubes of oyster sauce and garlic marinated beef gain smoky essences in a fiery hot sautœ pan. Then, they're paired with spiritedly dressed salad and sharp pickled onions. It feels like a "night on the town" in a single dish.

The French introduced the method of sautœing, "shaking the beef," to Vietnam. The Chinese brought oyster sauce and soy sauce. The Vietnamese practice of building layers of flavor by juxtaposing a hot, savory meat with a cool salad makes it their own. Although not traditional, I really like this prepared with pork, chicken, or even fish like salmon. They all hold up well to the intense sauce.

Makes 4 to 6 servings as part of a multi-dish meal

1	lb. (454 g.) Beef filet mignon, strip loin or other tender cut, 3/4-inch (2 cm.) cubes
2	tsp. Oyster sauce
2	tsp. Fish sauce (*nước mắm*)
2	tsp. Soy sauce
1	tsp. Coarsely ground black pepper
8	cloves Garlic, roughly chopped
1/2	cup Sliced red onions, 1/8 inch (0.3 cm.) thick, about 11/2 to 2-inch (3.8 to 5 cm.) pieces
2	Tbsp. Distilled white vinegar
2	Tbsp. Water
1/2	tsp. Granulated sugar
pinch	Kosher salt
2	bunch Watercress, picked into sprigs or 1/2 head green leaf lettuce. Torn into bite size pieces.
1	tsp. Dark soy sauce
1	tsp. Vietnamese caramel sauce (pg. 248) or dark brown sugar
2	tsp. Vietnamese chili sauce (pg. 198) or store bought
2	Tbsp. Vegetable oil

1. Marinate the Beef: Toss beef with oyster sauce, fish sauce, soy sauce, black pepper and garlic. Marinate for a minimum of 30 minutes.

2. Pickle the Onions: In a small bowl, combine the onions, vinegar, water, sugar and salt. Toss to dissolve the sugar and salt; marinate 10 to 30 minutes.

3. Getting Ready to Cook: Arrange watercress around inside perimeter of plate. In a small bowl whisk together the soy sauce, caramel, and chili sauce. Divide mixture into two small bowls.

4. Cook the Beef: To achieve the proper sear, you will need to cook the meat in two batches or two pans. Heat a large sauté pan (non-stick works well for this recipe) or wok over high heat; add 1 Tbsp. oil. Heat 15 seconds until smoke begins to rise from pan. Add half of the beef in an even layer, but do not shake yet! After pan's heat recovers (about 15 seconds) shake pan to redistribute beef helping it with a spatula. Cook, shaking pan and stirring occasionally, until somewhat browned, yet still pink inside. Slowly add the sauce mixture and cook, stirring rapidly, until sauce coats the beef, about 5 seconds. Transfer beef to center of serving plate; repeat with remaining beef and sauce. (if using the same pan, clean after cooking first batch) Sprinkle onions on top of beef.

We ordered shaking beef to accompany our freshly brewed beer. Within minutes, an insipid dish of the beef arrived. We sent it back with instructions to bring it back to life. The chef added sliced onions and peppers. It made all the difference. A few judiciously applied vegetables can turn a mistake into a miracle.

How and Why

1. Marinating the beef helps it brown better. The oyster sauce and soy sauce both brown quickly when heat is applied, especially in the presence of meat proteins.

2. Do not shake the pan right away to achieve the best sear. Although to sauté translates literally as "to jump," inexperienced cooks often shake the pan prematurely. Let the surface of the meat sear first, so it browns, instead of steaming.

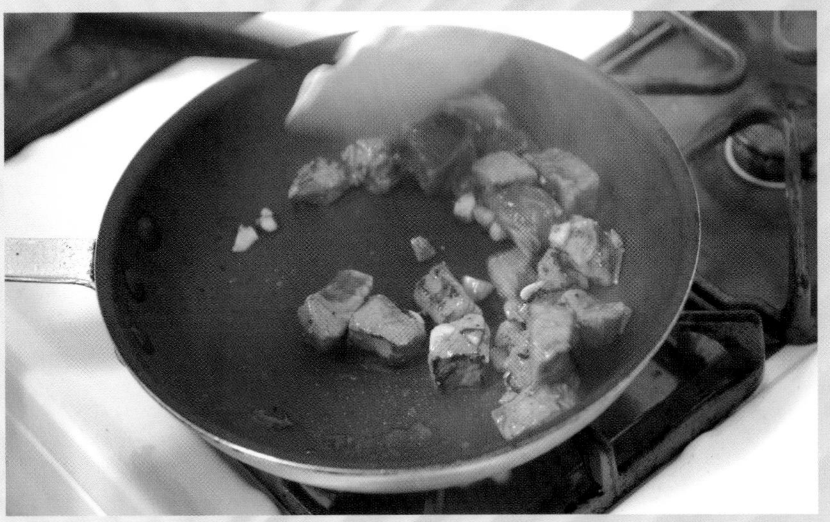

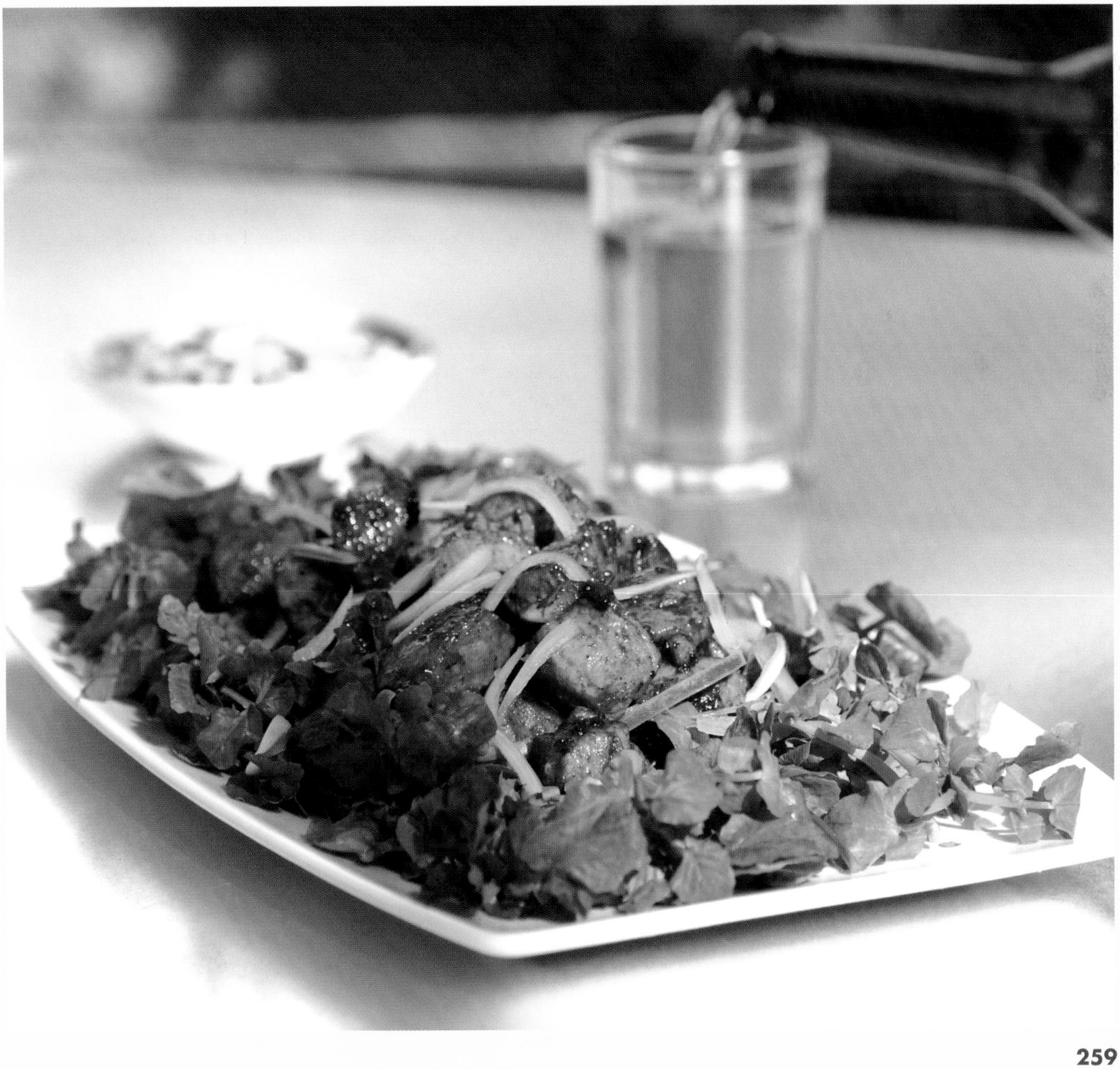

Lemongrass Beef Stew with Tomatoes and Star Anise

Bồ Kho

Cẩm-Vân Nguyễn, a friend and famous cooking teacher in Vietnam, invited me to work with her at her cooking school in Saigon during my last visit. This is an adaptation of her recipe. Annatto seeds provide brilliant orange color. This stew originated in the tropics but it seems custom made for a cold night. French baguettes are always used in Vietnam for mopping up the gravy, but the dish goes equally well over steamed rice or wide rice noodles.

Makes 4 to 6 bowls as a one-dish meal

BEEF STEW

2	lb. (1 kg.) Beef chuck or shank meat, 1¹/₂-inch (3.8 cm.) chunks
3	Tbsp. Fish sauce (*nước mắm*)
1	Tbsp. Vietnamese curry powder (pg. 113)
2	Tbsp. Granulated sugar
2	Tbsp. Minced ginger
¹/₄	cup Vegetable oil
2	Tbsp. Annatto seeds
2	cloves Garlic, minced
2	stalks Lemongrass, trimmed, cut into 3-inch (7.5 cm.) lengths and bruised lightly (pg. 102)
3	pieces Star anise

1   piece Cassia (Cinnamon), about 3 to 4 inches (7.5 to 10 cm.) long

¹/₂   lb. (227 g.) Carrots, peeled, cut into 1-inch (2.5 cm.) pieces on angle

2   medium Tomatoes, core and seeds removed, cut into 1-inch (2.5 cm.) chucks

1. Toss beef in bowl with fish sauce, curry powder, sugar, and ginger. Marinate for at least 30 minutes.

2. Combine oil and annatto seeds in 4 qt. (4 L.) saucepan, heat until they begin to sizzle (less than 1 minute) in hot oil. Remove from heat and rest for 10 minutes to infuse oil. Strain or scoop out annatto seeds with a slotted spoon.

3. Heat pan with annatto-infused oil, lemongrass, star anise and cassia; cook lightly for 2 minutes. Add garlic; cook until aromatic but not brown, about 30 seconds.

4. Increase heat to high, add marinated beef, and mix well. Cook stirring often, for 5 minutes. Add enough water to just cover the beef. Bring to a boil, and then lower to simmer.

5. Cook, uncovered, until meat is almost fully tender, about 1 hour. Taste; adjust seasoning with fish sauce, salt, and sugar. Stir in carrots and tomatoes; simmer for 20 minutes until the carrots are tender.

6. If desired (to prevent any unpleasant surprises), remove the star anise, cassia and lemongrass. Adjust thickness and flavor intensity by adding water. Add fish sauce or salt as needed.

GARNISHES, TABLE SALAD AND OTHER TABLE CONDIMENTS

1/2   medium Yellow onion, sliced into paper-thin rings, rinsed under cool water, dried well

8   leaves Vietnamese saw leaf herb (pg. 38), shaved thinly about 1/4-inch (0.6 cm.) slices or 12 sprigs of cilantro

8 to 12 sprigs Asian basil

2   medium Limes, cut into Southeast Asian style wedges (pg. 108)

2 to 4 lg. Crisp light baguette

4   lg. Red or orange chilies, thinly sliced, about 1/8 inch (0.3 cm.) thick

2   Tbsp. Vietnamese chili-salt (pg. 251)

ASSEMBLY OF STEW BOWLS

1. Divide stew into large deep bowls, top with sliced onions and sliced saw-leaf herb.

2. Serve with side dishes of sliced chilies and chili-salt.

3. Have plenty of light, crisp, warm baguettes on hand to sop up the gravy.

How and Why

1. Marinating the beef in the spices infuses it with aroma and color. When it is cooking, the meat does not absorb flavorings the same way.

2. Infusing oil with annatto seeds gives this stew its characteristic red-gold color. Alternately some add up to 1/4 cup of tomato paste in step three, adding both color and flavor.

Vietnamese Style Yogurt
Ya-ua/Sữa Chua

My first taste of Vietnamese yogurt a few years back instantly brought a smile to my face. It was so smooth and silky that it tickled my senses. The flavor was rich and light at the same time. The luxurious flavor of condensed milk is contrasted by the tart yogurt culture: pure balance. Hmmm, I wonder which came first, Yoplait or Vietnamese yogurt...

American style yogurt making requires clean glass containers. I found that plastic works just as well. Vietnamese yogurt should be made in individual, super-clean cups, since any agitation will soften the yogurt, undermining its special texture.

I could not get anyone to tell their secret on how to make it and there were no books I could find that had the recipe. So I did some preliminary research and Ari, my sous chef really led the charge in figuring this one out. A word of advice, FOLLOW THE RECIPE EXACTLY. The temperatures listed are there for a reason, certain bacteria need to grow, others not. Get organized and try this one—it's amazing.

Makes: 8, four oz. portions

1   (14 oz. / 396 g.) can Sweetened condensed milk
1¹/₂ cups Water
1¹/₄ cups Whole milk (room temperature)
³/₄   cup Plain yogurt (room temperature)

1. Plastic containers or cups, 6 to 8 oz.(177 to 237 ml) capacity, preferably with tight-fitting lids. Disposable plastic tumblers "party cups" work fine.
2. Ensure all equipment is very clean (sterile is best). Bring one gallon of water to boil (keep this at the ready). Whisk condensed milk and water in saucepan. Heat up to 185°–190°F (85°–88°C); remove immediately from the heat. Cool to 105°–115°F (40°–46°C).
3. Whisk whole milk and plain yogurt into cooled condensed milk mixture; transfer mixture immediately to small containers. Cover tightly with sterile covers (plastic wrap is fine).

4. Incubate:
- Cooler Method: (recommended) Transfer cups to small CLEAN cooler (spray with disinfectant and wipe dry), carefully pour boiling water in to cooler until fill level reaches 90 % up the side of yogurt mixture. Cover cooler; place in warm environment (most parts of the house will do, other than cold areas like garages or basements). Do not move or agitate until yogurt is fully set. Leave until set overnight. Transfer cups to refrigerator until completely set and cold.
- Blanket Method: Transfer cups to deep heat proof container (metal or glass and more than 1 inch taller than filled cups) carefully pour boiled water in container until fill level reaches 90% up the side of yogurt mixture. Wrap container with large blanket (several layers), place in warm environment, most parts of the house will do, not in a cold area like a garage. Do not move or agitate until yogurt is finished. Leave until set overnight.

5. Transfer cups to refrigerator until completely set and cold. DO NOT MIX IT UP. This will liquefy the yogurt.

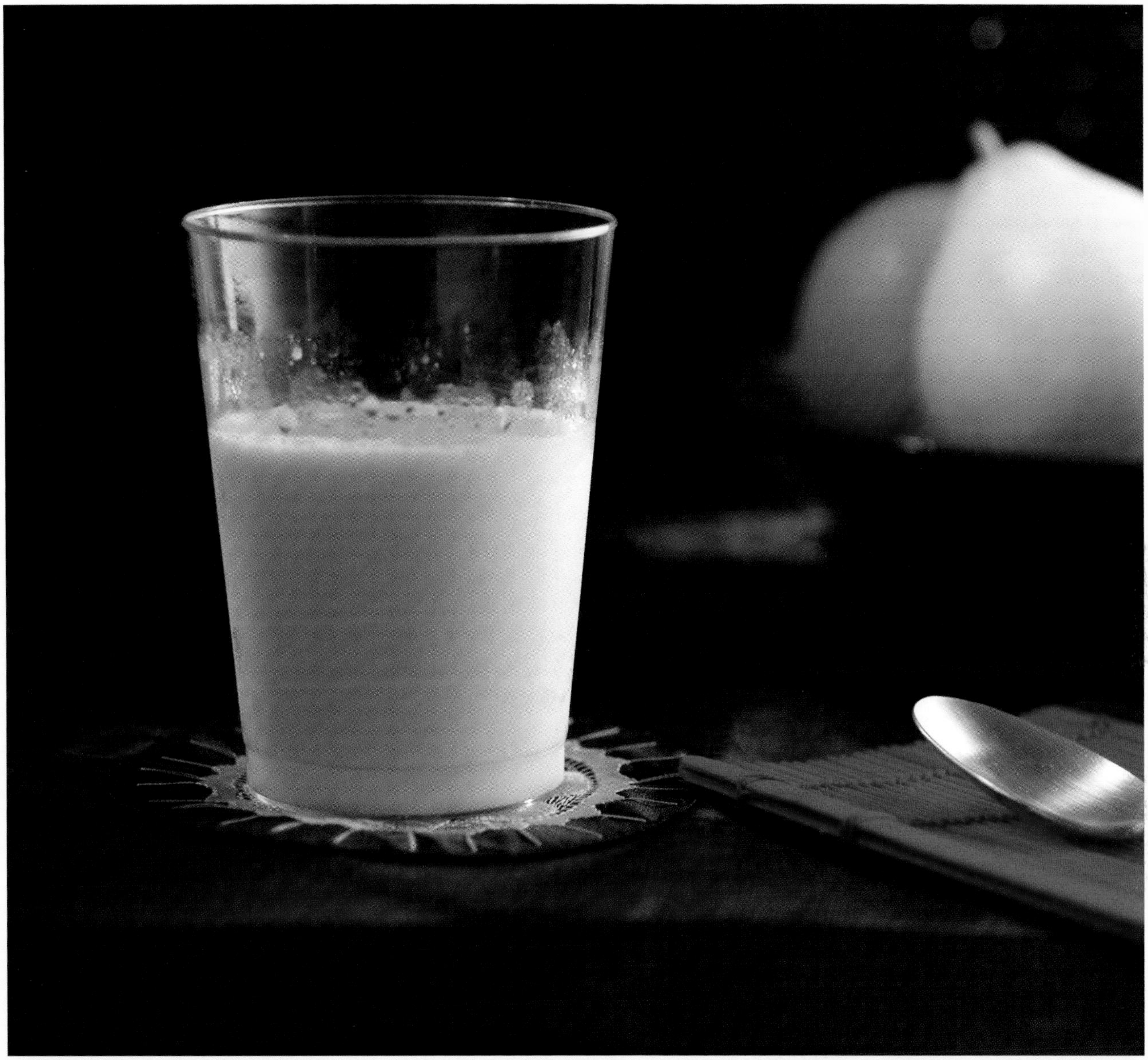

VIETNAM

How and Why

1. Make sure to have all the equipment clean. This precaution is needed to ensure that harmful bacteria will not interfere with culture process.

2. Boiling the milk makes for finer textured yogurt. Heating the milk denatures the whey proteins and allows them to form a fine matrix that is smoother.

Bananas and Coconut Milk with Tapioca Pearls

Chè Chuối Chưng

The banana flavor permeates this creamy coconut milk dessert "soup." This is a very common *chè* (sweet snack). Using the smaller variety of bananas known as "finger bananas" is ideal, but ripe, yet firm regular (Cavendish) bananas will suffice. Be unbound with your creative license: substitute slices of cooked sweet potato (adding to simmering tapioca after 10 minutes) or even taro in place of bananas for a change. You can serve it still warm, at room temperature, or chilled (the cooler it gets the thicker it will be, so you may want to thin it down when serving it chilled).

Tapioca pearls are made of tapioca starch. This recipe calls for the smallest size available as that is what is traditionally used. By all means, if you can only get another size, use it—just adjust the cooking tiem accordingly.

Makes 4 to 6 servings as part of a multi-dish meal

4   cups (1 L.) Water
1/4   cup Tapioca pearls, small variety (about the size
        of mustard seeds)
1   can Coconut milk (about 14 oz.)
4   lg. Pandan leaves, tied into one knot
1/2   cup Granulated sugar
1/2   tsp. Kosher salt
1   lb. (454 g.) Bananas, "baby" variety whole or large
        bananas cut on diagonal into 2-inch
        (5 cm.) pieces
1   Tbsp. Toasted sesame seeds or crushed
        roasted peanuts

1. Bring water to a boil in 4 qt. (4 L.) saucepan. Slowly sprinkle in tapioca. Stir well; simmer, stirring occasionally until almost completely translucent, about 20 minutes.
2. Add coconut milk, pandan leaves, sugar, salt and bring up to a simmer.
3. Add bananas, and return to a simmer for 1 minute.
4. Remove from heat and let the banana and pandan flavors permeate the coconut milk. Taste and adjust seasoning as needed with salt and sugar, it should have salty background note to contrast with the overall sweetness. Pull out pandan and squeeze out excess moisture into ché for maximum flavor extraction.
5. Serve warm, room temperature or chilled. Sprinkle with sesame seeds or peanuts right before serving.

How and Why

1. Simmering the tapioca pearls until they are almost completely clear yields a firm yet tender bite. Undercook these, and they are tough. Simmer until completely cooked, and they will over-hydrate and get gummy as they cool in the liquid.

2. Only simmer the bananas for one minute, so they hold together. As with the tapioca pearls, you must account for carry-over cooking, wherein residual heat continues to cook the item, in this case softening the bananas.

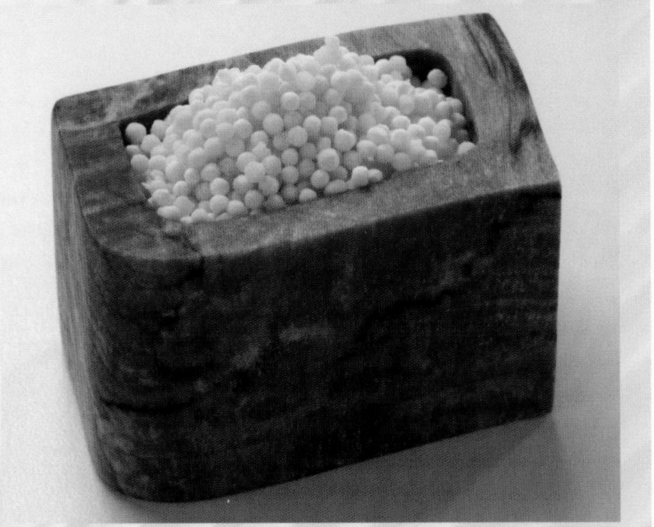

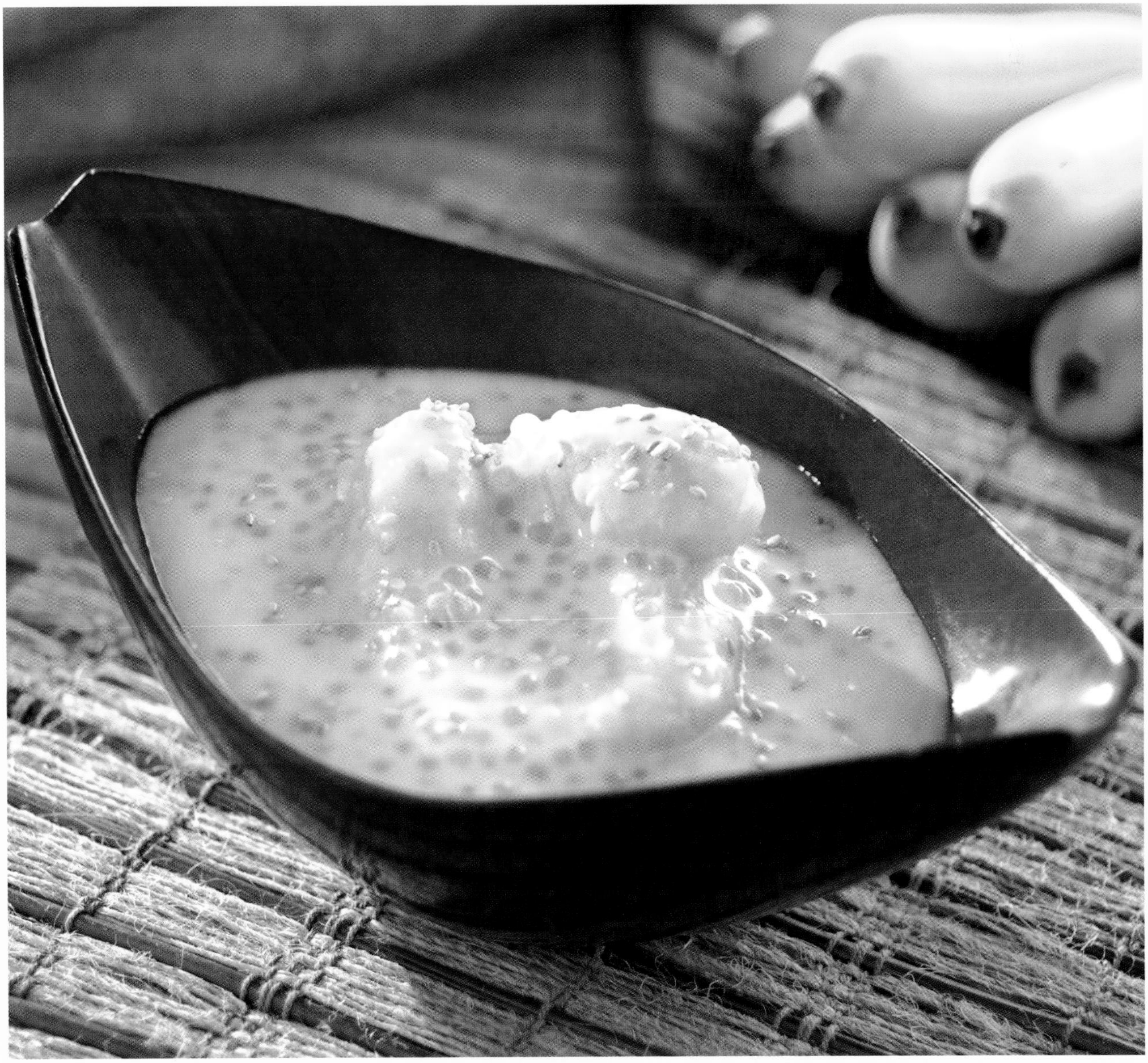

Avocado Smoothie
Sinh Tố Bơ

A cooling, soothing, creamy milkshake isn't the first thing that comes to mind when you think of an avocado—unless you're Vietnamese. In Vietnam the rich fruit is routinely pureed with milk, condensed milk and ice for a luxurious smoothie. *Sinh tố*, which translates as "alive elements" or "vitamins," illustrates how Vietnamese value food as nourishment. Feel free to use other fruits in place of the avocado, such as mangos, papayas or even more exotic fruits like jackfruit (or go wild with durian). Using frozen fruit works fine. I defrost them first to make sure the puree is not too thick.

Makes 4 to 6 servings

2   large Ripe avocado (Hass variety preferred),
         peeled and pitted
2   cup Milk
3/4 to 1 cup Sweetened condensed milk (to taste)
3   cups Crushed ice
pinch Kosher salt

1. Combine all ingredients in blender.
2. Begin on low speed and pulse the ingredient to achieve a smooth puree.
3. Be patient and stop blender, remove container from base and shake to remove air pocket.
4. Replace on blender base and puree again until velvety smooth, adding milk only if necessary to facilitate blending.

How and Why

1. Using crushed ice gives a more accurate measure and easier to puree. Air pockets between random sized ice cube leads to inconsistency, and the crushed ice breaks down more quickly in the blender.

2. Put the avocado in the bottom of the blender vase, so that it helps to start the puree. Puree this drink very smooth.

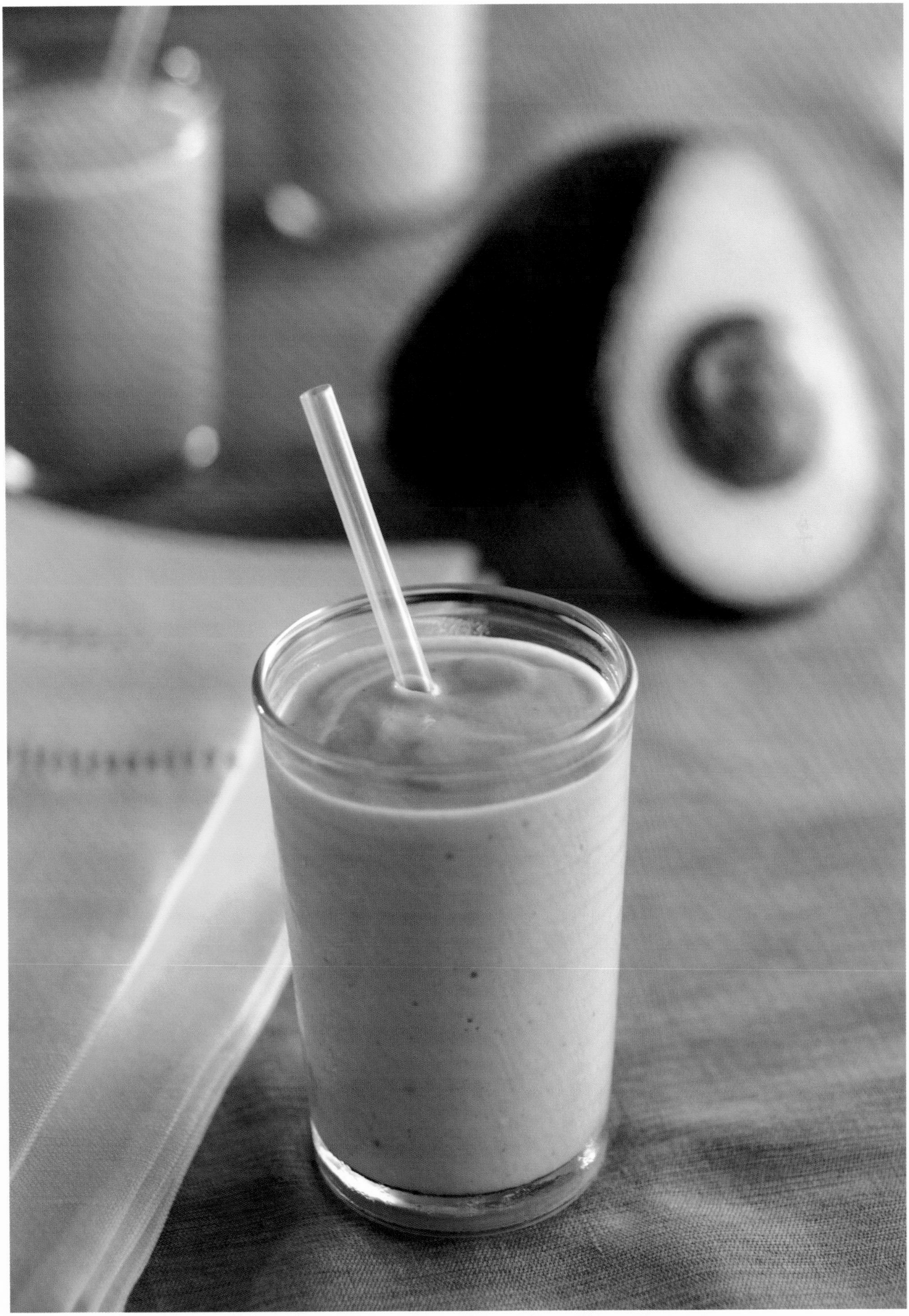

Vietnamese Coffee with Condensed Milk
Cà-Phê Sữa Nóng (hot)
Cà-Phê Sữa Đá (iced)

Imagine a triple shot of espresso, resting on top of a thick layer of sweetened condensed milk. Give this a stir, and the jet-black brew slowly gives way to a rich, chocolaty brown, bittersweet brew. Slowly sip the intense brew and begin to feel your palate and body come alive…this is Vietnamese coffee. *Trung Nguyến* is the most notable brand available in Vietnam (now sold in the U.S.), but many Vietnamese Americans prefer Café du Monde coffee from New Orleans, which has chicory root added to it. Either way, a dark roast and fine grind is essential to achieve the intensity for which Vietnamese coffee is famous.

There's a special device used for certain types of coffee. It's a single-serving metal brewer that perches right on the rim of the coffee cup. A screened brewing chamber holds the dark grounds. A twist of a screw in the center of the chamber releases the brewed coffee, allowing it to filter slowly through a screen at the bottom into the cup. If you ask for coffee with milk, *café sữa*, a thick layer of condensed milk will be spooned into the bottom of the cup before the brewing device is affixed. The slow rain of rich, intense coffee drips directly onto the condensed milk. They meld into a rich mixture. Once the coffee has all dripped through, a few strokes of your spoon stirs the sweet milk in, and a rich brown cup is ready for a slow sipping. Pour this concoction over ice for an iced coffee. Mmmmm, I'll be right back. I need to go make myself a cup right now.

Makes: 4 small but pungent servings (3 oz. / 88 ml. coffee each)

1/4 to 1/2 cup Canned condensed milk, room temperature
3/4 cup Finely ground coffee, French roast
    (espresso grind) (about 2 3/4 oz. / 75 g)
4 cups Boiling water

VIETNAMESE DRIP FILTER METHOD
1. Fill four coffee cups with condensed milk—1 to 2 tablespoons. in each. Place 3 tablespoons of ground coffee into each filter chamber of special Vietnamese coffee devices. Set the devices onto the cups.
2. Add 1/4 cup of boiling water; wait a moment while the grounds absorb some of the water. Top off with additional boiling water, close the covers of the devices, and steep two minutes.
3. Turn the central screws in the devices, releasing the coffee, and letting it slowly drip into cups.
4. Stir to incorporate milk. Enjoy hot, or pour over crushed ice.

BREW AND STRAIN METHOD
1. Bring water to boil and warm condensed milk to room temperature. Set coffee grounds in clean vessel, such as a tempered glass pitcher.
2. Pour water over grounds, cover and steep for 2 minutes. Strain through a very fine mesh strainer.
3. For hot coffee, divide milk among coffee cups. Top with brewed coffee. For iced coffee, combine coffee with milk, stir well to dissolve, cool to room temperature, and pour over crushed ice.

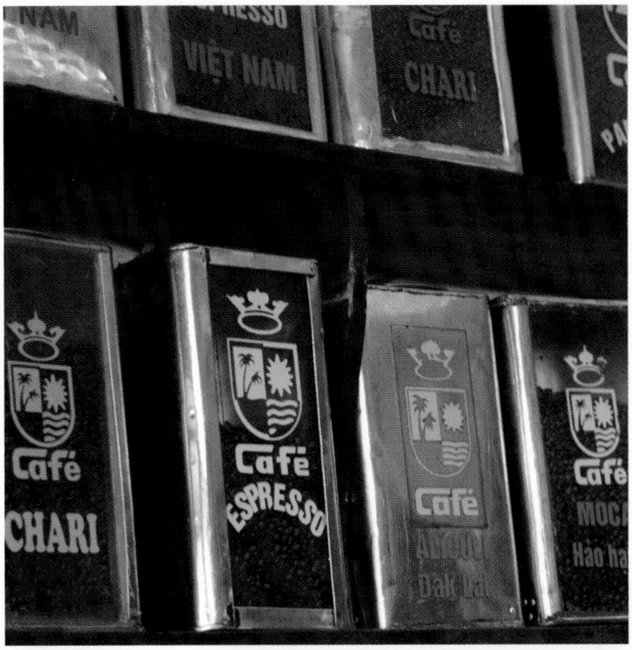
VIỆT NAM
CHARI
Café
CHARI
Café
ESPRESSO
Café
Café

How and Why

Dark roasted coffee that is finely grounds is essential for authentic flavor and color. The finer the grind the stronger the brew.

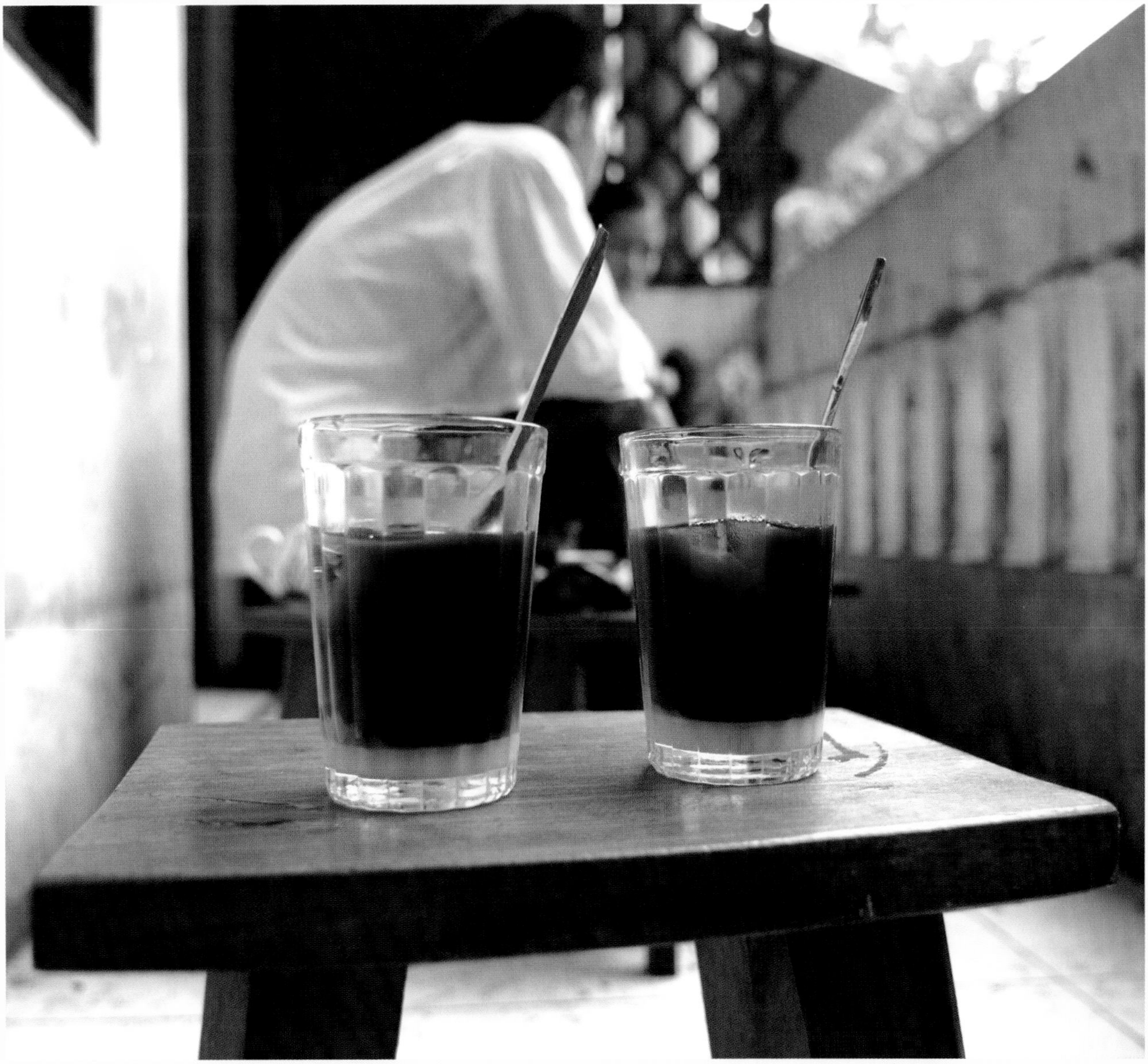

Malaysia & Singapore

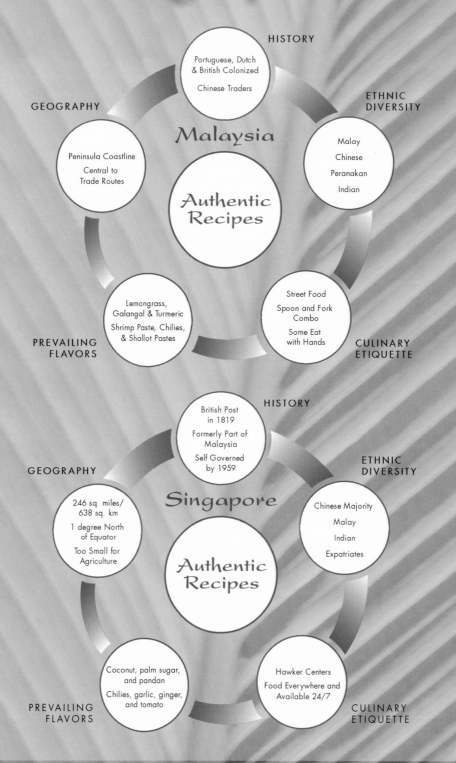

HISTORY
Portuguese, Dutch & British Colonized
Chinese Traders

GEOGRAPHY
Peninsula Coastline
Central to Trade Routes

Malaysia

Authentic Recipes

ETHNIC DIVERSITY
Malay
Chinese
Peranakan
Indian

PREVAILING FLAVORS
Lemongrass, Galangal & Turmeric
Shrimp Paste, Chilies, & Shallot Pastes

CULINARY ETIQUETTE
Street Food
Spoon and Fork Combo
Some Eat with Hands

HISTORY
British Post in 1819
Formerly Part of Malaysia
Self Governed by 1959

GEOGRAPHY
246 sq. miles/ 638 sq. km
1 degree North of Equator
Too Small for Agriculture

Singapore

Authentic Recipes

ETHNIC DIVERSITY
Chinese Majority
Malay
Indian
Expatriates

PREVAILING FLAVORS
Coconut, palm sugar, and pandan
Chilies, garlic, ginger, and tomato

CULINARY ETIQUETTE
Hawker Centers
Food Everywhere and Available 24/7

MALAYSIA
SINGAPORE

Melting Pot at the Crossroads of Asia

Malaysia and Singapore each possesses a culture that is uniquely its own; however, the foods from these neighboring culinary destinations are quite similar. This chapter will give insight into each culture separately, yet address their Culinary Identity™ together. Both made up of primarily Chinese, Malay, Nonya, and Indian ethnicities, these vibrant culinary cultures are a distinctive microcosm located in the heart of Southeast Asia.

Fortunately for travelers, English is spoken much more commonly in Malaysia and Singapore than in Thailand and Vietnam. English is Singapore's national language. Singapore's population is a colorful mixture of 74 percent Chinese, 14 percent Malay, and 8 percent Indian. The remaining residents include other races such as Eurasian, Indonesian, Filipino, and many expatriates. Malaysian ethnic diversity is more evenly distributed, with three major ethnic groups making up the majority of the population—Malays, 53 percent; Chinese, 32 percent; and the Indians, 10 percent. The remaining 5 percent are made up of the Orang Asli, or Original People, and hundreds of other tribes living mainly in East Malaysia.

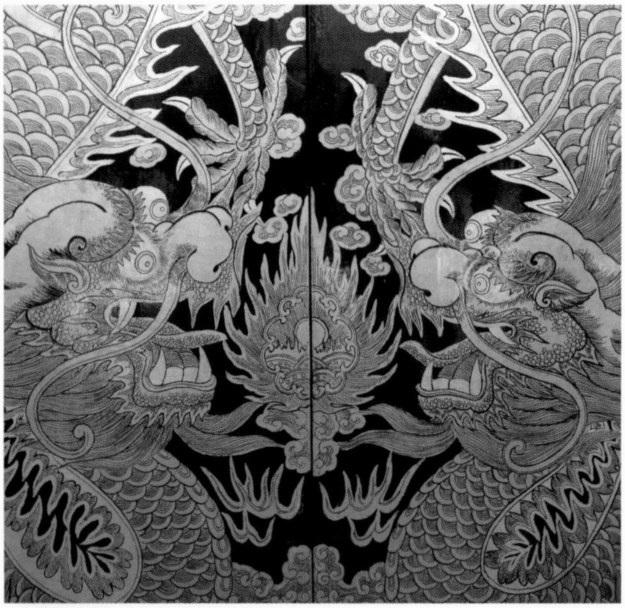

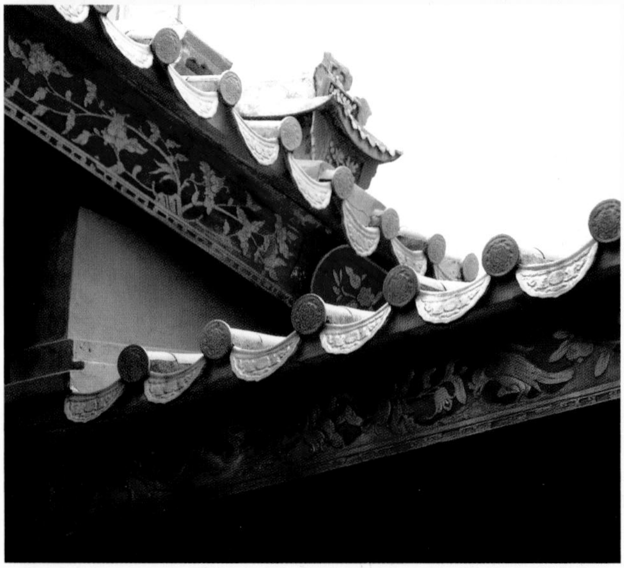

One peculiar phenomenon I see here is the frequent classification of cuisine and recipes by dialect or language. Normally foods are grouped by geographic origin or ethnic group. Chinese dialects include Hokkien, Hakka, Teochew, Cantonese, and Mandarin. They are associated with entire styles of Chinese cuisine, but here it's a geographic relationship, since most Hokkien people have origins in the Fujian Province, and Cantonese are from the Guangdong Province. Mandarin is spoken across China. Some culinarians use Mandarin to designate northern food, Cantonese for southern food, and subcategorize regions such as Shanghainese, Szechwan, and cuisine of Beijing.

Singapore may be a small island dwarfed by the long Malaysian peninsula and Eastern Island, but its culinary culture is huge. When it comes right down to it, many of the same dishes are available in both Malaysia and Singapore. Singaporeans may have invented the incredible dish Chili Crabs (pg. 314), but this saucy seafood excellence is also found in restaurants in Malaysia. Some dishes may have the same name in each country but reveal themselves differently. Such is the case with Hokkien Mee (pg. 338). The version most would call "Kuala Lumpur Style" from Malaysia involves extra-thick wheat noodles in a dark soy gravy with pork cracklings, yet order Hokkien Mee in Singapore and the cook will fire up the wok and stir-fry thinner egg noodles in a drier style with no dark soy sauce. Countless hours have been spent debating whose

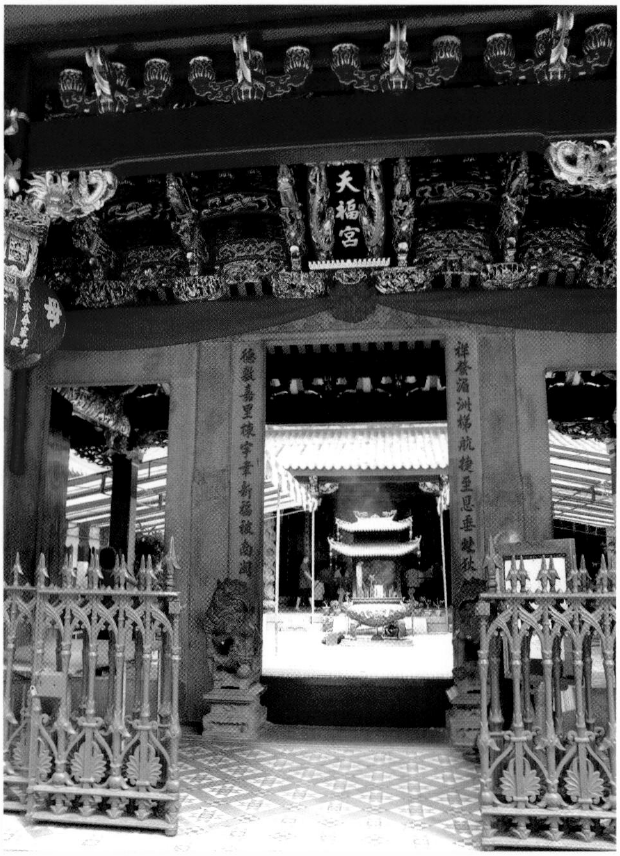
天福宮

cooks and chefs reign supreme. This can't be answered, but I am anxious to keep traveling through these sibling lands, discovering the people, places, and food they celebrate and argue over.

I've journeyed through Malaysia and Singapore's culinary landscape for nearly twenty years and continue to taste dishes I have not seen before. Some are new inventions, but many are from a traditional repertoire that is so vast that it is a never-ending quest to experience the flavors. So many ethnicities within the population, other welcomed outside influences, available raw ingredients, and locally crafted food products encourage a constant evolution of this food culture. Come take a journey with me through this chapter—a snapshot of history and the current state of culinary affairs—and discover what makes these two countries serious contenders in the battle for the best food on earth.

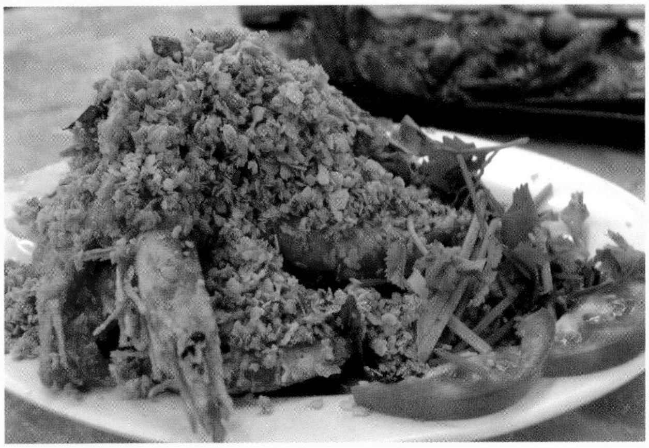

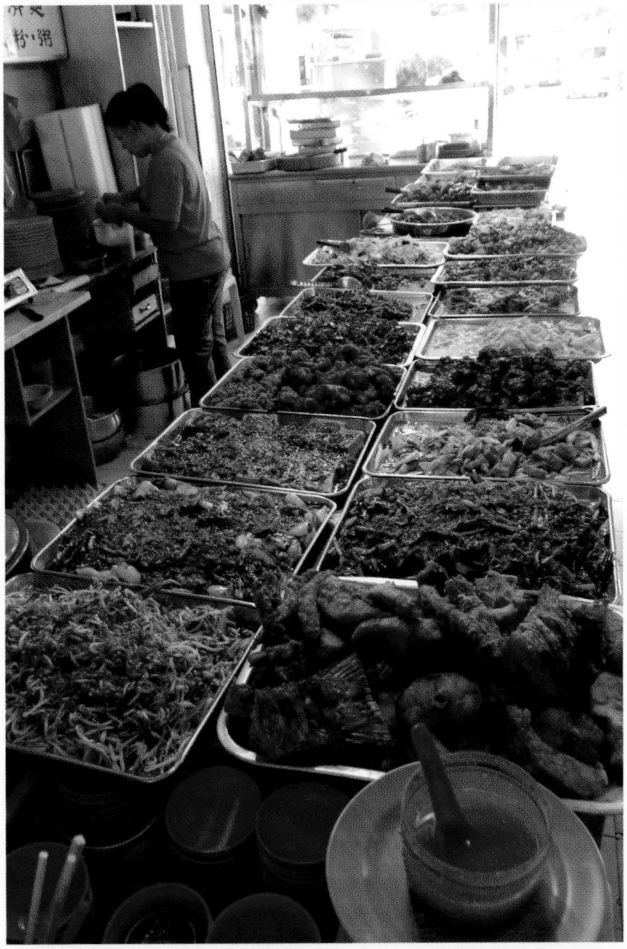

Hawker Centers

At every waking hour, food awaits. Often grouped in clusters, food stalls are commonplace in Southeast Asia. You may find a culinary treasure being offered on a street corner, down an alley, or on a village road. But it is when you gather from five to seventy-five stalls in one location that a "Hawker Center" is born. These food courts of Malaysia and Singapore are culinary meccas to locals and travelers alike.

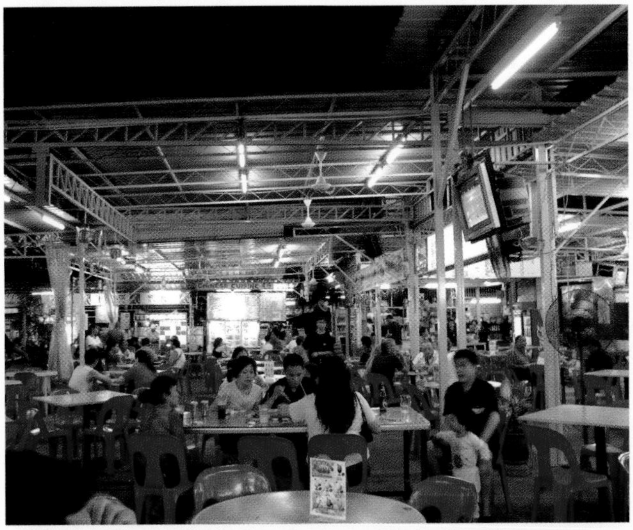

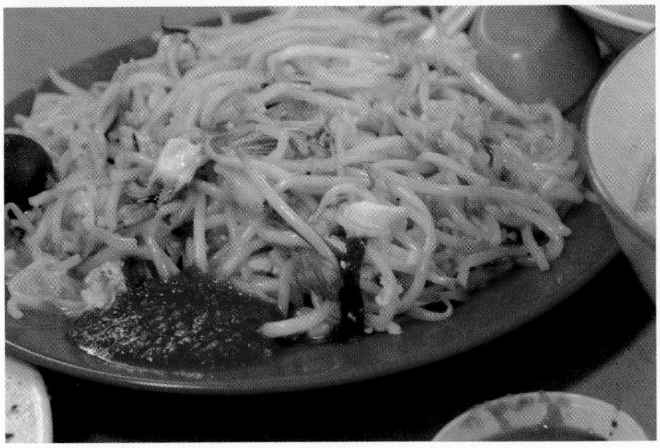

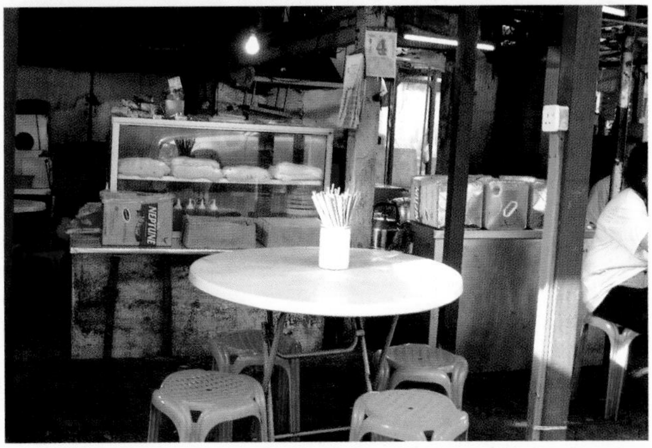

Most vendors have been cooking the same dish or few dishes every day for years. They're masters of their craft! Often a stall's specialty has been passed down from generation to generation. Each spends a whole career focused on preparing a regionally unique offering, building and maintaining that all-important reputation. She or he may have chosen Chinese-inspired Char Kway Teow (wok-charred rice noodles with green onions and local clams) (pg. 336), while others have focused on Malay Nasi Lemak (coconut rice with curries, cucumbers and crisp anchovies) (pg. 330), or possibly Indian Roti Canai (crispy flat bread paired with curry or dhal) (pg. 286). Even chicken wings are given the attention that they deserve; here they slowly roast them over a coal fire. A few Malaysian ringgit, less than one U.S. dollar, can get you a meal.

As impressive as the foods are, so are the logistics that make them possible. You enter the culinary arena in search of that certain dish you crave at the moment. You order your food and then sit on a flimsy plastic stool and wait at a rickety table nearby. Within minutes your food arrives—no receipt or pager needed. At your seat, your drink order will be solicited. Each center has at least one beverage hawker. They come to your table, take the drink order, and bring your selection back to you. The beverage menu invariably includes fresh fruit juices, beer, soda, shaved ice specialties, tea, and coffee.

Although clearly not a beverage, shaved ice is a category of refreshments unto itself. Dissimilar to the syrup-soaked shaved ice of Hawaii, these concoctions usually marry salty and sweet items all in one bowl. *Cendol,* a Malaysian specialty, begins with short and squiggly green pea noodles infused with pandan leaf in the bottom of a bowl. Cooked red beans are then added and topped with ice shaved as fine as snow. The layered mixture is then doused with thin coconut milk and drizzled with dark brown palm sugar syrup.

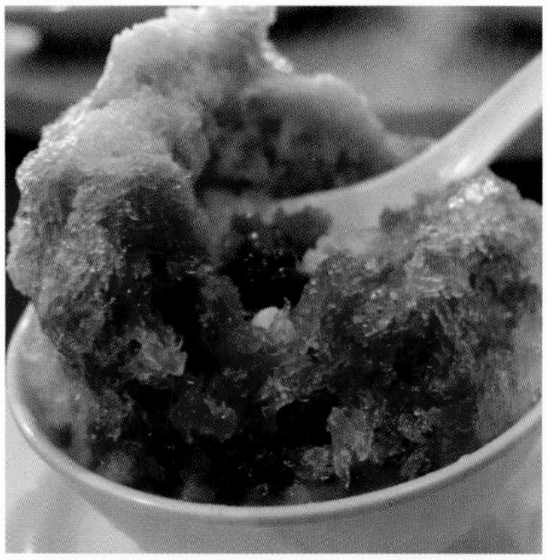

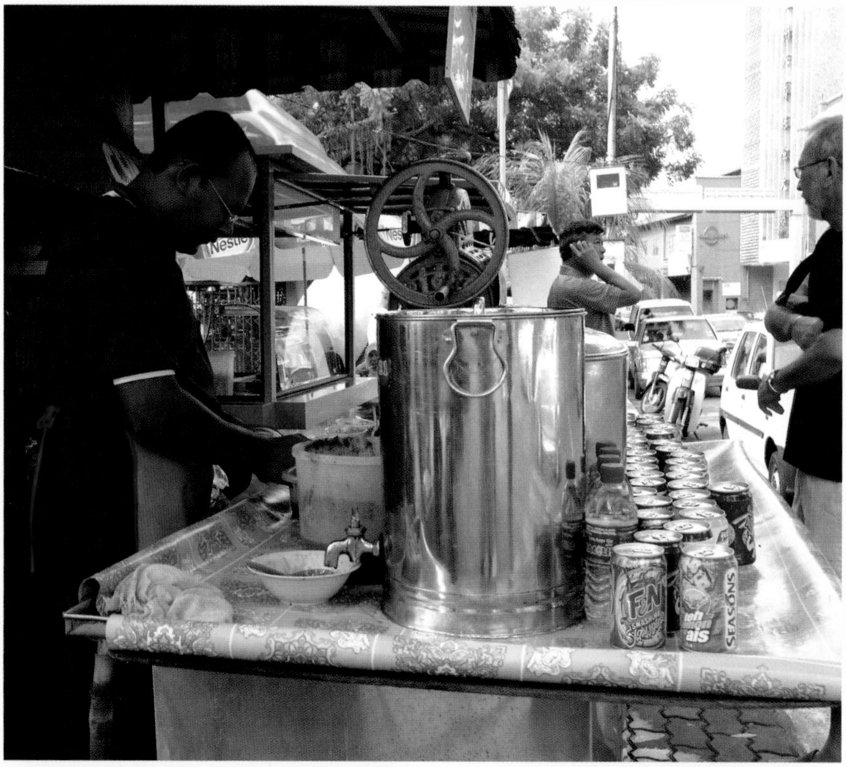
SEASONS

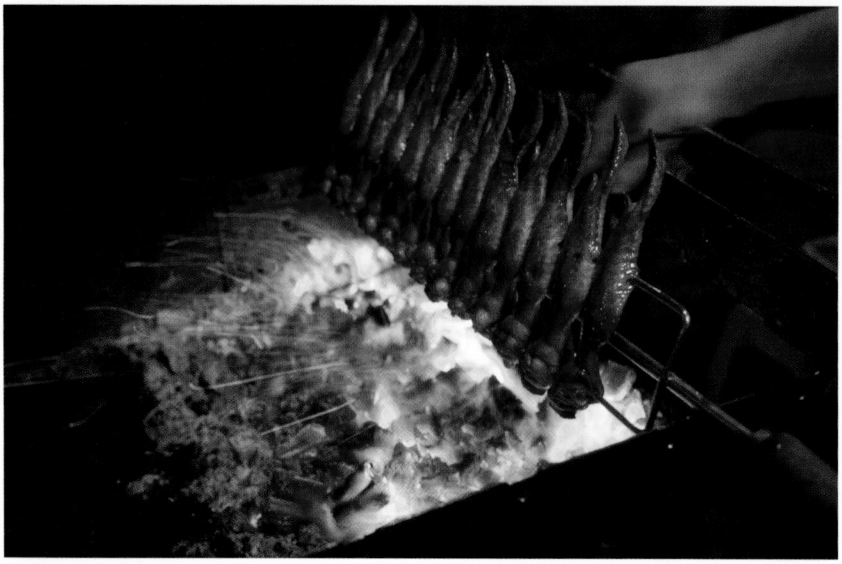

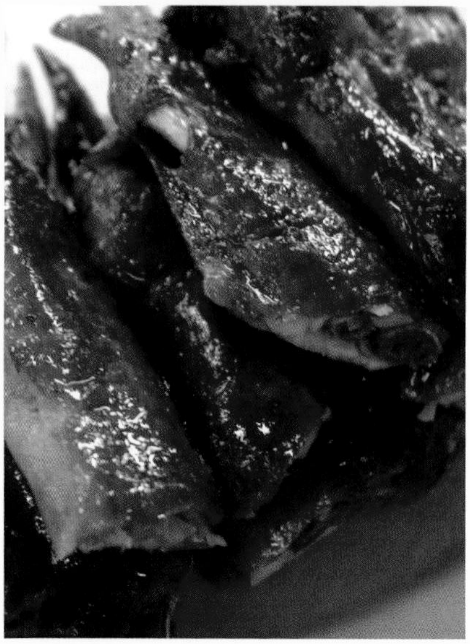

Malaysia

This is where my love affair with the foods of Asia began. Twenty years ago when I arrived in Malaysia, a food-focused multicultural country, I immediately knew I was in the right place. Even before we left the airport my Malaysian-born wife, Esther, and her brother, Glenn, began to plot where we were going to eat before heading to their mom's home. In Malaysia, where food is so central to their lives, breakfast discussions often center around what will be eaten for lunch or dinner. Malaysia has four major distinct ethnic groups—Malays, Chinese, Nonya, and Indians. The only challenging aspect is deciding what and where to eat. Although each group has retained its heritage, and traditional foods from each culture are available, some of the most memorable dishes are those that blend several of the cultures onto one plate.

The diversity of Malaysia is not only within the people. Gaze out the window of a chic café located on the top floor of a mega-mall that is selling the latest electronic gadgetry, and you are likely to see a rural neighborhood with wooden homes still built on stilts. Some trips I fly right into Kuala Lumpur's new airport. It's an hour's drive from the city center. Not for long, though. The government knows

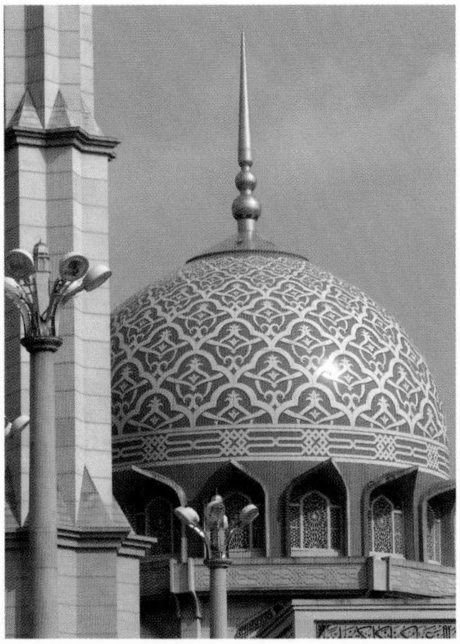

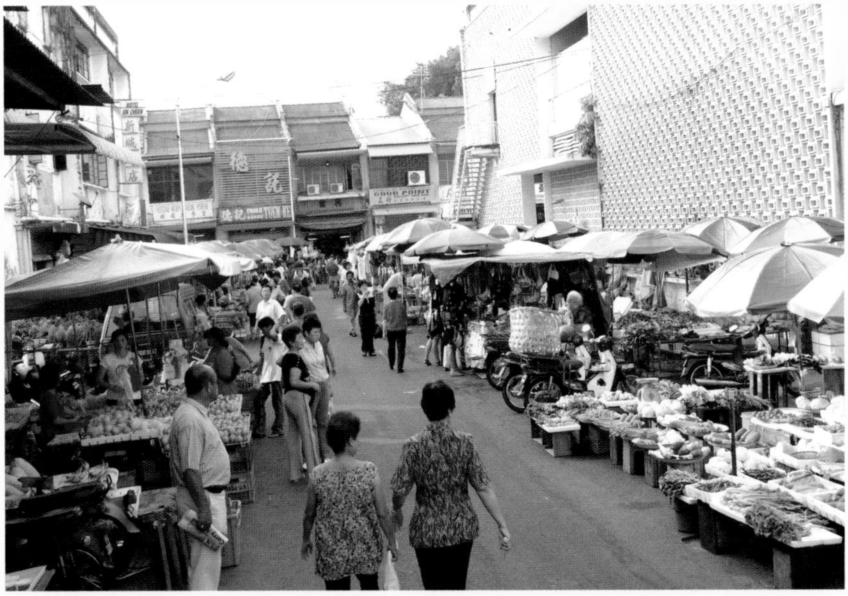

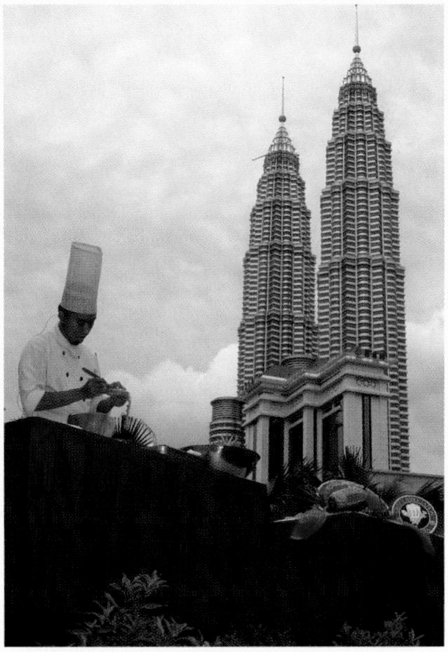

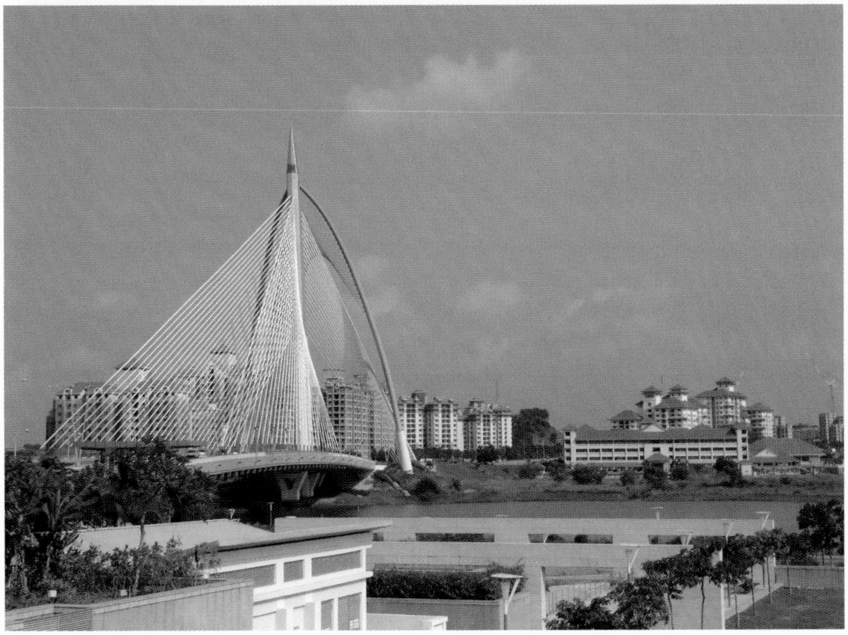

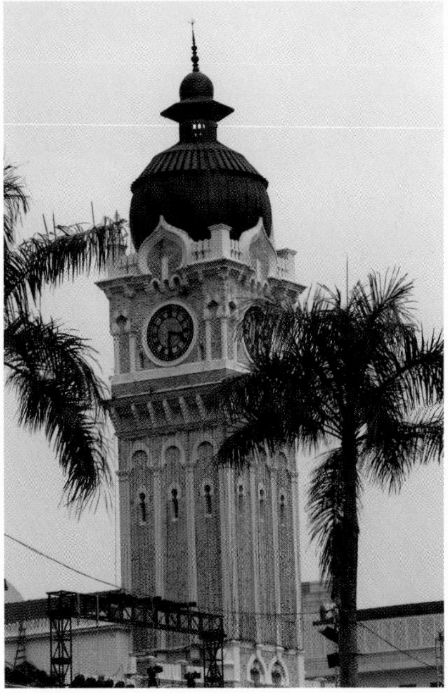

the city is rapidly expanding to fill in the tropical landscape that is now covered with palm rubber trees for oil and rubber production. This rapidly developing country is likely to be one of Southeast Asia's prominent economic powers in the next century.

Muslims refrain from eating pork. How they resist this succulent pig I will never know, yet I know that the Chinese devotion to the famed hog is still clearly evident in mostly Muslim Malaysia. Usually when going out for dim sum, you cannot avoid it, along with the copious use of shrimp—often in tandem. One dining experience at the Mandarin Oriental Hotel in Kuala Lumpur of drinking tea with these small bites changed the way I felt about halal food (conforming to Muslim law). The hotel, as many do, abided by the Islamic laws and served no pork. Led by my friend Chef Bong, the Chinese Executive Chef, they make a mind-blowing offering of dim sum without pork? No way? Yes way…big time. It was delicious!

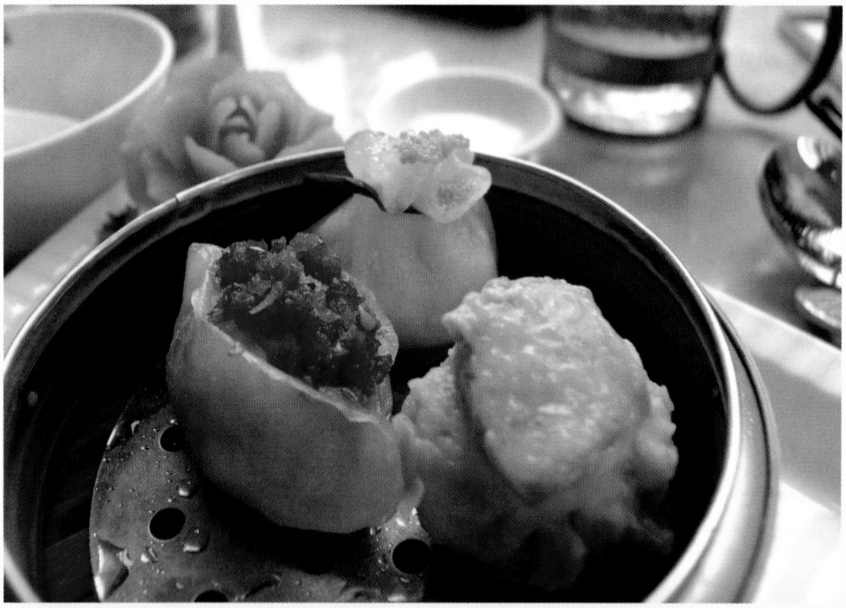

Geography

Malaysia's central location in Southeast Asia has made it a land of many cultures. Merchants and travelers from China, the Subcontinent, and Europe left their mark on Malaysia as they journeyed through this bustling port. Some stayed to farm the fertile land or to mine it for minerals.

Peninsular West Malaysia stretches down from southern Thailand into the South China Sea to the small island nation of Singapore. East Malaysia, made up of two island states, is four hundred miles east across the South China Sea sharing the island of Borneo with Brunei and Indonesia. These fertile Spice Islands, sometimes

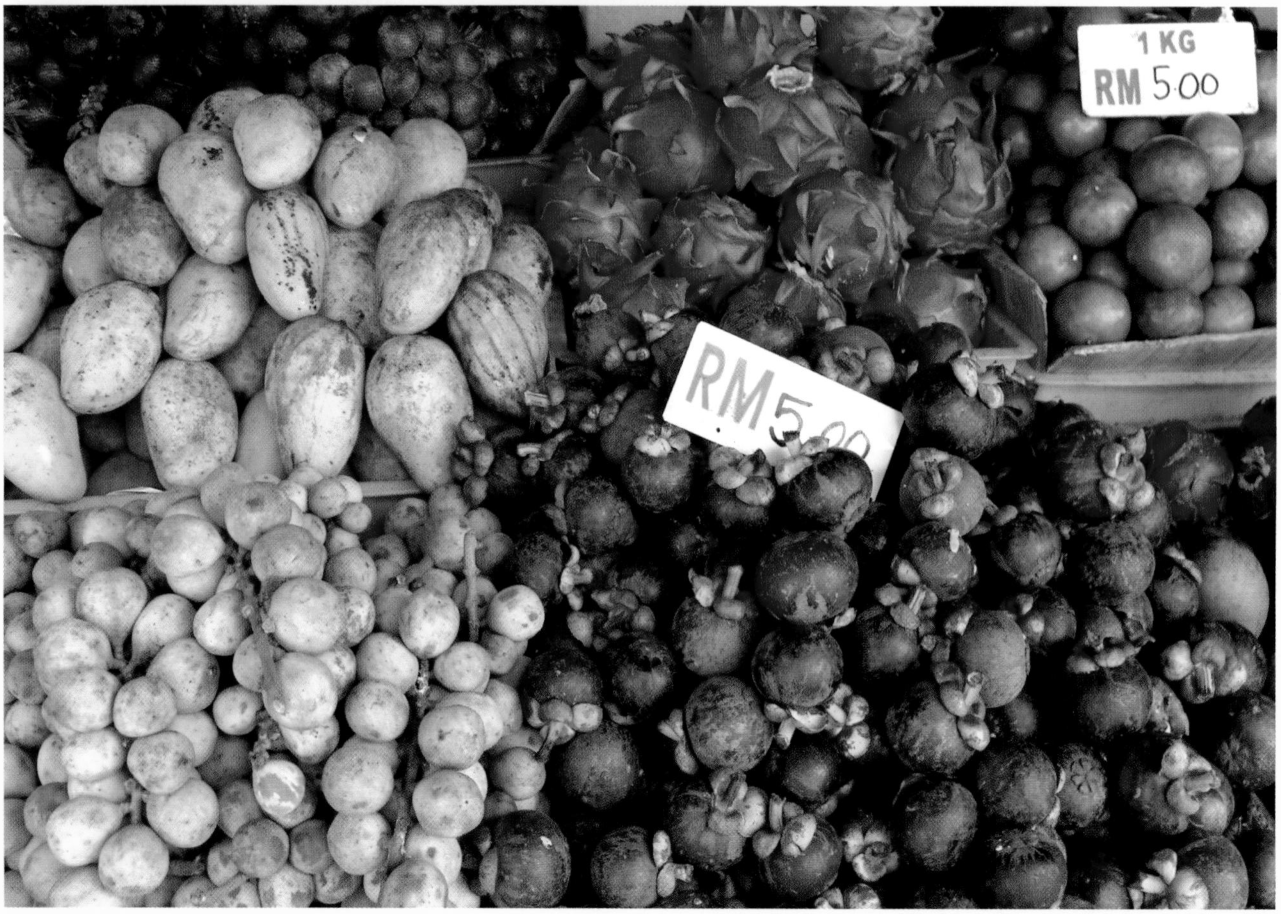
1 KG
RM 5.00
RM5.00

referred to as the Moluccas, are the origin of several indigenous aromatic spices: clove buds extend as unopened flowers on trees, and the yellow fruit of the nutmeg tree drops its hard seed covered with lacy mace (which is also used as a spice).

Many of the Malaysian states boast their own regional foods. The residents of Penang, the gastronomically rich island, are proud of their Penang *Laksa*, a hot-and-sour soup. On the way from Penang to the Malaysian capital city of Kuala Lumpur, I go out of my way to stop in the town of Ipoh, in the Perak state, to savor that region's classic rice noodle dish, *Ipoh sar hor fun* (pg. 306). Perak's hard water (high in salt and alkali) produces the most silky smooth rice noodles you will ever sample. These silky noodles bathe luxuriously in a light chicken broth with shredded chicken and scallions. A large platter of Ipoh stir-fried bean sprouts is a traditional accompaniment and should be crunched on intermittently. These countries have been passageways to the west and centers of spice production and trade in Southeast Asia for centuries. The tropical location, with a year-round average temperature of 82°F (28°C), provides an ideal growing climate for rice, coconuts, various palms, sugar cane, chilies, tamarind, and many unique fruits.

Rice is grown throughout the country and takes many different forms in Malaysian cuisine; it's steamed, fried, ground into flour, and often transformed into noodles. Sugar cane is also prevalent. The majority is processed into granulated sugar, but travelers to the region always fondly remember the joy of freshly squeezed cane juice sold at roadside stands throughout the peninsula. At these stands, the outer layer of the cane is removed by the fastidious vendors, and then the stalk is pressed through a pair of steel rollers, squeezing out a delicate, sweet, light green nectar.

Malaysia's expansive coastline yields a bounty of seafood. Fish, squid, crab, clams, and shrimp are the primary catches, but many other delicacies such as sea cucumber find their way to market. Much of the ocean harvest is dried and fermented for future use. As in most regions, the drying process was originally developed as a means of preservation, but continues today for reasons of culinary preference. Dried fish tastes delicious, and fermented shrimp paste lays an essential foundation flavor. And its preservative function still has relevance. Refrigeration is common in most modern homes, but not ubiquitous in villages across the country.

Ethnic Diversity

The spice trade brought Chinese people to Malaysia in search of fortunes. The British transported many Southern Indians to be laborers for tin mining and rubber planting. The indigenous Malays adopted much of the culture and cuisine from these newcomers. As the three major ethnic groups (Malay, Chinese, and Indian) converged, new ethnic identities were formed. The Straits Chinese, also known as the Peranakan, are made up of the Chinese men who took Malay wives when they came from China. These marriages flourished during colonial times in Malaysia. The men are referred to as the Babas and the women as Nyonyas. These families developed a sophisticated culture and cuisine. "Nyonya-ware" ceramics made in southern Chinese provinces of Jiangxi and Guangdong especially for the Straits Chinese are colorful remnants of early Peranakan culture. Pastel greens, dark blues, sun-bright yellows, and pinks are combined to form unique, ornately patterned Chinese-style plates, vases, and dishes.

The ingredients, cooking techniques, and culture that the Indians and Chinese brought with them from their homelands gave birth to new regional dishes, combining flavors to produce something uniquely Malaysian. Inexpensive, authentic vendor stalls often produce the best dishes. At the roadside, corner market, or shopping center, these hawkers are Malays, Chinese, and Indians working side by side.

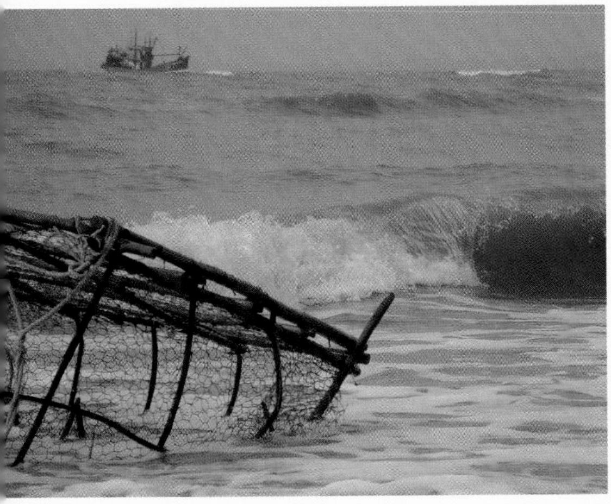

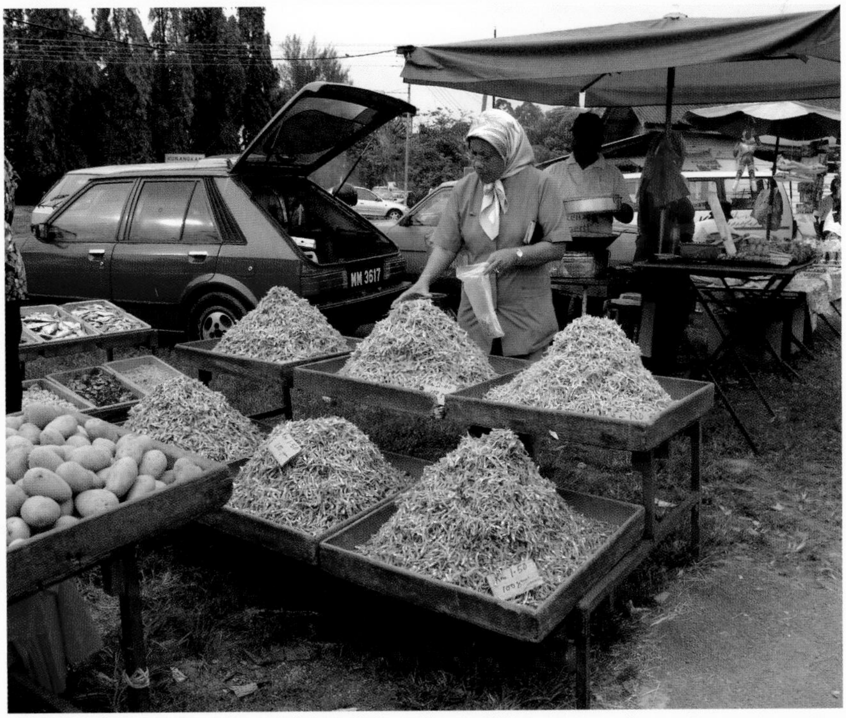
MM 3617

Singapore

Singapore has a well-deserved reputation for some of the best "food courts" in Asia. These indoor hawker markets bear little relation to the Western concept of food courts, which involve mostly nationwide fast-food outlets. The Singaporeans have been successful at bringing most of the independent hawkers from the streets and organizing them into more sanitary environments while maintaining the authentic characteristics of street food. Each stall still has a specialty that its owners have mastered. The hawker centers have also evolved into syndicated business ventures at über-chic malls like Vivo City's Food Republic.

Singaporeans' other national pastime is shopping. There are countless shopping centers generously appointed with serious restaurants, food courts, and gourmet supermarkets. It seems everyone in this country is a food fanatic and ready to spend Singaporean dollars for food in an instant. You can randomly ask a person for food insight and get a thoughtful response. Ask anyone, anywhere, where to find a good local shop serving the de facto national dish of fried crabs in a sweet spicy chili-tomato gravy, Singapore Chili Crab (pg. 314); they will politely claim to know who makes the best and where to try it. They will probably take the time to give you directions for how to get there. Singaporeans are friendly people with a strong national spirit and sincere desire to be hospitable, especially to foreigners.

Ethnic enclaves still exist. Some days I meander through the twisting aromatic alleys of Little India, gazing at ornate temples that tower above small shops selling densely sweet Indian treats. I stop on the edge of Little India at the two-story Tekka Centre. My first destination is usually a place serving *roti pratha,* a buttery, multilayered, flaky flatbread usually served with chicken coconut curry (pg. 290). As I peel back layer after layer of the roti, wiping up rich coconut gravy with the chewy bread, I watch the cast of characters waiting in the never-ending line for Biryani.

When I am in the mood for Hainanese Chicken Rice (poached chicken with fragrant rice and gingered chili sauce), I pay a visit to Maxwell Food Court, which makes the version I include on page 318. Afterward, I wander through Chinatown among the ornately decorated

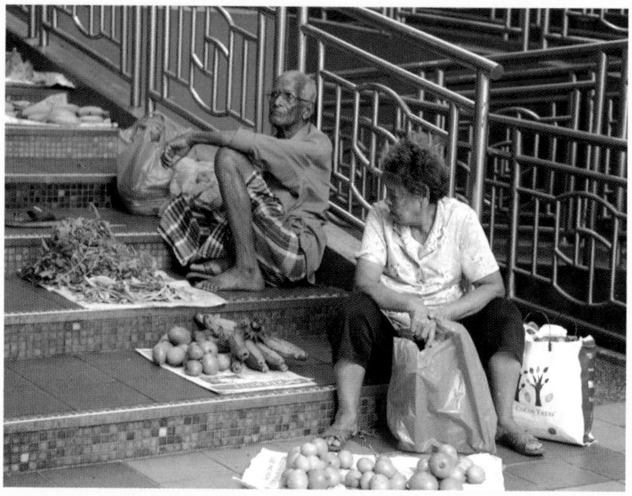

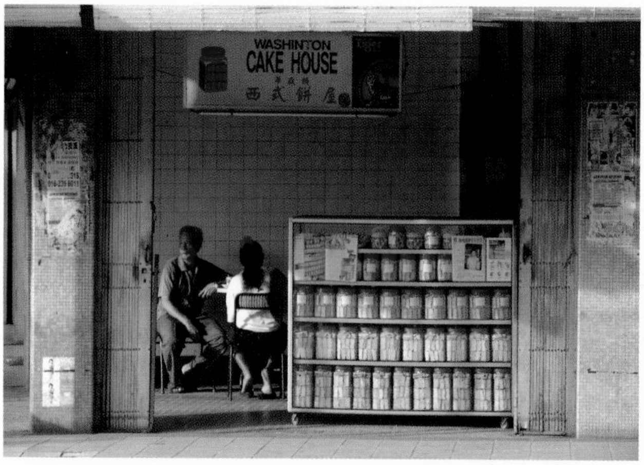
WASHINTON
CAKE HOUSE
西式餅屋

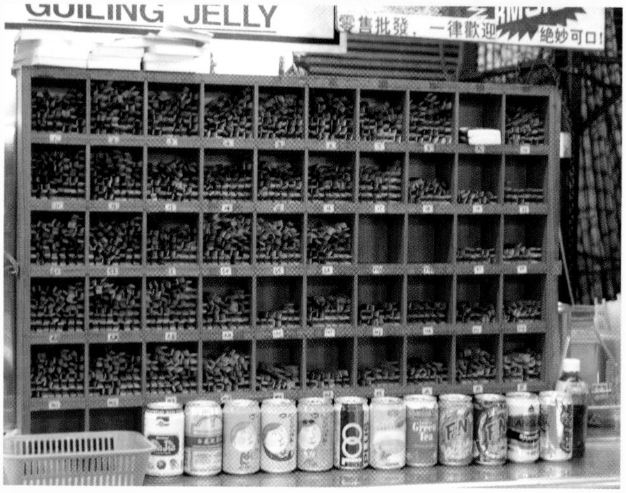
JELLY
零售批發，一律歡迎
絕妙可口!

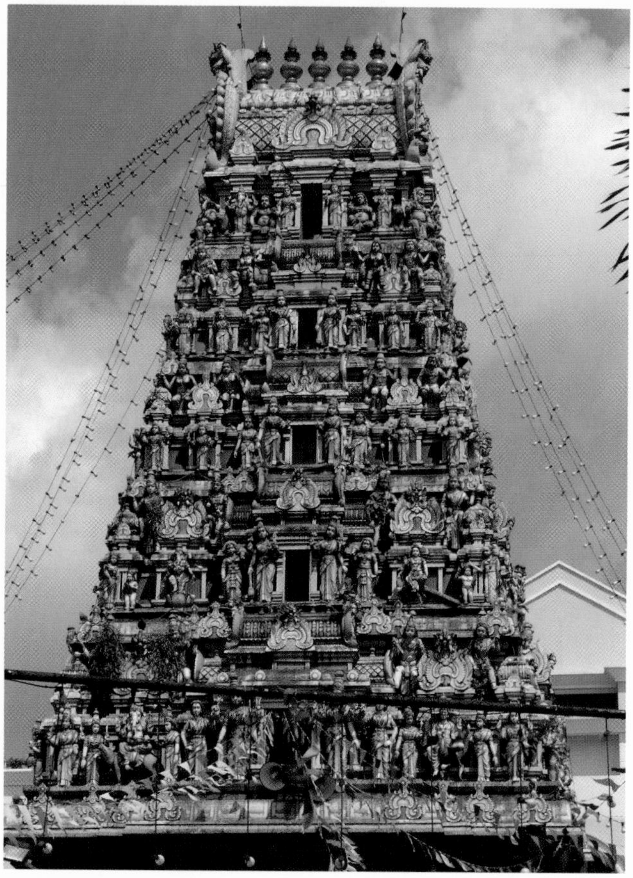

buildings with glowing red lanterns. Other times I feel the need to trace the ethnic origin of the Malay folks and explore the Kampong Glam, aka the Arab District. There I'll sample some Nonya cakes such as one of my favorites, the small spheres of coconut-crusted molten palm sugar dumplings, *Ondeh Ondeh* (pg. 350). If you want to do some serious damage on your credit cards, head to Orchard Road, which rivals the shopping opportunities of New York City's Fifth Avenue.

Geography

A modest 246 square miles (646 square kilometers) in total landmass, Singapore is made up of one main island and fifty-eight much smaller islands, all located only one degree north of the equator. Its tropical hot and humid climate year round is compensated for with highly air conditioned malls, office buildings, and homes. It may be fertile land, but lack of space makes agriculture unfeasible. Most raw ingredients are brought in from Malaysia, Indonesia, and elsewhere in the region. The long-established Port of Singapore is one of the busiest harbors in the world, so much so that their vast experience has led them to manage other ports around the globe. Look out into the harbor from one of the skyline's many luxury hotels, and you will see hundred of ships docked, coming, and going.

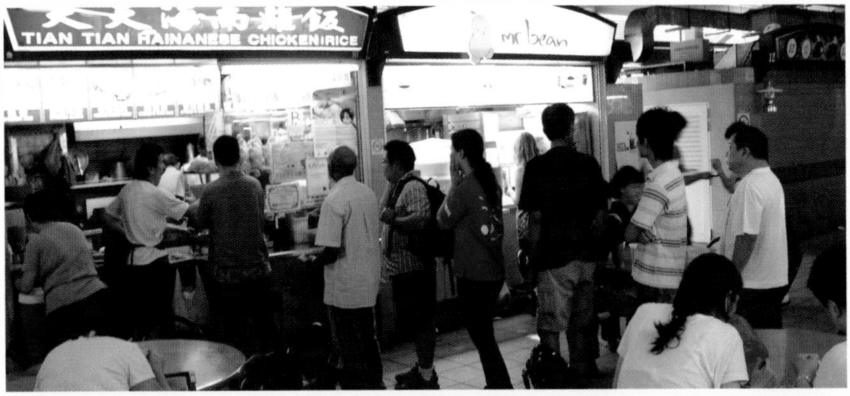
TIAN TIAN HAINANESE CHICKEN RICE
mr bean

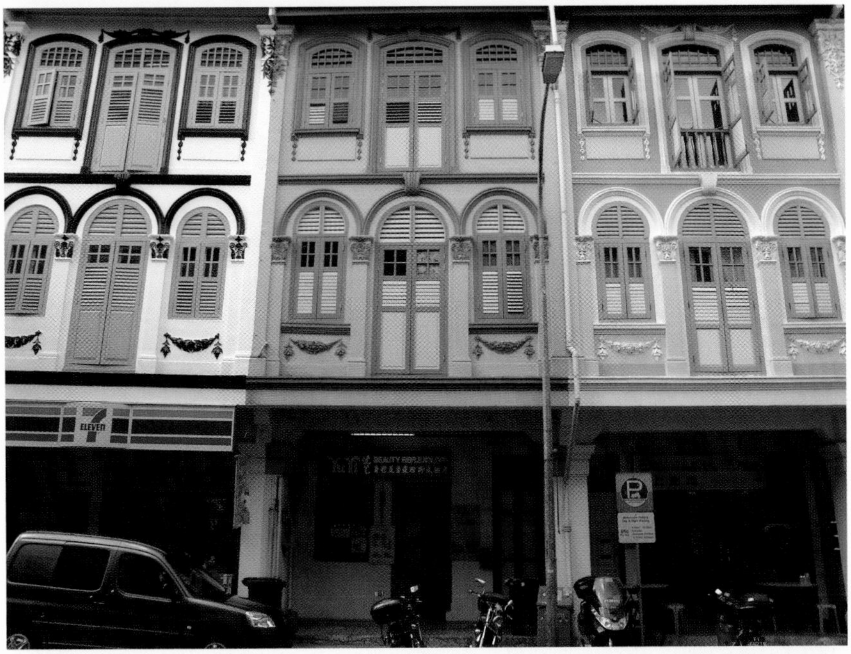
ELEVEN

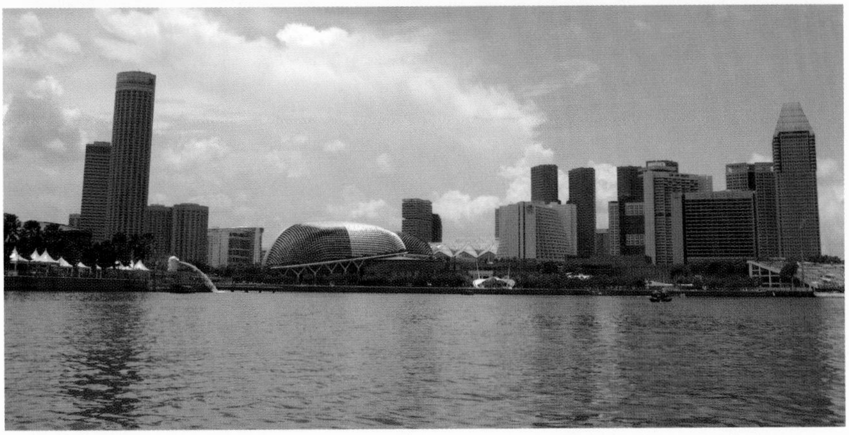

Ethnic Diversity

Ethnically Malaysia and Singapore are made up of the same stock, but the proportions are very different. While Malaysia still retains a high percentage of ethnic Malays (about half of the population), ethnic Chinese dominate Singapore, representing nearly three-quarters of the population there. The rest consists of Malays (about 14 percent), Indians (about 9 percent), and a small minority of Eurasians and Arabs. Four main languages are spoken in Singapore: English, Mandarin Chinese, Malay, and Tamil. Singaporean English is unique. To the casual ear it may sound like standard English, but pay attention and you will hear the fascinating unique blend known as "Singlish," which is an enticing mixture of an English accent, Chinese tonal clarity, and Malay slang.

Many of the Chinese immigrants came here from the southern regions of China. Most read and write one written language—Mandarin or Cantonese—but communicate verbally in two or three dialects. Hokkien is the most commonly spoken dialect (the main Chinese spoken language). As in Malaysia, Peranakan culture (Their cuisine is referred to as Nonya.) evolved when Chinese immigrant traders married local Malay women. This provided for a wonderful melding of cuisines.

The Parallel Cuisines of Malaysia and Singapore

Very different cultures, yet stunningly similar food offerings, characterize Malaysia and Singapore. The pantry that they draw upon for ingredients is primarily the same. The cooking techniques used vary in the same way as they do from region to region within the states of Malaysia, and foods shared by the two countries are presented similarly in both places. One major difference, though, is that pork is much more prevalent in Singapore, since its majority ethnic Chinese population does not follow the Muslim religion prevalent in Malaysia.

Prevailing Flavors

Flavor Foundation

Recurring ingredients and techniques give a snapshot of Malaysian flavor. Ethnic Chinese there combine garlic, pork, and thick soy sauce and then elevate these flavors in the inferno of the wok for succulent noodle dishes like *Char Kway Teow* (pg. 336) and *Hokkien Fried Mee* (pg. 338). Lemongrass, turmeric, galangal, garlic, and shallot converge in the spice mixture for beef *rendang*, (pg. 334) chicken *satay* (pg. 310), and *Otak Otak*, among other dishes common to Singapore and Malaysia. Classic curries are likewise built, with the addition of brilliant yellow turmeric and rich coconut milk.

Malay Sweets

Though desserts are not common in Malaysia, there are sweets made out of rice flour, coconut milk, palm sugar, and other flavorings. They are called *kueh*. These local cakes are steamed to create a type of sweet rice pastry eaten as a midday snack. Most *kueh* are steamed, though some are cooked on thin waffle irons, and others are deep-fried. Palm sugar (called gula melacca or melaka), coconut milk, and bananas are some flavorings used in *kueh*. Leaves from the pandanus plant (sometimes referred to as screw-pine) perfume and tint green versions of *kueh*. In lieu of rice flour, which is most common, Malays also make *kueh* with glutinious rice flour, tapioca starch, and sweet potato starch. They seldom use wheat flour.

A plate of shaved ice from a café or street food vendor counters the tropical heat in Malaysia and Singapore. Toppings for this sweet repast include sugar-stewed red beans, shredded coconut, jackfruit, opaque black cubes of honeyed agar-agar (seaweed gelatin), sweet creamed corn, and pearls of sago tapioca. Loving spoonfuls of dark amber palm sugar syrup, coconut milk, or condensed milk are poured over the shaved ice to complete the luscious scene. Pandanus leaves often lend their brilliant green color and flavor to mung bean noodles, as in the Cendol. This shaved ice concoction cools the soul on a hot tropical day: a bowl is filled with some of the tender squiggly noodles and cooked sweet adzuki beans, then topped with shaved ice, doused with thick fresh coconut milk, and drizzled with deep-brown palm sugar syrup.

Otak

280

LAKSA

What's *laksa?* I feel that the term is thrown around too loosely. At its most basic, it's one of a number of noodle soup dishes. I believe that there are three types of true laksa: asam laksa, laksa lamak, and katong laksa.

Katong

Asam laksa, or "sour laksa," is a pungent fish broth with fermented shrimp paste. It's made sour by the addition of locally grown tamarind fruit pulp and pineapple. Lemongrass, galangal, shallots, and red chilies are the primary aromatics in the spice paste that forms the broth's flavor complexity. The spices are fried to release their inner essences, and then the cooked paste is combined with a strong fish broth. In the finished soup, thick rice noodles float in the broth, garnished with chopped laksa leaves, pineapple shards, shredded mint, ginger flowers, and chili slices.

The most popular, my favorite, and the recipe included in this book is *laksa lamak*, or more commonly called curry laksa (pg. 302), a light, creamy, coconut lemongrass broth garnished with noodles. The coconut milk is simmered with an aromatic spice mixture to create a yellow, turmeric-tinted broth that coats resilient noodles. Fresh rice vermicelli and/or wheat-based egg noodles are most common, yet some cooks prefer fresh flat rice noodles. Pillows of deep-fried tofu (pg. 75) unleash a stream of spicy soup across the palate with every bite. The noodle soup is garnished with sliced fish cake, hard-boiled egg, shrimp, cockles (similar to tiny clams), and chopped laksa leaves. Small limes and a dish of chili sambal are served on the side, allowing guests to customize the flavor to their liking.

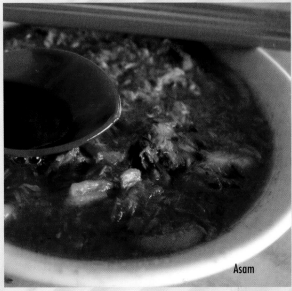
Asam

Singaporean *katong laksa* is very similar to laksa lemak, but is made with evaporated milk and eaten solely with spoon. The noodles are chopped, and its hearty ingredients are so substantial that chopsticks aren't required. This may be Singapore's favorite variety.

Broths vary, with offshoots like *Sarawak* laksa, *Johor* laksa, and *Penang* laksa to name a few. The noodles are also often a matter of personal preference. But one thing that all these variations have in common is the ever-present laksa leaf (pg. 38), also known as Vietnamese coriander or *rau ram*. Its pungent aroma and slightly sour taste are essential parts of the package.

Lamak

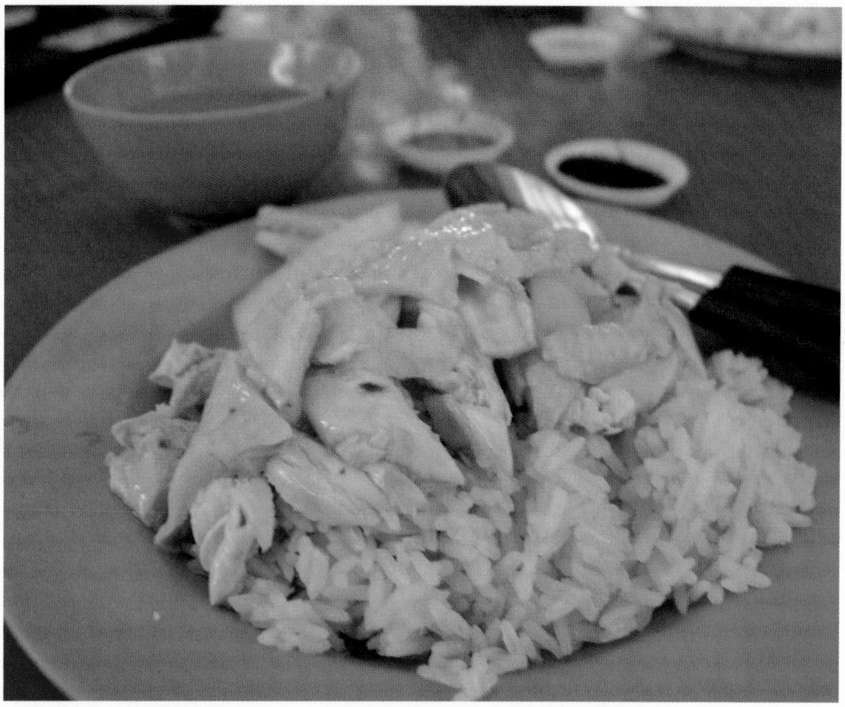

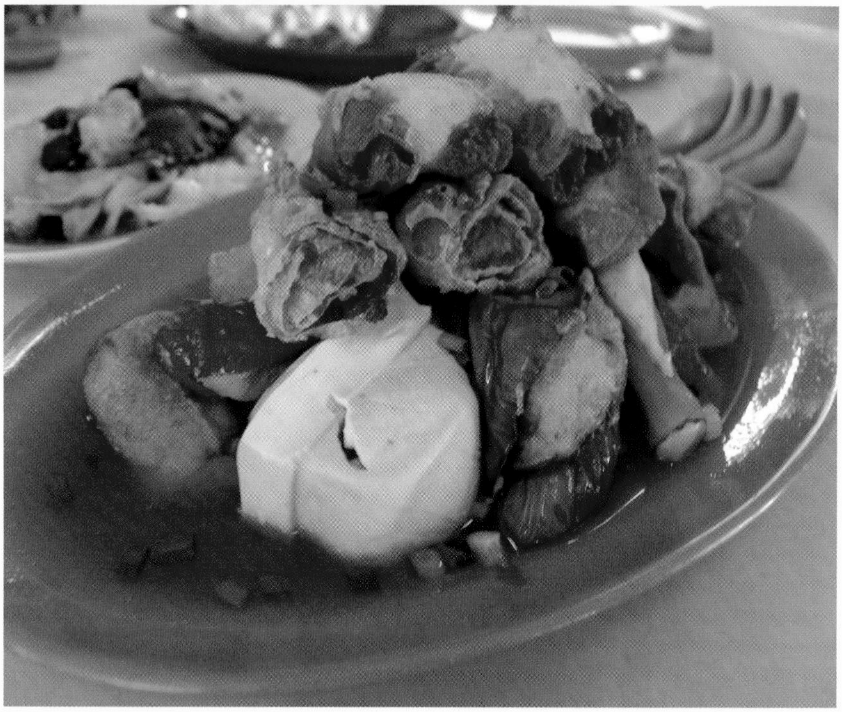

Chinese Influences

The Chinese created Char Kway Teow, a Malaysian favorite, (pg. 336) using flat rice noodles and local cockles. The Hokkiens from southern China's Fukien (Fujian) region created Malaysian specialties such as Hokkien Fried Mee (pg. 338) ("mee" means noodle), a dish of thick egg noodles in a rich soy gravy.

One breakfast food, *yong tau foo,* is comprised of several vegetables, tofu, and fish paste filling. The fish paste filling is the same mixture used to produce the fish balls common in Chinese soups (it's basically puréed fish, starch, and salt). Malaysian cooks pack okra pods, bell pepper wedges, and slender eggplants with the paste and then pan fry them or simmer them in broth.

Hainanese chicken rice (pg. 318) originated on the Chinese island of Hainan. It's now claimed as a national treasure in both Malaysia and Singapore. In it, chicken is poached in broth until just barely cooked through and still extremely juicy. The fat is skimmed off from the broth to be used for cooking the rice. The luscious chicken, which attains a resilient (some would say bouncy) skin, is served atop the "chickeny" steamed rice and accompanied by a sipping cup of the delicate cooking broth and a coarse garlic/ginger/chili sauce. Its simplicity (poached chicken, rice, broth, and a condiment) proves that "less is more," since the combination of these elements creates a strikingly memorable flavor immersion. The "yin-yang" concept of creating harmony through the proper pairing of opposites arrived along with Chinese settlers. Stir-frying and the ubiquitous wok are major Chinese contributions to Malaysia and Singapore's gastronomic environments.

Nonyas

southeastasianflavors.com Go to...

Poh piah, a fresh spring roll, is a clear example of how the Chinese spring roll was transformed into a Malaysian delight (pg. 294). The wrapper is prepared like a French crepe. The filling consists mostly of cooked jicama (known locally as bangkuang, turnip, or yam bean) and assorted vegetables. These moist, delicate rolls are assembled to order. Poh piah parties, where guests are invited to roll their own at a host's home, are a common social get-together.

Pong teh is another example of flawlessly combined Chinese ingredients and Malay techniques. The Chinese penchant for simmered, soy sauce–flavored stews melds with a Malay-derived pounded paste of shallots, garlic, and fermented brown bean sauce. Dried Chinese black mushrooms are simmered in this broth with pork or chicken and large chunks of potatoes (pg. 322).

Culinary Etiquette

First-time visitors to homes and restaurants in Malaysia and Singapore are often surprised to see such prolific

at first, but the oil acts as a cooking medium, sweetening the aromatics with an even transfer of heat. When the oil begins to seep out from the rempah, you know you have achieved a harmony of flavor. Although not traditional, one could drain the excess oil off the dish without ruining it.

The recipes that follow are found in both Singapore and Malaysia. Each recipe is packed with history, teeming with flavor, and easily prepared by even a modestly experienced cook. Take some time to read the page references for a full understanding of the recipe, its background, key ingredients, cooking techniques, and to plan a complete meal.

use of Western utensils. Chopsticks are customary for noodle dishes and Chinese or Malay dishes that are easily picked up. But usually the joint effort of a fork and a spoon is used to gather rice and sauce together. The fork is used to push the foods onto the spoon, from which the food is eaten. Indians, Malays, and Nonyas often eat with their fingers. Only the right hand is used. The left hand is considered impure, as it is used for bathing and washing.

Ask any Malaysian their ultimate enjoyment in life, and they are bound to respond, makan, "to eat." The word is both a verb and a noun. They makan several times a day, including very late at night. In Malaysia I observed that mealtime conversation invariably addresses what the next meal will be. "Good food is life" is the credo, though a Malaysian may express the sentiment in the converse: "Life is good food." If the "best" fried chili crab is one hundred kilometers away, chances are good that most Malaysians would prefer to drive the distance rather than risk a meal in an unknown place.

Rempah

Literally translated as "spice paste," the term *rempah* is popularly used to describe a pounded paste of aromatic ingredients which is cooked to bring out its essences. Most rempahs contain ingredients such as garlic, shallots, spices, rhizomes (like galangal and turmeric), lemongrass, chilies, and shrimp paste. The rempah can even be the primary thickener in Malay stews and soups. Shallots are less expensive than onions in these lands (I love this!), and they're used more extensively.

Blenders have replaced mortars as the tool of choice for making rempahs in modern kitchens, since the mortar method takes a long time. The blender result is good, but be careful not to over-purée it. Leave the mixture somewhat coarse, as it would be if it were made with a mortar and pestle (see page 105, regarding making spice paste).

As important as how the rempah is puréed is how it is cooked. Malaysians call the cooking stage of rempah "tumis" (pronounced two-meese). The amount of oil used in this frying of spice paste may be startling

283

Red Chili Sambal
Sambal Belacan

"Sambal," a term primarily used in Malaysia, Singapore and Indonesia, is essentially a chili-based condiment. The most common ingredients are chilies, garlic, shallots, and sugar, though many also contain shrimp paste, salt, and tamarind. Bottled versions can now be bought in the US. The Indonesian name for pestle is ulek ulek, this is where makers of chili paste coined the name "sambal ulek," sometimes spelled "sambal olek." Removing the veins and seeds from the chilies greatly reduces the spiciness of the dish. A capsicum's spice is located primarily in the veins; the seeds are guilty by association. If you desire more heat, by all means go with the traditional preparation of using the entire chili. Finishing the sauce with tamarind pulp yields a more liquid sauce with a slightly tart edge.

Preparing sambal is essential to learning about Singaporean and Malaysian cuisine, involves adding fresh red chilies (fresh, dried or both) and combination of shallots and garlic. These are pounded in a mortar to create a paste then usually fried in oil. In recent years, many modern homes have begun to use a blender to simplify this task. The *sambal* puree is fried until the oil separates out from the solids, becoming visible, and the rawness of the shallot-garlic flavor has softened.

Makes 1 to 1¹/₂ cups

12	Dried red chilies, remove stems and seeds
2	tsp. Malaysian shrimp paste (belacan), toasted (pg. 111)
³/₄	cup Vegetable oil (divided use)
¹/₂	lb. (14 g.) Long red chilies or other hot red chilies, roughly chopped (about 10) (pg. 44)
8	Shallots, roughly chopped (about 4 oz)
¹/₂	tsp. Kosher salt
¹/₂	tsp. Granulated sugar

1. Soak dried chilies in room temperature water 30 minutes; drain and squeeze out excess moisture.

2. Make a *rempah* by pureeing half of the oil, dried chilies, fresh chilies, shallots and shrimp paste in a blender until smooth.

3. Cook the rempah: Heat remaining oil in a wok or 2-quart (2 L.) saucepan over medium heat; add rempah. Cook, stirring constantly, until oil separates from solids, about 10 minutes. Stir in salt and sugar; adjust seasonings to taste. Serve with cucumbers on a sandwich, as a table condiment, or as a cooking sauce for shrimp (pg. 335).

How and Why

You can use a mortar and pestle or a blender to puree the chilies, however do not make the mixture too fine. Especially in a blender if mixture is too fine it does not fry well and the final sambal would not be the authentic texture.

Indian Clarified Butter
Ghee

Ghee is made differently from European clarified butter. Rather than being slow-melted and skimmed, butter for ghee is simmered until it clarifies. Any impurities and milk solids adhere to the bottom of the pot. It becomes slightly golden brown, and acquires a light nutty flavor. Pure butter ghee is also known as "usli ghee," and if you do not want to make it yourself, you can certainly buy some at Indian markets labeled as such.

Ghee is actually so prized in the Indian culture that it is used in ceremonial lamps as fuel, given to Brahmin (highest caste) newborn babies and children daily by the spoonful to promote intelligence, and of course, used in cooking, such as to roast spices for the topping of the coconut chutney (pg. 300).

Makes 1 1/2 cups

1   lb. (454 g.) Unsalted butter

1. Heat butter in 2 to 4 qt. (2 to 4 L.) saucepan over medium-low flame until melted.
2. Cook at a gentle simmer until the watery liquid at the bottom boils off, about 20 minutes. Keep an eye on the simmering butter, as it has a tendency to boil over. The milk solids should stick to the bottom and begin to brown.
3. Strain through fine mesh strainer into a heatproof container.

How and Why

Cook long enough to get a nutty brown flavor. The lactose and other elements in the butter turn light brown when cooked, giving ghee its unique nutty flavor.

Crisp Pulled Flatbread
Roti Canai (Malaysia) or Roti Paratha (Singapore)

Buttery, crisp-edged, yet possessed of distinctive elasticity and chew, this Malaysian descendant of Paratha bread from southern India takes some time to prepare, but is a fun project that's well worth the commitment. It's invariably served with a meat or vegetable curry stew for dipping (pg. 290) although my nephews Hunter and Garrett like dipping into granulated sugar. This same dough can be stuffed with all sorts of fillings.

For simple versions an egg is cracked in center, then some add sliced chilies and onion, and a very common version is called Murtabak when a dry curry is used a hearty filling, making it a complete meal. When fillings like eggs or lentil puree are folded in, they are stretched as for plain roti, and then topped with a flavorful mixture, folded in from all four sides, and then transferred to griddle. The Thais use a similar dough to create a sweet snack with sliced bananas drizzled with condensed milk.

It takes some practice to master the stretching, pulling and folding that gives this bread its signature texture. Before you make this dish for the first time, try to watch the video at www.southeastasianflavors.com to see me make it for you! A standing mixer can be used to eliminate some of the work of hand-mixing the dough. Use the "hook" attachment for best results.

Timing Note: This dough needs at least six hours to rest but can be made the day before.

Make 8 pieces

3¹/₂ cups 1¹/₄ lb. / 580 g.) All purpose flour
1¹/₂ tsp. Kosher salt
1 tsp. Granulated sugar
³/₄ cup Ghee, room temperature
    (divided use) (pg 285)
1 lg. Egg, beaten
³/₄ cup Whole milk
¹/₂ cup Water

1. Make the dough: Use you hands and a bowl or better yet a heavy-duty stand mixer with a paddle attachment: Combine flour, salt, sugar and ¹/₄ cup of the ghee. Rub together with fingertips (or run on low with dough hook) until mixture clumps. Add egg, milk, and water. Using one hand, mix until a cohesive dough forms. (Continue to mix with paddle until a smooth elastic dough is formed. Knead into a smooth, soft, elastic dough, about 8 to 10 minutes. It should be a bit sticky, but not wet. Cut into eight equal pieces, about 4 oz. each (113 g.). Form into smooth balls. Coat each ball with one teaspoon of ghee (yes…that much), slathering them well. Arrange in a single layer on a plate, cover lightly, and allow them to rest at room temperature for at least 6 hours (The dough can be made a day ahead up to this point, and kept in the refrigerator).

Murtabak is a stuffed version of this flatbread.

Step 3. Flatten dough into 6-inch circle and pull into paper-thin sheet.

2. Prepare your workspace: If the dough was prepared the day ahead, let come to a warm room temperature (Malaysia is tropical). So if your kitchen is cold, place the dough in warm area, or you can even microwave it for 10 second intervals. Warm dough is more elastic and easier to work with. Clean a 2-inch × 2-inch (.6m. × .6m.) surface, and coat it with a 12-inch circle (30 cm) of ghee (about 2 Tbsp). Coat hands liberally with ghee.

3. Stretch the dough into a sheet: Put 1 tsp. of ghee in center of the buttered work area; arrange one dough ball in the center. Press with your buttered palm to flatten dough into a 6-inch disk, less than 1/4 inch (0.6 cm.) thick, slightly thinner around edges. Choose a method, Traditional or Simplified, for stretching the dough:

This Singaporean hawker twists and pulls the dough pieces into a paper-thin sheet.

TRADITIONAL DOUGH STRETCHING METHOD
(Practice This Technique with Cloth Napkin First)
A. Place four fingers of your right hand underneath dough and your thumb on top, at the 5 o'clock position. Place four fingers of left hand on top of dough at 8 o'clock
B. Throw dough by moving right hand toward your left side, and then slapping it back onto table in one quick motion. Each time, as the dough sticks to the table, pull it back to stretch it further. The dough gets thinner as it's tossed and pulled. Repeat this until it become thin as possible without too many holes (a few are okay).
C. Systematically move your hands clockwise around dough perimeter each time you throw dough, allowing the disc to slowly rotate in your hands. This ensures an even stretch from all sides.
D. Make sure most of dough is paper thin by systematically moving around dough perimeter lifting thicker edges, pull outwards to thin and gently pressing against table to adhere.

MY SIMPLIFIED, FOOLPROOF DOUGH STRETCHING METHODS
A. In this method, the dough never leaves the table. Instead, you pull and stretch it from the center outwards. Make sure most of dough is paper thin by moving around dough perimeter with your fingertips and thumbs, lifting thicker edges, pulling outwards to thin, and gently pressing against table to adhere.
B. Systematically, slowly, work your way around the perimeter of dough circle pulling outwards to thin the dough. For the first few rounds, pull 3 to 4 inches (about 8 to 10 cm.) each time, making it thinner and thinner. As it gets thinner, it will be obvious where the thicker parts of the dough are. Focus on those areas. Keep going until you achieve a paper thin sheet. It should reach about 2 feet in diameter. Use the tips of your fingers to smooth those inevitably thicker parts paper thin.

Crisp Pulled Flatbread
Roti Canai (Malaysia) or Roti Paratha (Singapore)

SHAPE THE BREAD—A BIT MORE COMPLICATED:

PARATHA STYLE (Able to Cook Immediately)
Using two hands, fold top quarter of dough over itself, almost reaching middle of sheet. Fold top edge over again to meet the top edge. Then repeat with other sides to create a square multi-layered square of dough about 6 to 8 inches (about 16 to 20 cm.) Each time you fold, try to capture some air in-between layers.

SIMPLE: ROTI CANAI STYLE
(Needs to Rest But Has More Layers)
Form sheets into layered ropes: Drizzle the paper-thin dough sheet with 1 teaspoon of ghee. Using two hands, fold top quarter of dough over itself, almost reaching middle of sheet. Fold top edge over again until you create a 1 to 2-inch (3 to 5 cm.) wide long rope. Each time you fold, try to capture some air in-between layers. (Alternate, simple method: loosely roll dough, jellyroll-style, into a 2-inch (5 cm.) wide rope.)

Beginning from one end, coil up the rolled rope into a loose pinwheel. Pull the outer end into center, and tuck it in. Flip the coil over. Each coiled disc should resemble a turban, and be filled with pockets of air. Repeat with all remaining dough balls. Let them rest at least 5 minutes for gluten (protein) to relax. This will make flattening them easier, and result in a more tender flatbread.

COOK THE BREADS:
Heat a griddle or large sauté pan over low flame. Firmly flatten and spread one disc of dough until it is 7 inches to 8 inches in diameter or (18 to 20 cm.) The dough will be elastic, and may pull back a little: That's okay. Drizzle the griddle with a little ghee. Add one bread to the pan, and cook slowly, turning once, 3 to 4 minutes per side, rotating occasionally to ensure even browning. Cook until each side is deep golden brown, even if that means more cooking time than you expect. The first bread is always a "tester," telling you whether to raise or lower the heat. Transfer the breads to a work surface, and then use a clapping motion (careful it will be hot), slapping the bread together between your hands to separate the layers. Repeat with remaining roti, cooking as many as will fit in the pan at one time.

Serve with curry (pg. 290), other flavorful heavily sauced dishes, or use it as a flatbread for a warm sandwich.

Try to trap some air as you fold the dough into layers.

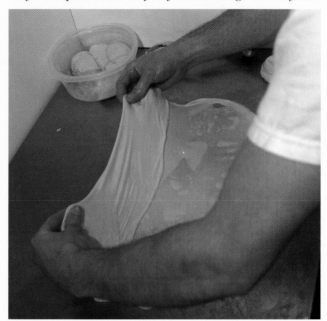

How and Why

1. When making the dough, have the ghee at room temperature, about 75°–80°F (23° to 26°C.) (it should be liquid). This ensures it mixes well into the dough. This will be important when forming the dough, since if it's too cold it becomes deceptively thick.

2. Resting dough after mixing allows you to stretch it as thin as possible. Kneading the dough forms layer of gluten protein, making the dough elastic. But the six-hour resting period allows the dough to relax again, enabling you to stretch it paper thin.

3. Pulling dough paper thin and drizzling with ghee creates multiple layers. The coating of ghee keeps the layers separate and traps moisture and air. This air expands during cooking, making the roti light and flaky.

4. Slap the cooked flatbreads to fully separate layers. The final stage of slapping the dough together separates the finer layers of dough that have adhered together (especially with round version above), increasing delicateness.

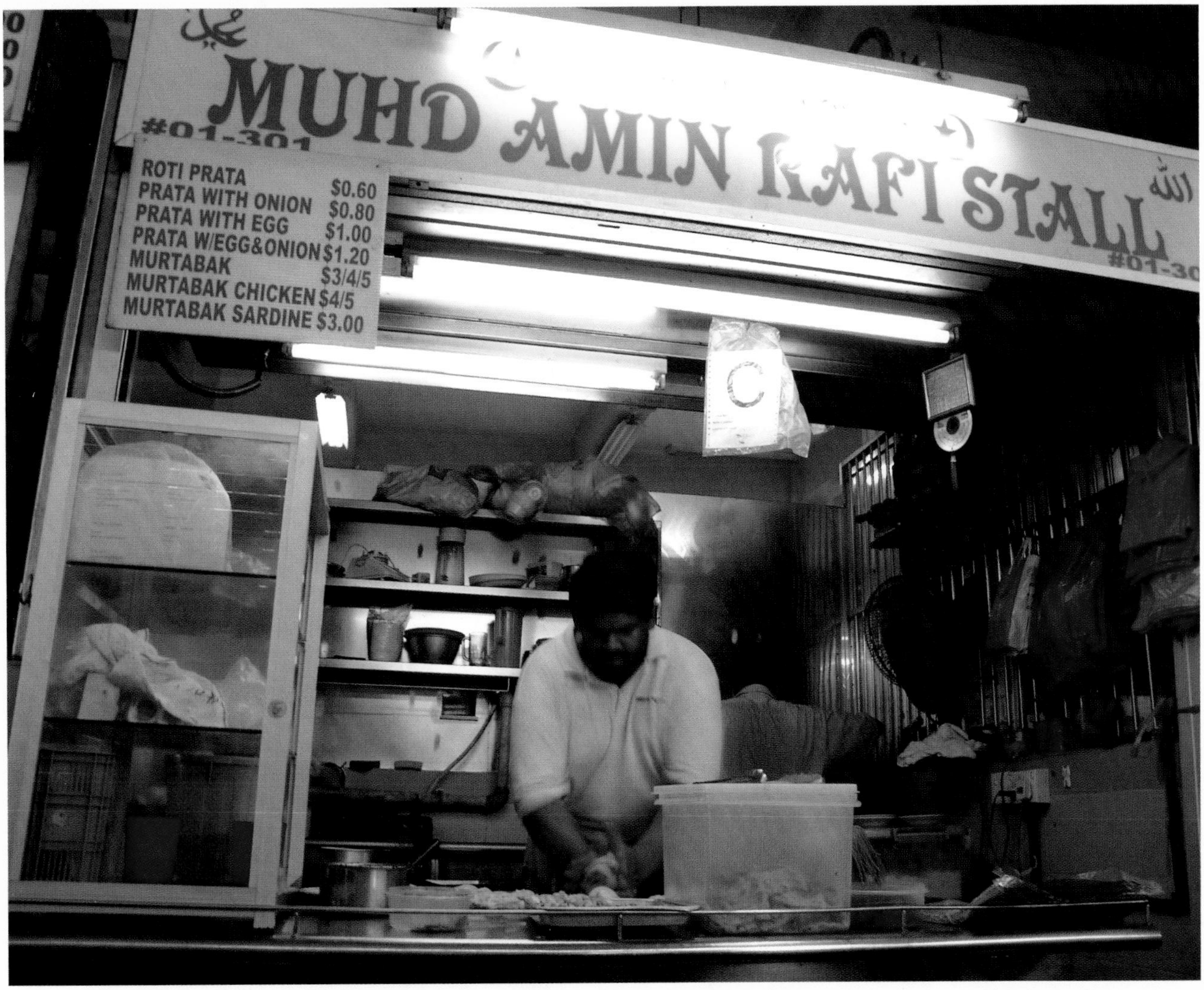
MUHD AMIN KAFI STALL
#01-301
ROTI PRATA $0.60
PRATA WITH ONION $0.80
PRATA WITH EGG $1.00
PRATA W/EGG&ONION $1.20
MURTABAK $3/4/5
MURTABAK CHICKEN $4/5
MURTABAK SARDINE $3.00

The Tekka Market in Singapore's Little India beholds a hawker stall that specializes in Roti Paratha.

Indian Chicken and Potato Curry
Kari Ayam

This Indian curry is almost always served for dipping with *Roti Canai* (pg. 286). But over rice, it's equally divine. Fresh curry leaves, available at Asian and Indian specialty stores, are the defining flavor in this simple little stew. Sometimes I like to add a stick of cinnamon, a few cardamom pods, and some cloves for a more complex flavor, and a squeeze of lime juice gives it a bright citrus note. You can try these and other options at your pleasure.

Makes 4 cups

1/2	cup (1/2 oz. / 14 grams) Dried red chilies, remove stems and seeds
4	medium Shallots, roughly chopped
3	cloves Garlic, roughly chopped
1	Tbsp. Minced ginger
2	lb. (.9 kg) Boneless/skinless chicken thighs or legs, halved
2	Tbsp. Malaysian Meat Curry powder or store-bought
2	tsp. Kosher salt
1/4	cup Ghee (pg. 285)
1/4	cup Curry leaves (optional)
1/2	cup Onions, 1/4-inch (0.6 cm.) dice
2	cups Chicken stock/broth or water
1	can (about 14 oz./ 414 ml.) Coconut milk
1	med. Gold waxy potato, peeled, cut into 1-inch (2.5 cm.) chunks
1/4	cup Tamarind pulp (pg. 109)

1. Soak the chilies: Soak chilies in 1/2 cup of room temperature water for 30 minutes, drain and squeeze out excess moisture.

2. Make the spice paste: Combine the soaked chilies, shallots, garlic, and ginger in a mortar, blender or food processor and pulverize into a paste.

3. Combine spice paste with chicken, curry powder, and salt. Marinate for 30 minutes.

4. Cook the curry: Heat a 4 qt. (4 L.) saucepan over medium heat with ghee, fry the curry leaves and onions until onions become translucent. Add marinated chicken, potatoes and stock and coconut milk, mix well and bring up to a boil, lower to a simmer

5. Simmer until chicken and potatoes are cooked through, about 20 minutes.

6. Finish the curry: Add and the tamarind, bring back up to simmer. Taste; season with salt. Adjust consistency with additional stock or water to taste. It should have the thickness of heavy cream.

Curry leaves have small firm leaves that are easily identifiable.

Creamy Coconut and Pandan Jam
Seri Kaya

Yes jam, that's what Malaysians and Singaporeans call this sweet-creamy custard. Maybe that's because they keep a jar of this on hand like westerns keep fruit jams, to spread on toast or fill a pastry. A classic use is making Kaya toast (pg. 292), where the jam is spread on grilled bread, sandwiched with slabs of butter, and eaten with poached eggs. Ice cream also revels in luscious spoonfuls of this pale golden coconut spread.

Makes 2 cups

1 cup Coconut milk
1 cup Granulated sugar
8 ea Pandan leaves, tied into a knot and bruised
3 lg. Eggs
3 Egg yolks
pinch Kosher salt

1. In small saucepan whisk together the coconut milk and 1/2 cup of sugar; add pandan leaves and bring to a boil, shut off heat and steep for 10 minutes. Pull out pandan leaves, squeezing to extract as much flavorful liquid as possible, discard leaves.

2. Combine eggs and yolks with remaining 1/2 cup of sugar in mixing bowl and whisk until smooth. (Sugar will not dissolve). Gradually whisk in the warm coconut milk.

3. Transfer to bowl over a double boiler. Cook custard gently, whisking *constantly* until mixture thickens considerably. Scrape down sides and bottom occasionally with rubber spatula so it does not overcook. This process will take 10 to 20 minutes or until it reaches a thick custard consistency. The custard is ready when whisk is removed and the trail of the tines clearly remains on surface for more than 10 seconds.

4. Remove and cool to room temperature. Transfer to container; store in refrigerator for up to a month.

How and Why

1. Slowly add hot coconut milk to avoid curdling. Bringing up the temperature of eggs slowly prevents their proteins from coagulating too quickly.

2. Make sure the bowl of the double boiler fits inside the rim of the pot so that at least 1/4 of it is below the top. This ensures that the custard is being cooked with steam.

3. Gently scrape entire interior of bowl with spatula with whisk when cooking over water bath to ensure even cooking. If parts of the custard are not stirred they will set into large semi-solid curds.

Coconut Jam Toast with Poached Eggs and Dark Soy Sauce

Kaya Toast

Ya Kun Kaya, the ultimate Singaporean kopitiam (coffee shop) focuses on tradition. Through a back window, I spied the old man, effortlessly toasting bread over glowing charcoal. Nuances of woodsy flavor can impregnate bread from the essence of smoke. Next, he slathers on creamy coconut custard. The aroma of pandan and coconut waft through the open window. He adds a generous helping of butter to the warm sandwich before closing it up, halving it, and sending it out to it's lucky owner.

Crunching down on the sweet sandwich and sipping dense black coffee with condensed milk is almost over-stimulation. But ethereally soft poached eggs push me over the edge with a sprinkle of white pepper and dash of dark soy sauce. Dip, crunch, sip....oh what a rhythm.

Since Malaysian coffee is not yet available in the USA you can substitute with either Thai coffee (pg. 182) or Vietnamese coffee (pg. 268). While we were testing recipes relentlessly my sous chef Ari discovered the wondrous taste of ginger snap cookies dipped in kaya.

Serves 4 for breakfast or snack

8   lg. Eggs, room temperature
2   qt. Water, boiling
8   slices White bread, optional to remove crusts
1/4 lb. (113 g.) Salted butter, sliced, about 1/8 inch (0.3 cm.) thick
1   recipe Kaya (creamy coconut and pandan custard) (pg. 291)
4   tsp. Dark soy sauce
as needed Ground white pepper

1. Cook eggs: Arrange eggs in a heat-proof container, small enough so they are stacked in two layers. Slowly pour 2 quarts (2 L.) boiling water over the eggs; cover tightly (it's no problem if some crack). Leave eggs undisturbed to cook for 20 minutes; drain. Gently crack eggs around entire circumference. Break the shells open over 4 shallow bowls, releasing the barely cooked egg gently. Cover with plastic wrap and keep in warm area.

2. Meanwhile make toast: While the eggs are poaching, toast eight pieces of bread, slather 2 tsp. of custard (*kaya*), onto each slice. Evenly distribute butter among four slices; sandwich with kaya-coated bread. Cut each sandwich into half and stack on plate.

3. To serve: Drizzle each dish of eggs with 1 tsp. of dark soy sauce and large pinch of white pepper. Serve with some strong coffee sweetened with condensed milk.

How and Why

1. Use large eggs (2 oz. / 57 g. each) to achieve the correct doneness. Each US standard size of eggs (jumbo, extra large, large, medium, small and pee wee) varies 1/4 oz. (7 g.) so if you use jumbo instead of large eggs there is an entire 1/2 oz. (14 g) difference and with small eggs that is enough to change the cooking time. I suggest adding/or subtracting 3 minutes time for smaller or larger eggs.

2. Make sure the eggs are room temperature, so they cook evenly. Room temperature eggs allow the boiled water to penetrate the egg evenly cooking it uniformly.

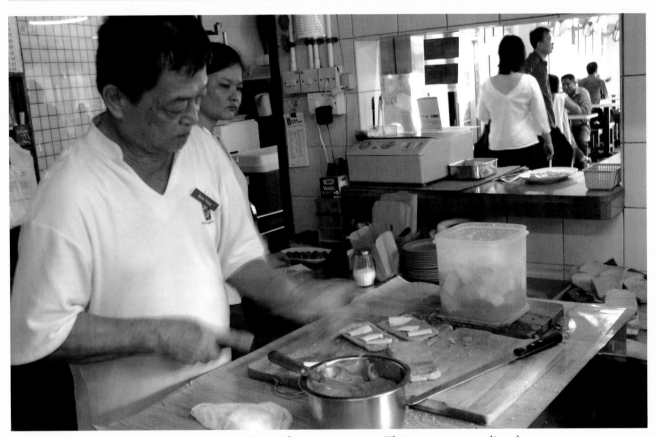

Note how he keeps the butter floating in water. This way you can slice them ahead yet keep them separated for easy assembly.

SCREW THE
FRENCH PRESS
WE'VE
GOT
THE
SOCK
Coffee prepared the same since 1944.

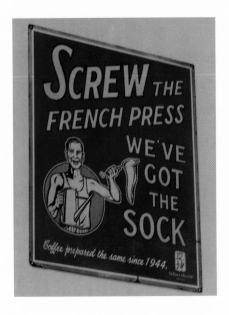

A metal loop is covered with cloth to form a cone that is used as the filter for brewing the rich coffee.

HOW WOULD YOU LIKE YOUR EGGS?
Wet and Runny
or
Runny and Wet
THE SAME MENU SINCE 1944.

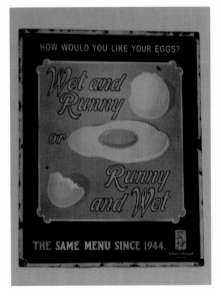

Ahhh, who needs options anyway. They know what's best!

MALAYSIA SINGAPORE

Soft Nonya Spring Rolls with Spicy Plum-Hoisin Sauce

Poh Piah

Chinese and Malay cultures marry in this variation on the spring roll to present a precious culinary experience. Their shape resembles gold bars, and is designed to attract prosperity. The filling is a simple stir-fry, which is rolled with some crunchy salad ingredients into thin, tender crepes.

In Malaysia and Singapore, a layer of sweetness in the rolls comes from a sauce called *tim cheong*, which is available only in the region. I have devised an easy substitute for that tangy, soy-based sauce, using a combination of readily available hoisin and plum sauces.

Although jicama is not often thought of as a vegetable for cooking (or even a vegetable for Asian cuisine), it actually stays pleasantly crunchy after cooking. Store-bought fried shallots, sold in Asian markets, are a finishing touch to the rolls, or you can fry your own (pg. 119). In Southeast Asia these rolls are party food: Hosts prepare the fillings and the crepes, and then let their guests roll their own. It's a fun start to the evening!

Makes 8 to 10 rolls

CREPES/WRAPPERS

1 1/2 cups Water
3   lg. Eggs
1/2   tsp. Kosher salt
1   Tbsp. Vegetable oil
3/4   cup All purpose flour

1. Make the crepe batter: Whisk together the water, eggs, salt and oil. Fold the flour into this mixture. Let batter rest for at least 1 hour. (For large batches—just place all the ingredients in a blender and hit it!)

2. Cook the crepes: Heat a non-stick 10-inch skillet (25cm.) over medium heat; wipe with an oiled paper towel. Lift the pan off the stove, add 1/4 cup of batter and tilt pan to coat. Place the pan back over heat, and cook until the pancake's

edges become dry and begin to release from the pan. A light browning on the pancake is ok. Remove the cooked crepe by inverting the pan over a plate (you may need to loosen it with a shake or a push first). Repeat with remaining batter (crepes can be made up to 8 hours in advance). Stack the crepes right on top of one another: they will not stick.

3. Wrap in plastic and keep covered until ready to use, they can be store in the refrigerator for a day or two then brought to room temperature before serving.

Some folks like to deep-fry the spring rolls. It's best to use a Chinese spring roll or Filipino style lumpia wrappers. The fresh wrapper recipe here is not made to be fried.

"TIM CHEONG" SAUCE

2	tsp. Chili-garlic sauce or minced long red chilies
2	Tbsp. Plum sauce
2	Tbsp. Hoisin sauce

1. Whisk together the chili-garlic sauce, plum sauce and Hoisin sauce. Set aside.

COOKED FILLING

2	Tbsp. Vegetable oil
5	cloves Garlic, minced
2	Tbsp. Ground bean sauce (pg. 53)
1/4	lb. (114 g.) Pork (leg or butt), cut into 1 × 1/4 × 1/4-inch (2.5 × 0.6 × 0.6 cm.) strips
1	lb. (454 g.) Jicama, julienne strips, about 1/8 inch (0.3 cm.) thick
2	tsp. Thick soy sauce (pg. 50) or 1 Tbsp. Dark soy sauce
5	tsp. Granulated sugar
1/2	tsp. Kosher salt
1/4	lb. (114 g.) Small shrimp, peeled, deveined, cut into 1/2-inch (1.3 cm.) pieces

1. Rinse the jicama julienne under water for a few minutes to rid it of excess starch. In a sauté pan or wok with a few tablespoons of vegetable oil, fry the garlic and ground bean sauce together over high heat until aromatic, 2 minutes. Add pork; continue to cook for 3 minutes. Add jicama, thick soy sauce, and sugar. Cook until the vegetables have released their juices, and the excess moisture steams out, about 10 minutes. The pan will be almost dry. Add shrimp, and cook 3 minutes more, until they are cooked through. Season to taste with salt; set aside to cool to room temperature.

UNCOOKED FILLINGS

8 to 10	leaves Green leaf lettuce, cleaned and dried, remove hard ribs
1	cup Bean sprouts, rinsed and dried
1	cup Julienne cucumber, Kirby variety preferred, seeded, bite size strips, about 1/8 inch (0.3 cm.) thick (pg. 81)
2	Scallions, chopped
1/4	cup Roughly chopped cilantro (leaves and stems)
1/4	cup Fried shallots (pg. 119) or store bought

Assemble the rolls: On a clean work surface, lay out a crepe, and spread 2 tsp. of tim cheong sauce, leaving a 1-inch (2.5 cm.) border. Place a leaf of lettuce to cover the bottom third of the wrapper. Top the leaf with bean sprouts, cooked filling, cucumber, scallions, cilantro, and fried shallots. Total filling should not exceed 1 cup. Starting from the edge closest to yourself, fold crepe over the filling. Then, fold in the sides, and roll it up as if it were a burrito, using gentle pressure to keep the crepe from breaking.

Soft Nonya Spring Rolls with Spicy Plum-Hoisin Sauce

Po Piah

A very elastic wet dough is rubbed on the hot griddle and quickly pulled back leaving a film behind that becomes the thin spring roll wrapper. These drier style wrappers are tougher and hence sometimes topped with the liquid from the cooked filling.

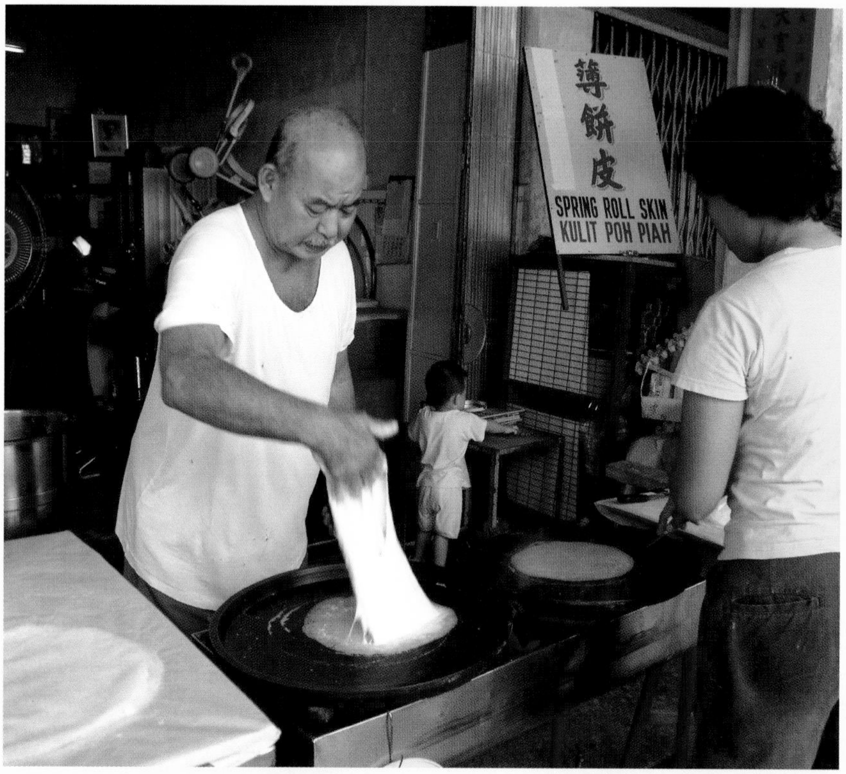
SPRING ROLL SKIN
KULIT POH PIAH

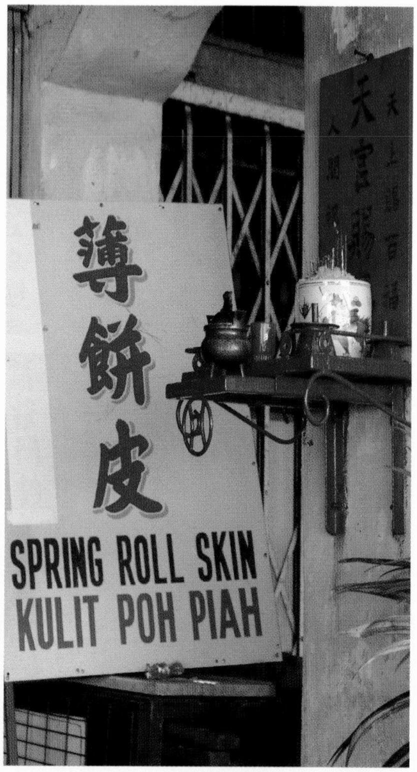
SPRING ROLL SKIN
KULIT POH PIAH

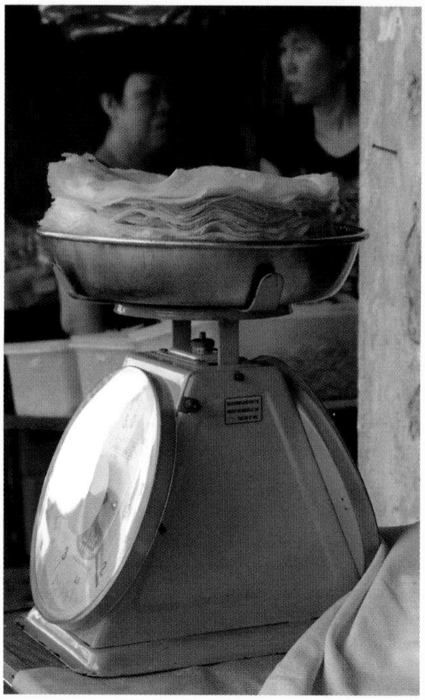

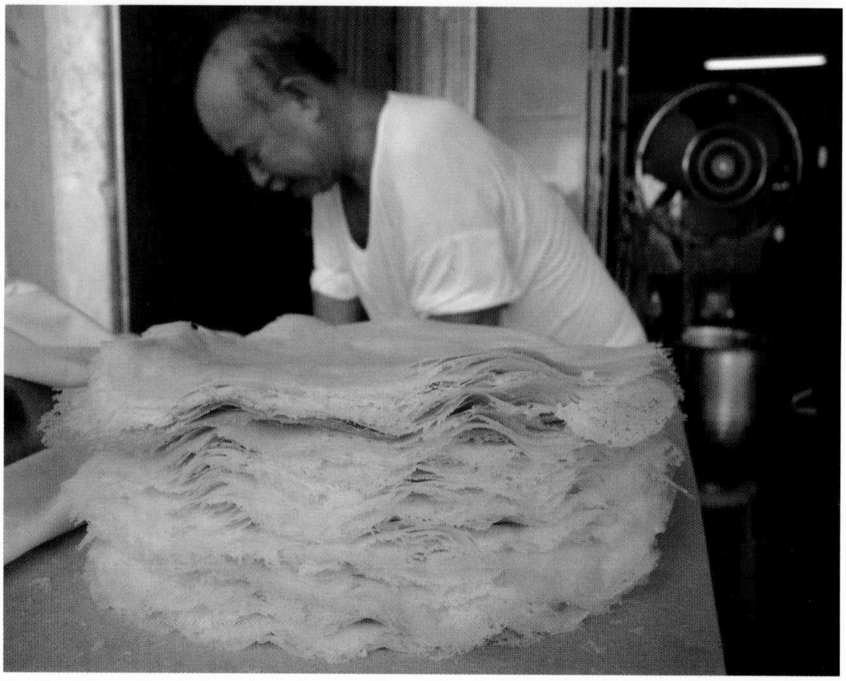

How and Why

1. Set the batter aside to rest for a more delicate flavor and stronger wrapper. Allowing the batter to rest hydrates the flour and relaxes gluten, improving the texture of the crepes.

2. Make sure to put the lettuce down first, to prevent the wrapper (crepe) from breaking. Laying a leaf of lettuce down serves two purposes: It prevents harder items like bean sprouts from puncturing the crepe, and keeps juices from making the crepe soggy.

3. Be careful not to roll too tight, or it will burst. The wrappers have some elasticity, and wrapping the roll tight makes it easier to eat. But pull too hard, and it will break.

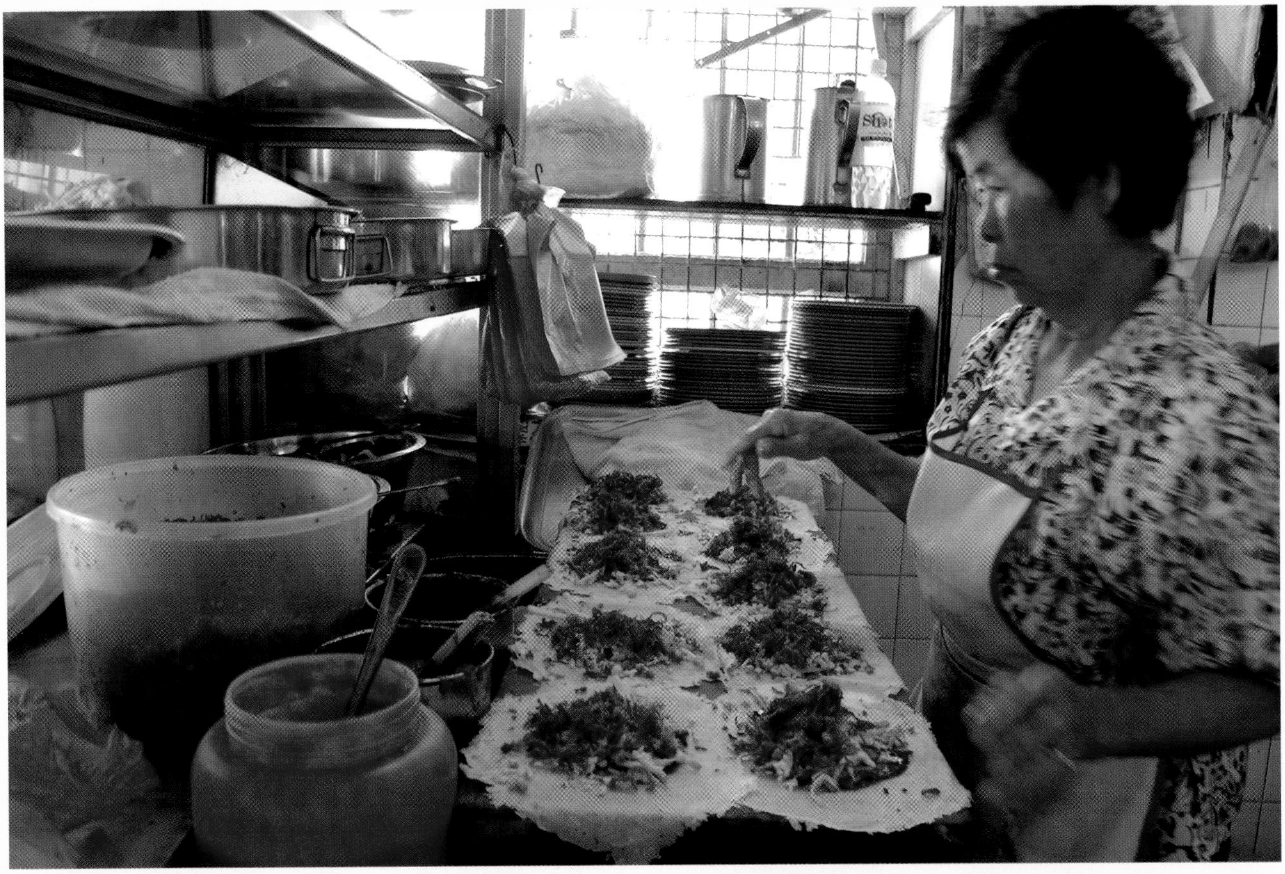

Don't be afraid to assemble them all at once.

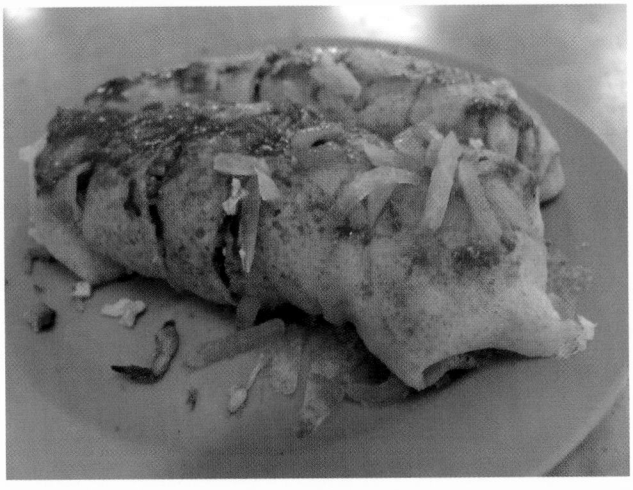

These are topped with some chili sauce and filling.

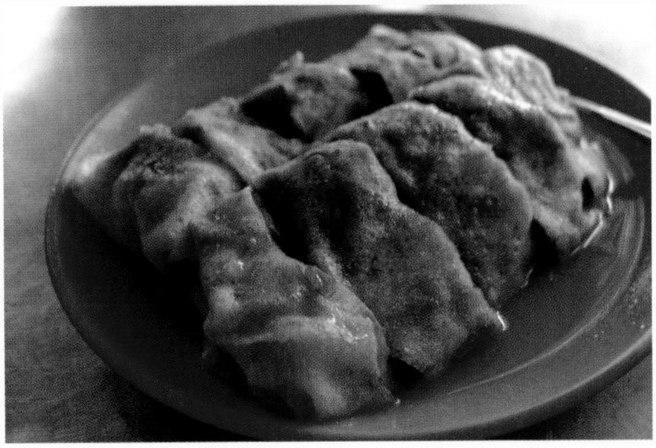

Some folks like to drench the wrappers. In this case it is more of a spoon and fork affair rather than eating them with your hands.

Spiced Split Pea Fritters with Coconut Chutney

Vadai

These savory "doughnuts" are quite addictive. They're very hearty, yet tender because they are made from finely ground beans, not flour. I recommend serving with Coconut Chutney (pg. 300). Though it's not authentic, I must admit I enjoy mixing some chili sauce into coconut milk to make another tasty quick dip for these.

Makes about 12 pieces

1	heaping cup (1/2 lb. / 227 g.) Split urad dhal (skinless black lentils) (pg. 74)
1	tsp. Kosher salt
1/4	tsp. Ground black pepper
1/2	Medium Onions, minced
1/4	cup Finely diced Long green chilies or other hot green chili (pg. 44) (See Southeast Asian Pantry for acceptable substitutions) (pg. 45)
14	Curry leaves, roughly chopped
1	tsp. Cumin seeds
1	Tbsp. Vegetable oil
12	sheets Parchment paper or aluminum foil, 3 × 3 inches (7.5 × 7.5 cm.)

1. Wash the urad dhal in three changes of water, cover with room temperature water and soak 4 to 8 hours.

2. Preheat a deep-fryer (or a pot with 6 cups vegetable oil) to 350°F. (177 C°) Drain dhal very well; combine salt, pepper and 1/4 cup of onions. Grind in food processor until finely ground (particles should be about the size of mustard seeds). Transfer to mixing bowl.

3. Add remaining 3/4 cup onions, chilies, curry leaves, and cumin to chopped dhal. Divide mixture into 12 equal portions, 2 tablespoons each (11/2 oz. / 42 g.).

4. Oil one side of parchment or foil. Place ball in center of oiled sheet, and then push a finger through the center until it touches the parchment, creating a doughnut shape. Flatten, if necessary, to 1-inch (2.5 cm.) thickness.

5. Gently transfer the fritters, parchment sheets included, into deep-fryer. After about a minute, carefully remove paper with tongs and continue to fry fritters until they are a deep brown color. Remove from oil, and drain on absorbent paper. Serve with coconut chutney (pg. 300).

How and Why

Grinding the dhal to the correct fineness ensures tender light and fluffy fritters. Coarsely ground dhal releases the steam that would otherwise puff the fritters.

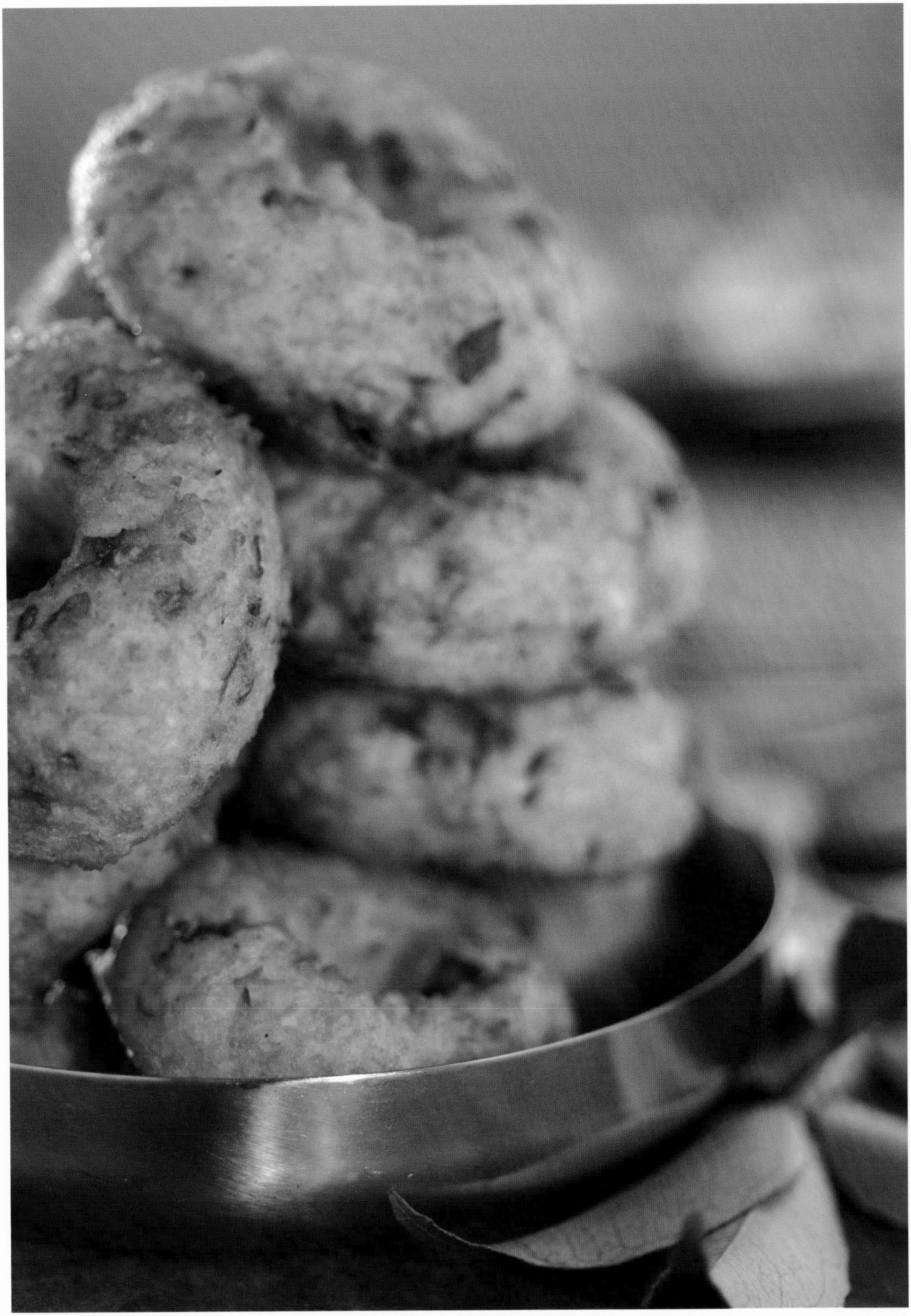

Coconut Chutney with Butter Fried Curry Leaves and Chilies

Kobbari Pacchandi

*C*hutneys are sauces and relishes whose name stems from "catni," which means "sauce." They can be fruity sweet-tart mixtures, spicy herbal purees, or, as in this recipe, delicate balances of fresh nuts and spices. For simplicity, buy frozen grated coconut in Asian food stores (comes in plastic pouches); use less water. This chutney pairs beautifully with Split Pea Fritters (pg. 298) or paratha (pg. 286), but people also love it with grilled meats and curries.

Makes 2¹/₂ cups

2 cups (about ¹/₂ coconut) Fresh Coconut Meat (pg. 115)	1 pinch Asafoetida (optional)
¹/₄ cup Roughly chopped, long green chilies or other hot green chili (pg. 44)	2 Tbsp Ghee (clarified butter) (pg. 285) or vegetable oil
1 cup (237 ml.) Water (divided use)	1 tsp Mustard seeds, preferably brown
1 tsp. Finely grated ginger	2 Dried red chilies, cut into ¹/₂-inch (1.3 cm.) pieces
1 tsp Kosher salt	8 Curry leaves (optional)

1. Make the coconut base: In a food processor, grind coconut, green chilies, and 1/2 cup of water until very fine (about 2 to 3 minutes). Season with ginger, salt and asafoetida. Spread this coconut mixture into a shallow serving dish, about 6 inches (15 cm.) wide.

2. Cook and add the spices: Heat ghee in a small pan; add mustard seeds, chilies and curry leaves. Fry until mustard seeds begin to pop. Carefully drizzle hot mixture over surface of coconut mixture. Do not mix in the oil. It is served this way, with the spiced oil floating attractively on top.

How and Why

Heating the ghee with spices extracts their full flavor. This traditional tempering (tadka) technique infuses the ghee with tons of flavor.

Curry Noodles in Coconut Broth

Laksa Lemak "Curry laksa"

Flavored with a classic Malaysian combination of lemongrass, galangal, chilies, candlenuts, shallots, garlic and turmeric, this dish gets its name from the word, "lemak," which indicates that that the dish is "rich," due to coconut milk. Fresh turmeric, a brilliant yellow rhizome that defines the color of the broth, is becoming more and more available in the US.

Makes 4 to 6 bowls as a one-dish meal

1/2 cup (1/2 oz. / 14 g.) Dried red chilies, stems and seeds removed

2 tsp. Dried shrimp

1/2 cup Vegetable oil

6 small Shallots, roughly chopped

3 cloves Garlic, roughly chopped

3 stalks Lemongrass, trimmed and sliced thinly, about 1/8 inch (0.3 cm.) thick

1 Tbsp. Finely grated galangal

4 Candlenuts or macadamia nuts or blanched almonds

1/4 tsp. Ground turmeric

1 1/2 tsp. Coriander seeds

1/4 tsp. Ground white pepper

1 qt. (1 L.) Light seafood or chicken broth

2 cans (14 oz. / 413 ml. each) Coconut milk

1 Tbsp. Granulated sugar

1 1/4 tsp. Kosher salt

1 lb. (454 g.) Cooked egg noodles, 1/8 inch (0.3 cm.) thick (mee) (pg. 64)

3/4 lb. (340 g.) Small shrimp, peeled and deveined

3/4 lb. (340 g.) Cooked fish balls or sliced fish cake (pg. 303)

1 pkg (4 oz. / 113 g.) Deep fried bean curd puffs, halved

2 cups Bean sprouts, trimmed and blanched

1 cup Cucumber, Kirby variety preferred, bite size julienne strips, about 1/8 inch (0.3 cm.) thick (pg. 81)

1/4 cup Laksa Leaves or Mint leaves, thinly sliced, about 1/8 inch (0.3 cm.) wide

2 to 3 medium Limes, cut into wedges (pg. 108)

1/4 cup Malaysian chili sauce (Sambal Belacan) (pg. 284) or store bought chili paste

Photo direct from the streets of Malaysia illustrates how small droplets of golden oil float on the coconut broth, do not skim these off, they are packed with flavor...and spice.

How and Why

1. If using a blender instead of mortar and pestle, add ingredients to the blender vase from wettest to driest, avoiding unnecessary added water. Starting the blender with the wet ingredients at bottom creates liquid base into which the drier ingredients can meld. This keeps the paste from becoming watery.

2. Fry the *rempah* (wet spice paste) enough to banish any raw flavor. Since this broth does not simmer long, it's necessary to fry the *rempah* long enough to soften the raw flavor notes first.

1. Make the spice paste (*rempah*): Soak chilies and dried shrimp in $1/2$ cup room temperature water for 30 minutes; drain, and squeeze out excess moisture. In blender, combine oil, shallots, and garlic; puree on lowest speed until semi-smooth. Add lemongrass, galangal, candlenuts, turmeric, coriander, white pepper, drained chilies, and shrimp. Puree again until the paste is semi-smooth.

2. Make the broth: Heat a 4 quart (4 L.) saucepan over medium-low heat. Add pureed chili paste, and fry over low heat until it is fragrant, and oil begins to separate from puree, 10 to 15 minutes. It should lose any raw aroma, and the raw flavor of the shallots also softens. Add stock; simmer 30 minutes. Add coconut milk and sugar; taste and season with salt as necessary. Bring back to a simmer.

3. Assemble the soup: Add fish balls and fried bean curd to broth; heat through. Reheat noodles in boiling water, drain well and divide among 6 bowls. Pour in the broth, and arrange the hot solid ingredients atop the noodles, topping each bowl with bean sprouts, cucumber and laksa leaves or mint. Serve with lime wedges and chili sambal (pg. 284).

The laksa leaf (Polygonum odoratum) *has a powerful, tart, peppery flavor hidden within the slender leaves.*

FISH CAKES, NO NOT FOR YOUR BIRTHDAY

One day you could begin the day with pancakes, then at lunch order a crab *cake*, followed by a slice of birthday cake for a late night party. Language is a peculiar thing and just as Americans have given treat the word cake as if it has multi-personalities Southeast Asians do as well. The fish cakes listed in the recipes is not a sweet cake (thank goodness) yet in its purest form a fine puree of fish, water and salt. Manufacturers usually add starch to bind it together. You can buy the paste in markets (very inconsistent quality) or buy it already formed into balls, discs or slabs and cooked. Even the frozen brand Dodo sold in the freezer section has a great texture and flavor.

Shrimp Broth with Noodles and Pork

Prawn Mee

This dish is all about the shrimp, or as they call them in Malaysia and Singapore the "prawns." Combining pork and shrimp in a single dish is very common in Asia. For this recipe, using the freshest head-on shrimp is critical. When made right, a rich shrimp essence come through, the soup acquires a characteristic red-orange color. Though it's red, it's not a spicy as it looks—that's what the side dish of fiery sambal belacan is for.

Makes 4 to 6 bowls as a one-dish meal

3   lbs. (1.3 kg.) Pork Ribs/Bones, 2 to 3-inch
         (7.5 cm.) pieces
1/2   lb. (227 g.) Pork Leg or loin, 2 × 1 × 4-inch piece
         (5 × 2.5 × 10 cm.)
2   lbs. (.9 kg.) Medium Shrimp, head on
1/2   cup (1/2 oz/14 g.) Dried red chilies, remove stems
         and seeds
1/4   cup Vegetable oil (divided use)
4   medium Shallots, roughly chopped
6   cloves Garlic, roughly chopped
1   Tbsp. finely grated ginger

2   stalks Lemongrass, trimmed and bruised
2   tsp. Kosher salt
2   tsp. Granulated sugar
1/2   lb. (227 g.) (229 g.) Chinese greens such as Choy Sum
1   lb. (454 g.)(457 g.) Wheat Noodles, fully cooked and
         cooled (pg. 116)
1   cup (229 g.) Bean Sprouts, trimmed and blanched
3   Tbsp. Fried shallots (pg. 119)
2 to 3 medium Limes, cut into Southeast Asian style wedges
         (pg. 108)—Calamansi or Key if available
1/4   cup Sambal Belacan (pg. 284)

1. Make pork stock: Combine pork ribs with 1 gallon of water. Bring to a boil; lower heat and simmer for 1 hour.
2. Cook and slice the pork leg: Lower the pork leg or loin into stock, and simmer until it is cooked through, about 20 minutes. Remove the pork from the stock, and plunge

it into ice water for 10 minutes. Transfer to a cutting board, and slice into 1/8-inch (0.3 cm.) thick slices; cover and reserve. Strain stock.

3. Peel and clean the shrimp, saving the heads and shells for broth. Soak dried chilies in 3/4 cup of room temperature water for 30 minutes, drain and squeeze out excess moisture.

4. Make the broth: In a blender, make a *rempah* by pureeing the first 2 tablespoons of the oil, shallots, garlic, ginger, and chilies. Heat a 4 qt. (4 L.) saucepan with remaining 2 tablespoons of the oil, add the shrimp shells and cook until color changes to a bright orange. Add puree (*rempah*) and cook over medium-low heat for 5 to 10 minutes, until the raw aroma dissipates. Add strained stock, lemongrass, salt and sugar and simmer for 15 minutes.

5. Puree and strain broth: Carefully transfer about half of the mixture, shells and all, to a blender. Puree well, and then add back to simmering pot; continue to cook for 10 minutes more. Strain this mixture: it should yield 2 1/2 qt. (2.5 L.) of liquid. If there is less than that, add water to achieve that volume. Adjust seasoning with salt to taste.

6. Blanch whole bunches of choy sum in boiling water; remove from water with a slotted spoon or skimmer, squeeze dry, and cut into 2 to 3-inch (5 to .75 cm.) lengths. Keep water boiling for later use.

7. To serve: Bring shrimp broth to a simmer. Cook shrimp lightly in the simmering broth, remove and set aside. Reheat noodles in boiling water, drain well and divide among 6 bowls. Ladle simmering broth over the noodles. On top of noodles, arrange sliced pork, greens, bean sprouts, and shrimp Sprinkle with shallots, and serve with lime wedges and sambal on the side.

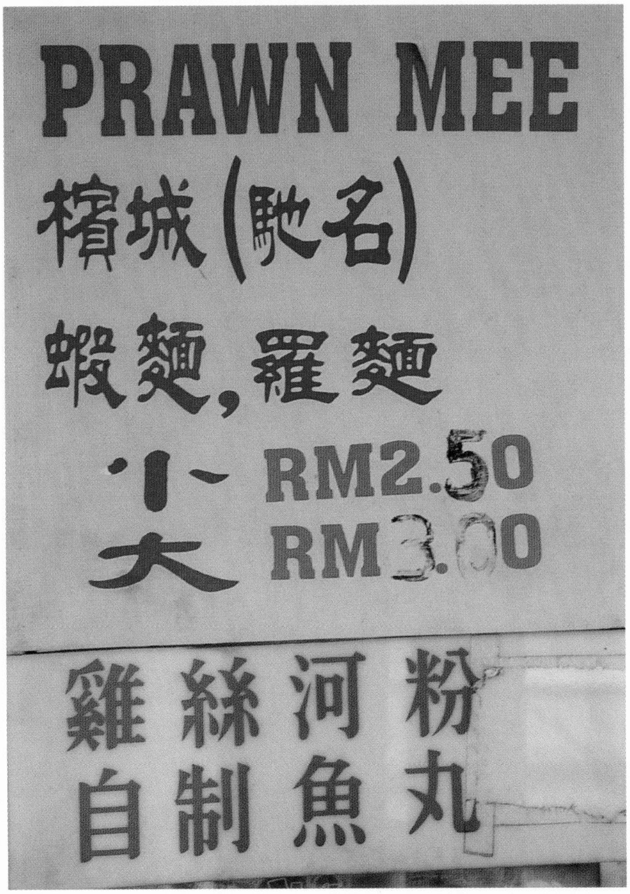
PRAWN MEE
檳城(馳名)
蝦麵,羅麵
小 RM2.50
大 RM3.00
雞絲河粉
自制魚丸

How and Why

1. Pork bones add depth of flavor. Using a pork stock as the base gives the soup a deep, rich flavor background, onto which the shrimp flavors build.

2. Using shrimp heads gives the broth depth of flavor and orange color. Try to find the freshest head-on shrimp. Those with a large amount of orange "fat" in their heads are the most prized for this.

3. Puree the shrimp for maximum color and flavor. This step is reminiscent of the technique for making shrimp or lobster bisque. The pulverization releases flavor and color from the shells into the broth.

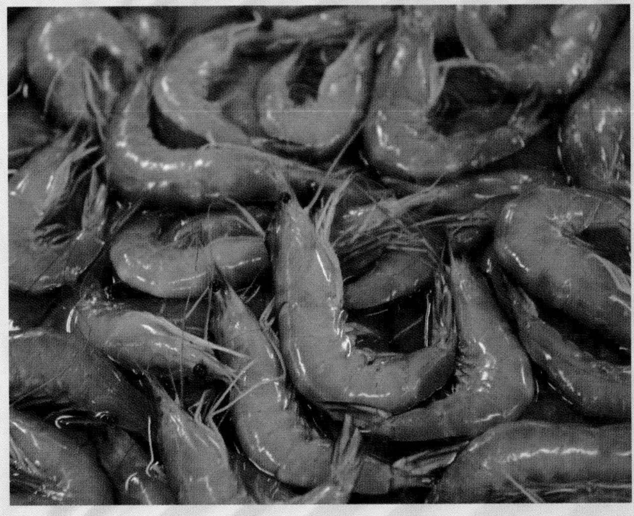

Chicken Soup with Rice Noodles, Asian Greens, and Chili-Soy Sauce

Ipoh Sar Hor Fun

The industrial town of Ipoh is justifiably famous for its unique style of chicken noodle soup. The noodles made there are so soft and supple, they yield to gentle pressure between the tongue and the palate. Some say it's the water. The way the water in New York is said to make their bagels' texture unique, or Paris' water for baguettes, Ipoh water is coveted for these noodles. I do recommend you making your own (no big deal [pg. 117]), but even if you don't, the soup from this place is outta this world. Locals eat it with stir-fried bean sprouts on the side.

This easy recipe takes some time. If you need a shortcut, poach chicken breast in store-bought broth and use it for this soup.

Makes 4 to 6 bowls as a one-dish meal

1	Medium Whole chicken (3 to 4 lbs/ 1.4 to 1.8 kg.)
1	2-inch (5 cm.) piece Ginger, lightly smashed
1	lg. Onion, cut in quarters
6	cloves Garlic, smashed
12	White peppercorns, crushed
2	tsp. Kosher salt

1. Make Chicken Broth: Place rinsed chicken in 2-gallon pot (8 L.), with just enough water to cover. Bring to a vigorous boil; lower to simmer. Skim off foam and impurities; simmer 15 minutes. Remove pot from heat, cover tightly, and leave undisturbed at room temperature for 45 minutes (an instant-read thermometer should read 165°F / 74 C° at the thickest part of the chicken).

2. Carefully lift chicken from poaching liquid and plunge into a large container/pot/bowl of ice water. Leave in water for 15 minutes to stop cooking and firm up meat. Using your hands, pull off skin and discard.

3. Pull meat off breast and thighs into 1/4 to 1/2-inch (.6 to 1.3 cm.) thick strips, transfer to covered container and reserve at room temperature (you will have more than needed for the recipe).
4. Combine bones, thighs and poaching liquid back in the pot. Add ginger, onion, garlic, peppercorns and salt; simmer one hour to make a broth. Strain through fine wire mesh sieve. Taste and season well with salt.

How and Why

Letting chicken cook slowly, away from the stove ensures moister chicken. The slow cooking of the chicken prevents dry meat caused by over-coagulation of proteins.

SOUP GARNISHES

1 lb. (454 g.) Rice noodles, fresh ribbon style, about 1/4 inch (0.6 cm.) (1.3 cm.) wide (*kway teow*), store bought or homemade (pg. 117)
1/2 lb. (227 g.) Small shrimp, shell-on
1/2 lb. (227 g.) Chinese greens such as choy sum
2 Scallions, chopped

1. Soak noodles in lukewarm water 10 minutes, drain; peel apart into individual strands. Poach shrimp in chicken broth until just cooked; peel, devein and halve lengthwise.
2. Blanch whole bunches of choy sum in boiling water; transfer to a bowl of ice water for 30 seconds, squeeze dry, and cut into 2 to 3-inch pieces (5 to 7 cm.).

TABLE SAUCE

4 to 6 ea. Thai bird chilies, or other small hot chilies, sliced thinly, about 1/8 inch (0.3 cm.) thick
1/4 cup Soy sauce

1. Combine soy sauce and chilies, spoon mixture into individual bowls for each person.

ASSEMBLY OF NOODLE BOWLS

1. Bring seasoned broth up to a near boil. Have all ingredients ready, and have a pot of water boiling to reheat the noodles.
2. Reheat noodles in boiling water for 15 seconds. Drain, and distribute into 4 to 6 Asian soup bowls. Top noodles with chicken meat, shrimp, and choy sum. Ladle about 1 1/2 to 2 cups of broth into each bowl.
3. Sprinkle with scallions; serve with small dishes of chili-soy sauce. This sauce is used for dipping the subtly-flavored chicken, but can also be added to the soup.

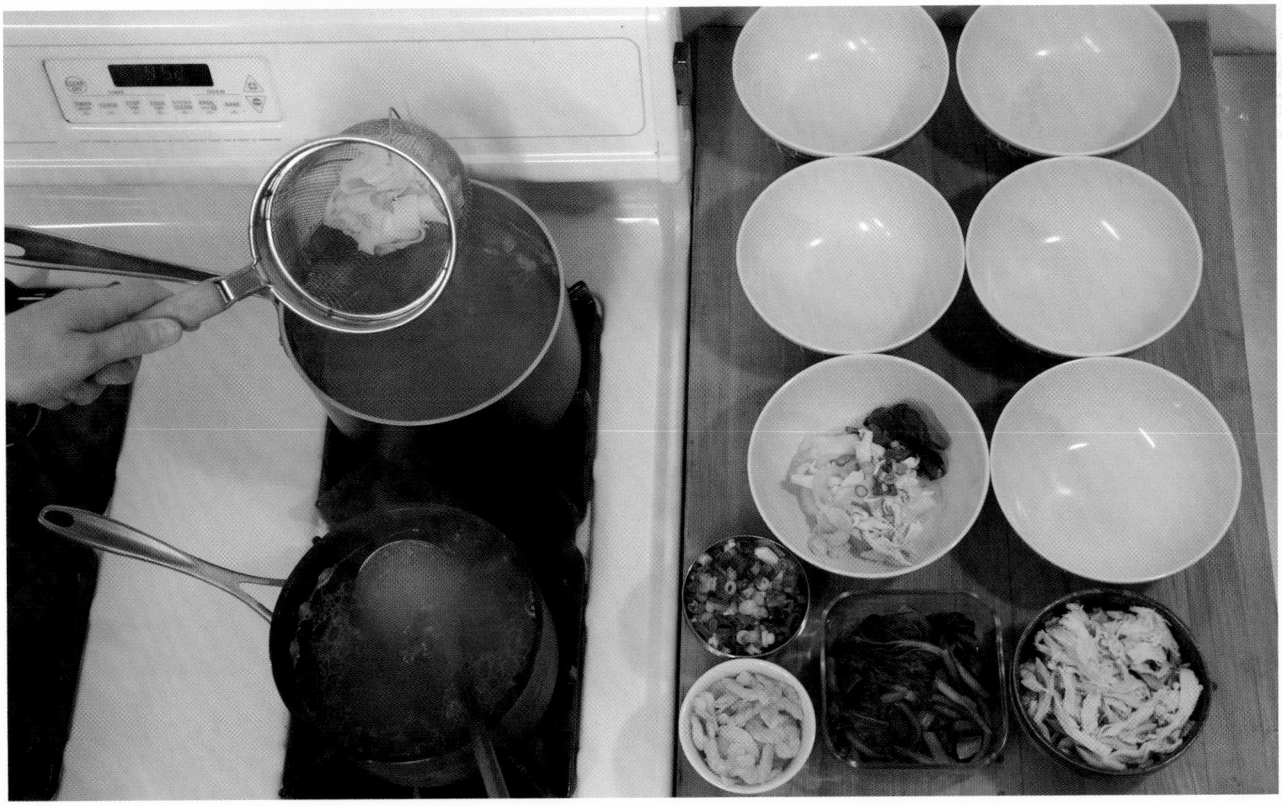

Get everything ready before assembling the noodle bowls.

Chicken Soup with Rice Noodles, Asian Greens, and Chili-Soy Sauce

Ipoh Sar Hor Fun

In Ipoh, Malaysia, this Kedai Kopi (Coffee Shop) is infamous for their Ipoh Sar Hor Fun.

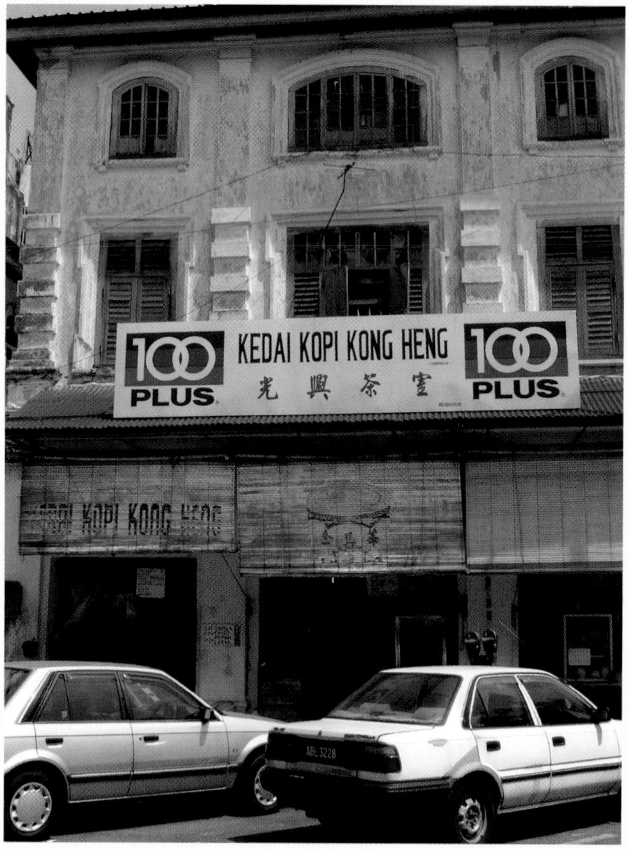
100 PLUS
KEDAI KOPI KONG HENG
光 興 茶 室
100 PLUS

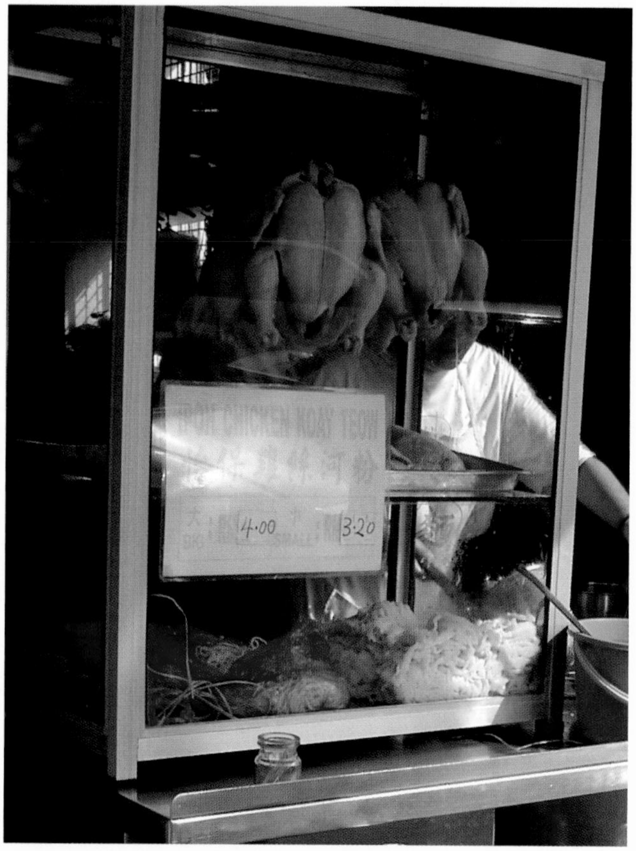
4.00
3.20

Poached chickens hang street-side at the ready to top luxurious bowls of noodles.

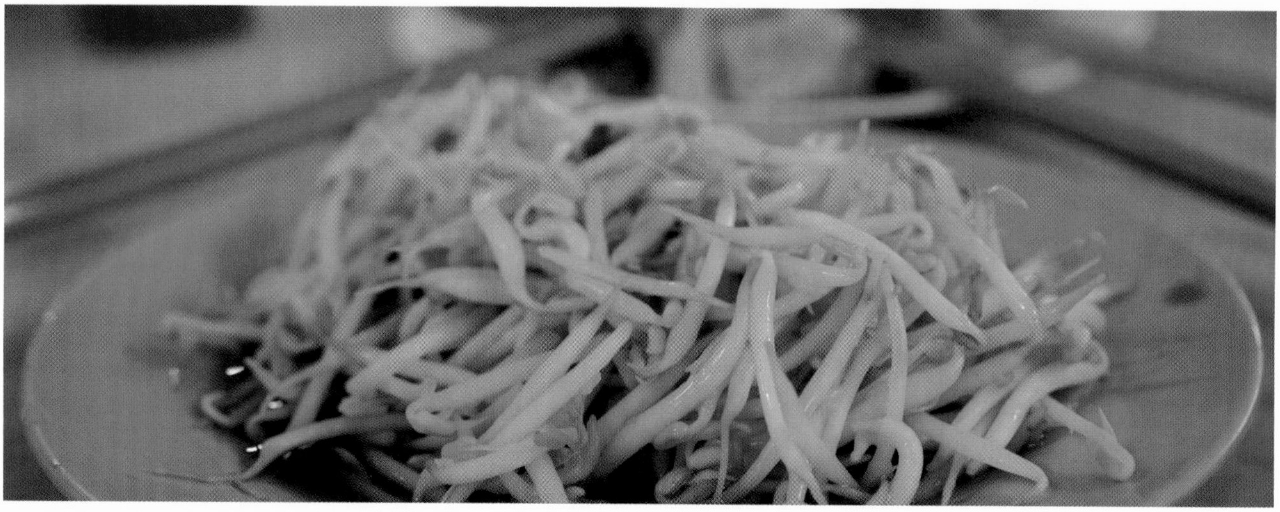

Piles of stir-fried bean sprouts are often served with the noodle bowls.

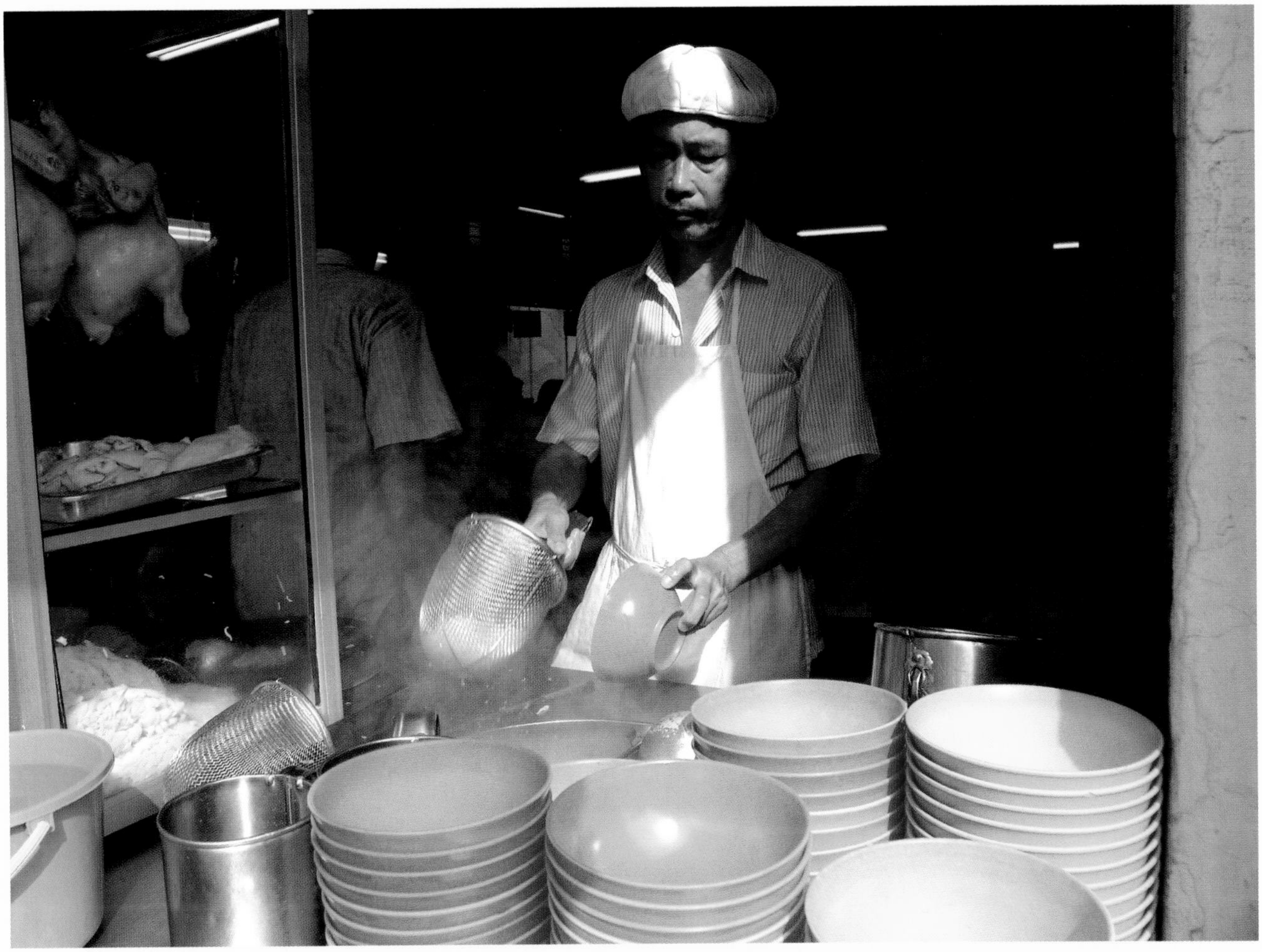

Bowl by bowl they churn out hundreds of bowls of noodles. Since everything is at the ready it only takes moments to receive your own bowl.

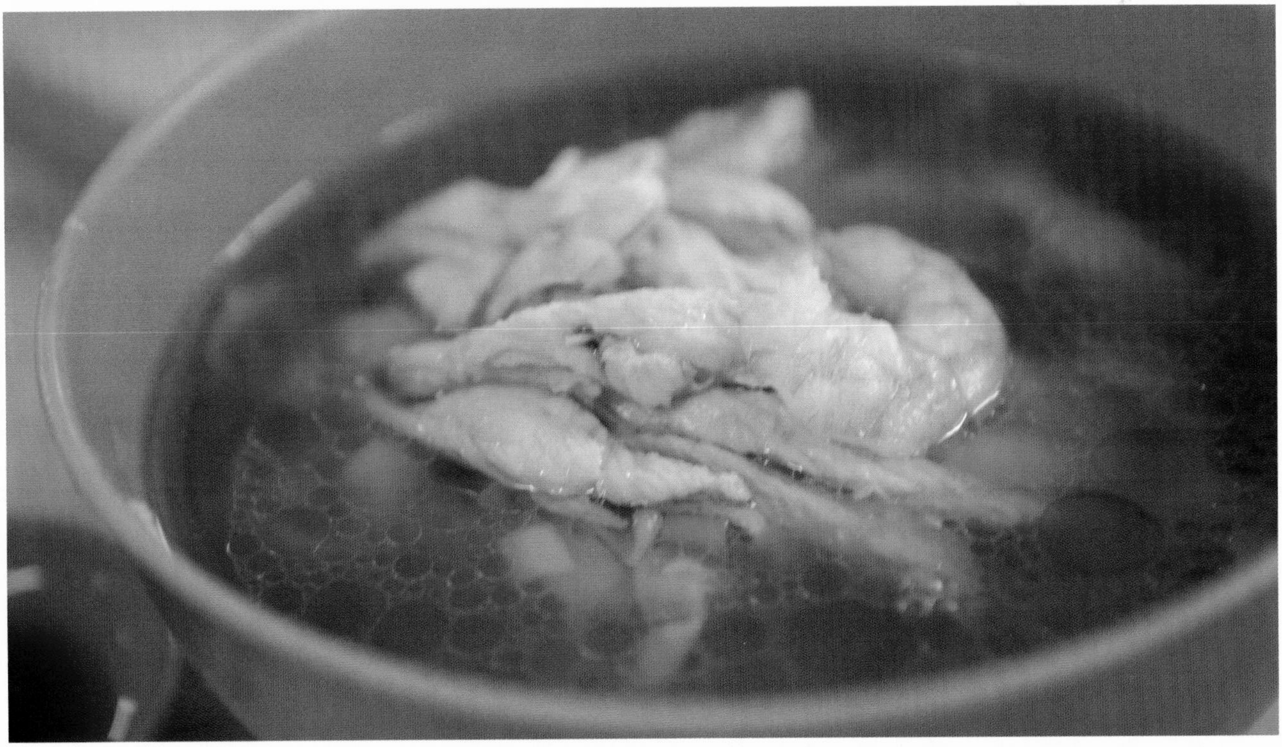

Many patrons request the noodles unadorned in order to savor the supple noodles without distraction.

Malaysian Chicken Satay
Satay Ayam

Fanning the glowing fire as he flipped skewers of golden-hued meat, increasing their alluring char, Lajis grudgingly revealed a secret to me: for special customers he adds ground-roasted peanuts to the marinade. At his hawker stalls in Kuala Lumpur, his cooks grill and serve mountains of this bamboo-borne snack, and pile them onto tables for guests to help themselves. At the end of the snack, customers simply count the number of skewers and pay accordingly: not too long ago they were ten cents a stick (peanut sauce, cucumbers and red onions included).

Here are a few more insider tips from the hawkers: Firstly, make a lemongrass basting brush. The woody tops of lemongrass stalks fray into fibrous bristles when pounded with the handle of a knife, creating a brush. Use this to apply juices and marinade to the meat as it grills. Soaking the skewers may not completely prevent them from burning on the grill but it sure slows them down. To really prevent burning, arrange the skewers so that their exposed ends hang off the edge of the grill. Make sure to push the coals to the edges of grill (pg. 111).

When Malaysians eat satay, they use their spent skewers to spear crisp cucumbers and onions and dip them in peanut sauce. They nosh, alternating between the spicy charred meat and the refreshing vegetables.

Makes 30 skewers

2	stalks Lemongrass, trimmed and sliced very thin, about 1/16 inch (.1 cm.)
4	cloves Garlic, roughly chopped
1	Tbsp. Finely grated galangal
1/2	cup Granulated sugar
2	tsp. Kosher salt
2	tsp. Ground turmeric
2	Tbsp. Ground, peanuts, roasted in dry pan (pg. 109) or ground fried peanuts
2	lb. (914 grams) Chicken thighs, boneless, fat on, skin-off, cut in 1/2 to 3/4-inch (1.3 to 2 cm.) squares
30	each Bamboo skewers, about 10 inches (25.4 cm.) long, soaked in warm water 1 hour
2	medium Cucumber, Kirby variety preferred, bite size pieces, about 1 inch
1/2	small Red onion, small bite size pieces, about 1/2 inch (1.3 cm.)
1	recipe Compressed rice cakes (*ketupat*), (optional) (pg. 312)
1	recipe Malaysian peanut sauce (*sos kacang*), (pg. 313)

1. Make the marinade: In a blender, puree lemongrass, garlic, galangal, and as much water as is necessary to facilitate blending, until it becomes a smooth marinade. Transfer to a bowl; add sugar, salt, turmeric, and peanuts. Pour marinade over chicken. Massage thoroughly (you may wish to use gloves or tongs, since the marinade will stain your fingers). Marinate covered in the refrigerator for 24 hours.

2. Skewer the satay: Pierce the marinated chicken onto skewers, aiming for the center of meat so that it lays flat on skewers. Arrange three to five pieces onto each skewer, leaving space at the blunt end of the skewer for handling.

3. Make the accompaniments: Wash cucumbers, trim off ends. Cut 1/2-inch chunks on varying angles to create odd bite-size wedges. Trim off the ends of the onions, cut into 1/2-inch (1.3 cm.) dice. Arrange on plate with compressed rice cakes.

4. Grill the satays: Grill over glowing coals or in a grill pan, turning often, until they are cooked through and the marinade has caramelized.

5. Serve with peanut sauce, compressed rice cakes, cucumbers and red onions.

Intense fire chars the outer edges of the satay creating an unparalleled flavor.

How and Why

1. Marinate overnight for the maximum flavor penetration and tenderness. The sugar and salt tenderize the meat and hold in the moisture when grilling it (a quick curing process).

2. Aim for the center of meat so that it lays flat on the skewer. This way more surface area is exposed, promoting even cooking.

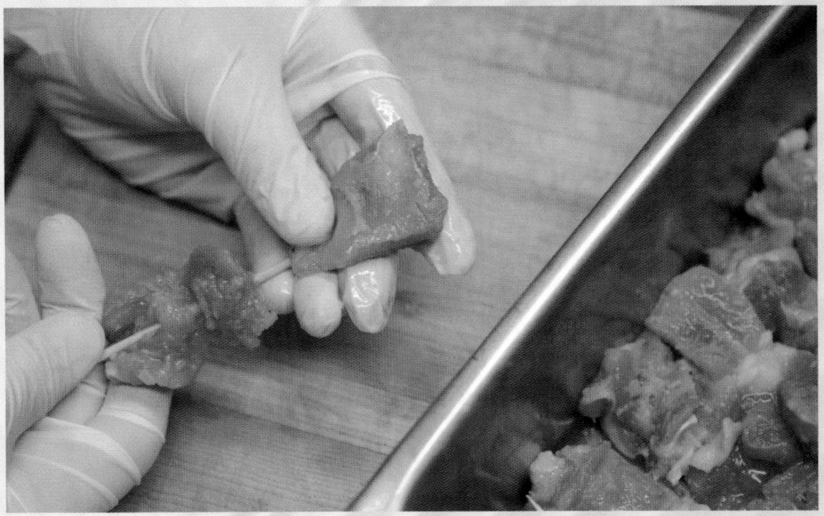

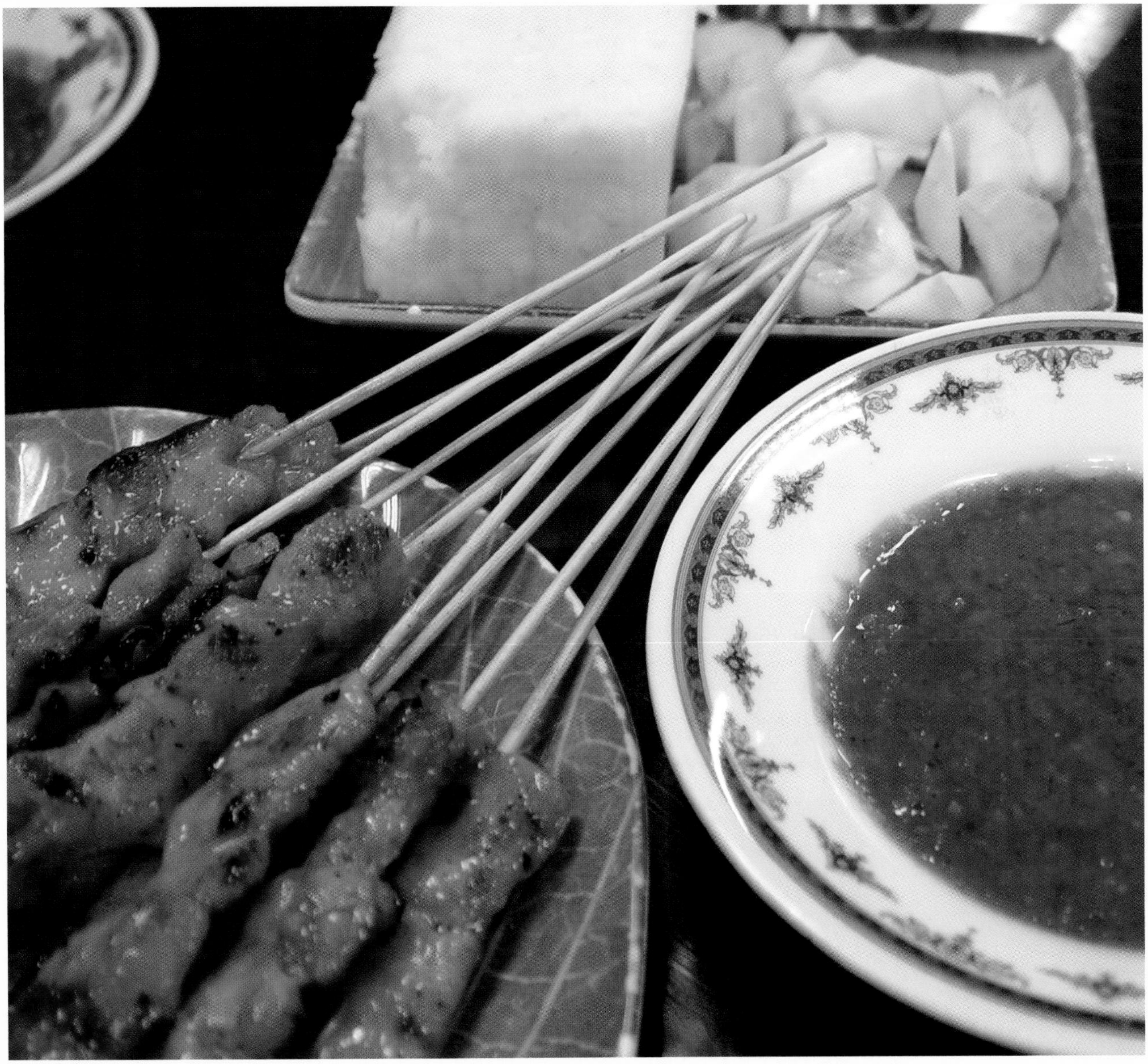

Pressed Rice Cakes

Ketupat

In Singapore and Malaysia, artisan cooks weave the palm fronds into small pouches for this dish. The pouch is with raw rice, pulled closed, and then boiled until the rice expands and compresses inside to form a tight cake. The cakes are cooled, cut into bite-size pieces, and eaten with satays and other flavorful dishes. I've created a more practical method for preparing the rice cakes, using standard baking pans. This is very authentic, albeit non-traditional. Many Malaysian cooks now prepare it this same way!

Makes 25 pieces

1   cup Long grain rice, such as jasmine
1¹/2 cups Water

1. Prepare the pans: Lightly grease an 8-inch × 8-inch × 2-inch baking pan (20 cm. × 20 cm. × 5 cm.) Line with plastic wrap, allowing a 4-inch (10 cm.) overhang on all sides. Have ready a second pan that stacks neatly into the lined baking pan (this will be used to weight down the rice).

2. Cook and mold the rice: Cook rice in covered pot or rice cooker using standard absorption method (pg. 106). After resting for 10 minutes, when cooking is complete, remove from heat and stir rice for 10 seconds slightly mashing some of the grains so they stick together after pressing.

3. Transfer rice into the prepared pan; spread into an even layer. Fold the overhanging plastic wrap over the rice, and then cover with an additional sheet. Top the rice with another pan, so that it's surface is completely pressed by the bottom of the inserted pan. Weight the top pan down with a 4-pound weight (¹/2 gallon of water (1.9 L.) or even a selection of canned goods). Set aside at room temperature for 1 hour, until rice is firmly set.

4. Unmold, cut and serve: Remove weight, remove top sheet of plastic and grip overhang of plastic wrap from bottom layer, pull up to remove rice from pan. Transfer to cutting board, remove all plastic wrap, and use a wet knife to cut into ³/4-inch (2 cm.) cubes. Arrange on a platter with cucumbers, red onions, and peanut sauce for dipping. When serving with satay, it's traditional to spear the rice and vegetables with aid of the spent satay skewers.

How and Why

1. Spraying or wiping pan with oil first helps the plastic wrap adhere. The oil acts like an adhesive making the plastic stick, I find I use this same technique for lining pans with parchment paper or plastic wrap.

2. Giving the rice a brief stir after cooking ensures that the cakes hold together. The slightly mashed grains act as a sort of glue.

Spicy Peanut Sauce
Sos Kacang

This is one of the first authentic Malaysian sauces I learned, It was back in the late 1980s and my then-Malaysian-food-guru, Mr. Lajis, had come to my mother-in-laws house to show me some of the secrets that made his six street food stands in Kuala Lumpur such booming successes. This sauce can be served after it's simmered only an hour, but full flavor is achieved only after a slow cook of several hours. Add small splashes of water as it simmers to maintain a medium-thick consistency. The flavorful oil that the spice paste was fried in will eventually rise to the surface, resist your temptation to skim this off. The oil is very flavorful and is not discarded.

Makes 3 cups

<table>
<tr><td>1/2 cup (1/2 oz. / 14 g.) Dried red hot chilies, stems and seeds removed</td></tr>
<tr><td>1 tsp. Dried shrimp</td></tr>
<tr><td>1/2 cup Vegetable oil</td></tr>
<tr><td>2 medium Shallots, roughly chopped</td></tr>
<tr><td>2 stalks Lemongrass, trimmed and sliced very thin, about 1/16 inch (.1 cm.)</td></tr>
<tr><td>2 tsp. Finely grated galangal</td></tr>
<tr><td>2 cloves Garlic, roughly chopped</td></tr>
<tr><td>1 1/2 cups Peanuts, roasted in dry pan (pg. 109) or deep-fried, ground finely</td></tr>
<tr><td>3 cups Water</td></tr>
<tr><td>3/4 cup Granulated sugar</td></tr>
<tr><td>2 tsp. Kosher salt</td></tr>
</table>

1. Cover chilies and shrimp with 1 cup room temperature water; soak 30 minutes. Drain well.

2. Make a semi-smooth spice paste (*rempah*) (pg. 105) by pureeing the oil, shallots, garlic, lemongrass, galangal, drained dried shrimp, and chilies in a blender.

3. Heat a 2-quart saucepan over medium heat. Add pureed rempah; cook on medium heat until mixture is fragrant and oil begins to separate out from it, about 5 to 10 minutes.

4. Add water and peanuts; stir well. Bring back to a boil, lower heat, and simmer 1 hour, stirring often. Add sugar and salt. Continue to simmer until "raw" flavor has dissipated, up to 2 hours, adding water as needed to compensate for evaporation.

How and Why

Oil will rise to the top of this sauce. Do not discard this oil. The oil is packed with flavor and it is traditional to have some oil floating on top.

Notice the difference in appearance between the pan-roasted nuts (top) and the deep-fried nuts (left).
Look at page 109 for more details on strategies for maximizing flavor.

Singapore Chili Crabs
Ketam Sos Chili

Chili crab is unofficially the national dish of Singapore, a food-obsessed where locals still debate which is "number one" into the wee hours of the night. This recipe, with its copious amount of gravy, is modeled after Mellben Seafood's version, which is served with piles of fried bread cubes to sop up the sweet, spicy gravy. A modern dish that fuses the best of the traditional (a Malay-style spice paste, rempah) and new (ketchup).

Yes, ketchup. After all, ketchup's ancestry can be traced back to Southeast Asia in the form of an Indonesian fermented sauce called "keciap." When the British brought this sweet concoction to their colonies in the New World, tomatoes became the dominant ingredient. Ketchup is now an authentic ingredient in chili crab. Not that they're using Heinz or Hunt's: "Asian" style ketchups like Lee Kum Kee are much deeper red, have less spices and tangy flavor.

Makes 2 to 3 servings as part of a multi-dish meal

1/4 cup (1/4 oz. / 7 g.) Dried long red chilies, stems and seeds removed

1/4 cup Vegetable oil, plus 2 Tbsp. extra for cooking crab

2 medium Shallots, roughly chopped

6 cloves Garlic, roughly chopped

1 Tbsp. Minced ginger

2 pieces Long red chilies or other hot red chilies, roughly chopped (pg. 44)

1 lg. Live Dungeness crab, about 2 to 3 lbs. (.9 to 1.4 kg.)

1 Tbsp. Cornstarch whisked together with 1/4 cup water

1 1/2 cup Water (divided use)

3 Tbsp. Ketchup, (preferably Asian style, such as Lee Kum Kee)

1 Tbsp. Ground bean sauce (pg. 53)

1 Tbsp. Granulated sugar

1/4 tsp. Kosher salt

1 lg. Egg, lightly beaten

1 Scallion, 2-inch (5 cm.) pieces, shaved thinly, rinsed under cool water

6 Sprigs cilantro

1 loaf White bread (soft baguette or other of your choice)

1. Make the spice paste: Soak dried chilies in 1/2 cup of room temperature water 30 minutes; drain (save water), squeeze out excess moisture. In a blender, puree soaked chilies with 1/4 cup oil, shallots, garlic, ginger, and chilies to create a fine spice paste (*rempah*). Add only as much water (use water from chilies), as needed to facilitate blending. (Alternately make the spice paste in mortar (pg. 104).

2. Prepare crab: Cut crab with by piercing through the center of the body with a knife, cutting through head. Pull off top shell; reserve. Pull off the feathery gills and bottom tail flap; discard. Cut entire crab in half from head to tail. Cut off both claws, cut body halves evenly in two so there are some walking legs on each piece. Rinse crab with cold water and drain very well. With heavy, blunt object (such as a mallet or the back of a cleaver) crack claw and thick legs to ensure seasoning penetrates.

3. Combine water and cornstarch; whisk well, and set aside.

4. Cook the crab: Heat a large skillet, wok or Dutch oven over high heat. Add 2 Tbsp. oil, heat briefly, and then add crab (drained of any moisture that has gathered); stir-fry for about 3 to 5 minutes, until crab begins to turn orange and a roasted aroma is perceivable. Add 1 cup water cover, and cook 3 minutes until crab is almost fully cooked. Remove crab from pot, and reserve in a warm place, along with any remaining liquid.

5. Add 2 tablespoons of oil to pan, add spice paste and cook until paste looses raw aroma, about 3 to 5 minutes. Add remaining 1/2 cup water, ketchup, ground bean sauce, sugar, and salt; bring to a boil. Stir cornstarch mixture (a slurry), and then drizzle in cornstarch slurry while rapidly stirring boiling sauce; cook until sauce thickens considerably. Add water as needed to maintain a thick and creamy sauce consistency.

6. Add crab back to pan, and cook, stirring constantly, until crab is fully coated with sauce. Transfer crab to a serving platter. Bring sauce up to a simmer; drizzle in eggs while stirring slowly to create small ribbons of eggs (like egg drop soup). Remove from heat. Taste and adjust seasoning with salt or sugar. Pour sauce over crab. Garnish with scallions, and serve with crusty soft-centered bread or steamed rice.

Sri Lanka crabs are prized for their meaty body and rich flavor. Here they are bound to prevent the cook from losing a finger or two.

How and Why

1. Cooking spice paste thoroughly makes a balanced sauce. Once the liquid ingredients are added to the cooked spice paste, it only cooks for a few minutes. The initial stage of cooking is necessary to soften the flavors of the aromatics.

2. Slowly stir the sauce as you add the eggs, to create small ribbons. Stir too fast and it will cloud the sauce with small flakes of eggs, a steady, slow stir allows the eggs to cook as they are drizzled in.

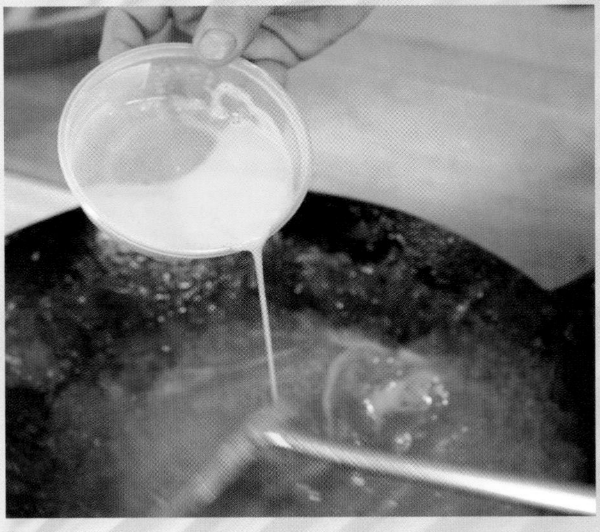

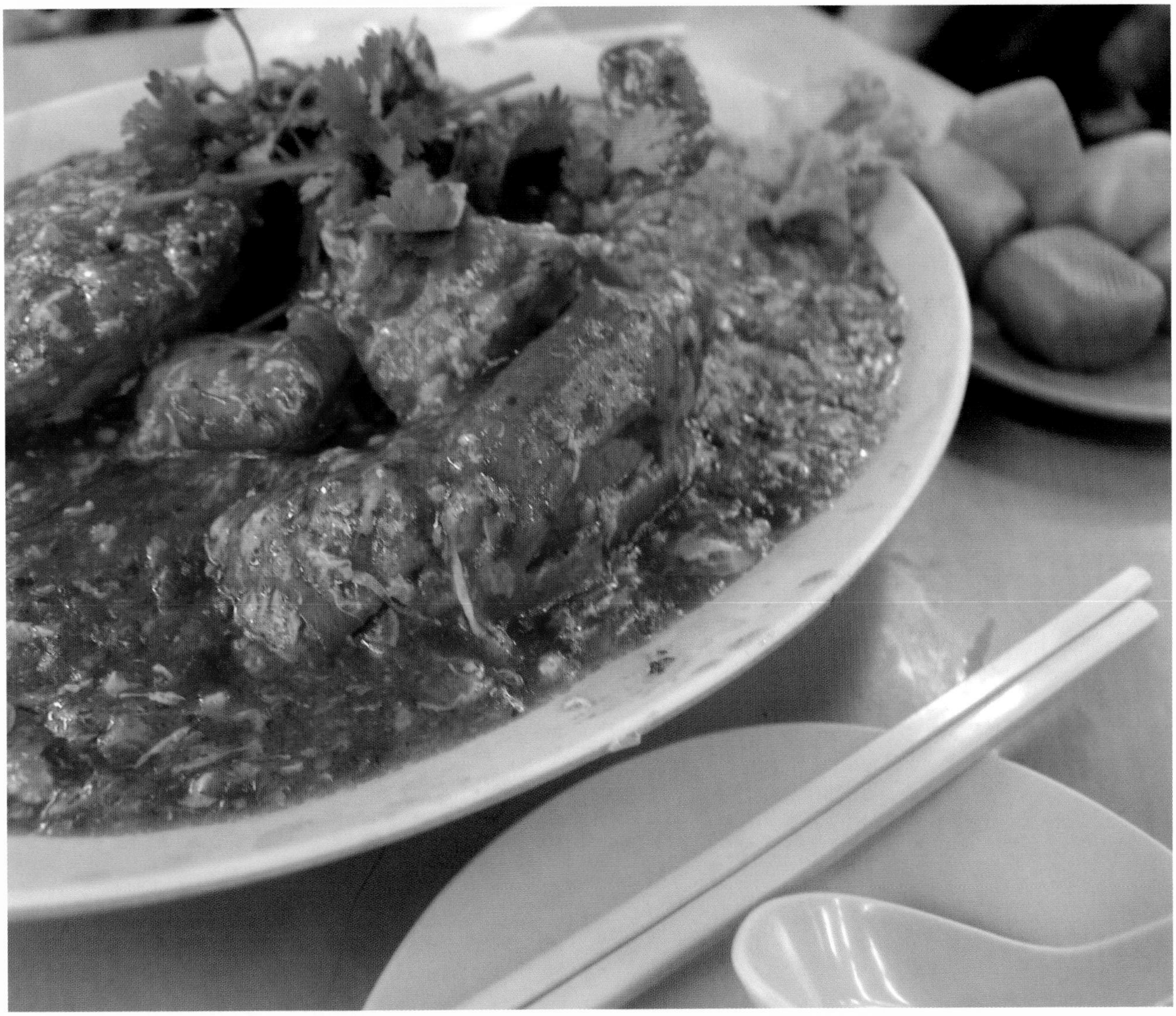

Mellben restaurant in Singapore serves their chili crabs with deep-fried buns for sopping up all the gravy.

Black Pepper Crab

Ketam Lada Hitam

My lips tingle just thinking about the spicy black pepper sauce that clings to this crab. Each time I make it, it brings back memories of "al fresco" dining on Singapore's east coast, where restaurants straddle the seashore. Uncompromisingly fresh crab is essential here: alive and kicking are the qualifiers. If that's not available, choose shrimp as an alternative. If you do, split the shrimp shells up the back, devien them, and shorten the recipe cooking time. This recent addition to Singapore's culinary cache uses butter in to soften the black pepper and garlic edge. I like to add a few teaspoons of oyster sauce to round out the flavor and help everything adhere to the crab

Makes 2 to 3 servings as part of a multi-dish meal

1	lg. Live Dungeness crab or other fresh crab, about 2 to 3 lbs. (.9 to 1.4 kg)
1/4	cup Vegetable oil
1/2	cup Water
2	Tbsp. Unsalted butter
2	Tbsp. Roughly minced garlic
4	tsp. Coarsely ground black peppercorns
1	Tbsp. Thick soy sauce or 2 Tbsp. dark soy sauce and omit the salt
2	tsp. Oyster sauce
1/4	tsp. Kosher salt
1	Tbsp. Granulated sugar
6	sprigs Cilantro

1. Prepare crab: Cut crab with by piercing through the center of the body with a knife, cutting through head. Pull off top shell; reserve. Pull off the feathery gills and bottom tail flap; discard. Cut entire crab in half from head to tail. Cut off both claws, cut body halves evenly in two so there are some walking legs on each piece. Rinse crab with cold water and drain very well. With heavy, blunt object (such as a mallet or the back of a cleaver) crack claw and thick legs to ensure seasoning penetrates.

2. Cook the crab: In a large skillet, wok or Dutch oven over high heat, heat oil for 1 minute, until it almost begins to smoke. Add crab (drained of any moisture hat has gathered); stir-fry 3 minutes until crab begins to turn orange, and a roasted aroma is perceptible. Add water; cover and steam 2 minutes until crab is almost fully cooked. Remove crab and any remaining liquid from pot; reserve.

3. Add butter, garlic, and black pepper to the pan; cook until garlic looses raw aroma, 20 seconds. Add crab back to pan, along with any juices that have collected. Stir in soy sauce, oyster sauce, salt, and sugar; cook, stirring, until crab is fully cooked and sauce is sticking all over crab exterior. If crab is cooked and sauce is not thick, remove crab, boil sauce until thickened, and then add crab back top pan and toss to coat.

4. Transfer to serving platter and garnish with cilantro sprigs.

How and Why

1. Buy fresh, live crabs to ensure freshness. Crustaceans such as crab deteriorate internally once dead.

2. Using one quick cut through the entire head of the crab is the most humane way to kill it. This technique kills the crab nearly instantly.

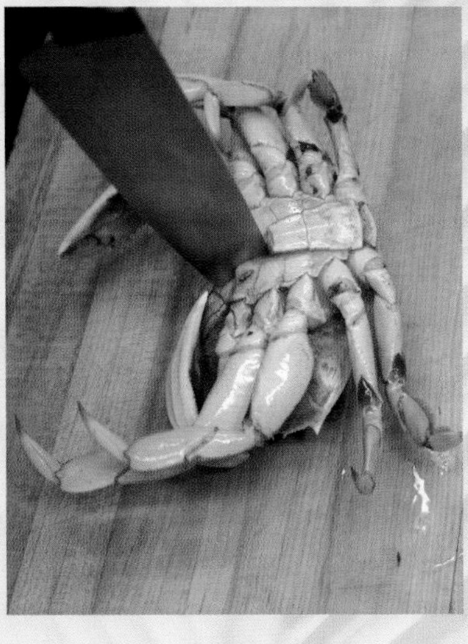

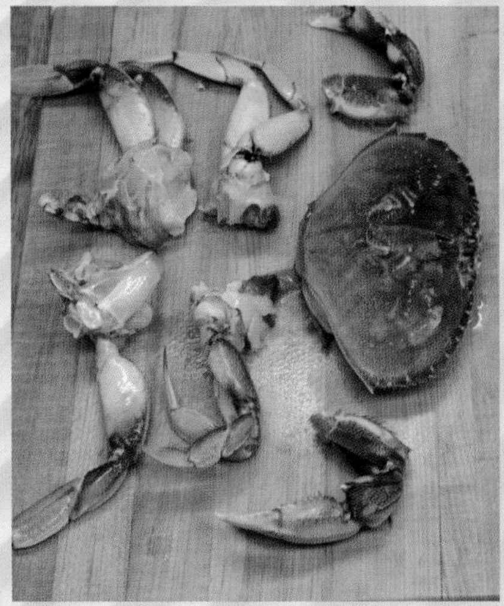

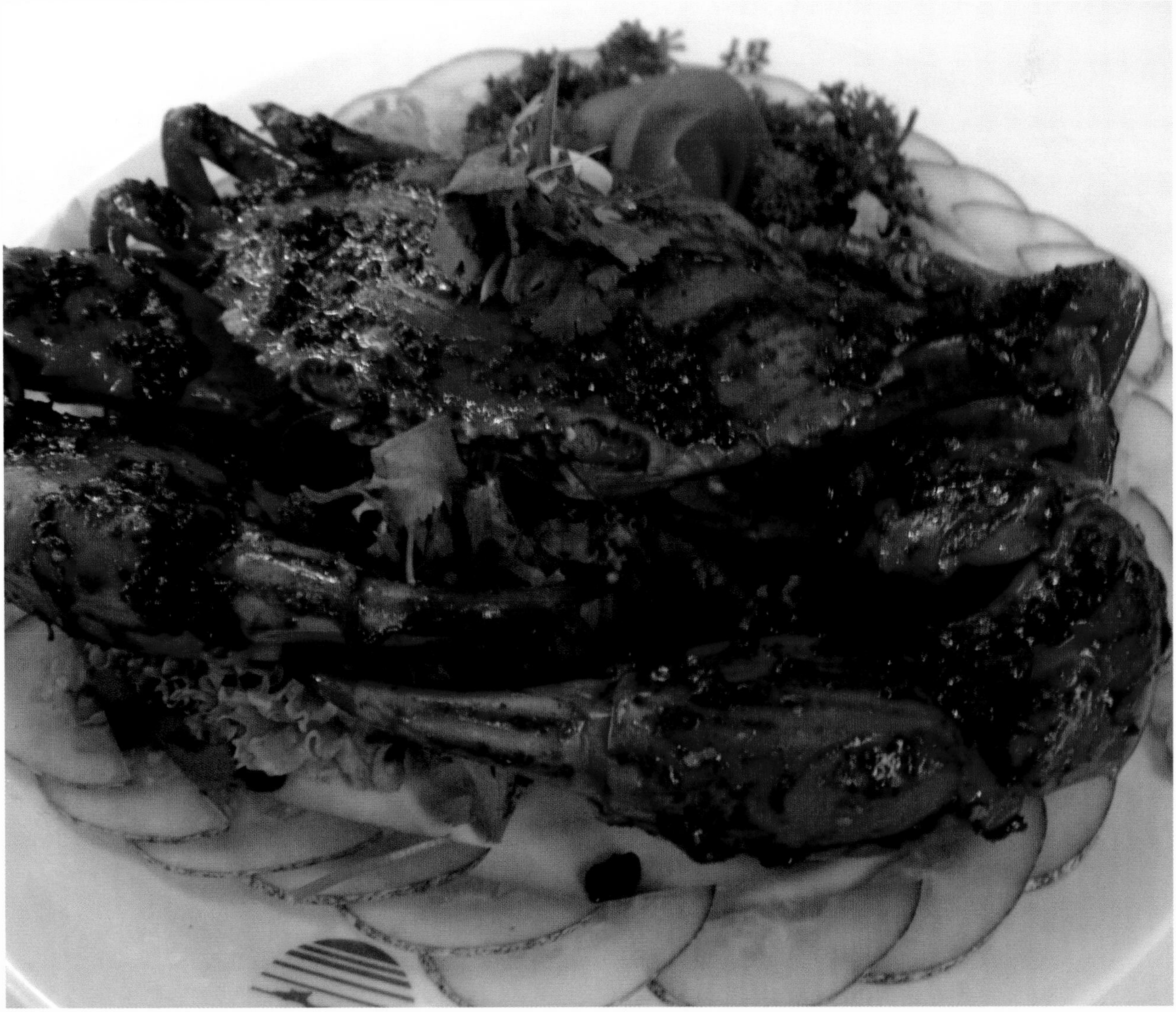

Long Beach Seafood serves a sedap (delicious) version of the black pepper crab.

Succulent Poached Chicken with Aromatic Rice and Ginger-Garlic Chili Sauce

Hainanese Chicken Rice

Hainanese chicken rice originated on the Chinese island of Hainan. It's now claimed as a national treasure in both Malaysia and Singapore. In it, chicken is poached until just barely cooked through, and still extremely juicy. The luscious chicken, which attains a resilient (some would say "bouncy") skin, is served atop "chickeny" steamed rice, accompanied by a sipping cup of the delicate cooking broth and a coarse garlic/ginger/chili sauce.

Its simplicity (poached chicken, rice, broth and a condiment) proves that "less is more," since the combination of these elements creates a strikingly memorable flavor immersion.

The fat that makes the rice so luscious is skimmed from the top of the chicken poaching liquid. But any chicken fat will do, so if you wish to render fat from the cavity of the bird, go ahead and use it.

Makes 4 to 6 servings as part of multi-dish meal

FOR POACHING THE CHICKEN

1   medium Whole chicken (3 to 4 lbs or 1.4 to 1.9 kg)., keep gizzard and neck, discard liver and heart or use for another recipe
1   Tbsp. Kosher salt
1   2-inch (5 cm.) piece Ginger, lightly smashed
3   Scallions, lightly smashed

MAKE BROTH AND POACH CHICKEN:

1. Place rinsed chicken in 2-gallon (8 L.) pot, with just enough water to cover. Bring to a vigorous boil; lower to simmer. Skim off foam and impurities; simmer 15 minutes. Remove pot from heat, cover tightly, and leave undisturbed at room temperature for 45 minutes (an instant-read thermometer should read 165°F / 74°C at the thickest part of the chicken).

Chicken rice is one of those simple dishes that rely on the best quality ingredients so choose your chicken wisely. Some folks like to serve thick soy sauce on the side to add a level of complexity to the flavor.

2. Carefully lift chicken from poaching liquid and plunge into a large container/pot/bowl of ice water. Leave in water for 15 minutes to stop cooking and firm up meat.

3. Cut chicken into eight major parts—2 breast, 2 legs, two thighs, two wings, transfer to covered container and reserve at room temperature. Strain broth through very fine mesh strainer (or cheesecloth lined sieve). Taste broth, and adjust seasoning with salt.

CHILI SAUCE

5   (about 1/4 lb. / 113 g.) Long red chilies or other hot red chilies, roughly chopped (pg. 44)
1   Tbsp. Finely grated ginger
4   cloves Garlic, finely minced
2   Tbsp. Distilled white vinegar and/or lime juice
1/2   tsp. Granulated sugar
1/2   tsp. Kosher salt
1/4   cup Chicken broth (use from poaching chicken)

1. If using a mortar: Pound or puree chilies, ginger, garlic in mortar until a paste is formed. Add vinegar, sugar, salt and broth; mix until dissolved. Taste and adjust seasoning with salt, sugar and vinegar.

2. If using a mini-food processor or blender: Combine chilies, ginger, garlic, vinegar, sugar, and salt. Pulse until a semi-smooth paste is formed. Transfer to a bowl; add broth, and mix until dissolved. Taste and adjust seasoning with salt, sugar and vinegar.

FOR THE RICE

1/4   cup Rendered chicken fat (skimmed from poaching chicken) or store bought
1   Tbsp. Minced, ginger
4   cloves Garlic, minced
2   medium Shallots, minced
2   cups Chicken broth (chicken poaching liquid)
11/2   cups Jasmine rice, rinsed in sieve until water runs clear, drained well
3   Pandan leaves, tied in a knot (optional)
1/4   tsp. Kosher salt

STOVETOP METHOD:

1. Heat a 2-quart (2 L.) saucepan with the chicken fat until it shimmers but does not smoke. Add ginger, garlic, and shallots; fry until the garlic begins to brown. Add chicken broth, add rice, pandan, and salt.

2. Bring to a boil, uncovered. Stir once, and then cover tightly. Lower flame to lowest setting, and simmer rice 20 minutes.

3. Remove pan from heat (do not uncover!). Allow rice to rest, covered, for 10 minutes, before fluffing gently with a fork or wooden spoon and serving.

How and Why

1. Letting chicken cook slowly, off the heat, ensures moist chicken. Slow cooking of the chicken prevents dry meat caused by over coagulation of proteins.

2. Plunge chicken into ice water bath for a resilient bite. The ice water not only shocks the skin into a delightful texture, but it also prevents residual heat from continuing to cook the chicken.

RICE COOKER METHOD:

Heat a 2 qt. (2 L.). saucepan with the chicken fat, add ginger, garlic and shallots and fry until the garlic begins to brown. Add 1 cup of chicken stock and bring to a boil. Pour this mixture into rice cooker, add rice, pandan, remaining chicken broth and salt. Even out rice surface with your hands. Turn the cooker on (or Follow manufacturer's directions). Fluff gently with a fork or wooden spoon.

CHICKEN BASTING MIXTURE

2   Tbsp. Soy sauce
2   Tbsp. Sesame oil

ACCOMPANIMENT

2   medium Cucumbers, preferably Kirby variety, peeled, halved lengthwise and sliced 1/4 inch (0.6 cm.) thick

TO ASSEMBLE CHICKEN RICE

1. Arrange cucumbers on a platter.

2. Leaving the bone in and skin on, hack chicken through bones into smaller pieces (trying to keep the precious skin intact). Cut breasts into 4 to 6 thick slices each; legs and thighs into 3 pieces each and wings in half. Arrange chicken atop cucumbers, and then spoon soy and sesame oil mixture over the chicken.

3. Serve hot broth in small bowls. Serve each guest an individual portion of rice, accompanied by a dipping bowl of chili sauce. Guests help themselves to the chicken and cucumbers family style, and slowly sip the soup as an accompaniment.

Soy and Spice Simmered Pork Shoulder: "Annie's Pork"

Se Bak

Annie Leong, my mother-in-law, has been my indispensable tutor in Malaysian cookery. This is one of her simple, delicious recipes, which is similar to the Chinese style of "red cooking" from the Fukian region. But this version takes on a distinctly Southeast Asian spin with its infusion of lemongrass and galangal. The star anise and cinnamon perfume the rich brown sauce with their kind aromas. If can you resist finishing it all and refrigerate for the next day make sure to remove the spice so they do not over flavor infuse their flavor. A pressure cooker works extremely well for this dish. Simply pressure cook 20 minutes to achieve ultra-tender pork. Steamed white rice and some sliced cucumbers complete the meal.

Makes 4 servings as part of a multi-dish meal
(easy to double and its gets better the next day)

1 1/2 lb. (227 g.) Pork shoulder or butt, cut into 2-inch (5 cm.) chunks (do not trim fat or skin)
3 Tbsp. Dark soy sauce or 1/4 Tbsp. Black/thick soy and 1 tsp. salt
2 Tbsp. Granulated sugar
4 medium Shallot, roughly chopped
2 cloves Garlic, roughly chopped

1/4 cup Vegetable oil
3 stalks Lemongrass, trimmed and bruised
4 slices Galangal, 1/4 inch (0.6 cm.) thick
1 stick "Cassia" Cinnamon (about 3 inches (7.5 cm.) long)
2 pieces Star anise

1. Marinate pork in soy sauce and sugar for at least 1 hour. In blender, mini-food processor or mortar, create a smooth paste with shallots, garlic and oil. (in mortar pound garlic first, then add shallots and pound until smooth, stir in oil and proceed)
2. Heat a 4 qt. (4 L.) saucepan over medium-low heat; add shallot mixture. Cook 5 minutes, stirring occasionally until raw aroma has dissipated. Add marinated pork (with any marinade), lemongrass, galangal, cinnamon and star anise. Add just enough water to cover (usually about two and a half cups).
3. Bring to a boil, and then lower to simmer. Cook until pork is very tender, about 1 to 1 1/2 hours. Adjust seasoning with soy sauce, sugar, and salt to taste.
4. Before storage remove the star anise and cassia so they do not overpower.

Annie Leong, one of my
Malaysian cuisine mentors.

How and Why

1. Marinating pork first will give it a deep brown color. The first step of saturating the pork with the dark soy sauce before adding all the liquid ensures it takes on a dark color and rich flavor.

2. Cooking the shallot mixture (*rempah*) in oil will mellow the harsh shallot and garlic flavor. This diminishes the sulfur compounds, and brings out natural sweetness in the shallots.

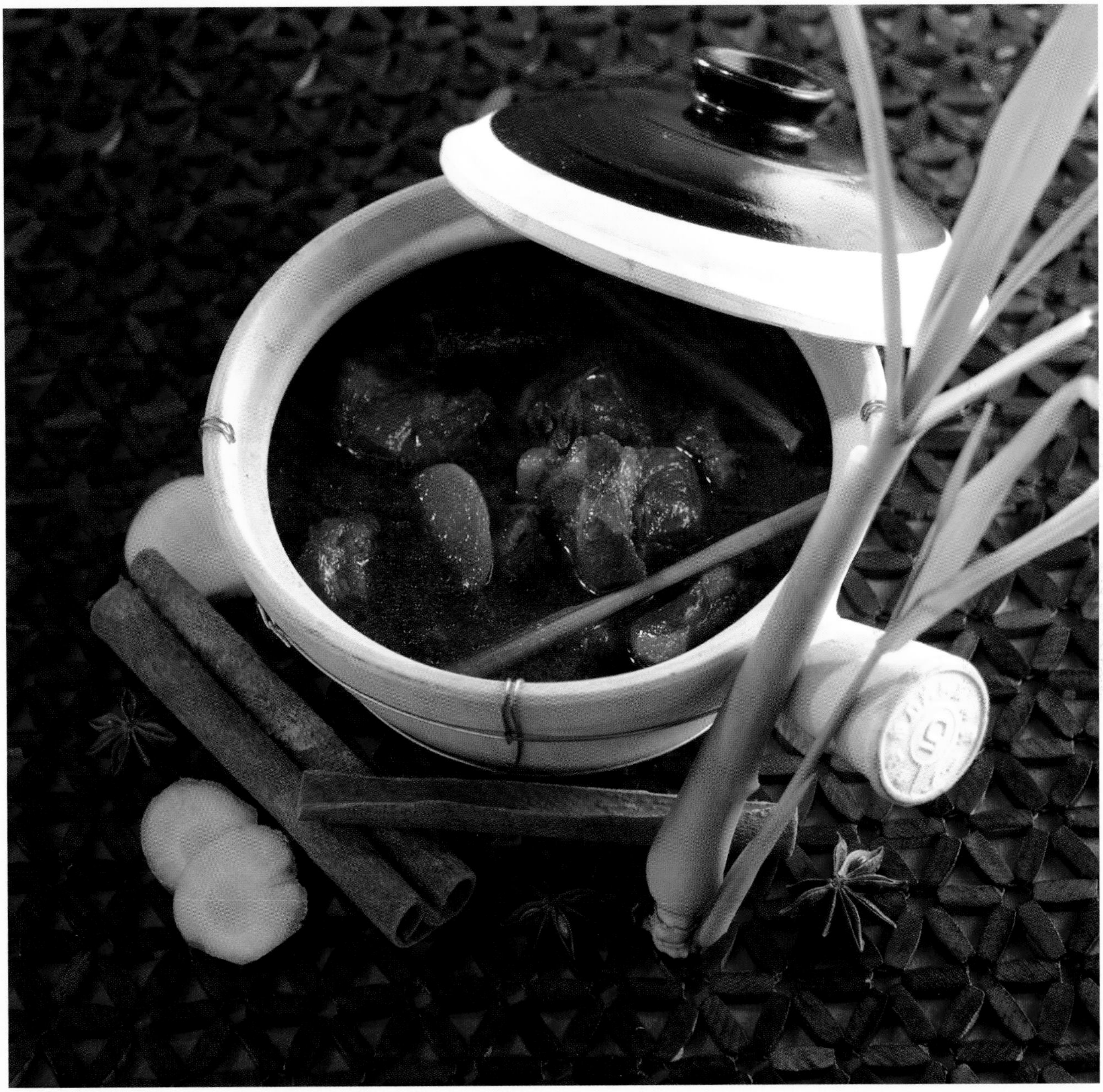

Chicken and Chinese Black Mushroom Stew

Pong Teh

This rich stew is always a great introduction to Malaysian food. Its rich sauce with mahogany potatoes and resilient mushrooms creates a stew that wouldn't seem all that unfamiliar to most Americans. A piquant pickle, "achar," which adds a punch of vibrancy to the finished dish, is a frequent accompaniment. Some families substitute pork shoulder for the chicken, a testament to the Chinese penchant for pork.

Makes 4 to 6 servings with steamed white rice

10	Dried Chinese black mushrooms (shiitake)
8	(about 2¹/₂ lbs. / 1.125 kg.) Chicken thighs, bone in, skin off
2	Tbsp. Thick soy sauce (or sub 3 Tbsp. dark soy and reduce regular soy by 1 Tablespoon)
2	Tbsp. Soy sauce
2	Tbsp. Granulated sugar
¹/₂	cup Vegetable oil
20	cloves Garlic, roughly chopped (³/₄ cup)
8	Shallots, roughly chopped (about 1 cup)
6	Tbsp. Ground bean sauce (*tau cheung*) (pg. 53)
1	lb. (454 g.) Gold (waxy) potatoes, 1-inch (2.5 cm.) chunks
1	recipe Malaysian pickles (*acar awak*) (pg. 324)

1. Soak mushrooms in 2 cups room temperature water until soft. Trim off stem; discard. Cut caps in half. Pour clear soaking liquid into a cup; discard any sediment. Toss chicken with soy sauces and sugar; marinate 1 hour, mixing once after 30 minutes.

2. Make Aromatic Base: Blend oil, garlic, and shallots into a semi-smooth puree.

3. Cook the Chicken: In an 8 qt. (8 L.) pot over medium heat, add the garlic/shallot mixture. Cook, stirring and scraping bottom often with wooden spoon until oil begins to separate, 5 to 10 minutes. Add brown bean sauce and cook 3 minutes, until rich aroma develops. Add mushrooms, potatoes and chicken (with marinade); mix thoroughly. Add enough mushroom soaking liquid to barely cover the chicken (add water if needed).

4. Bring to a boil, and then lower to simmer. Stew, stirring occasionally until chicken is cooked through, about 1 hour. Skim excess fat.

5. Taste sauce; adjust seasonings to taste. For a thicker sauce, mash some of the potatoes into the broth.

How and Why

1. Marinating the chicken in the soy sauces give it a rich color. Don't marinate too long as it will become dry and stringy.

2. Puree garlic and shallots coarsely for appealing texture. The shallot and garlic mixture is the primary thickener.

3. Fry until garlic-oil puree until it darkens and oil begins to separate. This indicates that the water has evaporated and the mixture has become sweetly, subtly flavored.

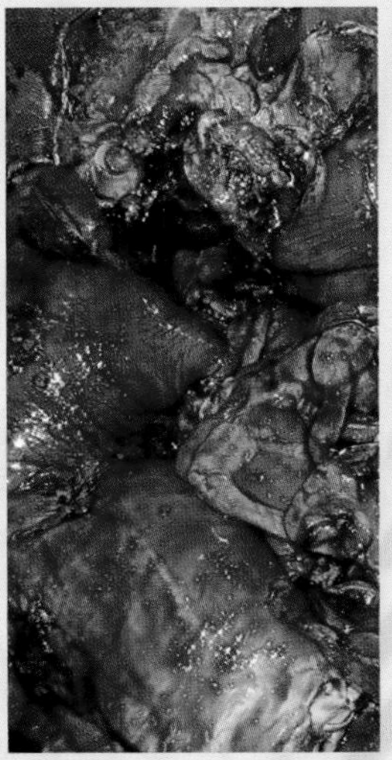

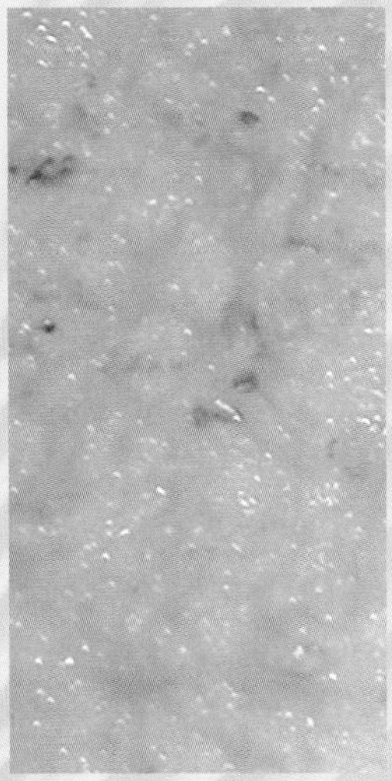

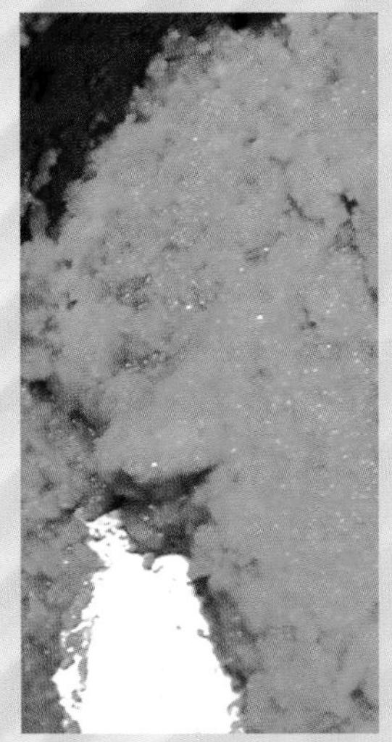

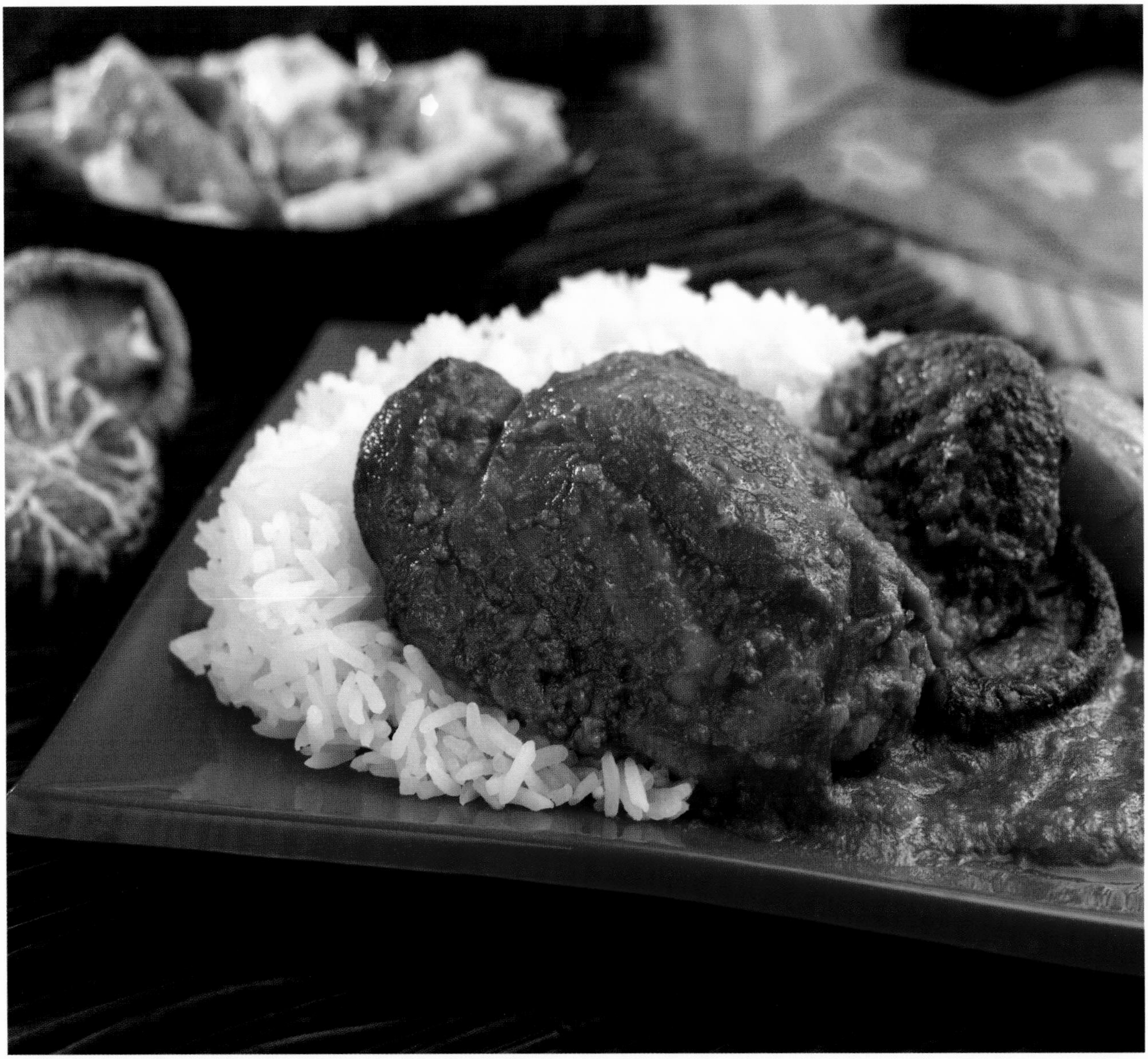

Mixed Vegetable Pickle
Acar Awak

This classic Malaysian pickle is vibrant yellow from turmeric, and sparkles with the flavor of lemongrass. On Chinese New Year the pickle accompanies the deep brown chicken stew (pong teh), it piquant flavor juxtaposes the savory and rich stew. I keep them in my refrigerator for a snack, tossed into salads or with other salty dishes that call for their sweet and sour crunch. If it's a nice sunny day, place the vegetables, after blanched in vinegar in step two, on a pan uncovered in the sun to dehydrate them for a couple of hours, this will create an even crisper pickle. Although they can be stored for up to one month, these pickles taste best in the first two weeks.

Makes 4 cups

1/4 cup (1/4 oz. / 7 gm.) Dried red chilies, remove stems and seeds

3 1/2 cups Distilled white vinegar (divided use)

1 cup Biet size carrot strips, about 2 inches (5 cm.) long and 1/2 inch (1.3 cm.) thick

1 medium Kirby cucumber, seeded, cut into bite size strips, about 2 inches (5 cm.) long and 1/2 inch (1.3 cm.) thick

1 cup Green cabbage strips, about 1 1/2 inch (about 3.9 cm) wide

1 cup Green beans pieces, about 1 1/2 -inch (about 3.9 cm) pieces

2 medium Red long chilies strips, about 1/2 × 2-inch (1.3 × 5 cm.) strips

1/2 cup Vegetable oil

2 medium Shallots, roughly chopped

2 cloves Garlic, roughly chopped

1 Tbsp. Finely galangal

2 stalks Lemongrass, trimmed and sliced very thin, about 1/16 inch (.1 cm.)

1/2 tsp. Turmeric powder

1/2 cup Water

1/4 cup Granulated sugar

1 tsp. Kosher salt

1/4 cup Peanuts, roasted in dry pan, roughly chopped (pg. 109)

1. Soak chilies in 1/2 cup of room temperature water for 30 minutes, drain and squeeze out excess moisture.

2. Blanch the vegetables: Bring 3 cups of vinegar and 1 cup of water to a boil in a 2 qt. (2 L.). saucepan. Simmer the vegetables in this liquid separately, cooking for times listed below.

    Carrots—30 seconds
    Cucumbers—10 seconds
    Cabbage—10 seconds
    Green beans—10 seconds

3. Retrieve from blanching liquid with a slotted spoon or wire mesh skimmer.

4. Cool and dry the vegetables: Drain vegetables well, and then spread out evenly on a baking sheet to cool. Press gently with paper towels to remove excess liquid. Air-dry for at least 30 minutes, and up to 2 hours (in the sun if possible—this will increase the crunch). Discard the vinegar mixture after blanching vegetables.

5. Make the rempah: In a blender, puree oil, soaked chilies, garlic, shallots, galangal, lemongrass, and turmeric until smooth. Heat large wok or a pot over medium heat. Add chili-spice puree, and cook until very fragrant, 3 minutes. Add remaining 1/2 cup vinegar, water, sugar, and salt. Bring to a boil.

6. Dress the vegetables: Remove rempah from heat. Add cucumber, carrots, green beans, cabbage, chilies and ground peanuts, stir to coat vegetables evenly. Taste and adjust seasoning as necessary with sugar, salt and pepper.

7. Transfer to glass or plastic containers, cover and store in refrigerator. Pickles should marinate at least 24 hours before serving

How and Why

1. Pay attention to the length of time cooking the vegetable for the best texture. The vegetables should remain crisp-tender so blanch them separately to ensure each is cooked to its perfect doneness.

2. Drying vegetables help keep the vegetable crisp and makes them last longer. Removing excess water from the vegetables keeps them crisper longer.

3. Fry the rempah (wet spice paste) enough top avoid the raw flavor. Since this broth does not simmer long, it is necessary to fry the rempah for enough time to soften the raw flavor notes first.

Fish Grilled in Banana Leaves with Tamarind Chili Sauce

Ikan Bakar Asam

My friend Lui brought her sister Veronica Ang Liew Kee, a seasoned Singaporean cook, over to teach show us the fine points of some of her best dishes. This recipe, and the Chicken rice (pg. 318), owe a debt of gratitude to Lui and Veronica's tutelage.

The juicy skate (called stingray in Asia) holds up well to intense flavors of the spice paste. Its sometimes-sharp flavor is calmed by the sweet, spicy, sour chili paste used here. Although it's called "grilled," the dish is often made on the stovetop on a hot griddle. This chars the outside of the leaves and imparts a smoky flavor. But grilling is the best method, so, if possible, fire up the grill for the most dynamic flavor.

Makes 4 to 6 servings as part of a multi-dish meal

1/4   cup (1/4 oz. / 7 g.) Dried red chilies,
     stems and seeds removed
6   med Shallots, roughly chopped
3   cloves Garlic, roughly chopped
5   (about 1/4 lb) Long red chilies or other hot red chilies,
     roughly chopped (pg. 44)
5   Candlenuts (pg. 63) or macadamias
1   Tbsp. Malaysian shrimp paste (*belacan*), toasted
     (pg. 111)
1/4   tsp. Ground turmeric
1/4   cup Vegetable oil
1/4 to 1/2 cup Tamarind pulp (pg. 109)
1/4   tsp. Kosher salt
1/4   tsp. Granulated sugar
4   piece Banana leaves, 12 inches (5 cm.) by 2 feet long
     (about 1 package of frozen leaves)
1   lb. (454 g. Firm fish (four 4 oz. / 113 g. portions)
     such as tilapia, sea bass, or skate (no thicker than
     1 inch (2.5 cm.)
1/2   cup Sliced onions, about 1/8 inch (0.3 cm.) thick
8 to 12 Kaffir lime leaves, bruised
2 to 3 medium Limes (Calamansi or Key if available),
     cut into Southeast Asian style wedges (pg. 108)

1. Soak chilies in 1/2 cup room temperature water for 30 minutes; drain, reserving soaking liquid. Squeeze out excess moisture from the chilies.
2. Make the spice paste (*rempah*): Puree soaked chilies, shallots, garlic, fresh chilies, candlenuts, shrimp paste, and turmeric in a blender until smooth. Add only as much water (use water from chilies), as needed to facilitate blending. (Alternately make the spice paste in mortar (pg. 104).
3. Cook the rempah: Heat oil in a wok or 2-quart (2 L.) saucepan over medium heat; add rempah. Cook, stirring constantly, until oil separates from solids, about 10 minutes. Stir in tamarind, salt and sugar; adjust seasonings to taste (it should be strong, as it will be seasoning fish).
4. Prepare the Banana leaves: Wipe with a damp cloth or paper towels to remove the dirt. Slowly pass the leaf over a medium-high stove flame or electric burner to soften. The color will change from light green to a dark, deep, shiny green with a waxy texture.
5. Place 2 Tbsp. of cooked rempah on each leaf; spread the paste to equal the dimensions of the fish pieces. Place fish on leaves; top with another tablespoon of rempah. Scatter onions and lime leaves over the fish, and then wrap the leaves around the fish to form a packet. A tight wrapping helps trap the steam to properly cook the fish.
6. Cook on grill, griddle, or sauté pan over medium-low heat, 3 to 5 minutes on each side, until leaf is charred and fish is cooked through. Use an instant read thermometer (135°F or 57°C) or sneak a peek to check doneness. Serve with lime wedges.

At right: *Ari is being shown how to toast the banana leaves to make them more pliable.*

At far right: *Cook the packets until charred on the outside and the fish is cooked through.*

How and Why

1. Toast the banana leaves to make them pliable. This makes it easier to fold them and helps them trap the steam better.

2. Wrap the fish tightly to capture the aromatic steam. Much of flavor is volatile, and escapes with the steam. So trap it and infuse the fish with the maximum amount of flavor.

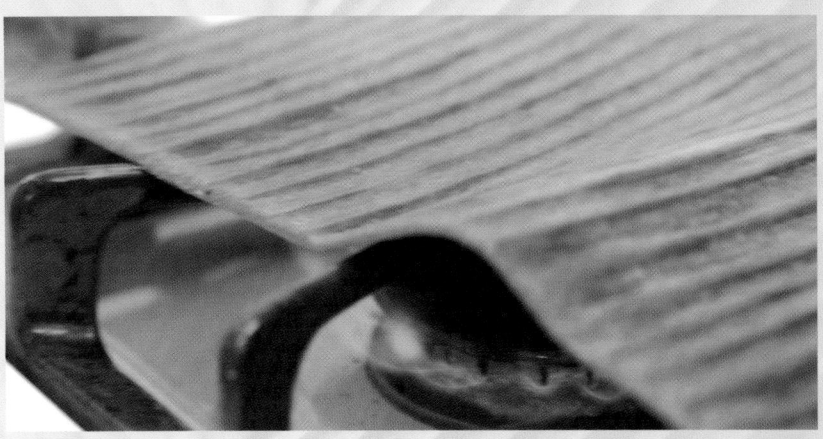

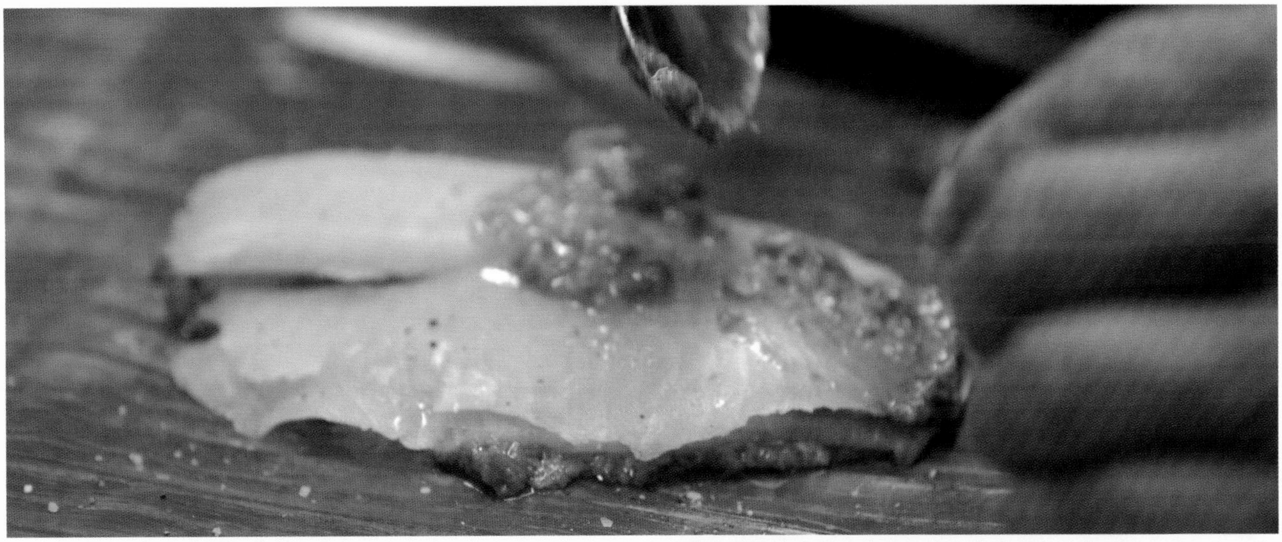

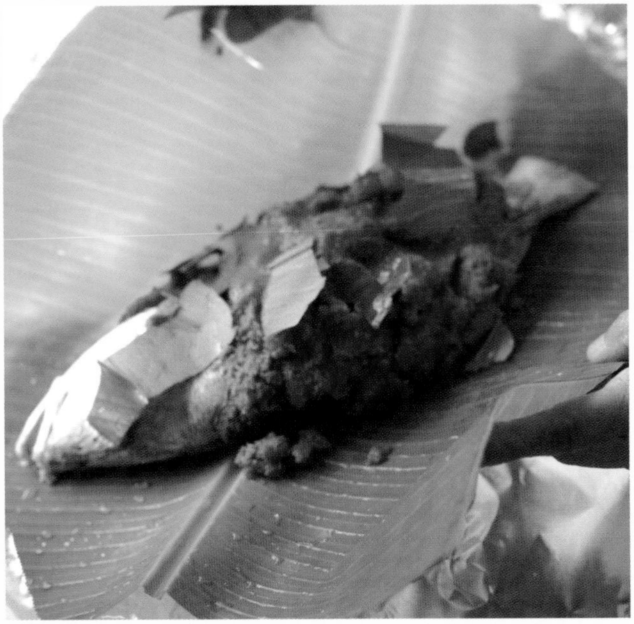

If you have a chance, try this recipe with whole fish. When cooked whole the meat is always more flavorful.

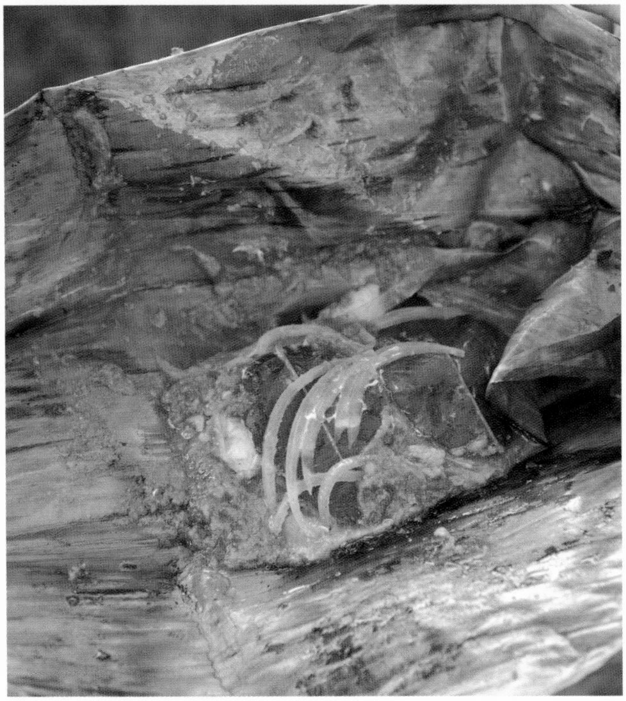

Spicy Portuguese Chicken Curry with Potatoes and Fried Ginger

Curry Devil

This Eurasian stew of deep red gravy is one of the few Portuguese-Asian fusion dishes. Fiery hot, it's best served with lots of rice. Angela Leong, my Portuguese sister-in-law, taught it to me years ago in Malaysia. A sprinkling of deep-fried shallot slices and ginger matchsticks add layers of aroma and eye appeal: an extra extravagance for the ambitious cook.

Makes 4 to 6 servings as part of a multi-dish meal

- 50 (1 cup / 1 oz. / 28 g.) Dried red chilies, remove stems and seeds
- 3/4 cup Vegetable oil (divided use)
- 10 medium Shallots, roughly chopped
- 8 cloves Garlic, roughly chopped
- 5 stalks Lemongrass, trimmed and sliced very thin, about 1/16 inch (.1 cm.) (pg. 102)
- 1/4 tsp. Ground turmeric
- 2 Tbsp. Finely grated ginger
- 2 Tbsp. Finely grated galangal (*luengkuas*)
- 1 Tbsp. Brown mustard seeds or yellow is adaquate
- 1 Medium Whole chicken, (3 to 4 lbs. or 1.4 to 1.8 kg.) cut into 8 pieces

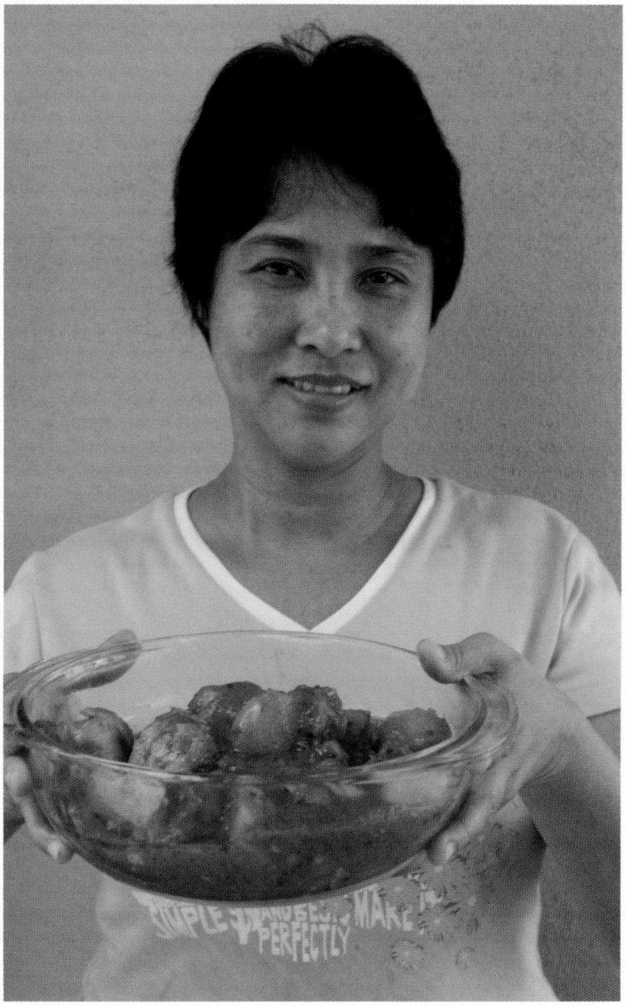
MAKE
PERFECTLY

- 1 cup Water
- 2 tsp. Kosher salt
- 1 lb. (454 grams) Gold waxy potatoes, 2-inch (5 cm.) chunks
- 1/2 cup Tamarind pulp (pg. 109)
- 2 Tbsp. Distilled white vinegar
- 2 Long red chilies or other hot red chilies, thinly sliced, about 1/8 inch (0.3 cm.) thick

1. Prepare spice paste (*rempah*): Soak dried chilies in 3/4 cup of room temperature water for 30 minutes; drain; squeeze out excess moisture. Puree these soaked chilies with 1/2 cup oil, shallots, garlic, lemongrass, turmeric, ginger, and galangal in a blender to fine spice paste Add water, only if needed, to facilitate blending.
2. Cook the curry: In a pan over medium heat, combine 1/4 cup oil with mustard seeds. Cook until seeds begin to make an audible popping sound, and then add spice paste; fry until the oil begins to separate back out of paste, about 15 minutes. The spice paste will become aromatic and lose its raw aroma.
3. Stew the meat and potatoes: Add chicken, stir to coat with paste, and cook 10 minutes; add potatoes and cook 5 more minutes, stirring often. Add water and salt. The cooking liquid should barely cover the chicken. Bring to a boil, lower to a simmer, and cover. Cook until chicken and potatoes are cooked through, about 30 minutes.
4. Finalize the seasoning: Add the tamarind and vinegar; stir well. Taste; adjust seasoning with salt and vinegar. Serve garnished with sliced chilies.

Fortunately I have access to lots of gifted cooks that have taught me the authentic flavors of Malaysia.

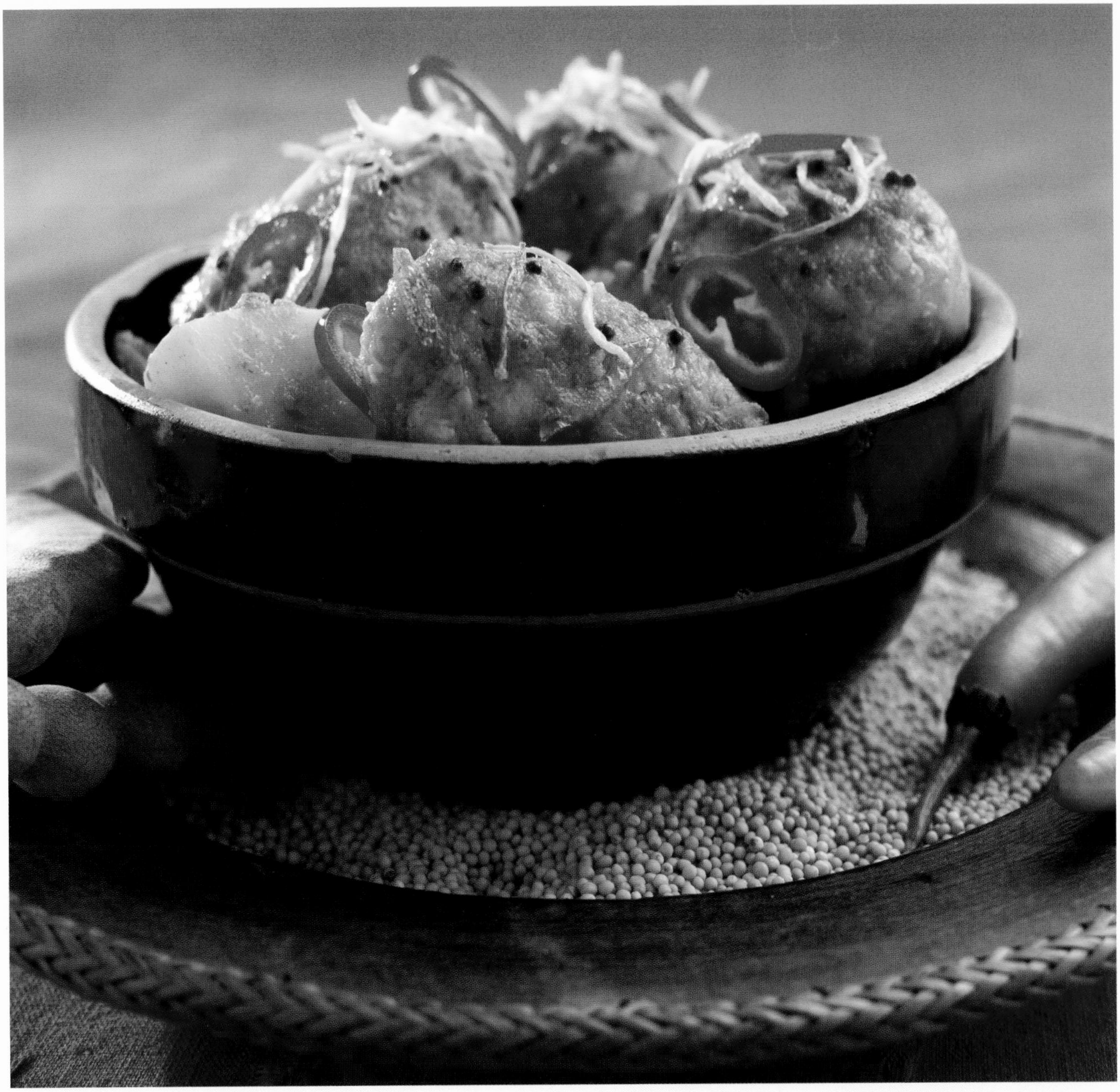

How and Why

1. Stir the spice paste more frequently as it reduces to prevent burning. As moisture evaporates from the cooking spice paste, the need to stir increases, since the mixture becomes tacky.

2. Cook the mustard seeds until they "pop" for full flavor development. Ethnic Indians throughout Southeast Asia use this technique, roasting the spice. The flavorful infused oil is often used to garnish the final dish. In this recipe, however, it becomes part of the sauce.

Fragrant Coconut Rice, Beef Curry, Shrimp Sambal and Crispy Anchovies

Nasi Lemak

"Nasi" is the Malay word for cooked rice and "lemak" indicates that coconut milk is used in the dish. "Nasi lemak" is actually a grouping of dishes on a single plate, with the coconut rice at the center. Each vendor has the opportunity to showcase some of her best dishes here. Most versions contain coconut rice, fried anchovies, boiled egg, cucumbers, and at least one curry. Some cooks will serve as little as three side dishes with the rice, yet others believe in variety. Sometimes over twelve side dishes are available. Sometimes the Malaysian cook will add a knotted leaf of the fragrant Pandanus plant (pg. 37). The technique of letting the rice rest after rinsing softens the grains and will ensure that the rice cooks evenly.

Makes 4 to 6 full meal portions (with sub-recipes listed below)

1/2 cup Dried salted anchovies (Ikan Billis)
1/4 cup Vegetable oil
4 to 6 Banana leaf pieces, cut into decorative shapes (optional)
1 recipe Coconut rice (*nasi lemak*) (pg. 332)
1 recipe Stir-fried Water Spinach (pg. 342)
1 recipe Beef Rendang (pg. 334)
1 recipe Shrimp Sambal (pg. 335)
3 lg. Eggs, hard-boiled, cut into 1/4's
1 small Cucumbers, preferably Kirby (pg. 80), sliced on angle into ovals, about 1/4 inch (0.6 cm.) thick
1/2 cup Peanuts, roasted in dry pan (pg. 109) or deep fried peanuts

PRE-PREPARATIONS

1. Fry the Fish: If still attached, pull of heads and remove innards, split in halves lengthwise, rinse fish in a mesh strainer or colander under cool running water for 5 seconds. Heat vegetable oil in wok over medium heat, add anchovies and cook stirring constantly until fish turn golden brown. Drain on paper towels.

TO ASSEMBLE

1. Line individual plates or platters with banana leaf.
2. Place 1/2–1-cup scoop of rice in center of leaf. Surround rice with portions of water spinach, beef rendang, shrimp sambal, egg, cucumbers, fried fish and peanuts.

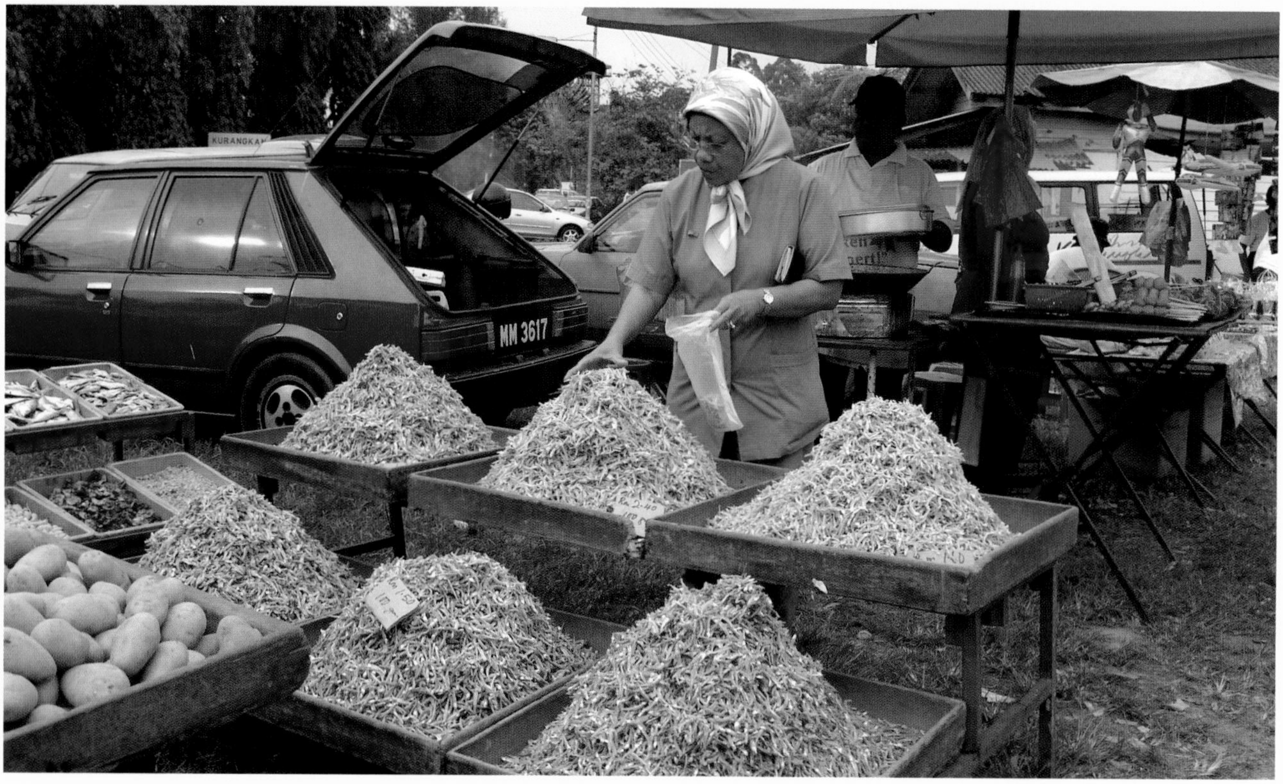
MM 3617

Piles of dried small fish (Ikan Billis) are being scrupulously selected at daily market in Melacca, Malaysia.

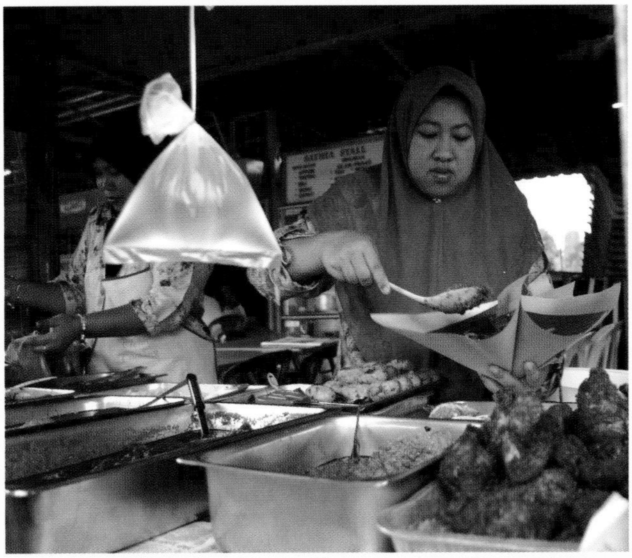
NASI LEMAK

A vendor in Ampang Jaya, Kuala Lumpur, Malaysia offers over a dozen different sambals and curries with her coconut rice. Here she packs a to-go order in a banana leaf and paper cone.

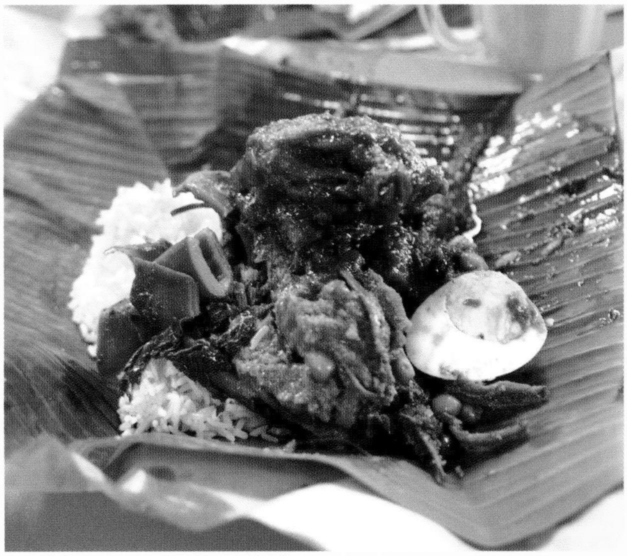

Here is breakfast, yes, breakfast. That to-go order was at 8 a.m. in the morning. Nasi lemak is traditionally a breakfast meal.

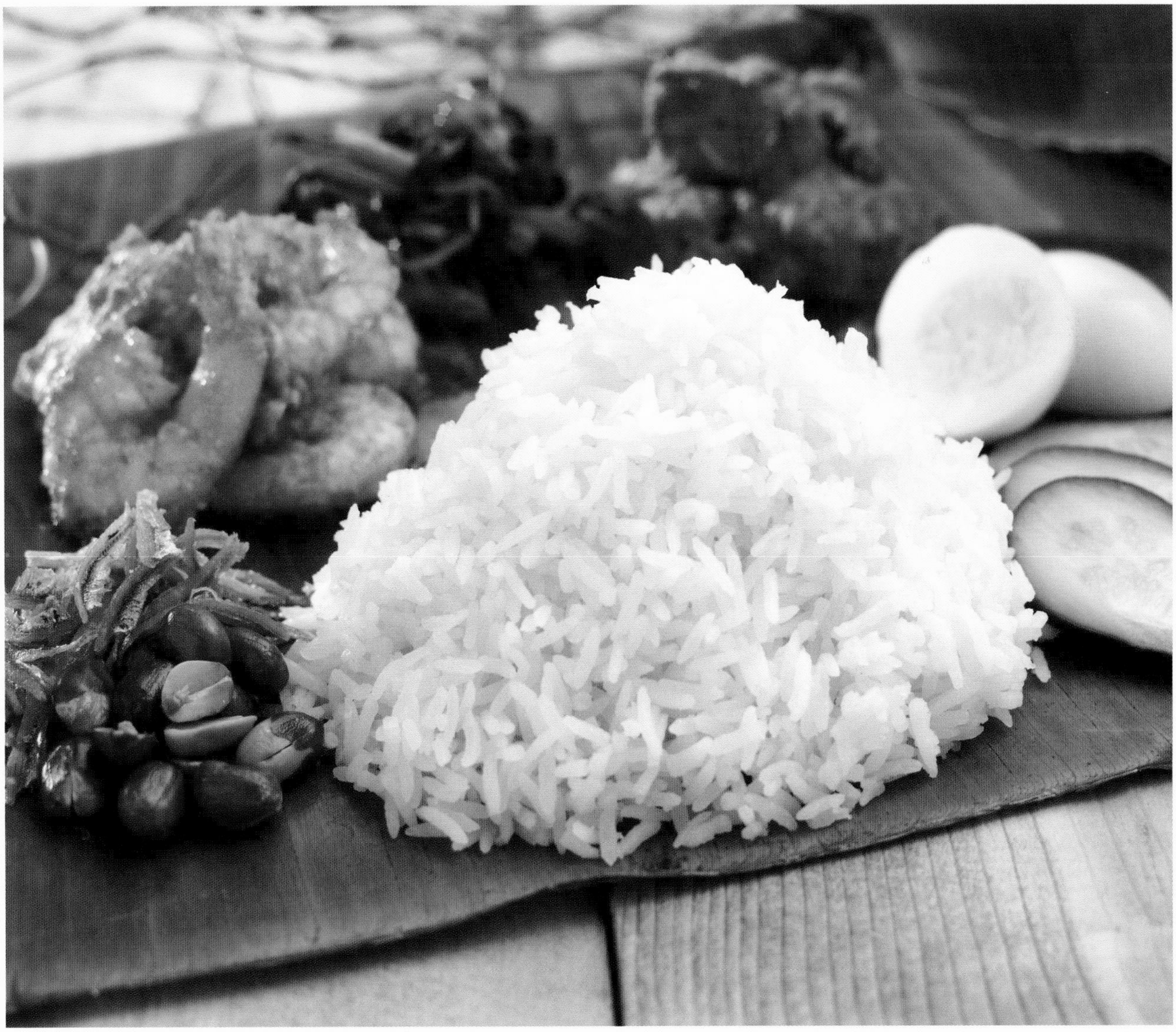

Fragrant Coconut Rice
Nasi Lemak

Each grain of rice is saturated with lightly sweet coconut milk. A knotted pandan leaf is commonly cooked in with the rice to perfume it. Coconut rice, usually served for breakfast, is usually accompaniment by fried peanuts (pg. 109), fried small fish (pg. 93), a hardboiled egg, chili sambal (pg. 284), and sliced cucumbers. In Malaysian and Singaporean eateries, guests select a myriad of curries, sambals, vegetables and other dishes to eat along with the rice. These determine the ultimate cost of the meal. Typically, the coconut rice is piled on a swatch of banana leaf, and all the other items are spooned on. Guests then eat right off of the leaf, or fold it up into a packet to go.

Serves 4 to 6 as part of multi-dish meal

2   cup Jasmine rice
1   cup Canned coconut milk
1³/4 cup Water

1. Rinse rice under running water in a strainer or fine sieve for 30 seconds, massaging gently to remove any talc or dust. Drain well, and then let the rice sit for 30 minutes before cooking.

2. In a saucepan with a tight-fitting lid, combine rice, coconut milk and water; stir. Add a knotted pandan leaf, if desired. Bring quickly to a boil, cover pan, lower heat, and simmer 20 minutes. Remove from heat, and allow the cooked rice to rest, covered, for 10 minutes.

3. Fluff gently with fork. Serve with traditional accompaniments (see headnote above).

Older coconuts are stripped of their husk before being split, and scraped and blended with water to create rich coconut milk (pg. 114).

How and Why

1. Using a strainer to rinse the rice helps measure the water accurately. If rinsed rice is tilted to remove excess water, some water inevitably remains hidden in pot (between rice grains or below the metal plate in the bottom of a rice cooker), so it is inconsistent; Draining in a sieve ensures that all excess moisture is removed before adding measured amount of water.

2. Do not uncover the rice immediately after cooking. When a rice cooker "pops" (an indicator of doneness based on moisture content), or a cooking pot is removed from the heat, the water has still not been completely absorbed, so the starchy rice is very hot and soft. Letting it rest allows excess moisture to be absorbed into the grains. The rice firms up, so it will fluff into separate grains.

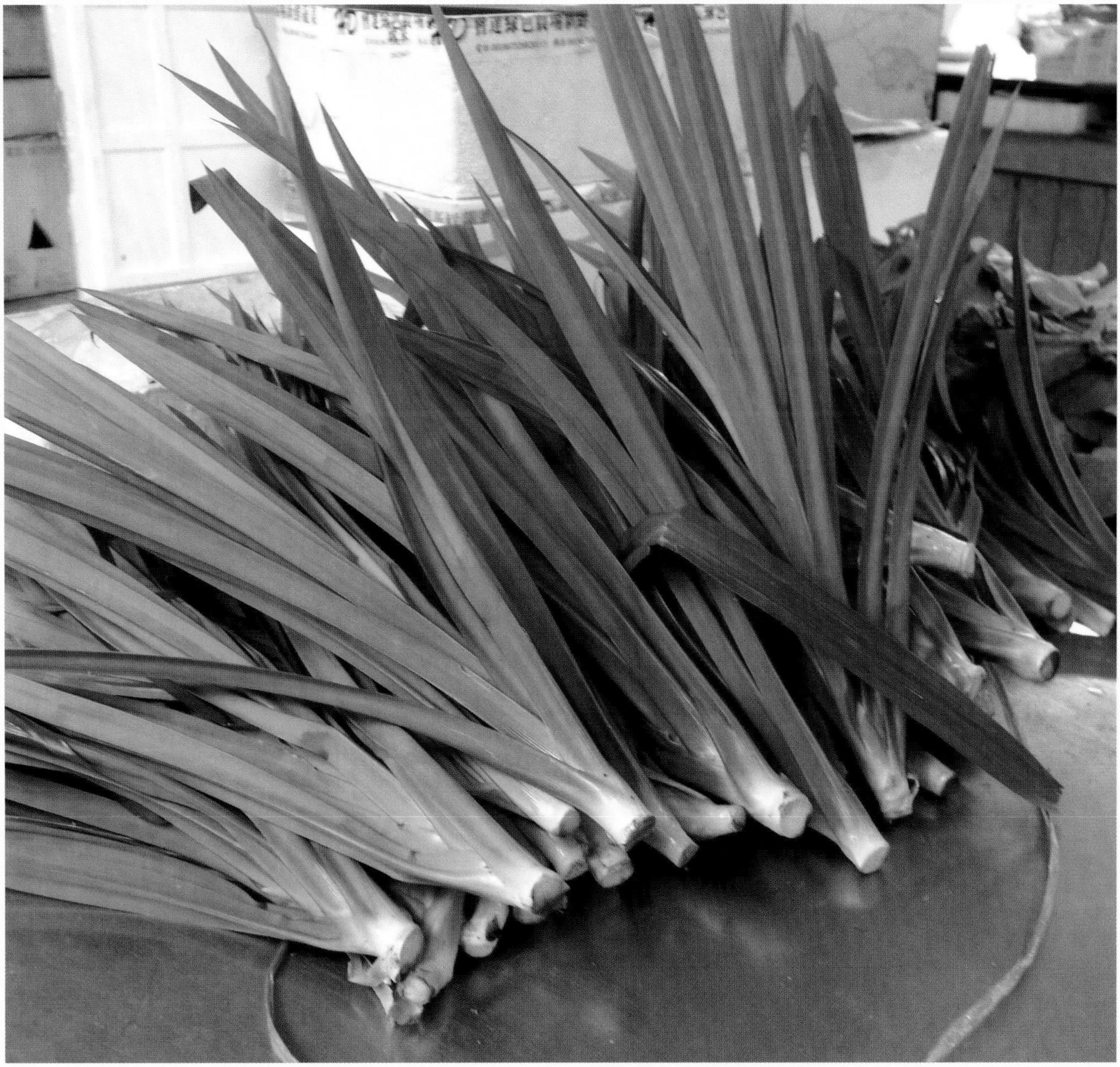

Piles of pandan leaves are destined to perfume large pots of steaming coconut rice.

Beef Rendang Curry
Rendang Daging Lembu

Layered with spices, this classic Malaysian stew is slow-cooked until the sauce concentrates into an intense, complex paste that coats the tender beef chunks. It's so dynamic in flavor that, to fully appreciate it, this curry needs to be tempered with calming forkfuls of rice between bites. I especially recommend coconut-scented rice, a classic part of Nasi Lemak.

Makes 4 to 6 servings as part of a multi-dish meal

1/2 cup	(1/2 oz/14 g.) Dried red chilies, remove stems and seeds
1/4 cup	Vegetable oil
5	medium Shallots, roughly chopped
5	cloves Garlic, roughly chopped
1	Tbsp. Finely grated galangal,
5	stalks Lemongrass, trimmed and sliced very thin, about 1/16 inch (.1 cm.)
4	Candlenuts or macadamia nuts, crushed
1/2	tsp. Black peppercorns, crushed
1	tsp. Ground turmeric
2	lb. (.9 kg.) Boneless beef chuck, 11/2-inch (3.8 cm.) pieces
2	tsp. Kosher salt
1	can (about 14 oz.) Coconut milk
1/2	cup Water
1	medium Lime, juiced
1/4	cup Toasted grated fresh coconut or unsweetened shredded coconut

1. Soak the chilies: Soak chilies in 1/2 cup room temperature water for 30 minutes; drain and squeeze out excess moisture.

2. Make the spice paste (rempah): In blender, puree oil, shallots and garlic into a semi-smooth paste. Add galangal, lemongrass, candlenuts, peppercorns and turmeric; puree until smooth. Stop and scrape down often, and add a drizzle of water, only if necessary, to facilitate blending—be patient.

3. Fry the rempah: Heat a 4 qt. (4 L.) saucepan or wok over medium heat. Add the spice paste (rempah) and fry until aromatic—at least five minutes The raw flavor and aroma of the shallots and garlic should subside.

4. Cook the curry: Add beef and salt. Cook five more minutes on the same heat. Add the coconut milk and water; raise heat to high. Bring to boil, and then lower flame to a simmer. Stew gently, stirring occasionally with a wooden spoon, until meat is tender and sauce is thick, about one and a half to two hours.

5. Adjust seasoning: When meat is tender, and the sauce has a slightly oily sheen, season with lime juice and grated coconut. Cook for an additional one or two minutes. Adjust seasoning with salt to taste.

How and Why

1. Add ingredients to the blender from wettest to driest, to avoid the need for added water. Starting the paste with the wet ingredients first gives you a liquid base, which will draw the dry ingredients into the puree.

2. Fry the rempah (wet spice paste) enough to subdue the raw flavor. Since this gravy does not simmer long, it is necessary to fry the rempah long enough to soften the raw flavor notes first.

Spicy Shrimp in a Sambal of Red Chilies and Tamarind

Sambal Udang

Sambal is a chili-based condiment used all over Southeast Asia. A "sambal" can also be a dish cooked using the spicy condiment. Shrimp is one ingredient that's frequently cooked into a "sambal." It's one of the classic dishes included in the Malaysian sampler platter called "nasi lemak," which pairs various stews and fried dishes with coconut rice (pg. 332). If you have homemade or store-bought sambal condiment in the house, this dish can be made in minutes.

Serves 4 as part of a multi-course meal

1	recipe Malaysian chili sambal (pg. 284)
1	lb. (454 g.) Medium or large shrimp, peeled and deveined
2	Tbsp. Tamarind pulp (pg. 109)
to taste	Granulated sugar
to taste	Kosher salt

1. In a large sauté pan, saucepan or wok, heat the Malaysian chili sambal over medium-high heat, stirring constantly until it begins to boil.

2. Stir in shrimp; continue to stir gently until shrimp are cooked through. Fold in tamarind pulp. Taste and adjust seasoning with salt and sugar

Stir-Fried Rice Noodles with Shrimp and Chinese Sausage

Char Kway Teow

Clouds of smoke from the sizzling wok announce this classic Malaysian street food. "Wok Hay" or "Breath of the Wok" is the searing effect of a seasoned cooking pot that gives this dish its characteristic smoky flavor— make sure to preheat your pan to get it very hot. Regular (often referred to as light) soy sauce adds much of the saltiness, while thick soy sauce lends the complex, molasses-like flavor. Do not double this recipe. Instead, make two batches. An overloaded wok won't create the right sear. If you cannot find fresh rice noodles in your local Asian market, dry rice noodles can be used or you can make your own (pg. 117). Soak 6 oz. dried rice noodles in cool water for 30 minutes; drain well. Boil until cooked, drain, rinse, and pat dry. Add cooked noodles in step 3.

Makes 4 to 6 servings as part of a multi-dish meal

1	lb. (454 g.) Rice noodles, fresh ribbon style, about 1/2 inch (1.3 cm.) wide (*kway teow*)
2	Tbsp. Vegetable oil (divided use)
1	Chinese sausage (*lap cheong*), sliced on angle, 1/8 inch (0.3 cm.) thick
4	tsp. Roughly chopped garlic
1	Egg, lightly beaten
1/4	lb. (113 g.) Small shrimp, peeled & deveined
2	Tbsp. Soy sauce
1	tsp. Thick soy sauce or 2 tsp. dark soy
1	Thai bird chili, minced or 1 tsp. Vietnamese chili sauce (pg. 199) or Thai Sriracha sauce (pg. 133)
1/2	cup Bean sprouts, trimmed
1/4	cup Chinese chives or scallions, green only, 1 1/2-inch (1.3 cm.) pieces
1/2	tsp. Sesame oil
to taste	Granulated sugar

1. Soak noodles in lukewarm water 10 minutes, drain; peel apart into individual strands. Have all ingredients ready, this stir-fry cooks quickly.

2. Heat a seasoned wok or 12-inch (30 cm) non-stick sauté pan over high heat for 3 minutes. Add vegetable oil and sausage. Cook, stirring constantly, until lightly browned. Sausage should be partly rendered releasing oil into bottom of pan.

3. Add the garlic; cook until garlic just begins to brown. Immediately add the eggs; rotate pan to spread the egg out into a thin sheet. Do not stir until eggs are set. Once they are cooked into a sheet, break them up into bite size pieces. Add the shrimp; stir-fry until it begins to turn pink, 10 seconds.

4. Add the noodles; fry without stirring until they soften and begin to brown (this can take a few minutes).

5. Add soy sauces and chili or chili paste; stir to coat noodles. Cook 15 seconds. Add bean sprouts, scallions and sesame oil; toss until the sprouts begin to wilt, about 3 minutes.

6. Taste and adjust seasoning with soy sauce and sugar.

7. Serve immediately, since the coveted "wok hay" dissipates rapidly.

How and Why

Preheat the pan and keep it over the highest possible heat to get the maximum "Wok Hay" flavor. The more intense the heat is, the more the dish will smoke, infusing the noodles with more flavor.

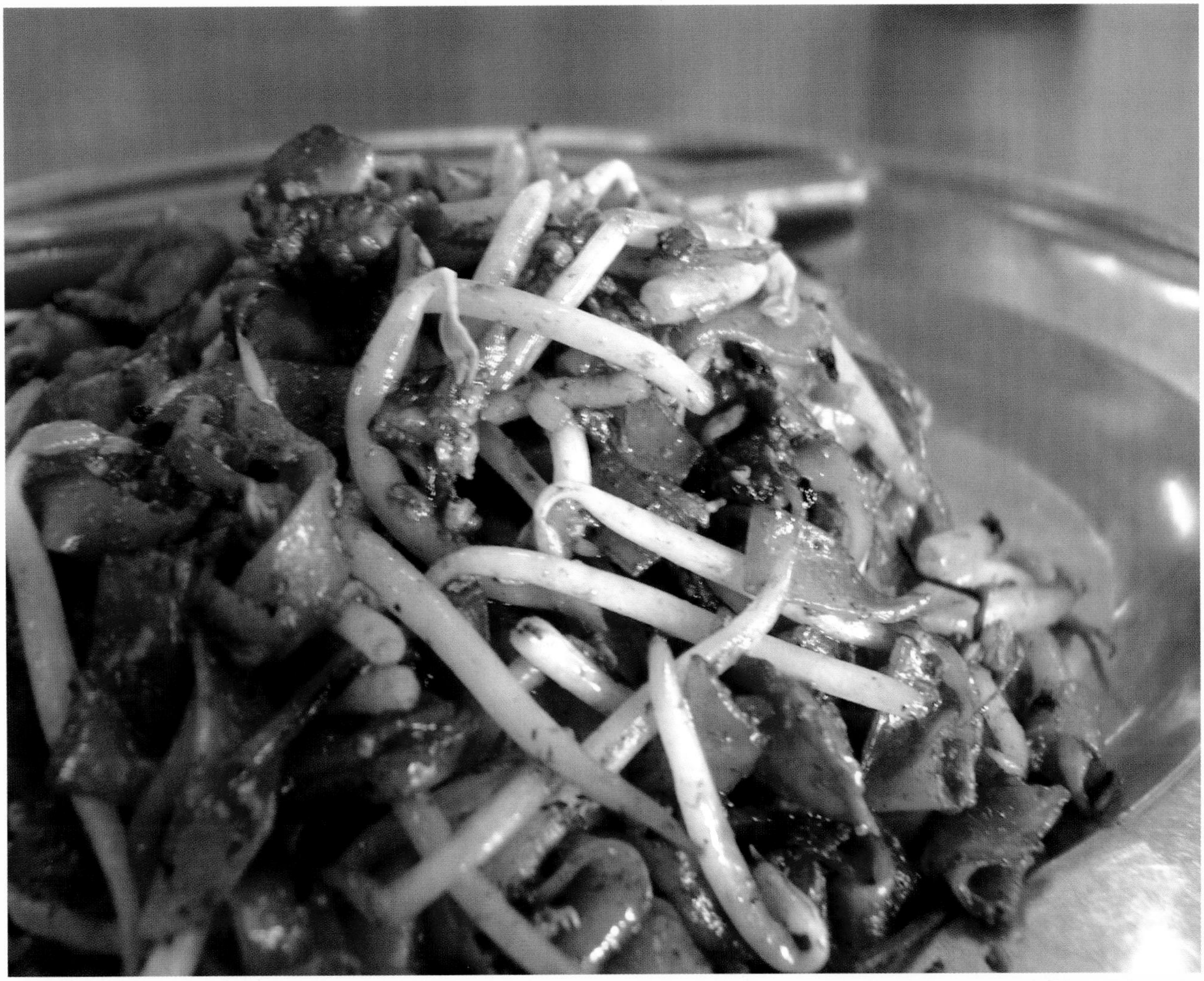

LAP CHEONG

Chinese sausage, called *lap cheong* (pronounced "lop shong"), are slender, red, dried sausages made from pork and pork fat (lots of it), seasoned with salt, sugar and rice wine. They gain a slight sour nuance from a fermentation process, but a touch of sugar in the recipe balances out that tartness. They should be stored in the refrigerator after opening even though they resemble dried sausages like pepperoni, which have preservatives that keep them from needing refrigeration. Chinese sausages have no such preservatives. Lap cheong are often sliced thinly, and then stir-fried into fried rice. They're essential to Malaysian Stir-fried Rice Noodles with Shrimp and Chinese Sausage (pg. 336).

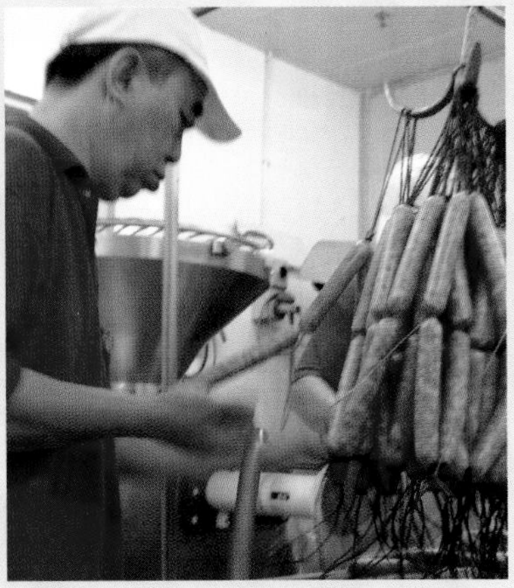

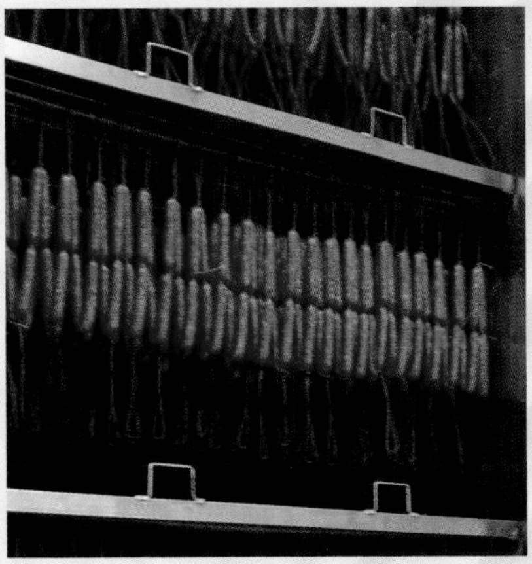

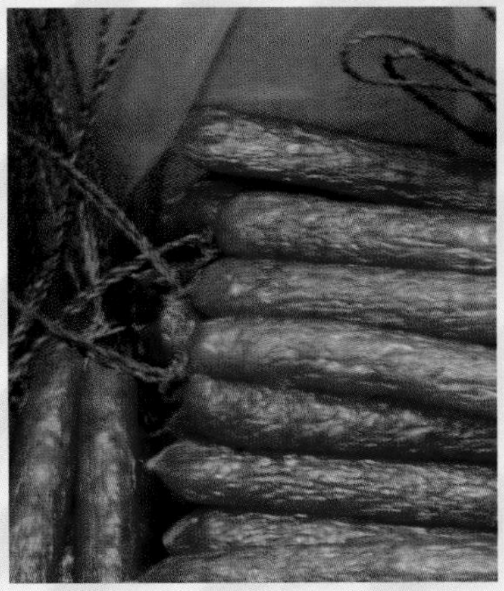

Stir-Fried Noodles with Gravy and Pork Cracklings

Hokkien Mee

As dark as midnight in the Cameron Highlands of Malaysia, these rich noodles are pure Malaysian comfort food. I usually get a dish as soon as I get off of the plane. Although it's authentically made with a molasses-like thick soy sauce (pg. 50), I've adapted it for the two types of soy that are widely available here. If you dont have the thick soy, reduce regular soy sauces to 4 teaspoons and add 3 Tablespoon dark soy sauce. You can prepare the recipe with vegetable oil instead of lard, and use store-bought pork cracklings, or simply omit the pork and still have a delicious wok of noodles. This dish is traditionally served with the Malaysian Red Chili Sambal on (pg. 284) but I love it with Pickled Green Chilies (pg. 120).

Makes 4 to 6 servings as part of a multi-dish meal

1	lb. (454 g.) Fresh thick egg noodles, about 1/8 inch (0.3 cm.) thick
3	Tbsp. Rendered pork fat (lard) or vegetable oil
2	Tbsp. Garlic, roughly minced
1 1/2	cups Chicken stock or broth
1	Tbsp. Thick soy sauce
2	tsp. Granulated sugar
16	ea Small shrimp, peeled and deviened
1 1/2	cups Choy sum or other Chinese greens, cut into 1 1/2-inch (about 3.8 cm) pieces
1/8	tsp. Ground white pepper
1/4	cup Pork cracklings or store-bought

1. Par-cook the noodles: Bring at least 1 gallon of water to a rolling boil. Add noodles, stir well and bring back to a boil, stirring occasionally to prevent sticking. Cook until noodles are almost, but not quite fully cooked and tender, about 8 minutes. (if using thinner noodles cook them less, thin "lo mein" style will only take about 3 minutes in boiling water) Drain and rinse under cool running water. Reserve at room temperature.

2. Make the stir-fry: Heat a wok or sauté pan over high heat. Add lard and garlic; cook until just beginning to brown. Immediately add chicken stock, soy sauces, and sugar; bring to a boil. Add cooked noodles, bring to a boil then cover wok and cook over high heat. After 2 minutes, stir noodles to coat evenly and replace cover.

3. Simmer: After one more minute, remove the cover and boil until gravy thickens and coats the noodles, about 5 minutes. There should be about 1/2 cup of gravy that gathers at bottom of wok. If it get too dry simply add splashes of water as needed.

4. Finish the dish: Add shrimp and greens. Cook, stirring constantly, until shrimp are cooked and greens are wilted, about 2 minutes. Taste and adjust seasoning as needed with soy sauces, sugar or salt. Add pork cracklings and white pepper, toss well. Transfer to platter; serve hot.

Pickled green chilies' (pg. 120)
sour taste is a perfect complement
to the rich soy gravy.

1. Using the right amount of pork fat (lard) provides characteristic flavor, and also thickens the sauce. Three tablespoons of lard may seem excessive, but this there as a more than just a cooking medium. The fat emulsifies the sauce as it boils down, increasing sauce body and depth of flavor.

2. Boiling the sauce vigorously helps create a stable emulsion, giving the sauce the proper body. Boil the sauce over a high flame to ensure that sauce will be smooth and even.

3. Add water as needed to keep noodles slathered in sauce. Remember that it is only water that evaporates, not the stock or soy sauces flavor so add back what has evaporated and not risk an overly concentrated sauce.

MALAYSIA
SINGAPORE

Yin Yang Noodles
Won Ton Hor Fun

This pairing of two kinds of noodles, thin rice vermicelli and wide, thick "kway teow" has a symphony of textures and flavors that awaken the palate. It's the favorite noodle dish of my wife, Esther, who longs for it since she immigrated from Malaysia. Charred resilient fine threads of rice noodle in silken garlic sauce provide a bed for brilliant jade greens and tender prawns.

"Wok hay," the smoky "breath of the wok" flavor (see sidebar page 100) prized in Asian cookery, is an essential component of this dish. So keep those flames up high. This stir-fry process moves quickly, so get organized. Read the method before starting, so you'll know where you're going. Serve the dish with pickled green chilies (pg. 120).

Makes 4 to 6 servings as part of a multi-dish meal

1/4 lb. (113 g.) Dried rice vermicelli
3/4 lb. (340 g.) Rice noodles, fresh ribbon style,
    about 1/2 inch (1.3 cm.) wide (*Kway Teow*),
    store-bought or homemade (pg. 67) or
    substitute dried wide rice noodles, cooked
1 tsp. Soy sauce
1 tsp. Dark soy sauce
2 cups (471 ml.) Chicken broth or stock (divided use)
2 Tbsp. Cornstarch
1/4 tsp. Kosher salt
1 Tbsp. Oyster sauce
1/4 cup Vegetable oil (divided use)
1 Tbsp. Coarsely minced garlic
1/4 lb. (113 g.) Pork shoulder, butt, leg or loin,
    bite size slice, about 1/8 inch (0.3 cm.) thick
1/4 lb. (113 g.) Small shrimp, peeled and deveined
1/4 lb. (2 cups/ 457 g.) Choy sum or other Chinese greens,
    cut into 2-inch (5 cm.) pieces
1 lg. Egg, lightly beaten
1/8 tsp. Ground white pepper
as needed Pickled green chilies (pg. 120)

How and Why

Thicken the sauce first, before adding eggs, to create large strands. If the liquid is not thickened, then eggs will break into small pieces.

1. Soak rice vermicelli in room temperature water for 15 minutes. Drain: toss with 1 tsp. light soy sauce. Separate fresh rice noodles (kway teow) into individual strands by peeling them apart; toss them with dark soy sauce.

2. Get Ready to Stir-fry: Whisk together 1/4 cup chicken broth, cornstarch, salt, and oyster sauce; set aside. Select large platter with sides that will hold in gravy. Line everything up in the order that you need it.

3. Fry the thin noodles: Heat 1 Tbsp. oil a wok or large sauté pan over high heat until it is smoky hot. Add drained thin vermicelli noodles; allow the noodles to cook undisturbed while they sizzle and brown, about 1 to 2 minutes. Flip the vermicelli like a pancake, and repeat browning on other side. You are looking for light brown crispy/chewy edges. Transfer this noodle "pancake" to a serving platter.

4. Fry the thick noodles: Add another 1 Tbsp. oil to the hot pan; swirl to coat. Add fresh wide rice noodles. Toss well, and then let noodles sit undisturbed until they sizzle and brown. Once they have become well browned on some edges, toss occasionally to attain browned, semi-crispy edges and charred flavor. Arrange these atop the thin noodles on the platter; cover loosely to keep warm.

5. Stir-fry the final dish: In same pan over highest heat, heat remaining 2 tablespoons of oil until it shimmers but does not smoke. Add garlic; cook until it just begins to brown. Add pork and shrimp; cook until they loose raw appearance. Quickly add chicken broth. Bring to a boil. Stir the cornstarch mixture, and rapidly mix it into boiling sauce; cook until it thickens considerably. Add greens and white pepper; cook 10 seconds. Turn off heat, add eggs, and give only a couple of stirs to create large ribbons of egg (wait about 5 seconds after stirring for the eggs to cook in hot sauce). Taste and adjust seasoning with salt.

6. Serve: Transfer stir-fry to the platter with the noodles, and serve immediately.

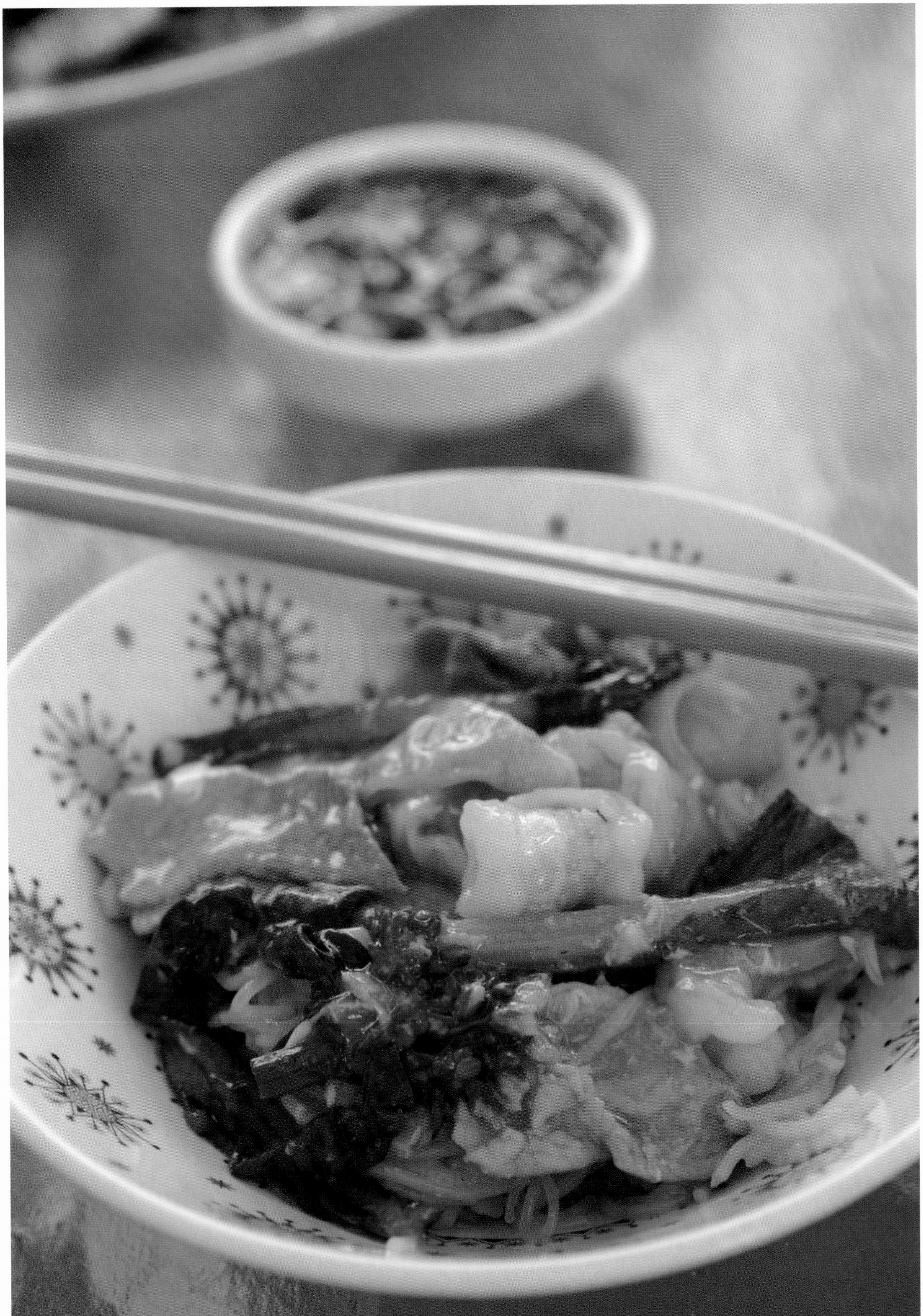

Stir-Fried Water Spinach with Garlic and Shrimp Paste

Kankong Belacan

Water spinach has as many aliases as a Cold War double-agent: "morning glory," "hollow heart spinach," "ong choy," and "kangkong" are just a few used in Malaysia and Singapore. This very popular green vegetable grows in shallow water all around Southeast Asia. Its unique structure allows for a peculiar preparation for cooking. The large top leaves hide tiny, tender baby leaves, or "leaflets" lower on the straw-like stem. Snap and pick the greens underneath each stem leaflet.

Makes 4 to 6 servings as part of multi-dish meal

2	Tbsp. Vegetable oil
1	tsp. Sesame oil
1	med. Long red chili or other spicy red chili, minced or pounded
4	cloves Garlic, roughly chopped
1	lb. (454 g.) Water spinach (pg. 76) (about 8 cups)
1	tsp. Malaysian shrimp paste (*belacan*), toasted (pg. 52)
as needed Kosher salt	

1. Heat vegetable oil in a large (10 to 12-inch / 25–30 cm.) sauté pan or wok over high heat until it shimmers, but does not smoke. Add garlic; cook until it just begins to lightly brown, less than a minute. Add shrimp paste, stir for a few seconds, and then immediately add the water spinach. Stir-fry often until leaves are wilted and cooked, about 3 minutes.

2. Thoroughly stir in the sesame oil. Taste; adjust seasoning with salt.

Be careful not to overcook greens. Anticipate carry over cooking. When you think the vegetable is almost cooked, remove it from the flame so that the residual heat in the pan (and the vegetable itself) can take it the rest of the way.

MALAYSIA
SINGAPORE

Vegetables in Nonya Coconut Curry

Sayur Masak Lemak

This creamy yellow curry is pure comfort food for my wife, Esther, whose mother, Annie, has cooked it for her whole life. The Malay term "lemak" indicates rich and creamy, from coconut milk. Various vegetables can be used, depending on availability. The most well suited is "Sawi" or Chinese mustard greens (not the same as the type from the southern U.S.). Feel free to use cabbage, choy sum, or any other green vegetable. If you cannot find fresh red chilies, substitute 6 dried long red chilies, soaked (pg. 45).

Makes 4 to 6 servings as part of a multi-dish meal
(about 3 1/2 cups)

- 1/4 cup Vegetable oil
- 4 lg. Shallots, roughly chopped
- 2 pieces Long red chilies or other hot red chilies, roughly chopped (pg. 44)
- 2 cloves Garlic, roughly chopped
- 1 tsp. Malaysian shrimp paste (*belacan*), or other fermented shrimp paste, toasted (pg. 52)
- 1 tsp. Ground turmeric
- 2 tsp. Minced ginger
- 1 stalk Lemongrass, trimmed, sliced very thin
- 1 1/2 cups Canned coconut milk (divided use)
- 1/4 cup Water
- 1 tsp. Kosher salt
- 1 tsp. Granulated sugar
- 1 lb. (454 g.) Chinese mustard greens, or other dark, leafy greens, cut into 2-inch (5 cm.) pieces (4 to 6 cups)
- 1/2 lb. (227 g.) Chinese eggplants, halved lengthwise, cut into 1 1/2-inch (3.8 cm.) lengths

1. Purée oil, shallots, and chilies in a blender until semi-smooth. Add garlic, shrimp paste, turmeric, ginger, and lemongrass; puree until semi-smooth. Add a drop of water, only if needed, to facilitate blending. This is a "rempah."
2. Heat a saucepan over medium heat. Fry the rempah until the oil begins to separate from the mixture, about 5 to 10 minutes (make sure raw shallot aroma and flavor is gone).
3. Add one cup of coconut milk, salt, sugar, and vegetables; bring to a simmer. Cook until all vegetables are tender.
4. Add remaining 1/2 cup coconut milk; bring to a boil, and then adjust seasoning with salt to taste. Serve with steamed rice.

The inner side of coconuts are pressed against sharp spiked heads as they rotate rapidly to shred the flesh which will be made into coconut milk (pg. 114).

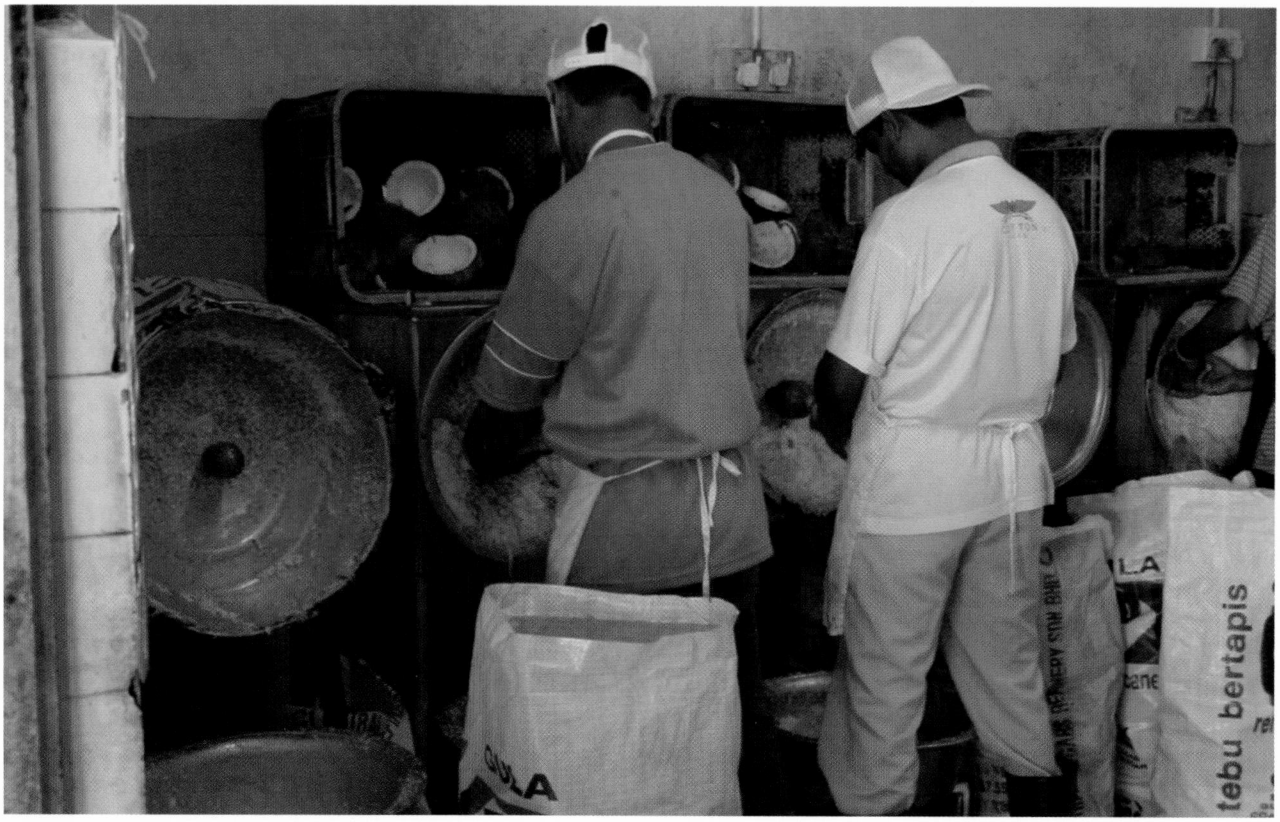

tebu bertapis

How and Why

1. First toast belacan (shrimp paste) for a deep flavor. Roasting the belacan softens its pungency and deepens its flavor.

2. Slice lemongrass thinly to eliminate long fibers. Make sure to slice lemongrass into slivers with a maximum width of 1/8 inch (0.3 cm.). Careless cutting will create unappealing texture in your curry.

3. Cook the spice paste, rempah, enough to eliminate raw flavor. Since there is such a short cooking time once liquids are added, it is necessary to cook the rempah very well beforehand.

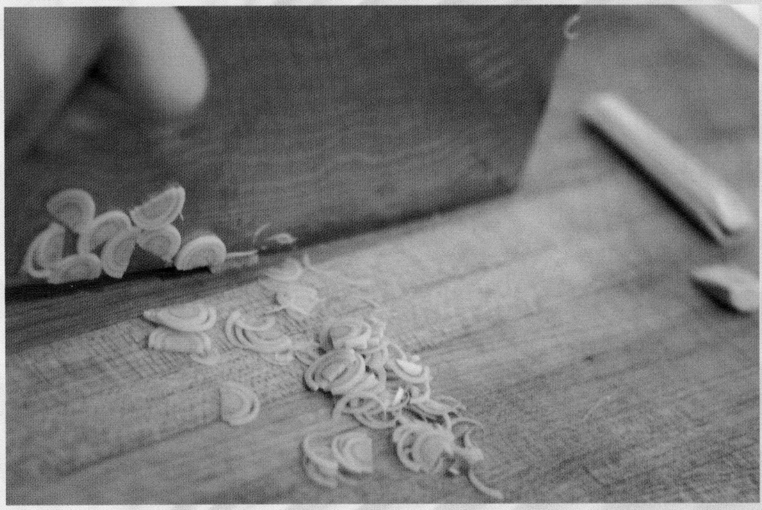

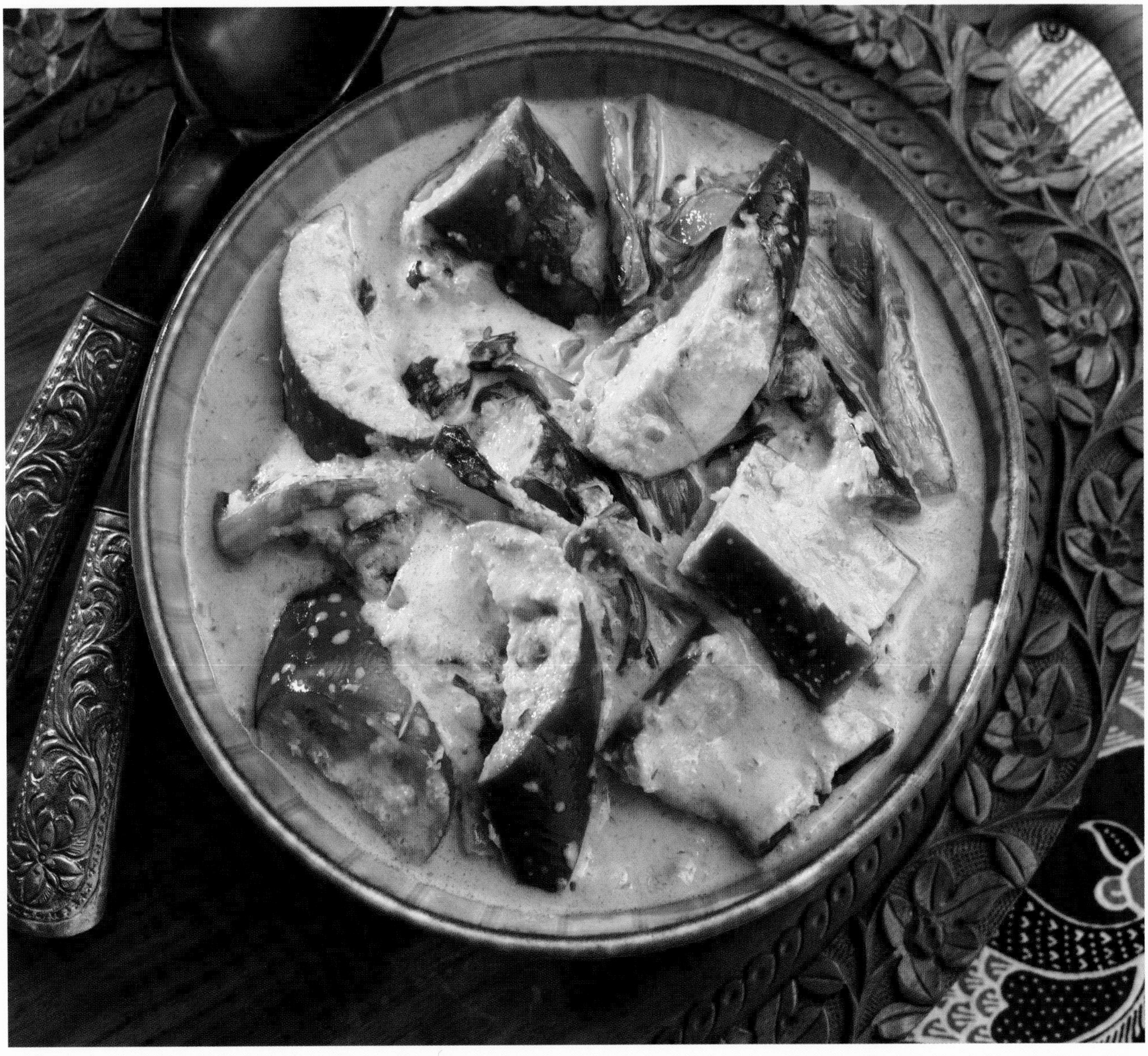

Nonya-Style Mixed Vegetables
Chap Chai

This is a treasure chest of vegetables and noodles, with different shapes, colors, and textures that glisten with flavor. Ground bean sauce (tau cheong) adds depth of flavor. To make it a vegetarian main course, use vegetarian oyster sauce or soy sauce, and omit the shrimp. To give the dish a more ornate look make lengthwise grooves in carrots before slicing, creating a flower-like shape. The sambal belacan chili paste adds a third dimension to this straight forward dish. The dish often includes dried bean curd.

Makes 4 to 6 servings as part of a multi-dish meal

6	Dried Chinese black mushrooms, soaked overnight, liquid reserved (pg. 82)
1/2	cup (1/2 oz. / 14 g.) Dried wood ear fungus, soaked 30 minutes, liquid discarded
1/4	cup (1 oz. / 28 g.) Dried lily buds, soaked 30 minutes
1	oz. (half of 2 oz. bundle / 28 g.) Dried cellophane noodles
1/4	cup Vegetable oil
2	Tbsp. Minced garlic
1	Tbsp. Minced ginger
2	Tbsp. Ground bean sauce or brown bean sauce
1	medium Carrot, sliced on angle, 1/8 inch (0.3cm.) thick
4	cups Green cabbage, 1-inch (2.5 cm.) pieces
2	Tbsp. Oyster sauce or soy sauce
1/2	lb. (227 g.) Small shrimp, peeled and deveined
1	cup Scallions pieces, 1½ inch (about 3.8 cm.)
1	tsp. Sesame oil
as needed	Sambal belacan (pg. 284)

1. Prepare the dried ingredients: Cut soaked mushrooms into halves and quarters, depending on size. Cut any hard nodules off from wood ear fungus, and cut the fungus into bite-size strips, 1/2 inch (0.6 cm.) thick. Cut hard ends off the lily buds, and tie the buds into individual knots. Cover the cellophane noodles with boiling water; soak for 5 minutes. Rinse in cool water, and drain well.

2. Cook the vegetables: Heat oil in a wok or large sauté pan over medium heat. Add the garlic and ginger; cook 1 minute until aromatic but not brown. Add the ground bean sauce; cook 1 minute more. Add carrots, cabbage, oyster sauce, mushrooms, wood ears, lily buds, and 1 cup of mushroom soaking liquid; cook stirring constantly until vegetables are tender, about 3 minutes.

3. Add shrimp; continue to stir-fry until cooked through. Fold in noodles, scallions, and sesame oil; cook until noodles are hot and tender. Taste and adjust seasoning with salt to taste.

How and Why

1. Slow-soak mushrooms for the best texture. Using room temperature water makes the softest texture.

2. Use the flavorful soaking liquid from the dried Chinese mushrooms. The wood ear mushrooms and lily buds, however, do not flavor their soaking liquid.

Purple Rice Pudding with Pandan
Pulut Hitam

In Malaysia and Singapore this snack is served warm or chilled. "Pulut hitam," the tough grained sticky rice, literally translates as "black rice." While teaching at the Culinary Institute of America I placed this on the breakfast menu as a hot cereal, garnished with fresh mango and coconut milk. Surprisingly, the dish developed a following that swore by it, reveling in their newfound breakfast every day at 6:00 AM.

Makes 6 to 8 servings as part of a multi-dish meal

1½ cups Glutinous black rice
6 cups Water
1½ cups Canned coconut Milk
5 Pandan Leaves, tied in a knot
¾ cup Granulated Sugar
⅛ tsp. Kosher Salt

1. Soak rice: Rinse rice, and soak at room temperature in enough water to cover by 1 inch (2.5 cm.) for at least one hour (ideally overnight). Drian well.

2. Cook the rice: Combine rice and water in a saucepan, bring to a boil, lower heat, and simmer 1 hour. Add coconut milk, pandan leaves, sugar and salt; return to boil and lower to simmer; cook until tender 10 to 15 minutes. Pull out panadan leaves, squeezing to extract as much flavorful liquid as possible, discard leaves.

3. Season and serve: Taste; adjust seasoning with sugar, salt and coconut milk. Serve immediately, or chill for later use.

This long grain dark-colored rice releases a gorgeous, deep purple color into the coconut milk mixture it is cooked in.

How and Why

Regulate the heat to avoid excessive moisture evaporation. Cook this rice at a low simmer so that it cooks but doesn't reduce. If it becomes too dry, add water (not coconut milk). It should have the consistency of creamy oatmeal or risotto.

Molten Coconut Pandan Rice Balls
Ondeh Ondeh

The Malaysian Peranakan cuisine is famous for sweet treats. This marriage of the aromatic pandan leaf with deep brown palm sugar and coconut is a harmonious combination familiar throughout Southeast Asia. Each of these tender yet slightly chewy confections oozes rich sugar syrup. Outside, stark white resilient strips of coconut encase the gem. Freshly grated coconut elevates this treat to its highest potential, but the moist unsweetened grated coconut sold in stores is fine. Malaysian and Singaporean cooks color the dough with green coloring for dramatic looks, but I don't. Pandan leaves are available fresh or frozen from Asian grocers. Pandan extract is available online (pg. 362). Making these take a bit of dexterity, just take your time until you get the hang of forming the sugar centered fragrant spherical dumplings.

Makes: About 30 pieces

1   cup Finely shredded coconut
Pinch Kosher salt, ground very fine
12   Pandan leaves or ¹/₂ tsp. pandan extract
1   cup Water
1¹/₂ cups (11 oz. /314 g.) Glutinous rice flour
¹/₂   cup Dark palm sugar (*gula melacca* or *gula jawa*), grated (pg. 58)
6   Banana leaf cups (pg. 353)

1. In medium bowl, combine salt and shredded coconut. Set aside.
2. Make pandan juice: Cut pandan leaves finely, the short way. Combine them in a blender with 1¹/₄ cups water, and puree into a smooth liquid, about 30 seconds; strain through very fine mesh sieve to extract all possible juice.
3. Make dough balls: In a mixing bowl, gradually stir pandan liquid into rice flour, working it into a stiff dough. If needed, add additional water to make dough pliable. Roll into tight, small balls, 1 teaspoon each. Use a finger to create a deep well into a dough ball. Fill with a ¹/₂ tsp. of palm sugar; pinch shut, making sure to create a solid seal. Roll gently in hands to form a round ball.
4. Cook: Bring 2 quarts (2 L). water to a boil. Add balls gently, stirring after 15 seconds to prevent sticking; cook these dumplings until they float (about three to five minutes). Spoon the cooked rice balls from pot, and deposit directly into grated coconut mixture; roll to coat.
5. Cool to room temperature in a single layer; serve in banana leaf cups or small dishes.

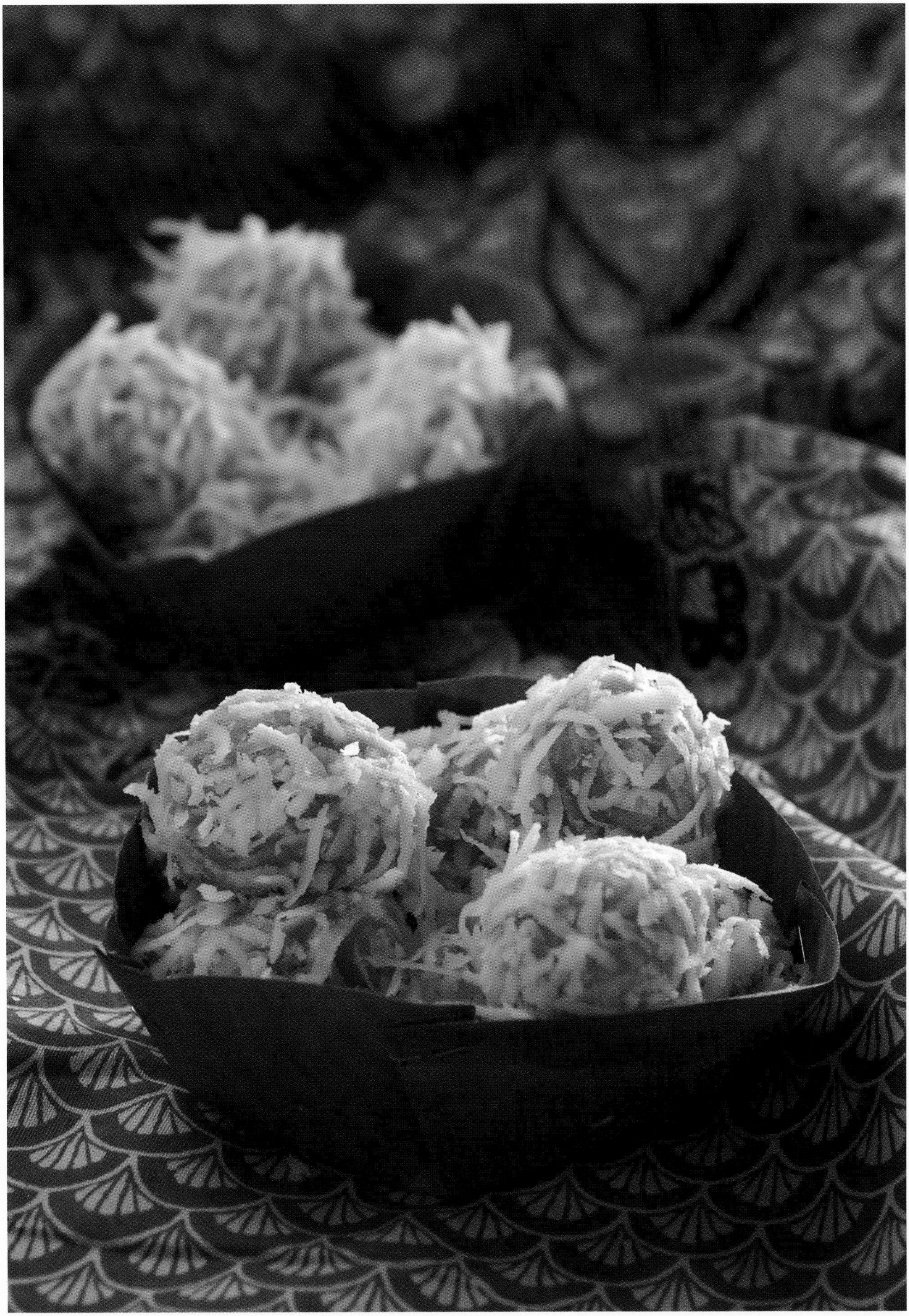

Molten Coconut Pandan Rice Balls

Ondeh Ondeh

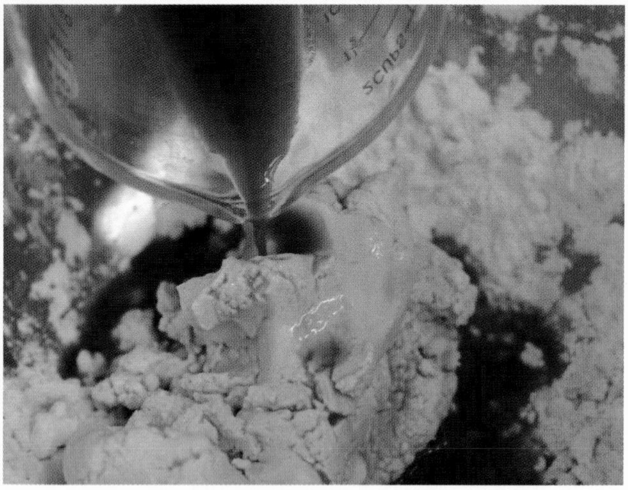

Be patient, the dough will come together, just knead it well. This rice flour based dough has a very different feel when compared to wheat dough.

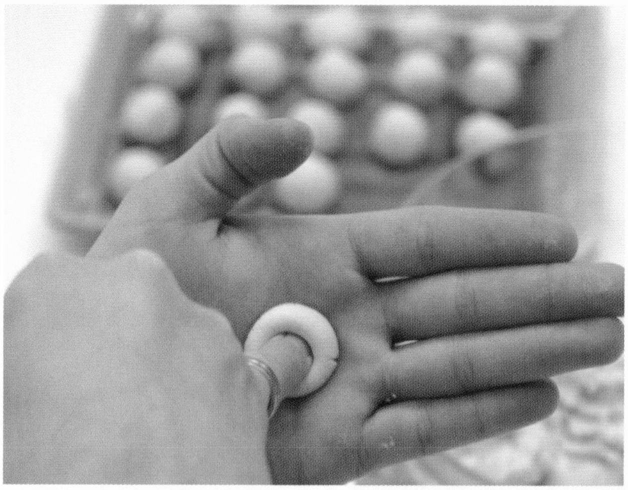

You can use your finger to create the dimple that is filled with the dark brown palm sugar.

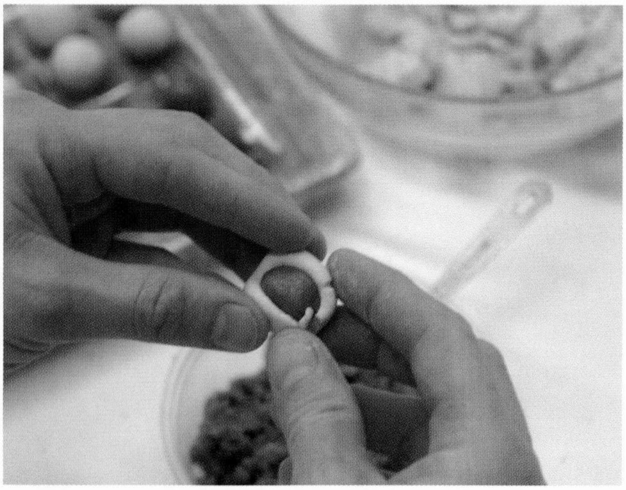

Slowly cinch the dough around the sugar to encase it fully. Pinch closed any gaps that remain.

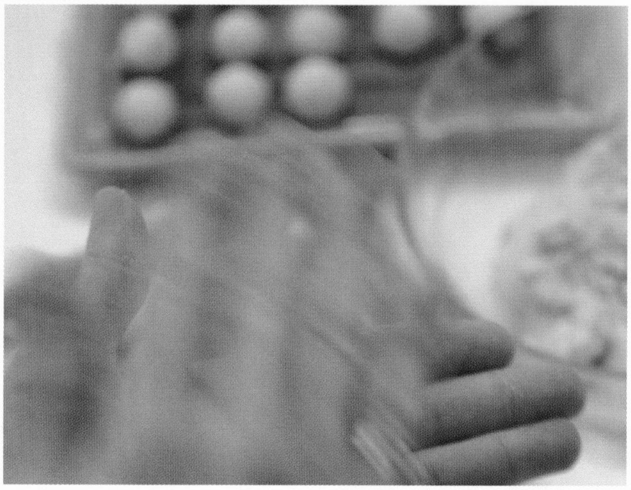

Roll gently to even out the dough and ensure a good seal.

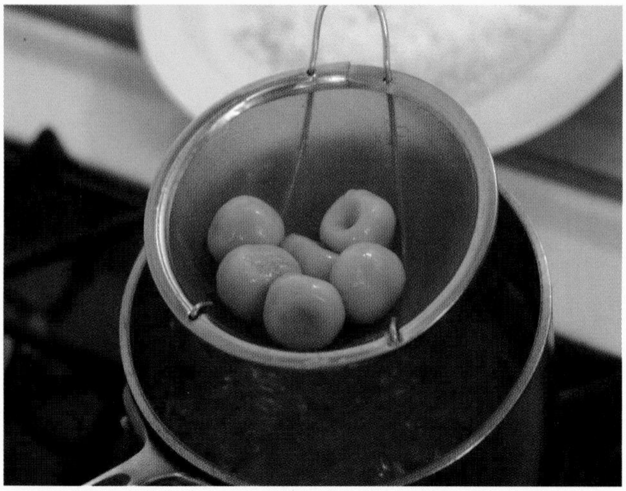

The sugar will liquefy as they boil so do not fret if they implode slightly.

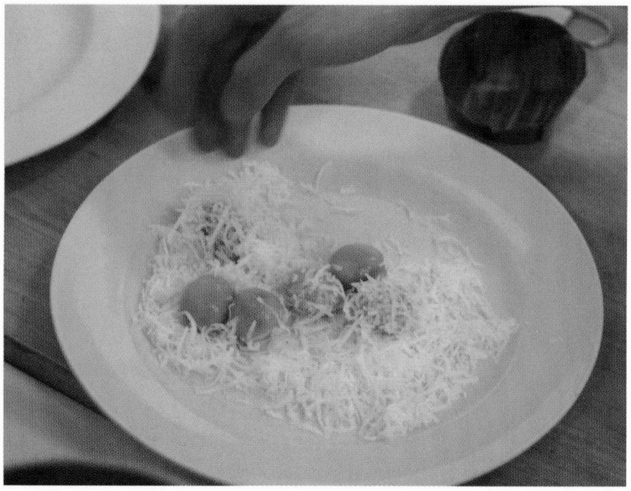

Freshly grated coconut is really worth the effort for these sweet treats.

How and Why

1. When straining the pandan juice, press very hard to ensure the most brilliant green color in the finished dessert.

2. Resting the dumpling after boiling creates the rite balance of chewy-tender dough. The dough firms up as the starches begin to re-crystallize.

Cut the leaves using a plate or bowl as the template, then fold them to pull up edges. This will need to be done in 5 or 6 places to form an actual cup.

Use a stapler to secure the leaf cup, yes, that's what is usually done. If you feel compelled to go all natural, you can use small bamboo skewers or toothpicks.

Feel free to serve other snacks or curries in these banana leaf cups.

Frothy Bittersweet Pulled Tea
Teh Tarik

The Mamak community of Malaysia and Singapore, descendants of Indian and Malay marriages, have invented a hot beverage commonly called "pulled tea." An ultra-strong brewed Orange Pekoe black tea, sweet from condensed milk, is dramatically tossed from one oversized stainless steel mug, to another in a long thin stream. This aerial agitation creates a nose-tickling foam on the sweet beverage, similar to the froth on a cup of cappuccino.

During this theatrical preparation the tea is not only poured from one vessel to another, but the mugs are pulled apart, creating a thin "thread" that connects the two vessels; hence the name: "pulled tea." Mamak are known for running excellent kopitiam (coffee houses) where they serve this sweetened tea along with foods such as roti canai/paratha flatbread (pg. 286) or lentil fritters (pg. 298).

Teh Halia Tarik is pulled ginger tea. To make it, just add one teaspoon of grated ginger to the tea leaves with each cup of tea you brew.

Makes 4 cups

4 cups Water, boiling
1/4 cup Orange Pekoe Tea (1 tablespoon per cup), preferably Ceylon (Sri Lanka)
6 Tbsp. Sweetened condensed milk (1 1/2 tablespoons per cup), to taste

1. In a teapot or other non-reactive container, pour boiling water over tea leaves. Steep 10 minutes (this makes a wickedly strong brew).
2. Strain tea into a large vessel with an easy-to-grip handle (such as a large measuring cup) containing the sweetened condensed milk.
3. "Pull" the tea by pouring it back and forth into another container in a long stream to generate froth. The longer the stream, the frothier the brew (at least 12 inches / 30 c.). Take your time and be careful, splatters from this can burn.
4. Serve the frothy tea quickly, before it deflates.

Orange Pekoe refers to a basic grade of tea, with little astringency, derived from the tender young leaves from the top of the tea plant.

How and Why

1. Use a high quality Orange Pekoe style tea such as to get the authentic color and taste. This black tea boasts strong flavor and deep color.

2. Reheat the tea before pulling it. The ten-minute brew time cools the tea to, as does the "pulling" process.

ALIF

RM 3.00	NASI PUTIH IKAN	RM 3.80	TOSAI BIA
RM 1.50	ROTI CANAI	RM 0.70	TOSAI MIN
RM 2.50	ROTI CANAI TELUR	RM 1.20	TOSAI TEL
RM 5.50	ROTI CANAI TELUR & BAWANG	RM 1.50	TOSAI MA
RM 6.00	MURTABAK AYAM	RM 4.50	ROTI NAN
RM 5.00	MEE GORENG	RM 3.00	BUTTER N
RM 6.00	ROJAK BIASA	RM 3.00	ONION NA
RM 4.00	ROJAK AYAM	RM 5.50	GARLIC N
RM 5.00	ROJAK MEE	RM 3.50	TANDOOR
RM 4.50 KE ATAS	MEE GORENG	RM 3.00	
RM 1.00	TELUR SEPARUH M	RM 0.60	

A thin stream of tea flows from cup to cup in this theatric frothing technique.

Acknowledgments

There have been hundreds of people who've made it possible for me to bring this book to life. My family and friends have put up with my obsession with Asia for years. Tour guides have led the way down back alleys, up lush green hills, and into the kitchens of Southeast Asia. Cooks and chefs took time out of their lives to explain dishes, and soy sauce makers revealed their techniques to me. I'm indebted to the late Barbara Tropp for showing me that you do not need to be Asian to become an expert on the region. Her book, *The Modern Art of Chinese Cooking,* is the first book I turn to for Chinese cuisine information, even to this very day!

I discovered the culture and cuisines of Southeast Asia when I was eighteen. I was taking a local college cooking class when I met Estrellita Leong, a classmate. Within months we were in love; we married, and she became my leader into the world of Southeast Asian flavors. Esther and her family in Malaysia continue to teach me about their culture and every aspect of the food system. Esther has had the patience of a saint during the months of development while my sous chef and I tested and retested hundreds of recipes in the kitchen studio connected to our Los Angeles home. A parade of chefs, student assistants, and advisors came through our home. Despite these challenges and the daily upending of our home life, Esther made everyone feel welcome and sacrificed much so that my work could get done. I cannot thank her enough.

We are a product of our environments. My family and friends helped me get to a place in my career where I was able to write a book. My family supported and encouraged me, even as I embraced a culture different than the one in which I grew up. I thank my mom and dad for bringing me into this world. My parents taught me good work ethics; my brother Dave (also a chef) bailed me out more than once when I was in need of culinary support. My other brother, Victor (an attorney), helped me with contracts and legal documents. And my dear sister Lisa's endless energy has always inspired me to push through the challenges that life presents, including the many I encountered in writing this book. Esther's sister, Pat, Pat's husband, Dave, and their kids, Hunter and Garrett, have been my friends and recipe tasters through it all. Pat: thanks for teaching me how to make great *sambal.* Dave and Hunter: thank you for helping me build my test kitchen.

When I finally decided to make this book a reality, I needed to assemble a team to make it happen. I was fortunate to meet a young chef, Ari Slatkin, who was completing his second degree in hospitality restaurant management. I was on the road, teaching about Asian cuisine for one of my clients, when this budding chef showed me that he was already hooked on Asian food and all it had to offer. Knowing we shared that passion, I hired him to be my sous chef. He has been my invaluable culinary support man ever since. Ari led much of the recipe development and was the lighting specialist during our photo shoots.

I called on my longtime editor and friend, Chef Jay Weinstein, to help craft my words. Jay, also a CIA-trained chef and author of several cookbooks of his own, had been the editor of the CIA's food magazine, *Kitchen & Cook.* He had edited more than a dozen articles I had written for it, so he knew how to let my voice come through while doing what he does best—writing and editing with the solid foundation of a professional chef. We traveled to Singapore together, and I could immediately see that this chef got it. He loves these foods and is as inquisitive as I am, so the partnership blossomed amid new discoveries in Asian cuisine. Jay and I have spent countless hours e-mailing, talking on the phone, and meeting on both coasts, honing and refining this book.

I have been taking photographs across Asia for years and have spent time honing my skills as a photojournalist. That's very different from studio photography. I had the great fortune to meet Dana Maione, the "Director of Light and Stuff," at her DMP Studio in Torrance, California. She tutored Ari and me in the basics of studio photography. Let's just say she pushed us up-to-speed quickly. She guided me in purchasing my studio equipment and led us step-by-step through the first round of photos for the book. David Miller, DMP's "Pixel Wrangler," is the backbone of the company and showed us how to control lighting and photo file management. Amber, their administrative assistant, kept us all in communication. Oh yeah, Pixel, the tiny dog with a big bark (small bite), cheered us on every day.

During the final stages of developing the recipes and content a slew of people came on board, even if it was just for a few days. From the local culinary schools came

Donna Whitehouse and Scott Lairson. Colleagues who jumped in to help during the last months, such as my friend and colleague and consummate professional Chef John Csukor, allowed me to continue working on the book. For the final hectic days, Chefs Paul Foster and Brad Kent were here for recipe testing and cooked much of the food in the photographs you find within the book—thanks, chefs. Mary Katherine Talley helped test the recipes—thank you. Christine-Thai Rimlinger and her family hosted numerous Vietnamese food fests where I was able to pick the brains of her friends and family and fortunately meet my Vietnamese language angel, Mai-Khanh, who not only translated all of the Vietnamese, adding the diacriticals (accents) to every page, she also evaluated the validity of several of the recipes. To Fah Vorarittinapa for her Thai language expertise, kop kum kop (thank you).

On the Road

Over the past two decades a network of friends and colleagues has made traveling in foreign lands possible. Some are officially in the travel business, and others just wanted to share their homeland. I usually start and finish my Southeast Asian travels in Singapore. It's the gateway to Asia: so well organized, you can count on everything going smoothly there. The first "culinary immersion tours" I led to Southeast Asia were hosted there. Those were hugely successful in part due to Janet Chee, my logistics authority. She is always a step ahead of our group and has become a close friend. I can rely on her to steer me to the best place for Champagne Pork Ribs (Por Kee Eating House) or the hottest dance spot (St. James Power Station). Joseph Wellesley, our main guide, was a calming presence, answering every question with a smile. Gary Low, the consummate professional driver, safely ferried us in the lap of air-conditioned luxury. The Singapore Tourism Board stepped up to the plate, helping me lead my first tour— simplifying logistics, reducing unnecessary costs, and supporting me whenever requested. They are top notch, and their Web site is a great resource. Recently, I've worked with International Enterprise Singapore, bringing food professionals to Singapore for journeys of discovery. The country's food manufacturing and quality control capabilities are exceptional.

Kwan Lui, the founder of At-Sunrice Global Chef Academy has involved me in the writing of curriculum and brought me in to teach at her campus. Phyllis Ong and the chefs at the school host countless visitors I have sent in, inviting them to tour their spice garden and cook in their kitchens. Thank you to Singapore's most-celebrated food personality, culinary diva Violet Oon, who writes about food, teaches cooking classes around the globe, and consults with numerous organizations. She always invites me into her cool flat and takes the time to show me a new culinary treasure. Pui San, a petite fireball of energy I met at a Foie Gras dinner, has led me into Chinese sausage factories, biscuit manufacturers, and fish ball shops. She is such a great spirit and friend. The Singapore National Museum has a permanent food exhibit (not many countries can boast that type of commitment to cuisine), and I'm grateful to their curator, Wong Hong Suen, for leading me through their exhibits.

Most of my in-laws still reside in Malaysia. They always put their lives on hold when I arrive, catering to my every whim. Esther's mom, Annie Leong, was the first person in Southeast Asia to teach me how to cook Malaysian foods. Glenn Leong, my brother-in-law, has spent countless hours shuttling me around Malaysia and Thailand in pursuit of the best version of one dish or another. I'm grateful for his wife, Irene's, patience when I whisk him away for my trips. Esther's brother, the late Kennedy Leong, is still alive in our hearts. I will always remember his passion for food and how he cooked his heart out for us alongside his dear wife Angela. Thank you to Aunties Autin and Ong for showing me secrets as you cooked great foods for us. My friends Sam and Lily Tan took the time to send some props for the Malaysian photography in our studio. A special thanks goes out to The Malaysian Tourism Board for helping me discover the mysteries of their country. The Colors of Malaysia festival was vibrant in colors and flavors.

The warm welcome I received in Thailand from my former student Fah Vorarittinapa's family brought that country into my heart. The first night, Teaw, Fah, and Fah's wife picked me up and brought me over for tom yum soup. The week her mom and dad spent with me was one of the most unforgettable weeks of my life. They treated me like family. I mentioned how I would like to learn about satay, and the next day I was sitting on the kitchen floor of a great cook learning it. These are truly amazing, kind people.

My Thai guide Yowgyut "Tik" and his family were extraordinary. My time with them taught me much about the food (including the Pumpkin recipe on page 170) and culture of Thailand. Tik translated for me during the entire time with Fah's family. He was our lifeline of communication.

Although we met at the CIA in Napa Valley, Thai cooking master Kobkaew Najpinij and her daughter Niphatchanok Najpinij "Ning" helped me greatly in Thailand, especially as I learned the intricacies of Thai curries. They introduced me to Thai expert chef David Thompson and his "right hand," Jane Alty, whom I worked with on their upcoming book on Thai street food. My gratitude goes out to my Thai carving masters, brothers Dumrongsak Nirund and Rawat Nirund at Chatuchuck market. They patiently taught me *kae sa luk*, the Thai art of fruit and vegetable carving. I thank them for their tutelage.

My first trip to Vietnam with the CIA was led by Marcia Selva of Global Spectrum. She and her team did an amazing job. Mai Pham was an incomparable culinary guide. Thanks go out to Dzoan Cẩm Vân Nguyễn and her son Khải for an intensive crash course in Saigon cooking. On my subsequent backpacking trip through Vietnam, my guide Lam took me to places I never would have seen (or found my way back from). Lugging me, my laptop, and my digital camera equipment on the back of his scooter, he weathered the hot sun, flat tires, and more to make my dream of seeing the salt fields of Vietnam a reality.

On my Vietnamese research trip for this book, **Tran Van Truong helped me in planning and made it the trip of a lifetime. He connected me with "Captain Cook" (pg. 254),** my guide through the south of Vietnam, who went beyond the call of duty. His cousin Phuong and daughter Ha Trieu Quyen Quyen helped prepare ingredients so we could cook each day, ensuring that I learned every moment. Thank you for becoming a friend and not keeping it just business. Sharing grilled field mice and beer with someone can bond people like nothing else. Mr. Cong, my central Vietnamese guide, had a scholarly approach that served me well, placing analogies and idiomatic expressions of daily life in context. In Hanoi, Mr. Phuong's inexhaustible appetite kept up with mine as we ate from morning to night.

Innumerable cooks shared their best recipes. I have credited as many as I could, along with their recipes, in the pages of this book.

Back in My Homeland

I'll be forever grateful to the Culinary Institute of America (CIA) for giving me my culinary education foundation, and later the opportunity to teach in Hyde Park and Napa Valley. I am honored to be part of the CIA family and treasure my continued work there. Martha Holmberg, then at *Fine Cooking* magazine, gave me my first shot at writing for a nationally distributed magazine; thank you. Thanks to all my editors since then, who have helped me become the writer I am today.

When I started my consulting firm, Chef Danhi & Co., in 2005, Wing Hing Foods, the leader in wheat noodles and dumpling wrappers, was first in line to partner with us. We continue to work together every month. Thank you, Kenny, for believing in me from the beginning. Jade, your friendship and customer relationships are cherished. Andy, thanks for your continued leadership. And Mark, thanks for your support with my recipe testing.

Lee Kum Kee, the maker of my favorite authentic Asian sauces, has also been on board since the beginning. They have provided me the tools and opportunities to expand my knowledge of Asian sauces, sending me to China to learn the traditional methods of making soy sauce, oyster sauce, and many other building blocks of flavor. They supported me in my testing of the recipes in this book. Winnie, thank you for leading the company to success and including me as part of the plan. Simon, your sales and marketing expertise are making an impact every day. Eliza, thank you for coordinating all the projects we work on together. Grace Chow, your spunky spirit always makes me smile. Ed Hsu, you're welcome to work in my kitchen any day. Gregorious, your support and eager attitude is valued. Anita Lim, your lightning speed (and tasty flan) does not go unappreciated. Thanks also to Andy Law and Betty Tsang for their help and company during my nationwide travels.

Melissa's World Variety Produce supplied countless shipments of bright red chilies, jade green Chinese broccoli, pounds of shallots, and numerous other items for testing the recipes and for the photos in the book. Robert Schueller coordinated the orders and deliveries on his way home. I also thank you for supporting me throughout the years, helping me find aromatic ingredients for my audiences and students to experience firsthand.

Sunkist Growers have helped growers of excellent citrus bring their crops to the world. Since most citrus is indigenous to Asia (pg. 84), Sunkist has proved invaluable, working together with me on several projects and sharing pummelos, grapefruits, and limes with me during my recipe testing. Thank you.

Paul Kurpe of Elite Spice, Inc., arranged a spice journey in India for me. That trip gave me a firsthand look at spice cultivation and processing. Ketan Mehta and his wife, Heena, were the most gracious hosts during my trip. Thank you. Leslie Krause and her talented team of R & D professionals helped us decipher the curry powders of Southeast Asia (pg. 112).

A big thank-you goes out to thousands of students that have passed through my classroom kitchens—you have inspired me to keep learning. My teachers and mentors along the way who have led by example—thank you for being role models for me. To educate is to change a person for life, and I feel privileged to be a teacher. And my gratitude goes to the many folks that I haven't listed here. So many people have impacted me (and hence this book) in wonderful ways. Thank you.

Asian Resource Guide

Asian Food Suppliers

Asia etc.—Asian product source for retail and wholesale.

http://www.asia-etc.com/

Import Food.com—On-line supermarket of exotic goods.

http://importfood.com

JFC International—Source for Asian products and equipment.

http://www.jfc.com/

Lee Kum Kee—A leading producer of Asian sauces.

http://www.lkk.com/

Melissa's World Variety Produce—Specialty produce purveyor for food service and retail.

http://www.melissas.com/

New Asia Cuisine—Here you will find a comprehensive guide to markets across the USA.

http://www.newasiacuisine.com

Temple of Thai—Offering Thai products, recipes, and information pertaining to Thai culture and culinary arts.

http://www.templeofthai.com

Wing Hing Food—The leader of Asian noodles in the USA.

http://www.winghingfood.com

Asian Specialty Stores

99 Ranch—A pan-Asian market chain serving states with large Asian communities. All the stores are clean and modern. They claim to be "America's largest Asian supermarket chain!" Though 99 Ranch caters mostly to Chinese shoppers, you can find ingredients for preparing all kinds of Asian cuisine. Stores feature live seafood tanks and "you buy, we fry" service. Most of their markets are in California.

www.99ranch.com

Asian Food Market/Center—In New Jersey for now, this growing chain of pan-Asian markets was started in 1992 by W. K. Chan.

www.asianfoodcenter.com

Dynasty Supermarket—Newest Asian food superstore in Manhattan's Chinatown.

http://www.dynastysuper.qpg.com/

H Mart—Korean-owned pan-Asian market chain on the East Coast and in the Midwest. Lots of Korean goods, but the shelves are also well stocked with Chinese and Southeast Asian staples.

www.hmart.com (click on "English" in the upper right-hand corner)

Kam Man Food Products, Inc.—New York's biggest Chinatown supermarket. Pan-Asian products. 200 Canal Street (at Mulberry) 212-571-0330.

http://nymag.com/listings/stores/kam_man_food_products/

Korin—Located in lower Manhattan, Korin is a great resource for all of your cutlery needs.

http://www.korin.com/

Marukai—Based in Los Angeles and Hawaii, the business began as an importer for Japanese food, furniture, household items, health foods, health and fitness items, and electronics.

http://www.marukai.com/

Mitsuwa—A Japanese grocery chain that took over when Yaohan went out of business. No Vietnamese ingredients, but you can get good prices on Japanese rice vinegars. Mitsuwa has locations in California, Illinois, and New Jersey.

www.mitsuwa.com

Mutual Trading Co.—The premier Japanese food, alcohol beverage, and restaurant supply specialist, providing the top brands to retailer and foodservice customers nationwide.

http://www.lamtc.com/

Uwajimaya—A pan-Asian chain of markets in Washington and Oregon. Has an on-line catalog that offers flours and soy sauces, but not much in terms of Vietnamese ingredients.

www.uwajimaya.com

Viet World Kitchen—Information and resources regarding Asian culinary supplies.

www.vietworldkitchen.com

The Wok Shop—Located in the heart of San Francisco's famous Chinatown, The Wok Shop is a family-owned and -operated business specializing in hard-to-find Asian cooking tools. Their unique stock of merchandise covers nearly every aspect of Asian cooking!

http://www.wokshop.com/

New Asia Cuisine—Here you will find a comprehensive guide to markets across the USA.

http://www.newasiacuisine.com

Asian Food and Culture

Asian Culinary Arts Institute—Dedicated to the preservation, understanding, and enjoyment of the culinary arts of the Asia Pacific Rim.

http://www.asianculinaryarts.com/

Country Studies—A comprehensive description and analysis of the country or region's historical setting, geography, society, economy, political system, and foreign policy.

http://countrystudies.us

Food Reference.com—An educational resource.

http://www.foodreference.com/html/thailand-cooking.html

Paknam Web Network—Promoting Thai life and culture to the world.

http://www.paknamweb.com/

Things Asian—Experience Asia through the eyes of travelers.

http://www.thingsasian.com/stories-PHOTOs/2306

US Central Intelligence Agency's World Fact book

https://www.cia.gov/library/publications/the-world-factbook/index.html

Vietnam VIP Tours—Travel and cultural information.

http://www.vietnamviptour.com/Minotities.php?g=1

Viet World Kitchen—Information and resources regarding Asian culinary supplies.

www.vietworldkitchen.com

Asian Food and Culture Educational

At-sunrice Global Chef Academy—This organization teaches classes to the professional chef, aspiring culinarians, and home cooks alike.

http://www.at-sunrice.com/

Culinary Institute of America—The CIA offers classes for the home cook and professional chef on all things Asian.

http://www.ciachef.edu/

Samui Institute of Thai Culinary Arts—Located on the island of Koh Samui. Southern Thailand's center for Thai food lovers and all those with an interest in food from Thailand.

http://www.sitca.net/

Thai Carving Institute—Located in Bangkok. They offer classes specializing in Thai fruit and vegetable carving.

http://www.carvinginstitute.com/

Asian Food Info

The Asian Grandmother's Cookbook—Compilation of traditional Asian recipes.

http://theasiangrandmotherscookbook.wordpress.com

Bangkok Beer Hunter—A reference for Thai beers.

http://www.bangkokbob.net

Bangkok Post—Leading regional news publication covering current events in Thailand.

http://www.bangkokpost.com/entertainment/restaurants/

Enjoy Thai Food—A Thai food blog.

http://www.enjoythaifood.com/khanomkrok.php

The Epicenter—An encyclopedia of spices.

http://www.theepicentre.com/Spices/spiceref.html

International Herald Tribune—International current events and news.

http://www.iht.com

The Last Appetite—Food history.

http://www.lastappetite.com

My Local Cuisine Blog—Food blog regarding authentic ethnic foods.

http://mylocalcuisine.blogspot.com

Pterodactyl Coffee—A coffee reference.

http://harryosoffdesign.com/fyi/coffee_info_coffeeFAQ.html

Rasa Malaysia—A blog regarding Malaysian food, culture, and travel.

http://www.rasamalaysia.com/

Real Thai Recipes—An adventure learning to cook Thai style.

**http://www.realthairecipes.com/recipes/
drunken-noodles/**

Samui Institute of Thai Culinary Arts—A Thai cooking and cuisine institute.

http://www.sitca.net/

The Star Online—A recipes reference and data base.

http://kuali.com/recipes/viewrecipe.asp?r=1603

Vietnam Tourism—A guide to food, culture, and travel in Vietnam.

**http://www.vietnamtourism.com/e_pages/
country/overview.asp?uid=1996**

Travel Resources

Air Asia—Providing transportation to most of Southeast Asia.

http://www.airasia.com

Fodor's On line—Providing travel information, transportation, guidance, and literature.

http://fodors.com/

Lonely Planet On line—Providing travel information, transportation, guidance, and literature.

http://lonelyplanet.com/

Malaysia Airlines—Providing transportation to most of Southeast Asia.

http://www.malaysiaairlines.com

National Geographic—Providing ethnographic information and adventure expeditions.

http://www.nationalgeographic.com/

North by Northeast—Travel guides.

**http://www.north-by-north-east.com/
articles/06_04_3.asp**

Safe Travel.com—Travel tips.

**http://safetravel.dot.gov/whats_new_
batteries.html**

Singapore Air—Providing transportation to most of Southeast Asia (Chef Danhi's favorite airline).

http://www.singaporeair.com

Thai Air—Providing transportation to most of Southeast Asia.

http://www.thaiair.com/

Vietnamese Embassy—Providing information pertaining to Vietnamese travel, culture, current events, and attractions.

http://www.vietnamembassy-usa.org

Printed Resources Used as References for the Development of This Book

Adams, Jane, ed. *China and Its Cuisine*. New York: Mallard Press, 1990.
ISBN: 978-0792452256

Agar, Charles, and Jennifer Eveland. *Frommer's Southeast Asia*. 4th ed. New Jersey: Wiley Publishing Inc., 2005.
ISBN: 978-0764578298

Alford, Jeffrey, and Naomi Duguid. *Hot Sour Salty Sweet: a culinary journey through Southeast Asia*. New York: Artisan, 2000.
ISBN: 978-1579651145

———. *Mangoes & Curry Leaves: Culinary travels through the great subcontinent*. New York: Artisan, 2005.
ISBN: 978-0679312802

———. *Seductions of Rice*. New York: Artisan, 1998.
ISBN: 978-1579652340

Aziz, Khalid, et al. *The Encyclopedia of Asian Cooking*. Ed. Jeni Wright. New York: Exter Books, 1984.
ISBN: 978-0671068011

Basan, Ghillie. *The Cooking of Malaysia & Singapore*. London: Hermes House, 2006.
ISBN: 978-0-681-28961-1

———. *Vietnamese Food & Cooking*. London: Hermes House, 2006.
ISBN: 978-1-84477-893-5

Bastyra, Judy. *Thai, the essence of Asian cooking*. London, UK: Hermes House, 2003.
ISBN: 978-0681923775

Bladholm, Linda. *The Asian Grocery Store Demystified*. California: Renaissance Books, 1999.
ISBN: 1-58063-045-6

Brennan, Jennifer. *One-Dish Meals of Asia*. New York: Times Books, 1985.
ISBN: 978-0060973582

————. *The Original Thai Cookbook.* New York: Perigee, 1984.
ISBN: 978-0399510335

Brissenden, Rosemary. *South East Asian Food.* Victoria: Penguin, 1971.

————. *Southeast Asian Food.* Singapore: Periplus Editions, 2007.
ISBN: 978-0794604882

Carmack, Robert, Didier Corlou, and Thanh Van Nguyen. *Vietnamese Cooking.* Singapore: Periplus Editions, 2003.
ISBN: 978-0-7946-5031-5

Carnegie, Celine. *Authentic Tastes of Southeast Asia.* New York: Barnes & Noble, 2007.
ISBN: 978-0-7607-8664-2

Cheong, Patsie. *Malaysian Delicacies: The best of Patsie Cheong.* Hong Kong: Seashore Publishing, 2003.
ISBN: 962-365-935-0

Ching, Lee Sook. *Cook Malaysian* 1980. Singapore: Times Editions, 2003.
ISBN: 978-9812324467

Choi, Trieu Thi, and Marcel Isaak. *Authentic Recipes from Vietnam.* Singapore: Periplus Editions, 2005.
ISBN: 0-7946-0328-9

Cost, Bruce. *Asian Ingredients: A guide to the foods of China, Japan, Korea, Thailand, and Vietnam* 1998. New York: HarperCollins Publishers 2000.
ISBN: 978-0060932046

Crawford, William, and Kamolmal Pootaraksa. *Thai Home Cooking.* New York: Plume, 1986.

Davidson, Alan. *Seafood of South-East Asia.* 2nd ed. California: Ten Speed Press, 2003.
ISBN: 978-1580084529

Davidson, Alan, and Helen Saberi. *The Oxford Companion to Food.* 2nd edition. Ed. Tom Jaine & Jane Davidson. New York: Oxford University Press Inc., 2006.
ISBN: 978-0192806819

Discovery Channel, and Francis Doral, ed. *Bangkok City Guide.* 4th edition. New York: Insight Guides, 2005.
ISBN: 978-9812582478

Discovery Channel, and Scott Rutherford, ed. *Insight Guide Vietnam.* New York: Insight Guides, 2005.
ISBN: 978-9812349842

Florence, Mason, and Robert Story. *Lonely Planet Vietnam.* Victoria: Lonely Planet Publications Pty Ltd., 2001.
ISBN: 978-1864501896

Greeley, Alexandra. *Asian Soups, Stews, & Curries.* New York: Macmillan Publishing, 1998.
ISBN: 978-0028612690

Hale, Glorya. *The World Atlas of Food: A Gourmet's Guide to the Great Regional Dishes of the World.* London: Spring Books, 1988.
ISBN: 978-0600559290

Harlow, Jay. *Chinese Cooking Techniques.* California: Chevron Chemical Company, 1987.
ISBN: 978-0897210935

————. *Southeast Asian Cooking,* California Culinary Academy Series. California: Chevron Chemical Co, 1987.
ISBN: 978-0897210980

Harpham, Zoe, and Wendy Stephen, eds. *The Essential Wok Cookbook.* California: Thunder Bay Press, 2002.
ISBN: 978-1571459763

Hemphill, John, and Rosemary Hemphill. *Herbs: Their Cultivation and Usage 1983.* London: Blandford Press, 1991.
ISBN: 978-0713714517

The Complete Step By Step Vegetable and Fruit Carving. Ed. Nidda Hongwiwat. Bangkok: Sangdad Publications, 1999.
ISBN: 978-9747162608

Hopgood, Honga Im. *Honga's Lotus Petal: Pan Asian Cuisine.* Utah: Gibbs Smith, 2007.
ISBN: 978-1-58685-893-3

Hsiang, Ju Lin, and Lin Tsuifeng. *Chinese Gastronomy.* New York: Pyramid Publications, 1972.
ISBN: 978-0515093261

Hsiung, Deh-Ta, and Nina Simonds. *The Food of China.* Sydney: Murdoch Books, 2001.
ISBN: 978-1740452847

Hutton, Wendy. *A Cook's Guide to Asian Vegetables.*
 Singapore: Peripolus Editions, 2004.
 ISBN: 978-0794600785

———. *Green Mangoes and Lemongrass: Southeast Asia's Best Recipes from Bangkok to Bali.* Singapore: Periplus Editions, 2007.
 ISBN: 978-0794602307

Hutton, Wendy, and Four Seasons Hotels. *Tropical Asian Cooking: Exotic Flavors from Equatorial Asia.*
 Singapore: Periplus Editions, 2002.
 ISBN: 978-0794600068

Isaak, Marcel, and Trieu Thi Choi. *The Food of Vietnam: Authentic Recipes from the Heart of Indochina.*
 Singapore: Periplus Editions (HK) Ltd., 1998.
 ISBN: 978-9625933948

Jaffrey, Madhur. *Taste of the Far East.* New York: Carol Southern Books, 1993.
 ISBN: 978-0517595480

Jue, Joyce. *Savoring Southeast Asia*, William Sonoma. Ed. Chuck Williams. Virginia: Time-Life Books, 2000.
 ISBN: 978-0737020434

Karim, Samad, and Hassim Ahmad. *Traditional Malaysian Cuisine.* Malaysia: Berita Publishing SDN. BHD., 1989.
 ISBN: 978-9679691399

Kong, Foong Ling. *The Food of Asia.* Singapore: Periplus, 2002.
 ISBN: 978-0794601461

Kongpan, Sisamon. *The Best of Thai Dishes* 1991. Bangkok: Sangdad Books, 2000.
 ISBN: 974-7162-62-8

Laursen, Therese Volpe. *From Bangkok to Bali in 30 Minutes: 175 Fast and Easy Recipes with the Lush, Tropical Flavors of Southeast Asia.* Boston: Harvard Common Press, 2003.
 ISBN: 978-1558322356

Law, Ruth. *The Southeast Asia Cookbook.* New York: Plume, 1995.
 ISBN: 978-1556114694

Le, Ann. *The Little Saigon Cookbook: Vietnamese Cuisine and Culture in Southern California's Little Saigon.*
 Connecticut: Insiders' Guide, 2006.
 ISBN: 978-0-7627-3831-1

Lee, Pamela, ed. *Fodor's Singapore.* 12th ed. New York: Fodor's Travel Publications, 2005.
 ISBN: 978-1400014767

Lee, Patricia. *Delicious Nyonya Kueh & Desserts.* Hong Kong: Seashore Publishing, 2004.
 ISBN: 988-202-190-5

Leong, Yee Soo. *The Best of Singapore's Recipes: Everyday Favourites.* Singapore: Marshall Cavendish International, 2005.
 ISBN: 978-9812326492

———. *The Best of Singapore's Recipes: Nyonya Specialties.*
 Singapore: Times Editions, 2004.
 ISBN: 978-9812326485

Loha-Unchit, Kasma. *Dancing Shrimp.* New York: Simon & Schuster, 2000.
 ISBN: 978-0684862729

———. *It Rains Fishes: Legends, Traditions, and the Joy of Thai Cooking.* California: Pomegranate Artbooks, 1995.
 ISBN: 978-0876543566

Lonely Planet. *Phrasebooks: Vietnamese.* Victoria: Lonely Planet Publications, 2006.
 ISBN: 978-1740592413

Lonely Planet, and Joe Cummings. *World Food Thailand.*
 Victoria, Australia: Lonely Planet Publications, 2000.
 ISBN: 978-1864500264

Lonely Planet, and Bruce Evens. *Thai Phrase Book.*
 Victoria, Australia: Lonely Planet Publications, 2004.
 ISBN: 978-1740592314

Lonely Planet and Simon Richmond. *Singapore 1991.*
 Victoria: Lonely Planet Publications Pty Ltd., 2003.
 ISBN: 978-1740593090

Malaysia Airlines. *Golden Gourmet.* Kuala Lumpur: Golden Boutique, 1987.

Marks, Copeland. *The Exotic Kitchens of Malaysia.* New York: Donald I. Fine Books, 1997.
 ISBN: 978-1556115264

McGee, Harold. *On Food and Cooking: The science and lore of the kitchen.* New York: Scribner, 2004.
 ISBN: 978-0684800011

Megel, Christophe, and Anton Kilayko. *Asian Tapas: small bites, big flavors*. Singapore: Periplus, 2004.
ISBN: 978-0794603144

Milligan, Angela. *Culture Smart! Singapore: A Quick Guide to Customs & Etiquette*. Oregon: Graphic Arts Publishing Company, 2004.
ISBN: 978-1558687899

Morris, Sallie, and Deh-Ta Hsiung. *The Practical Encyclopedia of Asian Cooking*. Ed. Jenni Fleetwood. New York: Lorenz Books, 1999.
ISBN: 978-0754809364

Mowe, Rosalind, ed. *Southeast Asian Specialties, A Culinary Journey*. Cologne: Konemann, 1998.
ISBN: 978-3895089091

Murdoch Books. *Food of the World*. London: Murdoch Books UK Pty Ltd., 2004.
ISBN: 978-1740455596

Nabnian, Carmack. *Thai Cooking*. Singapore: Periplus Editions, 2001.
ISBN: 978-0794650292

Nguyen, Ana Vinhanh. *Cooking with Ana: Vietnamese Cuisine*. Ho Chi Minh: Ho Chi Minh City General Publishing House, 2004.
ISBN: 0-9771074-0-x

Nguyen, Andrea. *Into the Vietnamese Kitchen: Treasured Foodways, Modern Flavors*. California: Ten Speed Press, 2006.
ISBN: 978-1-58008-665-3

Nguyen, Thanh Diep. *Feast of Flavours from the Vietnamese Kitchen*. Singapore: Marshall Cavendish International, 2005.
ISBN: 978-9812326775

Nitibhon, Wanvisa. *Thai Cuisine with Jasmine Rice*. Maryland: Eastland Food Corporation, 2000.
ISBN: 9747588676

Norman, Jill. *The Complete Book of Spices, A practical guide to spices & aromatic seeds*. New York: Viking Studio Books, 1991.
ISBN: 978-0140238044

Oseland, James. *Cradle of Flavor, Home Cooking from the Spice Islands of Indonesia, Malaysia, and Singapore*. New York: W. W. Norton & Co., 2006.
ISBN: 978-0393054774

Owen, Sri. *Noodles the New Way*. London: Quadrille Publishing Limited, 2000.
ISBN: 978-1902757476

Passmore, Jackie. *Asia: The Beautiful Cookbook*. California: Collins, 1990.
ISBN: 978-0002551151

———. *The Noodle Shop Cookbook*. New York: Macmillan Inc, 1994.
ISBN: 978-0025947054

———. *Williams-Sonoma: Savoring China*. Savoring Series. California: Oxmoor House, 2003.
ISBN: 978-0848726447

Pham, Mai. *The Best of Vietnamese & Thai Cooking*. California: Prima Lifestyles, 1995.
ISBN: 978-0761500162

———. *Pleasures of the Vietnamese Table*. New York: HarperCollins, 2001.
ISBN: 978-0060192587

Prieb, Roy, and Joann S. Chan. *Let's Go 1995 Thailand plus gateway cities*. Ed. Samantha Kent. New York: St. Martins Press, 1994.

QA International. *The Visual Food Encyclopedia*. New York: Wiley Publishing, 1996.
ISBN: 978-0028610061

Ray, Nick and Wendy Yanagihara. *Lonely Planet Vietnam*. 8th ed. Victoria: Lonely Planet Publications Pty Ltd., 2005.
ISBN: 978-1740596770

Reader's Digest. *Cook's Ingredients*. Ed. Adrian Bailey. New York: Reader's Digest Association Inc., 1990.
ISBN: 978-0895773562

Rosengarten, Fredric Jr. *The Book of Spices*. New York: Pyramid Books, 1973.
ISBN: 978-0515064902

Ross, Rosa Lo San, and Martin Jacobs. *Beyond Bok Choy*. New York: Artisan, 1996.
ISBN: 978-1885183231

Rowthorn, Chris, Sara Benson, Russel Kerr, and Christine Niven. *Lonely Planet Malaysia, Singapore and Brunei* 1982. Victoria: Lonely Planet Publications Pty Ltd., 2001. ISBN: 978-1864501889

Ruangkritya, Krissnee, and Tim Martsching. *Adventures in Thai Food & Culture.* Bangkok: Ratana-Nakorn Co, 1984. ASIN: B0006EJGPK

Sadsook, Victor. *True Thai: The Modern Art of Thai Cooking.* New York: William Morrow Cookbooks, 1995. ISBN: 978-0688099176

Schneider, Elizabeth. *Uncommon Fruits & Vegetables: a commonsense guide.* New York: Harper & Row, 1986. ISBN: 978-0688160647

See, Bernard, et al. *Famous Street Food of Penang: A guide & Cookbook.* Pung Kim Ying ed. Malaysia: Star Publications, 2006. ISBN: 983-9512-26-9

Simonds, Nina. *Asian Noodles.* New York: Hearst Books, 1997. ISBN: 978-0688131340

Solomon, Charmaine. *The Complete Asian Cookbook.* Massachusetts: Tuttle Publishing, 1992 ISBN: 978-0804817912

———. *Encyclopedia of Asian Food.* Massachusetts: Periplus Editions, 1998. ISBN: 978-9625934174

Sonakul, Sipban. *Everyday Siamese Dishes.* Thailand: Chatra Press, 1952.

Steinberg, Rafael. *Pacific and Southeast Asian Cooking.* Time Life Books ed. New York: Time Life Books, 1970. ASIN: B000GZQU94

Sterling, Richard. *Lonely Planet World Food Vietnam.* Victoria: Lonely Planet Publications Pty Ltd., 2000 ISBN: 978-1864500288

Stobart, Tom. *The International Wine and Food Society's Guide to Herbs, Spices, and Flavorings.* New York: McGraw-Hill Book Company, 1970. ISBN: 978-0070615656

Suan, Gek. *At a Nonya's Table.* Kuala Lumpur: C. B. Tan, 2002. ISBN: 981-04-5655-7

Su-Lyn, Tan. *Lonely Planet World Food Malaysia and Singapore* (Lonely Planet World Food Guides). Victoria: Lonely Planet Publications Pty Ltd., 2003. ISBN: 978-1740593700

Tan, Cecilia. *Foods of My Childhood: Penang Nyonya Cooking.* Singapore: Marshall Cavendish Cuisine, 2000. ISBN: 981-261-139-8

Tan, Florence. *Secrets of Nyonya Cooking.* Singapore: Times Editions, 2001. ISBN: 9812321217

Tan, Sylvia. *Singapore Heritage Food.* Singapore: Landmark Books Pte. Ltd., 2004. ISBN: 981-3065-76-1

Tan, Terry, and Christopher Tan. *Shiok: Exciting Tropical Asian Flavors.* Singapore: Periplus Editions, 2003. ISBN: 978-0794600952

Thompson, David. *Thai Food.* California: Ten Speed Press, 2002. ISBN: 978-0670867615

Trager, James. *The Food Chronology: A Food Lover's Compendium of Events and Anecdotes, from Prehistory to the Present.* New York: Henry Holt & Company, 1995. ISBN: 978-0805052473

Trang, Corinne. *Authentic Vietnamese Cooking: Food from a Family Table.* New York: Simon & Schuster, 1999. ISBN: 978-0684864440

———. *Essentials of Asian Cuisine.* New York: Simon & Schuster, 2003. ISBN: 978-0743203128

Tropp, Barbara. *The Modern Art of Chinese Cooking: Techniques & Recipes by Barbara Tropp.* New York: William Morrow & Company, Inc., 1982. ISBN: 978-0688005665

Vista Productions. *The Singapore Cookbook 2.* Singapore: Vista Productions, 1976.

Vista Productions LTD. *The Malaysian Party Cookbook.* Malaysia: Vista Productions LTD, 1977. ASIN: B000KAI8UY

Willan, Anne. *Perfect Asian Cooking.* London: Dorling
Kindersley Limited, 1997.
ISBN: 978-0751303896

Williams, Judy. *Thailand*, World Food Series. California:
Thunder Bay Press, 2003.
ISBN: 978-1592231317

Withey, Carl. *International Cuisine South-East Asia.*
London: Hodder & Stroughton, 2004.
ISBN: 978-0340857885

Wong, David, and Djoko Wibisono. *The Food of Singapore:
Authentic Recipes from the Manhattan of the East.*
Singapore: Periplus Editions (HK) Ltd., 1995.
ISBN: 978-9625930077

Wong, Julie, ed. *Nonya Flavours: A complete guide to Penang
Straits Chinese Cuisine.* Malaysia: Star Publications,
2006.
ISBN: 983-9512-17-x

Yee, Kenny. *Thai Hawker Food.* Bangkok: Book Promotion
& Service (BPS), 1993.
ISBN: 978-9748900995

Yee, Kenny, and Catherine Gordon. *Dos & Don'ts in
Thailand.* Bangkok: Booknet Co., Ltd., 2006.

Yeo, Chris, and Joyce Jue. *The Cooking of Singapore.*
California: Harlow & Ratner, 1993.
ISBN: 978-0962734564

Young, Grace, and Alan Richardson. *The Breath of a Wok.*
New York: Simon & Schuster, 2004.
ISBN: 978-0743238274

Web-Based Resources Used as References for the Development of This Book

Air Asia—**http://www.airasia.com**
Asia etc.—**http://www.asia-etc.com/**
Asian Culinary Arts Institute—
http://www.asianculinaryarts.com/
Asian Foods Online—**http://www.asianfoodsonline.com/default.asp**
The Asian Grandmother's Cookbook—
http://theasiangrandmotherscookbook.wordpress.com
Bangkok Beer Hunter—**http://www.bangkokbob.net**
Bangkok Post—**http://www.bangkokpost.com**

Country Studies—**http://countrystudies.us**
Crop Science Congress—**http://www.cropscience.org**
Enjoy Thai Food—**http://www.enjoythaifood.com**
The Epicenter—**http://www.theepicentre.com**
Fodor's Online—**http://fodors.com/**
Food Reference.com—**http://www.foodreference.com**
Import Food.com—**http://importfood.com**
International Herald Tribune—**http://www.iht.com**
JFC International—**http://www.jfc.com/**
The Last Appetite—**http://www.lastappetite.com**
Lonely Planet On line—**http://lonelyplanet.com/**
Malaysia Airlines—**http://www.malaysiaairlines.com**
Melissa's World Variety Produce—
http://www.melissas.com/
My Local Cuisine Blog—**http://mylocalcuisine.blogspot.com**
National Geographic—**http://www.nationalgeographic.com/**
North by Northeast—**http://www.north-by-north-east.com**
Paknam Web Network—**http://www.paknamweb.com/**
Pterodactyl Coffee—**http://harryosoffdesign.com**
Rasa Malaysia—**http://www.rasamalaysia.com/**
Real Thai Recipes—**http://www.realthairecipes.com/recipes/drunken-noodles/**
Safe Travel.com—**http://safetravel.dot.gov**
Samui Institute of Thai Culinary Arts—
http://www.sitca.net/
Singapore Air—**http://www.singaporeair.com**
The Star Online—**http://kuali.com**
Thai Air—**http://www.thaiair.com/**
Thai Carving Institute—**http://www.carvinginstitute.com/**
Temple of Thai—**http://www.templeofthai.com**
Things Asian—**http://www.thingsasian.com**
US Central Intelligence Agency's World Fact Book—
https://www.cia.gov
Vietnamese Embassy—**http://www.vietnamembassy-usa.org**
Vietnam Tourism—**http://www.vietnamtourism.com**
Vietnam VIP Tours—**http://www.vietnamviptour.com**
Viet World Kitchen—**http://www.vietworldkitchen.com**
Wikipedia—**http://www.wikipedia.org/**

Cultural Index

Vietnam

Foods of Southeast Asia Index

Techniques for Building Southeast Asian Flavors

Scientific Names of Pantry Ingredients

Aleurites moluccana (candlenuts), 63
Allium fistulosum (scallions), 46
Allium oschaninii (shallots), 46
Allium sativum (garlic), 46
Allium tuberosum (garlic chives), 46
Alpinia galanga (galangal), 34
Ananas comosus (pineapple), 90
Apium graveolens dulce
  (Chinese celery), 39
Arachis hypogaea (peanuts), 62
Artocarpus heterophyllus
  (jackfruit), 90
Auricularia polytricha
  (wood ear mushrooms), 83
Bambusa vulgaris
  (bamboo shoots), 79
Boesenbergia pandurata (krachai), 35
Borassus flabellifer (Asian Palmyra
  palm tree), 58
Brassica oleracea (green cabbage), 77
Brassica oleracea Alboglabra
  (Chinese broccoli), 77
Brassica rapa subsp. *chinensis*
  (bok choy), 76
Brassica rapa subsp. *pekinensis*
  (napa cabbage), 77
Brassica rapa var. *parachinensis*
  (choy sum), 76
Carambola (starfruit), 91
Carica papaya (papaya), 91
Cinnamomum aromaticum
  (cassia), 43
Cinnamomum cassia (cassia), 43
Cinnamomum verum, C. zelanicum
  (true cinnamon), 43
Citrus aurantifolia (key lime), 84
Citrus grandis (pummelo), 86
Citrus hystrix (kaffir lime), 36, 85
Citrus laifolia (lime), 84

Citrus microcarpa
  (calamansi lime), 85
Citrus reticulata (tangerine), 87
Citrus sinensis (oranges), 87
Cocos nucifera (coconut), 58, 60
Coriandrum sativum
  (cilantro, coriander), 38, 40
Cucumis sativus (cucumber), 81
Cucurbita maxima var. *akehime*
  (kabocha squash), 81
Cuminum cyminum (cumin), 40
Curcuma domestica (turmeric), 35
Curcuma longa (turmeric), 35
Cymbopogon citrates (lemongrass), 36
Durio zibethinus (durian), 90
Elettaria cardamomum
  (cardamom), 40
Elsholtzia ciliate
  (Vietnamese lemon balm), 39
Engraulis encrasicolus (anchovy), 48
Eryngium foetidum (saw leaf), 38
Ferula assafoetida (asafetida), 34
Garcinia mangostana
  (mangosteen), 89
Glycine max (soybeans), 74
Houttuynia cordata (fish mint), 39
Hylocereus undatus (dragonfruit), 91
Illicium verum (star anise), 43
Ipomoea aquatica (water spinach), 76
Ipomoea batatas (sweet potatoes), 80
Ixa orrellana (annatto), 40
Lactuca sativa (lettuce), 77
Lentinula edodes (Chinese black
  mushrooms), 82
Limnophila aromatica
  (rice paddy herb), 39
Manihot esculenta (tapioca), 80
Mentha × gracilis (spearmint), 39
Mentha spicata (peppermint), 39

Murraya koenigii (curry leaves), 37
Musa sapientum (bananas), 89
Nephelium lappaceum
  (rambutan), 91
Ocimum basilicum citriodorum
  (lemon basil), 38
Ocimum basilicum var.
  (Thai or Asian basil), 38
Ocimum sanctum (holy basil), 38
Oryza sativa (rice), 72
Pachyrhizus erosus (jicama), 80
Pandanus amaryllifolius
  (pandan leaves), 37
Perilla frutescens (perilla), 39
Persea americana (avocado), 81
Pimpinella anisum (anise seeds), 43
Piper nigrum (peppercorns), 42
Piper sarmentosum (wild pepper leaf
  or betel leaf), 37
Polygonum odoratum
  (Vietnamese coriander), 38
Shorea (wood of palm genus), 58
Solanum melongena (eggplant), 78
Solanum tuberosum (potatoes), 80
*Stolephorus baccaneeri, S. miarcha,
  S. purpureus* (stolephorus fish), 48
Syzygium aromaticum (cloves), 43
Tamrindus indica (tamarind), 57
Vigna angularis (adzuki beans), 74
Vigna mungo (urad dhal), 74
Vigna radiata var. *radiata*
  (mung beans), 74
Vigna sesquipedalis (long beans), 79
Volvariella volvacea
  (straw mushrooms), 82
Zanthoxylum piperitum
  (Szechwan peppercorns), 43
Zea mays (corn), 81
Zingiber officinale (ginger), 34

Tools for Building Southeast Asian Flavors

Personalities and Places Index

Photography Index
(Captioned)

Recipe Index by Country

INDEX

Vietnam (cont.)

Malaysia/Singapore

Recipe Index

INDEX

INDEX

INDEX

INDEX

Southeast Asian Flavors

ADVENTURES IN COOKING THE FOODS
OF THAILAND, VIETNAM, MALAYSIA, & SINGAPORE

To order, visit Web Site:

www.southeastasianflavors.com

or

send email to:

order@southeastasianflavors.com.

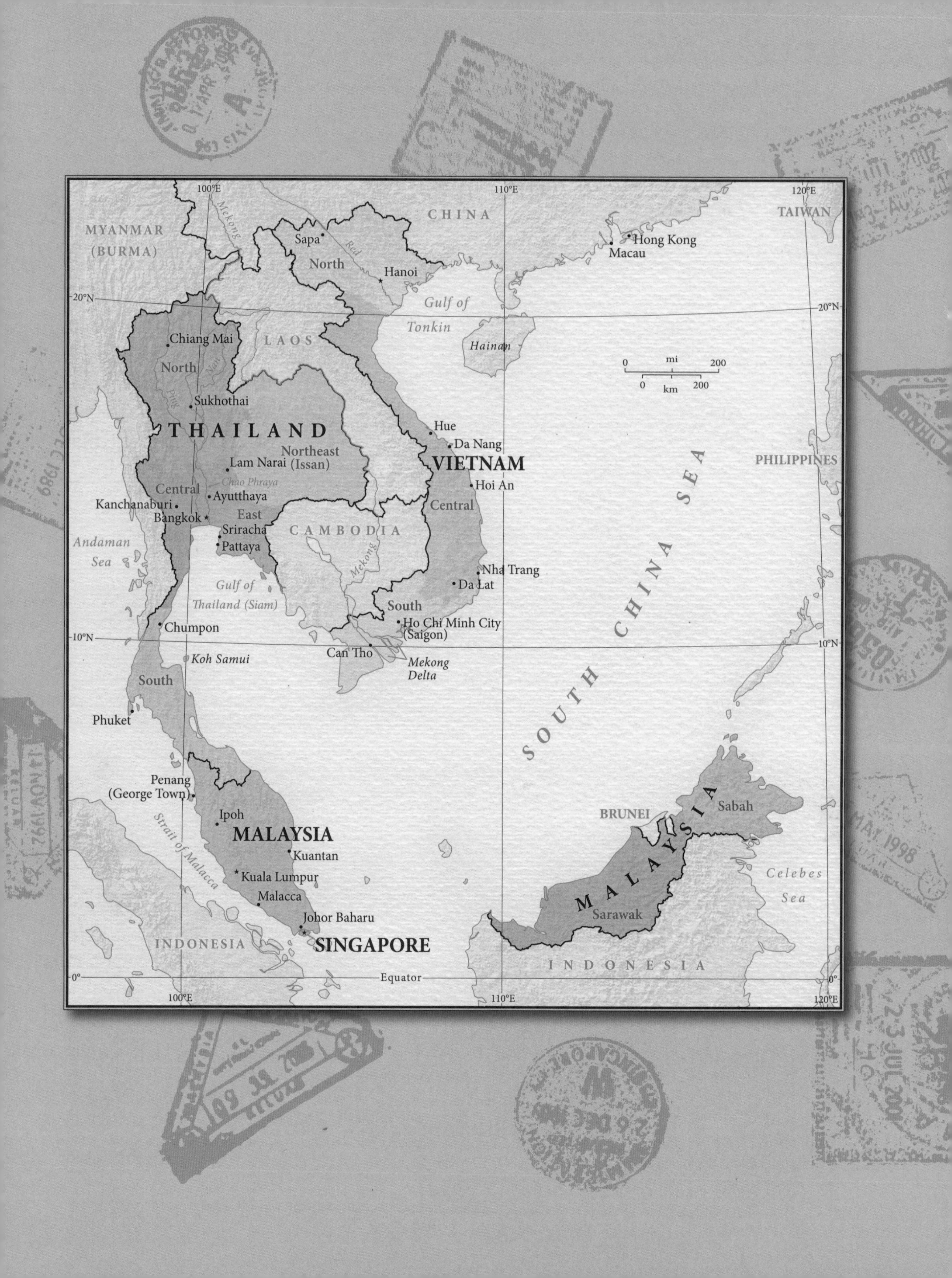
100°E
110°E
120°E
20°N
10°N
0°
Equator
CHINA
TAIWAN
MYANMAR
(BURMA)
Mekong
Red
Sapa
North
Hanoi
Hong Kong
Macau
Gulf of
Tonkin
Hainan
LAOS
Chiang Mai
North
Nan
Ping
Sukhothai
THAILAND
Northeast
(Issan)
Lam Narai
Chao Phraya
Central
Ayutthaya
Kanchanaburi
Bangkok
East
Sriracha
Pattaya
Andaman
Sea
Gulf of
Thailand (Siam)
CAMBODIA
Mekong
0 mi 200
0 km 200
Hue
Da Nang
VIETNAM
Hoi An
Central
Nha Trang
Da Lat
South
Ho Chi Minh City
(Saigon)
Can Tho
Mekong
Delta
Chumpon
Koh Samui
South
Phuket
SOUTH CHINA SEA
PHILIPPINES
Penang
(George Town)
Ipoh
MALAYSIA
Kuantan
Kuala Lumpur
Malacca
Johor Baharu
SINGAPORE
Strait of Malacca
INDONESIA
BRUNEI
Sabah
MALAYSIA
Sarawak
Celebes
Sea
INDONESIA